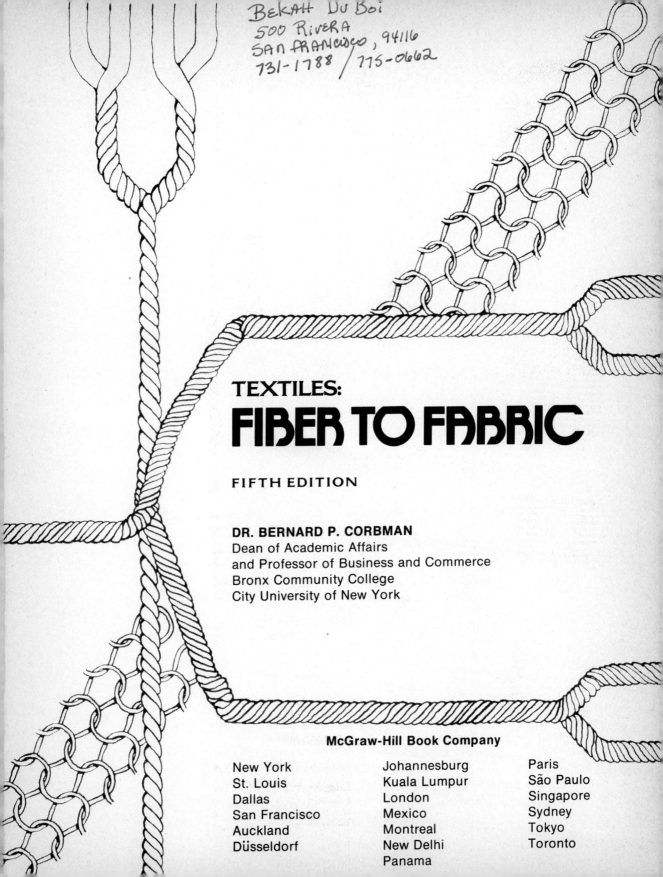

TEXTILES:
FIBER TO FABRIC

FIFTH EDITION

DR. BERNARD P. CORBMAN
Dean of Academic Affairs
and Professor of Business and Commerce
Bronx Community College
City University of New York

McGraw-Hill Book Company

New York
St. Louis
Dallas
San Francisco
Auckland
Düsseldorf

Johannesburg
Kuala Lumpur
London
Mexico
Montreal
New Delhi
Panama

Paris
São Paulo
Singapore
Sydney
Tokyo
Toronto

Library of Congress Cataloging in Publication Data

Corbman, Bernard P.
    Textiles: fiber to fabric.

    First ed. by M. D. Potter and 2d-3d by M. D. Potter
and B. P. Corbman have title: Fiber to fabric; 4th ed. by
Potter and Corbman has title: Textiles: fiber to fabric.
    Includes index.
    1. Textile industry and fabrics. I. Potter, Maurice
David, 1899–   Textiles: fiber to fabric. II. Title.
TS1446. P6 1975   677   75-1140
ISBN 0-07-013125-2

Textiles: Fiber to Fabric

4 5 6 7 8 9 0 DODO 7 8 3 2 1 0 9 8

The editors for this book were Mary Alice McGarry and
Zivile K. Khoury, the designers were Marsha Cohen and
Dennis Purdy, and the production supervisor was
Laurence Charnow. It was set in Century Expanded by
Textbook Services, Inc.

Printed and bound by R. R. Donnelley & Sons Co.

PREFACE

Textiles: Fiber to Fabric, Fifth Edition, blends both the revolutionary new developments in the textile field and the traditional background information necessary for a full understanding of this complex and fast-moving industry. This edition provides the basic information needed by (1) students who are preparing for careers in the textile industry—in manufacturing, retailing, purchasing, or promoting; (2) beginning workers who are employed in any phase of the textile complex; (3) consumers and home economists who need sound guidance in the selection and care of textile products; (4) teachers who need a complete basic text on textiles, adaptable to a variety of curricula and student needs; and (5) specialists who need an up-to-date reference book.

SCOPE OF THE BOOK

Textiles: Fiber to Fabric, Fifth Edition, continues to serve as a comprehensive survey of the textile field. It stresses consumer concerns with regard to comparison, selection, usage, and care of fabrics and merchandise as well as to the theory and processes underlying their manufacture.

New finishing processes such as shrink resistance and shrink-proofing, stain repellency and soil resistance, flame retardancy, and water repellency are surveyed. The discussion of permanent press finishes has been expanded. The wide application of "stretch" in fabrics is given considerable attention through discussions of stretch fibers, yarns, finishes, and the resultant stretch fabrics. The use of optical brighteners and their value are considered. New dyeing and decorating techniques are examined and their merits noted.

The several major strains of cotton fibers are identified, evaluated, and compared, as are the various forms of established, improved, and new varieties of rayon, nylon, polyester, acrylic, modacrylic, spandex, polypropylene, saran, and glass. A chapter on aramid has been added. The chapter on textured and stretch yarns has been updated, and more illustrations have been added.

In addition to the advancements made in weaving, such as the use of shuttleless looms, special attention is given to the continued growth of fabric construction by other methods. The chapter on knitting now includes the advances made in electronic techniques that increase the versatility of knitting. Nonwovens, tufting, Mali, Arachne, and Doweave are also covered.

In this edition, fabrics of all types are compared by performance, durability, care requirements, and related characteristics. Thus the student can develop an ability to select goods wisely. Discussions of the Permanent Care Labeling Rule and the Flame Retardancy Regulations have also been added.

Detailed descriptions and information are provided on apparel, such as sweaters and hosiery, and on home furnishings, such as rugs and carpets. The discussion of hosiery, for example, covers evaluation of various knitted constructions. The discussion of the various types of rugs and carpets, their methods of construction, the fibers used in their manufacture, and their merits have been expanded.

ORGANIZATION OF THE BOOK

The organization of *Textiles: Fiber to Fabric*, while following a distinct line of development, is by no means rigid. Each chapter is an entity unto itself, so that instructors may adapt the text to an outline appropriate for their particular textile course of study or group of students.

The sequence of chapters of the previous edition, which was based upon many years of teaching experience has been retained. The book opens with an introduction to the various fibers and tells how to identify them. Then the reader is taken through the logical, related sequence of chapters from fiber to finished fabric. For example, a chapter is devoted to spinning the fiber into various types of yarn. This is followed by treatment of fabric construction in a chapter on weaving, an expanded chapter on knitting, and a separate chapter on the less predominant, but growing, minor fabric constructions. Subsequent chapters review the many types of finishes, dyes and dyeing methods, and printing and flocking techniques.

Also included are the history of textile development, the methods of manufacture, and the characteristics, evaluations, and care of each type of textile. Comparative characteristics of all major fibers are presented in a summary chapter. Subsequent chapters of the book cover minor textile fibers, rugs and carpets, and care of fabrics, thus rounding out the reader's acquaintance with the field of textiles.

SPECIAL FEATURES

Textiles: Fiber to Fabric does not require a previous knowledge of textiles or a background in science. Its vocabulary is simple and direct. Where technical or chemical terminology is necessary, it is presented clearly and in an understandable manner. Technical theory, concepts, and methods are intermingled with practical information that the lay person needs and understands readily. The student is also provided with trademarks of fibers and finishes and with glossaries of significant fabrics.

Specific facts to be considered when purchasing such items as hosiery, sweaters, sheets, towels, and carpets are organized and presented for ready reference. The general care of fabrics is fully discussed, including detailed information on stain removal.

Illustrations. Illustrations help to make the more technical material understandable. A substantial number of photographs and diagrams are used to clarify new materials and to simplify complex industrial processes. Summary charts quickly identify and review the principal points covered and compare the specific items discussed.

Cross-References. Information in the text is organized so that the book can be used as a reference source as well as a classroom text. Although each topic is treated independently, cross-reference notations minimize repetition and enable the reader to find specific information, such as properties of fibers, description of fabrics and finishes, and the like.

End-of-Chapter Activities. There are two kinds of end-of-chapter activities. Review Questions provide an opportunity for classroom discussion and review and are based on the text material. Suggested Activities are also provided for selected chapters as appropriate. They give the student direction for enriching activities that will further increase his or her understanding of the subject.

Instructor's Manual and Key. The instructor's manual contains the answers to all Review Questions in the text. This manual also contains an extensive bibliography of reading and reference sources for independent study. Listed are current books, periodicals, trade journals, and brochures covering the entire textile area. Names and addresses of textile companies and other organizations that have educational material available are also provided. In addition, the manual offers helpful suggestions for teaching the course.

Bernard P. Corbman

ACKNOWLEDGMENTS

The fifth edition has entailed much research. The gathering and evaluation of material for this edition has been greatly facilitated by the kind cooperation of a great many companies and organizations, and by the officers and personnel acting in their behalf. Grateful acknowledgments are made to the following:

Allied Chemical Corporation: Edward A. Marinello, Publicity Manager; R. J. Richardson, Manager, Marketing Systems; R. J. O'Leary, General Manager, Plastic Film Department; Russell La Valla, Home Furnishings, Merchandising; Felix Murphy, Fabricated Products Division. *Alrac Corporation:* Dr. J. A. Gervasi. *Ameliotex, Inc.:* Arthur F. Cacella, Vice President and Laboratory Director. *American Apparel Manufacturers Association:* John Druckenbrod, Director of Public Relations; Bruce Eberhart. *American Dyestuff Reporter:* Herbert A. Stauderman, Publisher; Richard Consolas, Editor; Patricia R. Chin. *American Enka Company:* Donald R. Clarke, Technical Publications Coordinator, Marketing Technical Department. *American Rieter Company, Inc.:* John F. Dulken, Vice President and Sales Manager. *Amsco Division, Union Oil Company of California:* Charles R. Sheehan. *Amtech, Inc.:* L. V. Jones, Product Sales Manager-Textiles; Phil G. Hanel, Olefin Plastics TS&D. *Apex Chemical Company, Inc.:* Emil Baer. *Arkansas Company, Inc.:* Jules R. von Sternberg, President. *Batson Yarn and Fabrics Machinery Group, Inc.:* Hugh Ham. *Bemberg Industries, Inc.:* Robert L. McClure, Plant Manager. *The Bobtex Corporation, Ltd.:* J. A. Stenstrom, Assistant to the President. *Brunswick Corporation:* Perry H. Brown, Manager, Textile Applications and Technical Service. *Burlington Madison Yarn Company:* Thomas F. Carroll, Jr. *Carolina Mills, Inc.:* Leonard Moretz, President. *Celanese Fibers Marketing Company:* Marjorie J. Hefferon, Supervisor, Technical Writing; Juliet Blackburn Houston, Supervisor, Retail and Consumer Information. *Chas. S. Tanner Company:* Wm. F. Moore, Jr., Product Manager, Textile Auxiliaries. *CIBA-Geigy Corporation, Dyestuffs & Chemicals Division:* Frances C. Tharrington, Administrative Assistant. *Courtaulds North America, Inc.:* E. Attle, Manager, Staple Fiber Development. *Crompton & Knowles Corporation:* Ronald M. Torrence, Product Manager/Knitting Machinery. *Crown-Metro, Inc.:* Francis J. Scavitto, Technical Director. *David Gessner Company:* Eugene R. Massey, Assistant Sales Manager. *Deering Milliken, Inc.* *Dexter Chemical Corporation:* J. J. McGuinness, Vice President. *Diamond Shamrock Chemical Company:* C. H. Gillespie, Branch Product Manager. *Dow Badische Company:* John S. Mills, Product Publicity Manager. *Doweave, Inc.:* A. S. Martindale, Executive Vice President. *E. I. du Pont de Nemours & Company:* James Adshead, Jr., Public Affairs Manager; Tom Ellington, Textile Fibers Dept.; Peter P. Pritulsky, Technical Service Section, Multiservice Group; H. C. Miller, Jr., Sales Manager, Textile Chemicals. *Eastman Chemical Products, Inc.:* George T. Ford, Jr. *Edda Textile Machines, Inc.:* Erik B. Nagel, President. *Emkay Chemical Company:* Albert Malick D.Sc., President. *W. F. Fancourt Co., Inc.:* John M. Jester, Jr. *Federal Trade Commission:* Paul A. Jamarik, Supervisory Attorney for Textiles and Furs; Edward B. Finch, Assistant Director for Textiles and Furs; Charles A. Tobin, Secretary, Federal Trade Commission; John F. LeFevre, Attorney, Division of Rules and Guides. *Fibre Research Institute TNO, Delft, Holland:* Dr. H. J. Selling, Director. *Fibron Inc.:* Larry E. Clingan, President; W. Wayne Freed, Vice President of Marketing. *FMC Corporation:* Cynthia E. Bunitsky, Product Information, Fibers Technical Dept. *Freeport Kaolin Company:* Claud E. Westbrook, Jr. *Gabungan Koperasi Batik Indonesia:* Joesoef Moeid, Manager of Trade. *Gaston Country Dyeing Machine Company:* Gordon Hacker, Vice President and General Manager. *Globe Manufacturing Company:* M. Tosone, Technical Service. *Great Lakes Chemical Corporation:* Wayne R. Merriman, Manager of Business Development. *Harris Textile Machinery Company:* Stephen C. Harris, President. *Heberlein & Co. AG, Switzerland:* Hch. Teschudi; R. Dieter; F. Chavan. *Heberlein, Inc.:* Peter R. Wasmer, Vice President. *Hercules Inc.:* Stanley R. Nechvatal; T. Benton Sevison, Jr., Supervisor, Fibers Advertising. *Hoechst Fibers, Inc.:* G. P. Elden, Vice President of Marketing; Dr. William S. Wagner, Director of Development. *Humphrey Chemical Corporation:* S. Bruce Humphrey, President. *ICI*

Fibres, England: T. A. Hughes, Melded Products Business Area; Adrian W. Smith, Patents. *Indonesia:* Bustanil Arifin, Consul General (New York); Chairul Anwar, Industrial Attaché (Washington, D. C.); Rudy Lengkong, Industrial Attaché (New York). *The Kent Manufacturing Company:* Mike Risko, Vice President. *Leesona Corporation:* Ralph D. Fleming. *Man-Made Fiber Producers Association, Inc.:* Fisher A. Rhymes, Education Director. *Mather & Platt (Exports) Ltd., Manchester, England:* J. B. Ripley, General Machinery Division. *Metal Film Company, Inc.:* Alfred J. Green, General Manager. *Metlon Corporation:* Joseph B. Resch, Jr., Vice President. *Ministry of Foreign Trade & Supply, Government of India Central Silk Board:* K. I. Ahmed, Publicity Officer; D. A. Joshi, Joint Secretary. *Ministry of Industrial Development, Government of India, Central Silk Board:* S. P. Mediratta, Assistant Secretary, Liaison Office. *Minnesota Mining and Manufacturing Company:* Clark Duffey, Public Relations. *Modern Textiles Magazine:* A. H. McCollough, Publisher; Frank A. McNeirney, Managing Editor. *Monsanto Industrial Chemicals Company:* Charles R. Williams, Commercial Development Manager. *Monsanto Textiles Company:* F. C. Flindt, Technical Publications; G. D. Wilkinson, Supervisor, Technical Publications; John Lomartare. *Nan Sing Dyeing Works, Ltd., Hong Kong:* C. P. Wong, Assistant Mill Manager. *National Cotton Council of America:* Ford L. Boyd, Director, Printing and Audio-Visual Services. *Newton Filaments, Inc.:* William E. Higgins. *Sir James Farmer Norton, Salford, England:* J. R. Henshall. *Owens-Corning Fiberglas Corporation:* Robert P. Mulligan, Vice President, Decorative & Home Furnishings Division; F. A. Mennerich, Product Evaluation Manager. *Pardede Textile Industries, Indonesia:* Dr. T. D. Pardede, President; Dr. S. P. Napitupulu, Director. *Peter Zimmer America, Inc.:* J. Lee Gossmann, Executive Secretary. *Platt International, Ltd., England:* A. A. Chisholm, Product Manager, Open-End Spinning. *PPG Industries, Inc.:* Robert A. McLaughlin, Vice President and General Manager; E. M. Hunia, Product Development. *Repco Textile Machinery Company, Australia:* C. L. Burton, Assistant General Manager. *Rockwell International:* Frank A. Aschenbrenner, Vice President and Manager, ESP Operation; Robert W. Carlton, General Manager, Textile Machinery Divisions; John Denike, General Manager, Knitting Machinery Division; L. E. Bentz, Sales Administrator, TMW Products; R. E. Hilton, Advertising Manager; William J. Gardner, Marketing Services. *Sanitized Inc.:* Stewart E. Klein, President. *Scher Brothers, Inc.:* Martin Scher. *Scholler Brothers, Inc.:* Dr. E. C. Dreby 3d, Director of Laboratory. *Shirley Institute, Manchester, England:* Miss M. Sawbridge, Editor, *Textiles.* *Silk & Art Silk Mills Association, Ltd., India:* R. K. Bhatnagar, Secretary. *The Singer Company:* Terry Crumbliss, Sales Manager. *A. E. Staley Manufacturing Company:* John W. Lamprinakos, Application Manager, Textile & Converting. *Sulzer Brothers, Inc.:* Elisabeth Cauley, Advertising & Public Relations. *Taltex Ltd., Hong Kong:* K. Y. Hsu, Mill Manager. *Taylor Instrument Process Control Division/Sybron Corporation:* Robert H. Bonnett, Documentation Specialist. *Textile Alliance Ltd., Hong Kong:* Y. Koyama, Toray Industries Representative. *Textile Research Institute:* Henry J. Jansen, Secretary-Treasurer. *Textile World:* Richard B. Pressley, Senior Editor; L. A. Christiansen, Editor; Emily T. Sthreshley, Editorial Assistant. *Textile Systems Group:* L. P. Garrigan, Manager. *Thai Textile Organization, Bangkok:* Boonpob Bunyabhisand, Managing Director; Wichian Mokkhavesa, Deputy Director. *Thiokol Fibers Division:* J. P. Grochmal, Senior Product Manager. *Toray Industries, Inc.:* K. Hirai, Merchandising Manager; Jiro Nobe, Bangkok Representative; Takashi Yoshida, Senior Staff, Planning Dept. *Turbo Machine Company:* James N. Morgan, Vice President. *Ugaya & Co., Ltd., Hong Kong:* Robert M. Ugaya, Managing Director. *The Ullman Organization:* David U. Ullman, Vice President. *Union Carbide Corporation:* R. B. Forsyth, Product Manager, Advanced Materials Dept.; T. H. Newman, Research and Development Dept.; O. C. Trulson, Product Manager, Carbon Fiber Products; W. I. Lowe, Sales Coordinator, Fibers Dept.; W. Standerwich. *U.S. Department of Agriculture, Agricultural Research Service:* Dr. Harmon H. Ramey, Jr., Research Leader, Cotton Quality Laboratories; Mayer Mayer, Jr., Head, Machinery Development Investigations, Cotton Mechanical Laboratory. *U.S. Textile Machine Division of Dynamics Corporation of America, D.I.P.:* Anthony R. Summa, Marketing Services Manager. *Vikon Chemical Company, Inc.:* L. B. Arnold, Jr. *The Wool Bureau, Inc.:* M. J. Koroskys, Vice President, Product Development and Technical Services. *Zima Corporation:* Kurt Zimmerli, President. *E. I. du Pont de Nemours & Co.:* J. D. Barhydt, Public Affairs Dept.; H. E. Brokaw, Marketing Director, C. S. McCandlish, Jr., and A. R. Potter, Products Strategist, Industrial Fibers Div.

CONTENTS

1

TEXTILE FIBERS

under the microscope

Textiles have such an important bearing on our daily lives that everyone needs to know something about them. From earliest times, people have used textiles of various types for covering, warmth, personal adornment, and even to display personal wealth. Today, textiles are still used for these purposes and everyone is an ultimate consumer. You use textiles in some form even if you are not the direct purchaser. Included among consumers are merchandisers of many types, from the wholesale textile manufacturer and merchant to the sales force in any retail store. Many industries, such as the automobile industry, are important consumers of textiles in various forms. Some other consumers are homemakers, dressmakers, interior decorators, and retail-store customers, as well as students who are studying for these and various other occupations and professions in which a knowledge of textiles is of major importance.

The merchant, particularly, and all those who work for him must be thoroughly familiar with the merchandise they are handling if they wish to be successful. Only thorough knowledge will prevent the mistakes that are too often made in buying and selling.

REASONS FOR STUDYING TEXTILES

A study of textiles will show, for example, why certain fabrics are more durable and therefore more serviceable for specific purposes. It will explain why certain fabrics make cool wearing apparel as well as give an impression of coolness when used as decoration. The matter of cleanliness and maintenance must also be estimated before purchasing, when that is an important factor.

Complete knowledge of textiles will facilitate an intelligent appraisal of standards and brands of merchandise and will develop the ability to distinguish quality in fabrics and, in turn, to appreciate the proper uses for the different qualities. As a result, both the

1

consumer merchant and consumer customer will know how to buy and what to buy, and salespeople will know how to render good service to those consumers who have not had the advantage of a formal course in textiles.

In recent years, great strides have been made in the textile industry that have markedly influenced our general economic growth. The prosperity and growth of related industries, such as petroleum and chemistry, and dependent industries, such as retail apparel stores, have produced broader employment opportunities. Competition for the consumer's dollar has fostered the creation of new textile fibers with specific qualities to compete with well-established fibers. New fiber blends have been created to combine many of these qualities into new types of yarns with new trademarks. There are also new names for the fabrics made of these new fibers and yarns. New finishes have been developed to add new and interesting characteristics to fibers, yarns, and fabrics.

This welter of creativity and the myriad of trademarks present a challenge to the consumer, who is sometimes knowledgeable but frequently confused. Yet he need not be. Without being overly technical, this information can be easily understood and consequently very useful to the consumer in his business and personal life. All of this information can be adopted for such utilitarian benefits as economy, durability, serviceability, and comfort, as well as for such aesthetic values as hand (or feel), texture, design, and color.

In the study of textiles, the students' initial interest will become an absorbing interest when they discover the natural fascination of fabrics and their cultural associations, particularly when factual study is supplemented by actual handling of the textile materials. The subject will seem worthwhile as they become familiar with illustrative specimens and fabrics and begin to handle and learn to compare the raw materials of which fabrics are made as well as the finished consumers' goods.

SEQUENCE OF FABRIC CONSTRUCTION

In beginning the study of textiles, you should have in your hand a sample of a woven fabric. Note that it is constructed by interlacing sets of yarns that run lengthwise and crosswise. It is from the interlacing, or weaving, of yarns that such textile materials are made. A close examination of any one of these yarns will reveal the fibrous substance from which the yarn is made. Such yarns comprise a multitude of fine, hairlike fibers or filaments that have been separated, made parallel, overlapped, and twisted together by various processes.

There is a logical development of raw material into finished consumers' goods. Studying textile materials in the interesting sequence of "fiber to yarn to fabric" will help you understand the construction and ultimate qualities of the fabrics with which you will become familiar. Here are the steps in the manufacture of fabrics from raw material to finished goods:

1. Fiber, which is either spun (or twisted) into yarn or else directly compressed into fabric

2. Yarn, which is woven, knitted, or otherwise made into fabric
3. Fabric, which by various finishing processes becomes finished consumers' goods

KINDS OF FIBERS

The textile industry uses many different kinds of fibers as its raw materials. Some of these fibers were known and used in the earlier years of civilization, as well as in modern times. Other fibers have acquired varied degrees of importance in recent years. New fibers are being produced and tested daily. The factors influencing the development and utilization of all these fibers include their ability to be spun, their availability in sufficient quantity, the cost or economy of production, and the desirability of their properties to consumers.

Before 1960, the development of new fibers caused difficulty in the textile industry in terms of nomenclature, classification, and identification. The confusion was compounded by the trend of manufacturers to identify each of their fibers with a different trademark. Consumers became confused by these names and found it difficult and sometimes impossible to identify the fiber content of the products they saw in the stores. Often they did not know whether an identifying name represented a particular *kind* of fiber or a *trademark* for some kind of newly created fiber. Subsequently, the United States Congress enacted the Textile Fiber Products Identification Act, which became effective on March 3, 1960. This act requires that the labels of all textile products must show the fiber contents for amounts above 5 percent, both by fiber name and generic (or family) name, and that all fibers must be listed in descending order of their predominance, with the amount of each fiber indicated in percent by weight of the total fiber content. (The label must also indicate the name or registered number of the person or company marketing or retailing the product and, if the product is imported, the name of the country where it was manufactured.) To standardize this identification procedure, the Federal Trade Commission (FTC) assigned generic groups of man-made fibers according to chemical composition.

While this arrangement has brought about some standardization, clarification, and easier identification of fibers, the generic types do not provide for related groupings. Indeed, it has been found difficult by many authorities to arrange them into logical groupings by characteristics of types. One such grouping, as suggested by the Man-Made Fiber Producers Association, Inc., is cellulosic, synthetic long-chain polymers, and nonfibrous natural substances.

Table 1-1 identifies all fibers by type, name, and source or classification. It includes the author's suggested extension or modification of the association's grouping of nonfibrous natural substances into their derivations.

Natural fibers that occur in nature can be classified as *vegetable*, *animal*, and *mineral*. Vegetable fibers, found in the cell walls of plants, are cellulosic in composition. Animal fibers, produced by animals or insects, are protein in composition. The mineral fiber, asbestos, is mined from certain types of rock.

Table 1-1

CLASSIFICATION OF FIBERS		
TYPE	NAME OF FIBER	SOURCE OR COMPOSITION
NATURAL FIBERS:		
Vegetable	Cotton	Cotton boll (cellulose)
	Linen	Flax stalk (cellulose)
	Jute	Jute stalk (cellulose)
	Hemp	Hemp or abaca stalk (cellulose)
	Sisal	Agave leaf (cellulose)
	Kapok	Kapok tree (cellulose)
	Ramie	Rhea or China grass (cellulose)
	Coir	Coconut husk (cellulose)
	Pina	Pineapple leaf (cellulose)
Animal	Wool	Sheep (protein)
	Silk	Silkworm (protein)
	Hair	Hair-bearing animals (protein)
Mineral	Asbestos	Varieties of rock (silicate of magnesium and calcium)
MAN-MADE FIBERS:		
Cellulosic	Rayon	Cotton linters or wood
	Acetate	Cotton linters or wood
	Triacetate	Cotton linters or wood
Synthetic Long-Chain Polymers	Nylon	Aliphatic polyamide
	Aramid	Aromatic polyamide
	Polyester	Dihydric alcohol and terephthalic acid
	Acrylic	Acrylonitrile (at least 85%)
	Modacrylic	Acrylonitrile (35–84%)
	Spandex	Polyurethane (at least 85%)
	Olefin	Ethylene or propylene (at least 85%)
	Saran	Vinylidene chloride (at least 80%)
	Vinyon	Vinyl chloride (at least 85%)
	Novoloid	Phenol based novalac
	Fluorocarbon	Tetrafluoroethylene
	Alginate*	Calcium alginate
	Anidex*	Monohydric alcohol and acrylic acid
	Lastrile*	Acrylonitrile (10–50%) and a diene
	Nytril*	Vinylidene dinitrile (at least 85%)
	Vinal*	Vinyl alcohol (at least 50%)
Metallic	Metal	Aluminum, silver, gold, stainless steel
Rubber	Rubber	Natural or synthetic rubber
Protein	Azlon*	Corn, soybean, etc.
Mineral	Glass	Silica sand, limestone, and other minerals
	Ceramic	Minerals
	Graphite	Carbon

*Not presently in commercial production in United States; not covered in text.

Man-made fibers are derived from various sources. For instance, man has taken the natural material of cellulose from cotton linters and wood pulp, processed it chemically, and changed its form and several other characteristics into fibers of various lengths. These are classified as *man-made cellulosic fibers*. He has also taken the protein out of such products as corn, processed it chemically, and converted it into *man-made protein fibers*.

Synthetic fibers are another *group of man-made fibers*. Sometimes confusion exists regarding the terms "synthetic" and "man-made," and they may be incorrectly used interchangeably. All synthetic fibers are man-made; but not all man-made fibers are synthetics (as noted above, for example). Synthetic fibers have been and are still being created by research chemists as companies strive to imitate properties of other fibers, to develop other characteristics, or to combine certain properties. These fibers are synthesized by combining carbon, oxygen, hydrogen, and other simple chemical elements into large, complex molecular combinations or structures called *polymers*. Chemists, in fact, discover new chemical compositions and invent new substances that they form into fibers having certain desired characteristics.

Man-made fibers created from other sources are *mineral fibers*, *metallic fibers*, and *rubber fibers*. Glass fibers are produced by combining silica sand, limestone, and certain other minerals. Metallic fibers are produced by mining and refining such metals as aluminum, silver, and gold. Rubber fibers are made from the sap tapped from the rubber tree.

COMPOSITION AND STRUCTURE OF FIBERS

Each textile fiber has its own distinctive structural shape and markings that, under a microscope with a magnification of at least 100, provide aid in the identification of the fiber. Certain general observations also help to identify fibers without the use of a microscope. These differences in structure determine the various characteristics of the different fibers and explain why some fibers are to be preferred to others for certain uses. The illustrations in this chapter show cross-sectional and longitudinal photomicrographs of the various fibers.

THE NATURAL FIBERS

Vegetable Fibers

Of the several vegetable fibers, each derived from a different plant, two are recognized as major textile fibers. They are cotton, which grows in the seedpod, or boll, of the cotton plant, and linen, which grows in the stalk of the flax plant. (The minor vegetable fibers are discussed in Table 1-1 and Chapter 27.)

Cotton. Unlike other fibers obtained from plants, the cotton fiber is a single elongated cell. Under the microscope, it resembles a collapsed, spirally twisted tube with a rough surface. The thin cell wall of the fiber has from 200 to 400 turns of natural twists, or convolutions, to the inch. The fiber appears flat, twisted, and ribbonlike, with a wide inner canal (the lumen) and a granular effect. Chemically, the fiber contains

Figure 1-1 Cross-sectional and longitudinal views of cotton fibers under a microscope: *(a)* natural cotton fiber *(Courtesy U.S. Testing Co.)* and *(b)* mercerized cotton fiber. *(Courtesy U.S. Department of Agriculture)*

about 90 percent cellulose and about 6 percent moisture; the remainder consists of natural impurities. The outer surface of the fiber is covered with a protective waxlike coating, which gives the fiber a somewhat adhesive quality (see Figure 1-1*a*).

Because of the natural twist in cotton fiber, it may easily be spun into yarn. Some cotton fibers, however, look different under the microscope and do not have this natural twist. Such fibers have been subjected to the commercially important process of mercerization, which causes the naturally flat, twisted cotton fiber to swell and become straight, smooth, and round. The straightness of the fiber causes light to be reflected on the smooth surface and produces a lustrous effect that is commercially valuable. The resultant fabric is called *mercerized cotton* (see Figure 1-1*b*).

Flax. Under the microscope, the hairlike flax fiber shows several-sided cylindrical filaments with fine pointed ends (Figure 1-2). The filaments are cemented together at intervals in the form of markings, or nodes, by a gummy substance called *pectin*. The long flax filaments contain a lumen, or inner canal, which appears as a narrow line. The fiber somewhat resembles a straight, smooth bamboo stick, with its joints producing a slight natural unevenness that cannot be eliminated. Chemically, the flax fiber is composed of about 70 percent cellulose and about 25 percent pectin; the remainder consists of ash and woody tissue. From such fibers, linen yarns are produced. To the naked eye, linen yarns appear smooth, straight, compact, and lustrous. Flax fibers are more brittle and less flexible than cotton fibers.

Animal Fibers

There are several animal fibers, each obtained from a different source, but only two are recognized as major textile fibers. They are *wool*, which grows from the skin of sheep, and *silk*, which is unwound from the cocoon of a moth caterpillar known as the silkworm. (Minor *hair* fibers, such as camel, llama, alpaca, mohair, cashmere, vicuña, guanaco, and rabbit, are discussed in Chapter 13.)

Wool. Wool fiber is irregular and roughly cylindrical, tapered at the end, and multicellular in structure. Under the microscope, a cross section shows three fundamental layers—the epi-

Figure 1-2   Cross-sectional and longitudinal views of linen (flax) fiber under a microscope. *(Courtesy U.S. Testing Co.)*

Figure 1-3   Cross-sectional and longitudinal views of wool fiber under a microscope. *(Courtesy American Woolen Co.)*

dermis, the cortex, and the medulla (Figure 1-3). The epidermis, or outer layer, consists of scales or flattened plates ranging from 1,000 to 4,000 to an inch. These scales give the fiber its cohesive quality. They vary in type, from those having smaller, finer scales with smoother edges to those having coarser scales with irregular edges. The finer, softer, warmer fibers have more numerous and smoother scales. The thicker, coarser, less-warm fibers have fewer and rougher scales. The better fibers with more and finer scales are duller in appearance than the poorer quality wool fibers with fewer scales.

The second layer, the cortex, is the main fiber body. It gives the fiber strength and elasticity and consists of intermediate cells that hold the color pigment.

The innermost layer is the medulla, which consists of large spiral-shaped, air-filled cells. The medulla is discernible only in coarse and medium wools and only under high magnification. It is the central canal, varying in appearance from a narrow to a broad line or from a continuous to an interrupted line. Some wool fibers that have no cortical layer are compensated with a larger propor-

tion of medullary cells. This fact lessens the affinity for dyes, because the medulla has more fat than has the rest of the fiber. The finer wools, having no medulla, absorb dyes more readily.

Two striking characteristics of wool fiber are its susceptibility to heat and its felting property, which is caused by the horny epidermal scales. Because of this felting property, only pressure, heat, and moisture are required to make wool fibers into the type of fabric called *felt*.

Chemically, wool is the only natural fiber that contains sulfur. It is composed of the following basic elements in these approximate proportions: carbon, 49 percent; oxygen, 24 percent; nitrogen, 16 percent; hydrogen, 7 percent; sulfur, 4 percent. These elements combine to form a protein known as *keratin*.

Silk.   Raw silk fiber as it comes from the cultivated cocoon is called *bave*. Under the microscope, this bave appears somewhat elliptical. It is composed of the *fibroin*, consisting of two filaments, each of which is called a *brin*, held together by *sericin*, a gummy substance that gives the bave a rather uneven surface. As the sericin is removed by hot water, the two brin filaments appear clearly as fine and

Figure 1-4 Cross-sectional and longitudinal views of silk fibers under a microscope: *(a)* cultivated silk fiber *(Courtesy U.S. Testing Co.)* and *(b)* wild, or tussah, silk fiber. *(Courtesy U.S. Department of Agriculture)*

lustrous, somewhat triangularly shaped transparent rods.

Wild silk, or tussah silk, may be distinguished from cultivated silk by its coarse, thick form, which appears flattened. Cultivated silk is a narrow fiber with no markings. Wild silk is a broader fiber with fine, wavy, longitudinal lines running across its surface, giving it a dark hue under the microscope (Figure 1-4).

Chemically, the silk fibroin and sericin are composed of approximately 95 percent protein and about 5 percent wax, fat, salts, and ash.

Mineral Fibers

Asbestos. Asbestos is a natural fiber obtained from varieties of rock. It is a fibrous form of silicate of magnesium and calcium, containing iron, aluminum, and other minerals. It is discussed in detail in Chapter 27.

THE MAN-MADE FIBERS

Cellulosic Fibers

The three types of man-made cellulosic fibers—rayon, acetate, and triace-

tate—are derived either from the cellulose of the cell walls of short cotton fibers (called linters) or, more frequently, from pine wood. Pure cellulose appears as a formless white substance that is converted by chemical treatment and produced into fiber form. Paper, for instance, is almost pure cellulose.

Rayon. There are three varieties of rayon now commercially produced: viscose, cuprammonium, and high wetmodulus. These fibers have a glasslike luster under the microscope and appear to have a uniform diameter when viewed longitudinally. (The appearance of fine pepperlike particles on a cross-sectional view is an indication that the rayon has been delustered.) The rayon filaments differ in appearance according to the process used in their manufacture (Figure 1-5).

Viscose rayon, although produced in several forms, basically has a cross-sectional view under the microscope that is very irregular. These irregularities or wrinkles run the length of the fiber and appear as striations or fine lines in the longitudinal view on an otherwise glossy surface.

Viscose rayon is also produced in modified forms. *A high-tenacity* rayon fiber can be produced by causing the

Figure 1-5   Cross-sectional and longitudinal views of varieties of rayon: *(a)* dull viscose rayon *(Courtesy U.S. Testing Co.)*, *(b)* Krispglo bright viscose rayon *(Courtesy American Enka Co.)*, *(c)* Skyloft bright viscose rayon (cross section only), *(d)* cuprammonium rayon *(Courtesy U.S. Testing Co.)*, *(e)* Suprenka bright viscose rayon, (cross section only) *(Courtesy U.S. Testing Co.)*, *(f)* Avril high wet-modulus rayon *(Courtesy American Viscose Corp.)*, *(g)* Zantrel high wet-modulus rayon. *(Courtesy American Enka Co.)*

cellulose to coagulate rapidly, thereby forming a tough skin and making the fiber stronger. Other methods of modifying viscose rayon produce crimp in the fibers when they are treated chemically. Crimped Fibro is a trademark for one of these.

Cuprammonium rayon shows no markings; it is a fine, smooth, glossy fiber. The cross-sectional appearance is nearly round.

High wet-modulus rayon is another form of rayon. This type does not weaken significantly when wet, as ordinary viscose rayon does. This process is done by controlling the molecular structure to give maximum chain length and regularity in a fibril structure. There are two of

Figure 1-6   Cross-sectional and longitudinal views of *(a)* acetate fiber *(Courtesy U.S. Testing Co.)* and *(b)* dull acetate fiber *(Courtesy Celanese Fibers Marketing Co.)*

these rayons manufactured under the trademarks of Avril and Zantrel.

Under the microscope, Avril high wet-modulus rayon more closely resembles cuprammonium rayon than viscose. The fiber is relatively smooth, and its cross section is almost round. Zantrel is almost round to oval with dark flecks that give it a duller appearance.

Acetate. This fiber consists of a cellulose compound identified as an acetylated cellulose–a cellulose salt. As a result, acetate possesses different qualities from the rayons. The fiber comes in bright, semidull, and dull forms. Generally, the cross-sectional view of acetate is less irregular than viscose rayon, and it has a rather bulbous appearance with indentations. These indentations appear as occasional line markings or striations in the longitudinal view. The cross section can be regulated during the manufacturing process to produce flat or Y shapes. These changes vary the appearance and hand of the fiber (Figure 1-6).

Triacetate. This fiber consists of an acetylated cellulose that retains acetic groupings when it is being produced as triacetate cellulose. Its qualities are

therefore different from those of acetate. The cross-sectional view is much like that of the acetate fiber—bulbous with indentations. The longitudinal view appears straight and smooth, but it has heavy lines caused by the grooves in the surface. The fiber comes in both bright and dull forms (Figure 1-7). Arnel is a trademark for a triacetate fiber.

Synthetic Long-Chain Polymers

This group of fibers is distinguished by being synthesized or created from various elements into large molecules which are called *linear polymers* because they are connected in linklike fashion. The molecules of each particular compound are arranged in parallel lines or rows in the fiber, similar to the way fibers are arranged in yarn. This arrangement of molecules is called *molecular orientation*. The properties of such fibers are dependent upon their chemical compositions and kinds of molecular orientation. There are several distinct varieties of synthetic long-chain polymers. The fiber definitions that follow were set forth by the Federal Trade Commission in accordance with the Textile Fiber Products Identification Act.

Figure 1-7   Cross-sectional and longitudinal views of *(a)* triacetate and *(b)* dull triacetate *(Courtesy Celanese Fibers Marketing Co.)*

Nylon.   Nylon is a manufactured fiber in which the fiber-forming substance is any long-chain synthetic polyamide in which less than 85 percent of the amide linkages are attached directly to two aromatic rings. The elements carbon, oxygen, nitrogen, and hydrogen are combined by chemical processes into compounds which react to form long-chain molecules, known chemically as polyamides, and are then formed into fibers. There are several forms of nylon; each depends upon the particular chemical synthesis. They are nylon 4, 6, 6,6, 6,10, 6,12, 8, 10, and 11. There may be different types within each of these forms of nylon. For example, one trademark of nylon 6 is Cantrece, a bicomponent in which two varieties of nylon adhere as one.

While there are variations in the production of nylon, the basic microscopic appearance is generally fine, round, smooth, and translucent. It is produced in multilobal cross-sectional types also. It can be highly lustrous. If the nylon is semidull or dull, it will appear to be speckled under the microscope (see Figure 1-8).

Aramid.   Aramid is a manufactured fiber in which the fiber-forming substance is a long-chain synthetic polyamide in which at least 85 percent of the amide linkages are attached directly to two aromatic rings. This definition indicates a relationship to nylon; the difference is in the percentage of linkage of the carbon, oxygen, nitrogen, and hydrogen amide groups directly attached to the two aromatic rings. Aramid fibers are produced in different forms, each dependent upon the particular percentage of linkage or chemical synthesis. The fibers are smooth and straight but the cross section may be either round or peanut-shaped. Nomex and Kevlar are two trademarks for aramid fibers which are produced by Du Pont (see Figure 1-9).

Polyester.   Polyester is a manufactured fiber in which the fiber-forming substance is any long-chain synthetic polymer composed of at least 85 percent by weight of an ester of a substituted aromatic carboxylic acid, including but not restricted to substituted terephthalate units and para-substituted hydroxy-benzoate units. In producing such fibers, the basic elements of carbon, oxygen, and hydrogen are polymerized. Variations are possible in the methods of production, in the combination of ingredients,

Figure 1-8 Cross-sectional and longitudinal views of various kinds of nylon: (a) Enkalure bright nylon and (b) Enkalure II bright antisoil nylon (cross section only), (Courtesy American Enka Co.), (c) bright nylon and (d) semidull nylon (Courtesy E. I. du Pont de Nemours & Co.), (e) Enkaloft semidull nylon (cross section only) (Courtesy American Enka Co.), (f) Antron nylon (Courtesy E. I. du Pont de Nemours & Co.), (g) dull nylon 6 (cross section only) (Courtesy American Enka Co.), (h) "T" carpet fiber nylon. (Courtesy Celanese Fiber Co.)

Figure 1-9   Cross-sectional and longitudinal views of Nomex aramid. (Courtesy E. I. du Pont de Nemours & Co.)

and in the ultimate molecular structures of the fiber-forming substance. In general, polyester fibers are smooth and straight and the cross section is round (see Figure 1-10). But this general appearance may be altered to achieve certain characteristics, such as texture or light reflection. Sometimes the polyester fibers are speckled, indicating a delusterant. Avlin, Dacron, Trevira, Fortrel, and Kodel are examples of trademarks for polyester fibers.

Figure 1-10   Cross-sectional and longitudinal views of various kinds of polyesters: *(a)* Dacron and *(b)* Dacron (Type 62), *(Courtesy E. I. du Pont de Nemours & Co.)*, *(c)* Fortrel *(Courtesy Celanese Fibers Marketing Co.)*, *(d)* Kodel *(Courtesy Eastman Chemical Products, Inc.)*, *(e)* Blue "C" (longitudinal view only) *(Courtesy Monsanto Textiles Co.)*, *(f)* Enka *(Courtesy American Enka Co.)*, *(g)* Fiber 200, *(h)* "T" Carpet fiber (cross section only), *(i)* Eight-pointed star polyester (cross section only) *(Courtesy American Enka Company)*, *(j)* round polyester fiber (cross section only) *(Courtesy Hoechst Fibers Inc.)*, and *(k)* Pentalobal polyester fiber (cross section only) *(Courtesy Hoechst Fibers Inc.)*.

Figure 1-11   Cross-sectional and longitudinal views of various kinds of acrylics: *(a)* Acrilan *(Courtesy Monsanto Textile Co.), (b)* Orlon (staple) *(Courtesy E. I. du Pont de Nemours & Co.), (c)* Orlon (Type 42) and *(d)* Orlon (Type 21) *(Courtesy E. I. du Pont de Nemours & Co.), (e)* Creslan *(Courtesy American Cyanamid Co.), (f)* Zefran *(Courtesy Dow Badische Co.).*

Acrylic.   Acrylic is a manufactured fiber in which the fiber-forming substance is any long-chain synthetic polymer composed of at least 85 percent by weight of acrylonitrile units. By complicated processes, carbon, hydrogen, and nitrogen, the basic elements, are usually synthesized with small amounts of other chemicals (to improve the fiber's ability to absorb dyes) into large polymer combinations. Variations are possible in the methods of production, in the combination of ingredients, and in the ultimate molecular structures of the fiber-forming substance (see Figure 1-11). Varieties of acrylics are identified by such trademarks as Acrilan, Creslan, Orlon, and Zefran. Each of these has its own modifications, which have special properties to suit particular purposes.

Acrilan acrylic has a bean-shaped cross section; its longitudinal appearance is straight and smooth. It may be bright or semidull with speckles.

Orlon acrylic has a somewhat flat, dog-bone cross section; its longitudinal view is rather flat and smooth. Orlon is a semidull fiber.

Creslan acrylic fiber has an almost round cross section; its longitudinal appearance is straight and smooth. It may be bright or semidull with speckles.

Zefran acrylic fiber is composed primarily of acrylonitrile with a copolymer. Its cross section is almost round; its longitudinal appearance is smooth and straight. It may be bright or semidull with speckles.

Modacrylic.   Modacrylic is a manufactured fiber in which the fiber-forming substance is any long-chain synthetic

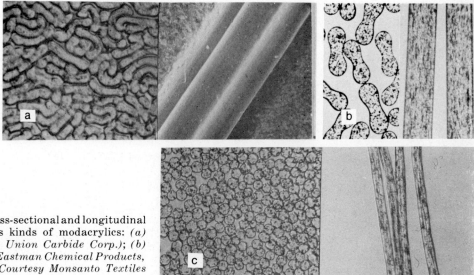

Figure 1-12 Cross-sectional and longitudinal views of various kinds of modacrylics: *(a) Dynel (Courtesy Union Carbide Corp.)*; *(b) Verel (Courtesy Eastman Chemical Products, Inc.)*; *(c) SEF (Courtesy Monsanto Textiles Co.)*.

polymer composed of less than 85 percent but at least 35 percent by weight of acrylonitrile units. As the definition indicates, variations are possible in producing this type of fiber. Modacrylics are made from resins that are copolymers or combinations of acrylonitrile and other compounds, such as vinyl chloride, vinylidene chloride, or vinylidene dicyanide. These chemicals are made of such elements as carbon, hydrogen, nitrogen, and chlorine, which are obtained from natural gas, coal, air, salt, and water. Trademarks of three modacrylics are Dynel, Verel, and SEF, which, in turn, have modifications (see Figure 1-12). A fourth modacrylic trademark is Elura, which is used for wigs.

Dynel modacrylic fiber is partly an acrylic and partly a vinyl chloride. The fibers are produced in several types and may vary slightly in shape from flat to dog-bone and oval; the surface is smooth. The fiber is semidull.

Verel modacrylic fiber is partly an acrylic and partly an undisclosed copolymer. It is produced in several types. The cross section is dog-bone, and the longitudinal view is straight and smooth. The fiber may be bright or dull.

SEF modacrylic fiber, a modification of Acrilan acrylic fiber, is semibright. The precise composition is not provided by the manufacturer.

Spandex. Spandex is a manufactured fiber in which the fiber-forming substance is a long-chain synthetic polymer comprised of at least 85 percent of a segmented polyurethane. As the definition indicates, variations are possible in producing this type of fiber. The basic elements of nitrogen, hydrogen, carbon, and oxygen are synthesized with other substances to ethyl ester compounds in polymer chains of soft segments or sections that provide stretch and hard segments that hold the chains together.

Figure 1-13   Cross-sectional and longitudinal views of varieties of spandex fibers: *(a)* Glospan (cross section only) *(Courtesy Globe Manufacturing Co.),* *(b)* Lycra (cross section only) *(Courtesy E. I. du Pont de Nemours & Co.),* and *(c)* Numa *(Courtesy American Cyanamid Co.)*

Trademarks of four varieties are Cleerspan, Glospan, Lycra, and Numa. The fibers are white and opaque with the exception of Cleerspan, which is translucent (see Figure 1-13).

Cleerspan spandex in cross section is a group of irregular-shaped clear filaments that are fused together at points of contact, which gives it a spongelike appearance. In longitudinal view, the fused multifilaments appear as a single straight fiber.

Glospan spandex looks similar to Cleerspan except that the multifilaments are more compactly fused, which gives a more solid appearance.

Lycra spandex also appears in cross section to be fused multifilaments. The individual filaments are speckled and dog-bone in shape. The longitudinal view is straight.

Numa spandex has a cross section showing fused, irregular-shaped filaments. These filaments tend to have minimal contact with each other, giving a more open appearance between them than exists in the other spandex fibers.

Olefin.   Olefin is a manufactured fiber in which the fiber-forming substance is any long-chain synthetic polymer composed of at least 85 percent by weight of ethylene, propylene, or other olefin units. As the definition indicates, variations are possible in producing this type of fiber. The carbon-hydrogen chains polymerized to produce this fiber are obtained from the cracking of petroleum. Polyethylene, the original olefin fiber, has been superseded by polypropylene.

Several types of polypropylene fibers are produced under different trademarks. Under the microscope, they are quite similar in basic appearance. The usual cross section of the fiber is relatively round, and the longitudinal view is straight and smooth. Some types may have speckles in both views, which indicates a delusterant. The cross section may be altered to give a desired appearance and hand to the fiber (see Figure 1-14).

Saran.   Saran is a manufactured fiber in which the fiber-forming substance is any

Figure 1-14 Cross-sectional and longitudinal views of an olefin fiber (Herculon polypropylene): *(a)* standard, *(b)* trilobal, and *(c)* delta. *(Courtesy Hercules, Inc.)*

long-chain synthetic polymer composed of at least 80 percent by weight of vinylidene chloride units. As the definition indicates, variations are possible in producing this fiber. Originally, it was produced as a copolymer of vinylidene chloride and vinyl chloride synthesized

Figure 1-15 Cross-sectional and longitudinal views of saran fiber. *(Courtesy Dow Badische Co.)*

from ethylene (from petroleum) and chlorine (from the salt of seawater). The fiber is smooth, round, and translucent (see Figure 1-15).

Vinyon. Vinyon is a manufactured fiber in which the fiber-forming substance is any long-chain synthetic polymer composed of at least 85 percent by weight of vinyl chloride units. This fiber is produced through the synthesis of the basic materials of chlorine, carbon, and hydrogen that are derived from salt water and petroleum. Variations are produced from copolymers (see Figure 1-16).

This fiber is limited to industrial use and to certain bonded fabric applications for consumer use since it has a very low melting point. It is consequently not treated in any detail in this text.

Figure 1-16 Cross-sectional and longitudinal views of vinyon fiber. *(Courtesy FMC Corp.)*

Novoloid. This is a generic term recently established by the Federal Trade Commission for any manufactured fiber containing at least 85 percent by weight of a cross-linked novolac. The composition is that of a phenolic aldehyde. The originator of this kind of fiber is the Carborundum Co., which manufactures Kynol novoloid fiber. It is produced in crimped and staple form for spun yarn for specialized industrial and uniform purposes. Because of this presently limited use, this fiber is not discussed further in this text.

Fluorocarbon. This fiber is polymerized from fluorspar and chloroform and is sold under Du Pont's trademark, Teflon. It is extremely difficult to dye and has excellent resistance to chemicals, mildew, bacteria, and insects. Another type is Halar, developed by Allied Chemical Corp. It has been found to have greater strength and better dyeability. Fluorocarbon is used primarily for industrial applications rather than for consumer fabric uses. Consequently, it is not defined under the Textile Fiber Products Identification Act and is not discussed further in this text.

Matrix Fiber. A matrix fiber is defined by the Federal Trade Commission as "a manufactured textile fiber that is essentially a physical combination or mixture of two or more chemically distinct constituents or components combined at or prior to the time of extrusion (i.e., produced in fiber form), which components if separately extruded would each fall within different definitions of textile fibers." Note that the matrix fiber is a physical *mixture* of its components. It therefore differs from bicomponent and biconstituent fibers which are comprised of two or more chemically distinct compositions. Both components of these fibers are whole but adhere to each other to form one fiber (pp. 61–62).

The first commercially produced matrix fiber is marketed under the trademark of Cordelan and manufactured by Kohjin International Corporation of Japan. This fiber should be labeled Cordelan matrix fiber (50% vinal, 50% vinyon). It is interesting to note that separately each component does not have the combination of required properties to be suitable for general consumer use. Yet, in matrix form this mixture gives Cordelan built-in flame resistance (though it is not flameproof), makes it self-extinguishing when removed from the flame, and provides other qualities which make it suitable for sleepwear and other kinds of garments.

The matrix fibers cannot be classified according to their appearance and characteristics as can other types of fibers which are treated in this book.

Graft Fiber. The Federal Trade Commission has been considering the classification or identification of manufactured fibers which are essentially graft copolymers. The proposal provides that where a fiber is "a graft copolymer, the components of which, if appearing as separate fibers, would each fall within different existing definitions of textile fibers as set forth...[in its rules], the fiber content disclosure as to such fiber shall... set out the components contained in the fiber by appropriate generic names specified... in order of their predominance by weight and... set out the respective percentages of such components by weight." An example of the proper way to label these fibers is 100% Graft Fiber [70% Acrylic, 30% Azlon].

The first commercially produced graft fiber is marketed under the trademark of Chinon and manufactured by Toyobo Co., Ltd., of Japan. It is a co-polymer graft fiber. According to the company it is made of 25 to 60 percent by weight of casein protein, and 40 to 75 percent by weight of vinyl monomer units, of which at least one-half by weight are acrylonitrile units.

The difference between the graft and matrix fibers is that the two or more components of the graft fiber are molecularly bonded to form a chemical hybrid from which the components cannot be subsequently isolated or regenerated by physical or chemical means. It is apparent that the appearances and characteristics of such graft fibers have limitless unique possibilities, although their present development and commercial production are in early stages and are relatively minimal. Consequently, further discussion is not provided in this text.

Mineral Fibers

Natural minerals such as silica sand, limestone, soda ash, borax, boric acid, feldspar, and fluorspar have been fused under very high temperatures into glass which can be processed into fiber.

Glass. Glass is a manufactured fiber in which the fiber-forming substance is glass. The fiber is smooth, round, translucent, highly lustrous, and quite flexible (see Figure 1-17). A well-known trademark is Fiberglas.

Figure 1-17 Cross-sectional and longitudinal views of glass fiber. *(Courtesy Owens-Corning Fiberglas Corp.)*

Ceramic. A new group of fibers not classified by the FTC is that of ceramic fibers. Most information regarding production and specific properties is lacking. The fibers are multifilament, are highly heat-resistant, and show excellent promise for aerospace applications. Two trademarks are Avceram and Fiberfrax.

Graphite. A fiber made from carbon derived from a cellulosic fiber, such as rayon, is produced for such highly specialized purposes as reinforcement in airplane and rocket structures, as well as for golf-stick shanks. Thornel and Magnamite are trademarks of such fibers.

Metallic Fibers

Metallic fiber is a manufactured fiber composed of metal, plastic-coated metal, metal-coated plastic, or a core completely covered by metal. This fiber is usually produced in flat, narrow, smooth strips with a gleaming luster.

Rubber Fibers

Rubber fiber is a manufactured fiber in which the fiber-forming substance is comprised of natural or synthetic rubber. The treated rubber is produced in cylindrical form, so that the cross-sectional view is round and the longitudinal surface is relatively smooth.

REVIEW QUESTIONS

1. Name five industries that are dependent upon or related to the textile industry, and indicate how they are related.
2. Name five areas of employment in the textile industry.
3. How can good knowledge of textiles be of value to the consumer?
4. (a) What are the two major groups of natural fibers? (b) Identify the fibers and their sources in each group.
5. What is meant by *generic fiber name*?
6. (a) Group the man-made fibers according to basic composition. (b) Identify the fibers in each group.
7. What is the difference between man-made fibers of natural nonfibrous substances and natural fibers?
8. How does the composition of man-made fibers of natural nonfibrous substances differ from man-made synthetic fibers?
9. (a) What are the basic provisions of the Textile Fiber Products Identification Act? (b) Who administers the law?

SUGGESTED ACTIVITY

Prepare a chart with drawings of the microscopic views of each of the man-made fibers.

2
TESTING FIBERS

identification of textiles

The Textile Fiber Products Identification Act requires that the manufacturers of cloth garments and household textiles attach labels to their products specifying the fiber content. These manufacturers are expected to know this information since it is they who tell the fabric producers the requirements for the fabrics they intend to purchase. Should a product manufacturer want to identify or verify the fiber content himself, he must be in a position to either make the appropriate technical analysis or refer samples to a testing laboratory.

The retailer, in turn, is held responsible under the act to see that labels or hangtags are attached to the textile products before he sells them. He must therefore rely on his vendor to provide him with properly labeled merchandise. Sometimes imported merchandise arrives unlabeled or sometimes labels become detached and lost. It is then the merchant's responsibility to have appropriate labels made and to attach them to the merchandise. Ready recognition and identification of fiber content in fabrics has become extremely difficult even for

knowledgeable and experienced merchants because of the growing variety of types of fibers, the blending techniques in yarn and fabric construction, and the finishes that affect the appearance and hand of the fabrics. If the fabric producer cannot provide the merchant with reliable information, he must either rely upon certain tests (performed readily, in some instances), send samples to his own testing bureau, or utilize the services of a testing company.

The consumer has the greatest handicap in identifying fiber content of fabrics. Should he lose the identification and/or care labels from a textile product, he may not know the composition of the fabric and therefore not know what to expect of it. Because he is usually not in a position to make a laboratory analysis, he must rely, insofar as he can, upon certain nontechnical tests.

THE NONTECHNICAL TESTS

There are several methods that do not require any special equipment for identifying textile fibers. Although they have certain limitations, they are useful because they are simple to perform and, under certain circumstances, provide ready identification.

Feeling Test

The feeling test requires perception if it is to be of any value. Skilled perception is acquired only after handling many different fabrics over a period of time. To understand what is meant by *feeling* a fabric, place your finger on a sample of wool. The heat generated by the finger remains in the area because wool is a nonconductor of heat. Consequently, wool fabric feels warm to the touch. If your finger is placed on a sample composed of the vegetable fibers—that is, cotton, linen, or even rayon—the heat of the finger passes off because such fibers are conductors of heat. These fabrics, therefore, feel cool to the touch. Limitations of this test become apparent as we examine and compare fabrics of different fiber contents.

Cotton. Cotton is cool to the touch and feels soft and inelastic.

Linen. Linen is cold and smooth and has a leathery feel.

Wool. Wool is warm to the touch and feels elastic and springy.

Silk. Silk is warm to the touch and feels smooth and elastic.

Rayons. Rayon filament fabrics feel cool, smooth, inelastic, and generally lack the body of silk. The staple fabrics may be given various textural qualities of the natural fibers but they generally lack their "life."

Acetate. Acetate filament fabrics feel smoother, a little warmer, more elastic, and more resilient than rayon. They also have more body and draping quality. The staple fabrics feel very much like rayon but may have a little more warmth and resilience.

Triacetate. Triacetate fabrics have the feel of acetate but are more resilient.

Nylon. Nylon filament fabrics feel very smooth, lightweight, elastic, quite resilient. Draping quality is good. Staple fabrics have a woollike hand.

Aramid. Aramid filament fabrics feel very much like nylon but tend to be stiffer and have less draping quality. The staple fabrics may either have a cottonlike or woollike texture but have a smoother hand.

Polyesters. Polyester filament fabrics feel very much like nylon but tend to be stiffer and, therefore, have less draping quality. The staple fabrics may have either a cottonlike or woollike texture. The cottonlike texture is smoother and a bit more slippery than fine cotton, and it is very resilient.

Acrylics. Acrylic fibers have the feel of wool but are much lighter in weight. Depending upon the manner of spinning the yarn, they may feel as soft as cashmere. Generally, they have a slippery or slick feeling that the natural fibers do not have.

Modacrylics. Although modacrylic fibers may be slightly stiffer than acrylics, they are actually very difficult to distinguish by feel.

Spandex. Since fabrics containing spandex fiber are usually made with other fibers, the fabric may have the feel of any of the other fibers. Such fabrics will have the additional characteristic of elasticity in the direction that the spandex fiber is running.

Olefins. Olefin fibers are extremely lightweight and very resilient. The hand of the polypropylene fiber is similar to that of the polyesters.

Saran. Saran fabrics are heavy, smooth, flexible, with a typical plastic feel.

Vinyon. Vinyon fabrics feel somewhat like saran fabrics.

Glass. Glass fabrics made of filament fibers are heavy, smooth, and somewhat lustrous. Fabrics made of staple have a soft, cottonlike hand.

Metal. Metal fibers have an obvious metallic luster and are smooth, flat, ribbonlike, and very flexible.

Rubber. Rubber fiber may be readily confused with spandex, depending on how it is made into yarn. However, rubber is much heavier.

Burning Test

To recognize the composition of fabrics by the burning test, the sample of fiber, yarn, or fabric should be moved slowly toward a small flame and the reaction to the heat carefully observed. One end of the sample should then be put directly into the flame to determine its burning rate and characteristics. After it is removed from the flame, the burning characteristics should continue to be observed and the burning odor noted. After the sample has cooled, the ash should be examined for characteristics such as amount, form, hardness, and color (see Table 2-1).

If both the lengthwise and the crosswise yarns in a fabric are known to be of the same substance, the sample may be tested as a whole. More than one kind of yarn, however, is sometimes used in a fabric. When the presence of different yarns is suspected, the lengthwise yarns should be separated from the crosswise yarns and each set should be tested separately. When it is believed that more than one fiber has been blended into a single yarn, the yarn should be untwisted and, with the aid of a magnifying glass and tweezers, the individual fibers separated. However, if biconstituent fibers (see page 62) are used, this is not possible.

One should also be alert to the possibility that finishing agents may have been used on the fabrics. These finishes can change the burning characteristics of the sample.

Special varieties of man-made fibers have also been developed. They are flame retardant and therefore cannot be adequately tested for identification by burning. Examples of these fibers are PFR rayon, Acele FLR acetate, Dacron FLR polyester, and SEF modacrylic.

Cotton. Cotton yarn blazes quickly when it comes in contact with the flame

Table 2-1

BURNING TESTS

NATURAL FIBERS

FIBER	APPROACHING FLAME	IN FLAME	REMOVED FROM FLAME	ODOR	ASH
COTTON	Scorches; ignites readily	Burns quickly; yellow flame	Continues to burn rapidly; has afterglow	Burning paper	Light, feathery, grayish; black ash denotes mercerized cotton
LINEN	Scorches; ignites easily	Yellow flame burns slower than cotton if yarns are heavier	Continues to burn	Burning paper	Feathery, gray ash
WOOL	Smolders	Small, slow flickering flame; sizzles and curls	Ceases flaming	Like burning feathers or hair	Crisp dark ash; irregular shape; crushes easily
SILK (pure dye)	Smolders	Burns; melts slowly; sputters	Supports combustion with difficulty; ceases flaming	Like burning feathers or hair, but less pronounced than wool	Round, crisp, shiny black beads; easily crushed
SILK (weighted)	Smolders	Burns with a glow	Burned part becomes briefly incandescent; then chars	Like burning feathers or hair	Screenlike skeleton of original sample

MAN-MADE FIBERS

FIBER	APPROACHING FLAME	IN FLAME	REMOVED FROM FLAME	ODOR	ASH
RAYONS Viscose Cuprammonium High Wet-Modulus	Scorches; ignites quickly	Burns quickly; yellow flame	Continues to burn; no afterglow as with cotton	Burning paper	Light, gray, feathery
ACETATE	Fuses away from flame; turns black	Flames quickly; fabric puckers, sputters, melts, drips like burning tar	Continues to burn and melt	Like vinegar	Brittle, hard, irregular black ash, difficult to crush
TRIACETATE Arnel	Fuses away from flame; turns black	Flames quickly; fabric puckers, sputters, melts, drips like burning tar	Continues to burn and melt	Like vinegar	Brittle, hard, irregular black ash, difficult to crush
NYLON	Fuses and shrinks away from flame	Burns slowly with melting	Flame diminishes and tends to die out	Somewhat like celery	Hard, round, tough, gray bead

Table 2-1

BURNING TESTS *(Continued)*				

MAN-MADE FIBERS

FIBER	APPROACHING FLAME	IN FLAME	REMOVED FROM FLAME	ODOR	ASH
ARAMID Nomex	Shrinks away from flame	Puckers and chars over 700°F	Self-extinguishing	None	Hard, black bead
POLYESTER	Fuses and shrinks away from flame	Burns slowly with melting	Burns with difficulty	Slightly sweetish	Hard, round, brittle, black bead
ACRYLICS Orlon	Fuses and shrinks away from flame	Flames rapidly; fabric puckers, sputters, melts	Continues to burn and melt	Faintly like burning meat	Brittle, hard, irregular, black bead
Acrilan	Fuses and shrinks away from flame	Flames rapidly and melts	Continues to burn and melt	Burning steak	Brittle, hard, irregular, black bead
Creslan	Fuses and shrinks away from flame	Flames and melts	Continues to burn and melt	Sharp sweet	Brittle, hard, irregular, black bead
Zefran	Fuses and melts	Sputters slightly; flames	Continues to burn and melt	Turmeric-like	Irregular black ash that crushes easily
MODACRYLICS Dynel	Fuses and shrinks away from flame	Burns very slowly with melting	Self-extinguishing	Sharp sweet	Brittle, hard, irregular, black bead
Verel	Fuses and shrinks away from flame	Burns very slowly with melting	Self-extinguishing	Sharp, similar to burning gun powder	Brittle, hard irregular, black bead
SEF	Fuses and shrinks away from flame	Shrinks, melts, smolders	Self-extinguishing	Sharp sweet	Hard, irregular, black bead
SPANDEX	Fuses but does not shrink away from flame	Burns with melting	Continues to burn with melting	Acrid	Soft, fluffy, black
OLEFIN Polypropyl- ene	Fuses, shrinks, and curls away from flame	Melts; burns slowly	Burns slowly with difficulty	Faintly like burning asphalt	Hard, round, light tan bead
SARAN	Fuses and shrinks away from flame	Burns very slowly with melting	Self-extinguishing	Acrid, sweet	Hard, black, irregular bead
VINYON	Fuses and shrinks away from flame	Burns very slowly with melting	Self-extinguishing	Sweet	Hard, black, irregular bead
GLASS	No reaction	Will not burn, melts at over 1500°F	Hardens	None	Hardens to glass

Table 2-1

BURNING TESTS *(Continued)*

MAN-MADE FIBERS

FIBER	APPROACHING FLAME	IN FLAME	REMOVED FROM FLAME	ODOR	ASH
METAL	No reaction, but coating may react as the polyester Dacron does	No reaction, but coating may react as the polyester Dacron does	No reaction, but coating may react as the polyester Dacron does	No reaction, but coating may react as the polyester Dacron does	Metallic ribbon
RUBBER	Smolders	Melts and shrivels away from flame	Self-extinguishing	Very disagreeable and pungent	Hard, brittle, black, irregular bead

because the cellulose ingredient is highly inflammable. The ash is light and feathery and has a vegetable odor similar to that of burned paper; mercerized cotton produces a black ash. Because cotton is highly inflammable, do not use cotton where its proximity to flame becomes a fire hazard unless it is treated with a fire-retardant finish.

Linen. Linen, when burned, produces an ash similar to cotton ash because both fabrics are of vegetable substance. Linen ash is also light and feathery and has the odor of burned paper. Although linen fabric burns somewhat more slowly than cotton because linen yarns are heavier, the pace of burning is not sufficiently different to aid in distinguishing linen from cotton.

Wool. Wool is slow to ignite and has a characteristic small, slow, flickering flame that sizzles and curls (see Figure 2-1). It can be extinguished easily, as the fabric ceases flaming when the fire is withdrawn. Wool ash is dark and crisp, and it falls into an irregular shape that can be crushed easily. The ash has a

strong animal odor resembling burning feathers or hair, which indicates the presence of an animal substance or of a fiber obtained from an animal. The characteristic odor of burned wool is due to the sulfur ingredient.

Figure 2-1 Wool does not burn readily. When the heat becomes sufficiently high, wool will smolder with a small, flickering flame. The fabric sizzles and curls. The ash is black, irregular, and crisp. (All the illustrations in this chapter are *Courtesy U.S. Department of Agriculture*)

a   b

Figure 2-2 *(a)* Pure silk burns with a small flame that soon dies, leaving an ash in the form of small, brittle, shiny black balls along the edge of the fabric. *(b)* Weighted silk burns without showing a visible flame. It chars and leaves a coherent ash, a skeleton of the original fabric.

Silk.   Pure silk also burns slowly and ceases flaming when the fire is withdrawn (see Figure 2-2a). The ash of silk appears in the form of round, crisp, shiny black beads that, like the ash of wool, can be crushed easily with the fingers. The ash has an animal odor less pronounced than that of wool, as silk does not contain sulfur.

In manufacturing, additional body is given to silk fabrics by weighting them with metallic fillers. Weighted silk burns without showing a visible flame. The burned part becomes incandescent; it chars and gradually smolders away, leaving a coherent ash that is a screen-like skeleton of the original fabric (see Figure 2-2b). The odor of the ash of weighted silk is similar to that of pure silk.

Rayons.   Like cotton, the rayons ignite quickly unless they either are fire-retardant types or are given a fire-retardant finish. They burn with a bright yellow flame, sometimes more rapidly than cotton because rayons are essentially purified cellulose. The odor of burning viscose, cuprammonium, and high wet-modulus rayons is like that of burning paper, also a cellulosic product. The ash disintegrates unless the fiber has been chemically dulled.

Acetate.   Acetate blazes as it burns. The edge of the fabric puckers and curls as the material fuses and melts into a hard mass (see Figure 2-3). Acetate sputters and drips like tar. The ash of acetate is hard and brittle, and is difficult to crush between the fingers. Because of the acetic acid used in the manufacture of acetate, the ash has an acid odor similar to that of vinegar.

Triacetate.   Triacetate is similar to acetate in both its chemical composition and its reaction to heat and flame. It flames quickly and then melts into a hard mass. As triacetate burns, it drips like burning

Figure 2-3 Acetate blazes as it burns. The fabric puckers, curls, and fuses into an irregular black residue that hardens when cooled.

tar. The ash is hard and brittle and has an acid odor like that of vinegar.

Nylon.   Nylon melts before it burns. As it burns, it shrinks from the flame and forms a hard, round bead that cannot be crushed between the fingers. While burning, it has a pungent odor.

Aramids.   The aramid fibers are highly flame-resistant. At temperatures above 700 degrees Fahrenheit, Nomex, for example, shrinks away from the flame. It puckers and chars but will self-extinguish when the flame is removed. The residue is hard.

Polyesters.   The polyesters fuse and shrink from the flame. They melt and burn slowly in the flame; when they are removed, they burn with difficulty. Kodel produces a slight soot. Dacron has a slightly sweetish odor; Kodel smells

faintly like burning pine tar. The ashes of polyesters are hard, round, black, and beady.

Acrylics.   The acrylic fibers Orlon, Acrilan, and Creslan melt, shrink away from the flame, fuse, and burn leaving a brittle, black, irregular-shaped bead. Their rate of burning is between that of cotton and acetate. Orlon gives off an odor that faintly resembles burning flesh; Acrilan smells a little stronger, like burning steak; Creslan has a sharp, sweet odor. Zefran flames rapidly and sputters slightly. The edges curl as the fabric blazes, leaving a black ash that can be crushed easily between the fingers. The odor is somewhat like the herb turmeric.

Modacrylics.   The modacrylic fibers, Dynel, Verel, and SEF, will not support combustion and do not flame. They melt, shrink away from the flame, and harden into a brittle ash. Dynel gives off a sharp, sweet odor; Verel has a sharp odor similar to that of burning condite or gunpowder.

Spandex.   Elastic yarns are usually combined with yarns of other fibers or are encased in a layer of other fibers. In both instances, the spandex fiber must be separated. Spandex fibers melt, fuse, and burn without shrinking away from the flame; they leave a soft, fluffy, black ash and give off an acrid odor.

Olefins.   The olefins that are polypropylene also shrink, fuse, and curl away from the flame. They melt and burn slowly, giving off an odor that faintly resembles burning asphalt. They have a hard, round, light tan bead.

Saran. Saran fiber burns very slowly. It melts, fuses, and shrinks away from the flame, leaving a hard, black, irregular bead. It stops burning when removed from the flame. The smell of burning saran is like that of slightly pungent melting paraffin.

Vinyon. Vinyon fiber fuses and shrinks away from the flame. It melts and burns slowly in the flame and self-extinguishes when it is removed. It gives off a sweet odor. The ash is a hard, black, irregular bead.

Glass. Glass fiber does not burn; it melts, however, at temperatures above 1500 degrees Fahrenheit.

Metal. Metallic fibers do not burn. However, the film that covers the metal will melt and burn with a slightly sweetish odor. The residue from this film will be a brittle, beady ash.

Rubber. Rubber fiber is usually covered with another fiber that must be removed for this test. Rubber melts, shrivels away from the flame, and is self-extinguishing. It leaves a hard, irregular ash and a very disagreeable pungent odor.

Limitation of Burning Test. It is apparent that many fibers have similar burning reactions that might cause doubt and occasional confusion. Nevertheless, the burning test provides a means of preliminary examination and elimination. It will separate and identify certain types or groups of fibers for technical testing when this is necessary.

THE TECHNICAL TESTS

Where laboratory equipment is available, much more reliable testing techniques may be employed. However, these require technical knowledge and skill, particularly in handling many of the chemicals.

Microscope Test

Identification by microscope, as studied in Chapter 1, is a reliable test that can be used to distinguish the fibers. Knowing what the fibers look like under the microscope will also help you understand other identification tests. Certain manufacturing and finishing processes, such as mercerizing and delustering, affect the appearance of a fiber under the microscope. Besides, a dark-colored fabric cannot be identified under the microscope because light which is necessary for identification cannot pass through a dark substance. The dyestuff must be removed, or stripped, by the use of a bleaching chemical, which is determined by the composition of the fabric. When stripping is essential and there is considerable doubt as to the composition of fiber, chemical tests are advisable.

Chemical Tests

In addition to the microscope, chemical tests are another technical means of identifying fibers. But chemical tests are not intended for the general consumer. Their value is demonstrated, however, by the fact that some consumer magazines and retail stores have their own laboratories for testing fabrics.

There are two chemical testing methods that may effectively be used:

stain and solvent. One stain technique is the double-barreled fiber identification (DBFI) procedure developed by the Atlantic Chemical Corp. Every commonly known fiber has its own distinct two-color reactions when treated with the stain. A fiber stained at the boil in the presence of dilute acetic acid will turn to a color specific only to that fiber; when that fiber is stained in the presence of a mild alkali, such as carbonate of soda, that fiber will turn to an entirely different color that is also specific only to that fiber. This double testing technique is the reason for the designation *double-barreled* stain identification. Examples of this identification include the following: acetate turns light green in acetic acid, but orange in dilute carbonate of soda; nylon stains beige in one bath, bright red in the other. Fibers in blends may likewise be identified, even to the type of particular fiber in a generic group, e.g., Orlon Type 42 among the Orlons in the acrylic group.

The solvent method of identification has become increasingly difficult as new fibers that are chemically very similar are developed and more fibers are blended and mixed in fabrics. There is no individual solvent or chemical identification for each fiber and no single solvent procedure for separating and identifying fibers in combinations. However, testing by solvents is very effective when it is used as a technique for eliminating and cross-checking.

In order to obtain accurate results, the fabrics to be tested should be thoroughly cleaned and the finishing agents should be removed. The fabric should be unraveled, yarns untwisted, and the fibers put in as loose a form as possible.

Distinguishing Animal from Vegetable Fibers with an Alkali. As strong alkalies destroy animal substances, a 5 percent solution of lye in water ($1/2$ teaspoon of lye in a glass of water) can be used to eliminate wool and silk fibers from a sample that contains a mixture of fibers. The action of this chemical (also known as caustic soda or sodium hydroxide) is hastened by boiling the solution before the sample is immersed. The wool and silk fibers will be completely dissolved. The vegetable fibers will not be affected; therefore, another test is necessary to identify those fibers.

Distinguishing Vegetable from Animal Fibers with an Acid. As dilute acids destroy vegetable fibers, a 2 percent solution of sulfuric acid may be used to distinguish vegetable from animal fibers. A drop of the solution is placed on a sample of the fabric, which is then placed between two blotters and pressed with a hot iron. The spotted area will become charred if the fabric is cotton, linen, or rayon.

Distinguishing Linen from Cotton. Before any chemical test is made to distinguish linen from cotton, all surface dressings should be removed from the samples by boiling them for a few minutes in a solution of dilute sodium hydroxide, about $1/2$ percent. Then any of the following tests can be made:

Immersing cotton and linen samples in a 1 percent solution of fuchsin in alcohol produces a rose-red color in both samples. After the samples have been washed and then immersed in ammonia, linen retains the red coloration, but cotton does not. This test is sometimes made with a 1 percent solution of magenta, a red dyestuff.

Cotton fibers are weakened more than linen fibers if samples are immersed in concentrated sulfuric acid for two minutes. After the samples are rinsed and immersed in weak ammonia, the cotton fibers dissolve, leaving the linen fibers unaffected.

When cotton and linen samples are immersed in a solution of iodine and zinc chloride (Herzberg's stain), cotton is stained reddish purple and linen is stained blue to purple.

When samples are immersed in a caustic soda solution, cotton remains white and linen turns yellowish.

Distinguishing Silk from Wool. If the fibers in a sample are known to consist of silk and wool, and identification of each is desired, the use of concentrated cold hydrochloric acid will dissolve the silk and cause the wool fiber to swell.

Distinguishing Rayons from Acetate. A solution containing equal parts of concentrated sulfuric acid and iodine (crystals) may be used to distinguish each of the different fibers. When samples are immersed in this solution, a dark-blue coloration indicates viscose; a light-blue coloration indicates cuprammonium; a yellow coloration indicates acetate. Another test to distinguish acetate from rayon, when both types are known to be used in a fabric, is to immerse the sample in a 50 percent solution of acetic acid.

The acetate dissolves; the rayons are not affected. All rayons will dissolve in a 60 percent solution of sulfuric acid or a concentrated solution of hydrochloric acid.

Distinguishing Acetate from Other Fibers. If a sample of acetate is immersed in an 80 percent solution of acetone (a chemical used in nail polish removers), the acetate fibers will dissolve but Arnel triacetate, Dynel modacrylic, and Verel modacrylic will swell.

Distinguishing Arnel Triacetate from Other Fibers. When a specimen of fabric or a blend of fibers is immersed at room temperature for one hour in a mixture of 90 percent methylene chloride and 10 percent ethanol (or methanol), Arnel and acetate will dissolve, but other commonly used fibers will be virtually unaffected. (Dynel, however, is softened and gains weight when similarly treated.) Arnel triacetate can be differentiated from acetate by immersing a sample of fabric or fibers in benzyl alcohol at 200 degrees Fahrenheit for one hour. Arnel is virtually unaffected, but the acetate completely dissolves.

Distinguishing Nylon from Other Fibers. Nylon can be distinguished from acetate by attempting to dissolve it in acetone. Nylon will not dissolve in acetone. If the yarn or fabric is thought to contain wool and/or nylon, the fabric may be immersed in a boiling solution of sodium hydroxide. The nylon is insoluble in such a solution, but wool will dissolve. In fact, nylon's insolubility in boiling sodium hydroxide makes it easily distinguishable from most other fibers. The only common solvents in which nylon is soluble are concentrated formic acid, phenol, and cresol.

Distinguishing Nomex Aramid from Other Fibers. An adequate specific chemical test for Nomex aramid fiber has not yet been devised. However, a fiber refractive index test which may be followed by a heat exposure (oxidation) test can be used to identify the fiber. The fiber should be immersed in a fluid having a refractive index of 1.670 (the same index as that of Nomex) and placed on a microscrope slide. Viewed under the microscope as the plane of light is rotated, undyed Nomex will become either invisible or barely visible. However, since this characteristic is also true of polyester, a further determination must be made. The material should be exposed to high heat or flame. Nomex aramid will degrade and char, whereas polyester will melt, drip, and form a hard bead (p. 28).

The fiber refractive index test can also be used if the Nomex aramid fiber is dyed. If the material is dyed a light color, the fiber will fade appreciably as the plane of light is rotated. If the material is dyed a dark color, the edges of the fiber will stand out sharply (due to the opaqueness of the dye) but then will fade away as the plane of light is rotated.

Distinguishing Polyester from Other Fibers. Like acetate and nylon, polyester is soluble in hot metacresol; however, unlike acetate it is not soluble in acetone, and unlike nylon it is not soluble in concentrated formic acid.

Distinguishing Acrylics from Other Fibers. Acrylic is often blended with cotton, wool, silk, rayon, acetate, nylon, and polyester. Even when not blended, acrylic may be mistaken for some of these fibers. Since acrylic fibers will dissolve in a 70 percent solution of ammonium thiocyanate at 266 degrees Fahrenheit at the boil but the other fibers will not, this test may be used.

Distinguishing Modacrylics from Other Fibers. Although a modacrylic is often used alone, it may be blended with other fibers. It is easily distinguishable, however, from other fibers by chemical tests. It is highly resistant to a wide variety of inorganic acids, bases, salts, hydrocarbons, and most organic solvents. With the exception of SEF, 100 percent solutions of acetone, cyclohexanone, and dimethylformamide are solvents in varying degrees. Other cyclic ketones and certain amines cause some solvent or swelling action at high temperatures. SEF is insoluble in boiling acetone; it swells and is partially soluble in dimethylformamide.

Distinguishing Spandex from Other Fibers. The characteristics and appearance of spandex fibers should make them readily identifiable. However, there is sometimes some confusion with the stretch yarns, including those made from rubber. In this case, a test for spandex fiber is to heat the specimen in dimethylformamide. Spandex fiber will dissolve in the solution at 200 degrees Fahrenheit.

Distinguishing Olefins from Other Fibers. Olefin and saran fibers are soluble in metaxylene at 282 degrees Fahrenheit at the boil. To differentiate between these fibers, saran fibers are soluble in dimethylformamide but olefin fibers are not. Olefin and saran fibers can also be separated by dissolving the saran in a solution of dioxane 1,4 at 200 degrees Fahrenheit; olefin fibers will not dissolve in this solution.

Distinguishing Polyethylene Olefins from Polypropylene Olefins.

Both polypropylene and polyethylene fibers will dissolve in decalin after a few minutes at the boiling point; however, polypropylene will not dissolve in cyclohexane as polyethylene will after ten minutes at the boiling point.

Distinguishing Saran from Other Fibers.

A 100 percent solution of acetone will not affect saran. At elevated temperatures, saran will dissolve in dioxan and cyclohexanone. Saran is also soluble in ammonium hydroxide.

Distinguishing Vinyon from Other Fibers.

Solvents for Vinyon HH are a 100 percent solution of acetone and a 50 to 50 solution of acetone/carbon disulfide, chloroform, chlorobenzene, or cyclohexanone. Since these reagents are also used to identify other fibers, Vinyon HH can be distinguished only by elimination.

Distinguishing Glass Fibers from Other Fibers.

Two specific solvents for quick identification of glass fibers are hydrofluoric acid and hot phosphoric acid.

REVIEW QUESTIONS

1. Why is the identification of fibers by labeling according to their substance important?
2. List the advantages and the limitations of the burning test when it is used to differentiate cotton, linen, wool, silk, rayon, and acetate.
3. Describe three tests used to differentiate cotton and linen.
4. Describe the differences between cotton and wool in the burning test.
5. What chemical processes would you use to distinguish (a) the animal fibers from the vegetable fibers, (b) cotton from linen?
6. What two positive tests permit identification of rayon and acetate?
7. What three tests differentiate silk from rayon?
8. Compare the effect of burning on acetate and on rayon in regard to flame, odor, and ash.
9. What chemical test differentiates acetate and Arnel triacetate?
10. What chemical tests differentiate nylon from other fibers? Describe the results.
11. How can acrylic fibers be differentiated from modacrylic fibers?
12. What chemical tests would identify the polyesters?
13. What chemical tests would identify the polypropylene fibers?

14. How would you differentiate spandex from rubber and stretch nylon?
15. What will dissolve glass fiber?

SUGGESTED ACTIVITIES

1. Prepare a chart of the burning characteristics of the man-made fibers.
2. As a consumer, which tests do you consider to be useful to you? Make several tests to prove your point.

3
YARN FORMATION

fiber to yarn

Primitive people discovered that a succession of fibers could be twisted into a continuous yarn. This was probably accomplished slowly and laboriously at first, but the greater strength thus produced and the many uses soon found for articles made from continuous yarns led to the invention of hand implements to aid and improve the process of twisting and spinning. Many such implements and methods are still used by the more primitive peoples in various parts of the world as well as by persons who are interested in reviving artistic handicraft. At the same time, it was necessary to invent simple methods of disentangling, separating, and arranging the fibers according to their length, other than by just using the fingers. Thus, crude methods of carding were invented to separate the fibers according to their length of staple.

STAPLE YARNS

Yarns can be made of staple fibers by any one of several techniques. The method used is dependent upon such factors as the manufacturer's preference of equipment, the economic implications, the fibers to be used, and desired properties of the yarn to be produced. Ring spinning is the oldest and most widespread technique. Open-end spinning has become an important method. Still newer methods have been developed, and experiments to find more effective and suitable processes continue.

Conventional Ring Spinning

The value and character of a yarn are determined by (1) kind and quality of fiber; (2) amount of processing necessary to produce fineness; and (3) amount of twist, which increases tensile strength in the finished yarn. The purpose of the yarn must be anticipated, as this determines the number and kind of manufacturing operations.

The formation of yarn from staple (short) fibers by spinning becomes possible when they have surfaces capable of cohesiveness. This quality is exemplified by the convolutions of the cotton fiber, the roughness of the flax fiber, and the scales of the wool fiber. Flexibility or elasticity permits the fibers to be twisted around one another. Uniformity of staple gives yarns a required evenness and improves the quality of the yarn.

Because the production of cotton yarn lends itself to a simple description of the manufacturing operations that make staple fiber into yarn, cotton fiber has been used in this chapter to illustrate the spinning process (see Figure 3-1). It must be remembered, however, that all other staple fibers pass through spinning operations, although, of course, there are differences that will be explained in the chapters dealing with the various fibers. One such difference occurs when long strands, or filaments, such as silk, are used rather than staple. In such instances, the required number of filaments is simply twisted together in a ropelike fashion as described in the paragraphs on the manufacture of silk yarns in Chapter 14.

The development of short fibers, or staple, into yarn, when stated in terms of basic manufacturing processes, is as follows: carding, combing, drawing out, twisting, and winding. As the raw fiber passes through these processes, it is successively called *lap*, *sliver*, *roving*, and finally *yarn*. Here are the manufacturing operations in which these stages occur:

1. Lap to card sliver by the carding process
2. Card sliver to comb sliver by the combing process (if the fiber is to be combed)
3. Sliver to roving by the drawing-out process
4. Roving to yarn by the drawing and twisting process
5. Yarn reeled on bobbins, spools, or cones by the winding process

Figure 3-1

(*a*) Cotton is thrown from bales (1) onto apron (2). Apron moves cotton to blending apron (3). Blending apron has sharp spikes that raise cotton until part of it is knocked off by roll (4). Some of the cotton stays on apron. The cotton knocked back by roll (4) continues to churn and blend until picked up again by apron. Another roll (5) strips off cotton that was not knocked back by previous roll (4). Cotton falls on conveyor belt (6) and is carried to next process. (*b*) Lint cotton falls on apron (1) and passes between feeder rolls (2) to beater cylinder (3). The rapidly whirling beater blades take off small tufts of cotton, knock out trash, and loosen up the mass. The two screen rolls (4) are made of screen material, and air is sucked out of them by fan (5). This draws the cotton from beater and condenses it on the surface of the screen rolls from which it is taken and passed on by the small rolls (6). Air suction through cotton takes out dirt and trash. Conveyor belt (7) passes cotton to another type of beater (8). (Beaters shown are typical of the many types used.) From beater, the cotton passes to a conveyor and is carried to picker. (*c*) Cotton in a loose mass enters picker, which is a series of beaters (2) and screen rolls (3) similar to those described under "opening" but progressively more refined. At the final output of beater and screen system (4), cotton has again been formed into a sheet, or lap. At this point, the "evener" operates to feed more or less cotton to make lap perfectly uniform as it is wound up into a lap roll (5) on winding rolls (6). Lap roll is then taken to the carding process. (*Continued.*)

BLENDING FEEDER

OPENER

PICKER

(d) The lap (1) from picker unrolls, and feed roll (2) passes cotton to the licker-in roll (3) (covered with sawtoothlike wire). The licker-in roll passes fiber against cleaner bars (4) and gives it up to large cylinder (5), which passes between the thousands of fine wires on surface of cylinder and on flats (6). The cotton follows large cylinder to doffer cylinder (7), which removes lint from large cylinder. The doffer comb (8) vibrates against doffer cylinder and takes lint off in a filmy web that passes through condenser rolls (9), coiler head (10), and then into can. The sliver may be passed from can to combing for further removal of foreign matter and parallelization of fiber or directly to drawing. (e) Six cans (1) that were filled at cards feed each drawing from delivery. The spoons (2) are connected so that if any one of the six slivers from can should break, the machine automatically stops. This prevents making uneven yarn later. Each of four sets of rolls (3) runs successively faster than preceding set. The last set runs approximately 6 times as fast as the first set; consequently, sliver coming out is the same size as each one of six going in, but it comes out 6 times as many yards per minute. The sliver is neatly coiled again in roving can (4) by coiler head. The sliver is now much more uniform and fibers are much more nearly parallel. The sliver is now ready for roving frames. In actual practice, drawing is usually repeated. (Continued.)

f

(f) The can of sliver (1) from drawing frames is fed between three sets of drafting rolls (2). Each following set of rolls runs faster than preceding set. This pulls sliver and thins it down, making fibers more nearly parallel. The spindle (3) turns flyer (5) and is driven at a constant speed. The front rolls (nearest flyer) are set at a speed that gives strand coming out of rolls a definite number of turns of twist per inch as it moves along between rolls and flyer. The bobbin (4) is driven by a source separate from gear that drives spindle and flyer. The bobbin is regulated to turn automatically at a speed sufficiently faster than flyer, which causes roving to wind on bobbin at same rate it is delivered by front roll. (g) The principle for spinning is the same as that used for roving except that the operation is more refined and a ring and traveler are used instead of the flyer. From bobbin (1) roving is fed between sets of drafting rolls (2) to draw strand down to its final desired size. The spindle (3) turns bobbin (4) at a constant speed. The front set of rolls is adjusted to deliver yarn at a speed sufficient to insert desired amount of twist as strand moves along. The traveler (5) glides freely around ring (6). The tension caused by drag of traveler causes yarn to wind on bobbin at same rate of speed as it is delivered by rolls. (All illustrations and copy courtesy of Bibb Manufacturing Co.)

g

Figure 3-2   Cotton going through the opening machine where the fibers are loosened. *(Courtesy Pepperell Manufacturing Co.)*

Opening and Blending.   When bales are opened at the mill, the compressed masses of raw fiber are loosened and exposed to the atmosphere (see Figure 3-2). Variation in the raw material is eliminated by mixing together parts of several bales and feeding the material into the opening machines. This blending of the raw material results in greater uniformity (Figure 3-3). Hard lumps in the fibers are loosened, and the heavier impurities—such as dirt, leaves, burrs, and any remaining seeds—are removed by three machines known as pickers: breaker, intermediate, and finisher. These machines clean and form the cotton into *laps*, or rolls; the laps are 40 inches wide and 1 inch thick and weigh about 40 pounds each (Figure 3-4).

Another technique has been developed that replaces the pickers (see Figure 3-5). A carousel revolves twelve bales of cotton in a circular path above four beaters that pluck the cotton from the bales. The cotton is moved by air pressure to an automixer where it is blended and then passed directly to the carding machine. It is not formed into laps.

Carding.   In the lap stage, the fibers are still in a tangled condition and contain waste material. Before this raw stock can be made into yarn, these impurities must be removed and the fibers must be straightened. Such straightening or smoothing is necessary for all natural staple fibers; otherwise, it would be impossible to produce fine yarns from what is originally a tangled mass. This initial process of arranging the fibers in a parallel fashion is known as *carding*. The work is done on a carding machine,

Figure 3-3   Automatic opening and blending of cotton fiber. *(Courtesy James Hunter Machine Co.)*

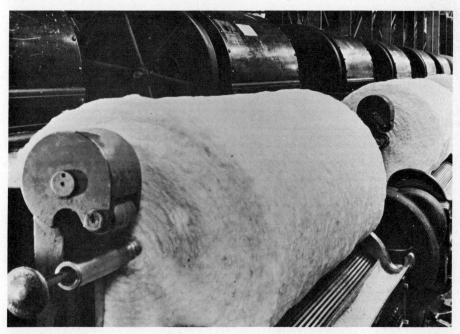

Figure 3-4   Cotton lap from the picker room where dust, leaf, twigs, and other foreign matter have been removed. *(Courtesy Pepperell Manufacturing Co.)*

Figure 3-5 *Karousel* opener plucks cotton from several bales on a rotating basis and passes fiber onto an automixer for blending and then carding. *(Courtesy American Rieter Co., Inc.)*

where the lap is unrolled and drawn on a revolving cylinder covered with very fine hooks or wire brushes (see Figure 3-6). A moving belt, also covered with wire brushes, is on top of this cylinder. The cylinder pulls the fibers in one direction, disentangles them, and arranges them parallel in the form of a thin film. This film is drawn through a funnel-shaped device that molds it into a round ropelike mass called *card sliver*, about the thickness of a broomstick (Figure 3-7). Card sliver produces *carded yarns* or *carded cottons* serviceable for inexpensive cotton fabrics.

Doubling. After carding, several slivers are combined (see Figure 3-8). This results in a relatively narrow lap of compactly placed staple fibers. The compactness of these fibers permits this cotton stock to be attenuated, or drawn out, to a sliver of smaller diameter without falling apart.

Combing. When the fiber is intended for fine yarns, the sliver is put through an additional straightening called *combing*. In this operation, fine-toothed combs continue straightening the fibers until they are arranged with such a high

Figure 3-6   Inside the carding machine, where the brushes clean and straighten the fiber. *(Courtesy Pepperell Manufacturing Co.)*

Figure 3-7   Sliver leaving the carding machine, where the cotton has been further cleaned and disentangled. *(Courtesy Pepperell Manufacturing Co.)*

Figure 3-8 Slivers are doubled to increase the density of the future cotton yarn. *(Courtesy Pepperell Manufacturing Co.)*

degree of parallelism that the short fibers, called *noils*, are combed out and completely separated from the longer fibers. (This procedure is not done when processing man-made staple fibers because they are cut into predetermined uniform lengths. Since these fibers do not need the combing separation, they are processed for spinning into yarns by the Direct Spinner, the Perlok Process, or the Pacific Converter, depending upon the desired end uses of the yarns. These techniques are discussed more fully in the description of spun rayon staple yarn in Chapter 15.)

The combing process forms a *comb sliver* made of the longest fibers, which, in turn, produces a smoother and more even yarn (see Figure 3-9). This operation eliminates as much as 25 percent of

the original card sliver; thus almost one-fourth of the raw cotton becomes waste. The combing process, therefore, is identified with consumers' goods of better quality. Since long-staple yarns produce stronger, smoother, and more serviceable fabrics, quality cotton goods carry labels indicating that they are made from *combed yarns* or *combed cottons*.

Drawing out. The combining of several slivers for the drawing-out process eliminates irregularities that would cause too much variation if the slivers were put through singly. The drawing frame has several pairs of rollers, each advanced set of which revolves at a progressively faster speed. This action pulls the staple lengthwise over each other, thereby producing longer and thinner slivers. After several stages of drawing out, the condensed sliver is taken to the slubber, where rollers similar to those in the drawing frame draw out the cotton further. Here the slubbing is passed to the spindles, where it is given its first twist and is then wound on bobbins.

Roving.   These bobbins are placed on the roving frame, where further drawing out and twisting take place until the cotton stock is about the diameter of a pencil lead. There are two stages of roving: intermediate and fine. The operations are identical, but each machine yields a finer product than the stock it received. *Roving* is the final product of the several drawing-out operations. It is a preparatory stage for the final insertion of twist.

To this point, only enough twist has been given the stock to hold the fibers together. Roving has no tensile strength; it will break apart easily with any slight pull.

Spinning.   The roving, on bobbins, is placed in the spinning frame, where it passes through several sets of rollers running at successively higher rates of speed and is finally drawn out to *yarn* of the size desired (see Figure 3-10). Spinning machines are of two kinds: ring frame and mule frame. The ring frame is a faster process, but produces a relatively coarse yarn. For very fine yarns, the mule frame is required because of its slow, intermittent operation. The ring frame, which is in general use now, is

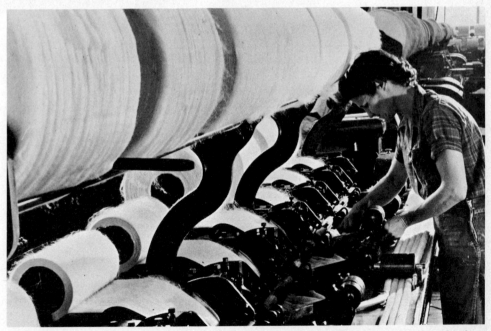

Figure 3-9 Combed slivers are combined as they leave the combing machine to further increase density and compactness of future yarn. *(Courtesy Pepperell Manufacturing Co.)*

Figure 3-10 On the spinning frame, the roving passes from the top through a series of rollers that draw out the cotton into a thread. The thread is twisted as it winds onto the bobbin. *(Courtesy Pepperell Manufacturing Co.)*

more suitable for the manufacture of cotton yarns for mass production. Its hundreds of spindles, whirling thousands of revolutions a minute, and its constant spinning action provide a fast operation. The ring spinning frame completes the manufacture of yarn (1) by drawing out the roving, (2) by inserting twist, and (3) by winding the yarn on bobbins—all in one operation.

Blending Fibers

When different types of fibers are combined or blended, the properties of the individual fibers are also combined, though modified, in the blended yarn. Blending has been done for many years to produce yarns for such fabrics as *union cloth*, which is made of cotton and wool. Fabrics made from some of the newer blends are sold under such trademarks as Cotron, a blend of cotton and rayon; Viyella, a blend of cotton and wool; and Cotdel, a blend of cotton and Kodel polyester. (The amount of fiber blended and the properties of the blend are discussed in the chapter dealing with the particular fiber.)

Blending may be done at any one of the fiber processing stages discussed. During the initial *opening* stage, appropriate amounts of each fiber can be weighed out and layers of them can be *sandwich blended* by spreading one on top of the other (Figure 3-12). Sections of the sandwich are then fed into a hopper or blending feeder for discharge into a mechanical mixer (Figure 3-13). When the fibers are *feeder blended*, each type of fiber is automatically weighed and fed directly from hoppers into a mechanical mixer.

When a lower percentage of one fiber is desired in a blend, it is *finisher picker blended*. Four of the breaker picker laps are blended together at the finisher picker stage and then fed to the carding machine.

Card blended fibers can be produced by feeding one lap of the different fibers into the carding machine to produce a blended sliver. However, this procedure does not produce a precise, well-distributed blend.

When the fibers are to be combed, the blending is not done until after the waste and the shorter fibers are re-

Figure 3-11 After spinning, yarn is sometimes reeled from bobbins into large skeins ready for bleaching, mercerizing, and dyeing. *(Courtesy Spool Cotton Co.)*

Figure 3-12 Sandwich blending by this battery of machines automatically weighs out fibers in layers on top of each other as they are conveyed on a belt moving from left to right. *(Courtesy Fiber Control Corp.)*

Figure 3-13 This beater blender controls removal of the blend from the sandwiching conveyor, maintaining the proportionate distribution of the fibers in the blend for discharge to the mechanical mixer. *(Courtesy Fiber Control Corp.)*

moved. Then, *drawing frame blended* fibers are produced by combined slivers of previously carded, combed, and parallelized fiber.

Sometimes fibers are *rove* or *spun blended*. This produces a rather random arrangement that is usually limited to the blending of colored fibers for such fabrics as tweed.

Yarn Twist. The amount of twist to the inch is an important factor in finished consumers' goods. It determines the appearance as well as the durability and serviceability of a fabric. Fine yarns require more twist than coarse yarns. Warp yarns, which are used for the lengthwise threads in woven fabrics, are given more twist than are filling yarns, which are used for the crosswise threads. To retain the twist in the yarns and prevent any tendency to untwist or kink, the yarns are given a twist-setting finish with heat or moisture, depending upon the kind of fiber used.

The amount of twist also depends upon the type of fabric to be woven:

1. Yarns intended for soft-surfaced fabrics are given only a slack twist. They are called *soft-twisted yarns*.

2. Yarns intended for smooth-surfaced fabrics are given many twists to the inch. Such *hard-twisted yarns* contribute strength, smoothness, elasticity, and some wrinkle resistance to fabrics.

3. Yarns intended for crepe fabrics (with rough, pebbly, or crinkled surfaces) are given a maximum amount of twist, which also adds wrinkle resistance.

Figure 3-14   From spools or cones, mounted on creel, separate yarns are wound on a warp beam. *(Courtesy Bibb Manufacturing Co.)*

The direction of twist may be observed by holding the yarn in a vertical position. If the spirals conform to the direction of the slope of the central part of the letter S, the yarn has an S twist; if they conform to the slope of the letter Z, the yarn has a Z twist (see Figure 3-15).

Permanent crepe effects, such as chiffon, georgette, crepe de chine, canton, and flat and French crepes, are produced by the use of hard-twisted yarns, some of which have left twist, others right twist. These yarns are placed alternately in the warp or in the filling, or in both. (Another satisfactory method of obtaining crepe effects during the construction of the fabric is by the use of slack warp yarns, which may or may not be wound on a separate warp beam. These yarns are held less taut than the other warp yarns and produce a permanent crinkled pattern. Seersucker and matelassé are produced in this way and prove very serviceable.)

Figure 3-15 The S and Z twists are diagramed here. The importance of the direction of the twist is illustrated in the diagrams of thrown silk threads shown in Chapter 14.

When the finished fabric is later washed or dyed, such yarns kink in different directions, producing the crepe surface.

Yarn Count. In the spinning process, there is always a fixed relation between the weight of the original quantity of fiber and the length of the yarn produced from that amount of raw material. This relation indicates the thickness of the yarn. It is determined by the extent of the drawing-out process and is designated by numbers, which are called the *yarn count.*

The standard for the yarn count in cotton is 1 pound of fiber drawn out to make 840 yards of yarn; the resultant thickness or size is known as count No. 1. If the yarn is drawn out farther, so that 1 pound makes twice 840 yards, it is identified as No. 2. Thus, a No. 2 yarn will be finer than a No. 1. A still finer yarn is No. 10, as it indicates that 1 pound of cotton is drawn out to 10 times 840 yards. The higher the number of the yarn count, the finer the yarn in size. Yarn counts up to 20 are called coarse yarns; 20 to 60 are medium yarns; above 60 are fine yarns. Up to 20, the count rises by single numbers. Only even numbers are used between 20 and 60. Above 60, the count rises by intervals of 5 until 100, after which an interval of 10 is used. The size of mercerized cotton sewing thread used for general purposes is No. 50 or No. 60. The very finest cotton yarns spun have been as high as No. 400, the product of 1 pound of cotton drawn out to a strand 336,000 yards long (almost 200 miles). Extemely fine yarns are difficult and costly to manufacture because of the greater care required in spinning and the greater amount of twist to the inch.

The size of yarn to be used in a fabric is determined by the purpose of the fabric. Yarns of varying sizes may be used to obtain the nubbed or novelty effects and rough textures characterized by ratiné, bouclé, or eponge.

There are presently different standards for yarn counts of different fibers. While the standard base of 1 pound is used for cotton, linen, and wool, the length of drawing for each of these fibers is different (see fiber chapter cited). Furthermore, yarn counts of such filament fibers as silk and nylon are designated according to denier, which is an entirely different system of measuring yarn diameter (see page 325). This difference has created an increasingly difficult situation in view of the greater number of fibers, the blending of these fibers into yarns, and the growth of international textile trade. There is a growing awareness of the need for a single common standard system of measuring yarn diameter.

The International Organization for Standardization (IOS) has adopted the Tex system and has established a fixed relationship between the weight and length of all yarns: one Tex equals 1 gram per thousand meters. The greater the weight, the thicker the yarn, and consequently the higher the Tex number.

This system was started in 1960 with the support of the American Society for Testing and Materials (ASTM), which proposed a three-stage approach to the changeover. During the first stage, technologists and yarn manufacturers were urged to familiarize themselves with the new system and to include Tex numbers in parentheses following the customary yarn count numbers.

After a period of time deemed sufficient, Tex numbers will be used as the regular designation and the former yarn count numbers will be in parentheses. Eventually, only the Tex number will be used.

Open-End Spinning

A relatively recent development in the production of spun yarn is the open-end, or break, spinning process. This technique was developed in Czechoslovakia at the Cotton Research Institute in Ústi nad Orlicí during the 1960s. Other countries, notably England, Japan, and the United States, subsequently developed similar machines. The technique has now reached acceptance as a commercially satisfactory process for spinning coarser yarns of counts of up to about 40.

The open-end spinning process begins with the carded sliver (combed sliver is not used), which is fed past a single-spiked roller or a succession of rollers, each advanced set of which revolves at a progressively faster speed, thereby completely opening up the sliver so that the fibers can be fed virtually individually into the spinning operation (this, in effect, breaks apart the sliver; hence, the terms "open-end" and "break"). As the fibers are thus separated, they are transported forward by an airstream and are collected as a thin layer in a groove on the inner surface of a funnel-shaped rotor, which rotates at a very high speed. The centrifugal force of the rotor builds up a multilayer of fibers which is peeled away from the collecting groove as it is simultaneously twisted by the rotation of the rotor and withdrawn continuously, thus being formed into a yarn (see Figure 3-16).

The primary difference between the conventional ring spinning and the open-end spinning is that in the latter the spool does not need to be rotated in order to put twist into the yarn. Furthermore, much larger spools can be wound, thereby providing very long lengths of knot-free yarn and consequent reduction in handling the spools. The system also allows for greater automation in yarn production and therefore provides greater production economy. Open-end spinning can produce yarn spun at a rate of 3 to 5 times that of the conventional

ring spinning. While the open-end spinning process provides better fiber elongation, the resultant yarn is only as even as a good ringspun yarn, but not better (see Figure 3-17). The yarn produced has excellent dyeability, particularly with bright shades. The system homogenizes blends very well, even better than ring spinning utilizing the same preparatory blending techniques.

On the other hand, open-end spinning has its limitations. It is not possible to spin yarns of 100 percent man-made (with the exception of rayon staple) or synthetic fibers on account of the fiber finish, which gets deposited in the rotor

Figure 3-16 *(a)* The turbine is opened and cleaned when the feed stock is changed on this open-end spinning unit. *(Courtesy Textile World and Carolina Mills, Inc.)* *(b)* High-speed photograph of open-end yarn formation in rotating rotor. *(Courtesy Shirley Institute, Manchester, England.)* *(c)* In open-end spinning, the sliver (at top of machine) is opened and the loose fibers are fed by an airstream into a turbine wherein its centrifugal force builds up layers of fibers which are twisted and drawn off (center) and wound on spools (bottom). *(Courtesy Platt International, Ltd.)*

Figure 3-17 *(a)* Magnified open-end spun yarn. Note similarity to conventional ringspun yarn. *(b)* Magnified ringspun yarn. *(Courtesy Shirley Institute, Manchester, England.)*

and causes clogging; and it is not possible to spin combed yarn. The yarn has a carded character and it has a rougher, sandier hand. The yarn counts are generally lower than 40, which limits their use to heavier, coarser fabrics, such as denims, towels, some poplins, and interlinings. Although open-end yarns are spun with 20 percent more twist, they are 15 to 20 percent weaker due to their coarseness. Also, the character of these yarns due to the twist formation is sufficiently different from that of ringspun yarns so that they cannot be mixed in manufacture.

From the point of view of the manufacturer's further concern, it is essential that the slivers be free of foreign matter in order to operate the open-end system effectively. The power requirements increase geometrically with the increase in spun yarn count. Also, the longer the staple, the larger the rotor must be, which in turn reduces the maximum turbine speed and thus the productivity.

Self-Twist Spinning

A more recently developed system created in Australia for spinning wool or woollike fibers is the self-twist spinning process. Pairs of rovings are drawn out on a succession of drafting rollers, the last set of which reciprocates axially, causing a rolling action of the strands as they emerge (see Figure 3-18). This sideways movement of the drafting rollers causes the strands to wrap around each other. The twist is held by the texture of the yarn and the relatively rough texture of the fibers in the yarn; sometimes additives may be used for cohesion. After the rollers complete their sideways motion in one direction, the movement is then shifted in the opposite direction. The resultant yarn therefore has alternating lengths of right- and left-hand twist (Figures 3-19 and 3-20). Under certain circumstances, depending upon the nature of the fibers used and the ultimately desired yarns, these self-twist spun yarns may subsequently be put through a further conventional spinning process to increase strength and produce yarns in which all the twist is in the same direction.

The self-twist process can spin worsted yarn of good quality up to 10 times faster than conventional spinning. Labor and power costs are considerably lower, and the self-twist spinning machine occupies much less floor space, thereby saving on capital costs.

Electrostatic Spinning

In the late 1960s, the Southern Regional Research Center of the U.S. Department of Agriculture in New Orleans, Louisiana, began exploration of a new approach to spinning. Mindful of the facts that each

Figure 3-18 Wool slivers are drawn out into roving form in preparation for self-twist spinning. *(Courtesy Repco Textile Machinery Co.)*

Figure 3-19 *(a)* Close-up of the four self-twisted yarns produced from eight spools of roving. *(b)* Eight spools of rovings are self-twisted in pairs producing four yarns of alternating S and Z twist. *(Courtesy Repco Textile Machinery Co.)*

Figure 3-20   Alternating S and Z twist created in the self-twist spinning process.

Figure 3-21   Primary yarn-spinning techniques: (1) Ring-spinning sliver is fed from delivery rollers through the traveler (a wire loop) onto the bobbin. As the rotation of the spindle drags the traveler around the ring, one turn of twist is inserted into the yarn. The drag of the traveler against the ring causes the traveler to lag behind the spindle and the twisted yarn is wound onto it. (2) Open-end spinning—an open sliver produces loose fibers which are fed by an airstream onto the inner surface of a funnel-shaped rotor driven at high speed. A thin layer of the fibers is deposited by the centrifugal force onto a collecting groove on the inner circumference of the revolving rotor. As this layer of fibers is peeled from the groove, twist is immediately inserted into it by the rotor's rotation, thus forming a yarn. (3) Comparison of ring spinning and open-end spinning showing that the latter method does not require the collecting package, or spool, to be rotated in order to insert twist into the yarn. (4) Self-twist spinning-pairs of rovings are drawn out into finer strands on a roller drafting system in which the front rollers move axially (sideways) causing the strands to roll over each other forming a twist—first in one direction and then in the other—as they are moved forward. Pairs of these twisted strands are brought together shortly thereafter in a manner that causes them to wrap around each other to form a "plied" yarn that has alternating S and Z twist at regular intervals along its length. (*Courtesy Shirley Institute, Manchester, England*)

bale of cotton may have as much as 8 to 12 percent very short fibers, and that a reduction in short-fiber content will result in an increase in yarn strength and a substantial improvement in spinning efficiency, researchers tried to develop a system that would improve the uniformity, strength, and appearance of cotton yarn. They also sought a more efficient and less expensive means of processing cotton fiber, which is more difficult to spin than other fibers.

The researchers began by exploring the possibility of removing the short cotton fibers from the longer ones by an electrostatic process. The principle is based upon the knowledge that widely differing materials can be separated from each other electrostatically. The idea of separating different sizes of the same material, and more particularly cotton, was a novel approach.

Ultimately, research showed that under carefully controlled conditions of humidity, it is possible to separate short fibers from long ones in an electrostatic field. The technique utilizes a nonuniform electrostatic field in which the gradient between the electrodes varies at a curved rate from minimum to maximum intensity. A mechanism was then developed to remove the short fibers from the long fibers as they passed through the electrostatic field and transport the desired long fibers by an air current. Thus, from the carded stage, the fibers are drawn out, or drafted, by rollers and are fed over rotating cylindrical electrodes of high field intensity which direct the long fibers to either an air current or an electrostatic field for transport to the combed sliver stage. The short fibers, which move more slowly, are carried by rotating electrodes of low field intensity to where they are removed to a receptacle (Figure 3-22).

Of far greater significance than the removal of short fibers is the fact that preliminary research with a modification of this electrostatic device has shown that it can replace all textile processing equipment from opening through spinning. Fed cotton from the bale, a small machine can produce a clean, relatively nep-free strand with excellent fiber orientation. The apparatus requires refinement, production rate is low, and there are still problems to overcome before a practical machine is developed. But the potential is exciting and this is perhaps the forerunner of a fundamentally new processing system of the future.

This electrostatic technique has been examined by some mill equipment manufacturers. One of the leading manufacturers has developed a commercially suitable machine. The process is considered to meet the initial objectives of lower cost of production, greater efficiency, and improved uniformity, strength, and appearance of yarns.

Twistless Spinning

Newer techniques for making yarns of staple fibers without the need for twisting them around each other to achieve cohesiveness and strength are being developed. The methods are basically designed to place the fibers parallel to each other, overlap them, and have them adhere together with the aid of a bonding agent that is removable after the yarns are constructed into fabrics.

DRAFTING ROLLS

BRUSH

SPRING LOADED FEED PLATE

WIPER

CYLINDRICAL ELECTRODE

PADDLE WHEEL DOFFER

AIR AND LONG FIBERS

a

SHORT FIBERS

CHARGED ELECTRODE

Figure 3-22 *(a)* Schematic diagram of electrostatic separation of long from short cotton fibers showing carded fiber drawn out and entering at the top, passing cylindrical electrodes attracting the long fibers that are drawn off through air ducts on either side at the bottom. The short fibers fall to the bottom at the center. *(Courtesy U.S. Department of Agriculture) (b)* Prototype fractionator for electrostatic separation of long and short fibers. *(Courtesy U.S. Department of Agriculture)*

b

Pavena System. The trademarked Pavena system was developed in the United States. There are two types of yarns made by this method: one has the trademark Paset, and the other has the trademark Pavil.

Paset yarn, made by the Pavena system, is produced by a novel patented process of drafting carded slivers to a predetermined relatively fine diameter; the resultant sliver is injected with a bonding liquid and dye to glue the fibers together and color them simultaneously. The strands are then dried, doubled, and drafted and bonded again, producing low-count yarns. At this stage, the fibers are *set* in the yarn. (The conventional drawing, slubbing, and ring spinning are eliminated.) The twistless set yarn is wound on bobbins and subsequently woven or knitted. The completed fabric is washed to remove the bonding substance and then otherwise finished.

Paset yarn is said to have a high breaking strength. In finished fabrics, the yarn possesses substantial bulk and filling capacity and has a good hand. It is further claimed that by utilizing Paset yarns, it is possible to use 30 percent less fiber without weakening the fabric. An infinite variety of colors can be achieved, particularly when fibers are blended in the yarn. Also, because of the structure of the yarns, the amount of napping of fabrics can be reduced and the same results can still be achieved as with conventionally constructed goods.

Pavil yarn, made by the Pavena system, is produced with the same drafting process as for Paset yarn. The sliver is also injected with a bonding liquid and dye to hold the fibers together and color them. The sliver is then ring-spun to produce the desired yarn count and wound on bobbins. After the yarn is woven or knitted into fabrics, the goods are washed to remove the adhesive.

Tek-Ja. There is under development at the Fibre Research Institute TNO in Holland another twistless process for making yarn. It is called *Tek-Ja*. Roving is drawn to a fine strand by a drafting system that also wets the parallel fibers to facilitate their cohesion and contraction. As the sliver leaves the drafting stage, the delivery rollers press inactive starch granules into it. The thin, flat fiber ribbon is then given a false (temporary) twist by a pneumatic air jet device. This wet yarn is wound onto a spool and placed in a low-pressure steamer where the inactive starch swells and spreads along the fiber surfaces to form an active adhesive film. The package is then dried. The entire process is said to be about 2 to 3 times faster than conventional ring spinning.

The glue in the yarn provides sufficient strength to enable it to be woven into fabric. The yarn is not suitable for knitting. After the cloth is woven, the adhesive is washed out. The fibers are then held in the yarn by the fabric structure. It is maintained that although these twistless yarns are generally weaker than comparable twisted yarns, fabrics made from each of the two types of yarns have similar strengths. Although the reasons for this are not clear, one factor appears to be that fabric strength is dependent upon the friction between the fibers at the cross-points of the weave.

Fabrics made of this twistless yarn have an attractive luster because the

Figure 3-23 *(a)* Highly magnified view of twistless yarns woven into a plain-weave fabric. The yarns can spread out easily to provide good cover. Lack of twist also enhances luster. *(Courtesy Shirley Institute, Manchester, England) (b)* Highly magnified view of ringspun yarns woven into plain-weave fabric. Yarns retain tightness allowing for spaces in the interstices. *(Courtesy Shirley Institute, Manchester, England) (c)* Principle of twistless spinning showing an adhesive (hare, starch) being applied to a drawn roving. Subsequent steaming causes fibers to be glued together without spinning. After weaving, adhesive can be washed out. *(Courtesy Shirley Institute, Manchester, England)*

fibers in the yarn are relatively parallel to each other, thereby providing a smooth surface. Also, since the fibers in the yarn are not bound together, they can be spread out to provide much better cover than can be achieved with twisted yarn (see Figure 3-23).

Aerodynamic Spinning

Another unique process is under development in West Germany by Herr Gotzfried. His aerodynamic spinning system passes continuous multifilament yarn (see page 60) together with staple fiber through a pneumatic device which causes the filaments to twist and curl, entrapping the staple fibers in the snarls. The yarn that is produced has an untwisted continuous multifilament core covered with twisted and entangled staple fibers. Such yarn, which is claimed to be similar in appearance to but stronger than ordinary spun yarn, can be produced about 4 times faster than yarns spun on the conventional ring spinning system.

FILAMENT YARNS

With the advent of man-made fibers, it became possible to produce endless, fine strands of fiber. These filaments are

Figure 3-24 Comparison of spun (left) and filament (right) yarns. *(Courtesy American Enka Co)*

produced by different methods, and they can be formed directly into yarn without the use of techniques to connect fibers together to form the required lengths (see Figure 3-24).

Wet Spinning

The first commercially successful method for the manufacture of man-made fiber was the *wet spinning* of the cellulosic fiber, rayon (see Chapter 15). This method is still used today. Essentially, the process involves the use of an appropriate liquid solution which is pumped through a small nozzle, which is called a *spinneret*, into a chemical bath that coagulates the extruded solution of endless strands of filaments. These coagulated continuous fibers are drawn out of the bath, purified by washing, dried, and then wound onto spools.

The construction of the spinneret may be varied according to the desired results. If the spinneret has one extrusion hole, then a *monofilament* yarn will be produced. If the spinneret has many holes, then a *multifilament* yarn will be produced. The size and number of the holes of spinneret may be varied. Thus the thickness, or denier, of the yarn is determined by the number and size of the filaments of which it is constructed. Also, the amount of twist given the processed yarn will affect its texture and strength.

Dry Spinning

Another method for the manufacture of man-made or synthetic fibers is *dry spinning*. An example of this is the process of making acetate (see Chapter 16). The process involves the use of an appropriate liquid solution which is pumped through a spinneret into an air chamber. The air reacts with the extruded streams causing them to solidify. These coagulated continuous fibers are then drawn out of the chamber, twisted and/or processed further, and then wound onto spools.

As in the case of wet spinning, mono-filament or multifilament can be produced, and the denier of the yarn will depend upon the number and size of the spinneret holes. Again, the amount of twist given to the yarn will determine its texture and strength.

Melt Spinning

A third method of manufacturing man-made or synthetic fibers is *melt spinning*. An example of this is the process of making polyester (see Chapter 19). Polymer chips obtained from previously reacted chemical combinations are melted and then pumped through a spinneret into an air chamber. The extruded streams cool and solidify into continuous filaments and are then drawn out of the chamber, twisted and/or processed further, and subsequently wound onto spools.

Monofilament and multifilament yarns of various deniers can be produced as is done with the the other extruded filaments. Texture and strength are also determined by the amount of twist put into the yarn.

Bicomponent Spinning

During the research of such synthetic polymers as nylon, various forms of the same polymer were created. While each variety had certain common characteristics, each also had certain different qualities. In the quest for yarns that would have combined certain desired properties of a particular synthetic fiber, a variation of melt spinning was devised. The technique involves the extrusion through a spinneret of two dif-

ferent types of the same polymer to produce a *bicomponent fiber*. For examples see Figures 3-25, 3-26, and 3-27.

There are three techniques of bicomponent fiber production. One method is the side by side extrusion through one spinneret hole of two varieties of the same polymer. As the two variants cool and solidify, they adhere together as one filament, one side of which is composed of one type of the polymer and the other side of which is composed of another type of the same polymer.

Another means of manufacture of bicomponent fiber is basically that of using one spinneret inside another. One variant of the polymer is pumped through the center, or core, spinneret while another is pumped through the outer, or surrounding, spinneret. Both varieties of the polymer emerge as one through the common hole of the surrounding spinneret so that the fiber is formed of a core of one polymer variant surrounded by a ring of the other variant.

The third method of composition of bicomponent fiber is the distribution of drops of one molten polymer variant into another molten form of the same

Figure 3-25 Semidull Cantrece bicomponent nylon: *(a)* longitudinal view and *(b)* cross-sectional view. The line running through the fiber indicates the demarcation of the two nylon components. *(Courtesy E.I. du Pont de Nemours & Co.)*

Figure 3-26 Type 57 Acrilan bicomponent acrylic fiber after crimp development. Note the helix direction reversal. Reversals of this type add greatly to fabric aesthetics. *(Courtesy Monsanto Textiles Co.)*

polymer. This composite mixture is then extruded through the single spinneret hole. The result is a matrix, or conglomerate, of minute, short strands of one fiber suspended inside another variety of the same fiber.

Biconstituent Spinning

Another variation of filament yarn production is *biconstituent spinning* (Figure 3-28). Essentially, the techniques used are the same as those for bicomponent spinning. The difference is that biconstituent spinning utilizes two *different* polymers that are combined and extruded in the same manner. One example is Monvelle, which is a biconstituent of nylon and spandex (Figure 3-29).

Fasciated Spinning

Numerous strands of filaments extruded from a spinneret may be tied together by binding staple fiber around them to form fasciated yarn (see Figure 3-30). (The designation is derived from its resemblance to a *fasces*—that is, a bundle of sticks bound around the handle of an axe and displayed as a magistrate's badge of authority during the Roman Empire.) The tying is accomplished by passing the filaments through a pneumatic device which causes staple fibers from a sliver produced by stretch-broken tow to wrap completely around the filaments, forming a bundle, or yarn. An example of a fasciated yarn is Rotofil.

The technique produces yarn at the very high speed of 500 to 1,000 yards per minute. Fasciated yarns look like conventionally spun yarns, are generally

Figure 3-27 Typical Herculon II polypropylene bicomponent fiber for apparel: *(a)* cross-sectional view and *(b)* longitudinal view.

Figure 3-28   Cross-sectional view of a biconstituent fiber of polypropylene core and nylon sheath. *(Courtesy ICI Fibres, England)*

Figure 3-29   *(a)* Photomicrograph showing filament cross-sectional structure of Monvelle nylon spandex biconstituent yarn. The nylon segments (shown in black) dye well with acid dyes, while the spandex segments are dye-resistant and therefore translucent. *(b)* Monvelle resembles a standard continuous-filament yarn—a factor which greatly simplifies knitting. Upon exposure to dry heat, boiling water or steam, however, the nylon and spandex segments comprising the yarn's filaments shrink to different degrees resulting in the power-packed torque-free helical (coil) crimp configuration shown here. *(Courtesy Monsanto Textiles Co.)*

Figure 3-30   Structure of a fasciated yarn. *(Courtesy Shirley Institute, Manchester, England.)*

less fuzzy, and have a higher luster and sheen than spun yarns. Although they have tactile characteristics similar to conventional ring-spun yarns, fasciated yarns are stronger.

Film Splitting

Filament fibers are also produced by melt extrusion of a polymer through a very wide die but with a very narrow slit to form a sheet of film. There are several methods of producing fiber from these sheets. The film may be stretched and oriented along its direction of extrusion and then either broken or cracked (technically called *fibrillating*) by mechanical means into a mat of fibers. Another technique is to emboss with a roller a fiber pattern of indentations of specific dimensions on the film and then mechanically to fibrillate the film to produce the fibers (see Figure 3-31). An example of a fibrillated yarn is Fibrilon olefin.

The same technique may also be used with bicomponent or biconstituent film.

Integrated Composite Spinning

In the late 1960s, father and son Emilian and Andrew Bobkowicz of Montreal, Canada, introduced an integrated composite spinning technique, which they called the *Bobtex ICS* process. It was aimed to take advantage of the most desirable features of both conventionally spun yarn and filament yarn. Since then, advancements in technique and yarn varieties have been made and are identified as ICS/MC yarn.

Polymer Filament Staple Yarn. There are two basic forms of these multicom-

Figure 3-31 *(a)* Fibrillated polypropylene yarn made by splitting the polymer sheath into a fishnet pattern which allows the yarn to widen and fill spaces in the woven or knitted fabrics. *(b)* Fibrillated polypropylene yarn produced by splitting very thin sheets of the polymer into narrow filament strips. *(Courtesy Textile World.)*

ponent spun yarns. One type is *polymer filament staple* yarn, which is produced by initially passing a monofilament or multifilament strand through a polymer or copolymer resin. The filament may be round, flat, fibrillated tape, or tubular monofilament, each of which may be highly oriented or of nearly crystalline structure (the latter aids acceptance and retention of the subsequent twist). The resin may be fed into the system either as a pellet, flake, or powder to be melted (as for melt spinning), or as a liquid polymer solvent, or as a polymer sus-

POLYMER

CARRIER

FIBER

FIBER

PRODUCTION SPEED
2,000 FPM

ICS SPUN YARN

BOBTEX ICS–INTEGRATED COMPOSITE SPINNING PROCESS

a

b

Figure 3-32 *(a)* Schematic diagram and *(b)* photo of an Integrated Composite Spinning machine for the production of polymer filament staple yarn. Monofilament of multifilament strand is fed through a molten polymer or copolymer resin. Staple fibers from the slivers are superimposed and press-bonded to the polymer coating. This is given a retained twist while still heated by a false-twist device and then cooled and wound on spools. *(Courtesy The Bobtex Corp., Ltd.)*

pension that is to perform the function of a heat and/or chemical bonding agent. As the filament is passed through one of these, it is coated with the polymeric substance. A predetermined variety and length of staple fiber is then superimposed upon and bonded by compression to the polymeric coated continuous filament strand. The ICS/MC yarn is then given a twist at high speed, cooled, and wound on spools (see Figures 3-32 and 3-33). This is all done in a continuous sequence of operations on one machine. Up to 2,000 feet of yarn can be spun per minute, depending upon such factors as yarn count, type of staple fibers, and polymeric bonding agent used. Experimental units have operated at speeds in

Figure 3-33 Stereoscan micrograph of longitudinal view of an ICS/MC polymer filament staple yarn showing fibers coated with the resin. *(Courtesy The Bobtex Corp., Ltd.)*

excess of 4,300 feet per minute, indicating that still higher speeds can be obtained in commercial machines.

Polymer Staple Yarn. The other type of ICS/MC yarn is the *polymer staple* yarn, which does not have a filament core. It is produced by extruding any type of polymer or copolymer directly from an extrusion die in various forms, including a continuous polymer strand, tube, or others. An outer texture of any preferred type or composition of staple fibers is superimposed upon the tacky polymer extrudate, consolidated into an ICS/MC spun yarn by compression, cooled, and given a twist at high speed in a continuous sequence. Up to 1,000 feet per minute can be spun, depending upon several variables.

Characteristics of Multicomponent Spun Yarns. In both of the ICS/MC yarn types the staple fibers can be superimposed onto one or both sides of the polymer matrix while the latter is under twisting torque to ensure a more even fiber deposition. Different types of staple fibers of different staple lengths and different colors can be used to incorporate desirable properties, effects, and appearances, as well as to enable the use of blends of lower-priced fibers to reduce raw materials costs. Further raw-material economies are realized since the finished yarn will contain 35 to 50 percent of a polymer resin in pellet form (e.g., polyolefin), which is lower in cost than the staple fibers used in conventional ring or open-end spinning. Production savings of as much as 50 percent of the cost of manufacturing spun staple

yarns at 4 to 10 times the speed are claimed.

Although it may be expected that the deposition of the staple fibers over the filament strand would be according to the desired arrangement, such as uniformly around a round substrate, that does not actually occur. This is a condition which may ultimately be altered. The polymer filament staple yarn tends to be flat or ribbon-shaped, probably because of the roller pressure exerted on the polymer as the staple is pressed into it. The cross-sectional shape of the yarn indicates a curl attributable to a combination of differential rates of cooling of the components and the twist put into the yarn. Also, the staple fibers tend to be concentrated on one side of the yarn at the central part of the curled cross section. The polymer substrate itself tends to split into several parts but is held together by the attached staple. Nevertheless, the ICS/MC yarn can have high tensile strength, depending upon the filament core (if used), the staple, the polymer substrate, and the drawing of that polymer. The twist further increases its tenacity. Abrasion resistance of ICS/MC yarn fabrics has been shown experimentally to be 2 to 3 times higher than that of fabrics from conventional yarns on the basis of tests performed on industrial ducks. It has little creep, which is generally controlled by the staple fiber characteristics. The yarn tends to be uniform in diameter but has varied stiffness along its length, possibly due to the twisting of the flattened polymer substrate.

Advantages and Disadvantages of Multicomponent Spun Yarns. The polymer filament staple yarn provides certain advantages over the polymer staple yarn. The former can be produced at a much higher rate of speed. It is stronger due to the inner filament core. It therefore is also less likely to break during production, which reduces downtime (loss of production due to interruption of operation). Because of this carrier component, which may be as low as 10 percent of the total yarn weight, low-cost short staple fibers may be used. The synergistic effect of the components of the polymer filament staple yarn is higher; the strength of polymer staple yarn depends primarily upon the length, strength, and proper parallel arrangement of the staple fibers used to optimize yarn strength during twisting, requiring higher quality and more costly card slivers as a feed material. The polymer filament staple yarn can be produced with short-staple card slivers, a continuous narrow fiberweb of any low-cost short or medium randomly arranged staple fibers, without involving carding, drawing, or roving operations. It can also be engineered to produce a wider variety of yarns of various compositions for a greater variety of purposes.

Blends. To obtain the desired characteristics of ICS/MC yarns, which can be produced without knots, certain amounts of each component are required. A minimum polymer resin content of 30 percent is needed for proper bonding and consolidation. A minimum outer staple fiber content of 35 percent is needed to produce a satisfactory fiber cover and acceptable yarn. As stated above for the polymer filament staple yarn, a filament content as low as 10 percent may be used. Within these constraints, a wide variety of general-purpose yarns can be produced. For example, general-purpose yarn for such uses as carpet or upholstery backing can be composed of 30 percent oriented polypropylene monofilament, 30 percent olefin resin, and 40 percent short-staple cotton, linters, jute, sisal, flax, etc. A low-stretch warp yarn for home furnishings or industrial fabrics can be made of 20 to 30 percent glass multifilament, 30 percent olefin resin, and 30 to 40 percent any staple fiber, depending upon desired texture and appearance. Woolen and worsted yarns with permanent press properties can be made of 10 to 30 percent nylon or polyester multifilament, 30 to 40 percent nylon or polyester resin, and 40 to 50 percent fine wool fibers. A low-cost, easy-care yarn for such applications as clothing, curtains, and upholstery can be composed of 30 percent nylon or polyester multifilament, 30 to 40 percent nylon or polyester resin, and as little as 30 percent silk staple. Fire-resistant ICS/MC yarns can be produced of 10 to 30 percent glass multifilament, 20 to 30 percent polyvinyl chloride resin, and 40 to 60 percent asbestos fibers. It is also possible to texturize ICS/MC yarns by giving them a permanent crimp.

TYPES AND CHARACTERISTICS OF YARN

There are various types of yarn, each having its own characteristics. These characteristics vary according to the construction and the treatment given in the manufacture of the yarn.

Ply Yarns

When two or more strands or yarns are twisted together, they are designated as *ply yarns*. They are termed two-ply, three-ply, and so on, according to the number used in their construction. A single yarn may be of relatively good quality; but where durability is all-important, ply yarns are preferable, assuming that the yarns have the same length of staple. Good-quality broadcloth for men's shirtings, for example, is made with ply yarns.

Yarn construction and yarn count are expressed in the following manner. The term 1/30s denotes the use of a single yarn having a yarn count of 30. In the same way, 3/30s denotes the use of a three-ply yarn—that is, three strands twisted together, each having a separate yarn count of 30. A three-ply yarn, indicated by 3/30s, would be equivalent to a single yarn having a yarn count of 10. In the same way, 2/10s (containing two single strands of 10s) is equivalent in size to 1/5s.

When the number of yards in a pound of cotton is to be calculated for any given size of yarn, the yarn count is multiplied by 840 yards. For example, if the required size of a yarn is 2/10s, the fraction should be reduced to 1/5s; then the 5 is multiplied by 840; and the result is 4,200 yards.

Doubled Yarns

Another type of yarn construction is the *doubled yarn*. This consists of two or more single strands treated as one in the weaving process, but the strands are not twisted together. The doubled yarn must not be confused with ply yarns, which are stronger because they are twisted. Doubled yarns are used for ornamental effect; they do, of course, contribute a certain amount of additional strength. Because doubled yarns have little twist, they produce luster and softness.

Novelty Yarns

The spinning process can produce decorative effects by varying the amount of twist or by twisting together yarns of different diameters, each of which may have different amounts of twist per inch. Such yarns can give fabrics almost limitless textural effects of various color combinations. Fabrics made of novelty yarns cannot generally be as durable as fabrics made of uniform yarns that have been evenly spun. A safe rule for the consumer is to remember that longer service may be expected from flat, smooth fabrics made from evenly spun yarns rather than from novelty yarns of complex character.

Slub Yarns. The consumer's desire for ornamental effects has popularized the production of yarns that are given only a small amount of drawing out. Such yarns, called *slub yarns*, have soft, untwisted areas at frequent intervals throughout their length. They are coarse, with slight twist, having varying diameters that show irregularities typical of an incomplete spinning operation.

If simulation of linen is desired, the use of slub yarns is easily understood. Where durability is a main consideration, their practicability is justly questioned, because a heavy yarn protruding

Figure 3-34 *(a)* Shantung, showing characteristic slub yarns in filling. *(b)* Tweed, showing characteristic slub yarns in warp and filling. *(Courtesy American Viscose Corp.)*

above the level of surrounding yarns is subjected to friction and the fabric soon shows signs of wear at those points after continued use. In the past, slub yarns were generally used in fabrics that possessed an especially compact construction and consequently were characterized by marked durability. Today, slub yarns do not always imply compact construction in the fabric of which they are a part. They furnish ornamental effects and are often used for that purpose in shantung and tweed (Figure 3-34).

Flake Yarns.   Flake yarns are variations of the slub yarns. The flake or slub effect is made by inserting soft, thick tufts of roving between binder yarns at intervals. The result is a flake yarn of varying thickness and softness, caused by the soft-effect ply held in place by the uniform binder. This type of yarn is limited to fancy-effect uses (see Figure 3-35).

Spiral Yarns.   The general appearance of a spiral yarn is that of a coarse yarn wound around a fine yarn, giving the effect of a spiral. The thicker yarn is given a slack twist and wound spirally around

the fine yarn (sometimes referred to as the *core yarn*), which is given a hard twist. Other names for the spiral yarns are *corkscrew* and *eccentric*. Spiral yarns may be made for different purposes. They may be constructed in such a way as to give the decorative spiral effect of a candy-cane pattern. Sometimes the core yarn is completely hidden by the spiraling outer yarn, as in the case of lastex where the core yarn is rubber while the outer yarn may be of cotton, nylon, or other textile.

Figure 3-35   Homespun fabric showing the soft, thick tufts of roving of the flake yarns.

Figure 3-36   Novelty yarns.

Ratiné Yarns. Ratiné yarns are a variation of the spiral yarn type, although the method of manufacture differs. The outer (effect) yarn and the core yarn are twisted in a spiral manner, but at intervals a longer loop is thrown out by the effect yarn, which kinks back on itself and is held in place by a third (binder) yarn. The binder is added in a second twisting operation going in the opposite direction of the effect yarn. The ratiné yarn's small loops on its surface give the yarn a taut, rough-surfaced effect. The technique may be applied to all major fibers and is popular for combinations of yarns made of such fibers as cotton and rayon.

Bouclé, Loop, or Curl Yarns. Bouclé, loop, or curl yarns are comparable to the ratiné yarn type, but in bouclé yarns the surface is softer and has a more pronounced novelty effect. This effect is accomplished by allowing one of the plies to remain slack during the twisting operation, causing it to twist on itself and form a loop. The size of the loop will vary depending on the speed of the rollers. These yarns are popular for knitted fabrics. They are also used to create fabrics with a looped pile to resemble fur, such as karakul, for trimmings and coating fabrics.

Nub, Knop, Knot, or Spot Yarns. Nub yarns are made by twisting the effect ply around the core ply many times within a very short space, causing bumps or nubs that may be spaced at intervals along the yarn. Variations are possible where, for example, two effect plies, each of different color, may be used, and the nubs arranged so that the colors are alternated along the length of the yarn. In some instances, nub yarns are bound by a binder or third thread; in other cases, the effects can be created without the binder.

REVIEW QUESTIONS

1. Describe the carding process and what it does to the cotton fibers.
2. Explain why a fabric woven from slub yarns may not wear well.
3. Why would it be difficult to make fabric directly from roving?
4. (a) What is meant by yarn count? (b) Why is it important?
5. How do filament yarns differ from yarns of staple fibers in the manner in which they are made?
6. In what way do differences in the raw material affect the formation of yarn?
7. Describe the combing process and what it does to the fibers.
8. What are the qualities that determine the choice of a yarn?
9. Explain the meaning of 1/60s, 4/20s, 3/30s.
10. Explain the difference between ply yarns and doubled yarns.
11. How is variation in yarns obtained in the spinning process?
12. How does twist in a yarn affect the finished fabric?
13. What kind of fabrics use yarns spun with a very slack twist?
14. What are the purposes and characteristics of the different types of novelty yarns?
15. How do open-end and conventional ring spinning differ?
16. How do twistless and integrated composite spinning differ?
17. Describe the electrostatic spinning process.

18. Differentiate between a bicomponent filament and a biconstituent fiber.
19. Describe a fasciated yarn.
20. What is film splitting?

SUGGESTED ACTIVITY

Prepare rough diagrams to illustrate the processes involved in the manufacture of yarn.

4 TEXTURED AND STRETCH YARNS

comfort, service, and appearance

The yarns discussed in Chapter 3 are made of fibers in their normal forms. While they are produced in many varieties to provide various effects, each yarn's characteristics are limited by the normal condition of the fiber's shape, its thickness, its length and surface texture, as well as such inherent qualities as elasticity, resilience, and warmth.

Consumers often wish that certain characteristics could be combined into one yarn for a particular kind of fabric. They welcome new, interesting, and useful properties in fabrics made from yarns that normally cannot provide these characteristics. Consequently, techniques have been developed that change the surface or shape and texture of the fibers and, in turn, affect the characteristics of the yarns. These *textured* yarns provide consumers with variations in fabric properties that they seek. For convenient identification, they may be grouped into three types: stretch, high bulk, and loop bulk.

PRODUCING FIBERS FOR TEXTURED YARNS

Textured yarns made of filament fibers may be produced either by the fiber producer, the throwster, or trade-texturizer who serves as an intermediary between the fiber producer and the fabric manufacturer, or the user-texturizer. The yarn may be textured from undrawn, partially drawn, or fully drawn filaments.

The primary source of textured yarns is from fully drawn filaments. Fibers such as nylon or polyester (the two major fibers that are textured) are produced by extrusion through small orifices in spinnerets (see Chapters 17 and 19) as tacky streams of filaments. Generally, there are about 34 filaments having a total initial diameter of about 600 denier. They are attenuated to about 150 denier by being drawn through a series of rollers. This process causes the molecules in the fibers to be longitudinally reoriented into a chainlike connected series and makes the filaments more uniform, stronger, and stable. The filaments are thus fully drawn, and the yarns are referred to as parent yarn (PY) or fully oriented yarn (FOY). Traditionally, the texturizer purchases the fully oriented yarn from the producer and processes it into the desired texture. This division of labor has additional built-in costs and results to some degree in lack of uniformity in the ultimate texturing process.

One alternative to this approach is to produce filaments without attenuating them after they emerge from the spinneret, thereby producing undrawn (UD) yarn. Since the fiber is not subjected to any significant linear orientation, it must be specially handled by meticulous packaging and by controlling the humidity, temperature, and oxygen to retain its viscous state. The fiber producer or texturizer subsequently draws and textures the yarn, but it must be done within a relatively short period of time of about two weeks in order to obtain the desired results. The fragility of this technique provides much risk.

The approach that is being more widely adopted is that of texturing from partially oriented yarn (POY). Fiber manufacturers produce filaments which are partially or incompletely drawn to yarns of about 450 to 245 denier, as may be desired. This drawing only partially aligns the molecules in the lengthwise direction of the fiber. These partially oriented yarns, sometimes called partially drawn yarns (PDY) depending upon the technique used, may be draw-textured by either the fiber producer itself, the trade-texturizer, or the user-texturizer. The conversion of the POY yarn

by *draw texturing* is done either by the sequential or the simultaneous method.

In the sequential method the fibers are drawn through rollers and the resultant 150-denier drawn yarn enters a heater unit attached to the texturing machine and then feeds into the appropriate texturing treatment. This procedure is the one more widely used. It is particularly more suited to draw texturing of nylon.

In the simultaneous system POY yarn is simultaneously drawn and textured in the first heater unit of the texturing machine itself and then subjected to final annealing, or curing, in a second heater zone. This method seems to be better for draw texturing of polyester.

Draw texturing from partially oriented yarn has been shown to be an adaptable technique. Although it has some aging and handling problems, it is less troublesome than draw texturing from undrawn yarn. As the denier of the POY yarn decreases, the yarn becomes more oriented and has greater stability. Consequently its aging period can be longer. In general, that period ranges between three and eight weeks. Longer delays could result in higher costs, create production problems, and reduce manufacturing efficiencies. Other advantages of the use of partially oriented yarn for texturing are lower production costs, more even yarn, and consequently greater ease and uniformity in dying.

Competition within the draw texturing field among fiber producer texturizers, trade-texturizers, and user-texturizers is likely to increase. This may be compounded by competition between draw texturing and texturing from the fully drawn yarn. The kinds and characteristics of the yarns produced are dependent upon the texturing processes.

STRETCH YARNS

There are five kinds of stretch yarns: (1) those made by giving a special mechanical heat-setting treatment to thermoplastic filament fibers, such as nylon or polyester; (2) those made of elastomeric fibers, such as spandex or rubber; (3) those made of bicomponent fibers, such as two different types of nylon produced as a single filament; (4) those made of biconstituent fibers, such as two different polymers produced on a single filament; and (5) those made of specially chemically treated natural fibers, such as cotton.

There are also several different techniques that are used in producing each kind of stretch yarn.

Heat-set Thermoplastic Yarns

The long, smooth, endless strands of man-made filament fibers, such as nylon, have varying amounts of natural ability to stretch when pulled and to spring back to their original sizes when allowed to relax. However, when subjected to certain methods that use heat to set crimp in these thermoplastic filament yarns, the crimp greatly increases their stretchability.

A *thermoplastic yarn* is one that can be put into any shape or position desired and, after being subjected to a predetermined level of heat for a specific period of time, will retain that shape despite washing, dry cleaning, stretching, or compressing. This heat-setting technique is employed in many ways, and depending on the method of manufacture and the fibers used, the properties of the yarn will also vary.

Thermoplastic stretch yarns have many advantages over untreated filament yarns. They have a soft touch and a dull appearance like that of wool rather than the sometimes undesirable sheen of some filament yarns. The resultant textural appearance of stretch yarns provides opportunity for desirable novelty effects. Fabrics or garments made of these yarns have a higher degree of absorbency and adsorbency than ordinary filament yarns, since stretch yarns provide loops and kinks to hold the moisture. This results in providing better perspiration conductivity and consequently increases comfort to the wearer. The pockets of air caused by the coils in the yarns also act as an insulative barrier, making the garment warmer.

Garments made of such stretch yarns wash easily and dry-clean readily. They are as strong and durable as garments made of yarns of similar fibers that have not been processed into stretch yarns. In fact, the stretch characteristic is more likely to result in less strain on the yarns, fabrics, and seams of garments during the ordinary stress of putting on, wearing, and taking off. The stretchability also provides greater comfort, shape retention, and wrinkle resistance and allows the garment to conform to the figure and to fit better. Solving the fitting problem is an advantage not only to the consumer but also to the manufacturer, who finds it more economical to produce fewer specific sizes, and to the retailer, who needs less space to store fewer sizes and finds it easier to fit the consumer.

There are four general types of heat-set thermoplastic yarns: coil, curl, crimp, and wavy. All are treated to provide a springlike or accordionlike characteristic to the yarn. The methods of accomplishing this vary, thereby giving different shapes to the yarns but producing somewhat similar effects.

Coil Types: Conventional Method. This method utilizes conventional twisting equipment with heat-setting techniques. It consists basically of untwisting nylon or polyester yarns, inserting a measured high twist (from 47 to 114 turns per inch depending upon the denier, or thickness), heat-setting the yarn in that condition in a high-pressure steam autoclave at approximately 260 degrees Fahrenheit for an hour or less, and then untwisting the yarns to a predetermined level. As a result, the torque or tendency to twist back to its heat-set condition causes the filaments to bulk up into a springlike condition. To give balance to the yarn, a set of filaments previously given an S twist is generally plied a few turns with a previously Z-twisted set of ends.

Helanca, a well-known stretch yarn introduced by the Heberlein Patent Corp. in 1947, is produced by this conventional method. It is now produced under license by many companies. This yarn can be stretched 3 times its relaxed length in heavier deniers and from 4 to 5 times in lighter yarns. Helanca has excellent recovery to its original size on release of the tension and will provide a snug fit and shape retention to garments made from it. It has a firm, crisp hand and a bulking power up to 3 times its uncoiled condition. Different types of Helanca stretch yarn are produced to meet specific requirements and end uses. They vary from high stretch to low stretch with high bulk.

Coil Types: False-Twist Method. Most of the world's stretch yarn is made by this method because it is more economical and much faster to produce. It is basi-

Figure 4-1 Schematic representation of false-twist coiling. *(Courtesy Heberlein & Co. AG)*

cally a technique of temporarily putting a very high twist in a multifilament yarn, heat-setting the yarn in this twisted condition, cooling it quickly, and then untwisting the yarn (see Figure 4-1). The operation is based on the principle that a stationary multifilament yarn that is held at both ends and twisted at the center by an eccentrically placed hook will develop equal amounts of twist in opposite directions on each side of the guide hook. The opposite direction of the twist in the yarn as it passes out of the false-twist spindle cancels out the twist in the yarn. However, since the yarn is made of a thermoplastic fiber that has been heat-set in a coiled condition, the yarn develops a coillike, bulky, springy character (Figure 4-2).

STATIONARY FALSE-TWISTED YARN

ROTATING 'FALSE-TWIST' SPINDLE

SPINDLE HOOK

a

UNTWISTED, COILED YARN FILAMENTS

ROTATING 'FALSE-TWIST' SPINDLE

SPINDLE HOOK

FALSE-TWISTED YARN

b

WIND-UP

SPINDLE HOOK

SPINDLE

HEATER

SUPPLY

TENSIONER

c

Figure 4-2 *(a)* Schematic representation shows insertion of false-twist in a stationary yarn. *(b)* Schematic representation shows insertion of false-twist in a moving yarn. As the yarn is drawn through the spindle, the twist is restricted to that part of the yarn reaching the spindle hook; it leaves the false-twist spindle with the filaments untwisted but coiled. *(c)* Schematic representation shows the false-twist texturing process. The untwisted yarn is given a false twist and is then heat-set just below the false-twist spindle. The spindle hook holds the twist below itself and permits the yarn to be untwisted above it as it leaves the false-twist spindle, but the heat-set coil in the filaments is retained. (Schematics drawn by Diane Corbman after *Stretch Woven Fabrics,* NI, Chemstrand Corp.)

On emerging from the false-twist spindle, the yarn has a built-in torque (or twist) in either the S or the Z direction, which depends upon the direction of the rotating spindle. Since fabrics made of yarns in this condition would be distorted, yarns of opposite torques are usually plied or sometimes doubled to provide balance.

The amount of stretchability and the texture of the yarn is dependent upon such factors as the denier, the amount of false twist used, the amount and method of heat applied, and the ply of the yarn. The principal varieties are as follows:

Helanca generally has less stretch than the other stretch yarns made by the false-twist method. It is used for sweaters and crepe-textured fabrics that need a more relaxed fit.

Fluflon yarn, produced on machines manufactured by the Leesona Corp., is usually made of nylon but could be made of other thermoplastic fibers. The yarn may be made into singles or plied. It has a high degree of elasticity, stretches up to 4 times its original length, and relaxes to its normal size. It has a very soft hand and a variety of uses.

Superloft, also produced on Leesona machines, is another trademark for stretch yarns made of any thermoplastic fiber. It has good bulk but less stretch than Fluflon.

Whitin ARCT, manufactured by the Whitin Machine Works, is a nylon stretch yarn. It can be stretched up to 5 times its relaxed length and, when relaxed, it can bulk up to 3 times its stretched diameter.

Cumuloft is a Monsanto Textiles Co. nylon stretch yarn. Its characteristics are the same as Whitin ARCT.

Figure 4-3 Yarns with reduced stretch; false-twist coiling with postsetting. (*Courtesy Heberlein & Co. AG*)

Saaba is a false-twist yarn that has been modified by a second heat-setting treatment at a lower temperature. The technique reduces the stretch but increases the bulk. The trademark is owned by Leesona Corp. (Figure 4-3).

Coil Types: Autotwist Principle. This process is similar to the false-twist principle. Two thermoplastic yarns are twisted around each other and then are passed over the surface of a heated tube to set them. The yarns are subsequently separated and the tension in them is equalized, but their coil, which provides the stretch characteristic, is retained (see Figure 4-4).

Duo-Twist is a trademark for a stretch yarn which is made by this process and developed by the Turbo Machine Co. (Figure 4-5).

Curl Types: Stress-curled Method. This is essentially an adaptation of the method of obtaining a random curl in a paper ribbon by pulling it between one's thumb and the edge of a dull blade (Figure 4-6).

Agilon is the trademark of the stretch yarn first developed by this process and patented by the Deering Milliken Research Trust. This thermoplastic yarn is softened by heating and passed with a slight pressure over a dull knife edge, which deforms the filaments by flattening one part of their curved surfaces. The actual contracting and stretching characteristic of the yarn is added to the fabric made from this yarn in the washing or scouring process, which is part of the finishing operation. The yarn develops very short sections of marked curl and torque, but since they change position at random, the net result is a balanced no-torque effect in the fabric (see Figure 4-7).

Agilon yarn is produced in monofilament and multifilament forms. It has an additional distinguishing feature in that a filament fiber, such as nylon, can have a staple fiber, such as cotton or wool, spun around it. Therefore, the textural characteristics can vary; Agilon yarn can simulate any kind of yarn made of any kind of fiber, whether smooth or rough, soft or harsh.

Depending on the denier and processing of the yarn, Agilon can stretch up to 3 times its length and return to its

Figure 4-4   Schematic representation of autotwist principle. *(Courtesy Heberlein & Co. AG)*

original length on release of the tension. Unlike some other stretch yarns, Agilon yarn does not immediately snap back with an almost rubber-band action after it has been released. It recovers its original shape more slowly. This gentle elasticity results in less strain on the fabric and no binding to the wearer, which insures increased comfort. Garments made of Agilon yarn include men's, women's, and children's hosiery, creped fabrics for women's blouses and lingerie, and pile fabrics, such as velvets, artificial furs, and fleeces.

Crimp Types: Stuffer Box Method. This process is essentially one of tightly cramming thermoplastic yarn into a container and heat-setting it in this

SUPPLY PACKAGES

Z TWIST
(ALTERNATE)

LONG (OUTER) PATH
105.5 INCHES

S TWIST

SHORT (INNER) PATH
97.0 INCHES

HEATER

SENSING ARMS

NIP ROLLS

WINDER
TRAVERSE

TAKE-UP
PACKAGES

BOBBIN
(UNWOUND)

TENSIONERS

WOUND
BOBBIN
(CLOCKWISE)

WOUND
BOBBIN
(COUNTERCLOCKWISE)

STRING-UP YARN PATH
Z TWIST
(RED OR GOLD BOBBIN)

STRING-UP YARN PATH
S TWIST
(GREEN OR BLACK BOBBIN)

Figure 4-5 Schematic Duo-Twist yarn pattern.
(Courtesy Turbo Machine Co.)

cramped condition, thereby forming a random zigzag crimp (Figure 4-8). There are several widely used varieties.

Ban-Lon yarn is licensed by Joseph Bancroft & Sons Co. The yarn is made of thermoplastic fibers that are permanently crimped by forcing them into a heated stuffing box. Ban-Lon yarn is composed of multifilament or staple fibers and has a soft hand with a dull appearance. It may impart a crepelike surface to the fabric. Ban-Lon has a moderate stretch and clings to the form. The yarn has a bulking capacity of 2 to 3 times its stretch diameter. It may be utilized in woven or knitted fabrics and is popular for men's socks and women's blouses and sweaters.

Figure 4-6   Schematic representation of edge curling. *(Courtesy Heberlein & Co. AG)*

Textralized yarn is also licensed by Joseph Bancroft & Sons Co. The method of production is similar but a finer denier yarn is used, producing a yarn that has greater stretch (up to 2 times its relaxed state) but the same bulking power. This yarn is used for both woven and knitted fabrics.

Spunized yarn is produced by the Hartford Spinners process from thermoplastic yarn in a laced-chain arrangement, passed through a stuffer box, and heat-set. The yarn is soft and quite bulky, but it has limited stretch.

Crimp Types: Gear Method. Another method of putting crimp into thermoplastic yarn employs the teeth on heated gear wheels. As the yarn is passed between the wheels, it is crimped into a jagged fashion in conformation to the gears and is heat-set. The permanently crimped yarn is then wound on spools (Figure 4-9).

Figure 4-7   *(a)* Helanca relaxed (left) and stretched (right). *(Courtesy Heberlein Patent Corp.) (b)* 40-denier Agilon nylon yarn with undeveloped crimp. *(Courtesy Deering Milliken Research) (c)* 40-denier Agilon nylon yarn, fully developed, showing the curled effect that provides its stretch property. *(Courtesy Deering Milliken Research)*

Figure 4-8 Schematic representation of stuffer crimping. *(Courtesy Heberlein & Co. AG)*

Figure 4-9 Schematic representation of gear crimping. *(Courtesy Heberlein & Co. AG)*

Crimp Types: IWS Crimp Method. IWS Crimp is related to the stuffer-box method; yet, it is different. It was developed by the International Wool Secretariat specifically to increase the crimp of some types of wool that do not have much crimp. The process is based upon the natural thermoplasticity of wool. The procedure is incorporated into the carding process for spinning wool sliver into yarn.

A device causes the fiber to be fed into the crimping zone 4 times faster than it emerges, causing the wool fiber to be compressed in its length and thereby becoming crimped. Steam is jetted onto the fiber to set the crimp permanently. The crimped fiber is then immediately moved into another chamber where high-velocity jets of hot air dry the fiber. The yarn of this crimped fiber, called Programmed Pile, is used for rugs (see Figure 4-10).

Wavy Types: Knit-Deknit Method. This technique requires that a thermoplastic yarn be knitted into a fabric and then heat-set. The yarn is subsequently unraveled from the fabric. The loops, formed in knitting and then heat-set, remain permanently in the yarn and give it a wavy or crimpy character (Figures 4-11 and 4-12).

CONVEYER BELT

STEAM JET

FEED PLATE

UNCRIMPED SLIVER

FROM BREAKER CARD

FEED ROLL

STEAM SET

DRYER

CRIMPED SLIVER

TO FINISHER CARD

BLOWER

a

b

Figure 4-10 *(a)* Schematic of the IWS Crimper operation for inserting additional crimp into wool sliver to be used for carpets. *(b)* Permanently increased crimp in a wool sliver is shown here as it emerges from the IWS Crimper. *(Courtesy The Wool Bureau, Inc.)*

Elastomeric Yarns

All these yarns are elastic because of the inherent nature of the basic fiber: rubber or spandex.

Lastex. Everyone is familiar with the elasticity of rubber. In fact, it is this characteristic that brought about the production of rubber yarn as the first stretch yarn. It has been produced for many years under the trademark Lastex. This yarn has a rubber core with a ply of cotton or some other yarn wound around it, thus combining the elasticity of rubber with the texture and hand of the other fiber, which hides the rubber.

Lastex elastic yarn can be produced in weights fine enough for sheer fabrics and laces and heavy enough for foundation garments. Stretched Lastex has a strong tendency to return to its relaxed condition, which makes it an excellent yarn for supportive or holding purposes. It is not affected by laundering or dry cleaning, but the use of chlorine bleach or excessive amounts of dry-cleaning fluid should be avoided. Over a period of time, Lastex loses its elasticity as the rubber tends to dry out and deteriorate. Fabrics of Lastex yarn are heavier than fabrics made of other types of stretch yarns.

Spandex. Spandex is a man-made fiber and has the distinctive property of stretching about 5 to 7 times its relaxed state without breaking. This high degree of elasticity, along with its relatively light weight and its resistance to most solvents (including the common dry-cleaning and laundering agents), make it

Figure 4-11 Schematic representation of knit-deknit routine. *(Courtesy Heberlein & Co. AG)*

Figure 4-12 A stretch high-bulk nylon yarn produced by the knit-deknit process. *(Courtesy Rockwell International)*

superior to rubber. Spandex fibers have a comfortable hand, wear very well, and retain their natural whiteness. They do not dye easily and may fade.

Spandex fibers, such as Lycra, are also produced as *core-spun* yarns. These yarns have a spandex core (which could be as little as 5 to 15 percent of the entire yarn) with a layer of any staple fiber spun around the core as it is held under a predetermined amount of tension. When it is relaxed after spinning, the spandex core returns to its normal length, which pulls the outer layer of spun fibers into a more compact formation. This technique can control the degree of stretchability of the core-spun yarn from a very low degree to twice its relaxed state. Since the core yarn is encased in a layer of staple fibers, the yarn takes on the hand and appearance of these fibers.

Spandex yarns differ from the heat-set thermoplastic stretch yarns in that they have a stronger pull or tendency to recover to original size. This provides more positive support to the body. They are therefore very useful for foundation garments, support hose, and swimsuits. They are also used for lingerie and outerwear, depending upon the type of yarn used, such as core-spun.

A variation of the use of spandex fiber that is under development has been called *intimate blend spinning*. This stretch yarn is composed of a spandex staple blended with any other staple fiber that is desired in the yarn by the fabric producer. As with other blends, the characteristics of the yarns and fabrics produced depend on the kind and the amount of fiber blended, the kind of spun yarn, and fabric construction.

Bicomponent Yarns

This yarn is made of a filament of two types of a man-made fiber extruded simultaneously through the spinneret opening (see page 61). The fibers adhere in siamese fashion. As the yarn is processed, one type, which shrinks more than the other, pulls on the other type attached to it and causes the whole filament to become distorted and crimped. Such yarns are free of torque. Cantrece, which is used for hosiery, is a nylon bicomponent yarn produced by Du Pont.

Biconstituent Yarns

This yarn is made of two different kinds of man-made polymers extruded simultaneously from the spinneret opening (see page 62). The polymers adhere together to form a single filament. In the production of stretch yarns, one polymer may be spandex, for elasticity, and the other nylon, for such purposes as added strength. One such yarn is Monvelle, produced by Monsanto Textiles Co. Other combinations are possible (Figure 4-13).

Chemically Treated Natural Fiber Yarns

Manufacturers of cotton fabrics have been interested for a long time in the development of yarns and fabrics that have stretch. The natural properties of cotton—cool hand, texture, absorbency, washability, and durability—could be enhanced by the addition of stretch capability. The competitive production of ingenious man-made stretch yarns has given great impetus to the experimentation and development of cotton stretch yarns. There presently are three techniques.

Figure 4-13   Longitudinal view of a biconstituent fiber of polypropylene core and nylon sheath. *(Courtesy ICI Fibres, England)*

Heat-set Thermoplastic Cotton Crimping Process. Cotton yarn can be treated with one of several polymeric chemicals, which gives it thermoplastic properties. The yarn is then processed by the same heat-setting and crimping methods that are applied to man-made thermoplastic yarns. Cotton yarns produced by this method have as high as 200 percent stretch, and fabrics woven of these yarns may have up to 100 percent stretch. The higher the thread count, the lower the stretch. Return to original size is not immediate and is generally about 75 percent, though it is completely restored by washing or dry cleaning.

Cotton Yarn Cross-Linking Process. Cotton yarn can be treated with a resin similar to the ones used for cotton wash and wear finishes. This resin is known as a cellulose cross-linking chemical. It gives cotton yarns and fabrics a "memory" and causes them to return to their original state (the same principle as wrinkle resistance). After the yarn has been treated, it is twisted and set with heat. It is subsequently *back-twisted* in the reverse direction. As the treated yarn tries to return to its original twist, it pulls itself up into tiny coils. This provides the springlike action of stretch.

A variation of this process is that of *false-twisting* the resin-treated cotton plied yarns, heat-setting them, and then untwisting the plies. The cotton singles retain their coiled characteristics and thus have the springlike stretch action.

At present, this process is relatively expensive and not too commercially feasible. Performance of the yarns and fabrics is similar to that of the heat-set thermoplastic crimping process.

Slack Mercerization Process. Another method used to provide stretch in cotton is to give the woven cotton fabric a special finish by the *slack mercerization* process. (This finish is discussed further in Chapter 8.) Essentially, it is a technique of passing the cotton fabric through caustic soda as the warp is held at constant tension while the width is allowed to relax. The resultant slack in the filling causes the yarns to contract. Under tension, the filling in the finished fabric may stretch 15 to 20 percent. The fabric returns to about 80 percent of its original size, and it is completely re-

Figure 4-14 Comparison of three types of 70-denier stretch and bulk nylon yarn: *(a)* modified nylon stretch yarn, also known as *set* yarn; *(b)* Ban-Lon Textralized nylon bulk yarn; *(c)* nylon stretch yarn. *(Courtesy American Enka Co.)*

stored by washing. The advantages of this method over the others are increased strength and low cost of production.

BULK YARNS

High-Bulk Yarns

The high-bulk yarns are relatively thick and soft, and they may also have the additional characteristic of stretch. They are always made of crimped staple synthetic fibers that are usually an acrylic, such as Orlon, Acrilan, or Creslan. Blends of these fibers can also be made with other synthetic as well as natural fibers. Some high-bulk yarns are spun with a slack twist, sometimes with crimped staple, to produce a soft, thick, spongy yarn; such yarns generally do not have much natural stretch. Frequently, high-bulk yarns are made by

Figure 4-15 Polyester bulk yarn textured on a single heater false-twist machine and then heat-set in an autoclave. *(Courtesy American Enka Co.)*

Figure 4-16 Comparison of *(a)* spun yarn: 16/1 cotton court, 50/50 blend of cotton/polyester staple; *(b)* textured yarn: 150/32 semidull luster (false-twist method) polyester filament yarn; *(c)* nontextured yarn: 150/32 semidull polyester filament yarn. *(Courtesy American Enka Co.)*

blending stretched fibers with fibers that have been stretched and relaxed. During the dyeing operation, the stretched fibers relax; and their contraction causes the other already relaxed fibers to crimp and curl. This produces a soft, thick, but lightweight stretch yarn. Agilon and Fluflon yarns may be produced as stretch high-bulk yarns.

High-bulk yarns have the soft hand of wool or cashmere. Although they are lightweight, they are warm because the crimped fibers form air spaces within the thick yarn providing insulation. High-bulk yarns have good water adsorbency; water droplets will accumulate on the surface of the fibers in the air spaces. The fabrics do not feel clammy when moist, and they tend to dry more quickly than wool fabrics. Garments made of high-bulk yarns wash and dry-clean readily. But they may pill—that is, form little balls of fiber on the surface of the fabric. To avoid this, garments should be turned inside out and washed gently. Light brushing with a very soft brush will help reduce the pilling. When knitted garments made of these yarns are washed, it is best to block them, since knitted garments of slack-twisted yarns tend to sag.

The durability of garments made of high-bulk yarns depends primarily on the durability of the synthetic fiber used and the amount of twist in the yarn. The more twist in the yarn, the greater the durability; however, the more twist, the less bulk in the yarn. Among the products made of high-bulk yarns are blouses and sweaters (Figures 4-14 to 4-16).

Loop-Bulk Yarns

These yarns are made of any of the continuous-filament fibers, such as rayon, acetate, nylon, or polyester. The textured appearance and hand of the yarns

Figure 4-17 Loftura Estron acetate textured yarn. *(Courtesy Eastman Chemical Products, Inc.)*

resemble that of cotton or fine wool. Yet the yarns have many of the desirable characteristics of the filament fibers used. There are variations in the technique of making textured yarns. They all involve the process of passing smooth filament yarn across high-pressure air jets that cause the individual filaments to loop up and become tangled so that a permanently textured surface of randomly situated tiny loops develops along the yarn. Different textures and effects are possible, depending on the size of the loops, the closeness of the loops, the yarn size, the amount of twist in the yarn, the number of plies, and the nature of the plies. Bouclé yarns can be produced; core and effect yarns can be made by twisting loop-bulk yarns around spun yarns.

Loop-bulk yarns are dull and have the fuzzy or rough appearance and texture of staple yarns. They have bulk without weight, which provides high cover power of 50 to 150 percent of the untreated filament yarn as well as opacity. These yarns have little stretch, depending upon the fiber used. Garments made of loop-bulk yarns launder and dry-clean readily, dry quickly, and need little or no ironing. The air spaces caused by the loops provide for moisture adsorption and some insulation, which makes the fabrics comfortable to wear. These fabrics will not pill, as will those made of some staple fibers, such as nylon or acrylic staple. Loop-bulk yarns are used for a wide variety of textile products, such as shirts, blouses, rugs (Figure 4-18).

Among the trademarks of loop-bulk yarns are the following:

Taslan, by E. I. du Pont de Nemours & Co.

Lofted Chromspun, by Eastman Chemical Products, Inc.

Loftura Estron, by Eastman Chemical Products, Inc. (see Figure 4-17).

Bulked Celaperm, by Celanese Corp. of America

Skyloft, by American Enka Co.

Figure 4-18   Schematic representation of jet crimping. *(Courtesy Heberlein & Co. AG)*

REVIEW QUESTIONS

1. (a) What are the properties of heat-set stretch yarns? (b) Give some common trademarks.
2. (a) Describe briefly each of the several techniques to produce heat-set stretch yarns. (b) Is one method better than another? Why?
3. (a) How are yarns of elastomeric fibers different from heat-set stretch yarns? (b) Name two elastomeric fibers.
4. What is meant by core-spun yarn?
5. How can cotton fiber be made into stretch yarn?
6. What is the difference between high-bulk yarns and loop-bulk yarns?
7. What are the main purposes of bulk yarns?

8. What is draw texturing?
9. Differentiate between (a) FOY, (b) UD, and (c) POY.

SUGGESTED ACTIVITIES

1. Obtain samples of heat-set stretch yarns and elastomeric yarns. (a) Compare them by examination for structure. (b) Compare their stretchability.
2. Obtain samples of high-bulk and loop-bulk yarns and identify their characteristics.

5

WEAVING

yarn to fabric

The second stage of development of fiber into fabric is the weaving process. Although there are other methods of cloth construction, that of weaving, or interlacing, yarns is used most frequently. The interlacing, or weaving, process probably became known before spinning. Primitive people may have observed the interlaced grasses and twigs in the nests of birds, and thus discovered how they could make clothing for themselves, baskets and nets, and thatchlike huts and fences. Or they may have seen rushes naturally interlacing as they grew. Spinning developed when people discovered that the raw materials could be improved before they were woven. In the course of time, rude looms were made, which were crudely simple and hand-operated. The modern power loom used in the textile industry today still contains essentially the same parts and performs the same operations as the simple hand-operated loom.

PREPARATION FOR WEAVING

In the weaving operation, the lengthwise yarns that form the basic structure of the fabric are called the *warp*. The crosswise yarns are the *filling*, also referred to as the *weft* or the *woof*. The filling yarns undergo little strain in the weaving process. In preparing them for weaving, it is necessary only to spin them to the desired size and give them the amount of twist required for the type of fabric for which they will be used.

Yarns intended for the warp must pass through such operations as spooling, warping, and slashing to prepare them to withstand the strain of the weaving process. These operations do not improve the quality of the yarn. In *spooling*, the yarn is wound on larger spools, or cones, which are placed on a rack called a *creel*. From this rack, the yarns are wound on a *warp beam*, which is similar to a huge spool. An uninterrupted length of hundreds of warp yarns results, all lying parallel to one another. These yarns are unwound to be put through a *slashing*, or *sizing*, bath. The slasher machine covers every yarn with a coating (for example, starch) to prevent chafing or breaking during the weaving process. The sized yarns are passed over large steam-heated copper cylinders that remove the moisture and set the size. They are then wound on a final warp beam and are ready for the loom.

ESSENTIAL WEAVING OPERATIONS

On the conventional loom, the warp yarns that are to run lengthwise in the fabric are wound on a cylinder called the warp beam, which is at the back of the loom. The warp also extends to a cylinder called the *cloth beam*, which is at the front of the loom and on which the fabric is rolled as it is constructed. Supported on the loom frame between these two cylinders (the warp beam and the cloth beam), the warp yarns are ready to be interlaced by the filling yarns that run in the width of the cloth, thus producing the woven fabric.

In any type of weaving, four operations are fundamental. They are performed in sequence and are constantly repeated. If these operations are carefully noted, the more varied and advanced constructions of fabric will be readily understood. The essential parts of the loom are the warp beam, cloth beam, harness or heddle frame, shuttle, and reed. These parts perform the following operations:

Shedding—raising warp yarns by means of the harness or heddle frame

Picking—inserting filling yarns by means of the shuttle

Battening—pushing filling yarns firmly in place by means of the reed

Taking up and letting off—winding the finished fabric on the cloth beam and releasing more of the warp from the warp beam

Shedding

On a primitive loom, the weaver had to raise each alternate warp yarn with his finger or with a stick to insert the filling yarns into the warp. Weaving was therefore a very slow process. The raising of the warp yarns formed an opening, or shed, through which the filling yarn was inserted. This first weaving operation therefore became known as *shedding*.

On the modern loom, simple and intricate shedding operations are performed automatically by the heddle frame. This is a rectangular frame to which a series of wires, called heddles, are attached. As the warp yarns come from the warp beam, they must pass through openings in the heddles. Each opening may be compared to the eye of a needle. The operation of drawing each warp yarn through its appropriate heddle is known as *drawing in*.

In the simplest weave construction, the heddle frame raises or lowers certain groups of alternate warp yarns so that the filling yarns alternate in passing under one group of warp yarns and over another. The heddle frame is better known as the *harness*, and that term is used hereafter in referring to the number of harnesses used for the different types of weaves (see Figure 5-1).

Figure 5-1 *(a)* Warp yarns pass through the eyes of the heddles (see enlargement) and are raised or lowered as one unit. *(b)* Warp yarns are evenly separated and held parallel as they pass between the teeth of the reed. *(c)* Looms such as this are capable of utilizing as many as sixteen harnesses to weave a wide variety of fabrics, e.g., lawn, poplin, oxford, sateen, denim, corduroy, and fancy weaves. Note the harness regulators at the top, the filling bobbins at the right to replace empty shuttle bobbins, and the tilted bar on the lower left for striking the shuttle through the shed. *(Courtesy Draper Division, Rockwell International)*

Figure 5-2 The bobbin of filling yarn lies inside the shuttle, and the yarn is pulled through a small opening in the side as the shuttle moves swiftly across the loom. *(Courtesy Steel Heddle Manufacturing Co.)*

Picking

As the harnesses raise the heddles, which, in turn, raise the warp yarns, the filling yarn is inserted through the shed by a small carrier device called a *shuttle*. The shuttle contains a bobbin of filling yarn, which emerges through a hole in the side as the shuttle moves across the loom (Figure 5-2). A single crossing of the shuttle from one side of the loom to the other is known as a *pick*.

The shuttle itself has often created problems of splintering and catching yarns, thus causing the loom to stop. This has led to certain modifications of shuttle structure, such as molding it from a nonsplintering plastic substance. Other alternatives are the shuttleless looms. One type has a fingerlike arm, or rapier, on both sides of the loom. The arm on one side feeds the filling yarn halfway through the shed of warp yarns to the arm on the other side, which reaches in and takes it across the rest of the way (Figures 5-3 and 5-4). Another type uses one long rapier device that reaches across the width of the loom to carry the yarn from one side of the loom to the other. A third type of loom uses an air jet to carry the filling yarn from side to side.

Battening

All warp yarns pass through the heddle eyelets and through openings in another frame that resembles a comb and is called a *reed*. With each picking opera-

Figure 5-3 Close-up of a filling yarn being transferred from one rapier to another midway across a shuttleless loom. *(Courtesy Draper Corp.)*

Figure 5-4 This shuttleless loom has fingerlike arms that extend from the disklike compartments on its sides and feed the filling yarn through the shed. Woven cloth is wound on a roll at the bottom front of the loom. *(Courtesy Draper Corp.)*

tion, the reed pushes automatically, or battens, each filling yarn against the portion of the fabric that has already been formed (see Figure 5-5). This third essential weaving operation is therefore called *battening*. It gives the fabric a firm, compact construction.

Taking Up and Letting Off

With each shedding, picking, and battening operation, the newly constructed fabric must be wound on the cloth beam. This process is known as *taking up*. At the same time, the warp yarns must be released from the warp beam; this is referred to as *letting off*.

SELVAGES

As the shuttle moves back and forth across the width of the shed, it weaves a self-edge called the *selvage* on each side of the fabric. The selvage prevents the fabric from raveling. It is usually made more compact and stronger than the rest of the fabric by using more or heavier warp yarns or by using a stronger weave. There are different kinds of

←HARNESS

←HEDDLES

←REED

←SHED

Figure 5-5 This loom in operation shows how the harness and heddles lift and lower units of warp yarns to form the shed through which the shuttle passes. The reed automatically moves forward to batten each newly woven yarn. (*Courtesy Crompton & Knowles Corp.*)

selvages. The kind of selvage used depends upon economy of production and the expected use of the fabric.

Plain Selvages

These selvages are constructed of the simple plain weave with the same size yarn as the rest of the fabric, but with the threads packed more closely together. Such selvages are fairly durable and firm.

Tape Selvages

The tape selvages are sometimes constructed with the plain weave but often are made of the basket weave, which makes a flatter edge. Tape selvages are made of heavier yarns or ply yarns, which provide greater strength.

Split Selvages

Split selvages are made by weaving a narrow width fabric twice its ordinary width with two selvages in the center. The fabric is then cut between the selvages, and the cut edges are finished with a chain stitch or hem.

Fused Selvages

These selvages are made on fabrics of thermoplastic fibers, such as nylon, by heating the edges of the fabric. The fibers melt and fuse together, sealing the edges. This technique is sometimes used to split wide fabrics into narrower widths or to prevent edges of jersey fabric from curling.

CONSTRUCTION OF CLOTH DESIGNS

In the textile industry, a pattern, or draft, of the weave to be used in the construction of a fabric is designed on cross-sectioned paper by the textile designer. A draft of the design is indispensable when setting up a loom for a particular weave or color effect, as it indicates the particular harness and heddle through which each warp yarn is to be drawn. The horizontal squares represent the filling yarns; the vertical squares represent the warp. The student may obtain a working knowledge of weaves by reproducing such designs on graph paper and then carrying out the actual weaving operations on a miniature loom made of stiff cardboard or a cigar box.

THREAD COUNT

The durability of a fabric depends on (1) the kind and quality of the fiber, (2) the tensile strength of the yarn, (3) the amount of twist in the yarn, (4) the use of ply yarns as compared with singles, and (5) compactness of construction. Compactness is one of the most significant factors when considering the durability of a fabric. It is determined by the closeness of the yarns after the fabric is woven. A closely woven fabric has a larger quantity of yarns than a loosely woven one and is therefore more serviceable. A garment made from such a fabric shrinks less in washing, slips less at the seams, and keeps its shape.

A fabric of compact construction has a high thread count. *Thread count*, also known as *cloth count*, is determined by counting the number of warp yarns and filling yarns in a square inch of fabric. These yarns are commonly referred to as *ends* and *picks*, terms that are synonymous with *warp* and *filling*, respectively. To ascertain the thread count, it is necessary to have a pick glass, sometimes called a thread counter, which is a magnifying glass mounted on a small stand with a square opening in its base. Through this opening, warp and filling yarns are magnified and counted. If the square opening is a $1/4$-inch size, the number of yarns counted in the quarter inch, when multiplied by 4, gives the number of yarns in 1 inch of the fabric. Some pick glasses have a $1/2$-inch square opening; others have a full square inch. The largest size minimizes the possibility of error in computation.

Thread count should not be confused with yarn count. Yarn count measures the degree of fineness in yarns; thread count measures the number of warp and filling yarns in a square inch of fabric. While these counts are separate devices of measurement, there is a direct relationship between them. Thick or coarse yarns will be used if coarse sheeting with a low thread count is to be constructed. These give the fabric greater resistance to hard wear.

Typical Thread Counts

Thread counts range from as low as 20 threads to the inch, used in tobacco cloth, to as high as 350 threads to the inch, found in typewriter-ribbon fabrics. An example of thread count used as a standard is illustrated by the summary of types of muslin and percale sheets in Chapter 11. With some finished goods, such as sheeting, thread count is sometimes given as a single number, which is the addition of warp and filling. A total thread count of 140 threads to the square inch, for example, means that each sheet must have 74 warp yarns and 66 filling yarns to the square inch. The first number indicates the warp; the second is the filling. Thus a 74×66 is described as a 140.

Balanced Construction

A fabric is said to be well balanced if the number of warp yarns and filling yarns are almost equal. For example, a piece of muslin with a thread count of 64×60 is considered well balanced. A piece of gauze with a thread count of 28×24 is also well balanced. In contrast, a broadcloth with a count of 100×60 has poor balance. Although good balance of warp and filling produces a fabric with good wearing qualities, a balanced construction is not always obtainable with certain staple fabrics. Broadcloth shirting, for example, uses approximately twice as many warp yarns as filling yarns. The nature of its construction, therefore, makes it impossible for it to be well balanced according to thread count; yet, it is a durable fabric if its thread count is high.

Sometimes, a fabric may have good balance in its thread count, but it may be altogether unsatisfactory because of weakness in either warp or filling yarns.

The factor of tensile strength of both sets of yarns must, therefore, always be taken into consideration when a fabric is being judged. Both yarn count and thread count determine the suitability and value of finished goods. A safe rule to remember is that a high-count fabric even with poor balance will give better wear than a low-count fabric with good balance.

A fabric's strength can be tested by grasping the fabric with both hands and pressing down and apart with the thumbs close together and parallel. This should be tried in both directions of the cloth. If the yarns are weak, the fabric will split, indicating low durability. If the count is low, the yarns will slide or spread apart into an elliptical opening, indicating weakness under strain or tension at points of stress, such as the seams.

CLASSIFICATION OF WEAVES

The manner in which groups of warp yarns are raised by the harnesses to permit the insertion of the filling yarn determines the pattern of the weave, and in large measure the kind of fabric produced. Weave patterns can create varying degrees of durability in fabrics, adding to their usefulness and also to their appearance. In a simple weave construction, consisting of the filling going under one warp and over the next, two harnesses are needed: one to lift the odd-numbered warp yarns, and a second to lift the even-numbered warp yarns. More than two harnesses are required for advanced weaves, and as many as forty for figured weaves.

Table 5-1

Basic Weaves			
WEAVE	CHARACTERISTICS	ADVANTAGES	LIMITATIONS
PLAIN	No distinct design unless yarns have contrasting colors	Maximum yardage; easily produced; inexpensive; strong; adaptable for direct printing and other finishing processes	Sleazy fabric if thread count is low
Basket	Basket pattern	Attractive; inexpensive; drapable; absorbent	Not durable for apparel; soils easily
Ribbed	Corded effects	Ornamental	Not serviceable if of inferior construction
TWILL	Distinct diagonal design	Strong, firm texture; increased drapability; interesting designs	Requires care to keep clean; develops shine
SATIN	Luster; interrupted diagonal design discernible with magnifying glass	Beauty contributed by luster; smooth; maximum drapability	Excessively long floats may snag and roughen fabric

The three basic weaves in common use for the majority of fabrics are plain, twill, and satin, with some variations (see Table 5-1). Important constructions are also obtained from the following weaves: pile, double cloth, gauze, swivel, lappet, dobby, and Jacquard.

Plain Weave

The plain weave is sometimes referred to as the tabby, homespun, or taffeta weave. It is the simplest type of construction and is consequently inexpensive to produce. On the loom, the plain weave requires only two harnesses. Each filling yarn goes alternately under and over the warp yarns across the width of the fabric (see Figure 5-6). On its return, the yarn alternates the pattern of interlacing. If the yarns are close together, the plain weave has a high thread count, and the fabric is therefore firm and will wear well.

As the manufacture of the plain weave is relatively inexpensive, it is used extensively for cotton fabrics and for fabrics that are to be decorated with printed designs, because the surface that it produces is receptive to a direct print. The appearance of the plain weave may be varied by differences in the closeness of the weave, by different thicknesses of yarn, or by the use of contrasting colors in the warp and filling. The last method gives the effect of a design. In addition, two variations of the plain weave afford simple decorative effects: the basket weave and the ribbed, or corded, weave.

a

a

b

Figure 5-6   The construction design for the plain weave resembles the familiar checkerboard. *(a)* The way in which filling yarns (black squares and yarns) pass under and over alternate warp yarns (white squares and yarns) is shown. *(b)* When fabric is closely constructed in the plain weave, there is no distinct pattern, as shown in this muslin.

Figure 5-7   *(a)* The basket weave is a variation of the plain weave. Two (instead of one) filling yarns pass under and over two (instead of one) warp yarns. This weaving method results in a simple, attractive pattern, so named because baskets have long been woven in this manner. *(b)* Monk's cloth shows how the interweaving of two filling yarns with two warp yarns constructs a loosely woven fabric with an attractive basket-weave pattern.

Fabrics in Plain Weave. In cotton: batiste, broadcloth, bunting, calico, cambric, challis, chambray, cheesecloth, chintz, crash, crepe, crinoline, cretonne, duck or canvas, flannelette, gingham, Indianhead, lawn, longcloth, muslin, madras, nainsook, oilcloth, organdy, osnaburg, outing flannel, percale, percaline, ratiné, seersucker, scrim, sheeting, tarlatan, voile.

In linen: airplane cloth, art linen, cambric, crash, dress linen, handkerchief linen, sheeting, theatrical gauze.

In wool: albatross, blanket cloth, challis, flannel, homespun, nun's veiling, tweed.

In silk, rayon, or other filament yarns: canton crepe, chiffon, crepe de chine, flat crepe, georgette, mousseline de soie, radium, taffeta, voile.

Basket Weave.   The variation of the plain weave known as the *basket weave* uses doubled yarns to produce the design that resembles the familiar pattern of a basket. Two or more filling yarns with little or no twist are interlaced with a corresponding number of warp yarns. They are woven in a pattern of 2×2, 3×3, or 4×4, instead of 1×1, which is the plain weave (see Figure 5-7).

Figure 5-8   The design for oxford cloth shows how a large filling yarn having no twist is woven under and over two single, twisted warp yarns.

a

b

Figure 5-9   *(a)* Drawing of a ribbed, or corded, effect running in the direction of the warp. *(b)* Drawing of a ribbed effect running in the direction of the filling.

The weave used in the popular oxford shirting varies slightly from the regular basket weave in that it has a 2×1 construction; but the size of the single yarn—a coarser yarn used as the filling—is approximately equivalent in size to the two separate warp yarns. As the coarser yarn has no twist, the fabric is of soft texture and has a degree of luster (see Figure 5-8).

Many variations of the yarn construction of the basket weave are possible. For example, there may be a 3×2 or a 5×3, and so on. The size or thickness of the combined warp yarns will, however, always equal the size or thickness of the corresponding filling yarns. This provides a certain degree of balance and pattern to the fabric.

The basket weave produces an attractive, loosely woven fabric that stretches easily and hangs well. It is therefore suitable for drapery and covering fabrics such as monk's cloth. Due to the characteristic looseness of construction and the low tensile strength of yarns that have little or no twist, this weave is not considered desirable for clothing purposes where the factor of durability is a primary consideration.

Fabrics in Basket Weave. In cotton: monk's cloth, hardanger cloth, oxford shirting or suiting, panama cloth, Shirley cloth.

In wool, silk, rayon or other filament yarns: shepherd's check or plaid.

Ribbed Effects. Ribbed, or corded, effects are further variations of the plain weave. The rib may be produced in the warp or in the filling by alternating fine yarns with coarse yarns, or single yarns with doubled yarns (Figure 5-9). Ribbed effects are popular, but the consumer should remember that sometimes inferior yarns are used in their manufacture,

Figure 5-10 *(a)* An example of a well-constructed ribbed fabric. *(b)* When too coarse a yarn is combined with fine yarns for a ribbed effect, the fine yarns adjacent to the rib soon break when subjected to strain or to heavy wear. *(Courtesy U.S. Department of Agriculture)*

especially when the yarns that make the rib are hidden in the thickness of the cloth. As these yarns do not show on either side of the fabric, sometimes extremely short-staple yarns or yarns with insufficient twist are used. A ribbed fabric will not be durable if the ribs are too pronounced, because the coarse yarns that produce the rib tend to pull away from adjacent fine yarns. Also, in ribbed effects, an entire yarn is exposed to friction, thus lessening the durability of the fabric (see Figure 5-10).

Fabrics in Ribbed Effects. Filling-ribbed fabrics include poplin and broad-cloth in cotton; bengaline, faille, taffeta, ottoman in silk, rayon, and other filament fibers. Warp-ribbed fabrics, usually referred to as *waled* or *corded*, include Bedford cord, piqué, and dimity.

Twill Weave

A distinct design in the form of diagonals is characteristic of the second basic weave, called the *twill*. Changes in the direction of the diagonal lines produce variations, such as the herringbone, corkscrew, entwining, and fancy twills (Figure 5-11). Increased ornamentation may be obtained by varying the diagonal

Figure 5-11 *(a)* The common herringbone twill. *(b)* The characteristic diagonal of the twill weave. *(Courtesy National Association of Wool Manufacturers)*

and yarn colors. The values of the twill weave include its strength and drapability. The diagonally arranged interlacings of the warp and filling provide greater pliability and resilience than the plain weave. Also, twill fabrics are frequently more tightly woven and will not get dirty as quickly as the plain weave, though twills are more difficult to clean when they do get soiled. The yarns are usually closely battened, making an especially durable fabric. Twill weaves are therefore commonly used in men's suit and coat fabrics and for workclothes, where strong construction is essential.

In the twill weave, the filling yarn interlaces more than one warp yarn but never more than four, as strength would be sacrificed by so doing. On each successive line, or pick, the filling yarn moves the design one step to the right or to the left, thus forming the diagonal. Whichever the direction of the diagonal on the face of the fabric, the design runs in the opposite direction on the reverse side.

When the direction of the diagonal starts from the upper left-hand side of the fabric and moves down toward the lower right, it is called a *left-hand twill*. When the direction of the diagonal starts from the upper right-hand side of the fabric and moves down toward the lower left, it is called a *right-hand twill*. Although there is no advantage of one over the other, the direction of the diagonal can aid in the recognition of the face of the fabric.

The *steepness* of the diagonal can indicate strength and durability in the fabric. In order to obtain a steep twill, more warp yarns must be used than filling yarns. And since warp yarns have a

Figure 5-12 Drawing shows a three-shaft twill —two warp yarns are interlaced with one filling yarn in each repeat. This is a right-hand, filling-faced twill because the diagonal moves from the upper right down to the lower left, and more filling than warp appears on the face of the fabric. It is also referred to as a one-up-and-two-down twill ($\frac{1}{2}$) because the warp goes over one and under two filling yarns.

higher twist and are stronger than filling yarns, the steeper the twist the stronger the fabric is likely to be.

Twill weaves are named according to the number of harnesses required to make the design. A three- or four-harness twill is frequently used. The word "shaft" may be substituted for "harness," as in *three-shaft* or *four-shaft twill* (Figure 5-12).

Twill weaves are also classified as *even* or *uneven* according to the number of warp and filling yarns that are visible on the face of the fabric. The even twill, for example, shows an equal number of warp and filling yarns in the recurring design, such as two over and two under. This pattern makes what is called a four-shaft twill, and it requires four harnesses.

Most twill weaves are uneven. An uneven twill may show more warp than filling yarns in the recurring design; this is called a *warp-face twill*. If more filling yarns than warp yarns show on the face, the weave is called a *filling-face twill.* Warp-face twills are generally stronger than filling-face twills because the stronger warp yarns on the face of the fabric can take more abrasion and wear. Warp-face twills generally have much more warp than filling yarns; consequently, such fabrics hold their shape better and drape better due to the warp's greater twist and resilience.

Twills are described in terms of the interlacing of the warp yarns over and under the filling yarns. An uneven four-shaft twill, for example, that has one warp yarn riding over three filling yarns is referred to as a three up and one down, or $\frac{3}{1}$. On the other hand, a three-shaft twill that has one warp yarn riding under two filling yarns is referred to as a one up and two down, or $\frac{1}{2}$ (see Figures 5-13 and 5-14).

Fabrics in Twill Weave. Wool fabrics are usually right-hand twills, such as broadcloth, cashmere, cheviot, covert, flannel, gabardine, mackinaw, melton, pilot cloth, serge, tweed, whipcord, and worsted cheviot.

Silk fabrics are also right-hand twills. They include foulard, merveilleux, silk serge, and surah.

Cotton fabrics are usually left-hand twills. They include canton flannel, covert cloth, coutil, denim, drill, gabardine, hickory shirting or hickory stripe, jean, khaki, middle twill, outing flannel, silesia, ticking, venetian cloth, and whipcord.

The twill weave is not used much in the production of linen, as linen yarns make a naturally strong fabric. However, it

Even ($2\frac{2}{2}$)

Uneven, Filling-Faced ($1\frac{1}{2}$)

Uneven, Warp-Faced ($3\frac{3}{1}$)

Figure 5-13 The basic diagonal of the left-hand twill weave. The direction of the diagonal and the number of harnesses used produce different surface designs.

Even (2_2) Uneven, Filling-Faced $(\frac{1}{2})$ Uneven, Warp-Faced (2_T)

Figure 5-14   Right-hand twills.

may be found in linen ticking, twill toweling, and towel drills.

Satin Weave

In basic construction, the satin weave is
similar to the twill weave but generally
uses from five to as many as twelve harnesses, producing a five- to twelve-shaft
construction. It differs in appearance
from the twill weave because the diagonal of the satin weave is not visible; it is
purposely interrupted in order to contribute to the flat, smooth, lustrous surface desired. There is no visible design

on the face of the fabric because the
yarns that are to be thrown to the surface are greater in number and finer in
count than the yarns that form the
reverse of the fabric. The satin weave
may have a warp-face or filling-face
construction.

Warp-Face Satin Weave.   Warp-face satin
is woven so that the warp may be seen on
the surface of the fabric. For example, in
a five-shaft construction, the warp may
pass over four filling yarns and under
one; in a twelve-shaft construction, the
warp may pass over eleven filling yarns

Figure 5-15   These variations of the twill weave show *(a)* and *(b)* broken twills (herringbone), *(c)* gabardine, and *(d)* corkscrew twill.

a   b   c   d

Point Design*   Yarn Layout

Figure 5-16 Warp-face satin weave. Point design (white squares indicate where warp yarns pass under filling yarns) and yarn layout of (a) five-shaft construction, warp floats interlace every fifth filling; (b) eight-shaft construction, warp floats interlace every eighth filling; and (c) twelve-shaft construction, warp floats interlace every twelfth filling.

and under one. Since the warp lies on the surface and interlaces only one filling at a time, the lengths of warp between the filling are called *floats*. These floats lie compactly on the surface with very little interruption from the yarns going at

right angles to them. Reflection of light on the floats gives satin fabric its primary characteristic of luster, which appears in the direction of the warp (see Figure 5-16).

The long floats found in the satin weave might be considered a disadvantage because they represent a minimum of interlacings, and therefore a potential weakness in the fabric. Furthermore, to increase the smoothness and luster of the fabric, the yarns are given a minimum of twist and are therefore relatively weak. The longer the float, the greater the chance that the surface of the fabric will snag, roughen, and show signs of wear. However, the luster makes the fabric suitable for dressy wear and the smoothness, for use as lining.

Satin-weave fabrics drape well because the weave is heavier than the twill weave, which, in turn, is heavier than the plain weave. More harnesses are used for satin weave, thus compressing a greater amount of fine yarn into a given space of cloth. This compactness gives the fabric more body as well as less porosity, which makes the fabric warmer. The quality of drapability also makes satin fabrics preferable for evening wear, and the warmth contributes to its value as lining material.

Designing a Satin Construction. When making a design for a satin construction, the interlacings on successive lines must be separated by a proper interval to avoid forming the contiguous diagonal. When the proper interval for any shaft construction is selected, the design will not repeat itself until the number of successive picks that make up the desired shaft have been interlaced. In a five-shaft construction, for example, the design begins to repeat on the sixth line; in an eight-shaft, on the ninth line; in a twelve-shaft, on the thirteenth line.

Fabrics in Warp-Face Satin Weave. In silk or rayon: damask, double-faced satin, duchesse, merveilleux, satin-faced crepe, slipper satin.

In cotton: damask, sateen, ticking, venetian cloth.

In linen: single and double damask.

Filling-Face Satin Weave. The filling-face satin weave is also called the *sateen weave*; however, this sometimes causes confusion because some cotton and rayon fabrics are also identified as sa-

teen. In this construction, the filling yarn lies on the surface of the fabric as it passes regularly over and under the warp yarns. For instance, a filling yarn may pass over four warp yarns and under one. The floats are consequently made up of the filling yarns, and the luster appears in the filling direction (see Figure 5-17).

Designing a Filling-Face Satin Construction. An eight-shaft construction illustrates here the rules that must be followed to select a suitable interval.

1. Arrange in pairs the numbers that will add up to the desired shaft number. For an eight-shaft filling-face satin, the shaft number is 8. The

Figure 5-17 Filling-face satin weave. Point design (black squares indicate where filling yarns pass under warp yarns) and yarn layout of *(a)* five-shaft construction, filling floats interlace every fifth warp; *(b)* eight-shaft construction, filling floats interlace every eighth warp; and *(c)* twelve-shaft construction, filling floats interlace every twelfth warp.

Figure 5-18 *(a)* Diagram of an eight-shaft filling-face satin construction. Each horizontal line of blocks represents a filling yarn or pick. The blocks covered by letters are the points at which the filling yarns interlace the warp yarns on each successive pick. In the eight-shaft warp-face satin construction, the filling is carried across the back, creating the float in the warp. The basic idea of warp-face satin can be seen when this diagram is turned sideways. *(b)* Satin cloth.

pairs are 1 and 7, 2 and 6, 3 and 5, 4 and 4.

2. Eliminate the pair that contains the number 1 and the number below the shaft number, which is 7 in this case. A contiguous diagonal would result if these intervals were used, producing the conventional twill weave.

3. Next, eliminate the pairs that have a common divisor and those that are divisible into the shaft number. This step eliminates 2 and 6, 4 and 4. The pair 3 and 5 remains. These numbers are the only intervals that can be used in an eight-shaft construction. If any of the eliminated numbers were used as an interval, the fabric would show no interlacing whatever for one or more warp yarns; in fact, there would be no fabric because it would fall apart.

Now that the only possible interlacings have been worked out, the design can be constructed (see Figure 5-18). For convenience, here the interlacing begins

in the lower left square, at *A*. The horizontal rows of squares represent filling yarns—that is, the successive picks on the loom. The vertical rows represent the warp yarns.

The interval to be used for this particular design could be 3 or 5; in this case, 5 has been selected. As this is to be an eight-shaft construction, the interlacing on the first pick will be 7 squares (warp yarns) apart at *B* and *C*.

To find the warp yarn that will interlace on the second pick, count 5 to the right, beginning with the square above the interlacing that is already started at *A*; thus, the interlacing occurs at *D*. Adjacent interlacing on the same line will be 7 squares apart, at *E*.

To find the warp yarn that will interlace on the third pick, start with the square above *D*. Count 5 to the right, and interlacing *G* is plotted. Adjacent interlacings will be 7 squares apart.

On the fourth pick, interlacing *I* is found by counting 5 to the right of the square above *F*; *J* is found by counting 5 to the right of the square above *G*, or 7 squares from *I*.

This same procedure determines the interlacing points on successive picks, additional interlacings always being 7 squares apart.

On the ninth pick, the design starts to repeat, which proves the accuracy of the construction of an eight-shaft weave.

Where it is not possible to plot subsequent interlacing by continuing to count to the right, because of the small area of the design, interlacings on successive picks can be determined by counting 3 to the left instead of 5 to the right. If the interval 3 had been used to count to the right, 5 would have been used to count to the left.

Fabrics in Filling-Face Satin Weave. In cotton: damask, sateen, ticking.

In linen: single and double damask.

Pile Weave

The pile weave is a fancy weave that also includes a plain or a twill construction. In contrast to the three basic weaves that produce a flat surface on a fabric, the pile weave introduces a decorative third dimension, creating an effect of depth. Its construction is especially desirable when softness, warmth, and absorbency are desired. Pile-weave fabrics are also durable if the proper yarns and adequate compact construction are used. In the manufacture of rugs, for example, a strong, tightly twisted staple with compact construction in the base cloth will withstand long wear.

Figure 5-19   *(a)* Drawing of pile weave as it looks after the wires that have raised the filling yarns have been withdrawn. *(b)* Drawing of cut pile which can be produced by using wires equipped with razorlike ends that cut the loops as the wires are withdrawn.

The pile is produced by weaving an additional warp yarn or filling yarn into the basic structure. The additional yarn, which forms loops at regular intervals, is drawn away from the surface of the fabric by thick wires. These loops may be cut or closely sheared, or left uncut if a loop surface is desired (see Figure 5-19*a*).

When the pile is produced by an extra warp yarn, the result is a warp-pile fabric, of which terry, carpet, and plush are examples. Fabrics are classified as plush when the pile is more than $\frac{1}{8}$ inch high. When the pile is produced by an extra filling yarn, the result is a filling-pile fabric, of which velveteen and corduroy are examples.

In certain cut-pile fabrics, the wires used to form the loops are equipped with razorlike ends, so that the loops are cut when the wires are withdrawn, thus producing the cut pile exemplified by velvet carpet (Figure 5-19b). Cut-pile fabrics are produced economically by constructing double-cloth fabrics, as explained in the following section, then cutting the two cloths apart.

Pile effects can also be created by using varying tension in the warp yarns. In the manufacture of rugs, such as chenille, wilton, velvet, and tapestry, various processes are used for pile effects, including hand knotting (see pages 538–539).

Cut-pile fabrics have certain limitations. They catch lint and spot easily. The grain or direction of the pile can be disturbed, causing the appearance of dark areas. In garment construction, the direction of the grain must be properly matched, otherwise there will be an impression of mismatched colors. Some cut-pile fabrics may be laundered, depending upon the fiber used, but they must be thoroughly rinsed so that they will not be stiffened by soaps or detergents. If they need be ironed, they should be pressed with a steam iron. To avoid crushing, ironing should be done on the wrong side. Uncut-pile fabrics may wear better but are not as soft or warm.

Fabrics in Pile Weave. In cotton: chenille, corduroy, duvetyn, frieze, plush, terry (turkish toweling), velour, velveteen.

In wool: frieze, plush, velour, rugs of all kinds.

In silk, rayon, and other filament yarns: chenille, frieze, fur fabrics, plush, transparent velvet, velour, velvets of all kinds.

Linen is seldom made in the pile weave.

Double-Cloth Weave

In the double-cloth weave, two fabrics are woven on the loom at the same time, one on top of the other. The fabric may have a plain weave on one side and a twill weave on the other. Each of the fabrics requires its separate sets of warp and filling yarns. They are combined by interlacing some of the warp or filling yarns or by means of a complete fifth set of stitching yarns. The surfaces of such fabrics may show different patterns or color on each side by varying the yarns as to color and size. A true double-cloth weave is never a pasted construction (Figure 5-20). *never glued together.*

Because the double-cloth weave produces two pieces of fabric combined into one, fabrics so woven are commonly regarded as strong and warm. Warmth, however, is due primarily to the insulative properties inherent in a fiber; bulk and thickness alone do not give warmth. Also, strength cannot be judged by mere

Figure 5-20 The double-cloth weave can be produced by either of two methods: (a) the V method or (b) the W method. Cutting the yarn that holds the two cloths together makes two separate cut-pile fabrics.

thickness or weight. It cannot be assumed that a double-cloth weave will have the qualities of warmth and strength; on the contrary, the fabric may be heavy, bulky, and needlessly expensive. Sometimes, this method of construction is chosen to use a cheaper material on the reverse side of the fabric, thus reducing the cost of a heavy fabric.

Fabrics in Double-Cloth Weave. In cotton: double-faced blankets, bathrobe blankets.

In wool: polo cloth, steamer rugs, overcoatings.

In silk and other filament yarns: upholstery fabrics of all kinds.

Gauze Weave

The gauze weave must not be confused with the weave used in manufacturing gauze bandages or cheesecloth; these materials are made with the plain weave. The true gauze weave construction produces a fabric very light in weight and with an open-mesh effect. Curtain materials and some cotton dress goods are woven with this weave. Such lightweight fabrics have a strength that could not be provided by the plain weave. In the gauze weave, strength is gained by the manner in which the yarns are interwisted: each filling yarn is encircled by two warp yarns twisted about each other.

The gauze weave is sometimes referred to as the *leno weave* because it is made on a leno loom, but the true leno weave is a variation of the gauze weave (see Figure 5-21).

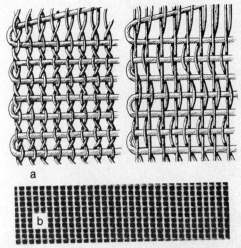

a

b

Figure 5-21   *(a)* Gauze weave (left) and leno weave (right). Note how the filling yarns in the gauze weave are encircled by two warp yarns twisting around each other, a construction that gives strength although the mesh is open. In the leno weave, the second of each of two warp yarns merely passes around the first yarn. *(b)* Marquisette, which is constructed with a leno weave. *(Courtesy U.S. Department of Agriculture)*

On the leno loom, the action of one warp yarn is similar to the action of the warp in the plain weave. The *doup attachment*, a hairpinlike device at the heddle, alternately pulls the second warp yarn up or down to the right or left with each passage of the shuttle. This causes the pair of warps to be twisted, in effect, around each filling yarn. The leno is sometimes used in combination with the plain weave to produce a stripe or figure on a plain background. Generally, the term "leno" is used synonymously with "gauze."

Fabrics in Gauze Weave. In cotton: grenadine, marquisette, mosquito netting, rice net, mesh shirtings.

Figure 5-22 Dotted swiss has a swivel-weave construction into which an additional warp thread is interwoven and subsequently clipped on *(a)* the reverse side of the fabric, producing intermittent dots on *(b)* the face.

In silk, rayon, and other filament yarns: bolting cloth, curtain madras, grenadine, marquisette.

Swivel Weave

The swivel weave is the method by which decorative effects, such as dots, circles, or other figures, are interwoven on the surface of a fabric while it is being constructed on the loom. The weaving of the design requires an extra filling yarn and additional small shuttles. A separate shed is made for these shuttles. While the fabric is being constructed, the row of small shuttles drops across the width of the loom, and each shuttle interweaves its separate design with a circular motion on a small area of the warp. A long thread is carried on the undersurface of the fabric from one design to the next. Different colors may be used in each of the designs because each figure is woven by its own shuttle containing its own miniature bobbin (Figure 5-22).

The decoration produced by the swivel weave is not considered durable, because the swivel yarns are cut when the fabric is completed and cannot be securely fastened. The cut ends roughen the undersurface of the fabric and may pull out if it is handled carelessly in laundering.

Fabrics in Swivel Weave. Dotted swiss, grenadine, curtain madras.

Lappet Weave

The lappet weave is also used to superimpose a small design on the surface of a fabric while it is being woven. In the lappet weave, the design is stitched into the fabric by needles that operate at right angles to the construction. Thus, the lappet weave is very similar to embroidery. The lappet design is made with one continuous additional warp yarn carried on the back of the fabric from one design to the next. Only one color is possible. The floating threads on the back are cut away when the fabric is completed, but the ends are fastened securely and will not pull out easily.

Fabric in the Lappet Weave. Dotted swiss produced by the lappet weave is superior to swivel-weave dotted swiss.

Figure 5-23   A twenty-harness dobby loom with a swivel for weaving fabric with small designs. *(Courtesy Draper Corp.)*

Dobby Weave

The dobby weave is a patterned weave used to construct designs that cannot be produced by the plain, twill, or satin weaves. The designs are simple, limited in size, and usually geometric in form. They are found in shirtings and tie fabrics. The dobby weave is created on a plain loom by means of a mechanical attachment, called a *dobby* or *cam*, which raises or lowers as many as twenty-four to forty harnesses containing the series of warp yarns that form the pattern (see Figure 5-23). Although a large number of harnesses is used in this construction, the design is always small and does not make use of long floats. The most familiar type of dobby weave is bird's-eye, the small diamond pattern that has an eye in its center.

Fabrics in Dobby Weave. In cotton: bird's-eye, huckaback.

In linen: cretonne, huckaback, mummy cloth.

In wool: granite cloth.

Jacquard Weave

In any of the weaves that have been described, the number of harnesses de-

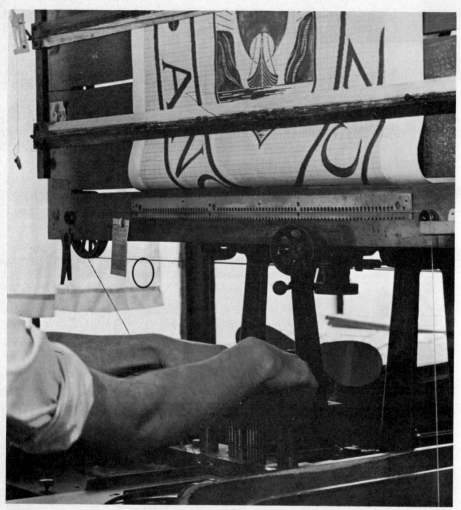

Figure 5-24 The card puncher has a paper design before him. Following a line of checks across the design paper, he inserts steel punches in the cardboards specified on the paper design. Each hole in the card controls the loom mechanism that raises the desired warp yarns in the fabric surface, thus producing the weaving design. *(Courtesy Textile World)*

termines the construction. For example, two harnesses are required for the plain weave, three or more for the twill, and five to twelve for the satin weave. As many as forty can be manipulated by the special attachment of the dobby. The dobby designs are not intricate, however. They are limited to straight lines, edges, steps, or small circular lines.

For curves, swirls, and large-sized figures, it was necessary to devise a different mechanism that would allow an unlimited range of intricate designs. This need is met by the Jacquard attachment, named after its inventor, Joseph Marie Jacquard, a Frenchman. The Jacquard mechanism controls thousands of heddles, which lift one or more warp yarns independently of others without the use of harnesses. Its action is similar to that of the player piano, where each note is governed by a hole on the music roll and is sounded when the hole passes over a certain opening.

The Jacquard design is first worked out on squared paper. Cards are then perforated to correspond with the design; they are laced together and placed on the Jacquard attachment (see Figure 5-24). The moving cards pass over a battery of needles mounted on top of the loom. Each needle controls a string, which, when released, picks up the heddle to which it is tied. The perforations on the cards allow the needles to drop through, and lift certain strings, which, in turn, lift single heddles independently of others (Figure 5-26). The preparation of a Jacquard weave is the most expensive part of its construction. Setting up the loom may take several weeks or months; but once set, the pattern to be produced can be used and reused for different materials. This is the most expensive form of weaving, and it is chiefly used for linen and upholstery materials.

Floats are inevitable in the Jacquard weave because of the elaborate designs. As in the satin weave, long floats may affect the wearing quality of the fabric; also, long cotton yarns exposed to friction cause lint. Compact construction of the fabric, however, offsets the tendency to friction and wear. The consumer should select the better-quality fabrics when purchasing those having the Jacquard weave, especially when purchasing linen damask because table linens receive hard wear and repeated washings.

Fabrics in Jacquard Weave. In cotton: damask, matelassé, tapestry.

In linen: single and double damask.

In wool: tapestry.

In silk, rayon, and other filament yarns: brocade, brocatelle, damask, and tapestry (Figure 5-25).

Figure 5-25 (a) Damask produced by the Jacquard. (b) Brocade produced by the Jacquard. (Courtesy American Viscose Corp.)

Figure 5-26 This Jacquard head loom in operation shows the laced cards at the top of the loom (see insert). The long, slanting strings control the heddles immediately below the cards. The heddles raise and lower the warp yarns in accordance with the pattern punched on the cards above; the filling yarns make the design as the shuttle passes across the loom. (*Courtesy Crompton & Knowles Corp.*)

DISTINGUISHING WARP AND FILLING

Persons who deal with fabrics, as well as the home sewing consumer, must be able to identify the warp and the filling yarns, because the direction of the warp determines the way in which the fabric should be cut when a garment is made from it. In a new piece of yard goods, the direction of the warp is easily distinguished. The length of the fabric indicates the warp yarns. Also, if a piece of the fabric shows part of the selvage, which is the firm edge of the cloth, then the yarns parallel to the selvage are warp yarns. The opposite yarns are the filling yarns. When a sample of fabric contains no selvage, the warp and filling may be identified by observation of the weave:

1. In plain weaves, a greater number of yarns running in one direction indicates the warp.
2. In twill weaves, the filling yarns run in the direction of the diagonal, which may be toward the right or toward the left.
3. In satin weaves, the floating yarns are more likely to be the warp yarns. When one runs a finger over the fabric in both directions, the finger will slide more easily in the direction of the floats. Usually the floats will be in the warp, unless the fabric is cotton. Cotton is more likely to have the floats in the filling.

When the name of the fabric is known, its characteristic features aid in distinguishing the warp and filling. For example, the ribs of dimity and of piqué run in the direction of the warp; the ribs of rep, faille, bengaline, and poplin in the direction of the filling. When colored stripes show in such fabrics as chambray, madras shirtings, and in some dress goods, the direction in which the stripe runs usually indicates the warp.

When the warp and the filling cannot be identified by the foregoing aids, the sets of yarns may be examined for the following characteristics:

1. Exerting tension on a sample by holding it in both hands and pulling, at the same time pressing with the thumbs and forefingers, will show which set of yarns is stronger. The stronger set will be the warp, because warp yarns have to withstand the tension of the heddles in the weaving process. The filling yarn, which emerges from the bobbin of the shuttle as it crosses the fabric, is under little tension.
2. When one set contains yarns of varying sizes, this set is usually the warp. Filling yarns are usually of the same size.
3. The set of yarns that can be more easily stretched is the filling.
4. Yarns of inferior quality are commonly used as filling in inexpensive fabrics. When both sets of yarns are carefully compared, the inferior yarn is usually the filling.
5. When a yarn has a hard twist, as in serges and overcoatings, it is generally the warp yarn.
6. Yarns with slack twist usually are the filling yarns. Yarns with little twist are used as filling when a soft, lustrous effect is desired.
7. If one set consists of thicker yarns, this indicates the filling, as the bulk produced by heavier yarns dispenses with the need for a great amount of twist.
8. If ply yarns are used, they probably indicate the warp.
9. In a napped fabric, the warp runs in the direction of the napping, be-

cause the fabric has been run through the machine in the direction of its length.

10. In light cotton or silk fabrics, a marked evenness between the yarns indicates the warp. This evenness is the result of the mechanical movement of the reed as it battens the filling yarns when the cloth is constructed. In patterned weaves, such as herringbone twill, the impact of the battening operation leaves small reed marks that distinguish filling from warp yarns.

IDENTIFYING THE RIGHT SIDE OF A FABRIC

For cutting and sewing purposes, it is necessary to identify the face, or right side, of a fabric. When the cloth is on a bolt, identification is easy because the fabric is wound or folded with the right side inside to keep it clean. Off the bolt, other characteristics may be observed. If one side of the fabric is shinier than the other, the more lustrous side is the face. If a printed fabric has a more distinct design on one side, that is the right side. When the fabric has a nap, the face is, as a rule, the fuzzier side. When slub yarns are used, they tend to be more outstanding on the right side. Recognition of the weave characteristics also helps.

Twill Weave

Since twills often have a diagonal with a distinct wale or ridge on the face, the right side may be identified in this manner. Even when there is no wale, the diagonal of the twill is likely to be more discernible on the face of the fabric. The cloth should be held so that the warp yarns run up and down.

Satin Weave

If the fabric is very smooth and lustrous, the fabric should be examined closely for floats, which would be on the face. By partially separating out a thread along the edge of the material, one could observe whether the yarn forms the characteristic floats of the satin weave. A magnifying glass will help.

Pile Weave

The prime purpose of the pile weave is to provide textural interest to the fabric. Therefore, the pile will be on the face of the fabric.

Fancy Weaves

The smoother sides of swivel and clip-spot weaves are the right sides. The back of the cloth will show the ends of the clipped yarns used for the design. The lappet weave usually has a trail thread passing on the back of the fabric from one design to the next in the row. The dobby designs, including piqués, are clearer and more outstanding on the face. Jacquard patterns, stand out from the background although the pattern is not always raised.

REVIEW QUESTIONS

1. Explain why lappet ornamentation is permanent and swivel is not.
2. Why are harnesses not required in the Jacquard weave?
3. Describe the basic operations of the weaving process, naming specific parts of the loom.
4. Compare the pile weave and its uses with the double-cloth weave and its uses.
5. Differentiate between plain weave, ribbed weave, basket weave, and twill.
6. Compare the advantages and disadvantages of the twill and satin weaves.
7. Which of the three basic weaves is (a) the most durable, (b) the most beautiful, (c) the most inexpensive to produce? Give reasons for the answers.
8. What weave would you prefer in a shirt, suit, curtains? Why?
9. Why was the Jacquard weave revolutionary in the weaving industry?
10. Contrary to common belief, why does the gauze weave embody strength?
11. Differentiate between damask and a fabric made by the dobby weave.
12. How can one identify the face of a fabric?
13. How can the warp be differentiated from the filling in a fabric?
14. (a) What is a swivel design? (b) On what kinds of garments would it be used?
15. (a) What is the selvage? (b) What are the different types? (c) Which is best and why?
16. Is it of any advantage to the consumer to know the basic differences between the three foundation weaves? Why?

SUGGESTED ACTIVITIES

1. Construct designs for variations of the plain and the twill weaves.
2. Construct a design for producing a ribbed effect in the warp.
3. Obtain samples of fabrics woven in each of the basic weaves described. Mount each fabric on a card and identify the weave.

4. Wind a piece of yarn or string around a square piece of cardboard, about 4 by 4 inches, so that on each side of the cardboard there are parallel yarns in close rows. These are similar to the warp yarns on a loom. Thread another piece of yarn of a contrasting color in a large needle. Insert it through the parallel rows to produce the weave pattern of the three foundation weaves.

6

KNITTING

yarn to fabric or garment

Knitting is the second most frequently used method of fabric construction. The popularity of knitting has grown tremendously within recent years because of the increased versatility of techniques, the adaptability of the many new man-made fibers, and the growth in consumer demand for wrinkle-resistant, stretchable, snug-fitting fabrics, particularly in the greatly expanding areas of sportswear and other casual wearing apparel. Today, the usage of knitted fabrics ranges from hosiery, underwear, sweaters, slacks, suits, and coats, to rugs and other home furnishings.

Hand knitting was an early invention. The earliest known knitted fabric was a pair of thick, hand-knitted wool socks found in an Egyptian tomb, which probably dated back to the fourth century B.C. But the art of knitting seems to have been perfected in Western Europe in the fifteenth century. The word "cnyt-tan" was first mentioned in English literature in 1492. Hand knitting spread rapidly throughout Europe within a few

generations. Primitive needles of bone or wood were first used, producing a coarse mesh. The Spaniards began to use steel needles, which produced a closer mesh and a more evenly knit fabric. In 1589, the Reverend William Lee, an Englishman, invented the first knitting machine, which knit 8 loops to 1 inch of width. As this construction was too coarse a mesh, he improved the machine so that it was possible to knit 20 loops to 1 inch. Today, the average is 28 loops; and the modern knitting machine still operates on the same general principles established by William Lee.

KNITTED CONSTRUCTION

Knitted fabrics may be constructed with a single yarn that is formed into interlocking loops by the use of hooked needles. The loops may be either loosely or closely constructed, according to the purpose of the fabric. Crocheting is knitting in its simplest form. A chain of loops is produced from a single thread by means of a hook. The interlocking loops of the knitted construction permit the fabric to stretch in any direction, even if low-grade yarn having little elasticity or yarn that lacks natural elasticity is used.

COMPARISON OF KNITTING WITH WEAVING

Woven fabrics are constructed by the interlacing of two or more yarns, which does not allow the fabric to stretch to any marked degree unless it is specially stretch-woven. If a certain amount of stretching is necessary, woven fabric must be cut on the bias—that is, in a diagonal direction. Even then the fabric can be stretched only in the direction of the diagonal cutting. The advantage of stretchability in knitted fabrics is an important consideration where fit and comfort are concerned—they fit the figure but do not bind it. Knitted fabrics also give warmth because of the insulative air pockets contained in this type of construction. Yet they are porous and provide "breathing" comfort because body movements cause the loops to expand and contract, thus pushing air through close-fitting garments. Knitted fabrics are very absorbent, light in weight, and wrinkle-resistant. It is usually unnecessary to iron them after laundering.

Certain kinds of knitted fabric have one serious disadvantage: if one of the loops breaks, a hole is made, which starts a run. This disadvantage can be eliminated by variation in the stitch, which protects the fabric from raveling if any single stitch is broken. Some knitted fabrics tend to lose their shape and sag. This tendency can be avoided by using a more closely constructed knit, giving the yarn a tighter twist, and using such special techniques as the double knit. Knitted fabrics may shrink considerably unless special techniques and shrink-proofing processes, such as Pak-nit or Perma-sized, are used. Also, unless the fabric is heavily napped or foam laminated, it is not windproof.

Evaluating Construction of Knitted Fabric

It will be recalled that thread count (the number of threads per square inch) is used to evaluate the construction of woven fabrics. The construction of knitted fabrics is evaluated by the number of stitches or loops that can be counted in any square inch. When the interlocking loops run lengthwise, each row is called a *wale*. A wale corresponds to the direction of the warp in woven fabrics. When the loops run across the fabric, each row is called a *course* (see Figure 6-1). A course corresponds to the filling, or weft. Thus, a knitted fabric having 40 loops or stitches in 1 inch of width, and 50 loops in 1 inch of length, is said to have 40 wales and 50 courses.

The construction of the knitted fabrics varies with the type, and each type has its own particular appearance and properties.

Some constructions, such as jersey and rib knitting, are made with a latch needle, which has a latch or swinging finger that closes onto the hook of the needle as it pulls the yarn through a loop to form a new loop. Other knits, such as the tricot, milanese, and simplex, are made with a spring-beard needle that has a fine, springy hook, which slightly

Figure 6-1 *(a)* A course in a plain circular-knit fabric. *(b)* A wale.

a   b

resembles a beard (Figure 6-2). This type of hook must be used with a sinker and a presser to close it as it forms the loop. However, because of its fineness, the spring-beard needle can be used in the knitting machine in much closer formation to produce more finely constructed fabrics with smaller loops.

The quality of the needle will affect the quality of the knitted fabric. If the thickness of the hook varies from one needle to the next, the stitches will vary in width. Also, if the needles vary in length, so will the loops. Obviously, these variations will affect the appearance, texture, and performance of the knitted fabric.

CLASSIFICATION OF KNITTED FABRICS

Knitted fabrics are divided into two general types: (1) those produced by weft knitting, where one continuous yarn forms courses across the fabric; (2) those produced by warp knitting, where a series of yarns forms wales in the lengthwise direction of the fabric.

Weft Knitting

There are three fundamental stitches in weft knitting: (1) plain-knit stitch, (2) purl stitch, (3) rib stitch. Novelty stitches are variations of these three stitches. The hand method of knitting is weft knitting. On a machine, the individual

Figure 6-2 *(a)* Working arrangement of a group of needles in its lead. *(b)* Latch needle. *(c)* Spring-beard needle. *(Courtesy CIBA Review)*

Figure 6-3 Stitch formation with a latch needle on a weft knitting machine: *(a)* the closed needle after drawing off a loop; *(b)* the needle latch opens as the finished loop slips over it onto the needle stem; *(c)* the thread caught and being drawn by the descending needle head; *(d)* the previously finished loop pushes the latch, closing the needle head while the new loop is formed; *(e)* the first loop slips over the needle head onto the newly formed loop. *(Courtesy CIBA Review)*

yarn is fed to one or more needles at a time (see Figure 6-3).

Plain-Knit Stitch. The *plain knit* is the basic form of knitting. It can be produced in *flat-knit* or in *tubular* (or *circular*) form. The flat knit is also called *jersey stitch* because the construction is like that of the turtleneck sweaters originally worn by English sailors from the Isle of Jersey; it is sometimes called

balbriggan stitch after the hosiery and underwear fabrics made in Balbriggan, Ireland. Plain flat knits may be shaped or full-fashioned.

The knitting is done with a row of latch or beard needles arranged in a linear position on a needle plate or in a circular position on a cylinder (Figure 6-4). All the needles are evenly spaced side by side and are moved by cams, which act on the needle butts. The spacing of the needles is referred to as the *gauge, gage,* or *cut.* As applied to many flat knits and some circular ones, gauge refers to the number of needles in $1^{1}/_{2}$ inches; for example, a 60-gauge machine would have 40 needles per inch. As applied to circular and flat machines that have needles adjustably or slidably mounted, *cut* refers to the number of needles per inch.

The plain knit is made by needles intermeshing loops drawn to one side of

Figure 6-4 *(a)* Section of a circular needle plate showing the arrangement of latch needles. *(b)* Section of a cylinder showing the arrangement of latch needles.

the fabric. These loops form distinctive vertical herringbonelike ribs or wales on the right (or face) side of the fabric. On the reverse (or back) side, the courses can be readily seen as interlocking rows of opposed half circles. This construction gives the face of the fabric a sheen, while the back is dull (Figure 6-5*a*).

The flat knit produces a relatively lightweight fabric compared with the thicker fabrics produced by other stitches. It has a high rate of production (up to 5 times faster than weaving), is inexpensive, and lends itself readily to variation in design by pattern devices. Single or double yarns may be employed.

As the fabric will stretch more in the width than in the length, the plain-knit stitch is widely used for underwear, gloves, hosiery, and sweaters. Most jersey sweaters are knitted with two-ply yarns, providing greater strength and shape retention (Figure 6-5*b* and *c*).

Purl Stitch. This construction is also referred to as the *links-and-links stitch* (after the German word "links," or *on the left*). It is made by needles using hooks on both ends to alternately draw loops to the front of the fabric in one course and to the back in the next course. The fabric looks the same on both sides and resembles the back of the plain knit. It is a slower and more costly technique (see Figure 6-6).

The use of double-hook needles enables ready changeover during fabric construction to include flat and rib stitches, which makes it possible to duplicate virtually any hand-knitted structure. It lends itself to the heavy, jumbo stitch that produces the familiar bulky effect. Because the purl stitch has cross-

Figure 6-5 *(a)* Plain knit, showing right (face) side at left and reverse (back) side at right. *(b)* Run-resistant circular knit. *(c)* Section of a garment knitted in the jersey stitch. *(Courtesy CIBA Review)*

wise stretch and excellent lengthwise stretch, it is widely used in infants' and children's wear.

Rib Stitch. Rib-knit fabrics have alternating lengthwise rows of plain and purl stitches constructed so that the face and back of the fabric appear alike. This is produced by having two sets of needles, generally at right angles to each other. Each set of needles alternately draws loops in its own direction, depending upon the width of the rib desired. For example, rib stitches can be 1 × 1, 2 × 2,

Figure 6-6 *(a)* Links-links double-latch needle with complete head and latch at each end. *(b)* Fabric made on a links-links flat knitting machine. *(Courtesy CIBA Review)*

2×1, 3×1, and so on. A combination of 1×1 and 2×2 is called an *accordion rib*. Rib construction is costlier because of the greater amount of yarn needed and the slower rate of production (see Figure 6-7).

The rib stitch has excellent width-wise elasticity, particularly in the 2×2 rib structure. This characteristic has resulted in its extensive use in apparel where snugness of fit is essential, such as wristbands of sleeves and waistbands

Figure 6-7 *(a)* Diagram of the rib stitch. *(b)* Fabric sample of 2×2 rib stitch.

of garments. It is also widely used for underwear and socks for men and children.

Variations of the rib stitch include the full-cardigan stitch, the half-cardigan stitch, the interlock stitch, the cable stitch, and the double-knit stitch.

The *full-cardigan stitch* is a bulky rib knit and is produced by one set of needles knitting and the other set of needles tucking on the first course. They reverse on the next course, with the plain needles tucking and the rib needles knitting. The fabric has the same appearance on both sides, looking like slightly stretched jersey fabric (Figure 6-8).

The *half-cardigan stitch* is a variation of the full-cardigan stitch. It is produced by one set of needles alternately tucking and knitting on alternate courses. The construction on the back of the fabric is the reverse of the face (Figure 6-9). A variation of this stitch is the

Figure 6-8 (a) Diagram of the full-cardigan stitch. (b) Fabric sample of full-cardigan stitch.

rack stitch, which has a herringbone pattern on the face.

The *interlock stitch* is also a variation of the rib stitch, resembling two separate 1×1 rib fabrics interknitted. To accomplish this, production is slow. The fabric is relatively heavy and is restricted to single yarns, which tend to pill more readily than ply yarns when spun from certain man-made fibers, such as nylon. The fabric has the same ap-

pearance on both sides, and the pattern scope is limited. The limited widthwise but excellent lengthwise extensibility of this stitch has been used to advantage for knit shirts and other sportswear. The fabrics made with the interlock stitch are extremely soft, firm, and absorbent (Figure 6-10a).

The *cable stitch* is formed by small groups of plain wales plaited with one another in ropelike fashion. One familiar form is made of two groups of three wales each, thus utilizing six needles. At regular intervals during the construction, the groups interchange their knitting actions, producing the twisted cable effect. The interesting appearance and textural effect has made this construction popular for outerwear, particularly sweaters (Figure 6-10b).

The *double-knit stitch* has become very popular. It lends itself to such apparel as sportswear and women's suits and dresses, and it is promoted for men's suits and slacks. The fabrics are knitted with two sets of needles producing an interknitted double-layered fabric. The knitted cloth has very desirable properties and characteristics customarily found in woven fabric as well as those found in knitted goods. Double-knit fabrics have firmness, body, and dimensional stability. This gives such fabrics hand and drape similar to that of woven cloth. Yet, the double knits are naturally shape retentive, wrinkle-resistant, and quite durable (Figure 6-10c).

There are several forms of double-knit construction. One type, called *double jersey*, looks like a fine-ribbed fabric on the face and a fine jersey on the reverse. The cloth is quite compact, yet a bit spongy.

Figure 6-9 (a) Half-cardigan stitch showing face side at left, reverse side at right. (b) Fabric sample of half-cardigan stitch.

Figure 6-10 *(a)* Needle set-out for interlock knitting. *(b)* Sample of cable stitch. *(c)* Sample of double-knit stitch.

Another type of double knit is *double piqué*. The surface of this fabric can vary to look like diamond or honeycomb piqué, or the reverse side of wale piqué. Double piqué is produced on circular machines. The Swiss double piqué is made with a smaller, finer loop than the French double piqué (Figure 6-11).

Warp Knitting

Warp knitting differs from weft knitting, basically, in that each needle loops its own thread. The needles produce parallel rows of loops simultaneously that are interlocked in a zigzag pattern. Warp knitting may be flat or tubular and can be produced in many varieties of patterns. It can yield cloth with a dimensional stability almost equal to that of woven fabric. Yet, a modern 28-gauge machine can produce a cloth 168 inches

Figure 6-11 *(a)* Swiss double piqué stitch *(b)* French double piqué stitch. *(c)* Fabric sample of French double piqué stitch.

Figure 6-12   Stitch formation with a spring-beard needle on warp knitting machine: (a) the needle returns after drawing off a loop; (b) the thread guide lays the thread over the needle stop; (c) the needle draws the thread to hook it; (d) the thread is pulled through the first loop to form another one. (Courtesy CIBA Review)

wide at a rate of 1,000 courses per minute—that is, 4,700,000 stitches per minute, or more than 40 square feet of fabric per minute. This speed coupled with the use of yarns of man-made fibers has resulted in a great production of warp-knitted fabrics that enjoy popularity (see Figure 6-12).

Consumers like warp knits because of their smoothness, possible sheerness, wrinkle and shrink resistance, strength, and abrasion resistance. Warp-knit fabrics, as compared with weft knits, also have certain other advantages. Warp knits will not ravel or run and are less susceptible to snagging. Quality is usually better; stitch definition, texture, and fabric cover are generally better than in weft knits. Warp knits have superior dimensional stability.

Products ranging from hairnets to rugs may be produced by warp knitting, depending upon the machine and technique employed. The seven types of warp knitting are tricot, milanese, simplex, raschel, ketten raschel, crochet, and weft-insertion warp.

Tricot Knit. The word "tricot" comes from the French word "tricoter," which means *to knit.* The tricot production began between 1775 and 1780 with the invention of the *warp loom* by an Englishman named Crane. Tricot knits are used in a wide variety of fabrics for such purposes as lingerie, blouses, dresses, and bed sheets.

The gauge in tricot knit is expressed in terms of the number of knitting elements per bar inch. They range from the coarsest of 14 to the finest of 44, with the most popular being 28 gauge. The lighter the gauge, the lighter the fabric and the greater its strength per ounce (Figures 6-13 and 6-14).

Figure 6-13   (a) Double-warp (two-bar) tricot. (b) Single-warp (one-bar) tricot.

Figure 6-14   Tricot fabric being woven on a high-speed warp knitting machine. *(Courtesy Allied Chemical Corp.)*

Tricot fabrics have many good attributes. They are porous and permit passage of water vapor and air for body comfort. They also offer bulk without undue weight. Tricot fabrics are soft, wrinkle-resistant, and have good drapability. They have controllable elasticity, and they do not run or fray. Tricot construction contributes to good abrasion resistance and high bursting and tearing strength. Other factors that contribute to the fabric's strength are the fiber and yarn structure.

Milanese Knit. The milanese stitch, though accomplished by a different technique, produces a fabric almost identical to tricot. (Tricot differs in that faint horizontal lines are discernible.) (See Figure 6-15.) Milanese fabrics are superior to tricot in smoothness, elasticity, regularity of structure, and split and tear resistance. Despite the apparent advantages of milanese fabrics, production has declined considerably due to the low production rates of milanese machines and their limitations in scope of patterns.

Figure 6-15 Diagram of the milanese stitch.

Simplex Knit. Simplex fabrics are produced with spring-beard needles on a machine that is essentially two tricot machines arranged back to back. The gauge ranges from 28 to 34 on fabrics of 84- to 112-inch widths.

Most simplex fabrics are made of cotton, are relatively heavy, and are double faced. They are used for such purposes as gloves, handbags, sportswear, and slipcovers. Eyelet and other openwork may also be produced on the simplex machine.

Raschel Knit. The raschel knit is made with latched needles rather than the bearded type used for tricot, milanese, and simplex. It ranks in importance of production with tricot, but it surpasses it in a variety of products, which range from veilings and laces to pile fabrics. The gauges of these materials are measured in terms of the number of needles per 2 inches. The finest gauges, used for elastic cloths, are 48 and 56. The 18 gauge is used for such products as outerwear and bedspreads. The great majority of these materials are made on a *pillar and inlay principle* that uses one bar of needles knitting ver-

tical rows of loops, or pillars, with each row connected by a horizontal inlay thread.

Raschel machines are extremely versatile. They can knit every type of yarn made of *any* kind of fiber, including metallic and glass, and in *any* form, whether staple or filament, standard or novelty. This versatility naturally extends the possible characteristics and properties of the fabrics produced.

Ketten Raschel Knit. This knit is also called the *chain raschel*. It is a variation of the tricot knit that produces a coarse gauge of 14 to 20 needles per inch on widths of 90 to 120 inches. The machine can be equipped to produce raised pattern effects in one or more colors by a *shell-stitch construction*. Since the ketten raschel knit is produced with bearded needles, the fabric is finer and has a better hand as well as superior elasticity and cover (see Figure 6-16).

Figure 6-16 These magnifications of warp-knit Nylsuisse fabric show variations from basic warp-knit stitches. (*Courtesy CIBA Review*)

Figure 6-17 *(a)* Magnified view of weft-inserted warp-knit fabric showing weft interwoven between the loops. *(b)* Magnified view of weft-inserted plain fabric showing weft interwoven between the loops. *(c)* Weft-insertion carriage for accommodation to knitting machine. *(Courtesy Crompton & Knowles Corp.)*

Crochet. This basic stitch is used in hand-crochet work employing a pillar chain. Using either latch or beard needles, this construction is used in a wide variety of fabrics ranging from nets and laces to bedspreads and carpets.

Weft-Insertion Warp Knit. Still another method of warp knitting is the weft-insertion process. The technique combines the advantages of weaving and warp knitting by inserting a weft yarn into a warp structure. The weft yarn dominates the appearance of the fabric and offers the opportunity for styling versatility because the weft can be of spun, slub, or textured yarns. The weft can also impart color variety, design, and pattern (see Figure 6-17).

Jacquard Knitting

Both weft and warp knitting can incorporate the Jacquard mechanism to produce multicolored designs. The Jacquard punched-card technique used in weaving can also be adapted to knitting. Cards control the selection or inhibition of the needles to produce the pattern.

Another technique for controlling the individual needles to produce the various types of knits and designs utilizes electronic or electromagnetic devices. A third means is the use of a strip of film encoded in a boxed fashion. The film is divided into successive opaque and transparent squares that act similarly to the holes in the Jacquard card or paper tape. A lens directs light through the moving film to phototransistors to select the particular needle for each stitch (see Figures 6-18 to 6-21 and 6-25).

Figure 6-18 The circular Jacquard knitting machine employs spools of yarns of various colors (see insert) to obtain the design governed by the action of the punched tapes shown connected around the middle of the machine. *(Courtesy Wildman Jacquard Co.)*

Pile Knitting

The production of *pile knits* has grown since 1955, with the development of acrylic, modacrylic, and olefin fibers. Weft and warp knitting machines pro- duce imitation fur fabrics and rugs that are similar in appearance to woven fab- rics but are more flexible and have bet- ter drape. These fabrics are lightweight and easy to care for. They usually can be

Figure 6-19 *(a)* This Morat Patronik 500 unit reads freehand designs, fabrics, photographs, or pattern grids in any combination of up to seven colors or shades. The pattern information is stored on magnetic tapes which activate the needles of the circular knitting machine. *(b)* This Morat unit controls the selection of needles for Jacquard knitting by a light directed through moving film that has the design translated into opaque and transparent squares. The light passing through the transparent squares contacts phototransistors which activate the particular needle selection. This device permits the use of up to seven colors in one design. *(Courtesy Sulzer Bros., Inc.)*

Figure 6-20 *(a)* Circular Jacquard knitting can be accomplished by this Morat Patronik 200 system which, left to right, uses a semiautomatic scanner that records a rough pattern sketch of up to six colors (done in colors, black-and-white, or representative symbols) and translates that pattern onto paper tape, a paper tape reader, and a compact computer which transmits the design to the needle-controlling mechanism in this knitting machine. *(b)* Close-up of the punch tape reader of the Morat Patronik 200 semiautomatic pattern scanning and knitting system. *(Courtesy Sulzer Bros., Inc.)*

Figure 6-21   *(a)* This 48-feed double knitting machine is capable of producing an infinite variety of patterns varying from plain fabric and intermediate Jacquards to very large and complex Jacquards controlled by either magnetic tape (on the right) or a solid-state electronic pattern control system. *(b)* Enlargement of additional manual controls for simple mechanical operations without use of electronic feature. *(Courtesy Knitting Machinery Div., Rockwell International.)*

laundered and cold tumble-dried. The pile should then be combed or brushed.

Production of Pile Knits.   The techniques for knitting pile fabrics are quite complicated. The slower and more common method uses a plain knit with heavy yarn for the background and a carded sliver for the pile. As the needles pull the ground yarn to form loops, they catch and draw the sliver through, causing the fibers to get locked into place as the stitch is tightened. Production runs from 5 to 11 yards per hour.

A faster method uses circular-knitting units operating on a cutloop and ground-yarn principle (Figure 6-22). Another technique is the cut-pile and ground-yarn method on a raschel machine.

To simulate natural fur coats, the materials are processed through the following special finishes:

1. *Heat setting*, to preshrink the fabric in length, giving it stability and expanding the diameter of the pile fibers. (If the fabric is made by the uncut-loop method, it must be napped to cut the loops prior to heat setting.)
2. *Tigering*, which uses a roll of wire brushes to remove loose fibers from the face of the fabric.
3. *Rough shearing* by helical knives (similar to those of a reel-type mower) to the desired height.
4. *Electrofying*, a polishing technique that gives a desired luster by comb-

Figure 6-22 The needles of this circular-pile knitting machine form loops from the ground yarns as they come off the spools and draw the carded slivers from the cans through these loops, causing the fibers to get locked into the stitches and forming the pile effect. *(Courtesy Wildman Jacquard Co.)*

ing the fabric in both directions with a heated, grooved cylinder.

5. *Wet application* of certain chemicals, such as silicones and various resins (depending upon the pile fiber), to

further increase the smoothness and luster.

6. *Electrofying* a second time to bring out the luster.

7. *Finish shearing*, a light shearing to

Figure 6-23 Closeup side view of knitted pile fabric *(Courtesy CIBA Review)*

remove loose fibers raised by a previous treatment.

8. *Embossing*, sometimes done instead of shearing when the fabric is to simulate the curl of such furs as karakul, Persian lamb, or broadtail. The fabric may first be processed through an offset and swirling machine with rows of narrow rotary wire brushes, which permanently deform the lay of the fibers in adjoining strips and cause variations in light reflection. The fabrics are then passed under heated embossing steel rollers that are cut to resemble the natural curl of the fur they are intended to imitate. The curl is permanently heat-set into the fabric.

The imitation fur fabrics, which must be labeled as required by law, are much less expensive than genuine fur fabrics. They are soft, resilient, durable, and warm. When not made of wool, they cannot be damaged by moth larvae. They may be dry-cleaned or laundered, depending on the construction (Figures 6-23 and 6-24). Of course, on close examination, they do not have the same appearance or luxuriance of genuine fur.

Figure 6-24   These furlike coats are made of knitted pile fabric of Acrilan acrylic fiber. They are warm, lightweight, and washable. *(Courtesy Monsanto Textiles Co.)*

Figure 6-25   A Jacquard knitted sweater of Orlon Sayelle acrylic fiber. *(Courtesy E. I. du Pont de Nemours & Co.)*

KNITWEAR

To provide greater insight, understanding, and appreciation of the knitting techniques and the characteristics and properties of knitted fabrics, such representative knitwear as hosiery, underwear, and outerwear will now be considered. This discussion should be of particular use and value to the retailer as well as to the consumer, for whom some suggestions are also given regarding the care of such garments.

Hosiery

Before the sixteenth century, the Anglo-Saxon word "hosa" designated a woven cloth garment that covered the lower portion of the body as well as the legs. As knitting was popularized and practiced to a great extent throughout England and Scotland, it soon became customary to knit the leg coverings separately by hand. In the course of time, these garments became known as stockings. Wool was used for such hand knitting.

When William Lee invented the knitting machine, the English queen encouraged him to adapt it to the knitting of silk stockings rather than wool ones because she feared that such a machine would take away the livelihood of the wool hand-knitters. But credit for the later development of machine-knit silk stockings must be given to France, as Lee was invited to that country to set up his machines there when the queen of England failed to grant him a patent. Misfortune still followed Lee, and he died in France before the full value of his knitting machine became apparent.

Hosiery is a major product of knitting, and its cost is often a large item in the clothing budget of the consumer. The construction of hosiery should be of interest because it has a bearing on the serviceability of the article. In most cases, the better-constructed hosiery is well worth its extra cost, provided it is given proper care in wearing as well as in laundering.

Yarns Used for Hosiery. The selection of hosiery yarn depends upon the purpose for which it is to be used. Different types of hosiery are available for sportswear and dresswear for women, children, and men. The yarns may be made of spun staple or filament, and they may be textured. The fiber used will also contribute particular characteristics to the hosiery.

Cotton. Cotton is suitable for hosiery because it is soft, absorbent, and dries quickly. It has less tendency to run when a thread is broken. The durability of cotton hosiery is enhanced when it is made of lisle and mercerized yarns.

Wool. Wool is desirable for some hosiery because of its warmth. The high absorbency of wool is another good feature. Of course, the grade of the wool yarns used has an important bearing on the quality and price of the hose.

Rayon. This was the first man-made fiber to be used for hosiery. But it does not possess the elasticity or strength necessary to produce good-looking, fine hosiery for women.

Nylon. Nylon has proved to be the outstanding fiber for hosiery. Before nylon was developed in 1940, silk had always been the most popular fiber for hosiery because of its strength, elasticity, and pleasing, soft, luxurious texture. Because nylon filament yarn is stronger and more elastic than silk, it has become the first yarn acceptable for fine hosiery in place of silk. Nylon has a greater resistance to abrasion and outlasts silk in the heels and toes of stockings. It lacks the absorbent quality of silk, however. Nylon filament hosiery snags easily and, once a thread is broken, a run develops quickly unless the hosiery is constructed with a run-resistant stitch.

Nylon yarn can be spun into fine deniers, so that a large variety of styles, types, and weights of women's nylon hosiery can be made. At first, the full-fashioned construction was used, but the use of the circular-knit construction on high-count needle machines has increased because nylon can be preset by heat. A preboarding operation stabilizes the nylon stocking fabric against distortion of stitch by subjecting it to conditions higher in temperature than those that will be subsequently encountered.

One kind of nylon developed by Du Pont especially for women's hosiery is Cantrece. Its characteristics, as described on page 384, are a little different from the conventional nylon. Cantrece has greater resilience and fit regardless of the size and shape of the leg, and the fit does not diminish even after continued wear. The superior resilience and fit reduces the straining and wearing effect of stress at the ankle, calf, and knee. Cantrece has a soft, matte finish. It retains a wrinkle-free appearance without letdown or looseness throughout its entire wear-life.

Another fiber that was developed especially for women's hosiery by Monsanto is *Monvelle*, as described on page 384. The dye-resistant spandex constituent in this nylon/spandex biconstituent produces superior translucency and elasticity in combination with the inherent strength and elasticity of nylon.

The nylon staple can also be spun into woollike yarns, which are usually knitted into men's hosiery. Spun nylon hosiery is soft and warm, and the yarn is even more abrasion-resistant than nylon filament yarn; therefore, spun nylon hosiery is very durable and will wear for a very long time—it will, in fact, outwear all other hosiery. Spun nylon hosiery launders easily and does not shrink. The one big disadvantage of this type of hosiery is its tendency to cause the feet to perspire.

Nylon is the most common fiber used to produce yarns that have stretch characteristics, as described in Chapter 4. One trademark of nylon stretch yarn used for hosiery is Agilon. Stretch nylon hosiery has fewer size ranges, fits well without binding, and is durable.

Spun Acrylic. These yarns are often made into men's hosiery, but they do not have the abrasion resistance and wearing qualities of spun nylon. They have low absorbency and a cashmerelike feel but will not produce durable hosiery.

Spandex. Spandex yarns, both covered and uncovered, are particularly well suited for support hosiery for men and women, including women's sheer dresswear.

Types of Hosiery Construction. There are two basic types of hosiery construction: full-fashioned and circular (or seamless). While a third type, cut-and-tailored, has been generally discontinued, features of it are retained in hybrid constructions utilizing the two basic methods.

Full-fashioned Hosiery. Full-fashioned hosiery received its name from the narrowing process performed during the knitting operation to shape the hose to fit the leg. The fabric is knitted flat. Loops are dropped at appropriate points between the knee and the ankle, thus tapering the width of the stocking. Stitches are also dropped to shape the instep and the heel. When the selvages are joined together, the stocking is fully shaped. The joining produces a noticeable seam on the back of the hosiery.

Small dots, called *fashion marks*, appear on both sides of the seam indicating where the stitches were decreased during the narrowing process. Lines, or wales, radiate from these fashion marks. All parts of full-fashioned stockings have the same number of loops to the inch (see Figure 6-26a and b).

A variation in the method of constructing full-fashioned hosiery employs the thermoplastic properties of nylon. The entire leg and foot are knitted to the same width, but progressively tighter stitches are utilized for the graduated body shape. After seaming, the stocking is placed on a *board shape* and heat-set to the desired leg shape. This technique eliminates the fashion marks and radiating wales.

Circular-Knit Hosiery. The most popular form of hosiery construction is circular knit from hem to toe and therefore has no seam. Circular-knit hosiery is sometimes called *seamless hosiery*.

There are the same number of stitches in the width of circular-knit hosiery from top to toe. The shaping is accomplished by gradually reducing the size of the loops from the top to the toe. The heel and toe are shaped by a circular *fashioning* mechanism that drops successive courses in the knitting process (Figure 6-26c and d). In women's hosiery, two or three gores, or segments, will appear in the heel unless it is knitted to have the same sheerness as the leg. This may be called *nude heel*. The toe section may be made in a similar manner. Children's and men's hosiery usually have two-segment gore heels.

To imitate the full-fashioned hosiery, circular-knit hosiery is given a

Figure 6-26 *(a)* and *(b)* Diagrams show fashion marks in full-fashioned stockings and illustrate the method of narrowing in full-fashioned stockings. *(c)* and *(d)* Diagrams show tuck stitch, used in seamless stockings to imitate fashion marks, and illustrate the method of narrowing in seamless stockings. *(Courtesy American Bemberg Corp.)*

mock seam and additional stitches are knitted at the back of the leg. Since the hose is heat-set on a board shape, it provides excellent fit (see Figure 6-27). Circular-knit hosiery eliminates the problem of unsightly twisted or crooked seams on the back of the leg, and it imparts the bare-leg appearance preferred by most women.

A variation of the circular knit is the *fashioned seamless stocking.* This is now in limited production, usually for certain kinds of hosiery specialities. Fashioned seamless hosiery is knit on a special flat machine. The hose is started at the toe, where only a small number of needles is used. As the stocking is widened from ankle to calf and finally to hem, one needle at a time is added to obtain the full-fashioned effect. The added stitches form a V at the back of the leg, which identifies fashioned seamless hose. The fashioned seamless construction makes a comfortable stocking because the seam in the foot is eliminated.

Figure 6-27 At left, unfinished, seamless stocking just off a circular knitting machine. At right, the same stocking after being heat-set on a board shape. *(Courtesy CIBA Review)*

Hybrid Construction of Hosiery. Stocking leg shapes are sometimes cut out of lace machine fabrics as well as from raschel or Jacquard knitted fabrics. These cut blanks are then joined to welts and feet made from other circular- or flat-knitted fabrics, which produces such hosiery as lace stockings and sweater-set hose. Other varieties combine plain stockings or knee-high hose with sewed or topped-on lace, elastic, or plain welts.

Women's Hosiery. Nylon is the most popular textile for hosiery among women. Nevertheless, many women find fault with the durability of their nylon hosiery. For greater service, the following factors should be considered when purchasing nylon hosiery.

Types of Stocking Fabric. The manner in which hosiery is knit has a great deal to do with its durability, appearance, and fit. There are two main types of knit: plain and mesh. The *plain knit* of which most hosiery is made has several advantages. It stretches in both directions, has a smooth clear texture, and provides unequaled sheerness. The outstanding disadvantage of the plain knit is that a break in any loop can cause a run.

The *mesh knit* can be produced in a variety of patterns. Usually, the fabric is of a run-resistant construction. The yarn can snag but will develop only a hole in the fabric rather than a run because the loops are interlocked. Since most mesh-knit fabrics are less stretchable than plain-knit, special attention should be given to proper fit to avoid unnecessary strain on any part of the stocking. A half-size larger stocking is recommended to make up for this lack of stretch. Mesh-knit hosiery is not as smooth or as sheer and flattering to the leg as plain-knit, but it tends to be more serviceable.

Another type of mesh hosiery is the *micromesh knit.* Because this hosiery is constructed with the loops knitted in one direction, the stocking will run in only one direction: from the foot toward the welt.

Sheerness of Hosiery. The sheerness of nylon hosiery depends on the fineness (denier) of the yarn used and the closeness (gauge, for full-fashioned, and needles, for seamless hosiery) of the stitches or loops (see Figure 6-28). The term "denier" indicates the weight of the nylon yarn. The higher the denier, the heavier or thicker the yarn; the lower the denier, the finer the yarn. Nylon deniers most commonly range from 7 (the finest yarn) through 10, 12, 15, 20, 30, 40, 50, 60, and 70.

The term "gauge" refers to the closeness or fineness of the loops across the width of the full-fashioned stocking. The gauge, which indicates the number of stitches or loops per $1^{1}/_{2}$ inches across a knitted row, may range from a low of 39 through 42, 45, 48, 51, 54, 57, 60, 66, 75, and 90. Since each needle makes a loop, the more needles used, the more loops there will be and the finer the gauge. Since a high gauge uses more and finer stitches, it uses more nylon yarn and gives greater strength to the stocking. The higher the gauge and the finer the stitch, the greater the wearing quality and snag resistance.

In seamless hosiery, the closeness of the loops is measured in terms of *needles* on the circular stocking knitting machine. Like gauge, the higher the number of needles, the closer and finer the knit. Sometimes, a seamless stocking

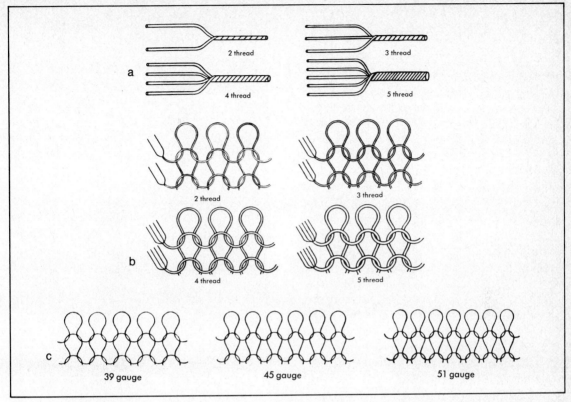

Figure 6-28 *(a)* Construction of a hosiery yarn. *(b)* Total size of hosiery yarn affects sheerness of the stocking. Hosiery of deniers of 30 and above are made of such multifilament yarns. *(c)* Relative fineness of 39, 45, and 51 gauge. *(Courtesy American Bemberg Corp.)*

is also referred to by its equivalent gauge count—that is, a 400-needle count is similar to 51 gauge, a 432-needle count is as closely knit as 54 gauge, and a 474-needle count is similar to 60 gauge.

Gauge affects the appearance and durability of hosiery, but it is the combination of denier and gauge that determines the sheerness of the hose. For example, 45-gauge, 15-denier hosiery is sheerer than 51-gauge, 15-denier hosiery, but the 45-gauge stocking will probably not wear as well because it is not so closely knitted. Likewise, 54-gauge, 15-denier hosiery should wear even better because of the greater number of stitches to each $1\frac{1}{2}$ inches of the stocking. When comparing hosiery deniers and gauges, similar components must be used. Each stocking is a combination of the quality of knitting, the quality of the yarn, the denier of the yarn, the gauge, and the construction features. The following facts are helpful when purchasing hosiery:

15 denier, 51 gauge—filmy and supersheer, for evening wear

20 denier, 51 gauge—sheer weight, desirable for evening wear

30 denier, 51 gauge—average weight, for afternoon or business

40 denier, 45 gauge —duty weight, often preferred for daytime wear at home

60 to 70 denier, 45 gauge—service weight, best for outdoors and for extra long wear

Construction of Hosiery.   For hosiery to wear well, it must be properly constructed. The fact that strong nylon yarn is used, or that a high gauge is employed in knitting the stocking, does not automatically ensure long-wearing hosiery. The seams in full-fashioned hosiery should be straight, sturdy, narrow, and trim, with no raw fabric edges showing. Nylon thread should be used because it assures long-wearing and fast-drying fine seams. When correctly sewed, the heel reinforcing, welt, and fashion marks will match on both sides of the seam. The *welt*, or hem, should be 3 to 4 inches long to permit firm anchoring of the garter. The welt should be sufficiently wide and elastic to fit the thigh without binding. It should measure 7 to 8 inches when flat and should stretch to about 12 to 13 inches to be comfortable on the average leg.

There should be a well-constructed *shadow welt*, or *afterwelt*, directly below the welt, which gives added strength to the upper part of the hosiery by taking up the garter strain. Just below the welt or the shadow welt, there should be a row of *run-stop stitching* around the stocking, which discourages runs starting in the welt from running into the body of the stocking. This stitching can be made in several ways, such as by interlocking the loops during the knitting process. (See Figure 6-29.)

Figure 6-29 Construction of full-fashioned hosiery.

Reinforcement in the toe, heel, and sole is desirable for greater durability and should be in proportion to the weight and style of the hosiery. Some styles of sheer hosiery are made with little or no reinforcement. Fortunately, nylon is strong and can withstand unusual rubbing and abrading before it will wear through.

The *volume* of the stocking is another important consideration. Since nylon hosiery has unusual two-way stretch, flat measurement alone is not sufficient to assure that the stocking is correctly sized. Good construction requires that stockings should conform to standard leg-form sizes. This volume should not be skimpy but rather should be adequate in both girth and length of the foot, leg, and thigh.

Table 6-1

WOMEN'S HOSIERY SIZE—BASED ON SHOE SIZE AND SHOE WIDTH

SHOE SIZE	SHOE WIDTH			
	AAA or AA	A or B	C or D	E or EE
4	8½	8½	9	9
4½	8½	9	9	9½
5	9	9	9	9½
5½	9	9½	9½	9½
6	9½	9½	9½	10
6½	9½	9½	10	10
7	9½	10	10	10½
7½	10	10	10½	10½
8	10	10½	10½	10½
8½	10½	10½	10½	11
9	10½	11	11	11
9½	11	11	11	11

Regardless of the quality of construction, no hosiery will give proper service unless the wearer selects the correct foot size in accordance with the width and size of her shoe, and the correct leg length (see Tables 6-1, 6-2, and 6-3).

When stretch nylon yarns are used, the top of the welt should measure 12 to 13 inches across. A narrower width would tend to bind, while a wider width would not provide sufficient elasticity and snugness. The stocking should be able to stretch about 7 inches at the instep, otherwise strain in this area might result in holes at splicing and sole reinforcement points.

Grading of Hosiery. Hosiery is graded as *first quality, irregulars, seconds,* and *thirds*. Stockings are classified as irregulars if there is an irregularity in dimension, size, color, or knit, but without any breaks, runs, tears, or mends in the fabric or yarn. Seconds and thirds

Table 6-2

WOMEN'S HOSIERY LENGTH—BASED ON STOCKING SIZE

STOCKING SIZE	STANDARD LENGTH		
	Short	Medium	Long
8½, 9	28″	30″	...
9½	28″	31″	34″
10	...	31″	34″
10½, 11	...	32″	34″

have a substantial number of imperfections, including runs, mends, and defects in the yarn, fabric, or finish.

Pantyhose. Pantyhose has become the most popular form of hosiery worn by women and girls. It is generally knitted of nylon in various sheernesses and is also produced as support pantyhose in combinations of nylon and spandex yarns. The legs of pantyhose are

Table 6-3

HOSIERY RUNS AND BREAKS—CAUSE AND CORRECTION	
CAUSE	POSSIBLE CORRECTION
Too much pull from garters. Lack of elasticity of garter or sharp edge on garter clasp.	Wear longer stockings. Have elastic and garters in good condition.
A skimpy welt or not enough elasticity in welt.	Buy stockings with plenty of stretch in the hem or those with a special stretch-top feature.
Stocking too tight or too long.	Buy stockings with more ample tops and of correct length. Garters should never be put into sheer leg fabric or shadow welt.
Too sheer a stocking for the occasion.	Wear stockings of heavier denier yarn or higher gauge knit.
Improper fastening of garter.	Always fasten garters into hem of stockings. Garters fastened into sheer leg fabric, shadow welt, or on the seams frequently result in tears and runs. Handle hose carefully.
Snags or pulled threads.	Avoid contact with sharp or rough objects, as broken or rough fingernails or toenails, zippers, crinoline skirts, and the like. Buy stockings that fit the leg more snugly. Loose, poorly fitting stockings are more readily snagged.
Strain at knee.	Buy longer stockings.
Excessive strain and wear above heel reinforcement.	Buy larger foot size.
Reinforcement too thin.	Buy hosiery with heavier reinforcements. Use lightly reinforced hosiery or sandal-foot types only for more dressy occasions.
Stocking snagging on rough shoe lining.	Have shoe lining repaired. Wear shoes with snug-fitting heels.
Stocking too short in foot, causing runs in toe reinforcing.	Buy larger-sized stockings.
Runs above toe reinforcing when too-long stocking is folded under.	Buy smaller-sized stockings.
Insufficient reinforcement.	Buy hose of heavier denier or more heavily reinforced in toe.
Reinforcement worn through.	Buy stockings more heavily reinforced or of heavier denier for the occasion. Check rough shoe linings.
Friction from bunions, calluses, or similar abrasion.	Take proper care of feet.
Friction from arch supports.	Buy hose with heavier foot reinforcements.

Figure 6-30 Nylon pantyhose are placed on leg forms and are then heat-set so as to permanently retain the leg contour. *(Courtesy Burlington Industries, Inc.)*

circular-knit and tapered to conform to the shape of the leg and foot according to predetermined size. The toe of each knitted leg is seamed closed in a manner that should provide both comfort and good appearance. Each stocking is then put on a flat, leg-shaped frame and permenently heat-set to the knitted size (see Figure 6-30). Matched pairs of leg blanks are then slit in the panty area, a crotch is inserted, and the garment is sewn together. An elastic band is sewn around the top of the pantyhose; this band should have sufficient relaxation and elongation to insure maximum com-

fort and fit. The pantyhose are subsequently dyed, given a final inspection, and packaged.

The size designations for pantyhose, as shown in Table 6-4, are set according to such characteristics as the height and weight of the consumer. However, these size classifications vary somewhat among manufacturers. The construction and yarn used are factors. For example, a Monvelle nylon/spandex yarn may be used to produce four general sizes because of this yarn's inherent elastic characteristics, whereas another nylon or nylon/spandex yarn may require five of more size classifications. The package generally provides the consumer size information.

Men's, Children's, and Infants' Hosiery. Men's, children's, and infants' hosiery, with minor exceptions, are circular-knit and are made of any of the various kinds and combinations of yarns, in many styles and color effects.

Stretch yarns are very popular in men's and children's hosiery. Sizes of

Table 6-4

SAMPLE OF WOMEN'S PANTYHOSE SIZES		
SIZE	HEIGHT	WEIGHT*
A (petite)	5 ft—5 ft 3 in	95–115 lb
B (average)	5 ft 3 in—5 ft 7 in	115–135 lb
C (tall)	5 ft 7 in—5 ft 9 in	135–160 lb
D (large)	5 ft 9 in—5 ft 11 in	160–180 lb

*If weight exceeds that shown for height, use next larger size.

Table 6-5

MEN'S AND CHILDREN'S HOSIERY SIZES					
SHOE SIZE	MEN	CHILDREN AND INFANTS	SHOE SIZE	MEN	CHILDREN AND INFANTS
1	...	4			
1½	...	4	7½	10½	6
2	...	4	8	10½	6½
2½	...	4	8½	11	6½
3	...	4½	9	11	7
3½	...	4½	9½	11	7
4	...	4½	10	11½	7
4½	...	4½	10½	11½	7½
5	9	5	11	12	7½
5½	9½	5	11½	12	7½
6	9½	5½	12	...	7½
6½	10	5½	12½	...	8
7	10	6	13	...	8

SOURCE: Courtesy National Association of Hosiery Manufacturers.

small, medium, and large provide the consumer with greater shopping ease and wardrobe flexibility for the family (Table 6-5). Such hosiery is comfortable and tends to fit the leg better, reducing or eliminating the sagging problems.

Dyeing of Hosiery. Most stockings are dip-dyed, or piece-dyed. This method is satisfactory if proper care is taken to ensure evenness of color, for the flesh background quickly reveals inadequately dyed hosiery. By stretching the seamed part of the stocking, the consumer can tell whether the dyeing was well done. Unevenness of color indicates poor or incomplete penetration of the dye. Hosiery is sometimes yarn-dyed. Ingrain stockings are made from yarns that were dyed before knitting. The amount of ingrain hosiery produced

today is very small. A richer color results, but the hosiery is not as durable as when piece-dyed.

Care of Hosiery. Hosiery should be washed after each wearing, as perspiration could weaken the fiber. Great care is necessary in washing, as rough skin or sharp fingernails cause snags that eventually result in runs. Rings should be removed when hosiery is being handled. Lukewarm water with suds made from mild soap or soap flakes should be used, and the suds squeezed through the hose. The hosiery should be thoroughly rinsed in clear, warm water. Cantrece nylon should be rolled quickly in a towel and then hung on a smooth rod in the same manner as other nylon hosiery. Stockings should never be wrung or twisted. When drying, they should not be exposed to the direct heat of the sun nor hung near a hot radiator or stove. These precautions apply to all types of hosiery. For wool stockings, the additional precautions for washing any wool fabric should be observed. Besides careful washing, the following suggestions will help lengthen the wear of hosiery:

1. Purchase at least two pairs of stockings of the same color, to match pairs when a single stocking has been damaged.
2. Keep stockings in a separate box, when not in use, to prevent contact with anything that may mar their texture.
3. Select the proper size of hose according to well-fitted shoes. The stocking should be at least $1/2$ inch longer than the wearer's foot.

Outerwear

Knitting has long been employed to produce sweaters and shirts. These garments may be constructed in several ways. Front, back, and sleeve sections may be flat-knit and subsequently seamed together. The seamed, flat-knit sleeves may be stitched to a body that has been circular-knit. Sweaters and blouses may also be full-fashion knitted, with the full-fashioned marks showing the contour shaping of the sleeves in the area of the shoulders (Figures 6-31 and 6-32).

Heavier-weight garments, such as jackets, may be constructed of double-knit fabrics that have been cut and sewn as is customarily done with woven fabrics. Such double-knit garments should have the same general contours and fit

Figure 6-31 Full-fashioned fabric made on a flat-knit machine *(Courtesy CIBA Review)*

Figure 6-32 Full-fashioned goods being flat-knitted with the aid of a racking mechanism. Note the two needle bars and the thread feed. (*Courtesy CIBA Review*)

as those of garments made of woven fabrics while providing wrinkle resistance, greater stretch, and shape retention capability—particularly when made of such man-made stretch fibers as polyester.

The type and method of knitting used are dependent upon many factors, including cost of production, the kind of garment (such as a cardigan or pullover), the kind of fiber (such as wool or one of the acrylics), and the kind of yarn (such as bulk or stretch). The techniques vary, depending upon the particular combination of these factors.

While these factors are discussed in various sections of the text, several other considerations should be kept in mind when selecting a sweater or knitted shirt. The quality of the ribbing at the sleeves and waistband should be such that these areas are not binding but elastic, shape retentive, and well finished. Seams should be straight and buttons should meet buttonholes properly to avoid puckering and unevenness. The grosgrain tape backing the buttons and buttonholes should be well-placed and secure. Shoulders of a sweater or a knitted shirt should fit comfortably.

Underwear

There are several factors that cause knitted underwear to differ from other knitted goods. The fiber and yarn used in underwear should be soft and able to absorb perspiration so that the body will be comfortable in all seasons. The stitch must offer sufficient cover and yet provide enough porosity for body ventilation. In order to provide proper fit, construction must allow for changes in dimension due to the finishing processes.

Underwear is made principally on circular-knit machines in various gauges. Most T-shirts and lightweight summer fabrics are made with the plain stitch on weft machines. The range of lightweight summer to heavyweight winter fabrics generally results from combinations of yarn size and needle spacing and the use of one set of needles, as in the plain knit, or two sets of needles, as in the rib knit. So-called fleece-lined fabric used in some underwear, as well as sweatshirts, is constructed of a plain knit employing an extra soft-spun, thick yarn. The yarn is knitted into the back of the fabric in longer course-wise loops and then brushed to produce a soft, fuzzy nap.

Rib fabrics used for underwear are usually of the 1×1 construction. Other ribs used are the 2×2 and, sometimes, the alternating front and back or *panel rib*, which are not as elastic as regular rib knits. Some better quality underwear is made on the Interlock machine, which simultaneously interknits two 1×1 fabrics.

The quality of underwear depends not only upon the fiber, yarn, and knitted construction but also upon the cutting, trimming, finishing, and sizing operations. The consumer should observe the evenness and neatness of the seams. The size should be full and protected against shrinking by such processes as Permasized or Pak-nit (as described on page 184).

REVIEW QUESTIONS

1. How does the construction of knitted fabrics differ from that of woven fabrics?
2. What is the chief advantage gained by the knitted construction?
3. Why is a knitted fabric always a warm fabric?
4. (a) What is a disadvantage of the knitted construction? (b) How can it be eliminated?
5. How would you evaluate the construction of knitted fabrics?
6. Compare the designations for construction and sheerness of full-fashioned and seamless hosiery.
7. What are the characteristics of the basic types of weft knits?
8. What are the advantages of the double-knit construction?
9. What are the characteristics of the basic type of warp knits?

10. How is pile knitting accomplished?
11. (a) What are the types of hosiery construction? (b) Which is preferable, and why?
12. How would you judge a pair of women's stockings?
13. (a) What is meant by gauge of hosiery? (b) What is meant by denier?
14. How will the gauge and denier of nylon hosiery influence a consumer's choice?
15. What is the difference between mesh and micromesh hosiery?
16. How will the fit of shoes affect the wear of hosiery?
17. Why is it important to examine the reinforcements of hosiery?
18. What are the average lengths of hosiery for women?
19. What considerations should be given to the care of hosiery?
20. Compare cotton, wool, rayon, nylon, and acrylics for use in men's hosiery.
21. What factors should one consider when selecting a sweater?
22. (a) What is fleece-lined underwear? (b) How is it made?
23. How are fabrics simulated to look like fur?

7 MINOR FABRIC CONSTRUCTIONS

tufting, Mali, Arachne, felting, bonding, braiding, netting, lace, Doweave

Some methods of fabric construction that have been in existence for a long time have been of relatively minor importance due to their limited practical application. Yet, they retain a place of significance in the textile industry. Felt, braid, net, and lace are all examples of these.

More recently, relatively new techniques of fabric construction have been developed. Perhaps the most important of these is tufting, as evidenced by its dominance in carpet construction. Other methods are the Mali, Arachne, and Doweave techniques, as well as newer felting and bonding methods for producing nonwoven fabrics.

TUFTING

The technique of tufting was developed by the early settlers of the southeastern United States. They worked wick ends (trimmed off their homemade candles) into fabrics to give them pile or tufted designs. These became popularly known as candlewick bedspreads. During the 1930s, machinery was developed to mass-produce such fabrics for cotton rugs, robes, and bedspreads. However, tufting was of little significance until 1950, when the first broadloom carpet was made by this technique. Today more than 90 percent of the carpets are produced by this method. Tufting has also been adapted to the manufacture of blankets and upholstery, and there is much promise for its widespread use for these purposes.

Method of Manufacture

Tufting is done by punching extra yarns into a ground fabric of desired weight and yarn content. Rows of needles, each of which carries a yarn from a spool held in a creel, simultaneously punch through the horizontally held fabric to a predetermined distance. As the needles are withdrawn, hooks move forward to hold the loops, thus forming uncut pile. When

Figure 7-1   Loop-pile tufting. (a) Each time the cloth is fed forward, the tufting needle pushes the yarn through the cloth to form a loop pile. The pile hook moves forward and catches the loop as the knife moves with it to cut progressively the rearmost loop on the hook. (b) The needle inserts the yarn through the fabric to form a loop pile. The hook grasps the loop, holding it in place as the needle is retracted. The height of the loop can be determined and adjusted by the combined depth of needle thrust and hook placement level. (Courtesy The Singer Co.)

cut pile is desired, knives that are attached to the hooks move in scissorlike fashion and cut the loops as the needles are drawn up. The fabric moves a predetermined distance forward each time the needles are retracted (see Figure 7-1).

The tufts of yarn are held in place by their own blooming, or untwisting, and by the shrinkage of the ground fabric in the finishing process. In rugs, where there is much abrasion, the back is coated with latex to hold the tufts.

Tufting is extremely rapid and therefore economical. A fabric can be tufted as rapidly as 3 yards per minute; a length of blanket fabric can be made in two minutes; a rug can be tufted at about 645 square yards per minute. Both cut and uncut pile may be combined.

Sculptured and textural effects can be obtained by controlling the depths of the individual needle punchings. (See also pages 533–534.)

MALI FABRIC-FORMING SYSTEMS

Several years ago, another method of constructing fabrics was invented. The principle was developed in East Germany by Heinrich Mauersberger, who had been trying to improve a knitting machine. One day he observed his wife mending a threadbare tablecloth with an ordinary sewing machine. She reinforced the cloth by passing it back and forth as the needle moved up and down stitching the fabric. This gave him the idea for his machine, Malimo. (The name was derived from "Ma," the first two letters of his last name, "li" from his home town of Limbach, and "mo" from the German word "molton," meaning the flat, napped woolen fabric known in English as "melton").

The machines have been successfully operated in several European plants and several major American fabric mills are also using them. There are three types of machines which can be used: the Malimo, which produces flat fabrics; the Malipol, which produces pile fabrics; and the Maliwatt, which fortifies nonwoven fabrics.

Malimo Technique

Essentially, the Malimo constructs a fabric by placing a layer of warp yarns over a layer of filling yarns and locking the crisscrossed layers together with a multiple needle and thread system, using an interlocking chain stitch (see Figure 7-2). This procedure is done at the rate of 1,200 to 1,400 stitches per minute. As many as 144 filling yarns, or picks, at a time can be fed directly into the machine from creels. This contrasts sharply with the single bobbins used in the shuttle of the conventional loom. It is also possible to produce Jacquard patterns. The Malimo machine is capable of producing fabrics up to 63 inches wide at speeds of 2 to 3 yards per minute—a rate of about 20 times that of the conventional loom.

In addition to the speed and economy of production, Malimo fabrics constructed in this manner do not ravel and have exceptional resistance to tearing. Since the warp and filling are under less tension than in a loom, it is possible to use yarns with less twist. Also, the need to strengthen the warp yarns by slashing is eliminated. Conventional finishing procedures are used.

Variations in fabric construction are possible. For instance, a two-yarn system or a backing fabric may be used in place of warp threads, and either an interlocking chain stitch or a plain chain stitch may be used, depending upon the desired fabric characteristics. They can be made to resemble closely woven or knitted goods. By varying the counts of filling and warp yarns and the gauge and length of the stitch, an infinite number of fabric weights, constructions, and design effects are possible. The wide range of fabrics produced by the Malimo machine has many uses, including coats and other wearing apparel, blankets, draperies, upholstery, and industrial purposes.

Malipol Technique

Pile fabrics are constructed on the Malipol machine. A backing fabric, or scrim, of either woven, knitted, or Malimo structure is conveyed at full width and under proper tension to the stitching area (Figure 7-3). Stitching needles then pierce the fabric, and, with the aid of pile sinkers, the stitching yarn is converted into pile loops of predetermined height on one side of the fabric. The stitching or pile yarns can be fed into the machine from beams or creels. Pile heights may be varied from $3/64$ inch to 1 inch. Depending upon yarn count and constructions, the Malipol machine is capable of constructing pile fabrics up to 67 inches wide at rates of more than 100 yards per hour.

Figure 7-2 These diagrams illustrate the Malimo technique. *(a)* The warp yarns are laid on the filling yarns and the unconnected yarns are joined with an interlocking chain (tricot) stitch to form a solid, ravel-free Malimo fabric. *(b)* The filling carrier moves back and forth across the width of the fabric being formed and places the group of filling yarns on constantly moving filling-hook chains. *(c)* The needles knit the filling and warp yarns together by looping or stitching them together with a third yarn. *(d)* This side view cross-sectional diagram shows how the filling and warp are stitching together by the Malimo fabric-forming technique. *(Courtesy Crompton & Knowles-Malimo, Inc.)*

Figure 7-3 Side view cross-sectional diagram shows how a pile fabric is constructed from a flat backing fabric by stitching loops into it to form a Malipol pile construction. (*Courtesy Crompton & Knowles-Malimo, Inc.*)

Figure 7-4 Side view cross-sectional diagram illustrates the Maliwatt technique of stitching a yarn through a batt of loose fibers in order to form a feltlike fabric. (*Courtesy Crompton & Knowles-Malimo, Inc.*)

Exceedingly dense pile can be obtained by this technique. The loops can be cut to form cut-pile fabrics and, since the pile yarns are firmly stitched into the backing fabric, the pile cannot be readily pulled out. Colored stitching yarns may be used to create stripe designs. Fabrics produced include pile linings, imitation furs, blanket materials, floor coverings, and upholstery.

Maliwatt Technique

By overstitching fiber batting or card webs, the Maliwatt machine rapidly forms a firm fabric (Figure 7-4). A batt or web of loose fibers is conveyed by a lattice arrangement to the stitching area where it is compacted and interlaced with either an interlocking chain stitch or a plain chain stitch, depending upon the desired fabric characteristics. Addi-

tional variations can be achieved through the use of a wide range of yarn counts of any type of fiber.

Maliwatt fabrics, which can be produced as wide as 100 inches, can retain the natural fluffiness of the fibers by regulating the stitching. Feltlike fabrics with various degrees of stiffness can be obtained by impregnating various substances or by using finishing techniques. The fabrics produced are used for interlinings for garments and for industrial purposes.

ARACHNE FABRIC-FORMING SYSTEM

The Arachne machine system was developed in Czechoslovakia in the early 1960s as an economical, highly automated method of fabric formation. It is essentially a technique of stitching webs of fiber with spun or continuous filament

STEP 1. PENETRATION—NEEDLES MOVE FORWARD INTO THE WEB FASTER THAN THE LATCHES WITHIN THE HOLLOW NEEDLE STEM. WEB MOVEMENT IS STOPPED BY THE CLOSING COMB AT THE START OF PENETRATION.

STEP 4. KNOCK-OFF—WHEN THE NEWLY FORMED STITCH IS PULLED THROUGH THE PREVIOUS STITCH, IT (THE PREVIOUS STITCH) IS KNOCKED OFF THE HOOK.

STEP 2. LAPPING—THE WARP ENDS ARE FED TO THE NEEDLE HOOKS BY MEANS OF YARN GUIDES.

STEP 5. DRAWING-OFF—AS SOON AS THE HOOK ENTERS THE KNOCK-OFF COMB, THE WEB MOVES FORWARD. HOW FAR DEPENDS ON THE COURSE SETTING, I.E., THE NUMBER OF COURSES THE OPERATOR WANTS PER INCH.

STEP 3. CLOSING—THE RETRACTING NEEDLE HOOK MEETS THE ADVANCING NEEDLE LATCH. THE CLOSED HOOKS DRAW THE YARN THROUGH THE PREVIOUS STITCH. THE FIBER WEB IS BRACED AGAINST THE PULLING MOTION OF THE STITCH FORMATION BY THE KNOCK-OFF RAIL.

Figure 7-5   How the Arachne system works. These five steps outline the basics of the Arachne method. How fast the machine works depends on two things: (1) weight of the web being fed in and (2) how many stitches per inch you want.

yarn in such a manner as to form stable fabrics (see Figure 7-5). Two dissimilar webs can be stitch-knitted together for such varied purposes as to produce a fabric with a reversible color effect or reversible fiber characteristics. A web may also be stitched to a woven fabric to make an insulating outerwear fabric.

There are several other attributes of the Arachne system. A wider range of fibers can be processed into fabrics than is possible with chemical or heat bonding. New and reprocessed fibers in batch or blend form can be used. Waste fiber from the various yarn-producing processes can be utilized, thereby conserving resources and achieving greater economies. The Arachne machine can handle in one hour as much as 176 pounds of waste, to produce fabrics of up to 98 inches in width and about 200 yards in length.

The process has two stages. In the first stage, a batt is formed of any predetermined thickness, density, and weight from any kind of fiber or fiber blends depending upon the properties desired of the fabric. The batts are produced in rolls of up to 24 inches in diameter. They are successively joined together by overlapping and intermeshing to form one continuous web that passes through the stitching machine. The second stage of the process is dependent upon the kind of fabric desired.

Arachne Stitch-Knitting

In the second stage, the Arachne machine stitch-bonds the webs of cross-laid fibers to form a fabric. The stitch may be chain, tricot, plain, or sateen. The type of stitch used will influence the fabric strength and quality. A wide range of fabrics may be produced. These may be used for dresses, jackets, outerwear, blankets, insulating industrial fabrics, and backings.

Arabeva Stitch-Knitting

The Arabeva technique is similar to the Arachne except that the fibers in the web are laid parallel across the width of the batt and no yarns for stitching are used. The stitching needle moves forward, penetrates the fiber web, and then, as it is pulled back, the needle hook grasps fibers in the web, holds them by a special device on the hook, draws the tangled fibers as a loop out of the web, and forms a chain stitch through the previously pulled loop of fibers. Fabrics made by the Arabeva technique are used as insulating linings for clothing, resilient interlinings, and heat and sound-insulating backings for industrial and building purposes.

Araloop Stitch-Knitting

Araloop produces loop-pile fabrics. There are two techniques. One method utilizes a backing fabric which is stitch-knitted of a tricot construction. In this procedure the needle penetrates the backing and then the web, grasps the yarn, pulls it over sinkers which determine the loop-pile length, and then pulls the yarn through the fabric passing through the previous stitch to form a tricot construction on the back of that fabric. Materials made by this technique are used for such purposes as towels, blankets, and upholstery.

The second method of constructing Araloop fabrics is more economical than the first. Instead of a backing fabric, a fiber web is used. As the web is stitch-knitted by means of a chain stitch, pile loops are constructed on one side with the aid of sinkers, while the other side is stitched as is done in the Arachne construction. These fabrics are used for such purposes as upholstery, outerwear linings, and floor coverings.

Araknit Stitch-Knitting

The Araknit technique produces warp-knit rib fabrics. It is an adaptation of the Arachne process but does not use a web. The kind of stitch may be varied depending upon the desired results. Araknit fabrics may be used for outerwear, home furnishings, and industrial purposes.

FELTED FABRICS

The art of producing fabrics directly from fibers matted together began before spinning and weaving were invented. History records that the patron saint of the felt industry, Saint Feutre of Caen, France, put wool fibers in his sandals to make them more comfortable during his long walking trips. The pressure, moisture, and heat from his feet caused the fibers to interlock into a matted layer. Today, felt is made from wool with or without the admixture of another animal fiber, vegetable fiber, or man-made fiber. Modern techniques have evolved and are still being developed to improve the quality and usefulness of such fabrics. Depending upon whether felt or some related type of fabric is being manufactured, these techniques will be different.

The Felting Process

Felting was originally based upon the physical characteristics of the crimp and scaly surface of wool fibers that cause them to cling and intermesh and allow them to be pressed into a compact fabric. In the wool felting process, two carding operations make the fibers parallel and of even thickness in the form of a fine web. Several webs may be built up until a sufficient amount of weight or thickness has accumulated. Timing is important during these processes, so that the web will not be broken or have weak areas. The mass, or batt, may then be cut, and the edges trimmed to the desired width. Finished felt may vary in thickness from a few thousandths of an inch to 3 inches. Any thickness can be obtained by superimposing batts on one another and felting them together. Batts are usually about 40 yards long and 60 to 90 inches wide; their weights vary from 18 to 50 pounds.

The batts are evenly sprinkled with warm water, passed over a steam box to warm the fibers thoroughly, and then pressed between two rollers. The top roller rests on the batt and, with an oscillating motion, exerts the pressure that, combined with moisture and heat, produces the final felting action.

After the batts have been processed, they are allowed to drain and cool off for about twenty-four hours. The timing for each raw material or blend used in the felt is very important. The felt is then dampened with a suitable lubricant, such as a soap and soda combination, for the *fulling* process, by which it is subjected to a pounding action with hammers. The fulling time varies from five minutes to half an hour. The longer the felt is fulled, the firmer it will be. But this operation cannot be continued too long, or the quality of the felt will be

CHAPTER SEVEN   MINOR FABRIC CONSTRUCTIONS   161

spoiled. Final operations include washing, stiffening, ironing, brushing to raise a nap, and shearing to produce a smooth, even surface. Felt may be made water-repellent and may be flameproofed or mothproofed. It may be dyed against fading, perspiration, cleaning, and washing.

Before 1952, it was believed that felt could be made only from wool or fur. Then technicians at DuPont created a process for making felt from man-made fibers by carding, cross-lapping or air dispersion, followed by passing the batt through a needle punching machine containing numerous barbed needles. (Needle-punched felt is now made of virtually every kind of fiber.) This machine forces fibers into a three-dimensional entanglement that gives the necessary adhesion, structure, and body to the fabric. Controls are provided for uniformity, density, and hardness. A shrinking treatment further contributes to these properties. Felts made by this process are resistant to mildew, rot, chemical degradation, and abrasion.

Types of Felt

There are two basic types of felt: wool and fur. These fibers may be combined with other fibers in various proportions to produce wool- and/or fur-blended felts. Formed fabrics that do not contain wool or fur are not truly felt.

Wool Felt. In most satisfactory grades of wool felt, at least one-half of the fiber comprises wool, as the wool fiber surpasses all others in the physical quality of cohesiveness that makes this type of fabric construction possible. Short-staple wool fiber, or noil, is used for felt; but the finer the grade of staple used, the stronger the felt. Some lower-priced grades of felt are also made chiefly from wool. Other felts are made by combining cotton, kapok, or rayon with wool. These felts may be distinguished from fur felt by the dull appearance, harder feel, and comparatively rougher texture.

Acetate, nylon, and acrylic fibers are also blended with wool. They contribute cross-dyeing color effects and improve the fabric's drapability. These blends also reduce the finished felt's tendency to shrink.

Fur Felt. The short fibers of such fur-bearing animals as the rabbit, muskrat, nutria, and beaver are important in the manufacture of felt for hats. Fur felt is usually made from a mixture of fibers, and the better grade contains beaver. Fur contributes softness, smoothness, resilience, and water repellency.

Properties of Felt

Felt has no warp, filling, or selvage, which simplifies its use in garment construction. Because it does not have a system of threads, it will not fray or ravel. On the other hand, its structure makes sewing difficult; hidden mending of tears and holes is impossible. Because it is made without twisted yarns and without interlacing, felt has little tensile strength and, when it tears, it does so in a ragged, fuzzy manner. It has practically no elasticity or draping quality. However, felt can be cut or blocked into any shape. It has good resilience and will retain its shape unless subjected to undue tension.

Wool felt has high thermal-insulating properties, and it provides warmth. It absorbs sound and shock, and is more impervious to water than untreated woven or knitted fabrics. Since wool felt shrinks, it should be dry-cleaned.

Uses of Felt

The properties of felt affect its application. Lack of tensile strength and drapability limit the use of felt as a general clothing fabric, but it is especially adaptable for blocking into hats. Felt is also suitable for such articles as slippers, shoe insoles, earmuffs, pennants, and table padding. Because of its insulative and noise absorptive properties, felt has various industrial uses.

FORMED (NONWOVEN) FABRICS

To differentiate them from felt, other nonwovens are defined by the American Society for Testing and Materials as fabrics constructed of fibers held together "by bonding or the interlocking of fibers or both, accomplished by mechanical, chemical, thermal, or solvent means, and the combination thereof."

The history of nonwovens began in the 1930s when a few textile firms began experimenting with cotton waste fibers. Significant commercial production began during World War II. The development of man-made fibers and bonding agents gave added impetus to this segment of the textile industry. In the course of this development, cognizance was taken of the detractive and even negative connotation of the term "nonwovens." Consequently, reference to these materials as *formed fabrics* has been widely encouraged and used.

Methods of Manufacture

The processing and manufacture of formed fabrics vary with the fibers and bonding agents used. The fibers include cotton, wool, acetate, rayon, nylon, polyester, acrylic, and glass. Generally, a combination of fibers is employed. The staple, which is usually not waste, ranges from $1/12$ to 6 inches in length. The fibers are processed through a series of opening, conditioning, and blending operations, and through the addition of appropriate resin, rubber, acrylic, or other bonding agents. Webs or layers of fiber are then formed.

Web Formation. Web formation is dependent upon the particular technique employed.

Parallel-laid Web. Fibers are passed through carding machines that put them into parallel alignment. Thin webs of parallelized fiber, produced by successive machines and running in the same direction, are laid on each other to form a multilayer web. This technique produces a fabric which has high lengthwise strength but low crosswise strength. The fabrics produced are used chiefly for disposable products.

Cross-laid Web. After fibers are passed through a carding machine to form thin webs of parallelized fiber, the webs are crisscrossed successively on each other. This technique is more costly to produce, but the fabric has greater crosswise strength than the parallel-laid web type.

Random-laid Web.   Loose fiber is blown onto a rotating, perforated drum. Internal vacuum causes the fiber to adhere to the drum, forming a heavy matte that is then passed to a licker-in, or rotating drum with teeth, which breaks up the web. These particles are blown onto a second vacuum drum, forming a highly uniform web of randomly placed fibers. The thickness of the web can be regulated as required. Fabrics from these random-laid webs have uniform weight (Figure 7-6).

Wet-lay Web.   This method is based upon paper-making technique. Fibers are mixed with certain chemicals, processed through beaters and pulpers, and then passed onto a wire screen. The excess moisture is drawn off, leaving a web that is then compressed in a manner similar to other formed fabrics.

High-velocity Sprayed Web.   This technique is used with thermoplastic fibers. They are first sprayed onto a belt, which produces a random web. Subsequently, heat and pressure are applied to the web causing the fibers to fuse.

Bonding the Web.   There are three principal methods of bonding the fibers in the web to form fabrics. Because the method used and the particular binder applied affect the characteristics of the finished fabric, the intended use of the fabric must be anticipated beforehand.

Resin Bonding.   If the fibers are absorbent, the web may be saturated with a suitable bonding agent either by spraying, printing, padding, or by immersing in a bath just before it is passed between two rollers that compress the web and squeeze out the excess liquid. The web is then dried and heat-cured at temperatures ranging from 200 to 400 degrees Fahrenheit, depending upon the material used.

Gelatin Bonding.   The fibers may be adhered together by a gelatinous substance. One such example is the BAR fiber, which is a cellulose derivative. The fiber in staple form is blended with the web component fibers. Upon contact with water, the BAR fibers dissolve into an amorphous gel which coagulates at the random intersections of the fibers in the web. Subsequently, the web is compressed and dried.

Thermoplastic Bonding.   Thermoplastic fibers with a low melting point may be blended into either a nonthermoplastic fiber web or a web composed of thermoplastic fibers that have a high melting point. The web may then be either calendered or embossed by passing it between rollers heated to the low melting point of the added thermoplastic fibers that fuse and bond with the other fibers.

Spun Bonding.   So-called extruded fabrics are made of polymeric fibers (spun from spinnerets) which are electrostatically charged and caused to fall randomly in web-form on a moving belt and then bonded together by heat or chemical reaction. The fabric produced is one of continuous filaments randomly crisscrossed. One such fabric is Reemay, which is made of polyester fiber bonded by heat and pressure (see Figure 7-7). Tyvek, made of polyethylene, and Typar, made of polypropylene, are similarly

Figure 7-6 Random-laid web (14) is formed by this combined Rando-Feeder and Rando-Webber from dry fiber stock (1) utilizing airflow and conveyor belts. (*Courtesy Curlator Corp.*)

Figure 7-7 The flexibility of Reemay may be predetermined by the use of crimped polyester fibers as shown in (*a*) the microscopic view. (*b*) Microscopic view of a sheet of Reemay shows a nonwoven fabric of thermoplastic polyester fiber bonded by heat. (*c*) The triple exposure photo shows the high strength and shape retention of Reemay nonwoven fabric despite tension in different directions. (*Courtesy Du Pont Magazine*)

produced. Another trademark, Cerex, which is made from nylon, is bonded by the use of hydrochloric acid vapor.

Melding. Bicomponent fibers may be fused together by the process of melding, which is similar in technique to that of spun bonding. The bicomponent fibers are comprised of two polymer components which melt at different temperatures. The components may be extruded in sheathed core or in side-by-side form. Typical of these fibers, which are also referred to as *composite fibers* and *heterofils*, are Cambrelle fibers and filaments, produced by Imperial Chemical Industries, Ltd. By means of a carefully controlled heating process, which the company refers to as *melding*, the component with the lower melting point melts and welds (hence, *melds*) to the fibers with which it is in contact.

The heterofils may be used alone or in blends with homofilaments such as nylon, and as the proportion of homofilaments increases, the tensile strength tends to decrease while the tear strength, softness of hand, and resilience improve. Goods are produced containing both staple-length fibers and continous filaments. Staple products are sometimes reinforced by incorporating a scrim or by needling, which is also used to produce a tuft pattern. Napping may be done to the web prior to melding to produce fabrics for such purposes as blankets and overcoating. Other staple products are used as upholstery, wall coverings, and floor coverings.

Continuous filament melded fabrics find uses as durable primary backings for tufted carpets and in soil stabilization applications. Another continuous filament fabric to which cellulose flock is adhered, known as Melcel, is used for disposables.

Composite Bonding. There are two types of composite formed fabrics. One is the scrim reinforced material, referred to as *SRM*. This is made of webs of fiber laminated in sandwich fashion to an inner scrim-core composed of nylon or other suitable fiber. The other is the tissue fiber laminate, referred to as *TFL*. Webs of tissue are print-bonded to a core of low-twist filament rayon yarns.

The nature and number of the layers of webs or tissues determine the tensile strength, tear resistance, and drape of the fabric. The scrim reinforced material generally has higher strength and tear resistance, but the tissue fiber laminate has greater drapability. Both types are used for such purposes as disposable surgical drape pack components.

Stitch-Through Bonding. Thermoplastic thread may be used to stitch laminated webs together. The application of

heat causes the thread to soften, shrink, and bond to the web structure, making it more compact.

Printed Adhesive Bonding. A web of filament or carded staple fibers may be spread on a belt printed with a pattern of thermoplastic adhesive. With partial curing of the adhesive, it releases from the belt and adheres to the web. The adhered web passes through a heating stage which softens the adhesive and causes it to shrivel together. The coalesced adhesive forms a backing and forces all the fibers upward to form a pile-faced fabric. The pile pattern and texture are determined by the pattern of the printed adhesive. The fabric can be thermoformed and heat-laminated. Variations are possible, depending upon such factors as type of fiber, web orientation, adhesive pattern, amount of fiber adherence, and coalescing ratio.

Needling the Web. Formed fabrics are also produced by inserting barbed needles in fiber webs. As the needles penetrate the web, they force some fibers downward and thereby entangle them with the randomly laid horizontal fibers. As the needles are pulled up, the entanglements increase. The number of needles, the type of barbs on them, the angularity of the needles, and the depth of penetration determine the characteristics of the fabric produced.

Finishing Formed Fabrics

Finishing techniques for formed fabrics are limited. Dyeing is usually done after the fabric has been formed. They may be calendered for smoothness or embossed for textured effects. They may also be printed or flocked. Softness may be added to improve the hand.

Characteristics of Formed Fabrics

The particular set of properties that a formed fabric may have is dependent upon the combination of factors in its production. The range of characteristics is wide. The appearance of formed fabrics may be paperlike, feltlike, or similar to that of woven fabrics. They may have a soft, resilient hand, or they may be hard, stiff, or boardy with little pliability. They may be as thin as tissue paper or many times thicker. Formed fabrics may be translucent or opaque. Their porosity may range from high, free airflow to minute to impermeable. Their strength may range from low tear and burst strength to very high tensile strength. They may be fabricated by gluing, heat bonding, or sewing. The drapability of formed fabrics varies from good to none at all. Some formed fabrics have excellent launderability; others have none. Some may be dry-cleaned.

While these fabrics already have many desirable properties, research is being conducted to produce formed fabrics that would meet or perhaps exceed the qualities of woven cloth.

Uses of Formed Fabrics

The properties of formed fabrics offer both unique and limited applications. Their newness, however, has met with understandable consumer hesitancy. Further developments and consumer education are likely to broaden their application. Today they are being used for apparel, such as aprons, skirts, and caps; home furnishings, such as napkins, draperies, towels, and sheets; medical applications, such as bandages and bed pads; and industrial purposes, such as filters, insulation, and packaging.

BRAIDING OR PLAITING

Another form of fabric construction is the diagonal or lengthwise interlacing that is most familiar as the method of braiding or plaiting long hair. Braid is formed on a braiding machine by interlacing three or more strands of yarn so that each strand passes over and under one or more of the others.

Braids are divided into two types: (1) flat braids, in the form of strips or narrow flat tapes; and (2) round braids, tubular in form, which may be hollow or have a center core of some material. Both types of braiding are produced from any of the textile fibers, as well as from metal threads, tinsel, straw, wire, or leather. This principle of fabric construction is used for making shaped articles, such as straw hats and small rugs; narrow fabrics, such as ribbons and braids for millinery and accessory dress materials; cords and tapes, such as fishlines, shoelaces, wicks, parachute and glider cords, and elastic of various types; and cord coverings for tires, tubing, hose, wires, and cables.

NETTING

Netting is an open-mesh form of fabric construction that is held together by knots or fused thermoplastic yarns at each point where the yarns cross one another. The mesh varies in size and type, and ranges from the very open fishnet to the finest and most delicate lace designs. The open-mesh construction is characteristic of both nets and laces. The true lace construction is always made with a design. *Bobbinet,* which is a machine-made net with a hexagonal mesh and no design, is not a true lace (see Figure 7-8).

LACES

Laces were first made only by hand, and hand laces have always been highly prized as trimming for apparel and as decorative pieces for the home (Figure 7-9). Unusually beautiful and intricately designed laces are retained in families as heirlooms and are displayed in museums as works of art. Real laces, such as needlepoint, bobbin (pillow), darned, crocheted, and knotted are now duplicated so expertly by machine that the average consumer is not able to determine whether a lace is machine-made or handmade. Linen yarns are generally used for expensive laces, but cotton, silk, rayon, and other yarns are used for other qualities and types.

Types of Laces

Lace may be made by knotting or looping, braiding, stitching, or twisting. Many of the lesser-known laces are made by hand; among them is macramé, which

Figure 7-8 Diagram of Bobbinet construction. *(a)* The yarn (on the brass bobbin) is twisted around each of the warp threads in turn. *(b)* Increase the number of such bobbins so that there is one for every second end on the warp (left to right diagonal) and add a second set that moves across the other (right to left) diagonal. *(c)* A regular net of hexagonal form is created. *(Courtesy Shirley Institute, Manchester, England)*

Figure 7-9   The art of making lace by hand. [*Courtesy Press Agency (Yorkshire), Ltd.*]

Figure 7-10   Macramé lace of knotted heavy yarn may be made into such garments as this vest. (*Courtesy American Enka Co.*)

enjoys fashion popularity from time to time. Machine-made laces are made on the Leavers, Nottingham, Bobbin, and Schiffli machines.

Macramé Lace. Macramé differs from other laces in texture and appearance. It is generally made of heavy yarn knotted into relatively large designs. Unlike most other laces, it is used for such purposes as ladies' hats, handbags, belts, and vests (Figure 7-10).

Leavers Lace. The Leavers machine, which was invented in 1813, was developed to incorporate the Jacquard princi-

ple and other improvements. Today, it can produce the most intricate patterns from any type of yarn into fabrics up to 10 yards wide. Leavers machines produce laces that are used to a great extent in the dress industry (Figures 7-11 to 7-13).

Nottingham Lace. The Nottingham machine produces a coarser fabric than the Leavers. Its large overall patterns are used for such purpose as tablecloths.

Bobbin Lace. The Bobbin machine employs the braiding principle. The lace produced has a fairly heavy texture, with an angular appearance and a uniform count. Bobbin lace lacks the fine texture and flowing lines of the laces produced by other machines.

Figure 7-11 *(a)* Detail of a Leavers lace edging. *(b)* Small area of the Leavers lace edging enlarged to show structure in greater detail. *(Courtesy Shirley Institute, Manchester, England)*

Schiffli Lace. Although the Schiffli design closely resembles lace, it is produced by an embroidery technique on the Schiffli machine developed in St. Gall, Switzerland. It is produced now by Swiss descendants from St. Gall living in the northeastern part of New Jersey, around Union City.

The machine was named *Schiffli*, which means "little boat," because of the shape of the shuttle. It employs 682 to 1,020 needles to produce fine and intricate designs in appliqués and embroideries on all kinds of fabrics, particularly sheer fabrics such as batiste, lawn, and organdy. The pattern is controlled by punched cards similar to those used in the Jacquard loom. The finished material has the appearance of expensive handwork but costs much less. The fabrics produced range from narrow trimmings to widths of up to 15 yards, including pile construction.

Uses of Laces

Laces may be classified according to their uses into the following categories:

Allover lace has the design spread over the width of the fabric and repeated in its length. Many kinds of design motifs and colors are used. The fabric can be produced in widths of more than one yard that are devoid of scallops. The fabric comes in bolt form and is used for blouses, dresses, and evening wear.

Flouncing comes in 12-to 36-inch widths and is used for ruffles. It has a straight top edge and is scalloped at the bottom.

Galloon has scalloped edges on top and bottom. It comes in widths of up to 18 inches and is used either as a banded appliqué on a fabric or as an insertion between two pieces of fabric.

Insertion may be sewn either between two pieces of fabric or to the top or bottom edge of a single piece of fabric.

Figure 7-12   A lace dress. *(Courtesy International Institute for Cotton, Manchester, England)*

Figure 7-13   The thin, circular brass bobbins swing to and fro, making a Z-twist movement about the warp yarns to produce Leavers and Nottingham laces. *(Courtesy Shirley Institute, Manchester, England)*

Figure 7-14 *(a)* Detail of a raschel lace curtain fabric. *(b)* Small area of the raschel lace curtain fabric enlarged to show structure in greater detail. *(Courtesy Shirley Institute, Manchester, England)*

Beading is a narrow galloon, insertion, or edging lace that has openings through which ribbon can be interlaced.

Edging comes in widths of 18 inches or less and has a straight top edge and a scalloped bottom. It is used to trim such garments as dresses, blouses, and lingerie.

Medallion is a single-lace design that is used as an appliqué on a ground fabric for dresses, blouses, lingerie, or napkins.

DOWEAVE

In the late 1960s, Norris F. Dow of Pennsylvania developed a weaving system utilizing three sets of yarns instead of the customary two. The technique is based upon a method of weaving cane for such purposes as chair backs and seats. His system was sufficiently unique to warrant a United States patent.

Methods of Construction

In the basic construction of a Doweave fabric, one yarn runs horizontally, the second yarn runs on a bias at a 60 degree angle to the first, and the third yarn runs in the opposite direction of the second and also at a 60 degree angle to the first, forming a triaxial interlocking, as opposed to the 90 degree biaxial interlocking of the conventional weaving technique. As the process is repeated, hexagonal interstices are formed rather than the squares of the conventional construction.

Variations of the basic construction are possible. For example, the horizontal yarn may be woven over and under alternate pairs of parallel bias yarns. The effect produces interstices that are parallelogram in shape. This variation produces a closer construction. Other variations produce fabrics of even closer constructions and different appearances (Figures 7-15 and 7-16).

Fabric Characteristics of Doweave

Fabrics constructed of the basic Doweave are very stable. For example, fabrics made of glass fiber cannot slip or slide. The porosity of the fabric will be determined by the diameter of the yarns and the closeness of the construction. When the fabric is constructed of yarns snugly compacted together, the hexagonal interstices are approximately twice the diameter of the yarn. Therefore, minimum porosity is about one-third of the fabric area. The weave imparts uniform resistance to stretch in all directions. However, if the yarns are very greatly compacted together, they tend to bend or crimp, and this gives the fabric some degree of stretchability.

The variations in construction alter the fabric characteristics. Surface appearance, porosity, and stretchability can be changed. For example, the variation which produces a parallelogram effect has a porosity of about $12^{1}/_{2}$ percent, stability in the horizontal direction, and stretch in the vertical direction.

Uses of Doweave

Fabrics of Doweave construction are primarily used for industrial purposes, such as conveyor belts, reinforcements for plastics, and aerospace accessories. Its various design and stretch possibilities suggest apparel and home furnishings applications.

Figure 7-15 (a) Illustrations of locked-intersection characteristics of Doweave triaxial fabrics, and conventions used for yarn identifications as seen from obverse side. (b) Plan view of the first basic position for weaving the first-variant weave. (c) Plan view of the first basic position for weaving the basic weave; alignment of warp yarns preparatory to shed formation. (d) Plan view of second step in weaving cycle for basic weave; shed formation. (Courtesy Textile Research Institute)

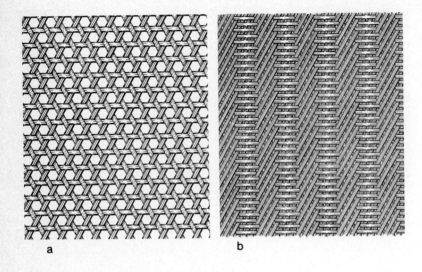

Figure 7-16 Doweave triangularly formed fabric: *(a)* basic weave; *(b)* variant weave. *(Courtesy Doweave, Inc.)*

REVIEW QUESTIONS

1. Describe the felting process.
2. Why is wool preferred in making felt fabric?
3. Why are fur fibers used in the production of expensive felt hats?
4. How is felt used for industrial purposes?
5. How does net differ from woven fabric?
6. What characteristics limit the use of felt for garments?
7. How do bonded formed fabrics differ from felt (a) in construction, (b) in fiber content?
8. What are the important properties of formed fabrics?
9. What limitations do bonded formed fabrics have?
10. Indicate some uses for formed fabrics.
11. Compare tufting to the pile weave (a) in construction, (b) in properties.
12. (a) Describe the Malimo construction. (b) What are its main advantages?
13. (a) What is the Arachne system? (b) What are its advantages?
14. Differentiate between spun bonding and melding.
15. For what purposes is the braided construction used?
16. Why are at least three strands required in braiding?
17. Why is braiding confined to the production of shaped articles?
18. Distinguish net from lace.
19. Compare the kinds of laces made on the several types of lace machines.
20. Describe the uses for lace.
21. What is macramé?
22. What is Doweave construction?

8

FINISHING PROCESSES

appearance and serviceability

Newly constructed fabric as it comes from the loom does not represent finished consumers' goods. It must pass through various finishing processes that make it suitable for many different purposes. Finishing enhances the appearance of the fabric and also may add to its serviceability and durability, thus increasing its value. Familiarity with finishing processes enables the consumer to recognize and judge quality in fabrics. The untrained purchaser is influenced too readily by quantity rather than by quality. He is likely to choose the large, the bulky, the heavy. As manufacturers and retailers conduct their businesses to meet existing demands, textile fabrics are finished to a large extent to satisfy this type of purchaser. This explains why many fabrics are "oversized" and others are weighted. If fabric is not properly constructed and if finishing processes try to conceal inferior construction or to simulate superior quality, the durability of the finished product is questionable.

This does not mean that finishing is intended to deceive the consumer, for no type of finish should be considered as spurious until the purpose of the fabric has been determined. A sustained demand for a particular kind of finished fabric usually explains its continued production.

CONVERTING GRAY GOODS

Finishing processes have assumed such great importance in the textile industry that this phase of textile manufacturing is generally undertaken by a highly specialized group of middlemen called *converters*, even though some firms have integrated conversion into their operations. Conversion of *gray goods*, or goods "in the gray," includes the various types of finishing processes as well as subsequent dyeing and printing.

The converter contracts for a volume purchase of gray goods and then converts this unfinished product into finished consumers' goods in accordance with either solicited demand, based on orders taken by his selling force, or with anticipated demand, which is an estimate of the immediate market.

The term "gray goods" does not imply that the fabric is gray in color. It is another form of the term "greige goods," originally applied only to unfinished silk fabrics, but now used to denote any unfinished fabric as it comes from the loom.

KINDS OF FINISHING PROCESSES

Finishing may take many forms, for it must be adapted to the kind of fiber and yarn used in the fabric and, most important of all, to its intended purpose. One type of gray goods may emerge from a certain finishing process in a form suitable for curtains, while the identical gray goods put through other finishing processes can be used for dress material.

Even the factor of thread count, so important in the evaluation of a fabric, can be changed by the kind and amount of finishing. Cotton can be given the soft finish required for such fabrics as batiste, nainsook, and lawn, the napped finish required for flannelette and duvetyn, the hard stiffened finish typical of cambric and linene, or the lustrous effect of chintz.

The most common finishing processes are listed here. The list does not represent a sequence, nor are all the processes applicable to all kinds of gray goods. Some fabrics must be put through more than one process. Some of the first-named operations are essential preparatory processing for other final finishes, since each fabric is given its own characteristic finishes.

Singeing or gassing
Bleaching
Mercerizing
Slack mercerizing
Ammoniating
Shrinking
Fulling
Tentering
Crabbing
Decating (or decatizing)
Stiffening (temporary and permanent)
Weighting
Calendering
Glazing
Schreinering
Embossing
Moiréing
Ciréing
Beetling
Napping
Gigging
Shearing
Crepe and crinkled effects
Shape-retentive finishes
Water repellency
Soil repellency
Soil release
Waterproofing
Absorbent finishes
Flame retardants
Mothproofing
Mildewproofing
Antibacterial finishes
Slip resistance
Antistatic finishes
Heat-reflectant finishes
Foam laminating
Fabric-to-fabric bonding

Singeing or Gassing

If a fabric is to have a smooth finish, singeing is one of the first essential preparatory processes. Practically all cotton fabrics, except those that are to be napped, are singed. Spun rayon fabrics are also frequently singed, but wool, silk, and man-made fibers are not because they would form unsightly rough melt balls on the surface of the fabric. Singeing burns off lint and threads as well as all fuzz and fiber ends, leaving an even surface before the fabric passes through other finishing processes or a printing operation.

Singeing is accomplished by passing gray goods rapidly over gas flames,

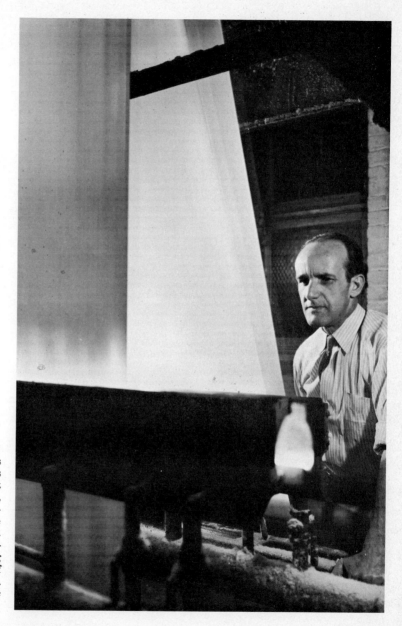

Figure 8-1 As the gray goods pass through the open gas flames of two infrared platens at over 100 yards per minute, hair, fuzz, and lint are singed simultaneously from both faces of the fabric. Singeing produces a smooth fabric surface—prerequisite to flawless dyeing—and eliminates the problem of balling in spun rayon fabrics. *(Courtesy United Piece Dye Works)*

usually two burners to a side, at a speed of 100 to 250 yards per minute (see Figure 8-1). After the cotton cloth leaves the burners, it is pulled through a solution of

an enzyme, squeezed out in a heavy mangle, and usually allowed to lie for several hours to allow the enzyme to digest the starch with which the warp yarns were sized. Rayons sized with gelatin do not need any enzyme treatment. In some plants, the singed goods pass directly into a steamer where the sizing is digested rapidly by the heat and moisture.

Singeing may also be done in the yarn stage, especially when the yarns are to be used for fine-quality cotton goods. Usually such yarns are fully mercerized, and singeing in this case is referred to as *gassing*. Mercerized gassed yarns are sold in the trade as *lisle*. Lisle hosiery was of major importance in both men's and women's styles, but it is being replaced by stronger nylon, polyester, and polypropylene.

Bleaching

If cloth is to be finished white or is to be given surface ornamentation, all natural color must be removed by bleaching. This is also necessary if discoloration or stains have occurred during the previous manufacturing process. Bleaching can be done in the yarn stage as well as in the constructed fabric. The kind of chemicals to be used depends upon the kind of textile fiber of which the fabric is composed. When cloth has been bleached for finishing, it is called *bleached goods*.

In the case of cotton goods, 85 percent of these fabrics are bleached by continuous peroxide methods. In this system, the singed goods are put through a rapid de-size steamer, washed, impregnated with a mild 3 percent solution of caustic soda, and pulled up into the top of a huge J-shaped container (called a *J-box*) that is equipped to maintain a temperature close to 212 degrees Fahrenheit. The J-box is big enough to hold

the goods for at least an hour. After this time period, the fabric is hauled out of the J, given a hot wash, impregnated with a 2 percent solution of hydrogen peroxide, and put in a second J for another hour. Washing follows, and the fabric goes to the dryers fully bleached. Variations on this process include single-J methods, faster routines, and combinations of peroxide and chlorine bleaching.

Some fabrics are bleached by the older method of first boiling off the goods in *kiers*, which are large steel vessels that hold about 5 tons of cloth. The goods are boiled for 12 hours under pressure in a 3 percent solution of caustic soda plus soap and sodium silicate. Then they are washed with cold water, pulled out of the kier, washed again, and "soured" by passing them through a weak solution of sulfuric acid to neutralize the alkali. After another washing, they are passed into a 2 percent solution of sodium hypochlorite and piled into bins or pulled up into J-boxes. After laying there about an hour, they are thoroughly washed, given a "white sour" by running them through a weak solution of sulfur dioxide in water, washed again, and dried for finishing.

All bleaching processes reduce the strength of the fiber. If durability is more important than appearance, the consumer should select gray goods rather than bleached material. With continued laundering, gray goods will gradually become quite white as natural impurities are washed out and the sun bleaches them.

Sunlight is still the primary bleaching aid for fine linens, which are spread out on the grass for several weeks with intermediate washings between grassings. This process is known as *grass bleaching*. The longer the linen remains in the sunlight, the whiter it gets; however, it correspondingly weakens. Commercially, wool is bleached by *stoving*, a process of exposing the scoured fabric to the fumes of burning sulfur. The material is further whitened by immersing it in a bath of hot hydrogen peroxide for several hours and then thoroughly rinsed. Silk also responds well to peroxide. Both silk and wool tend to yellow with age, and a touch-up with peroxide will restore the whiteness.

Man-made fibers as a class require less preparation to whiten. However, not all are easy to bleach. There is little foreign matter in these fibers, but some are inherently off-white and are difficult to whiten. Rayon and acetate are both easy to bleach with either peroxide or chlorine-based bleaches.

Nylon and Zantrel rayon do not respond well to ordinary bleaches. A stronger oxidizing agent, such as peracetic acid or sodium chlorite, is required. The latter is less harmful to the fiber and, in fact, it is beginning to be used extensively in cotton bleaching.

The other man-made fibers respond to chlorine or peroxide. The polyesters and the acrylics (Orlon, Acrilan, Creslan, and Zefran) may be bleached with chlorine. Zefran should not be bleached with peroxide; Verel modacrylic should not be bleached at all. Glass fibers are inert to chemical attack for all practical purposes and do not need bleaching.

In addition to the usual bleaches, mills sometimes utilize *optical bleaches*. Actually, optical bleaches are not true bleaches but flourescent white chemicals that are absorbed into the fabric and give off a bluish white light, thereby hiding the yellowish hue.

Mercerizing

Mercerizing is an important preparatory process for cotton fabric. It is also used in the finishing of linen. The fabric is usually singed before mercerizing, but mercerizing can either precede or follow bleaching. Mercerizing causes the flat, twisted, ribbonlike cotton fiber to swell into a round shape and to contract in length. The fiber becomes much more lustrous than the original fiber, and its strength is increased by as much as 20 percent (see Figure 8-2). Its affinity for direct, vat, and reactive dyes is much greater. Sometimes mercerizing is done

Figure 8-2 *(a)* The highly magnified cotton yarn shows its appearance before gassing and mercerization. Note the dullness of the yarn and the fuzz on its surface. *(b)* The highly magnified cotton yarn shows its appearance after gassing and mercerization. Note the smooth, lustrous appearance and absence of fuzz.

at low concentrations solely to improve the dye pickup. The improvement more than pays for the cost of processing.

Mercerization can give cotton broadcloth a silklike appearance and cause cotton damask to be mistaken for linen. When lisle yarn or high-quality mercerized yarn is used, a silklike luster results.

The process consists of passing the fabric through a cold 15 to 20 percent solution of caustic soda. It is then stretched out on a tenter frame where hot-water sprays remove most of the caustic. A special washer at the end of the tenter removes the balance of the alkali. The process is continuous. Good results require adequate saturation, sufficient tension (caustic soda induces a 20 percent shrinkage if the fabric is relaxed), and thorough washing.

Durene Finish. This is a standardized process of mercerizing that utilizes a fine quality of cotton yarn. Manufacturers who maintain standards established by the Durene Association of America are allowed to label their product "Durene Yarns." These yarns are made of fine long-staple combed cotton and are always of two-ply construction.

Slack Mercerizing

In order to maintain and expand the important position of cotton in our economy and have cotton keep up with the growth of man-made fibers, the U.S. Department of Agriculture, at its Southern Regional Research Center in New Orleans, Louisiana, embarked upon an experimental program to impart the property of stretch to cotton. During the early 1960s, an extension or variation of the principle of mercerization was one of the techniques developed (as well as others described on pages 85–86). The technique has been applied to yarn as well as to woven and knitted fabrics. It is also used in producing woven fabrics with stretch in the filling direction.

To obtain stretch in the filling direction only, cotton fabric is held under tension in the length, relaxed in the width, and treated with a strong cold caustic soda solution for about one minute. It is then washed in clear water (at or near boiling temperature) and dried. This slack mercerization causes contraction of the yarns not held under tension (in this case, the filling yarns). Subsequently, the dried fabric will stretch from 15 to 20 percent in the filling direction with about 80 percent recovery, in inverse relation to the compactness of construction. Complete recovery occurs with laundering (Figure 8-3).

This amount of stretch allows comfort and easy movement to the wearer. It is considered adequate for such apparel as shirts, blouses, and dresses. It also provides better-fitting cotton fabrics, despite the lack of complete stretch recovery. Stretch fabrics made by slack mercerization can have 4 times as much abrasion resistance as can untreated fabrics.

Improved stretch and recovery can be obtained by treating the slack mercerized fabric with a wash and wear or cross-linking resin. When a resin is used, however, the fabric loses from 30 to 50 percent of its strength, but techniques are being developed to reduce this loss.

Figure 8-3   *(a)* Cotton filling yarn and *(b)* cotton fiber in this photo were removed from cotton twill fabric after slack mercerization. Note the crimp in the yarn and in the fiber. *(c)* Cotton filling yarn and *(d)* cotton fiber shown here were removed from plain-weave fabric after slack mercerization. *(Courtesy U.S. Department of Agriculture, Southern Utilization Research and Development Div.)*

Slack mercerization of knitted goods has been primarily applied to all-cotton hosiery. The hose are loosely knit to about twice the normal length and from 25 to 30 percent less than the normal width. They are then slack mercerized, which causes about 50 percent reduction in the length only and provides a permanent lengthwise stretch quality. The hose are then bleached and dyed. These socks have the properties of good cotton. They have a good hand, are absorbent, and do not bind, but rather cling lightly to the leg. While the hose tend to "grow," or sag, somewhat during a day's wear, they recover their shape with washing.

Ammoniating

The newer ammoniating process for cotton yarn and fabrics, as well as for yarn and fabrics of rayon, has many advantages over mercerizing. The process is less expensive, has little or no polluting consequences, results in fewer imperfections, produces greater strength of 40 to 50 percent over untreated cotton as compared to the 20 percent increase by mercerization, and increases yarn smoothness, thereby improving abrasion resistance and knitability. Like mercerizing, ammoniating increases luster, dimensional stability, and affinity for dyes. Improved hand contributes wrinkle-shedding ability, and the process contributes to effective permanent press characteristics of cross-linked cotton fabrics.

The process consists of passing the yarn or fabric through a weak solution of ammonium at −33°C (where swelling and shrinkage occur) and then rapidly passing it through hot water as it is stretched about 5 percent more than its original length. It is then dried in hot air and packaged. This process is licensed as *Prograde* by a Norwegian firm, the Tedeco Textile Development Co. The trademark *Duralized* identifies the ammoniated process of Cluett, Peabody & Co., Inc. The company's combined compressive-shrinking (Sanforized) and ammoniated process is identified by the trademark Sanforset.

Cotton fabrics that are ammoniated and subsequently cross-linked present a greater competitive challenge to synthetic fiber fabrics. They retain their smooth appearance, are more absorptive and therefore more comfortable. They have better heat resistance and will not be quickly degraded by a hot iron. They are nonpilling, do not readily snag, have good dimensional stability and shape retention, have a pleasing luster, and dye well.

Shrinking

Fibers spun into yarn are under constant tension during the weaving process. Their physical condition is changed, but not permanently fixed: the fibers tend to revert to their natural state, causing shrinkage. The yarns are made to assume a final condition by shrinking the fabric in a preparatory finishing process that minimizes subsequent shrinkage, such as immersion in cold water, followed by hot water, steaming, or a chemical treatment. Any such method permits the manufacturer to label his product as preshrunk. But even when textile fabrics are preshrunk, they are liable to further shrinkage when washed. The amount of additional shrinkage that may occur after washing must be clearly stated on the label.

To realize maximum preshrinkage in finishing, the fabric must be given a preshrinking operation in which no tension is exerted while the fabric is damp. General adoption of such preshrinking methods for all fabrics is not feasible. Additional expense is incurred, and in some cases prized qualities inherent in certain fabrics are sacrificed.

In general, the factors that control shrinkage are the stability of the fiber and the construction of the fabric. Construction is based on the type of weave, the amount of twist in the yarn, the thread count, and the yarn count. For example, percales shrink from 3 to 8 percent, depending upon thread count, and flannelettes may shrink 10 percent or more. In terms of fitted garments, a 3 percent shrinkage of a man's shirt would reduce the collar from size 15 to $14\frac{1}{2}$; a 5 percent shrinkage in a woman's dress would reduce size 16 to 14 in general fit and to size 12 in length. The final finishing process also affects shrinkage; for example, a water-repellent quality in a fabric offers resistance to subsequent shrinkage.

If the label on a fabric mentions shrinkage, the fabric must conform to rulings on shrinkage issued by the Federal Trade Commission. One important provision states that if a product is to be labeled preshrunk or shrunk, the label must specifically indicate how much additional shrinkage is to be expected. Formerly, a manufacturer's label reading "fully shrunk" or "will not shrink" or "shrink-proof" did not guarantee that substantially more shrinkage would not take place with continued laundering.

A machine known as a *laun-derometer* is used to make washing tests in testing laboratories. A similar, though larger, machine is used for determining shrinkage. Measured distances are marked in indelible ink or with fine threads on unwashed samples of the fabric, which are washed in boiling water in cylinder machines. After an interval, the samples are removed, dried, and pressed. Any change in the measurements marked on the samples determines the amount of shrinkage.

Compressive Shrinkage. Compressive shrinkage was originally developed for woven cotton fabrics. A standardized method was first patented by Cluett, Peabody & Co., Inc., under the trademark of Sanforized finish, which reduced the residual shrinkage in cotton and linen to not more than 1 percent. Tests have been developed to ensure that proper application of this process conforms to this standard. The fabric is deliberately shortened in both width and length, resulting in a tighter and closer weave and, consequently, a higher thread count. The process is carried out on a machine about 65 feet long in the following manner:

1. Normal shrinkage is determined by subjecting a test sample of the fabric to ordinary washing conditions, using the U.S. government wash test as the standard.

2. Careful measurements before and after the wash test indicate how much the fabric shrinks in length and width.

3. The compressive shrinkage machine is set to shrink the fabric to the exact dimensions that the wash test indicated.

4. The fabric is dampened with pure water and live steam, which soften it in preparation for the adjustments to be made in length and width.

5. The width is adjusted by a stretching action, in which the fabric is gripped along its selvages.

6. The fabric is then held firmly against a heavy wool blanket, which is under controlled tension.

7. As the tension of the blanket is relaxed to the desired measurements, the fabric shrinks uniformly in length.

8. The fabric is then carried around a heated drum while drying, and the surface finish is restored.

9. A sample is tested again to make certain that additional shrinkage will not exceed 1 percent.

A process similar to this is identified by Springs Mills, Inc., under the trademark of Springshrunk. It also has a maximum residual shrinkage of 1 percent.

Another method of mechanical shrinking, somewhat similar to compressive shrinkage, is Rigmel, which was developed and patented by the Bradford Dyeing Association. A cotton fabric is put through a standard wash test to determine the precise potential shrinkage in inches per yard, and it is subsequently shrunk to planned dimensions that anticipate a residual shrinkage of a 1 percent maximum.

Rayon fabrics may also be preshrunk by a process known as Sanforsetting. This term has a resemblance to the term "Sanforized," which shrinks cotton up to 1 percent. Both processes are trademarked by the same company and are somewhat similar. Sanforsetting, however, has a residual shrinkage of not more than 2 percent.

Compressive shrinkage techniques have also been developed for cotton knitted goods. The Compax Corp. developed and patented the trademark process of Pak-nit, which guarantees less than 1 percent shrinkage in length. The process compacts the fabric in a specially designed machine by running it through rollers operating at progressively slower rates of speed, which causes overfeeding of the fabric and consequent lengthwise compression. In effect, this compression forces fabric shrinkage in advance, thus eliminating the usual shrinkage due to finishing and laundering.

A related shrinkage-control technique for cotton knitted goods is the Redmamized finish developed by F. R. Redman Co. The fabric is dampened and stretched widthwise to reorient the knitted loops, and then dried in a tensionless state by blasts of air, which causes a permanent shortening of the loops. A shrink-proofing process developed for, and applied to, knitted cotton goods that has proved to be effective is the Permasized finish.

A compressive shrinkage process called Sanfor-Knit has been developed for all-cotton and cotton/polyester circular-knit fabrics. The system uses a simulated torso to test the comfort level of finished garments such as men's knitted underwear. The technique is regulated through a three-part process: a compressor shrinkage system, a unique Knit Picker testing system, and knit technology. Cluett, Peabody & Co., the licenser, states that comfort standards are assured by controlling side-by-side dimensions of the knitted garment, and knit problems are identified and remedied by the system while improved dimensional stability, elasticity, and hand are achieved.

Cylinder Method. This method for shrinking wool uses two perforated cylinders, which steam the fabric as it is rolled off one cylinder and rewound on the other. The steamed fabric is then wound loosely around a wood roller, where it dries and cools slowly and naturally.

London Shrinking. London shrinking is a cold-water process of preshrinking wool fabrics. Lengths of wool fabric are retained between wet blankets for about twenty hours while the moisture of the blankets penetrates into the fibers of the cloth. The cloth is then dried slowly and subsequently subjected to a hydraulic pressure of about 3,500 pounds. Cold-water shrinking originated in London. It is considered one of the best methods.

Chlorination Process. This is a chemical method of treating wool so that the fabric will be shrink-proof. The wool fabric is treated with a dilute solution of calcium or sodium hypochlorite. Some of the scales of the fibers are removed, causing fusion of the outer and inner parts of the fibers (see Figure 8-4). As a result,

Figure 8-4   The effect of chlorination on wool fiber serations: *(a)* unmodified, *(b)* slightly modified, *(c)* modified, *(d)* severely modified. *(Courtesy CIBA Review)*

shrinkage decreases. When this protective scaly covering is removed, however, the felting quality is lessened and the durability of the fabric is affected; but, luster and affinity for dyes are increased. Steaming of fulling does not have this result. Chlorinated wool is chiefly used in woolen underwear, socks, and sweaters. Among the trademarks for this process are Harriset, Hypol, Kelpie, Kroy, Sanforlan, Schollerizing, and Protonizing.

A variation of this process is Drisol, which utilizes the action of chlorine gas from sulfuryl chloride to shrink-proof wool.

Another chlorination process that also incorporates a resin treatment has been developed through the joint efforts of the International Wool Secretariat and Wellman Industries, Inc. The process, called Wel-Set, is applied to wool top (worsted) sliver for knitted goods. It is claimed that not only is the finished fabric shrink-proof, but contrary to other chlorination processes, fiber strength is slightly increased.

Chemical Treatment. A method that works on wool fiber in much the same way as the chlorination processes is based on treating the wool in a solution of potassium permanganate, which is also nearly saturated with common salt. The salt confines the reaction of the permanganate to the surface of the wool. Excellent shrinkage control is possible. The process is called the McFee method, named after the inventor who is connected with the Commonwealth Scientific Research and Development Institute in Australia.

Resin Treatment. By adding certain thermosetting resins (mostly based on melamine) to wool fabrics, shrinkage can be controlled to a considerable extent. The resin is cured in the fiber and tends to prevent slippage of the fibers past each other in any wet processing. The hand of the fabric may be affected, and shrinkage control cannot be predicted for all types of fabric. The goal is a residual shrinkage of 2 percent, but these resin systems are not much used at this time. Trademarks for the process include Resloom, Lanaset, and Pacifixed.

Another method developed for controlling the shrinkage of wool is the *Wurlan* process. This method was developed by the Western Regional Research Center of the U.S. Department of Agriculture. Wool fabric is passed through a diamine, squeezed out, and then passed through a solution of a diacyl chloride. By a process of interfacial polymerization, a nylon-type resin is formed on the surface of the wool fibers. The film is extremely thin and needs no further treatment. Other polymers can be applied in the same way. Among these are the polyurethanes, polyureas, polycarbonates, and polyesters. The process has been commercially successful in a small way. Based upon this technique, J.P. Stevens & Co. introduced a washable-wool process under the trademark Stevens H_2O. The maximum residual shrinkage in the first three washes is guaranteed not to exceed 3 percent, with negligible shrinkage thereafter. The garments are automatic-machine washable. They should be washed in warm water in a normal wash cycle, spun dried, and dried further by hanging the garment on a line.

A process which guarantees a maximum residual shrinkage of 1 percent for any type of open-width knitted goods or bonded fabrics of cotton, cotton blends, wool, polyester, and polyester blends is *Micrex*. This method utilizes a compressive or a combined compressive and resin shrinkage-control technique, depending upon the type of fabric and its construction. The compression renders the fabric

tension-free and the resin on the fabric, when subjected to infrared curing in an oven, causes the material to be permanently set. A similar process is Shrink-No-Mor.

The International Wool Secretariat developed a process called *Superwash*, which makes wool garments home machine washable and dryable. The process is a continuous procedure of chlorinating, treating with a proprietary resin, drying, gilling, drafting, and spinning worsted yarn. Such yarn has good performance characteristics when properly spun, knitted, finished, and dyed with reactive dyes for which a high affinity is developed. Superwash process knitted garments have a maximum shrinkage of 3 percent in the length and 1 percent in the width. The soft and resilient hand and bulk of the wool are retained, as are the weight and moisture regain or absorbency, appearance, and comfort. The durability and insulative qualities of wool are also unaffected.

Fulling

The process of fulling, an important operation in the finishing of wool fabrics, actually operates as a preshrinking process for wool. The fibers are cleaned, scoured, and condensed by a combination of moisture, heat, soap, and pressure. Sometimes, chemicals are added to increase the adhesion of the fibers. The condensing is a natural result of the felting property of wool fiber—shrinkage takes place because the fibers are drawn together. As a result, the fabric has a fuller, more compact body.

Figure 8-5 After being relaxed during dyeing and finishing, all fabrics are coaxed back to normal width on a tentering frame. The endless chain of mechanical fingers, or tenter-frame clips, grips the fabric selvages on entering the machine, which has been set for the narrowest width of the fabric. Gently but firmly, the fingers stretch the fabric to a predetermined width as it passes down the widening 60- to 120-foot length of the tenter over live steam and subsequently heat, which dries and sets the fabric. (*Courtesy United Piece Dye Works*)

Tentering

This process is applied at various stages of finishing. Usually, the fabric is wet when it is run into a tenter; drying and evening of the fabric width are the primary purposes of tentering (see Figure 8-5). The tenter frame consists of two endless chains carried in rugged rails with a distance between them that can be adjusted. The chains are equipped with clips or pins, which grip the selvage of the fabric and carry it into the heated housing where a blast of hot air removes any moisture. Pin frames are mostly used on woolens or knitted goods; clip frames are favored for cotton. The tiny holes or marks of the clips are sometimes noticeable in the selvages of yard goods. Tentering is a continuous operation in that the goods enter one end of the frame, which is usually 90 feet long, and emerge from the other. The frame is equipped in most modern plants with devices that straighten the filling and keep it at right angles to the warp, thus avoiding biased goods. (See Figure 8-6.)

Crabbing

In finishing wool fabrics, a stretching process called *crabbing* passes the cloth over rollers into hot water or steam. The fabric is then put into cold water, after

Figure 8-6 Uneven tension of the filling yarns can result in bubbling when relaxation shrinkage subsequently occurs unevenly in dry cleaning or steam pressing. The problem cannot always be corrected by pressing, expecially when the finish, which had a stabilizing effect on the fabric, has been disturbed. *(Courtesy CIBA Review)*

which it is pressed. This process is similar to tentering, as the fabric is stretched or loosened where necessary and finally set at the width at which the warp and filling yarns are in proper relation to each other. Consequently, there is no hidden strain on any portion of the fabric. Crabbing also prevents the formation of creases or other forms of uneven shrinkage in subsequent finishing operations.

Decating

A finishing process that may be applied to wool fabrics to set the nap and develop the luster is called *decating*, or *decatizing*. In wet decating, the material is tightly wound on a perforated iron roller and immersed in a trough of hot water that is circulated through the fabric. In dry decating, steam is used instead of hot water. Decating may be applied to rayon and other man-made fabrics to improve the hand, color, and luster of the fabric, or to overcome uneven or blotchy dyeing.

Temporary Stiffening

Cotton and linen can be given stiffness, smoothness, weight, and strength by immersion in a solution of starch. This process is commonly known as *starching*. A small amount of starch in consumers' goods (especially cotton fabrics) helps to retain freshness while they are on the dealers' shelves. Cotton fabrics that are usually starched are organdy, lawn, voile, and buckram. Some starching is acceptable, but the consumer should avoid purchasing fabrics that have too much starch because it could conceal inferior construction. Starch fills in the openings in the constructed cloth, creating an appearance of greater compactness; thus, a low thread count is not immediately discernible at the time of purchase. If a fabric loses body after one or more washings, it has been overstarched.

Excessive starching can be detected by rubbing the fabric between the hands, which causes the starch to come off in the form of a fine powder. An absolute test for any starching can be made by touching the fabric with a drop of weak iodine; if starch is present, a blue color appears.

Other substances used for stiffening fabrics are flour, dextrine, glue, shellac, fats, wax, and paraffin. The starches give weight; glue gives stiffness; fats give softness; wax and paraffin produce luster. Starch that is baked brown before using is known as *dextrine*, or *British gum*; in this form, it gives a soft dressing to a fabric.

Cotton fabrics are sometimes stiffened with clay chalk, barium sulfate, calcium sulfate, or magnesium sulfate to make them especially heavy and close in texture. Some stiffenings, such as starch, make cotton fabrics susceptible to mildew, but this tendency can be offset by the addition of zinc chloride to the sizing bath.

In addition to starch, soluble oils and fats are often used to modify the stiffness of the starch and to develop a more pleasing feel to the fabric. In some cases, the starch is applied to the back of the goods only in an operation called *back starching*. This finish is used for low-count printed goods that require considerable loading but also must retain a bright print pattern. Cheap mattress ticking is often finished in this manner. Along with the starch, these finishes require a lot of talc, China clay, sulfonated oil, and a binder to hold the starch in the fabric.

Other terms used in referring to temporary stiffening are "sizing" and "dressing." While both terms are generally used today in preparing the warp for weaving, the term "dressing" usually applies to the warp of wool.

Permanent Stiffening

Permanent stiffening effects can be achieved by chemical processes that change the cellular structure of the fiber. By this method, sheer and medium-weight cottons are given stiffness, which sometimes lasts throughout the life of the fabric. These processes are known by specific trademarks. They vary in method, in the chemicals used, and in the degree of permanency of the final finish. All have the property of making the fabric smoother, and it soils less easily because dirt tends to slide off rather than to cling. As a result, fabrics with permanent sizing usually require less laundering and may therefore last longer. Some of these permanent finishes are as follows:

Ankord. Ankord, a starchless finish given to cotton and rayon gray goods, increases tensile strength, improves luster, and reduces shrinkage.

Basco. This starchless finish increases strength and gives permanent luster and a linenlike appearance to fabrics.

Clearight. This is a starchless process that imparts lasting crispness. Clearight is generally used on sheer fabrics.

Kandarized. This is a process which imparts a permanent crispness and an abrasion resistance.

Saylerizing. Saylerizing is a starchless finish similar to Bellmanizing. It gives permanent crispness to medium-weight as well as to sheer cottons.

Sheercroft. Sheercroft is a starchless finish that imparts crispness and increases luster, giving cotton a linenlike appearance.

Staze-Right. This finish gives luster and crispness to organdies and marquisettes and is resistant to washing and dry cleaning.

Trubenizing. Trubenizing is a patented process that prevents wilting in collars and cuffs. Fabric made of acetate yarns is used to interline the collars and cuffs, which are then immersed in acetone and pressed with a hot iron; the result is a permanent stiffness that does not require starching. This process also gives rise to the term "fused" collars and cuffs.

Weighting

Silk may be treated with tin salts to increase the weight of the fabric and improve its hand and drape. The weight and body of the fabric are increased by immersing it in a solution containing metallic salts. The salts permeate the yarns and become a permanent part of the fabric but cannot be detected by handling. If excessive metallic salts are used in the weighting, they eventually weaken the fabric. The Federal Trade Commission has issued specific regulations with respect to kinds of weighting and their proper labeling.

Only low-grade wool fabrics are weighted. As much as 40 percent additional weight can be obtained by felting extremely short wool fibers into the fabric. These fibers, called *flocks*, are obtained when wool fabrics are washed, brushed, and sheared. An excessive amount of flocks can be detected by brushing and shaking the fabric vigorously. Careful examination of the selvage will also reveal flock particles. Treating wool fabric with magnesium chloride causes an excessive water content, referred to as "watered stock."

Napped cotton goods may also be adulterated by adding flocks. These flocks, forced into the fabric under air pressure, can be detected by brushing and shaking.

Calendering

Calendering is essentially an ironing process that adds sheen to the fabric. The method varies according to the type of finish desired. Calenders are heavy machines made up of at least two rolls (see Figure 8-7). One is usually of chilled steel; the other, of a softer material like wool paper, cotton fiber, corn husks, or combinations of cotton and corn husk. The rolls are supported in vertical frames. Plain rolling calenders may have as many as seven rolls—four steel rolls and three corn husk or cotton rolls. The steel rolls may be equipped to be heated by gas or steam. When the calendar is in operation, the goods pass rapidly between the nips formed by the rolls. This is done at an average rate of 150 yards per minute, and under pressure of 40 to 60 tons and sometimes as much as 100 tons; the goods are then wound up on the back of the machine.

Another type of calender that is used to produce glazed finishes is the friction calender, which is geared so that the highly polished, hot steel roll goes faster than the goods passing through the nip.

Some rolling calenders are set up to pass the cloth through one nip several times so that the pressures built up in the calender nips are transferred to three or four layers of cloth at once. This operation is called *chasing*, and was once highly favored for broadcloth shirtings. Unfortunately, to get the best effect of this process, it has to be done after shrinking the fabric, and it invariably stretches the fabric so that it cannot be guaranteed to have only 1 percent residual shrinkage.

Figure 8-7   Close-up of a rolling calender showing cloth passing through the nip formed by the heavy rolls, which exert a smoothing and pressing action. *(Courtesy Pepperell Manufacturing Co.)*

Glazing

A stiff polished or glazed surface can be obtained by the application of starch, glue, mucilage, or shellac followed by friction calendering. The process makes a fabric resistant to dust and spots and minimizes shrinkage. This finish is found principally on chintz. Vita-glaze is a typical trademark.

Wool fabrics are sometimes calendered or polished. The process adds a soft luster. Typical are wool broadcloth and sheen gabardine. (See Figure 8-8.)

Figure 8-8 *(a)* Untreated wool fabric showing heavily crimped fibers that are not aligned longitudinally and are devoid of luster. *(b)* Uncurled, parallelized, and highly lustrous wool fibers after treatment with Wool Lustering Agent CIBA. *(c)* Schematic drawing of a lustering machine. *(Courtesy CIBA Review)*

Schreinering

Schreinering is an inexpensive method for imparting luster to low-priced cottons. Steel rollers, finely engraved with lines and exerting a pressure of 4,500 pounds, impress on the fabric diagonal ridges ranging from 125 to 600 to the inch. Reflection of light from these ridges gives the fabric a lustrous effect somewhat similar to that produced by mercerization. But the luster produced by schreinering is not permanent, because the imprinted ridges disappear with repeated launderings. This finish is suitable, however, for lingerie fabrics and for linings and sateens, as the slightly rough surface produced by the diagonal ridges reduces the tendency of fabrics to cling. If the fabric has been mercerized, the additional schreinering produces a luster simulating that of silk.

Embossing

The process of producing raised figures or designs in relief on surfaces of fabrics by passing the cloth between heated engraved rollers is known as *embossing*.

The process can be applied to fabrics made of all types of fibers with the exception of wool. This finish is permanent when applied to fabrics made of thermoplastic fibers. It is not permanent when applied to untreated fabrics made of natural fibers or man-made fibers that are not thermoplastic; however, if these fabrics are treated with certain chemical resins, the embossing is considered to be permanent. To preserve the embossed finish of such fabrics, they should be washed in lukewarm water with a mild soap, never be bleached, and be ironed on the wrong side while damp.

When plainwoven fabrics treated with these chemical resins are embossed, they can resemble fabrics that are generally more expensive. The decorative effects also enhance the beauty of the cloth. Various trademarks, such as Picolay and Clokay, have been given to particular fabrics of this type. There are also other trademarks, such as Everglaze, which apply to a group of fabrics similarly treated to produce a variety of effects.

Moiréing

Attractive, lustrous wavy designs known as *moiré* can be produced by a process that is essentially one of minute surface embossing or pressing of a fabric with crenellated, or ridged, rollers. The best moiré results are obtained on fabrics that have rib effects in the filling. The pattern is imprinted on the raised filling yarns by rollers, which exert over 100,000 pounds pressure to the square inch. The luster is produced by the divergent reflection of light on the impressed lines of the design (see Figure 8-9).

Figure 8-9   The best moiré results are obtained by imprinting the pattern on ribbed fabrics. Luster is produced by divergent reflections of light on the design. (*Courtesy FMC Fibers Div.*)

The technique requires the fabric to be cut lengthwise in two. The matched halves are rolled up on separate wooden rolls, or shells, passed over a wavy ridged bar under considerable tension, and wound up together. They are then put through a heavy, heated steel calender, and the patterns that have been induced in the goods by shifting the filling locally over the crenellated bar are embossed on the goods. The reason for cutting the fabric in two is that no two looms weave exactly alike, and it is upon the exactness of the spacing of the filling threads in the original piece that good moiré depends. Patterned moiré is done by passing the goods over a rubber roll engraved in relief with the pattern, while at the same time a brush engages the outside surface of the fabric and shifts the filling at the outlines of the engraving. The width of the moiré stripes is determined by the width of the crenellations in the bar used.

A moiré pattern on a rayon fabric is not permanent. Silk holds the pattern longer but will gradually diminish. Dry cleaning is recommended.

On acetate, moiré is definitely permanent because acetate fabrics have a melting reaction when subjected to the heat of the moiréing process, thus conforming and hardening to the pattern as the cloth cools. A similar condition can be obtained with nylon because of its tendency to melt and to hold a shape.

An entirely different method of moiréing cotton is obtained by treating the fabric with a chemical and then embossing the cloth. The moiré is permanent provided the fabric is cared for properly. It should be washed with a mild soap in lukewarm water and should never be bleached.

Ciréing

The ciré process may be applied to silk and rayon, usually satins and taffetas. Wax or a similar compound is applied to the fabric, followed by hot calendering. The result is a supergloss almost metallic in appearance.

Beetling

Beetling is a common finishing process for linen. The yarns are flattened by the impact of wooden mallets (see Figure 8-10). This hammering actually closes the weave and gives the cloth a firm, flattened, lustrous appearance. All table linen is put through this process, but dress linens are never beetled.

Beetling differs from calendering. The smoothness and gloss obtained by the calendering process are the result of horizontal pressing and are not permanent; in beetling, the action which is

Figure 8-10 "Beetles" are great wooden blocks used to beat the cloth for as long as sixty hours to give Irish linen its permanent sheen. (*Courtesy Irish Linen Guild*)

performed is a vertical impact that permanently flattens the yarns.

Cotton fabrics can be made to simulate linen by beetling, as the process gives cotton the firm feel and lustrous appearance of linen.

Napping

A napped fabric should not be confused with a pile-weave fabric. In the pile weave, the thickness is a true third dimension produced by loops from an extra warp of filling yarn. In the napped fabrics, the thickness is only a surface fuzziness that is the result of a brushing process. When a fabric is to be napped, the yarns intended for the construction of the cloth are given only a slack twist in the spinning process.

The fuzzy finish produced by napping makes a soft fabric, which provides warmth because of the insulative air cells in the nap. The thicker the nap, the more air cells, and the warmer the fabric. In men's suitings, where long wear is desired, a napped surface acts as a protection against objectionable luster. The fact that stains can be removed easily from a napped surface is an additional advantage. On the other hand, napping may also serve to cover up a sleazy construction and weaving imperfections. It is generally considered that excessive napping tends to weaken the fabric, especially where a heavy nap has been produced.

Single napping signifies that both sides of a cloth have been napped in one direction; double napping signifies that both surfaces have been napped in opposite directions, which produces greater surface density, increased firmness, and greater warmth. Flannelette, wool flannel, suede cloth, and duvetyn exemplify napped fabrics. Cotton and spun rayon fabrics are napped when a soft, fuzzy surface is desired.

Vegetable burrs called *teasels* have been used for napping finer grades of wool fabrics (Figure 8-11). Long cylindrical rollers containing closely set wires, which act like brushes, also perform the teaseling operation. As the brushes slide over the revolving fabric, they pull the

Figure 8-11   The teasel, a dried flower head with stiff, hooked bracts, has been used to produce the fuzzy surface on napped fabrics.

top fibers and raise the protruding ends above the surface of the cloth in the form of a fleecelike nap. If a heavy nap is desired, teaseling is repeated several times.

Gigging

Wool fabrics may be napped, or they may be subjected to a raising process called *gigging*. The fabric is first saturated with water. When the fibers of a moist wool fabric are raised, they tend to curl and shrink. When brushed in one direction, a smooth and lustrous appearance results.

Shearing

Pile-weave fabrics and fabrics that have been napped are usually sheared to give an attractive smooth surface to the cloth. Shearing levels all surface irregularities caused by the plucking action of the teasels in the napping process. Shearing is done by a cylindrical machine having rotating spiral blades whose action resembles that of a lawn mower. After shearing, the fabric is automatically brushed in order to remove the sheared ends of the yarns. (See Figure 8-12.)

wool only

Figure 8-12 A rotating spiral blade shears irregularities from napped and pile fabrics. A brush (shown in lower part of photo) removes the sheared ends. *(Courtesy National Associated Wool Industries)*

Crepe and Crinkled Effects

Permanent crepe effects are obtained by using hard-twisted yarns in the weaving process, as described in Chapter 5. Crepe surfaces can also be produced by certain finishing processes, but the results are not so satisfactory. One finishing method imprints a crinkled effect by means of engraved rollers, similar to that produced when the thumbnail is drawn across tissue paper. The finish disappears with repeated washings, however.

In another finishing method, caustic soda is impressed on the fabric in the form of figures or stripes. The fabric is then washed. The part imprinted with the soda shrinks, and the other part puckers. A similar effect is obtained by using strips of wax in place of the caustic soda. Plissé crepes are produced by these methods. The degree of permanency of these crepe effects can be detected by pressing the thumb heavily on a portion of the fabric and stretching it sideways at the same time. The difficulty with which the pressed portion will be smoothed, leaving no or little ripple on its surface, will indicate the relative permanency of the crepe (Figure 8-13a and b).

A chemical method gives a crepe effect to silk by treating the fabric with concentrated sulfuric acid for a few minutes, followed by rinsing and neu-

Figure 8-13 *(a)* Seersucker shows crinkled effect obtained by the use of slack warp yarns. *(b)* Matelassé shows crinkled effect produced by the Jacquard. *(Courtesy American Viscose Corp.)*

tralization with a weak alkali. There is a decrease in luster and a slight loss in strength. This method calls for careful manipulation, because too long an exposure in the acid injures the silk.

A permanent crinkle may be obtained on a fabric that will melt, such as nylon. The fabric is put through a hot roller on which there are raised figurations. The contact of the fabric against the raised hot surfaces causes it to melt and pucker at those points.

Crepe fabrics tend to stretch and shrink when subjected to any wetting operation.

Shape-retentive Finishes

Unlike wool, silk, and man-made thermoplastic fibers, the cellulosic cotton, linen, and rayon fibers do not have good resilience. Fabrics of cellulosic fibers lack the ability to retain their shape —they wrinkle and crush easily. To make them competitive with other fibers in a market that demands easy care for apparel, a variety of shape-retentive finishes has been developed.

The initial process was for the purpose of making spun rayon fabrics *wrinkle-resistant*. This was followed by

similar treatment for cotton and linen. With further development, chemical finishes were added to cotton fabrics for what has become known as *wash and wear* cottons. A further extension of this is the development of *permanent press*, which is used on cotton and cotton-blend fabrics as well as wool and wool/nylon blends.

Wrinkle-resistant Finishes. These finishes are also sometimes referred to as crease-resistant finishes. Actually, the term "crease-resistant" is a misnomer since the purpose of this finish is to prevent deformation of the fabric by undesirable and unintentionally introduced folds and rumples. The purpose is to keep the fabric flat and smooth as compared with creases or pleats that are deliberately placed in a fabric. Some finishes are more wrinkle-resistant than others, but fabrics treated with any of these finishes tend to smooth out when properly hung after wearing.

Durable wrinkle-resistant finishes have been developed for cotton and linen and, to a lesser extent, for rayon. These finishes are all based on resins or reactants that will combine chemically with the fiber through a process known as *cross-linking*, whereby adjacent molecular chains of cellulose in the fiber are linked or tied together to provide greater molecular rigidity and to prevent intermolecular slippage. The original chemical finish used was urea-formaldehyde; then came melamine formaldehyde and a host of variations on both basic chemicals including formaldehyde. These had a distinct disadvantage of giving off a fish odor, particularly when wet.

Many reactants are based on vinyl sulfones and on epichlorohydrin. The latter confers only wet wrinkle-resistance, although experimental work has produced a technique that provides both wet and dry wrinkle-resistance. In the meantime, dry wrinkle-resistance is obtained by aftertreating the fabric with a resin like dimethylolethylene urea.

All of these finishes reduce by 30 to 50 percent the tensile and tear strength of the fabrics to which they are applied, as well as reducing the abrasion resistance. This is due to the resultant brittleness of the fiber caused by the cross-linkage of the molecular chains. Also, the fiber becomes less absorptive and garments of such finished material are less comfortable in humid weather. The U.S. Department of Agriculture and other interested groups are now working on other techniques that will produce the desired wrinkle-resistant effect without cross-linkage and the concomitant disadvantages.

The durability of a finish depends upon its quality, the amount of fabric saturation, the care in applying and oven-curing it, as well as the care with which the consumer follows the instructions on the garment label. Of the many patented processes on the market, several of the better known are as follows:

Anticrease Finish. In the Anticrease process, a solution of formaldehyde resins is baked into the cloth, penetrating the fibers and resulting in a softened, flexible fabric. Fabrics so treated are not absolutely wrinkle-resistant, but they resist crushing, recover easily, and tend to shrink less in laundering. Because of the added weight of the resin, drapability is increased. This finish may be used on cotton, linen, rayon, and acetate.

Bounce. This is a permanent wrinkle-resistant finish for cottons.

Marafin. This finish imparts crease resistance as well as shrinkage control for rayon, cotton, and blended synthetic fabrics.

Perma-Pressed. A wrinkle-resistant process applied to cotton fabrics.

Prestwick. This is a permanent formaldehyde type of finish that imparts wrinkle resistance and dimensional stability to cottons, rayons, and blends.

Unidure. This finish is applied to spun rayons to avoid excessive wrinkles. Wrinkles that do occur will hang out. Unidure adds body to the fabric and improves the brightness and fastness of color. It also reduces shrinkage and stretch and is not affected by dampness and wilting weather.

Vitalized Finish. The Vitalized finish, also known by its English trademark, Tebelized, is a patented wrinkle-resistant process similar to the Anticrease finish. It gives additional "vitality," or elasticity, by the use of synthetic resins. It is applicable to both cotton and linen cloth. Fabrics so treated are heavier and shrink less. Washing or dry cleaning does not affect the finish.

Wat-a-Set.   This is a wrinkle-resistant finish for cotton fabrics.

Wrinkle-Shed.   This process gives cottons an excellent wrinkle-resistant property. It is difficult to wrinkle such cotton fabrics, and any wrinkles will hang out overnight.

Zeset.   This wrinkle-resistant finish also provides dimensional stability to cotton and rayon fabrics. The finish is not chlorine retentive, and white fabrics will not yellow when bleached.

Although silk is a naturally resilient fiber, pure silk fabrics may develop wrinkles from wear which will not readily hang out. To overcome this, processes have been developed to impart a high degree of wrinkle resistance even under very humid conditions. For example, one method developed by Kanegafuchi Spinning Co. (Kanebo) of Japan treats the silk fabric with a proprietary gas (probably ethylene oxide) for several hours. The process is said to increase strength retention, whiteness of material exposed to sunlight, and shrink resistance.

Wash and Wear Finishes.   These are also referred to as drip-dry finishes. They are of the same types as the wrinkle-resistant finishes. Garments made of fabrics with wash and wear finishes will dry smooth and need little or no ironing after washing, depending upon the quality of the finish and the construction. The fabrics have a good, soft hand and a neat appearance. Wash and wear finishes have been used primarily on broadcloth and oxford shirting but are also applicable to other types of cotton fabrics.

Each company has its own trademark for its drip-dry finish, and its effectiveness depends on the particular process. Among the most widely advertised finishes are AMC—Bradford, Arrow Wash-and-Wear 100% Cotton, Belfast, Dri-Smooth, Manhattan Mansmooth, Minicare, Sanforized Plus, Van Heusen Vantage All Cotton, and Vanalux.

Garments made of fabrics treated with drip-dry finishes usually may be commercially laundered. The primary advantage, however, is that such garments launder easily at home and need no ironing. This tends to increase their wear since home laundering is less harsh. In some cases, it is advisable to use a mild soap. Since some wash and wear finishes cause yellowing when a chlorine bleach is used, labels should be carefully read before using a bleach. Do not wring the garments or spin-dry them in a washing machine or in a dryer. Rinse them well, hang them on wooden or plastic hangers, buttoned and straightened out, and allow them to drip-dry. Metal hangers may cause rust stains.

Not all drip-dry finishes produce the same results. Some garments tend to pucker at the seams when they dry; some require quick, light ironing with a cool iron. Since the care of drip-dry finished garments varies with the particular finish, read the instructions on the garment tag to determine which is best suited to your needs. In any event, follow the care instructions for most satisfactory results.

It should be noted that not all fabrics that have drip-dry characteristics have a wash and wear finish. Some fabrics (see later chapters) are constructed either entirely of thermoplastic man-made fibers or of such fibers in blends with natural fibers. The extent to which garments made of such fabrics will drip-dry and have shape retention is dependent on the inherent properties of the fibers and on the proportion of thermoplastic fibers in the fabric—not on the finish.

Permanent-Press Cotton Finishes. The latest development in shape-retentive finishes is the *permanent press*, also referred to as *PP*, *durable press*, and *delayed*, or *deferred, cure*. This is the outgrowth of the manufacturers' difficulty in shaping wrinkle-resistant goods—that is, pressing creases into trousers and putting pleats in skirts made of such material. To overcome this difficulty, processes have been developed so that, generally, the fabric is treated or sensitized with the finish but not cured or set for permanent shape-retention until after the garment has been constructed.

Presently, all the finishes contain some type of cross-linking chemical, which reduces by 30 to 50 percent the strength and durability of all-cotton fabrics. The permanent crease represents another particularly weak area with further reduced abrasion resistance. In dyed goods, this weakness will first appear as a light-colored streak. One way

to lessen abrasion is to launder the garment inside out, since this will reduce the wear on the crease.

Since the cross-linkage occurs only in cellulosic fibers, the loss of strength can be reduced by blending cotton or rayon with polyester fiber. A blend of at least 50 percent polyester fiber with 50 percent cotton or rayon is required for significant strength retention. A blend of 65 percent polyester fiber with 35 percent cotton will result in only about 10 percent strength reduction due to the finish. The polyester fiber also improves the abrasion resistance, hand, and appearance, as well as color and styling potential.

There are a number of permanent press finishes on the market, and they may be readily identified by their trademarks. As indicated in the descriptions that follow, their methods of processing and their characteristics vary. These trademarks apply to all-cotton, cotton/polyester, and rayon/polyester blends, and the ultimate properties are affected accordingly.

Koratron. The Koratron Co., Inc., was the pioneer in this field, introducing a permanent press finish commercially in 1963. The patented process, utilizing the cross-linking chemical imidazolidone and produced under the trademark of Permafresh 183, impregnates the fabric at the mill or finishing plant. The cloth is dried at low temperature so as not to obtain a chemical reaction that would cure or set the finish. The sensitized goods are then shipped to the garment manufacturer.

Under strict quality control of Koratron, the manufacturer cuts and sews the garments, oversizing them up to a half size. This is done to offset shrinkage during oven-curing. Koratron sensitized zippers, waistbanding, and pocketing material are used. The garments are pressed into shape with specially designed pressers. Pants, for example, are pressed with the proper roundness at the waist, shape at the hip, smoothness at the seams, and sharpness at the crease. At this point, the curing occurs and produces a "memory-shaping," or shape-retentive, quality. The garments, placed on special hangers, are then put on a conveyor and passed through an oven where heat of about 320 degrees Fahrenheit permanently sets the shape given on the pressing machine. Quality testing is maintained by washing and drying samples of garments 5 times and evaluating them for smoothness of surface, lack of puckering, smoothness of zipper area, sharpness of crease, overall appearance, and dimensional stability.

Sta-Prest. This is a trademark of Levi Strauss & Co., which employs the Koratron process under license.

Super-Crease. This is the trademark of the patented process developed by J. P. Stevens & Co., Inc. It utilizes a sulfone cross-linking chemical that eliminates chlorine-retention and unpleasant odors. The hand of the fabric is not affected (see Figure 8-14).

The process is similar to the deferred-cure method described previously. The fabric is padded with the sulfone chemical that cross-links with cellulose when the fabric is passed through an alkaline solution. The cloth can be Sanforized. After the garment is cut, sewed, and pressed, it is oven-cured for permanent shape-retention.

Dan-Press. This is the deferred-cure process of Dan River Mills, Inc. To overcome shrinkage during the process, trousers, for example, must be oversized $1/4$ inch at the inseam and at the waistband. Dan-Press fabrics are made of cotton and polyester blends, which have greater strength and abrasion resistance than all-cotton fabrics.

Coneprest. This is a precured process of Cone Mills, Inc. It differs from the deferred-cure technique in that the fabric is treated with a resin and completely cured at the mill. The usual shrinkage from oven-curing occurs at this time. Sometimes, fabrics are given an added Sanforized-Plus treatment for greater shrinkage control.

The completely treated and cured fabric is shipped to the manufacturer, who cuts and sews garments to size. Intended crease lines are then sprayed with the Coneprest solution. Because of the solution, the sprayed area of the fabric temporarily loses its wrinkle-resistant quality. The garment is then pressed at an appropriate temperature above 325 degrees Fahrenheit at a predetermined pressure ranging from twenty-five seconds to three minutes. This technique recures the finish and produces a permanent crease and a shape-retentive garment.

Sharp/Shape. This is a precured process of Everprest, Inc. The finished fabric is shipped to the manufacturer for cutting and sewing into garments. Permanent press is achieved with special press

Figure 8-14 Super-Crease finish provides permanent creasing of cotton and cotton/polyester blended fabrics. It is durable to both home and commercial laundering, with or without chlorine bleach. Both pairs of slacks shown were washed innumerable times, but never ironed. Pair at left was treated with Super-Crease; pair at right was not, although it was made of identical fabric. *(Courtesy J. P. Stevens & Co., Inc.)*

equipment, and no further curing is required. The process is considered to be especially effective for stretch fabrics of cotton and cotton/nylon blends.

Kara Set.   This is a delayed-cure process by Refined Products Co. of Millmaster-Onyx Corp. The technique utilizes two separate cross-linking carbamate reactants, Kara Set 1 and Kara Set 4, to which are added finishing components that reinforce and complete the process. Effective curing is accomplished after subjection of the treated garment to a temperature of 350 degrees Fahrenheit for at least three minutes.

The process has been found to be suitable for 100 percent cotton fabrics and high-percentage cotton blends, such as 85/15 cotton and nylon fabrics. It also is well suited to knit goods since the chemical compound is not affected by the usual knit-goods finishing procedures. Sensitized fabrics may be compressively shrunk or given schreinered or friction effects. The finished fabrics are said to have good flex and abrasion properties and good tensile strength because the process has a low degradation effect on cotton.

Onyxset.   This finish is identical with Kara Set but is sold through Onyx Chemical Co., another subsidiary of the same parent corporation.

Ranedare Press.   This is a water-repellent finish which also imparts durable press properties to fabrics with at least 50 percent polyester fiber blended with cotton. It is a product of Metro-Atlantic, Inc.

Tanapress.   This is a durable press finish which utilizes a thermoset resin.

Wicaset P.E.P.   This is a permanent press finish by Wica Chemicals, Inc.

Never-Press.   This process, developed by Wamsutta, is a somewhat different approach to achieving permanent press. Fabrics are woven with a prescribed balance of warp and filling yarns of a predetermined blend. They are subsequently given a special resin finish and completely cured. The fabrics, which have a maximum residual shrinkage of 1 percent, are shipped to the manufacturer for cutting and sewing into garments. Durable creases are set on the pressing machine under the prescribed procedure of 250 degrees Fahrenheit for fifteen seconds with steam.

Ameriset.   This permanent press finish, developed by the American Laundry Machinery Industries, is applied to finished garments by placing them for twenty minutes in a gas chamber where a vapor of formaldehyde and sulfur dioxide permeates and cross-links the cellulose fibers. It is equally suited to wovens and knits.

Since the fabric is not pretreated with chemicals or resins, all findings, thread, pockets, and trimmings, as well as the fabric of the entire garment are given the permanent press characteristics. Shrinkage is virtually nonexistent and the fabrics have good abrasion resistance. The finish may be available to local clothing retailers and neighborhood establishments for servicing home-sewers.

Modifications of Permanent Press Finishes. Modified and new approaches are being developed to reduce or eliminate problems of strength loss, abrasion resistance, and color degradation. Among these are methods which would alter the molecular structure of cotton fiber so as to increase its strength. For example, scientists of the U.S. Department of Agriculture have found that the fiber construction can be oriented by swelling with sodium hydroxide without tension and allowing the cotton to shrink, then stretching the yarn while it remains in the caustic soda. This technique has been found to increase the strength of the permanent press cotton so that it is equal to that of untreated cotton after twenty launderings.

Pretreatment of cotton and cotton/polyester fabrics with liquid ammonia has been found to improve luster, tensile strength, wrinkle resistance, flex life, and hand of goods that are subsequently cross-linked.

A steam cure followed by a dry cure of cross-linked cotton has also been shown to be effective and, importantly, to provide about 300 percent greater abrasion resistance than the conventional method.

A different approach is the use of polymer sizing on yarns for cotton fabrics. Subsequently the goods are given the conventional dry-cure resin treatments. As a result, greater tensile strength and edge abrasion resistance of the permanent press fabrics are achieved.

It should be noted that all the permanent press trademarks that have been discussed refer to all-cotton or cotton-blended fabrics that have been chemically treated to obtain the desired shape-retentive effect with easy care and no ironing requirements for the consumer. There are, however, fabrics constructed wholly or partly of thermoplastic fibers, such as triacetate, nylon, polyesters, and acrylics, which have their own inherent permanent heat-setting characteristics. They are frequently sold under specific trademarks, such as Burmi-Crease and Estrel. The degree of shape retention depends upon the kind and amount of thermoplastic fiber used as well as the quality of the thermosetting technique. The labels on such garments may state that no ironing is necessary; those on others may advise little or no ironing.

Another approach is a heat-setting technique using three-dimensional forms, as for dresses. Such garments have no darts or seams other than for the attachment of sleeves which are also heat-set. However, this method makes garment alteration very difficult if not sometimes impossible without introducing darts or seams.

Durable Press Wool Finishes. Wool has its own natural memory. It is elastic, resilient, and tends to return to its original shape after tension or compression is exerted. The Wool Bureau has sponsored a process that will add long-lasting creases or pleats to wool fabrics, as well as retain the natural quality of wool.

The process requires that the crease area of the garment be sprayed with a chemical reducing agent, such as monoethanolamine sulfite, which temporarily inhibits the wool's resilience. When the garment is pressed, the heat resets the wool's memory with this crease so that the fabric always tends to return to the new creased condition. Moisture increases this reaction, and, when wet (worn in the rain, for instance), the crease tends to become sharper.

The International Wool Secretariat (IWS) has issued licenses for the pretreatment of wool fabrics to be permanently creased or pleated. The goods are padded in a solution of urea and diethanolamine carbonate, dried, and then pressed in an electrically heated (rather than steam) press. After this pretreatment, creases or pleats may be put into the fabric with the conventional steam press and then dried in the press for about one minute.

Going a step beyond this, IWS has devised a technique for imparting a stretch characteristic to wool fabrics given their permanent press finish. A reducing agent is added to the resin. After being padded, the fabric is taken up with warp tension onto a roll. This causes crimp interchange. The roll is covered with a polyethylene film to retain the moisture and rotated for one hour. It is then dried on a tenter frame with a minimum of filling tension and cured at room temperature for twelve to twenty-four hours. Subsequent finishes are applied as usual.

The Commonwealth Scientific and Industrial Research Organization (CSIRO) has developed a durable press finish for heavy and lightweight machine-washable wool garments at its laboratory in Geeling, Australia. Made with suitable zippers, pockets, linings, and thread that will not shrink, the wool garment is pressed to locate the creases and to smooth the fabric. Then it is dry cleaned to remove surface contaminants, such as scouring detergents, oils, and dirt. Subsequently, a polyurethane resin is added to the dry-cleaning solvent in the machine. The solvent is evaporated, leaving a 2 percent resin deposit on the garment. The garment is immediately pressed again and placed into a curing oven, which cures the resin, makes the wool shrink-resistant, and sets the creases. Several companies have been licensed to use this process.

The Western Regional Research Center of the U.S. Department of Agriculture has developed a somewhat simpler process. Wool garments are shrinkproofed with an emulsion containing a modified polyurethane resin and a cross-linking agent. The impregnated fabric is dried at a temperature below the curing temperature of the resin. The treated fabric is made into garments which are then sprayed with a 4 percent solution of sodium bisulfite in water to absorb 30 to 40 percent of the weight of the fabric. The moist garment is then steam-pressed and finally oven-cured for about fifteen minutes. This finish is said to be durable through at least ten launderings and tumble dryings.

Permanent press finishes, such as are used with cellulosic blend fabrics, achieve excellent durable press results in wool/cellulosic blends, provided the wool is shrink-proofed. The cellulosic component reacts in the usual manner so that while shape retention is achieved, the physical properties of strength and abrasion resistance of the cotton or rayon are reduced. Consequently, a high-strength synthetic, such as nylon or polyester, is needed as a third component to improve the fabric.

Water Repellency

A water-repellent fabric is one that will resist absorption and penetration of water for a given period of time, depending upon the length of exposure and the force of the water. Eventually, however, water will penetrate even a water-repellent fabric (Figure 8-15).

These fabrics have qualities not found in truly waterproof fabrics. They are porous, which permits the body to breathe, and are therefore comfortable. The hand and appearance of the fabric is good and very much like the untreated fabrics.

Figure 8-15 In this water repellency test, after sufficient "rain" has fallen, the moisture in the cup set beneath each fabric swatch is withdrawn into a graduate and measured carefully to determine how much water—if any—has penetrated the fabric. *(Courtesy Dow Corning Corp.)*

Penetration of water through a fabric is dependent upon the kind of fiber in the fabric, the tightness of the yarn twist, the compactness of the construction of the fabric, and the finish used to discourage water from soaking through the yarns and pores of the fabric. Some fibers, such as nylon and the polyesters, are hydrophobic—that is, they do not readily absorb water. Other fibers, such as cotton and rayon, absorb water readily. Consequently, the more hydrophobic fibers used, the more inherently water-repellent the fabric will be. For this reason, raincoats are often made of a 100 percent polyester fiber, such as Dacron, or of a polyester/cotton blend.

Some fabrics are specifically made with a cotton yarn that, when wet, will swell sufficiently to close the pores of the fabric so that the tightened construction will resist water penetration. One such fabric is Shirley cloth, which is made of low-twist three-ply cotton yarn with an oxford-weave construction.

Since the effectiveness and durability of water-repellent finishes vary, labels should be read carefully. A garment labeled as *shower-resistant* will protect the wearer from a light rain but will be penetrated by a heavy rain after fifteen minutes. A garment labeled as *rain-resistant* will provide protection for a few hours of exposure in a moderate rain. A garment labeled as *storm-resistant* will resist water penetration for many hours. It should also be noted that greater water repellency will be obtained when a double thickness of water-repellent fabric is used—for instance, across the shoulders. Also, seams should be sewn with water-repellent thread; untreated thread will carry water through the garment to the clothing worn underneath.

The quality and durability of the water-repellent finish are very important factors. These may be determined by recognition of the kind of finish used and the care instructions given to the wearer. There are three general types of water-repellent finishes: nondurable, semidurable, and durable. The least expensive are the least durable.

Nondurable Finishes.   This type of water repellent finish is usually based on a paraffin wax-aluminum acetate emulsion that is applied to the goods in a simple padding and drying operation. One development in this type has been the substitution of zirconium salts for aluminum to give even better repellency. Although these finishes have excellent ratings of water repellency, they will withstand only very light laundering, will lose their repellency with repeated washings, and, generally, will not tolerate dry cleaning. Examples of effective but nondurable water-repellent finishes are Aquarol AX, Aridex WP, Crestdri, Dryon, Picotex, and Repelex.

Semidurable Finishes.   These are wax and/or salt solutions which can be emulsified off the fabric in laundering. They are, however, resistant to dry cleaning. In the long run, therefore, they become more costly to the consumer than durable-finished products. Examples of effective semidurable water-repellent finishes are Bishopel, Dryon A-B, Nalan W, and Repello DC.

Durable Finishes.   There are several types of durable water repellents, and the degree of effectiveness and durability varies for each. One of the first, based upon a pyridinium compound, is applied to cotton, linen, and viscose rayon fabrics. This type of finish permeates the fiber and becomes part of it. It also endures repeated washings as well as dry cleanings. Other advantages claimed are that stains and spots can be sponged off with a damp cloth, that the fabrics resist perspiration and wrinkling, and that the finish manifests a softness of texture that improves the fabric's appearance.

Another type of durable water repellent is based on a combination of melamine resins and stearamides and is used on cotton, rayon, and blends containing these fibers. These have excellent repellency and good tolerance to laundering and dry cleaning.

Silicone compounds are excellent water repellents. Application of this finish to the fabric results in coating the individual fibers of the yarn. Water and water-borne substances, such as beverages, bead up and roll off the fabric. The finish is usually more resistant to dry cleaning than to laundering, and instructions on hangtags should be closely observed. Depending upon additional treatments, fabrics may also have a soft hand and be wrinkle-resistant. Examples of effective durable water-repellent finishes are Aerotex, Hydro-Pruf, Norane, Ranedare, Syl-Mer, Zelan, and Zepel.

Soil Repellency

A group of fluorochemical finishes which act as water repellents are also soil or

Figure 8-16   Spilled milk lies on the surface of a fabric treated with Scotchgard stain repeller. *(Courtesy 3M Co.)*

juices, coffee, tea, mustard, catsup, sodas, alcoholic and nonalcoholic beverages, and fats, as well as soil from perspiration, inks, and grass, mud, and motor oil satisfactorily wash or dry-clean out. The finishes applied by pad-dry-cure processes are similar to those used for wash and wear resins. They are generally effective through many cleanings, and some are durable for the life of the garment. Soil-repellent finishes of this type are identified by such trademarks as Fybrite, Scotchgard, Visa, and Zepel (see Figure 8-16 and Table 8-1).

There are stain repellents that can be applied to the fabric or finished textile product by the consumer. For a discussion of these, see Chapter 29.

stain repellents. These finishes, which are applied to a wide variety of fabrics for clothing and home furnishings, are effective against water- and oil-borne stains. Soil from food such as fruit

Soil Release

Finishes have been developed that will facilitate the removal of dirt or stains

Table 8-1

STAIN RESISTANCE AND REMOVAL COMPARISONS ON TREATED AND UNTREATED GABARDINE				
STAIN	UNTREATED		SCOTCHGARD TEXTILE TREATMENT	
	STAIN RESISTANCE	STAIN REMOVAL	STAIN RESISTANCE	STAIN REMOVAL
FRUIT JUICES (Water base, low viscosity)	Fair	Easy	Excellent	Easy
CATCHUP (Water base, high viscosity)	Poor	Medium	Excellent	Easy
WHISKEY (Alcohol, water base)	Poor	Medium	Excellent	Easy
GRAVIES (oil-water emulsion, low viscosity)	Poor	Difficult	Excellent	Medium
OLIVE OIL (Oil base, low viscosity)	No resistance	Very difficult	Excellent	Easy
MAYONNAISE (Oil base, high viscosity)	No resistance	Very difficult	Excellent	Medium

SOURCE: *Courtesy 3M Co.*

from fabrics treated with a permanent press finish (Figures 8-17 and 8-18). This is particularly important since permanent press cloth ordinarily is not as strong as untreated fabric and harsh washing treatment reduces the durability of the fabric and causes fuzzing and frosting (fading) at creases and areas of greater abrasion wear. Furthermore, since permanent press fabric which contains polyester is prone to retention of oil stains, soil-release finishes are particularly helpful.

Waterproofing

For a fabric to be truly waterproof, it must be completely sealed with a substance that is insoluble in water. The familiar rubber-coated garb of police officers and firefighters is a good example. Older methods include coating the fabric with linseed oil to produce the well-known fisherman's slicker; oiled silk is produced by a similar process.

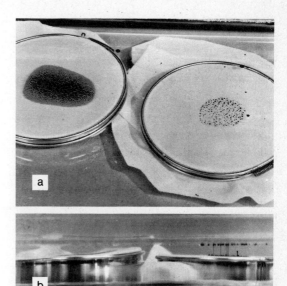

Figure 8-17 *(a)* During ten-minute cycle (normal washing cycle is twelve minutes) with no agitation, stain release chemical in permanent press fabric on right forces dirty motor oil out of the fabric. *(b)* Cross section shows the stain literally popping out of the treated fabric and rising to the surface of the wash water. *(Courtesy 3M Co.)*

Figure 8-18 Four photomicrographs showing spontaneous release of an oil stain from a yarn treated with a durable press plus soil release finish when the yarn is immersed in a detergent solution at 75 degrees Fahrenheit. *(Courtesy 3M Co.)*

Modern waterproofing materials include the vinyl resins, which do not oxidize and crack as readily as rubber. Synthetic rubbers are also more durable to outside influences than natural rubber. The fabrics used in most of today's waterproof materials are cotton and nylon. The latter, coated with vinyl resins, has largely superseded the heavy canvas tarpaulins used to protect merchandise in transit.

The *Koroseal* waterproofing process can be applied to any finished fabric except acetate. It makes fabrics impervious to water, wind, moths, and mildew, and resistant to acid, grease, sunlight, perspiration, and stains. Koroseal fabrics do not contain any rubber or oil; consequently, they will not deteriorate by cracking, sticking, or peeling and therefore serve a multitude of uses. The coating applied to the surface of the fabric is polyvinyl chloride, a plasticized white powder, which is obtained by compressing two gases—acetylene from coal and limestone, and hydrogen chloride from salt. The result is a tough, stretchable plastic coating having unusual properties.

A waterproofing finish that claims superiority to vinyl and acrylic coatings is sold by Kenyon Piece Dyeworks, Inc. under the trademark of *K-Kote*. Treated fabrics will not crack, and they can be either machine washed or dry-cleaned. Water-borne spots can be removed with a damp cloth, and the fabric requires little or no ironing because of the wash and wear quality given by the finish. K-Kote is neither brittle in cold weather nor tacky in hot weather, and it is durable enough to last the life of the garment to which it is applied.

The slick, or satiny, effect is usually applied to the outer side of the fabric, with a more subdued finish on the inside. Both sides feel the same. One variation has a clear finish on the outside and a colored finish, which takes the place of a lining, on the inside. In any case, the fabric is soft, pliable, and has a natural hand—that is, there is no obtrusive tactile awareness of coating.

K-Kote has been applied to nylon and blended fabrics for the outerwear and raincoat markets; however, it has also been found applicable to almost any kind of material. For example, it has been used to coat silk, cotton, and blended fabrics in home furnishings.

Absorbent Finishes

To increase the absorbency of cellulosic fibers, which improves their effectiveness and comfort for such uses as towels and undergarments, ammonium compounds may be applied to cotton, linen, and rayon fabrics.

The absorbency of nylon 6 and nylon 6,6 may be increased by treating them with a solution of nylon 8, which is more absorbent. This process is known as Nylonizing. Another finish used to increase nylon absorbency is known as Nylonex. Hysorb is a compound of surfactants and synthetic resins used to give absorbent properties to fabrics of other man-made fibers.

The *Fantessa* process applied to polyester fabrics renders the fibers adsorptive. That is, although the fibers do not absorb more water, they do wick, or adsorb, the water along their surfaces as a result of a change in the molecular surface structure. This capillary action

Table 8-2

ZEPEL—PROTECTION AGAINST COMMON FABRIC STAINS		
SOILS & STAINS	WET STAINS	DRIED STAINS
GREASE, FAT	Small residue may remain after blotting with dry tissue	Completely removed with solvent or by dry cleaning
INK STAINS Fluid Ink	Rolls off; remainder blots off with water: no residue	Completely removed by laundering
Ball Point Ink	Partly removed with solvent; some residue	Partially removed with solvent or by dry cleaning
GRASS STAINS	Partially removed with water and/or alcohol; small residue may remain	Almost completely removed with water, alcohol, or by laundering
FRUIT, FRUIT JUICE	Rolls off or blots off with water; no residue	Completely removed with water and detergent or by laundering
PERSPIRATION	Wipes off with water; no residue	Completely removed with water and detergent or by laundering
COFFEE, TEA	Rolls off or blots off with water; no residue	Completely removed with water and detergent or by laundering
COSMETICS Liquid or Cream Deodorant	Rolls off or blots off with water; no residue	Completely removed with solvent or by dry cleaning
Lipstick	Blots off with solvent; some small residue	Almost completely removed by laundering or dry cleaning
Hair Oil	Blots off or blots off with solvent; no residue	Completely removed by dry cleaning
MUD	Residue wipes off with water	Completely removed with water and detergent or by laundering

SOURCE: Courtesy E. I. du Pont de Nemours & Co.

eliminates the disadvantage of clamminess in the treated polyester fabrics, making them suitable for such uses as active sportswear, blouses, dresses, and shirts. The Fantessa process has no adverse effect on the other characteristics of the fiber.

Flame Retardants

Although textile finishes have generally been introduced to the market by individual companies as a consequence of competitive initiative and scientific research, consumer protection against textile fire hazards was primarily the result of strong reaction from consumers and consumer-interest groups against serious and sometimes fatal accidents to wearers of such explosively flammable apparel as "torch" sweaters, sleepwear, and children's cowboy chaps made of fabrics, such as napped rayon, which ignite readily and flare up quickly. In 1953, Congress enacted the Flammable Fabrics Act as a consumer protection measure. This legislation was designed to remove these products from the market.

As a result of greater consumer awareness and increased consumer-interest-group pressures, the federal act was amended in 1967. The revision covered a broad range of products: apparel (excluding footwear, gloves, hats, and interlinings); all types of interior furnishings for the home, office, and places of assembly; and "related material," such as synthetic film and foam, paper, plastic, and rubber "which may reasonably be expected to be used" for apparel and furnishings. Jurisdiction over the law was initially under the Department of Commerce in cooperation with the Department of Health, Education and Welfare and with the Federal Trade Commission. In 1972, however, the Consumer Product Safety Commission was established to administer the act.

The National Bureau of Standards is responsible for testing and recommending to the commission flame-retardant standards for the various areas of textile coverage. Upon acceptance and promulgation of the standards by the commission, appropriate fabrics and garments must be labeled to comply with standards and to inform the consumer. In response to these standards, the industry has taken three approaches to flame retardation of textiles: chemical finishes, modified man-made and synthetic fibers, and new flame-retardant fibers.

Flame-retardant Finishes. A wide variety of flame-retardant chemical finishes has been developed for application to fibers and fabrics. However, some of the compounds affect the hand of the fabrics, causing them to become harsh and somewhat stiff. Some finishes have unpleasant odors. Also, some finishes lose their effectiveness in washing or dry cleaning, although some may be restored or reprocessed. It has also been found that in laundering fabrics with flame-retardant finishes, some nonphosphate soap and detergent residues, as well as minerals in the water, block the effectiveness of these finishes. However, rewashing in phosphate detergents removes the blocking residues and restores the flame-retardant quality. But here, again, is another disadvantage: these phosphates pollute the water.

Among the more effective flame-retardant finishes are ammonia-cured tetrakis - hydroxymethyl - phosphonium hydroxide (THPOH) and tetrakis-hydroxymethyl-phosphonium chloride (THPC); several halogen phosphorus, nitrogen phosphorus, boron phosphorus, and antimony compounds; and inorganic salts. Since flame-retardant finishes are generally specific to certain fibers and since the durability to washing and dry cleaning varies, labels should be noted and observed (see Figure 8-19).

Modified Flame-retardant Fibers. The second approach to flame retardation of textiles is the creation of flame-retardant fibers by the addition of certain chemicals to existing fiber spinning solutions. Celanese Fibers Marketing Co. has produced a flame-retardant acetate, *D-107*, and a flame-retardant triacetate, *D-108*. Fabrics and garments made of these fibers self-extinguish when the external source of ignition is removed. Such fabrics can be processed in the conventional manner and have a good hand.

Avril FR rayon, a type of high wet-modulus rayon that has greater strength than ordinary rayon (see pages 447–448) is a flame-retardant fiber produced by FMC Fibers Division. It is intended for blends with cotton to obtain greater strength, improved hand, and reduced odor, as well as flame-retardance uniformity which is superior to that obtained with an all-cotton composition.

Figure 8-19 An untreated cotton dress (left) bursts into flames, while a dress treated with THPC flame-retardant finish (right) is resistant to the lighted candles. *(Courtesy U.S.D.A. Photograph)*

Safyr, also marketed by FMC, is a flame-retardant acetate fiber. It is particularly well suited for knit goods.

Acele FLR is a flame-retardant acetate produced by Du Pont. It is marketed to meet sleepwear standards.

Dacron D-489 FLR is a flame-retardant polyester also made by Du Pont.

Flame-retardant Fibers. The third approach to flame retardation is the development of special flame-retardant fibers.

Nomex aramid, produced by Du Pont, is one of the earliest synthetic high-temperature-resistant fibers. It is used primarily for industrial purposes where high strength and flame retardation are needed.

Modacrylics in several forms (see pages 447–448) have been produced to meet the flame-retardant requirements of such garments as children's sleepwear. Dynel, Verel, SEF, and Orlon FR are typical modacrylics in this category. However, due to certain limitations inherent in these fibers, manufacturers are using them in blends to obtain better hand, bulk, absorbency, laundering performance, and styling effects. To achieve satisfactory flame retardation, the dominant fiber in such blends must be modacrylic.

Kynol, a phenolic fiber produced by the Carborundum Co., is highly flame- and heat-resistant. It is used for a wide variety of fabrics (sometimes blended with Nomex aramid), primarily for industrial garments, fire-entry suits, and related uses.

Boron-nitride fiber, also made by the Carborundum Co., is very highly fire-resistant. It is used for protective clothing and equipment.

Thornel, a graphite fiber, was developed by the Union Carbide Corp. It is used for reinforcement and fire-resistant applications to industrial, military, and aerospace purposes.

Glass fibers, such as Fiberglas (see page 491), are also used for reinforcement and fire-resistant purposes.

Mothproofing

Wool fabrics are sometimes mothproofed as one of the finishing operations to the cloth by impregnating the yarns with a chemical. Of all these preparations, tests seem to indicate that the most effective are Mitin FF, Eulan CN, and Lanoc CN. These are fast to other finishing processes as well as to dry cleaning, but are only moderately fast to washing.

Simple home methods of moth-damage prevention comprise daily brushing of apparel after wearing, frequent exposure to sunlight, and dry cleaning before placing the garments in airtight storage and cold storage at a maximum temperature of 40 degrees Fahrenheit. For additional protection, various commercial compounds are available for use in the home. Among these are naphthalene and paradichlorobenzene (moth balls, flakes, and cakes). These do not act as a repellent, as is commonly thought. They will actually kill the moth, eggs, and larvae, provided the closet, chest, or package containing the wool fabrics is airtight. The atmosphere must be thoroughly saturated for these substances to be effective. The container should be hung above the clothes so that the vapor will flow down over them.

Many sprays are also available. Some of these, such as Atomoth, Berlou, Boconize, Larvex, and Ya-De, contain ei-ther a fluoride or silicofluoride. These are very stable to exposure to light and air and are not removed by dry cleaning. They are, however, water-soluble and also may give rise to white markings when the fabric is rubbed. They also may cause a harshening of the fabric's hand. Products containing carbon tetrachloride, such as Moth Gas, are also effective. Others containing arsenic, such as Per Mo, are poisonous to humans as well as to moth larvae.

Mothproofing agents containing DDT or dieldrin may not be used by the consumer because of their water-polluting and toxic effects on wildlife as well as humans. The Environmental Protection Agency will, however, allow their use when applied in a "closed system" which will not produce concomitant pollution. One such permissible finish which contains dieldrin is Drewclad. It is applied in conjunction with acid dyebath processing.

Another method of mothproofing is the work of a U.S. Department of Agriculture scientist, Dr. Roy Pence, who has discovered what he calls *antimetabolites*. These substances, which can be applied easily to wool, make the fiber useless to the moth larva as food. Consequently, it starves to death before it has consumed enough fiber to damage the fabric.

Mildewproofing

Cellulosic fibers are particularly susceptible to mildew; silk and wool are also susceptible, but to a lesser extent. Such untreated fabrics will become stained, malodorous, and eventually deteriorated by the fungus if allowed to remain in a moist condition for a period of time.

Shower curtains or other cotton fabrics may be mildewproofed at home by soaking the material in very soapy water, then, without rinsing, dipping it into a solution of copper sulfate. Antiseptics, such as boric acid and carbolic acid, also prevent rapid growth of the mildew fungus.

One compound that is not easily washed out is a 0.05 percent solution of phenyl mercuric acetate in water. This is one of the most effective mildewproofing agents.

Certain organometallic compounds, such as of tin and copper, are powerful mildew retardants. Copper imparts a greenish color to fabrics. Certain resins based on melamine formaldehyde, such as Mel-Tron 80 of Crown Chemical Corp., are also valuable for mildewproofing. The Arigal process, developed by CIBA-Geigy, is another example. Rotproofing, an extension of mildewproofing, is very important in agricultural applications.

Antibacterial Finishes

Chemical antiseptic finishes impart a self-sterilizing quality to a fabric. The appearance and feel of the fabric are unchanged, and no chemical odor remains. Dry cleaning does not impair the finish. Cyana-finish, Hygienized, Perma-fab, Sani-Age, Sanitized, and Vita-Fresh are trademarked names which exemplify these finishes.

Slip Resistance

In fabrics that have a low thread count, the warp yarns sometimes slip along the filling yarns. Unusual wear or strain on some part of a fabric may cause the same action, known as *slipping*. It is not frequent with rough-surfaced fabrics made of hard-twisted yarns. Permanent firmness can be given to fabrics by immersing them in synthetic resins, then stretching and drying them under tension. The deposit of resin at the points of interlacing in the weave prevents the yarns from slipping. This treatment is advantageous for smooth-surfaced rayons, as the smoothness of the synthetic yarn causes it to slip and fray. Fabrics labeled "slip-resistant" should be examined closely for thread count, as the resinous coating may be used to create an effect of compact construction. One such finish is Estralok A of Crown Chemical Corp.

Antistatic Finishes

Wool and such synthetic fibers as nylon, acrylic, and polyester develop static electricity from the friction caused by wearing and general use. As a result, the fabrics attract dirt particles, cling and climb, crackle, even spark, and cause very minor but discomforting shock to the user. Some companies do apply antistatic treatments, sometimes in combination with other finishes which may have antistatic components in them. One form of Zepel is such a finish. These vary in effectiveness and durability. Some synthetic fiber producers are making types of fibers which have built-in antistatic properties. There are several household products used in laundering that provide nondurable antistatic properties. Among these are Downy, Final Touch, Nu Soft, and Sta Puf.

Heat-Reflectant Finishes

It may be desirable to conserve the heat of the body if conditions are cold or to

Figure 8-20   Aluminum particles used as a heat-reflective finish on lining fabrics are easily removed by rubbing action during dry cleaning if not held securely enough to the cloth by the binder. The dark color of the fabric (top) shows through the partially removed finish. *(Courtesy CIBA Review)*

protect it from the heat if conditions are hot. For cold conditions, a properly treated fabric with a metallic substance faced toward the body will reflect its radiated heat back to the body rather than permit it to escape. For hot conditions, the same treated material with the face outward will reflect the outside heat away from the body. Similar considerations apply to insulating a window, a room, or a tent.

One such excellent finish, developed by Deering Milliken Research Corp., is sold under the trademark of Milium. A fabric to be used as a lining can be coated with this resinated metal (usually aluminum) spray, which adds less than an ounce to the weight of the lining and does not interfere with the porosity or pliability of the fabric. Tests using a wind velocity of 15 miles an hour have shown that a wool outer fabric with a Milium satin lining is approximately equal in warmth to an untreated satin lining plus an $8\frac{1}{2}$-ounce wool interlining with the same outer fabric. Another similar finish is Temp-resisto. The quality and durability of the finish depend upon the quality of the resin and its ability to withstand

darkening and removal by laundering or dry cleaning (see Figure 8-20). The degree of reflectiveness is also affected by the closeness of the weave. A sleazy, open construction will result in much loss of reflective ability since the heat will pass through the open pores.

A variation of the metallic heat-reflectant technique involves the application of an extremely thin metal foil to a woven fabric so that the foil conforms to the surface contours of the fabric and is ruptured at its interstices. The degree of air permeability may vary, depending upon the closeness of the weave. Developed in England as Flectavent, it is produced in this country under the trademark of Foylon. Another process that applies aluminum foil to fabric is Scotch-Shield (see Figure 8-21).

Figure 8-21   Scotch-Shield brand aluminized film Type 103, a 5-millionths-thick film of aluminum, assumes the texture of the material to which it is bonded. *(Courtesy 3M Co.)*

Figure 8-22 Cross section of washable knitted nylon velour (top) laminated to a foam backing. *(Courtesy CIBA Review)*

Foam Laminating

The heat-insulative properties of dead or trapped air spaces have been formerly limited to the nature of the fiber, yarn, and fabric construction. The principle has been extended to the application of a solid foam to woven and knitted fabrics (Figure 8-22). One type is the ether urethane foam commonly found in furniture upholstery; similar types are ester urethane foam and LF70 heat laminatable ethers. The foam thicknesses generally range from $1/16$ to $1/8$ inch and have an accepted range standard of 40 to 60 air cells per linear inch (Figure 8-23).

Since the bulk of foam laminates is air, separated by extremely thin walls of urethane, its outstanding features are the insulative properties combined with light weight. Foam sheets are warmer than the equivalent thickness of unlaminated fabrics or any fiberfilled quilted materials. The degree of insulation depends upon the small cell size of the foam and upon its thickness. Skimping on the thickness could neutralize the insulative effect. Since fabric porosity is an important factor for body comfort, the foam can be produced in a manner that provides for some of the air spaces to be continuous so that the moisture can gradually pass through the material. This permits natural regulation of body temperature and tends to prevent overheating or chilling from moisture collection.

Figure 8-23 A solid bun of urethane foam is peeled into a sheet of foam for lamination to a fabric. *(Courtesy Nopco Chemical Div.)*

Figure 8-24 The waffle pattern of Nopco-Foam on the back of this fabric facilitates better draping quality. The foam is heat-bonded to the fabric. *(Courtesy Nopco Chemical Div.)*

The draping quality of foam-laminated fabrics varies depending upon the thickness of the foam, its density, and its fabrication. Techniques imparting special designs, such as the waffle pattern, and patterned application of bonding adhesives have been developed for improved pliability and drapability with reduced bulky or "ballooning" appearance (see Figure 8-24). Foam laminates move readily with the fabric to which they adhere as well as with body movements. They possess sufficient stretchability to reduce binding and increase action comfort—both distinct advantages when applied to stretch fabrics. Foam laminates have good dimensional stability, shape retentiveness, and resiliency.

Generally, foam-laminated fabrics may be laundered if the base fabric is launderable. They may also be dry-cleaned. Temporary swelling, possible peeling, or deterioration that might result from the application of dry-cleaning solutions depends upon the quality of the foam and the care taken in applying it to the fabric. While urethane foams do tend to discolor, this problem is being met by new dyeing methods as well as such hiding techniques as flocking and printing, by other surface treatments on smooth-faced or polished foam, and by sandwiching the foam sheet between two fabrics. However, the sandwiching technique gives the fabric a heavier hand.

Urethane foams can be odorless. They are nontoxic, nonallergenic, and can be safely worn without fear of skin irritation.

The two basic methods of adhering the foam to the fabric are *flame* or *heat bonding* and *adhesive bonding*. The method used is dependent upon the manufacturer's objectives. Flame bonding requires the use of either an ester urethane or an LF70 ether foam sheet that is sufficiently heated (about 250 to 300 degrees Fahrenheit) to melt its surface immediately before it comes in contact with the cloth and is pressed between two rollers (see Figure 8-25). The tacky foam surface unites with the fabric and produces a material with a cloth face and a foam back. This method is very fast (40 to 70 yards can be processed per minute), but an additional cost allowance must be made for some foam burn-off. Heat laminating must be done after such processes as preshrinking; otherwise, there will be puckering and possible delamination. Other processes, such as repellency finishes, must be applied after heat laminating to ensure proper adherence.

A modification of the heat-bonding process applies the same basic technique to a thin ether urethane foam sheet ($\frac{1}{32}$ inch thick) sandwiched between two layers of cloth. The method competes with fabric-to-fabric bonding techniques.

Adhesive bonding of ether urethane foam to fabric may be accomplished by applying a resin, usually an aqueous acrylic, with a spray or roller before pressing the cloth and foam between rollers.

Figure 8-25 Nylon fabric heat-bonded to urethane foam with the added feature of a permanent heat-pressed design. *(Courtesy American Enka Co.)*

For increased "body breathing" comfort and better drape and hand, the adhesive may be applied as dots, lines, or scattered patterns. Special finishes, such as repellencies, may be applied to the fabric before laminating. Adhesive lamination is slower—about 20 to 25 yards per minute. Additional time is required for curing, but there is no burn-off loss. There is a greater chance that adhesive-bonded cloth and foam will separate when washed or dry cleaned, depending upon the care exercised in processing.

To encourage consumer confidence and provide consumer protection against loss of fabric dimensional stability and foam peeling, several producers formed the Bonded Fabric Council. Quality control was established through the International Fabricare Institute (IFI) which administers a program of testing laminated and bonded fabrics submitted for certification by participating bonders. The standards used are those set forth by the American Society for Testing and Materials. Samples, along with the test findings, are forwarded to the Better Fabrics Testing Bureau which tests some of the samples, as well as random production samples, in its own laboratory. Fabrics that pass these tests are certified, and consumer hangtags with the identification "Perma-Ply Bonded Fabric" are authorized.

Should certified bonded fabrics shrink excessively or delaminate, the bonder is responsible for reimbursement to the consumer for the retail price paid. If the performance records of the IFI indicate excessive returns, the organization can call for a hearing to consider cancellation of the bonder's participation in the program.

Urethane foams are sold under a variety of trademarks that are owned by either the foam producers or the laminating processors. The end product will be affected by both the nature of the foam and the method of bonding.

Curon. This foam is heat-laminated. Reeves Bros., Inc., produces the foam, laminates knitted and woven fabrics with it, and also licenses other mills and converters to process fabrics under this trademark. A waffle design Curon is produced for greater drapability.

Nopco-Foam. This foam is sold by the Nopco Chemical Company. They produce it in flat, waffle design, and smooth or polished form. Mills and converters heat-bond it to their fabrics and merchandise the laminated fabrics under their own trademarks.

Vomar. This is a trademark owned by the Allied Polymer Corp. for a foam made by Nopco. It is merchandised by various fabric firms.

Scott Apparel Foam. Manufactured by the Scott Paper Co., this foam is sold to mills and converters for laminating to knitted and woven fabrics. It may be laminated by heat or adhesive. Some fabricators feature this foam under their own trademarks. However, the quality control standards have been set up by Scott.

Astrotex. This trademark is owned by Princeton Knitting Mills for its fabrics laminated with Scott Apparel Foam.

Bondaknit. Abasco Fabrics, Inc., merchandises its knitted fabrics that are bonded to Scott Apparel Foam under this trademark.

Feathalite. Guilford Woolen Fabrics, Inc., uses this trademark for its woven fabrics laminated to Scott Apparel Foam.

Chem-Stitch. This is the trademark owned by Hicks and Otis for a process that applies a pattern of specially formulated adhesive-bonding, low-density, high-loft ether urethane foam. It produces a permanent quiltlike effect on the face of the fabric that is both wash and dry-clean resistant. The process is licensed to converters.

Fabric-to-Fabric Bonding

This technique uses specially developed adhesives that effect a permanent bond between two fabrics. It can be applied to a wide variety of fabrics of different fibers, constructions, and textures (see Figure 8-26). The original soft hand and drapability of the fabric combination is retained after washing or dry cleaning. The process gives dimensional stability to knitted goods and produces a self-lined fabric. The latter factor contributes to fabric shape retention, opacity, and lower garment construction costs, as

Figure 8-26 *(a)* Knitted woolen bonded to nylon tricot. *(b)* Woven worsted bonded to rayon jersey. *(c)* Ribbon fabric bonded to acetate jersey. *(d)* Raschel-knitted rayon bonded to acetate jersey. *(Courtesy Coin Sales Corp.)*

well as to unusual styling possibilities. Sheer, lacy fabrics may also be given opacity and drape by bonding a lining to them.

The process has gained wide recognition and has been adopted by leading mills under such trademarks as Coin, which is advertised as a two-faced fabric. Other trademarks include Everline, Lockline, and Perma-Line.

REVIEW QUESTIONS

1. Describe one important preparatory finishing process for smooth-surfaced fabrics.
2. Name six finishing processes for producing luster.
3. In each pair of the following finishes, which type is preferable and why? (a) Waterproof or water-repellent; (b) fireproof or flame-resistant.
4. (a) What is the purpose of weighting? (b) Why would it be unwise to buy a heavily weighted silk garment?
5. Explain two finishing methods by which a crinkled effect is achieved.

6. (a) What is the result of beetling? (b) How does it compare with schreinering?
7. How is starch used in finishing fabrics?
8. (a) Explain the calendering process. (b) What is chasing?
9. How may a finishing process deceive the consumer?
10. Discuss shrinkage, telling (a) why it occurs, (b) whether it can be prevented entirely, (c) methods preferable for cotton, (d) methods preferable for wool.
11. (a) Discuss the advantages of napping. (b) Name the disadvantages, if any.
12. (a) What fabrics are naturally wrinkle-resistant? (b) How can this quality be produced in other fabrics?
13. (a) What method of bleaching is preferable? (b) Is there any advantage in buying unbleached fabrics?
14. Why are finishing processes necessary?
15. Explain tentering and crabbing.
16. What is meant by a drip-dry or wash and wear garment?
17. How effective is the drip-dry finish?
18. How are fabrics embossed?
19. Under what circumstances will embossing on fabrics be permanent?
20. Differentiate between mercerizing and slack mercerizing in terms of their effect on cotton.
21. What is ammoniating?
22. Differentiate between wrinkle-resistant and permanent press finishes in terms of properties and limitations.
23. Is it possible to treat wool fabrics so that garments made of them will be washable and shape retentive?
24. What are the essential provisions of the amended Flammable Fabrics Act?
25. What is the principle of each of the two types of heat reflectants?
26. (a) What is foam lamination? (b) Describe its effectiveness.
27. What are the characteristics of bonded fabrics?
28. (a) Name four *modified* flame-retardant fibers. (b) Name six *inherently* flame-retardant fibers.
29. How can a consumer impart antistatic properties to garments?

SUGGESTED ACTIVITIES

Visit the yard-goods department of a large retail store. Obtain the names of the finishes of ten different fabrics by noting the labels. Describe the fabrics' appearance and finish characteristics.

9

DYEING

finishing with color

As textile fibers have been examined and tested for their differential qualities and as the spinning and weaving processes have been explained, the qualities of durability and serviceability have been constantly stressed. When the yarn is made into fabric, the interesting and intricate constructions begin to add beauty of appearance as well as serviceability. The various finishing processes suggest additional means of enhancing the appearance of the newly formed fabric. It remains for the dyeing and printing processes to provide lasting beauty and delight to the eye. Both these processes add color to fabrics, and color delights by stimulating or soothing. Dyeing and printing differ in the method by which color is applied to fabric. In the dyeing process, fiber, yarn, or fabric is impregnated with a dyestuff. In printing (described in Chapter 10), a pattern or a design is generally imprinted on the fabric in one or more colors by using dyes in paste form or some related means.

SELECTION OF DYE

To select the proper dye for a fiber, it is necessary to know which dyes have an affinity for the vegetable, animal, or man-made fibers. In general, the dyes used for cotton and linen may be used for rayons, but acetate requires a special class of dyes. When a dye colors fabric directly with one operation of impregnation, without the aid of an affixing agent, the dye is said to be a *direct dye* for that fiber. Direct dyes are the easiest to produce, the simplest to apply, and the cheapest in their initial cost as well as in application. They are not, however, as colorfast to light and washing as some other dyes. The term "bleeding" describes dyes that run in washing. When dye rubs off a fabric exposed to the friction of wear, it is termed "crocking."

Requirements for colorfastness differ. Fastness to *light* is important in draperies, for example, as they must stand strong light daily but do not need to be washed frequently. Fastness to *washing* is important in dress fabrics and household linens because they must undergo frequent washings. Therefore, both the kind of fiber to be dyed and the intended use for the fabric enter into the selection of the dye.

NATURAL DYES

Primitive people obtained dyes from flowers, nuts, berries, and other forms of vegetable and plant life, as well as from mineral and animal sources. These sources have provided such natural dyes throughout civilization. They are no longer used in quantity by the dyeing industry, but they are still used in Oriental countries to a certain extent for rug dyeing and in many parts of the world for native handicraft.

The principal vegetable dyes are fustic, sumac, catechu or cutch, madder, henna, saffron, logwood, indigo, and alizarin. Animal dyes, such as cochineal, squid sepia, lac, and tyrian purple, are obtained from species of fish and small insects. Minerals provide such dyes as prussian blue, chrome yellow, and iron buff.

SYNTHETIC DYES

Although synthetic dyes were first derived from coal tar in 1856, they were not developed in the United States to any great extent until World War I, when the supply of imported synthetic dyes was cut off. Since then, the United States has built up a dye industry that is unsurpassed. Innumerable dye compounds made from coal tar have now supplanted natural dyes. These synthetic dyes are constantly being improved

as to beauty of color and colorfastness. Lasting beauty of color is an important factor in consumers' finished goods. Durability of color depends on (1) selection of the proper dye for the fiber to be dyed, (2) selection of the method of dyeing the fiber, yarn, or fabric.

The synthetic dyes may be categorized into about fourteen classes. The classification is based upon the particular type of chemical composition of the dye and/or the method of its application (see Table 9-1).

Basic (Cationic) Dyes

The first coal-tar dye was a so-called *basic* dye. It was developed to give many bright shades for silk and wool. The chemical agent that binds the dye to a fiber, which otherwise has little or no affinity for the dye, is known as a *mordant*. Cationic dyes are used with a mordant for cotton, linen, acetate, nylon, polyesters, acrylics, and modacrylics. A fluorescent basic dye which imparts extremely bright shades has been developed in a wide range or colors. It is suitable for acrylics and certain polyesters.

When used on natural fibers, basic dyes are not fast to light, washing, perspiration, or atmospheric gases; they tend to either bleed or crock. They give good fastness and bright shades to acrylics for which they are principally used. Basic dyes are frequently used as an aftertreatment for fabrics that have been previously dyed with acid colors.

Oxidation Bases

These are one of the oldest of synthetic dyes. Aniline black, one of the most intense and fastest blacks available, is an example of this group. Excellent browns are also available for printing. They are used primarily for cotton and can be applied with oxidizing agents and careful processings to wool, silk, and acetate.

Acid (Anionic) Dyes

Acidification of basic dyes led to the creation of acid dyes that are used mostly on wool and silk. They are also being more widely used for dyeing acetate, nylon, acrylics, modacrylics, and spandex. These anionic dyes have also been found useful in printing chlorinated wool and silk.

Acid dyes are inexpensive and fairly fast to light, but they are not fast to washing and have only fair fastness to dry cleaning. They have low resistance to perspiration.

Wool may be given increased fastness to both light and washing by boiling the fabric in a chromate solution after the first dyebath. This is called *afterchroming*.

Acid-Milling Dyes

A further development of the acid colors was the acid-milling dyes, which have superior wetfastness, good lightfastness, and less tendency to bleed onto surrounding white areas.

Acid-Premetalized Dyes

These are another outgrowth of the acid dyes. Carrying one or two molecules of chromium bound to the dye in their structure, they require a strong acid bath to get the color into the fabric. The metal improves the colorfastness, which is greater than for acid or acid-milling dyes. Acid-premetalized dyes are used a great deal on wool, nylon, and acrylics. The colors are good, though no brilliant blues or greens are obtainable.

Neutral-Premetalized Dyes

These dyes have one molecule of metal, usually chromium, bound to two molecules of dye to improve fastness properties. The shades are not so bright as acid colors. These dyes are used on wool, silk, nylon, acrylics, modacrylics, and vinylidene-derived fibers. Since the generally good fastness properties are similar for all these fibers, the neutral premetalized dyes are used for their blends.

Mordant or Chrome Dyes

These dyes are related to acid dyes but are more complex. They require the addition of sodium or potassium bichromate in the dyebath or after the dyeing is completed to obtain the mordant or binding action of the chrome. They are the fastest dyes to wet processing available for wool and are therefore principally used for wool requiring maximum fastness. They are also used with less effective fastness for cotton, linen, silk, rayon, and nylon. They provide a wide range of colors that are duller than the acid dyes.

Substantive Direct Dyes

This group is one of three types of direct dyes, all of which dye cellulosic fibers directly and without a mordant in bright, full shades. Some direct dyes may be used on wool, silk, and nylon. They are applied to cotton or rayon from a water solution, and when salt is added, the color is forced out of solution onto the fiber. The dye colors often have only fair fastness to light, poor fastness to washing, and are not very bright. They are often referred to as *commercial colors*, a term that indicates that the dyes are not the best available for the purpose.

Developed Dyes

This is another group of direct dyes. In addition to their primary use for cellulosic fibers, they are also used to color wool, silk, and nylon. The process requires a base to be dyed on the goods. This is followed by a *diazotizing* process, whereby the dye is chemically changed and treated with a fresh set of chemicals, called *developers*, that form the completed dye. Developed dyes are fairly fast to washing because they have been literally built into the fiber.

Azoic Dyes

This is the third group of direct dyes that is further identified as naphthol and rapidogen types. They are quite fast to washing and vary from poor to excellent lightfastness. Azoic dyes are used to a very great extent on cotton and for special purposes on nylon and acetate. The method of applying these dyes is somewhat similar to that of developed dyes, as it involves diazotizing. The fabric is first immersed in naphthol, which impregnates the fibers; it is then dipped into the diazotized color bath. The dyeing is followed by thorough soaping and rinsing. Naphthol or azoic dyes are sometimes referred to as *ice dyes* because ice is frequently used to bring the dyes to a low temperature and assure efficient dye for-

mation. A complete color range is available, but these dyes are used primarily for bright reds, yellows, and blacks.

Disperse Dyes

These dyes were developed originally for dyeing acetate fibers and have since found wide use in dyeing triacetate, nylon, polyester, acrylic, modacrylic, and olefin, as well as cellulosic fibers. While they are not soluble in water, they are supplied in a finely ground form that will disperse in water. The particles will dissolve in the fibers and, by this action, the fabric is dyed. Disperse blacks are usually made by a process similar to the one described for developed direct dyes.

Other shades are dyed just as are direct dyes except that salt is never added to the dyebaths. The disperse dyes have one weakness, particularly in the blue shades: they are susceptible to nitrous oxide gas in the atmosphere and will gradually fade to a pink color. Inhibitors applied at the dyehouse can slow down the fading process. Peculiarly enough, disperse blues applied to nylon do not gas-fade. The disperse dyes as a class are fairly fast, except that the ones least sensitive to gas-fading on acetate are the least lightfast.

Sulfur Dyes

Sulfur dyes, first made in 1879, are used for cotton and linen. These dyes are fast to washing, light, and perspiration, but they have one weakness: excessive chlorine bleaching will strip the color.

Sulfur dyes are insoluble in water and must be made soluble with the aid of caustic soda and sodium sulfide. (One or two manufacturers produce sulfur dyes that have been made water-soluble.)

Sulfur dyeing is done at high temperature and with a large quantity of salt, which helps to drive the color into the fabric. After immersion in the dyebath, followed by rinsing, the fabric is oxidized to the desired shade by exposure to the air or, chemically, by the use of potassium bichromate and acetic acid. The oxidizing process must be carefully controlled because penetration of the dye is retarded by premature oxidation. Also, oxidation changes sulfur to sulfuric acid, which may be harmful to the fabric. Excess chemicals and excess dye must be completely removed by thorough washing. Sulfur dyes penetrate more thoroughly than any other dye because of the high temperature and the alkalinity of the dyebath. They are excellent for khaki and for the heavy piece goods used in workclothes. Sulfur dyes produce dull colors, such as navy, brown, and black. They are used for black more than any other dye. If stored for a great length of time, fabrics become tender.

Vat Dyes

The first synthetic vat dye was an indigo created in 1879. Vat dyes are the fastest dyes for cotton, linen, and rayon. They also may be applied to wool, nylon, polyesters, acrylics, and modacrylics with the use of a mordant. Vat dyes are not only resistant to light and to acids and alkalies, but are also equally resistant to the strong oxidizing bleaches used in commercial laundries. In this respect, vat dyes excel sulfur dyes, which are not fast to chlorine washing.

A label stating that a garment is vat-dyed is not a guarantee that the fabric is absolutely fast to washing if it is of brilliant color. The name "Indanthrene" on labels indicates that a special type of dye has been used that is particularly fast to light and to washing. This type was among the first of the synthetic vat dyes.

The old-fashioned method of fermenting and steeping indigo in a vat gave vat dyes their name. They are prepared today on the same principle, but they are chemically purer and the process is shorter. Vat dyes are expensive because of the initial cost as well as the method of application. They are insoluble pigments; but they are made soluble in water by the use of a strong reducing agent, such as hydrosulfite dissolved in the alkali, sodium hydroxide. The fabric is immersed in this solution. Subsequent exposure to air or immersion in an oxidizing bath (bichromate) restores the dye to its insoluble form as a part of the fiber.

Reactive Dyes

This interesting class of colors was the first really new development (1957) since the vat dyes. There are now several varieties of reactive dyes, which actually react with fiber molecules to form a chemical compound. While these dyes were first designed for cellulosic fibers, types are now available for wool, silk, nylon, acrylics, and blends of these fibers. Some advantages of reactive dyes are their excellent fastness to light and washing and their brilliant shades, which are rivaled only by acid dyes on silk.

There are several chemical ways of combining the dye with cellulosic fibers, and all have about the same potential. The dyes can be applied from alkaline solution in a one-step process of pad and dry, or they can be applied from neutral solutions and then alkalized in a separate run. Heat is also used to develop the shade. In all cases, the fabric is well soaped after dyeing to remove any unfixed dye (color that has combined with the water in the dyebath and is of no value in the dyeing of the goods).

Pigment Dyes

These dyes utilize a technique of coloring that has become increasingly important. The colors, confined to light shades, bright colors, and such metallic colors as gold, are usually applied to cotton cloth but are also used on fabrics of man-made fibers. Actually, they are not true dyes because they have no affinity for the fiber and are applied and held to the fabric with resins, which are then cured at high temperatures.

Pigment dyeing gives excellent lightfast colors and generally good all-around fastness. However, if the shade is too deep, the color will crock. Great improvements in the pigments and resins have made it possible to dye in much darker shades than was possible at first.

Colorless Dyes

These so-called dyes are also called *fluorescent whiteners* or *optical brighteners*. The whiteness is really caused by absorption of ultraviolet light and reflection of visible blue light. Optical brighteners are available for cotton, acrylics, wool, acetate, and nylon. They may be applied during bleaching, before resin finishing, or with the resin.

Though lightfastness varies, it is generally fair depending upon the compound and the fiber to which it is applied. Washfastness also varies but is generally good; further brightness buildup occurs from washing the fabrics in household detergents.

SELECTION OF DYEING METHOD

Textiles may be dyed at any stage of their development from fiber into fabric by the following methods:

Stock dyeing, in the fiber stage

Top dyeing, in the combed wool sliver stage

Yarn dyeing, after the fiber has been spun into yarn

Piece dyeing, after the yarn has been constructed into fabric

Solution pigmenting or dope dyeing, before a man-made fiber is extruded through the spinneret

Stock Dyeing

Stock dyeing refers to dyeing a textile fiber in a loose condition before it is spun. This is done by putting it in large vats and circulating dye liquor through the mass of fiber at elevated temperatures (see Figure 9-1). Although the dye liquor is pumped through the fiber in large quantities, there are areas where the dye does not penetrate completely. However, in subsequent blending and

Figure 9-1   Cotton staple being stock-dyed in a kettle containing 1,000 pounds of fiber. *(Courtesy Pepperell Manufacturing Co.)*

spinning operations, these areas are so mixed with the thoroughly dyed fiber that an overall even color is obtained. In stock dyeing, which is the least expensive method of coloring, the color is well penetrated into the fibers and does not crock readily. Stock-dyed fiber does not spin as readily as undyed fiber because it loses some of its flexibility, but lubricants added in the final rinsing overcome most of this difficulty.

Woolens are often stock-dyed. The completeness of this method is reflected in the expression "dyed in the wool," which is used to attribute the quality of thoroughness. Stock dyeing produces mixture effects and color blends, of which oxford suitings and tweed homespuns are examples.

Top Dyeing

One step nearer to the finished yarn than stock dyeing is what is called *top dyeing* in the worsted industry. *Top* is wool that has been combed to take out the short fibers, then delivered from the combs in a ropelike form about $1\frac{1}{4}$ inches thick. The top is wound on perforated spools and the dye liquor is circulated through it. Very even dyeing is possible with this method.

Table 9-1

DYE CLASS	GENERAL DESCRIPTION	USES	FASTNESS	
			Light	Washing
Basic (Cationic)	First synthetic dye (1856); organic base dissolved in inorganic acid. Limited use today, except some used for acrylics. Complete color range; colors bright	Cotton (with mordant), wool, silk, nylon, polyesters, acrylics, modacrylics. Direct printing on acetate; discharge printing on cotton	Poor; selected types excellent on acrylics	Poor on natural fibers; good on others in wide range of shades
Oxidtion Bases	One of earliest synthetics; aniline black, still one of the most intense and fastest blacks available. Excellent browns for printing	Primarily for dyeing cotton; also wool, silk, acetate. Direct, resist, and discharge printing	Excellent	Very good
Acid (Anionic)	Originated from basic dye acidification; complete color range	Primarily for wool and silk; also acetate, nylons, acrylics, modacrylics, spandex; some rayon, polyester, and polypropylene. Printing on chlorinated wool, silk, acetate	Generally very good; range poor to excellent	Poor
Acid-Milling	Similar origin to acid dyes. Complete color range; duller than acid dyes	Same as acid; also stock and top dyeing	Generally very good; range poor to excellent	Good
Acid-Premetalized	Require strong acid bath; based on structure of one or two molecules of chromium to one molecule of dye; metal assists dye fastness; blues and greens duller than acid dyes; tendency to dye unevenly on nylons	Suitable for carpeting, decorative fabrics, women's wear, swimwear of wool, nylon, acrylic fabrics	Good to excellent	Fair to good
Neutral-Premetalized	Derived from acid dyes based on structure of one molecule of metal (usually chromium) bound to two molecules of dye; shades fairly bright but less so than acid colors; fastness similar for various fibers	Wool, silk, nylons, acrylics, modacrylics, vinylidene-derived fibers; blends of these fibers due to similar fastness properties for various fibers	Very good to excellent	Fair to good
Mordant (Chrome)	Related to acid dyes; require addition of chrome derived from potassium or sodium bichromate; fairly complete color range but duller than acid dyes	Primarily for wool requiring maximum fastness: carpeting, decorative fabrics, men's wear; also silk, nylons, cellulosic fibers. Printing on wool and silk.	Good to excellent, depending on depth of shade, dyeing method	Good

DYES AND THEIR CHARACTERISTICS

			FASTNESS			
Hot Pressing	Dry Cleaning	Gas Fading	Staining (Bleeding)	Perspiration	Crocking	Seawater
Not affected	Mostly poor; good on acrylics	Not susceptible	Bleeds easily on wool, silk; good resistance on man-made fibers	Generally poor; some blues good; good on acrylics	Good resistance on acrylics	Very poor; good on acrylics
Not affected	Very good	Not susceptible	Very good	Good	Very good	Not affected
Not affected	Good	Not susceptible	Bleed easily; stain adjacent fibers	Fair	Excellent	Fair
Not affected	Good	Not susceptible	Good resistance; generally will not stain adjacent fibers	Fair to good	Excellent	Good
Not affected	Good	Not susceptible	Generally good resistance to staining other fibers	Good	Good to excellent	Fair to good
Not affected	Good	Not affected	Generally good resistance	Good	Good to excellent	Good to excellent
Not affected	Fair to good	Not affected	Considerable staining of adjacent fibers, particularly silk, nylons; more resistant to cellulosics	Generally good; some greens fair	Fair to good	Good

Table 9-1

DYE CLASS	GENERAL DESCRIPTION	USES	FASTNESS	
			Light	Washing
Substantive Direct	Dye cellulosics directly; some dye wool, silk, nylons; union dyes for cotton/wool blends. Complete shade range; colors duller than basic or acid dyes	Primarily for cellulosic fabrics. Some good for cotton wool blends; some for better quality fabrics. Much used for printing on dischargeable dyed backgrounds	Good to excellent	Poor
Developed	Dyes processed using copper salts, copper resin compounds to develop new dye in fiber. Used for cellulosics, wool, silk, nylons. Complete shade range; colors duller than basic or acid dyes	Same as substantive dyes	Good to excellent	Fair
Azoic (Naphthol and Rapidogens)	Also known as insoluble azos and ice colors; ice helps to reduce temperature of bath to facilitate dyeing. Complete shade range; yellows, reds, blacks most used. Bright shades at moderate cost	Primarily for cotton goods; limited use on acetate, nylons. Extensive printing use since colors are dischargeable and work with other groups	Good to excellent, depending on type, shade, depth	Good; some sensitive to chlorine bleach
Disperse	Developed for acetate (1922). Insoluble in water; supplied in paste or finely powdered form; particles disperse in water and dissolve in fibers. Good shade range	Primarily for acetate; also triacetate, nylons, polyesters, acrylics, modacrylics, olefins, as well as cellulosic fibers. Wide use in apparel, decorative fabrics. Used for dyeing and printing	Fair to excellent, depending on fiber	Fair to good; better on polyesters than on on acetate or nylons
Sulfur	First created in 1879. Generally insoluble in water. Complete shade range except for true red; colors not bright	Applicable to stock, yarn, piece goods; used for heavy woven and knitted cotton goods as well as linen and jute. Some printing	Poor to fair for yellows and browns; good to excellent in darker shades	Poor to good; most sensitive to chlorine bleach
Vat	Synthetic indigo original (1879). Insoluble in water; require reduction to apply. Incomplete but adequate shade range	Primarily for cotton; also wool. Generally for workclothes, outerwear, sportswear, decorative fabrics, awnings. Much used for prints	Generally excellent	Good

DYES AND THEIR CHARACTERISTICS *(Continued)*

FASTNESS						
Hot Pressing	Dry Cleaning	Gas Fading	Staining (Bleeding)	Perspiration	Crocking	Seawater
Good	Good	Not affected	Good resistance	Good	Very good in most shades on cotton, rayons	Poor to good, depending on color
Good	Good	Not affected	Good resistance	Good	Very good in most shades on cotton, rayons	Poor to good, depending on color
Good	Good	Not affected	Fair, sometimes stain adjacent whites; some bleed in peroxide bleach	Generally good	Depends on dyeing technique and aftertreatment	Good
Some color change possible	Good	Poor to good resistance, depending on fiber. Blues and violets on acetate very sensitive, less sensitive on nylons and polyesters	Stains wool badly	Good	Good	Good
Good	Good	Not affected	Fair to good, depending on shade, depth, aftertreatment	Good	Poor to good, depending on shade, depth	Good
Generally good; some color change with certain dyes	Good	Generally not affected; a few are susceptible	Good resistance	Good	Fair to good, depending on dye, depth of shade	Good

Table 9-1

DYE CLASS	GENERAL DESCRIPTION	USES	FASTNESS	
			Light	Washing
Reactive	First available in 1957; several varieties. Form chemical combination with fiber, distinguishing class from others. Produce brightest shades on cotton	Primarily for cotton apparel, decorative fabrics for bright colors; where good all-around fastness is important. Applicable to stock, yarn, piece goods, printing. Some suitable for wool, silk, nylons acrylics, and blends	Good to very good on most fibers; poor to moderate on nylon	Good; generally sensitive to chlorine bleach
Pigment	Generally organic coloring materials; all insoluble in water with no affinity for fiber. Fixed on fiber with resinous binders and cured at high temperatures. Complete shade range in bright colors	Primarily for printing cotton of all weights; also rayon, acetate, nylons, polyesters, olefins	Very good to excellent	Good
Optical Brighteners (Colorless Dyes)	Also called fluorescent whiteners. Brightness caused by absorption of ultraviolet light and reflection of visible blue light. Applied during bleaching or in the final finish (before resin finish or with the resin)	Much used on cotton; also wool, acetate, nylons, acrylics	Fair	Varies but generally improves with build-up of whiteners in household detergents

Data based upon Dye Chart originally prepared by *Textile World*.

Yarn Dyeing

When dyeing is done after the fiber has been spun into yarn, it is described as yarn dyeing. There are several methods of yarn dyeing. The purpose is to have the dyestuff penetrate to the fibers in the core of the yarn; this is similar to the penetration of the fibers in stock dyeing. Cloth made of dyed yarns is called yarn-dyed.

Yarn-dyed fabrics are usually deeper and richer in color. Yarn-dyed fabrics intended for laundering must be quite colorfast, or bleeding could occur. The primary reason for dyeing in the yarn form is to create interesting checks, stripes, and plaids with different-colored yarns in the weaving process. Chambrays, for example, are usually woven with a colored warp and white filling. Other combinations of different-colored yarns are checked gingham, shepherd's check, plaid, seersucker, and heather mixtures.

Skein (Hank) Dyeing. Yarn may be prepared in skein, or hank, form and then dyed. The loose arrangement of the yarn allows for excellent dye penetration. The skeins are hung over a rung and immersed in a dyebath in a large container.

YES AND THEIR CHARACTERISTICS *(Continued)*

FASTNESS

ot Pressing	Dry Cleaning	Gas Fading	Staining (Bleeding)	Perspiration	Crocking	Seawater
Not affected	Good	Not susceptible	Good resistance	Good	Good	Good; some fair, particularly in chlorinated pool
Good	Good, if properly bound	Majority not susceptible; a few sensitive	Good	Good	Good for light to medium shades; very poor for dark shades	Good
Not known to be affected	Not known to be affected	Not known to be affected	Not affected	Not known to be affected	Not known to be affected	Not known to be affected

Skein-dyed yarn is used to a considerable extent for suiting and dress goods.

Package Dyeing. Yarn wound on spools, cones, or similar units and then dyed is referred to as *package-dyed yarn* (see Figure 9-2). The packages of yarn are stacked on perforated rods in a rack and then immersed in a tank wherein the dye is forced outward from the rods under pressure through the spools and then back through the packages toward the center to penetrate the entire yarn as thoroughly as possible. Most carded and combed cotton that is used for knitted outerwear is package-dyed.

Warp-beam Dyeing. This method is similar to package dyeing. Yarn is wound onto a perforated warp beam, immersed in a tank, and dyed under pressure. It is used when fabrics are to be woven with dyed warp yarns (Figure 9-3).

Space Dyeing. Yarn that is space-dyed is dyed at intervals along its length. One procedure is the knit-deknit method whereby the yarn is knitted on either a circular or flatbed knitting machine set to produce the desired size of loop. The knitted cloth is then dyed, and it is subsequently deknitted. The dye penetrates the loops of the yarn but since it

Figure 9-2 Another form of yarn dyeing is package dyeing, whereby the packages, or spools of yarn are stacked on a rack (right) and then immersed in a vat of dye (left). *(Courtesy Burlington Institute, Inc.)*

does not readily penetrate the areas of the yarn where it crosses itself, alternating dyed and undyed spaces appear. Variations in hue and heather effects are possible in the fabric subsequently produced.

Another more recently introduced technique, the *OPI Space-Dye Applicator*, produces multicolored space-dyed yarns. It was designed for use on knitting and carpet yarns. The yarns are dyed intermittently as they run at high speeds of up to 1,000 yards per minute through spaced dyebaths with continuous subjection to shock waves produced by compressed air assuming supersonic velocities. The compression effect resulting from this shock wave creates a residual humidity in the yarn sufficiently low to avoid the need for intermediate drying before subsequent operations of winding, etc.

Piece Dyeing

The great bulk of dyed fabric on the market is dyed in the piece. This method gives the manufacturer maximum flexibility for his inventory to meet large or small demands for a given color as fashion requires. Where yardage warrants it, fabrics are dyed in continuous-range machines. Small lots of fabrics of all fibers are dyed in batches. Piece dyeing is thoroughly satisfactory as regards levelness, penetration, and overall fastness, assuming that the proper dyes have been used.

Fabric may be piece-dyed whether it is composed of only one kind of fiber or yarn or of blends of different fibers or combinations of different yarns. When the fabric is made of one kind of fiber or yarn, then dyeing is relatively uncomplicated because the one appropriate dye is used. However, when the fabric contains a blend of fibers or combination of different yarns, then there are required special procedures which employ different dyes that are each specific for the particular fibers used. These procedures are called *union dyeing* and *cross-dyeing*.

Union dyeing. This process of dyeing piece goods made of different fibers or yarns may be readily accomplished. Although different fibers may require different dyes to obtain the same color, this may be done by putting the appropriate color dye that is specific to each type of fiber into one dyebath.

Cross-dyeing. Cross-dyeing of goods may be accomplished in any one of several ways. The results produce varied effects. One method is a combination of stock dyeing or of yarn dyeing with subsequent piece dyeing. Cross-dyeing produces varied effects. For instance, either the warp or the filling yarns may be stock-dyed or yarn-dyed, one set of yarns being left undyed. The fabric is piece-dyed after weaving; thus, color is given

Figure 9-3 Warp-beam dyeing, a form of yarn dyeing, is done by steeping the yarns on a warp-beam in a dye vat. Note the perforations in the warp-beam cylinder through which the dye is forced and circulated to obtain thorough yarn dyeing (see insert). *(Courtesy Gaston County Dyeing Machine Co.)*

to the undyed yarn in a second dyebath, and the yarns that were originally stock-dyed or yarn-dyed acquire some additional coloring, which blends with the piece-dyed portion of the fabric.

If yarns of vegetable fibers have been combined with yarns of animal fibers in a fabric that is to be piece-dyed, two separate dyebaths must be used. The fabric is dipped into both solutions, each of which affects the fiber for which it has an affinity. This provides colorful effects.

A mordant can be included in a single dyebath to cause the dye to adhere to the fiber for which it does not have an affinity. Thus, the more expensive method of cross-dyeing, requiring two dyebaths, need not be used.

Still another method of cross-dyeing is to immerse a fabric composed of two different types of fibers into one dyebath containing two different dyes, one specific for each of the fibers. For example, a fabric composed of viscose rayon and acetate yarns may be cross-dyed in this manner. When the fabric is removed from the dyebath, the viscose rayon yarns will be one color, and the acetate yarns will be another color.

Beck Dyeing. Long yardages of cloth that are to be dyed on a continuous process are very often beck-dyed by passing the fabric in rope form through the dyebath (Figure 9-4). The rope of cloth moves over a rail onto a reel which immerses it into the dye and then draws the fabric up and forward to the front of the machine. The process is repeated as long as necessary to dye the material uniformly to the desired intensity of color.

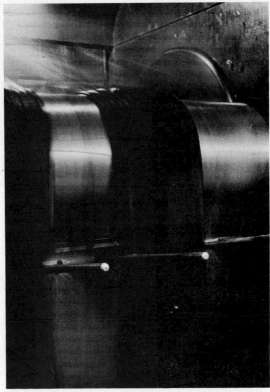

Figure 9-4   Close-up of fabric in rope form being fed into dyebath at rear. *(Courtesy Burlington Industries, Inc.)*

Jet Dyeing. Fabric may be jet-dyed by placing it in a heated tube or column where jets of dye solution are forced through it at pressures of up to 300 pounds per jet. The dye is continually recirculated as the cloth is moved along the tube at speeds of up to 300 yards per minute. The fluid moves faster than the cloth so that the cloth floats through the tube without touching the walls. This method is not only fast but also very thorough, and crease and rope marks may be avoided.

Figure 9-5 Fabric may be piece-dyed on a jig, whereby the cloth is immersed into troughs of dye and subsequently rewound into rolls. *(Courtesy Burlington Industries, Inc.)*

Jig Dyeing. This method utilizes the basic procedure of beck dyeing. However, in jig dyeing, the fabric is held on rollers at full width rather than in rope form as it is passed through the dyebath. This open-vat process is repeated until the desired shade is obtained (Figure 9-5).

Pad Dyeing. Like jig dyeing, *padding* dyes the fabric as it is held at full width. The fabric is passed through a trough containing dye and then between two heavy rollers which force the dye into the cloth and squeeze out the excess.

Cold Pad-Batch Dyeing. This technique is a variation of *pad dyeing*. It is used for wool piece-goods to overcome certain disadvantages of beck-dyeing them in light, bright shades. Wool fabric is immersed in the dye liquor at room temperature. After the excess liquor is squeezed out by the pad rollers, the roll of fabric is wrapped to prevent drying. It is then rotated slowly for up to forty-eight hours to obtain uniformity of dye application. The fabric is then washed in a mild alkaline solution to remove the liquor additives and unfixed dyes. Finally the cloth is extracted and dried.

Vacuum Impregnation. Imparting color to fabric by vacuum impregnation differs from the methods described above in that it depends upon an initial lack of air followed by the use of normal air pressure to impregnate the fibers with the dye. It is based on certain important principles. One of these is that air entrapped in the substrates of the textile fibers in the fabric and in the folds of the fabric itself hinders the passing of dye through to the fiber sites. Also, normal atmospheric pressure can be substituted for the higher pressures generally used, and the concomitant cost of developing and using the higher pressures is eliminated.

In the vacuum impregnation process, air is evacuated from the dye tank to near-zero pressure, the fabric is then covered with the dye liquid while it is in this vacuum state, and then the system is opened to allow return to normal atmospheric pressure. As a result, there is instantaneous wetting, virtually complete saturation of the fabric, and impregnation of the dye into the fibers. The high degree of saturation and impregnation occurs because the swift change from the vacuum to normal atmospheric condition causes the liquid dye to rush in and fill the voids, unhindered by the resistance of the entrapped air. In effect, when the vacuum condition is suddenly changed to normal or even a bit higher, the pressure created is so comparatively great that the dyestuff is literally forced into the fiber. The vacuum impregnation technique has special value for fabrics made of fibers that are not easily wetted, since the coloring is primarily dependent on the sudden pressure that causes the penetration of the dye into the fibers. The method can be applied subsequent to certain finishes, such as wrinkle-resistant resins, because they do not block the dye impregnation process.

Solvent Dyeing. All the dyeing techniques discussed in previous sections depend upon dissolving the dyestuffs in water. These aqueous solutions have their limitations with regard to such factors as the relative dye solubility in water, dye liquid viscosity, and the water permeability of the fiber. Recent techniques have used other liquids, such as ammonia, perchlorethylene, and trichlorobenzene, which have been found to be superior dye vehicles. These liquids are better dye solvents, and they penetrate better a wide variety of man-made and synthetic fibers. Furthermore, the exhausted solvents are recoverable, are thereby nonpullutive, and are less expensive means of dyeing.

Solution Pigmenting, or Dope Dyeing

In producing man-made or synthetic fibers, a great deal of time and money can be saved if the dye is added to the solution before it is extruded through the spinnerets into filaments. This method also gives a greater degree of colorfastness. A process called *solution pigmenting*, or *dope dyeing*, has been used with varying degrees of success for man-made fibers ranging from rayon through saran and glass fiber. Effective results have been obtained.

Two outstanding examples of the solution pigmenting process for acetate fiber are Chromspun and Celaperm. The former is the trademark for the process developed by the Tennessee Eastman Co.; the latter is the trademark for a similar process developed by the Celanese Corp. of America. These solution pigmenting processes were developed to overcome problems in dyeing acetate yarns and fabrics where grays and blues would gas-fade. The pigment colors are the fastest known—much faster than any of the customary dyeing techniques. Therefore, where warranted, they are to be preferred when fastness to almost any known factor is important.

Chip Dyeing. Special dyes may be added to the polymer for the production of such fibers as nylon prior to melt-spinning of the chips. The dyestuffs are resistant to the reducing action of the polymer under high temperatures. Such dyes will not fade, crock, or run.

TESTS TO DETERMINE COLORFASTNESS

Beauty of color in any fabric is of no value to the consumer unless the dye may be considered fast under the conditions in which the fabric will be used. Color must meet such tests as washing, ironing, steaming, perspiration, strong light, and dry cleaning. The U.S. government tests fabrics for colorfastness to maintain and enforce trade standards. Retail stores often have laboratories for testing consumers' goods both to maintain merchandise standards for their own protection and to give their customers proper value for the price paid. The consumer may also test fabrics for color-fastness at home. Garments will retain a fresh, new appearance and give additional wear if they are properly

cleaned at home or at a commercial cleaner in accordance with the results of the tests to which samples of the garment's fabrics have previously been subjected.

Fastness to Washing

The usual method for determining fastness to washing is to wash and then iron under a white cloth a sample of the fabric while it is still wet. If the dye bleeds on the cloth, the color cannot be considered fast. Home washing is not a rigorous enough test for fabrics that will be washed in commerical laundries. A better test is to immerse the sample in water containing a bleach, such as Clorox, because similar strong compounds are used in the laundries (Figure 9-6).

Figure 9-6 Swatches of colored fabric are put into containers of water and soap or detergent and are rotated in this Launder-Ometer to test color-fastness to washing. *(Courtesy Atlas Electric Devices Co.)*

Fastness to Ironing

To test for fastness to ironing, iron the sample with a very hot iron. After the sample has cooled, compare it with the original fabric. If the color is unchanged, the fabric is fast to ironing.

Fastness to Steaming

To test for fastness to steaming, place a sample between the folds of a white cloth, and steam it over a teakettle. If the color is fast, it should be unchanged, and no dye will show on the white cloth.

Fastness to Light

To test for fastness to light, cover half a sample of fabric with opaque paper and expose it to outdoor light for perhaps twenty days. Then compare both halves. If the exposed portion shows perceptible fading, the fabric is not fast to light. A more specific time for exposure cannot be given, because the intensity of sunlight varies in different localities. Usually, resistance to exposure of twenty days is considered good.

This test is performed in a much shorter time in textile testing laboratories by the use of the Fade-Ometer, an apparatus having very strong electric lamps or a special carbon-arc light (see Figure 9-7). If a fabric can withstand an exposure of forty hours in this machine with no perceptible loss of color, it is said to have superlative fastness to light. A fabric has good fastness to light if it withstands an exposure of thirty hours.

Fastness to Perspiration

To test for fastness to perspiration, soak a sample of the dyed fabric for ten minutes in a weak acid, such as a dilute acetic acid solution. Do not rinse. Roll the sample in a piece of undyed cloth. Permit gradual drying, and leave the material rolled for a few days. If comparison with the original color shows that the shade of the dyed fabric has changed, or if the dye appears on the cloth in which the sample was rolled, the color is not fast to perspiration.

The effects of both acid and alkaline perspiration can be determined by the standard government test, which recommends the use of two solutions. *For acid perspiration:* 10 grams sodium chloride; 1 gram lactic acid, U.S.P. 85 percent; 1 gram disodium orthophosphate, anhydrous. Make up to 1 liter with water. *For alkaline perspiration:* 10 grams sodium chloride; 4 grams ammonium carbonate, U.S.P.; 1 gram disodium orthophosphate, anhydrous. Make up to 1 liter with water. Samples of the dyed fabrics are placed against pieces of undyed cloth and left for a few days in each solution. The pieces of dyed fabric and undyed cloth are then squeezed and allowed to dry. Any staining denotes poor fastness to perspiration.

Fastness to Crocking

To test for fastness to crocking, rub dry and wet samples against a white cloth. If the color does not rub off on the white cloth, the color is fast to rubbing or crocking (Figure 9-8).

Fastness to Gas Fading

Flames from heating appliances cause nitrogen in the atmosphere to unite with oxygen, forming nitrogenous compounds that cause some acetate dyes to lose

Figure 9-7 The Fade-Ometer is used for testing colorfastness to sunlight. Samples of fabric are exposed to the rays of the machine for a period of hours or days. After removal, the samples are compared with an unexposed piece of fabric to determine the extent of loss of color. *(Courtesy Atlas Electric Devices Co.)*

Figure 9-8 This Crockmeter drags one colored fabric across another to determine if dye will rub off. *(Courtesy Atlas Electric Devices Co.)*

color if the fumes come in contact with the fabric. This is known as *gas fading* or *acid fading* in acetate; blue is especially susceptible. An antifume finish of an alkaline nature can be applied to a fabric to minimize gas fading by the use of an inhibitor in the dye. Fabrics can be tested to determine the permanency of their antifume finish by exposure for about twenty hours in a chamber containing the combustible fumes of a gas burner.

REVIEW QUESTIONS

1. Explain the difference between dyeing and printing.
2. Explain the importance of dyeing from the consumer's point of view.
3. What two factors enter into the selection of a dye?
4. What types of fabrics need to be colorfast (a) to washing, (b) to light, (c) to perspiration?
5. What are the essential differences between stock, yarn, and piece dyeing?
6. Explain the terms (a) crocking, (b) bleeding, (c) gas fading.
7. Discuss both the limitations and the advantages of direct dyes.
8. (a) What is a mordant? (b) Explain how it is used in dyeing.
9. Discuss the advantages and the limitations of acid dyes.
10. Why is salt often put into a dyebath?
11. What happens to sulfur-dyed fabrics if stored for a long time?
12. (a) What is vat dyeing? (b) When would it be used?
13. What is meant by an optical brightener, or colorless dye?
14. What characteristic is common to yarn dyeing and skein dyeing?
15. (a) What is solution dyeing? (b) What are its advantages?
16. Identify and briefly describe the several methods of yarn dyeing.
17. Why may warp yarns be dyed in the fiber stage or in the yarn stage instead of using the piece-dyeing method entirely?
18. What factors determine the durability of a dye?
19. What is the difference between union dyeing and cross-dyeing?
20. What kinds of dyes are used primarily (a) for the animal fibers, (b) for the vegetable fibers, (c) for man-made fibers?
21. Explain how to test colorfastness (a) to light, (b) to washing, (c) to crocking.
22. Identify and briefly describe the several methods of piece dyeing.

10

PRINTING AND FLOCKING

color, design, and decoration

The yarns produced in the spinning process create some form of decoration in the fabric. In the formation of the fabric, decoration is also obtained by the pattern of the construction. The checkerboard pattern of the plain weave, the variations of the basket weave, the diagonal of the twill weave, and the luster of the satin weave produce simple designs. This type of decoration becomes more elaborate as fabric construction advances to the use of the third dimension in the pile weave, to the open-mesh lacelike effect of the lappet weave, and to the intricate effects of the Jacquard weave, as well as to the various knits and other types of fabric formation.

When fabric passes through finishing operations, it is given lustrous effects that contribute further to its final appearance. Other finishing processes create the additional effects of soft napped surfaces and the crinkled designs seen in matelassé, seersucker, and similar crepes. Dyeing makes an important contribution to fabric decoration by the many beautiful colors it produces and the color harmonies obtained by combinations of the various dyeing methods. Fabric can be still further enhanced by printing color designs on the finished cloth.

DISTINGUISHING PRINTING FROM DYEING

To know whether a fabric has been dyed by immersion or whether the color has merely been printed on the cloth, examine the outline of the design. On the printed fabric, the outline or edges of the design are sharply defined on the right side. The entire design seldom penetrates to the back of the cloth.

On sheer fabrics, the design may show up favorably on the reverse side because dyestuffs will penetrate sheer construction. Such fabrics may intentionally simulate woven designs, which use yarn-dyed warp and filling. Examine some of the raveled yarns. If the design has been imprinted, the yarns will show areas on which the color is not equally distributed.

DYES USED FOR PRINTING

Most classes of dyes are adaptable to one or more of the various types of printing. The choice depends on the purpose for which the goods will be used, the fiber or fibers involved, and what the potential customer would be willing to pay. Good fastness properties in prints are available, and there is no reason why the consumer should settle for less than satisfactory fastness.

Of the various dye classes, the *vat*, *reactive*, and *naphthol* colors will generally produce the needed fastness properties for most purposes. Another class, called *pigment* colors, are not truly dyes but are of utmost importance in printing. These colors are fixed to the fiber by means of resins that are very resistant to laundering or dry cleaning. The pigments themselves are among the fastest known colors to all normal influences. For light to medium shades they are unbeatable; but for full or dark shades they are impractical because the colors are not really absorbed by the fiber and will crock, or rub off. This problem may be solved by improved resins, better pigments, or more effective anticrock agents.

For cotton printing, vat and reactive dyes are used. Pigments and some naphthols are also used. Very cheap prints can be made with basic colors mixed with tartar emetic and tannic acid, but today's domestic market has scarcely any room for such prints. Silk is usually printed with acid colors; wool, treated with chlorine to make it more receptive to color (and to prevent shrinking), is printed with acid or chrome dyes.

METHODS OF DECORATION WITH COLOR

One form of applying color decoration to a fabric after it has otherwise been finished is called *printing*. Fabric that is to be printed must be singed, bleached, and cleaned. The methods producing color designs are as follows:

Block printing
Roller printing
Duplex printing
Discharge, or extract, printing
Resist printing
Stencil printing
Screen printing (flat and rotary)
Transfer printing
Blotch printing
Warp printing
Photo printing
Batik dyeing
Tie dyeing
Airbrush painting
Polychromatic dyeing
TAK dyeing
Electrostatic printing
Differential printing
Composition or paste designing
Flocking

In most of these methods, the dye is imprinted on the fabric in paste form, and any desired pattern may be produced. The dyes are usually dissolved in a limited amount of water to which a thickening agent has been added to give the necessary viscosity to the print paste. Originally, corn starch was much favored for this purpose in cotton printing; today, gums or alginates derived from seaweed are preferred because they are easier to wash out and do not themselves absorb any color (which would be subsequently washed out in the final soaping and printing). Furthermore, the gums allow better penetration of color, which is important to good printing. Most pigment printing is done without thickeners, as such; the thickening is obtained by mixing together resins, solvents, and water to produce the necessary viscosity for printing.

Block Printing

Block printing is the hand method and the oldest method of printing designs on fabric. It is not commercially important because it is too slow—printed fabric cannot be produced inexpensively in large enough quantities by the hand-blocked method. Block printing has usually been done in countries where labor is less costly than in the United States. Today, fabric is block-printed only in comparatively short lengths of material. Block printing is found chiefly in decorative pieces for the home or in expensive linens for upholstery purposes.

To make hand-blocked prints, the design must first be carved on a wooden or metal block. The dyestuff is applied in paste form to the design on the face of the block. The block is pressed down firmly by hand on selected portions of the surface of the fabric, imprinting the carved design as many times as desired on a specific length of cloth. To obtain variation of color in the same design, as many additional blocks must be carved as there will be additional colors. The portions of the design that will appear in different colors must be separately imprinted by hand before each design is complete. The more colors used, the more valuable and expensive the hand-blocked print will be, because of the enhanced beauty of design as well as the labor involved in the hand printing.

Hand-blocked prints can be recognized by noting slight irregularities in the detail and in the repetition of the design and by comparing areas for slight variations in color. These irregularities are now imitated by machine printing, however. They give machine prints the characteristic appearance of expensive hand-blocked prints.

Roller Printing

Roller printing is the machine method of printing designs on cloth by engraved rollers. It turns out color-designed fabrics in vast quantities at the rate of thousands of yards an hour. This method of producing attractive designs is relatively inexpensive when compared with any hand method. It is a machine counterpart of block printing. In roller printing, engraved copper cylinders or rollers take the place of the hand-carved blocks. Just as there must be a separate block for each color in block printing, so must there be as many engraved rollers in machine printing as there are colors in the design to be imprinted. With each revolution of the roller, a repeat of the design is printed.

Originally, the design for each of the rollers was engraved by hand with an awl; then a skilled craftsman duplicated the artist's design onto copper

Figure 10-1 The high fidelity of a print pattern depends on the accuracy of the engraving and registration of the copper rollers. Separate rollers for each color in the fabric design are outlined by pantograph, then hand-etched, polished, and chrome-plated. *(Courtesy United Piece Dye Works)*

rollers (see Figure 10-1). Today, the engraving is frequently done by *pantograph* transference. Separate photographs on individually sensitized copper plates are taken for each color of the design. An artist then paints the appropriate color of the pattern on each plate. The engraver traces the outline of the design on the plate with one arm of a pantograph, which simultaneously cuts the design (with a diamond needle on its other arm) into the curved surface of a copper roller. Next, a chemical resistant is coated over the areas of the roller that will print the color, and the roller is treated with acid. The acid etches the unprotected areas; the protected raised areas are the design pattern to be used for color printing.

Another method of reproducing a design on a roller is by photoengraving. A film of a photograph pattern is placed over a sensitized roller. After exposure, the roller is etched. This technique reproduces the photograph's detail and shading.

Each roller is polished for uniform smoothness so that the dye will spread evenly on the raised areas. They are then locked into precise positions on the machine. The number of rollers used depends upon the number of colors in the design, and as many as sixteen rollers can be employed.

Each of the engraved rollers first comes in contact with a companion roller that has been submerged in the dye paste to be used for its part of the design. A sharp blade, called the *doctor blade*, scrapes the excess dye from the roller. As the fabric passes under the engraved rollers, the design is imprinted on it. A mordant is generally used in the dye paste to fix the color (Figure 10-2).

Duplex Printing

Duplex printing simulates a woven pattern by printing the fabric on both sides. The fabric may be passed through the roller printing machine in two separate operations or through a duplex printing machine in a single operation. Duplex printing produces an equally clear outline on both sides of the fabric. The design is applied so skillfully by careful registration of the printing cylinders that the result may be mistaken for a woven design. But the difference can be detected by raveling a yarn.

Figure 10-2   In roller printing, engraved copper rollers transfer print design to fabric. Note color pans and furnisher-rolls supplying color to the rollers. In the foreground are counterweights controlling doctor blades (hidden from view by copper rollers), which continuously removed excess color from the engraving. *(Courtesy United Piece Dye Works)*

Discharge Printing

In the discharge method of printing, fabric is often dyed in the piece and then printed with a chemical that will destroy the color in designed areas. Sometimes the base color is removed and another color printed in its place, but usually a white area is desirable to brighten the overall design. When properly done, discharge printing is thoroughly satisfactory; however, the discharged areas may literally fall out of the fabric if the goods are not thoroughly washed after printing (a rare situation today). The usual method of producing discharge prints is to print the design, such as polka dots, with a paste containing caustic soda and sodium hydrosulfite. A steaming follows and then there is a good washing to remove the by-products of the reaction.

Resist Printing

In resist printing, bleached goods are run through cylinders that print a pattern on the fabric in the form of a resist paste—a resinous substance that cannot be penetrated when the fabric is subsequently immersed in a dye. The dye will affect only the parts that are not covered by the resist paste. After the fabric has passed through a subsequent dyeing process, the resist paste is removed, leaving a pattern on a dark ground. In the discharge method, the fabric is first dyed and the color is then extracted by an imprinted chemical; in the resist method, a resist paste is first imprinted and the fabric is then dyed. The durability of the fabric is not affected by the resist method.

Stencil Printing

Stencil printing originated in Japan. Its high cost limits its use and importance in the United States. In stencil printing, the design must first be cut in cardboard, wood, or metal. The stencil may have a fine, delicate design, or there may be large spaces through which a great amount of color can be applied. A stencil design is usually limited to the application of only one color and is generally used for narrow widths of fabric (Figure 10-3).

Screen Printing

Originally, this technique was referred to as *silk-screen printing* because the screens were made of fine, strong silk threads. Today, they are also made of nylon, polyester, vinyon, and metal. Screen printing is done with the use of either flat or cylindrical screens.

Flat Screen Printing. The artist's design is copied onto a series of very fine, flat screens, one for each color to be printed.

Figure 10-3 The lacquer used in this stencil print curled and became brittle after the inferior plasticizer was leached out during dry cleaning. *(Courtesy CIBA Review)*

Each screen's design may be drawn by hand and a coating of lacquer or other impermeable substance applied to all parts of the screen that are not part of its design. More usually, today, the design is photographed and a negative is used for each sensitized screen to opaque, or block out, those areas not part of the screen's color design. Each screen is then fitted onto a wooden or metal frame.

The fabric to be printed is attached to a backing spread on a long table. A screen representing one color of the design is set by hand over the fabric in the first position by metal brackets on the sides of the table to hold it in place (Figure 10-4a). The printing paste, or dye, is poured on the screen and forced through its unblocked areas onto the fabric with a rubber-edged squeegee (Figure 10-4b). The frame is then raised and placed on the next section of the fabric, and the operation is repeated until the entire length of the cloth is printed with that one color. This process must be repeated for each color to be used in the design (Figure 10-4c and d).

Whereas the hand screen printing is time-consuming and limited to relatively short lengths of 60 yards of fabric, electronically controlled automatic machines screen-print hundreds of yards of cloth at rates of up to 450 yards per hour. By this method, the back of the fabric to be printed is coated with an adhesive, which causes it to adhere to a backing on a rubber conveyor belt that serves as the tabletop for the printing operation. A series of flat screens, one for each color, is set in frames with automatically operated squeegees and is placed above the belt. As the fabric advances, the screens are automatically lowered to the cloth and the appropriate color is properly applied with automatically regulated squeegees. The cloth is continuously fed into an oven to be dried. The modern flat screen printing machine is very expensive, but it will print up to twenty colors in one run. The versatility and production rate of this method, however, compensate for its initial high cost (Figure 10-5).

The chief advantages of screen printing are that the colors can be produced in brighter, cleaner shades than are possible with roller printing and the designs to be repeated can be much larger. The technique also lends itself to experimental and creative designs. Short runs of unique designs provide an exclusive pattern often sought by couturiers and interior decorators. The process is slower than machine roller

Figure 10-4   *(a)* In hand screen printing, the fabric to be printed is laid out on a table and a screen for each color of the design is precisely placed. *(b)* Two men work together passing the squeegee to each other as they force the dye through the screen. *(c)* Each screen of the series is progressively moved to succeeding sections of the fabric to repeat the same color of the design. *(d)* The hand screen-printed fabric is hung on a rack above the printing table to air-dry. *(Photos Courtesy CIBA-Geigy Corp. and Printex Corp.)*

printing; therefore, it is not quite as economical for large-sized yardages. However, the automatic flat screen printing machines now available have cut down the cost differences considerably. Printers so equipped are no longer looked upon as small-yardage operators. Most roller printing plants today have auxiliary flat screen printing machines to get out samples and intermediate-sized yardages that are not profitable on the roller machines.

In screen printing, it is possible to have designs consisting of squares, circles, and ovals because the areas not to receive the dye are painted out by the lacquer. If clearly defined geometric designs were attempted in cardboard or metal stencils, obviously, the cut area would fall away.

On a knitted fabric, such as jersey, flat rotary and screen printing and transfer printing are the only printing methods that can be used. Other methods smear the dye, as a knitted fabric stretches when it receives the impact of the rollers.

Rotary Screen Printing. A printing machine that utilizes seamless cylindrical screens made of metal foil was originally developed in Holland. This process is called *rotary screen printing.* The machine employs a rotary screen for each

Figure 10-5 *(a)* In automatic screen printing, electronic controls set each screen on the fabric, release a measured amount of the appropriate color, and run the squeegee on a rail passing over the screen. *(b)* The fabric is automatically moved along on a conveyor belt successively from one screen to the next to receive different parts of the colored design. *(c)* The fabric passes under the last of a series of screens before being moved into the dryer. As many as twenty screens may be employed to obtain as many colors. *(d)* The automatic machine screen-printed design is inspected as it leaves the dryer. *(Photos Courtesy CIBA-Geigy Corp. and Printex Corp.)*

Figure 10-6 Rotary screen printing combines the basic principles of the roller and the screen printing techniques. *(Courtesy Textile World)*

color, as in flat screen printing, and the design for each rotary screen is made in a manner similar to automatic flat screen printing. As the fabric to be printed is fed under uniform tension into the printer section of the machine, its back is usually coated with an adhesive, which causes it to adhere to a conveyor printing blanket. Some machines use other means of gripping the cloth firmly in place. The fabric passes under the rotating screens through which the printing paste is automatically pumped from pressure tanks. A squeegee in each rotary screen forces the paste through the screen onto the fabric as it moves along at rates of up to 100 yards per minute. The cloth then passes into a drying oven.

Rotary screen printing combines the advantages of roller and flat screen printing techniques (see Figure 10-6). Rotary metal screens are lightweight in contrast to the heavy copper rolls, and they cost less. They give color depth that is similar to or as good as that of flat screens. Prints of various types and intricate designs with shadings of up to twenty colors can be obtained with a high degree of accuracy and sharpness.

Rotaries operate continuously rather than starting and stopping as the flats do. Production output is considerably higher than it is on flat screen machines.

Transfer Printing

This process was originally developed in England. Transfer printing transfers thermoplastic ink designs from a roll of paper to the fabric. The technique is similar to that of transferring decals, but in this process, the patterns are transferred by the application of heat and pressure. Consequently, the technique is sometimes referred to as *heat-transfer printing*.

The process can print fabric at much higher rates of speed than screen printing. Production costs are reduced and pollution problems are eliminated since no aftertreatments, such as washing off, steaming, ageing, or drying, are necessary. Clarity of design and brightness of color are good. Fastness varies; for example, wetfastness of most of the dyes on polyester is good, and high lightfastness on such fabrics is obtainable. However, wetfastness on nylon is not so good. Fastness varies with shade, the fiber in the fabric, wear, and cleaning processes. Good results are possible, but correct dye selection for the pattern is imperative.

Transfer printing consists of printing disperse-dye patterns primarily by gravure, sometimes with flexographic processes, limited lithographic, or specially adapted rotary and flatbed screen printers onto specially prepared paper. The patterned paper is pressed by a calender onto the fabric while subjected to dry heat. The disperse dyes sublimate (vaporize) in pattern form directly onto the fabric.

Transfer printing is applicable to a wide range of synthetic materials, particularly polyester fabrics. The original process was called Thermocrome. Others now available are Transfaprint, Sublistatic, Holtset, and Decotherm. The trademarks refer either to the transfer machine or the transfer paper.

A special transfer printing technique has been developed for wool and cotton blends, which may also be applied to wool/nylon and some wool/modacrylic blends, as well as to all-nylon fabrics. The original process is Fastran, a trademark for the system. The goods are padded with an aqueous bath containing Fastran powder which contains sulfamic acid, a locust bean gum derivative that holds a moisture film over the material during transfer, and surfactant derivatives that facilitate high-level dye absorption. After the fabric or garment (placed on a plastic frame to hold its shape) is prewetted by the padding process with a 5 percent solution of the powder to about 2 to $2^1/_2$ times its original weight, the transfer-print paper is placed over it and is covered with a silicone-rubber sheet. This sandwich is then placed in a steam or dielectric heated press where the heat converts the water to steam, which is sealed in by the silicone-rubber sheet. The print vaporizes and migrates from the paper to the fabric. The amount of color transfer is extremely high—that is, 90 percent or better. The process is completed with a simple afterwash. The Fastran process may also be used for dye-discharging from previously colored fabric, fluorescent whitening, mothproofing, flameproofing, and embossing.

Among the advantages of transfer printing is the fact that it can be applied to both woven and knitted fabrics, including circular-knitted goods around the circumference, without slitting the material. Transfer printing can also be done on cut-and-sewn and fully fashioned garments. Transfer printing is so effective that it gives knitted goods the appearance of woven designs. The system can be installed in a knitter's plant and at a lower cost than flat bed and rotary screen equipment. A large inventory of dyes and chemicals is obviated. Yet, a wide range of patterns in a great many colors, including rich and deep shades, may be produced. There is also less waste and considerable savings on dyes and auxiliary agents.

Blotch Printing

Blotch prints may have a colored background as well as a colored design, and both may be printed at the same time. This method is used chiefly for cottons and linens. Any one of several methods of application, such as block, roller, or screen, may be used.

Warp Printing

Warp printing is roller printing applied to warp yarns before they are woven into fabric. Fine white or neutral-colored filling yarns are generally used for weaving so that the design on the warp will not be obscured. This method produces designs with soft, nebulous, but striking effects. Great care must be taken to keep the warp yarns in their proper position so the outline of the design will be preserved. Warp printing is used for expensive cretonnes and upholstery fabrics.

A variation of warp printing is *Vigoureux printing* or *melange*. Utilizing a variation of roller printing, horizontal or cross-striped designs are printed on the ropelike wool tops or slubbings. Subsequently, when the tops are spun into yarn, the stripes are attenuated and pulled apart so that they appear as scattered flecks of color in the woven cloth.

Photo Printing

In photo printing, the fabric is coated with a chemical that is sensitive to light. Any photograph may be printed on the fabric. The results are the same as when printing photographs on paper. All details can be reproduced if the photographer and technician are careful.

Batik Dyeing

The resist-dyeing process, whereby designs are made with wax on a fabric which is subsequently immersed in a dye to absorb the color on the unwaxed portions, is known as *batik dyeing*. It has been done in the Orient, notably India and to some extent in Japan, for many centuries. However, it is on the island of Java in Indonesia where the term "batik" originated and where high technical and artistic skill of batik print really developed. Originally limited to execution by noblewomen, the technique is now a flourishing industry, particularly as a cottage industry where natives do batik dyeing in their small houses.

There are two methods. The technically more difficult and more artistic designs are drawn by hand. The patterns are generally in geometric, floral, bird, or animal motifs, but the artist's imagination may introduce other fanciful designs. The motif is drawn on cotton cambric. Then melted wax mixed with a resin is traced on the areas not to be dyed with a *tjanting*, which is a small instrument made of a short, straight reed handle to which is attached a small, funnel-shaped copper cup with one or more spouts (see Figure 10-7a and b). When the tjanting is refilled by scooping the hot, liquid wax from a copper pan kept over a burner, the worker blows into the spout to eliminate any blockage and allow the wax to flow. The application of the wax must be done on both sides of the fabric. This hand method of making the design is a slow process, which may take as long as one month to produce $2\frac{1}{2}$ yards. When an artist makes a large, individual picture which may be used for such purposes as wall hangings, it may take six months to one year to complete.

The faster method of designing is done with a *tjap*, or stamp, of a pattern made of fine copper strips soldered together. The tjap is pressed onto a pad of cloth saturated with liquid wax. The wax picked up by the stamp is then applied to the cambric (Figure 10-7c and d). The design may be intricate, but it is repetitious and limited in artistic quality. However, about 25 to 40 yards of cloth can be printed in one day.

After each application of wax, the fabric is dipped into dye to obtain the particular color desired. Only that portion of the fabric that is not covered by the wax will absorb the dye, as the wax coating on the rest of the cloth serves as a resist. After the dye has been fixed and the material dried, the cloth is boiled and rinsed to remove the wax. Any traces of wax remaining on the fabric are then scraped off. This procedure is repeated

Figure 10-7 *(a)* The tjanting used for batik designs is held by the bamboo handle. The copper cup holds the wax and resin mixture, which passes through the narrow spout to trace the waxy substance forming the design on the fabric. *(b)* Using a tjanting, hand batik designs are slowly and carefully traced with melted wax which resists the dye when the fabric is subsequently put into a dyebath. *(c)* The tjap used for block batik dyeing is made of copper strips formed into intricate designs. *(d)* Using a tjap, a batik design is stamped repeatedly with melted wax which resists the dye when the fabric is subsequently dyed.

as many times as there are different colors to be obtained to complete the design composition.

The primary colors used are red, yellow, and blue, although some designs are black and white. Various light and dark shades of brown, green, violet, orange, and pink are also used. Sometimes, in the last application of color, the wax is permitted to crack, and the last dyestuff partially penetrates the other dyed portions, producing the multicolored design characteristic of batik.

The American method differs from the Oriental in that light colors are applied first, followed by the wax; the deeper shades are then built in. In the Oriental method, the dark shades are applied first, and the portions to be kept light are waxed.

There are three qualities of cambric that are used for batik-dyed fabrics. The best is *primisima*, or fine. The second, which is the most extensively used, is *prima*, or medium (moderately fine). The third is *mori biru*, or coarse.

Tie Dyeing

The results of tie dyeing are sometimes similar in appearance to batik, but the designs are made differently. The dye is resisted by knots that are tied in the cloth before it is immersed in the dyebath. The outside of the knotted portion is dyed, but the inside is not penetrated if the knot is firmly tied. Partial penetration occurs when the knot is not tight, causing gradations and irregularities of color that produce indistinct but attractive designs. The process is repeated as many times as desired by making new knots in other parts of the cloth and immersing the fabric in additional dyebaths. This gives a characteristic blurred or mottled effect, the result of the dyes running into each other. Like other hand methods, tie dyeing is expensive. Because the method creates interesting designs, the patterns are imitated in roller printing.

Airbrush (Spray) Painting

Designs may be hand-painted on fabric, or the dye may be applied with a mechanized airbrush, which blows or sprays color on the fabric. Airbrush painting is used when surface coloring is to be done quickly and economically; for example, designs on tablecloths. Direct, acid, or vat dyes dissolved in water, alcohol, or other organic solvent may be used.

Polychromatic Dyeing

As the term implies, polychromatic dyeing is a multicoloring process. The effect resembles printing but does not use printing machinery. The method, developed and patented by ICI Dyestuffs Div.,

Figure 10-8   As fabric is passed under the jets of this polychromatic dyeing machine, streams of dyes are ejected onto it producing multicolored patterns. *(Courtesy Harris Textile Machinery Co.)*

applies several dyes in one operation in a manner that produces such designs as random splashes of several colors, tiedye abstracts, and multicolored stripes. The application of the dyes is done by controlled direction of the flow of dye liquors onto continuously moving openwidth fabric. The streams of dyes are applied through jets set in bars above the width of the cloth (see Figure 10-8). The number of jets, their size, their placement, and fabric speed determine the pattern. The number of possible designs is enormous, and each can be reproduced again based upon the required factor combinations. The jets, which can be moved from side to side according to the pattern desired, direct the streams of dye over an inclined plane which directs the streams as they fall onto the fabric. The cloth then passes between heavy rollers where it is padded to force the dye through to the back of the material. The result is a

Figure 10-9 Random pattern achieved by polychromatic dyeing. *(Courtesy Textile World and Castle Creek Prints)*

predetermined multicolored pattern equally visible on both sides of the fabric, similar in appearance to duplex printing (Figure 10-9).

The double-sided design is applicable to drapery and other materials where both sides of the fabric are to be exposed. The combination of thorough penetration of the dye and variable multicolors is also useful for a wide range of thick fabrics for such use as blankets, towels, corduroy, and velvet. The materials may be woven, knitted, tufted, or flocked of such fibers as cotton, rayon, nylon, and polyester.

Polychromatic dyeing has several other advantages. The process is fast; it can make designs at speeds up to 30 yards per minute. It is versatile. It is economical because designs can be quickly

set and altered once the patterns have been catalogued. No expenses need be incurred to produce screens, rolls, or other printing equipment.

TAK Dyeing

"TAK" is an acronym for a machine invented jointly by a German rug manufacturer, Textil Ausrustungs Gesellschaft, and a machinery supplier, Edward Kuesters. Although it was originally made to produce random color patterns on carpets, it can also be used for a wide variety of fabrics, such as terry cloth, velvet, and various upholstery materials.

The TAK dyeing process is a continuous technique for randomly dropping or sprinkling dye liquor on a fabric to produce multicolored patterns. Streams of dye run from a trough under a doctor blade into individual channels. The doctor blade oscillates, breaking up the streams into drops and scattering them over a predetermined width. As the drops fall toward the continuously moving open-width fabric, they hit protruding fingers, or drop cutters, which move across the width of the cloth on a rotating chain (see Figure 10-10). Two or more rows of drop cutters may be used, depending upon the desired pattern and color combinations. The fabric is then padded to force the dye into it.

TAK dyeing can be done to gray goods or predyed material to achieve the pattern and desired background. The variety of patterns that can be obtained is infinite. Each pattern is dependent upon factors of the machine, the dyebath, and the fabric. For example, the machine may regulate the speed of the dye application, the speed of the fabric, the movement of the doctor blade, and the tilt of

Figure 10-10 Close-up of the TAK process. Controlled streams of dye liquor fall from grooves onto drop cutters, and the drops hit the fabric which travels underneath this application. *(Courtesy Textile World)*

the drop cutter; the dye may vary according to its viscosity and its wetting agent; the fabric may vary in construction and in absorbency. These factors can all be noted, catalogued, and programmed for automated reproduction. The process is not only versatile, but it can also be used in place of some more expensive printing techniques at a considerable cost saving.

Electrostatic Printing

A Swiss firm, Heberlein & Co., patented in England a process of mixing a finely powdered dye with a carrier, such as a natural or synthetic resin, that has high dielectric properties for electrostatic printing. The dye is spread on a screen bearing the design, and the fabric is passed into an electrostatic field under the screen, which is held about $^1/_2$ inch above the cloth. The dye-resin mixture is pulled by the electrostatic field through the pattern area onto the material. The dye is initially fixed by infrared heat. The fixation is subsequently reinforced by whatever process is most suitable for the kind of dye used.

Differential Printing

The Du Pont Co., Ltd., of England has developed a technique of printing tufted material made of yarns having different dyeing properties. This technique of differential printing is especially associated with screen printing of carpets tufted with differential dyeing yarns. Up to a ten-color effect is possible by judicious selection of the yarns, dyestuffs, and pattern. For example the design can consist of a solid-color background with superimposed motifs, which may have contrast-color areas of differentially dyed colors.

Composition or Paste Designing

The rollers used to imprint color by means of dyes, chemicals, or resist pastes can also apply lacquer or colored paste to fabric as small designs. Modern adhesives make such designs very resistant to normal laundering. Substances that can be baked into the fabric are also used for this decorative effect. When this is done, the designs become so much a part of the cloth that they may be considered permanent, seldom being destroyed by washing or dry cleaning (Figure 10-11).

Figure 10-11   Pasted designs, like the dots in this fabric, may disappear in laundering if an inferior adhesive is used. *(Courtesy U.S. Department of Agriculture)*

Flocking

The technique of adhering minute pieces of fiber, called *flock*, to form designs on fabric has been used to a limited extent for about 600 years. It has become more widely used in recent years because of modern methods. Using a suitable adhesive (instead of a dye), a design is roller-printed onto a fabric. Then, flock of cot-

Figure 10-12   Pattern flocking, using different-colored flock and controlling the deposition of each to certain areas, can be done on a substrate that is coated with a design of an adhesive. *(Courtesy Modern Textiles Magazine)*

ton, wool, viscose rayon, or nylon is applied to the fabric in a manner that causes it to adhere in an upright position and produce a pilelike, velvet-textured design. The flock is usually of colored fiber, thereby adding to the decorative appeal (Figure 10-12).

Cotton and wool waste fiber are often ground or random-cut into flock. However, since such production results in uneven and angular ends that do not affix as well as straight ends, precision-cut flock of rayon and other man-made fibers (such as nylon and acrylics) are preferred. The flock generally ranges in length from $2/25$ to $1/4$ inch.

Flocking may be accomplished by a *mechanical* method of beating the underside of the adhesive-coated fabric with rotating multisided beater bars as the flock is sifted onto the surface of the fabric. The fabric's vibrations, produced by the beater bars, cause the flock to flow over the surface of the fabric and stand erect those fibers that do not land flat on the adhesive. Continued vibration causes the erect fibers to penetrate deeper into the adhesive, and, as more fibers fall on the already erect fibers, they become similarly oriented and build up a pile effect (Figure 10-13). With this method (which has the advantage of being relatively inexpensive), the fibers become more deeply imbedded and, therefore, more permanently attached. However, since many fibers adhere at various angles, the flocking may not be as dense as desired.

Another technique utilizes an *electrostatic* principle. As the flock is sifted onto the fabric, it passes through an electrostatic field, or electrically charged air space. This directs and propels the fibers in the longitudinal direction of the

SCHEMATIC DIAGRAM OF MECHANICAL FLOCKING

FLOCK HOPPER

BRUSH AND SCREEN FOR SIFTING

ADHESIVE-COATED SUBSTRATE

TO OVEN FOR DRYING ADHESIVE

BEATER BARS

Figure 10-13 The beater bars' vibration of the fabric causes the flock to flow over the surface of the cloth, stand erect, and penetrate into the adhesive-coated fabric, producing an inexpensive pile design. *(Courtesy Modern Textiles Magazine)*

current toward the fabric, which causes them to stick to the adhesive in an erect position (Figure 10-14). This method can produce a denser flocking because the fibers uniformly adhere upright to the fabric. However, it is a more expensive technique, requiring more complicated apparatus and better-quality flock.

Depending upon the background fabric, or substrate, the depth of the pile, the flock used, and the pattern, flocked fabrics may be created for various purposes. Flocking is used for household goods such as curtains, draperies, carpeting, and wearing apparel.

The *Giroud process* is a different mechanical method (see Figure 10-15).

Figure 10-14   Closeup view of an electrostatic flocking unit showing nylon flock being propelled onto a woven jute substrate. *(Courtesy Modern Textiles Magazine)*

Figure 10-15 Schematic diagram of ground flocking process. Tow (bottom left) is fed into a channel of predetermined width where a knife slices uniform lengths of flock which are forced in vertical position along the fiber guide. Adhesive coating is applied to the fabric (top right) and the coated fabric meets the fiber which adheres to the cloth. The flocked fabric is subsequently returned and fed into a curing oven. (*Courtesy American Dyestuff Reporter*)

Sheaves of fiber, such as tow, are fed into a device which holds the fibers vertically and cuts them into predetermined, uniform lengths. The cutting operation is regularly repeated causing continuous horizontal pressure against the fibers. While remaining aligned in a vertical position, the flock is continually moved horizontally in a feeding guide toward a conveyer belt on which is a fabric substrate coated with an adhesive. As the flock comes in contact with the adhesive, it is implanted in it to form a very erect, compact, dense pile superior to that possible by other methods. The flock may be cut to any length and may be made of any type of fiber, including glass and metal.

Table 10-1

DECORATION OF FABRICS BY PRINTING AND DYEING		
TYPE OF DECORATION	HAND METHOD	MACHINE METHOD
Block printing	Design carved on blocks; dye applied to block; block pressed on fabric	Similar blocks pressed on fabric by machine; design tends to be more regular
Roller printing		Design etched on roller; companion roller transmits dye to etched roller, which transmits it to fabric
Duplex printing		Design printed back to back on both sides of fabric; gives effect of woven pattern
Discharge printing		Bleached goods first dyed; chemical bleach printed on fabric; color discharged
Resist printing		Resist paste put on fabric; fabric dyed; paste removed
Stencil printing	Design cut in stencil; color applied over stencil	

Table 10-1

DECORATION OF FABRICS BY PRINTING AND DYEING *(Continued)*		
TYPE OF DECORATION	**HAND METHOD**	**MACHINE METHOD**
Flat screen printing	Design sketched or photographed on sheer silk, nylon, polyester, vinyon, or metal screen; background of design opaqued; color applied to screen as stencil and forced through screen	Similar screens; up to twenty set in electronically controlled machine that regulates speed of operation, amount of dye forced through each screen, fabric movement
Rotary screen printing		Cylindrical seamless metal screen; dye paste forced through screen as it rotates on moving fabric
Transfer printing		Thermoplastic ink designs transferred by heat and pressure from paper to fabric
Blotch printing	Direct application by block, screen, etc.	Direct application by roller, screen, etc.
Warp printing		Engraved rollers print design only on warp yarns; fabric then woven, using white or neutral filling yarn
Vigoureaux or Melange		Warp printing of wool tops or slivers
Photo printing	Photographs printed on sensitized fabric	
Batik dyeing	Design put on fabric; wax deposited on background of design; fabric dyed; wax removed	
Tie dyeing	Fabric knotted or tied in parts with string; dipped into dye; fabric untied	
Airbrush (Spray) painting	Mechanized airbrush applies surface coating	
Polychromatic dyeing		Streams of several dyes applied to continuously moving fabric
TAK dyeing		Randomly sprinkled droplets of several dyes distributed on continuously moving fabric
Electrostatic printing		Dye attracted by electrostatic field through patterned screen onto fabric
Differential printing		Screen printing of differential dyeing yarns of tufted fabric
Composition or paste designing		Lacquer figures or colored paste glued or baked on surface of fabric
Flocking		Very short, usually colored fibers adhered to fabric in design effect, conforming to pattern of adhesive applied with roller

REVIEW QUESTIONS

1. How can spinning and weaving processes produce decoration (a) in fabrics, (b) in finishing processes?
2. What is meant by block printing?
3. Explain roller printing and duplex printing.
4. Differentiate between discharge and resist printing.
5. Why is the discharge-printed fabric the least desirable?
6. What is the difference between a blotch and a duplex print?
7. How could one determine whether a color design is printed or woven?
8. How do screen printing and stenciling differ?
9. Compare the methods of rotary screen printing and automatic flat screen printing.
10. What are the values of transfer printing?
11. Describe warp printing and its result.
12. How does Vigoureux printing differ from warp printing?
13. Compare and contrast the batik method and the resist method of decoration.
14. (a) How are composition or paste designs made? (b) Are composition and paste designs durable?
15. Describe tie dyeing, and explain why it is expensive.
16. (a) Describe the flocking techniques. (b) How effective and durable are they?
17. How can batik and tie dying imitated on a machine be detected?
18. What are the several methods of hand decoration with color?
19. Why are most fabrics machine-printed?
20. What are the characteristics of a well-printed fabric?
21. How is polychromatic dyeing different from spray painting?
22. What is TAK dyeing?
23. How does electrostatic printing differ from flock printing?
24. (a) Is differential printing really a printing technique or is it a dyeing technique? (b) Why?

11

COTTON

a natural cellulosic fiber

Cotton is a fiber that grows from the surface of seeds in the pods, or bolls, of a bushy mallow plant. It is composed basically of a substance called *cellulose*.

VEGEATABLE

HISTORY OF COTTON

Cotton has been cultivated for more than 5,000 years. Archeological finds indicate cotton was grown and used for textile purposes in the Indus Valley by 3000 B.C., in Mexico by 3500 B.C., in Peru by 2500 B.C., and in the southwestern United States by 500 B.C. Fragments of fiber and bolls dating from 5800 B.C. were found in Mexico, although there is a question as to whether cotton was used as a textile that early. Cotton was used extensively in the Medo-Persian Empire and may have been used in ancient Egypt as well. It was introduced into the Mediterranean countries by the Arabs and into other parts of Europe by the Crusaders. The use of cotton in England is mentioned in writings of the thirteenth century, although its use did not become general until the first half of the sixteenth century. In the United States, cotton was cultivated by the colonists in the early seventeenth century. The impetus of the industrial revolution, represented in the cotton industry by the invention of the carding machine and the spinning mule in England and by the invention of the cotton gin in the United States, resulted in vastly increased cotton production and manufacturing. Today cotton fields extend across the southern United States from Virginia to California.

Cotton fabrics have been so well known and so extensively used throughout the world for hundreds of years that the spinning of the cotton fiber into yarn, the wearing of cotton fabric, and many of the finishing processes used for cotton goods come first to mind and naturally serve as foremost examples in a study of fiber and fabric. Cotton has been of service to mankind for so long that its versatility is almost unlimited

265

and new uses are constantly being discovered. It can be depended on to serve many purposes. Not only is cotton a textile in its own right, but some of its by-products form the base for some of the man-made textile fibers.

KINDS AND TYPES OF COTTON

Different kinds and types of cotton are grown in various parts of the world. Some of their basic characteristics differ. Variations among cotton fibers also occur because of growth conditions including such factors as soil, climate, fertilizers, and pests. The quality of cotton fiber is based on its color (degree of whiteness), length (or staple), fineness, and strength. Usually, the longer fibers are finer and stronger.

The particular kind of cotton is often identified by the name of the country or geographical area where it is produced, and although a major portion of the world's cotton is Upland type, it is still known by the place of production whether Brazil, Zaire, Greece, Pakistan, Russia, Syria, Turkey, Uganda, or San Joaquin Valley. The quality is associated with the name. The following are the better known kinds and types of cotton used in the United States.

Upland Cotton

American Upland cotton constitutes over 99 percent of the United States cotton crop and is used for many fabrics either wholly or as a component of blends with man-made fibers. The particular kind of Upland cotton from which these fabrics are made is important because the quality and characteristics vary among the kinds.

Generally speaking, Upland cotton fibers are fairly white, strong, and dull, and range in staple length from $7/8$ to $1 1/4$ inches. The Upland cottons are usually categorized as short-, medium-, and long-staple. The short-staple cottons are less than 1 inch and are produced in Oklahoma and central and west Texas. Lankart, Lockett, Paymaster, Rilcot, and Western Stormproof are the principal cultivars. The medium-staple cottons are $1 1/32$ to $1 3/32$ inches in length and are produced in the Southeast, the Mississippi Valley, and the low valleys of Arizona and California. The principal cultivars are Coker, Deltapine, and Stoneville. The long-staple cottons are $1 1/8$ inches or longer and are grown in the high-altitude areas of the Southwest. Acala 1517 is the primary cultivar. The cotton grown in the San Joaquin Valley of California has a staple length from $1 3/32$ to $1 5/32$ inches. The fiber is stronger than the other Upland kinds.

American Pima

American Pima cotton is grown in the upper Rio Grande Valley of Texas, in New Mexico, Arizona, and southern California. The cultivars, Pima S-3 and Pima S-4, account for most of the acreage. The staple length is from $1 3/8$ to $1 1/2$ inches and the fiber is fine, strong, lustrous, silky, and creamy-brown-white in color. American Pima fiber is used primarily for sewing thread although a small amount is used in high-quality broadcloth and other fabrics where silky smoothness, softness, and luster are desired.

Egyptian

Egyptian cotton is imported into the United States in small quantities. Menoufi and Giza 68 are the cultivars used to produce most of the exported crop. The fibers are light brown, fine, strong, and $1^1/_4$ to $1^1/_2$ inches in length. They are used in the same applications as American Pima.

Giza 45 is exported in limited quantities. The fiber is light brown, fine, strong, and $1^3/_8$ to $1^5/_8$ inches in length. It is used in applications where fine yarns or strong yarns are required.

Asiatic

Asiatic cottons are produced in India, China, and the Near East. For the most part these are coarse fibers less than 1 inch in length. The major usage in the United States is in surgical supplies.

Sea Island

Sea Island was once the quality cotton. It derived its name from the sea islands off the coast of South Carolina and Georgia. Changing fiber demand plus pests have reduced the production of this long, fine fiber to the point where only a few hundred bales are grown in the West Indies.

FROM FIELD TO MILL

Cultivating Cotton

Cotton can be cultivated only in warm places, which is the reason for its cultivation in the southern part of the Unit-

ed States. Cotton requires about two hundred days of continuous warm weather with adequate moisture and sunlight; frost is harmful to the plant. The ground must be thoroughly plowed, and the soil pulverized. In the United States, usually in March or April, carefully selected cottonseeds are planted in rows. Approximately thirty-five days pass before the seeds develop. The plants require careful fertilization.

The cotton plants must be protected from being crowded out by weeds. A variety of techniques is employed depending upon such factors as topography, soil texture, frequency of cultivation, and necessity of irrigation. The plants are generally thinned out and weeded when they are from 5 to 7 inches tall. This may be done by hand or by mechanical rotary hoes. Flame cultivators, which throw out small flames from jets set low to the ground between the rows of young cotton plants, are sometimes used to burn the thin-stemmed weeds and grass and leave the stronger, woody cotton plants unharmed. Some farmers use geese as cultivators since the geese voraciously eat the young weeds and grass but do not bother the cotton plants. Chemicals specifically developed to kill certain weed and grass seeds are often spread or sprayed on the ground at the time the cotton is planted. Other chemicals are sprayed on weeds after they emerge, but care must be taken to avoid contact with the cotton plants as they could be damaged.

Buds appear a few weeks after the plant emerges. They begin to bloom as creamy white blossoms about three weeks later in June or July. These blossoms change to pink and then to reddish

Figure 11-1 This mechanical picker can pick cotton bolls from two rows at one time. *(Courtesy Deere & Co.)*

purple. Within three days their petals fall off, leaving the ripening seedpod. The fibers that grow from the surface of the seeds cause the pod to expand to about an inch in diameter and to an inch and a half in length to form the cotton boll. During this period, the plant is subject to attack by many insects (in particular, the boll weevil that lays its eggs inside the buds), which, when they are hatched, feed inside the maturing boll. To protect the plants, insecticides are sprayed by hand, tractors, or airplanes.

The cotton bolls grow to full size by August or September, a month and a half to two months after the blossoms first appeared. When fully grown, the cotton plant may be from 3 to 6 feet in height. Its wide green leaves conceal some of the bolls, which begin to burst with fleecy white cotton fiber. This indicates that the cotton bolls are ready for harvesting.

Harvesting

Not all cotton bolls open at the same time. Only those that burst, thus exposing the fiber, are ready for picking. Consequently, a hand-picked cotton field must be gone over several times. When mechanical pickers are used, the bolls are left on the plant until they are all mature. Although some leaves will have fallen off by then, the plants are defoliated by spraying them with a chemical, causing the remaining leaves to wither and fall. The full, ripe bolls are then picked by machine, one or two rows at a time (see Figure 11-1).

Ginning and Baling

When the raw cotton is harvested, it contains seeds, leaf fragments, dirt, and other material that must be removed before the fiber can be baled. Cottonseeds alone constitute approximately two-thirds of the weight of the raw cotton when first picked. The seeds are removed by the cotton gin. (The cotton gin was invented by Eli Whitney in 1794. Whitney's invention was not immediately accepted, and he suffered serious financial loss. It was subsequently promoted by others, and it became a major impetus in the growth of the cotton industry. The invention of the cotton gin also led to the dominance of the southern United States as a cotton producer.)

Essentially, the cotton gin has rows of revolving saw-toothed bands that pull the fiber away from the seeds as well as remove other extraneous material. The cottonseeds are one of the valued by-products. The cotton fiber is compressed into rectangular bales, which are covered with jute or polypropylene bagging and bound with iron bands. These bales weigh about 500 pounds each (see Figure 11-2).

Figure 11-2   *(a)* Shown in the drawing are the following basic principles of the cotton gin: (1) Seed cotton enters gin. (2) Roll throws seed cotton against bars. (3) Saw teeth take cotton up and against bars. (4) Bars near saws on both sides let lint pass through but hold back seed. (5) Seed falls into conveyor. (6) Lint on saw-tooth is struck by blast of air, and (7) blown into lint cotton conveyor pipe. *(Courtesy Bibb Manufacturing Co.)* *(b)* Cotton fiber, which has entered the cotton gin from a pneumatic conveyor, is here seen falling on covered gin saws after sand and coarse soil have been removed. The saws separate the seeds from the fiber; the fiber is removed from the sawtooth by a blast of air and is whisked toward the back. The seeds then fall into a conveyor at the bottom of the machine. *(Courtesy National Cotton Council of America)*

BY-PRODUCTS OF COTTON

The raw cotton passes through several cleaning processes before it is baled as well as after it is unbaled at the cotton mill. As a result, the grower obtains valuable by-products that amount approximately to one-sixth of the entire income derived from the cotton plant. Cotton is therefore important because of its contributions to other industries as well as to the textile industry.

Cotton Linters

Linters are the short, fuzzy hairlike fibers that remain on the seeds after they have been separated from the fiber in the cotton gin. The cotton linters are removed by a second ginning process. They are used in the manufacture of rayons and acetates, plastics, shatterproof glass, guncotton, photographic film, fast-drying lacquers, and for other purposes.

Hulls

The hulls, which are the outside portion of the cottonseeds, are obtained after the linters have been removed. The hulls are rich in nitrogen, an important plant food, and are used as fertilizer and also in the manufacture of paper, plastics, cattle feed, and as a base for explosives.

Inner Seeds

The meat of the seed inside the hull yields *cottonseed oil*, which is used in cooking oils and compounds and in the manufacture of soap. The residue of the inner seed becomes cattle feed.

PROCESSING, BLENDING, AND MIXING COTTON

As observed in Chapter 3, cotton fiber may be spun alone or blended with other fibers in making yarns. Cotton yarns are also combined or mixed with other yarns in making fabrics. These techniques contribute to fabrics such desirable cotton properties as softness, strength, absorbency, and affinity for color.

FINISHING COTTON FABRICS

The finishing processes given to cotton were reviewed in Chapter 8. They may be summarized as follows:

Ammoniating—for strength, abrasion resistance, luster, and affinity for dyes

Antibacterial finish—for hygienic protection

Beetling—for flattened effects

Calendering—for luster

Compressive shrinkage—for maximum preshrinking

Crepe effects—for wrinkle resistance and textured surface

Drip-dry—for no ironing

Embossing—for decoration

Flame retarding—for fire inhibition

Full bleaching—for clear whiteness

Glazing—for luster

Insulating—for warmth

Mercerizing—for strength, luster, and affinity for dyes

Moiréing—for variable luster and variable pattern

Napping—for softness, warmth, and increased absorbency

Permanent pressing—for easy care

Preshrinking—for serviceability

Schreinering—for luster

Singeing—for smoothness

Slack mercerizing—for stretch

Stain repelling—for easy care

Stiffening—for smoothness and body

Water repellency—for resistance to water and rain

Weighting—for bulk

Wrinkle resistance—for retention of appearance

The types of dyes used for cotton and their degree of fastness to light and to washing were explained in Chapter 9.

Simulating Linen

Cotton yarn can be spun to simulate the irregularities characteristic of linen fiber. The fabric is woven in the damask and other patterns usually associated with linen fabrics and is then sized, beetled, and calendered similarly to linen.

Simulating Wool

Cotton fibers can be treated with chemicals to give them the roughness characteristic of wool fibers. The fibers are spun into thick yarns to increase the similarity. The finished fabric is napped

or roughened to produce a woollike surface. Because Peruvian cotton fiber has crimp, an inherent similarity to wool fiber, it is sometimes mixed with American Upland cotton to simulate wool.

Simulating Silk

The highest quality of cotton fiber, when spun to a high yarn count and then mercerized, simulates silk. The use of the satin construction in weaving produces a silklike luster. The cotton fabric may be singed and calendered to smooth its surface and to increase the luster. Cotton fabrics are frequently schreinered to obtain an added lustrous effect.

EVALUATING COTTON FABRICS

Manufacturers now place labels on finished consumer's goods to give such information as the thread count, fiber content, expected shrinkage, permanency of crispness (if any), fastness of dye to strong light, washing, dry cleaning, and general instructions on the maintenance and care of the fabric. Such labels are designed to protect and help the consumer. If he understands them, he can estimate how long the fabric or garment that he is purchasing may be expected to give good wear. These labels also protect the manufacturer from the consumer's possible misunderstanding of the quality and durability of a fabric and from complaint if it is improperly handled when washed or dry-cleaned.

The information gained in previous chapters of this book concerning the essential qualities of the fibers and their spinning into yarn and construction into

Figure 11-3   Diagram of inner layer of an enlarged cotton fiber shows how fibrils crisscross and double back. This structure contributes greatly to the strength of cotton. *(Courtesy CIBA Review)*

fabric can now be applied to the purchase of consumers' goods.

Strength. Cotton fiber is relatively strong due to the intrinsic structure of layers of crisscrossed, minute, spiraled fibrils that compose the fiber cell (see Figure 11-3). Strength is also determined by the character of the cotton yarns, which should be of long staple and tightly twisted. Compact construction, represented by high thread count, helps a fabric keep its shape and give longer wear. A sample of the fabric may be tested for strength by holding it in both hands and pressing down firmly with the thumbs while pulling. If the cloth gives easily, it will not stand the strain of wear. Strength can be substantially improved by mercerizing.

Amount of Sizing. If a cotton fabric is oversized, rubbing or tearing a sample swatch will cause shedding of excess starch. Holding the fabric to the light will reveal defects in construction that may have been concealed by sizing. Washing a sample will remove excess sizing, showing sleazy construction. An absolute test for starch is made by dipping a sample in a very dilute iodine solution; a dark-blue color indicates starch.

Elasticity. Cotton fiber has very little natural elasticity. This characteristic can be altered to varying extents by hard-twisting fibers into creped yarns and by using fabric construction techniques such as knitting. Recently, the slack mercerization technique has been used to give cotton fabrics some stretch in the warp and/or filling, thereby reducing the binding characteristic of the cotton fabrics.

Resilience. The tendency of cotton fabrics to wrinkle easily may be offset by finishing processes that give a wrinkle-resistant quality.

Effect of Heat. Cotton will withstand moderate heat. If pressed with an iron that is too hot or if a hot iron is allowed to remain too long in one place on the fabric, it will scorch and ultimately burn. It is therefore best to either iron cotton material that has been dampened or use a steam iron.

Heat Conductivity. Cotton fabrics make excellent summer clothing because cotton is a good conductor of heat. Crisp, clean, fine cotton fabrics look cool as well as feel cool. Napped or pile-weave cotton fabric has a warmth-giving quality.

Absorbency.   Once the outer protective cuticle of the fiber is broken down by finishing processes, such as kiering and mercerizing, the fiber becomes very absorbent. Cotton fiber is composed primarily of cellulose, which is very absorbent. Its hollow center, or lumen, aids in conveying moisture. Such factors as the amount of twist in the yarn will also affect the absorbency, since a low-twisted yarn will be more absorbent than a high-twisted one. Fabric structure, such as a pile weave, will affect absorbency. Also, the compactness of the weave influences the absorbency because the looser the structure the more absorbent the fabric will be.

Cleanliness and Washability.   Although cotton attracts dirt particles because of its roughness, this disadvantage is offset by the washability of the fiber. Cotton fabrics are not injured even in strong, hot solutions of alkalies; therefore, they can stand laundering with strong soap. They withstand rough handling.

Drapability.   Cotton does not have the body and suppleness required for good drapability. However, this can be enhanced by sizing and finishing. The nature and compactness of the weave can also improve the drapability.

Reaction to Bleaches.   Cotton may be safely bleached with ordinary household bleaches. However, the bleach should be put into the rinse water after washing so that it is thoroughly mixed and diluted to avoid the oxidizing or yellowing that may be caused by overconcentration from sodium hypochlorite bleaches, such as Clorox and Rose-X. Labels on wash and wear fabrics should be observed since some of these finishes are chlorine retentive—they turn yellow when subjected to sodium hypochlorite bleaches. Bleaches containing sodium perborate, such as Snowy, are safe.

Shrinkage.   A great amount of shrinkage will occur if cotton fabric is loosely woven and stiffened with starch, which is usually lost in washing. Preshrinking finishing processes minimize shrinkage in cotton fabrics.

Effect of Light.   Cotton fiber oxidizes, turning yellow and losing strength from exposure to sunlight over a protracted period of time. Cotton fabrics should therefore be shaded from direct sunlight.

Resistance to Mildew.   Cotton fabrics, especially sized fabrics, mildew readily when permitted to remain in a damp condition. New processes, in many cases, offset this tendency to mildew.

Resistance to Moths.   Cotton is not digestible by moth larvae, so the fabric will not be attacked by moths. But in fabrics containing cotton and wool, the larvae may damage the cotton to get at the wool.

Reaction to Alkalies.   Cotton is not harmed by alkalies. In fact, a solution of sodium hydroxide is used to mercerize cotton, making it stronger, smoother, and more lustrous.

Reaction to Acids. Cotton is not damaged by such volatile organic acids as acetic acid (vinegar). However, it is tendered if such nonvolatile organic acids as oxalic and citric (found in orange, lemon, and grapefruit juices) are allowed to remain on it, particularly if heat is also applied. They should therefore be rinsed with cool water as soon as possible. Concentrated cold or diluted hot mineral acids, such as sulfuric acid, will destroy cotton.

Affinity for Dyes. Cotton has a good affinity for dyes. It is dyed best with vat dyes, which provide good colorfastness. Fastness of dye to washing can be tested by washing a sample in hot water. Fastness to light can be tested by exposing a sample to light for a week or more. Penetration or thoroughness of dye can be tested by raveling a yarn and examining its unexposed surfaces.

Resistance to Perspiration. Acid perspiration has a slightly deteriorating effect on cotton.

CONSTRUCTION OF SHEETS AND PILLOWCASES

As sheets and pillowcases are important items in the family budget, the labeling of them is explained here. The references are based upon nomenclature related to cotton construction but serve as a basis for cotton/polyester blended permanent press material as well. (It may be noted that sheets and pillowcases are also made to a limited extent of linen, silk, acetate, and nylon; the constructions vary from plain to satin.)

Thread Count

Sheets and pillowcases are labeled as belonging to one of seven types: backfilled, 112, 128, 140, 180 carded, 180 combed, and 200. The figures are obtained by adding the number of warp yarns per square inch and the number of filling yarns per square inch, which represent the thread count. The higher the count, the closer and more uniform the weave; the more compact the weave, the greater the resistance to wear.

Types including backfilled, 112, 128, and 140 are known as *muslin*, which is made from cotton yarns that have been carded but not combed. Of these types, 140 represents the best quality, giving greater durability, because such sheets and pillowcases are made from good-quality carded cotton yarns that are coarser and heavier and more compactly constructed than the first three types. Heavy muslin sheets and pillowcases are practical and economical because they are moderately priced and withstand wear longest, particularly when subjected to hard laundering.

Types including 180 carded, 180 combed, and 200 are known as *percale*. Percale is woven from fine-quality long-staple cotton yarns. In the case of 180 carded percale, the fabric is woven with 180 carded threads to the square inch. The 180 combed percale is woven with 180 combed threads to the square inch. Combed yarns are smoother, more lustrous, and stronger than yarns that are merely carded. The 180 combed percale is therefore superior and a little more expensive than the 180 carded percale. The 200 percale, woven with 200 combed threads to the square inch, is constructed of the finest cotton yarn and is considered the most luxurious of cotton sheets and pillowcases. The thread count is high in all percale fabrics because of the fineness of the yarns and their compact construction. Such yarns make lightweight cloths of fine texture, desirable for summer use. There is a gain in luxury but a slight sacrifice in durability because, all other conditions being equal, the heavier fabric gives the longer wear.

Sheets and pillowcases are generally labeled. But you can always examine them for quality. By holding the fabric up to the light, you can determine whether it is firmly, closely, and uniformly woven. It should look smooth. Lengthwise and crosswise threads should be of the same even thickness, rather than thick or thin in spots. There should be no weak places, knots, or slubs, and the yarns should run straight and unbroken (see Figure 11-4).

Selvage

Sheets and pillowcases should be made with a tape selvage into which extra threads are woven. The selvage should be firm and strong, clean, neat, and with no loose threads.

Weight

Many weights of sheets and pillowcases are available, varying from $3\frac{1}{4}$ to $5\frac{1}{4}$ ounces per yard. But good weight should be the result of compact construction, not of excessive sizing. Government regulations on sheets permit a certain amount of sizing depending on the grade of the sheet. In the lowest grade of sheet, an excessive amount of sizing may be used to give the material greater body. Since this washes out, leaving the sheet thin and sleazy, it is advisable for the consumer to test sheets for sizing by rubbing parts of the sheet together over a dark surface. If much of a white powdery substance comes out, the sheet is "loaded" or sized. A label reading "no weighting" on a sheet indicates there is no overdose of sizing.

Length and Width

Sheets should always be long enough and wide enough to tuck underneath a mattress—at least 6 inches on all sides. The better grades of sheets are torn to size to make certain that the length is absolutely even; therefore, the size is given as a torn size, which means before hemming. After hemming, sheets are shorter; top hems are usually 3 inches wide on muslin, 4 inches wide on percale sheets; bottom hems are 1 inch wide on both types. After washing, there is another decrease in length of approximately 5 inches, or 5 percent, due to shrinkage. Sheets for standard-length beds should be 108 inches long. As about 10 inches must be deducted from the stated torn size for hems and shrinkage allowance, 98 inches remain for use. The average mattress is 74 inches long and 6 inches thick. Thus, 6 inches will be left for tucking under when a sheet is used to cover the mattress directly, and when used as an upper sheet, there will be a sufficiently wide turnover to protect blankets. Larger queen-size beds require sheets from 113 to 120 inches long; sheets for king-size beds should be at least 122 inches long. When the sheets are made of cotton/polyester permanent press

GRADE		WEAVE OR THREAD COUNT	POINTS TO CONSIDER IN BUYING	PRICE
	Back-filled muslin	Woven with less than 112 threads to each square inch	Loosely woven; excess starch washes out, leaves sheets sleazy	Lowest
	Light-weight muslin	Woven with not less than 112 threads to each square inch	Wears well considering low price. For limited household service	Low
	Medium-weight muslin	Woven with not less than 128 threads to each square inch	Strong; gives satisfactory wear. Widely used for everday household service	Medium
	Heavy-weight muslin	Woven with not less than 140 threads to each square inch	Sturdy; longest wearing muslin. Used where durability is prime consideration, as in hospitals, many hotels, etc.	Highest price muslin
	Percale (carded)	Woven with carded yarns, not less than 180 threads to each square inch	Lightweight; durable. Smooth, pleasant to sleep on, easy and economical to launder	Medium
	Percale (combed)	Woven with all combed yarns, not less than 180 threads to each square inch	Lightweight; extremely strong and durable. Soft and unusually smooth; easy and economical to launder	Medium
	Finest quality percale	Not less than 200 threads to each square inch	The finest, most luxurious sheets available. Light, fine, soft texture, beautiful appearance. Made of finest all-combed yarns	Highest price percale

Figure 11-4   Types of muslin and percale sheets. *(Courtesy Cannon Mills Co.)*

fabric, however, they will be shrink-resistant and therefore need not be as long as when made entirely of cotton. For example, cotton/polyester sheets for standard-length beds need be no more than 104 inches long.

Careful consideration should also be given to the width of sheets. For a double bed, a sheet should be 81 to 90 inches wide. Extra-wide double and queen-size beds require sheets 90 inches wide; a king-size bed requires a sheet 108 inches wide. A three-quarter bed requires a sheet 72 inches wide, and a single bed, a width of 63 to 72 inches.

There are also fitted, or contour, sheets, the corners of which conform to the shape and size of the mattress. These sheets, as a rule, are preshrunk. Contour sheets are sized according to the mattress of the type of bed as listed:

Cot
Youth
Three-quarter
Daybed
XL Twin
XL Full
Queen
King
Super
XL Super

The sizes of pillowcases vary and purchase should be related to the size of the pillow to be covered (see Table 11-1). In general, a pillowcase should be about 10 inches longer than the pillow and about 2 inches greater in circumference. The hems are usually 3 inches wide.

CONSTRUCTION OF TERRY TOWELS

The primary function of a terry towel is to absorb moisture from wet skin. It must, however, be strong enough to withstand the strain of the rubbing and pulling, twisting and tugging of the user and of constant laundering. A terry towel, therefore, should be constructed of an uncut pile with a sound underweave (see Figures 11-5 and 11-6). One cannot purchase towels merely by a brand name because the name identifies only the manufacturer, not a particular quality of terry towels. A company may manufacture many different grades and qualities of terry towels under the same brand name.

Weave

The underweave, which supplies the strength of the towel, should be firm, close, tight, and preferably of a twill weave. It is difficult to examine the weave because the loops hide it. It can be more readily seen in the plain portion or near the hem or selvage of the towel. To examine the weave better, the towel should be held up to the light. If light shows through in tiny and regular pinpoints, the weave is uniform and good; if the light shows loose and open spots, then the weave is poor.

The loops of the pile absorb the moisture, and they should be closely packed. In a well-constructed towel, the moisture absorbed remains in the surface pile and does not reach the underweave. A better-quality towel, therefore, will absorb more moisture and dry faster after use. Another consideration is that the longer the pile, the greater the absorbency of the towel. Also,

Table 11-1

TYPICAL PILLOWCASE SIZES	
PILLOW	PILLOWCASE
20 × 26″	42 × 36″
20 × 28″	42 × 38½″
22 × 28″	45 × 36″
22 × 30″	45 × 40½″

Figure 11-5 The magnified views show (a) single-crop and (b) double-crop construction in terry cloth. (Courtesy Dundee Mills, Inc.) (c) The enlarged view shows how the loops, or uncut pile, in terry cloth are formed. (d) The enlarged cross section shows how terry loops are formed on both sides at the same time. (Courtesy Cannon Mills Co.)

Figure 11-6 (a) The loops do the drying, and (b) the ground weave does the wearing. (Courtesy Cannon Mills Co.)

Figure 11-7 Three types of selvages: *(a)* fast, *(b)* overedged, and *(c)* hemmed. *(Courtesy Cannon Mills Co.)*

loosely twisted loops are more absorbent than tightly twisted ones. On this point, however, personal choice must be a factor, since some people prefer soft towels with loosely twisted loops or cut-pile for the soft velour effect, some prefer medium-soft towels, and others prefer a rough, hard towel with tightly twisted loops. In a well-constructed towel, good absorbency may be expected, since the close weave will result in a close, thick pile.

Hem and Selvage

The hems of the towel should be sewn with small close stitches and finished with the edges either back-stitched at the corners or turned and continued across the width of the hem. There are three types of satisfactory selvages, if properly made. One is the fast selvage, which is the ordinary type of selvage found on any fabric. It should be closely woven. The second is an overedged selvage, and the third the hemmed selvage (see Figure 11-7).

Length and Width

Terry towels are divided by size into five groups: guest, small, bath, extra large, and beach. The guest towels are 11 × 18 inches. The small size, used for hands and face, are from 16 × 26 to 18 × 36 inches. The bath size are from 20 × 40 to 22 × 44 inches. The extra-large bath towel is 24 × 46 to 25 × 48 inches. The beach size is 35 × 70 to 36 × 72 inches.

REVIEW QUESTIONS

1. (a) What are the by-products of the cotton plant? (b) For what are they used?
2. How would you judge cotton fabrics?
3. Name the more important varieties of cotton grown in the United States, according to their quality.
4. What climate is necessary for the growth of cotton?
5. Discuss the advantages of cotton fabrics.
6. How can cotton be made to simulate (a) linen, (b) wool, (c) silk?
7. What is the difference between muslin and percale?
8. (a) How are sheets labeled? (b) What is the basis for labeling?

9. (a) How may the strength of a fabric be determined? (b) How may the amount of sizing be determined?
10. (a) Why are long fibers separated from short fibers? (b) How may the consumer identify finished goods made from long staple?
11. Name some of the finishing processes used for cotton fabrics.
12. (a) What is ginning? (b) What are linters? (c) What are hulls?
13. Why is the more expensive method of vat dyeing used for such an inexpensive fiber as cotton?
14. (a) What determines the strength of a terry towel? (b) How can the consumer determine whether a towel is strong?
15. (a) What determines the absorbency of a terry towel? (b) How can the consumer determine whether a towel will be absorbent?
16. What care should be taken when laundering cotton fabrics?
17. What characteristics does cotton contribute to blends or mixtures in yarns and fabrics?

SUGGESTED ACTIVITY

Obtain three samples of fabrics used in cotton clothing. Attach to each a record showing the name of the fabric, kinds of yarns, weave, thread count, and finish. State the uses and relative durability of each sample.

12

LINEN

a natural cellulosic fiber

Linen yarn is made from fibers removed from the stem of the slender flax plant. These fibers, held together under the stem's bark principally by a gummy substance (*pectin*), form the body of the flax plant. The flax fiber is composed basically of the woody substance, *cellulose*.

HISTORY OF LINEN

Belgium/Ireland

The fiber obtained from the stem of the flax plant was probably the first textile fiber to be used. Historical records show that linen cloth was produced and used far back in antiquity, the earliest record being the use of flax for fish nets by the Neolithic lake dwellers of the Stone Age some ten thousand years ago. The Bible contains references to the use of linen. The bodies of early Egyptian kings and nobles were swathed in yards of delicate linen, indicating that the art of spinning and weaving had reached a high state of perfection in that country six thousand years ago. Such linen burial wrappings have been found to be in good condition, proving the amazing durability of the flax fiber.

Linen has always been considered the fabric of luxury. In some ancient countries, linen was used only for ceremonial purposes, as the symbol of purity. The descriptive phrase "pure linen" is customarily used to describe all-linen fabrics. Linen always looks cool, crisp, and clean, and gives an attractive and immaculate appearance to the persons and objects it adorns.

Fine-quality linens still retain the reputation of luxuriousness and expensiveness. The flax plant must be grown in countries where there is plenty of cheap labor as well as natural facilities for extracting the fiber. Even the manufacture of the fiber into fabrics requires unusual care throughout each process to retain the strength and beauty of the fiber.

The seed of the flax plant is valuable as the source of *linseed oil*, which is used in the manufacture of paints, varnishes,

Tow

linoleum, oilcloth, patent leather, and oiled silk. To obtain the seed, flax must be allowed to overripen. As overripening destroys the value of flax as a textile fiber, the method of raising the plant is influenced by the purpose for which it is required.

FLAX-PRODUCING COUNTRIES

The countries that produce flax of various grades are Australia, Austria, Belgium, Czechoslovakia, France, Germany, Ireland, The Netherlands, New Zealand, Poland, Scotland, and the U.S.S.R. Flax is grown in Canada and in the United States (Michigan, Minnesota, and Oregon), but chiefly for its seed.

QUALITIES AND GRADES OF FLAX

Courtrai flax, which comes from the Lys district in Belgium, produces the finest and strongest yarns. The water of the Lys River in Belgium and of the Scheldt River in The Netherlands is free from minerals and has proved especially desirable for decomposing the woody tissues of the plant, a necessary step in treating the flax fiber.

Belgium has a reputation for producing the best quality of linen, but Ireland is noted for the best workmanship. Irish linen is also prized for its fine white color and strength. The flax is spun while it is wet, and the cloth is grass-bleached, two processes reserved for good-quality linen.

Scotch linen is lighter in color than Irish linen. It is used extensively in making heavy-grade fabrics, such as twine and canvases for tarpaulins.

French linen ranks high. It is characterized by fine designs and the use of round yarns, as the cloth is not put through the beetling process.

Russian flax is used for medium and coarse yarns, which are dark gray in color. Russian linen sometimes cracks because the fiber is not as carefully processed as in the countries that have a reputation for fine-linen production.

German linen is generally of medium grade. Austria, Czechoslovakia, and Poland also produce medium-quality flax.

FROM FIELD TO MILL

Cultivating

The flax plant requires deep, rich, well-plowed soil and a cool, damp climate. Prematurely warm weather affects the growth and the quality of the fiber. Level land with a plentiful supply of soft, fresh water is essential. As the soil in which flax is grown must be enriched for six years before it will yield a good harvest, only one crop in seven years can be raised on a specified portion of land. The crops, therefore, must be carefully rotated. Shorter periods of rotation have been tried with success.

The flaxseeds are sown by hand in April or May. When the plants are a few inches high, the weeds must be pulled by hand with extreme care to avoid injury to the delicate sprouts. In three months, the plants become straight, slender stalks from 2 to 4 feet in height, with tapering leaves and small blue or white flowers. The plant with the blue flower yields the finer fiber. The white-flowered plant produces a coarse but strong fiber.

Figure 12-1   Flax is pulled from the ground at harvest time but not cut. *(Courtesy Irish Linen Guild)*

Harvesting

By the end of August, the flax turns a brownish color, which indicates that the plant is about to mature; it is ready for harvesting. There must be no delay at this stage; otherwise, the fiber will lose its prized luster and soft texture. The plants are often pulled out of the ground by hand; however, there is a machine which can efficiently pull the flax. If the stalk is cut, the sap is lost; this loss affects the quality of the fiber. The stalk must be kept intact, and the tapered ends of the fiber must be preserved so that a smooth yarn may be spun. The stalks are tied in bundles, called *beets*, in preparation for extraction of the fiber (Figure 12-1).

Preparation of the Fiber

The seeds and the leaves are removed from the stems of the flax plant by passing the stalks through coarse combs. This process is called *rippling*. The bundles of plants are then steeped in water. The plants are weighted down with heavy stones to insure complete immersion. This allows the tissue or woody bark surrounding the hairlike flax fiber to decompose, thus loosening the gum that binds the fiber to the stem. This decomposing or fermentation is called *retting*.

Dew Retting.   Dew retting is the method used in the U.S.S.R. The flax straw is spread on the grass and is exposed to the atmosphere for three to four weeks. This method produces strong flax, dark gray in color.

Pool, or Dam, Retting.   This method is used in Ireland. It requires less time than dew retting, from ten to fifteen days. As stagnant pools of water are used, this method sometimes causes over-retting, which is responsible for brittle and weak flax fibers. Pool retting darkens the flax, giving it a bluish gray color (Figure 12-2).

Stream Retting.   This method produces the best quality of flax fiber, as the process of fermentation can be retarded and easily controlled. Bundles of flax straw are weighted down in streams of cool, soft running water for five to fifteen days. This method, which produces strong, superior linen of a pale yellow color, is used extensively in the River Lys in Belgium.

Figure 12-2 Bundles of flax stacked in a retting dam. *(Courtesy Irish Linen Guild)*

Chemical Retting. Chemical retting can shorten the retting process, but chemicals will affect the strength and color of the flax fiber. Soda ash, oxalic soda, and caustic soda in warm water, or boiling in a dilute sulfuric acid solution are the chemical methods used.

Vat, or Mechanical, Retting. This method shortens the retting process and is used primarily in France, Northern Ireland, and the United States. The flax is immersed in wooden vats of warm water at temperatures ranging from 75 to 90 degrees Fahrenheit, which hastens the decomposition of the woody bark. The flax is removed from the vats and passed between rollers to crush the decomposed bark as clean water flushes away the pectin, or gum, and other im-

purities. Linen produced by this method is more susceptible to mildew.

Retting only loosens the woody bark. If flax is not retted enough, the removal of the stalk without injury to the delicate fiber is difficult. If flax is over-retted, the fiber is weakened. The retting operation, as well as all other processes for producing linen fabric, therefore requires great care.

MANUFACTURING PROCESSES

Breaking

The stalk becomes partially separated from the fiber when the wet plants are laid in the fields to dry (Figure 12-3). When the decomposed woody tissue is

Figure 12-3   After retting, flax is shaken out by hand and spread in the fields to dry. This can be done by machine as well as by hand. *(Courtesy Irish Linen Guild)*

dry, it is crushed by being passed through fluted iron rollers. This *breaking* operation reduces the stalk to small pieces of bark called *shives*.

Scutching

The scutching machine removes the broken shives by means of rotating wooden paddles, thus finally releasing the flax fiber from the stalk. This operation can be done by hand as well as by machinery.

Hackling

The simple combing process known as hackling straightens the flax fibers, sep-arates the short from the long staple, and leaves the longer fibers in parallel formation (see Figure 12-4). For very fine linen, hackling is usually done by hand and is repeated, a finer comb being used with each hackling treatment. Coarse linen is hackled by machine. (See Figure 12-5.)

Spinning

The short-staple flax fibers, called *tow*, are used for the spinning of irregular linen yarns. Tow is put through a card-ing operation, similar to the carding of cotton staple, which straightens the fibers and forms them into a sliver ready

Figure 12-4   After scutching, the fibers for very fine linen are sometimes hackled by hand by drawing them over successively finer sets of steel combs to remove pieces of straw and disentangle the fibers. *(Courtesy Irish Linen Guild)*

Figure 12-5 The hackling machine is used to produce coarser linens. The hanks of flax suspended at the top of this machine are being hackled by the horizontal rows of combs that pass down behind them. *(Courtesy Irish Linen Guild)*

for spinning into yarn. The long-staple fibers are used for fine linens. These are called *line*, sometimes *dressed flax*. Line fibers are from 12 to 20 inches in length. They are put through machines, called *spreaders*, which combine fibers of the same length, laying them parallel so that the ends overlap. The sliver thus formed passes through sets of rollers, making a rove for the final spinning process, which inserts the necessary twist.

Although flax is one of the strongest fibers, it is inelastic and requires a carefully controlled, warm, moist atmosphere for both methods of spinning.

Dry Spinning.   Dry spinning does not use moisture. It produces rough, uneven yarns, which are not especially strong. These yarns are used for making coarse, heavy, and inexpensive linen fabrics.

Wet Spinning. This method requires a temperature of 120 degrees Fahrenheit, which is conducive to the production of soft, fine, even yarns. By passing the roving through hot water, the gummy substance on the fiber is dissolved, permitting drawing out the roving into a fine yarn of high yarn count.

Linen Yarn Count

The standard measure of flax yarn is the *cut.* If 1 pound of flax fiber is drawn out to make 300 yards, the yarn is known as No. 1s. When drawn out to make twice 300 yards, it is labeled No. 2s. The higher the yarn count, the finer the yarn. Exceptionally fine linen yarns for fine laces have been spun as high as 600s.

CONSTRUCTION OF LINEN FABRICS

The inelasticity of the flax fiber presents a problem in the weaving process because the fiber breaks easily under strain. A dressing, applied to the warp yarns by passing them over rotating brushes, helps linen yarns to withstand the strain of being lifted by the heddles during weaving. A very moist atmosphere is also required.

General Applications

Linen fabrics usually have a balanced or squared construction, with the exception of double damask and certain sheer linens. The thread count, therefore, is always expressed as one number.

With the exception of some toweling, linen is seldom made in the pile weave.

The pile weave increases absorbency, and this quality is already possessed to a large degree by any linen fabric. The twill weave is seldom used, as the fiber possesses natural strength; for the same reason, ply yarns are not necessary. The plain, satin, and Jacquard weaves are predominant. The twill weave, however, is used for linen drills in the South American market.

Damask Table Linens

Fine table linens are always woven with the Jacquard construction; there are two kinds of construction, depending on the weave. The designs in damask result from the manner in which the warp yarns pass over the filling yarns. The background is always the same on both sides.

A five-shaft satin construction on the Jacquard loom is used for *single damask linen.* Most single damasks have the same number of warp and filling yarns, and the thread count ranges from 100 to 200 to the square inch. Some better single damasks have more filling than warp yarns, being overwefted by about 10 to 15 percent more filling than warp. But the cheaper qualities are usually underwefted—that is, some skimping is done with respect to the equalization of filling and warp.

The weave used for *double damask linen* is an eight-shaft satin construction on the Jacquard loom. There are twice as many filling yarns as warp yarns, which gives greater distinctness to the pattern. The pattern is further enhanced by the increased luster resulting from the longer floats. The thread count ranges from 165 to 400 to the inch.

Figure 12-6   The construction and appearance of *(a)* single damask may be compared with *(b)* double damask. Double damask is superior to single damask only if good yarns and quality construction are used.

Originally, double damask linen was considered superior to single damask. Today, the weave alone does not produce a superior product, because inferior yarns as well as high-quality yarns are used in all weaves. Double damask may range in quality from mediocre to excellent, and is superior to single damask only if good yarns and quality construction with higher thread count are used (see Figure 12-6).

If single and double damasks having thread counts approximately the same are compared, the single damask is preferable because shorter floats give greater serviceability. The threads hold more firmly. A double damask with a thread count less than 180 threads is not advisable for home use.

FINISHING PROCESSES

Linen is generally scoured before it is given a finish, and the finish used depends upon the intended purpose and use of the fabric. The most common treatment given to linen is bleaching.

Bleaching

Linen is usually bleached in the piece except when it is to be used for such purposes as yarn-dyed fabrics and dress linen. The two methods used are *grass bleaching* and *chemical bleaching*.

Grass bleaching produces the finest results. It is accomplished by spreading the linen out in the fields so that it is gradually bleached in the sun. This process is time-consuming but less injurious to the linen; it is therefore considered more desirable (Figure 12-7*a*).

Although chemical bleaching is the method chiefly used, it may adversely affect the durability of the finished fabric owing to the weakening effects of the chemicals. The process requires boiling the linen in a lime solution for eight to ten hours to remove such impurities as

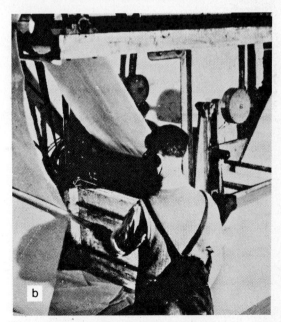

Figure 12-7   (*a*) Fine Irish linens are laid "on the green" for sun bleaching, which produces the best results. This process is seldom used today. (*b*) Today chemical bleaching is chiefly used, though not for the finest linens. (*Courtesy Irish Linen Guild and British Information Service*)

wax, then rinsing it in water, bleaching it with hydrochloric acid, washing the fabric again, and then treating it with caustic soda to neutralize any acid that remains (Figure 12-7b).

Bleaching produces four grades in the finished product: fully bleached, three-quarters bleached, half or silver bleached, and quarter bleached. Unbleached linen makes a fifth grade. A fully bleached linen fabric is less enduring than any other grade. Unbleached linen is the strongest because the natural strength of the fiber has not been weakened by the bleach. It is sometimes called gray linen or brown linen.

union linen
Linen.

Other Processes

The natural characteristics of linen are enhanced by the following finishing processes, which are discussed in detail in Chapter 8.

Beetling—for flexibility and uniform thickness

Calendering—for luster and smoothness

Mercerizing—for luster

Sizing—for added body

Wrinkle resisting—for resilience and easier care

Linen is never napped. The fiber does not lend itself to this process, nor would napping be desirable for long-staple yarns of hard surface. Where some crease resistance is obtained by reducing the yarn to short staple, the strength of the linen, which is its chief attribute, is sacrificed. Thus, any fuzz-iness in a linen fabric indicates the use of short staple or the presence of another fiber.

DYEING LINEN

Linen is seldom yarn-dyed. The surface of the natural flax fiber is hard and nonporous and is, therefore, impenetrable to dyes. The cells of the fiber are held together with tissue that can be broken down only in a severe bleaching process. Highly colored linens, therefore, will not give lasting service because they must have been fully bleached to absorb the dye. The colors are therefore usually pastel or dark but dull shades.

EVALUATING LINEN FABRICS

The term "linen" has long been used to refer to such household necessities as tablecloths, napkins, towels, pillowcases, sheets, and decorative coverings. Every consumer knows that these articles are not necessarily made of pure linen. They may be made of cotton, spun rayon, polyester, or even of linen mixed with such fibers. It is, however, always an ideal to possess pure linens, because they satisfy a desire for the beautiful and the luxurious and may remain in families as heirlooms. When linens are chosen wisely, their additional cost is well worthwhile. There is no doubt that linen is still the best fabric for table covering because of its durability as well as its exceptional beauty when thus displayed.

There are several well-known trademarks that are recognized as representing fine-quality linen. Moygashel, produced by Stevenson & Sons, Ltd., enjoys a reputation for excellent quality. Meadow Bleach and Yorkflax, produced by York Street Flax Spinning Co., Inc., and McBratney linens, of Robert McBratney & Co., Inc., are also fine-quality linens. The Irish Linen Guild has promoted its quality products under the Irish Linen label.

Even when a fabric is labeled "pure linen," it is necessary to know whether the yarns are line or tow. Fine linen fabrics, such as high-grade table damask and dress linens, are usually made of line, the long uniform staple. Line may be distinguished from tow by untwisting and examining the length of the fibers. The popular peasant linen is made of tow, but it is constructed with a very fine weave.

Pure linen is free from lint; therefore, the presence of lint indicates adulteration with cotton, or possibly oversizing. Cotton yarns are frequently mixed with linen to produce inexpensive fabrics. The name Union Linen is given to a fabric of which half or more is cotton. Linene is a name for an all-cotton fabric that simulates linen.

Strength. Linen is especially durable being two to three times as strong as cotton. Among the natural fibers, it is second in strength to silk. In linen, weight may be considered a criterion of durability. Damask weighs from 4 to 7 ounces to the square yard.

Amount of Sizing. As excessive sizing indicates the probability of poor construction or imperfections in weave, a sample may be tested for oversizing by holding it to the light, by rubbing, or by washing.

Elasticity. Linen has no significant elasticity. It is, in fact, the least elastic of natural fibers. In order to fit comfortably, linen garments should neither bind nor pull at the seams.

Resilience. Linen fiber is relatively stiff and has little resilence. Therefore, it wrinkles easily, which somewhat offsets its otherwise excellent qualities as a fabric for summer apparel. But it is possible to buy dress linens that have been given one of the patented wrinkle-resistant processes described in Chapter 8.

Due to its stiffness, linen fabrics should not have creases pressed firmly into them. Deep repeated folds, as in tablecloths, should be avoided because these creases eventually cause the otherwise strong yarns to crack and break long before they ordinarily would.

Heat Conductivity. Linen is most suitable for summer apparel, as it allows the heat of the body to escape.

Absorbency. When absorbency is the main consideration, linen is preferable to cotton. It absorbs moisture and dries more quickly. It is therefore excellent for handkerchiefs and towels.

Cleanliness and Washability. Linen launders well and gives up stains readily; its softness is enhanced by repeated washings. Since linen can be boiled and made sterile, it is desirable for surgical dressings and bandages. Bacteria do not thrive on linen because of its hard, smooth surface. Because of its stiffness, linen must be thoroughly damp when it is ironed, or a steam iron may be used.

Reaction to Bleaches. Linen does not stain as readily as cotton, but it is also more difficult to bleach. Like cotton, it is weakened by sodium hypochlorite bleaches.

Drapability. Linen has more body than cotton and drapes somewhat better.

Shrinkage. Linen does not shrink a great deal; in fact, it shrinks less than cotton.

Effect of Heat. Linen scorches and flames in a manner similar to cotton.

Effect of Light. Linen is more resistant to light than cotton, but it will gradually deteriorate from protracted exposure.

Affinity for Dyes. Linen does not have good affinity for dyes. However, it is possible to obtain dyed linen that has good colorfastness. When buying colored linens, look for the words "Guaranteed Fast Color" on the label or get a guarantee of colorfastness from the store. If a label states that the fabric is vat-dyed, it has been given the fastest color possible to withstand washing.

Resistance to Mildew. Like cotton, linen is vulnerable to mildew.

Resistance to Moths. Also like cotton, linen is not damaged by moths.

Reaction to Alkalies. Linen, like cotton, is highly resistant to alkalies. Linen may also be mercerized.

Reaction to Acids. Linen is damaged by hot dilute acids and cold concentrated acids. Cold dilute acids will not harm linen.

Resistance to Perspiration. Acid perspiration will deteriorate linen.

REVIEW QUESTIONS

1. Why is linen a desirable fiber?
2. Why is linen not used as frequently as cotton?
3. What disadvantages may there be in the use of linen fabrics?
4. Why are linens expensive?
5. What kind of climate is necessary for the growth of flax?
6. Which retting method is used in Russia? Ireland? Belgium?
7. Which method of retting produces the finest linen?
8. From what part of the flax plant is the fiber taken?
9. What are line and tow?
10. Would you prefer a cotton blouse to a linen blouse? If so, why?
11. (a) What country grows the flax plant for its seed? (b) Purpose?
12. Why should the short fibers be separated from the long fibers?
13. (a) What characteristic of the linen fiber makes it difficult to spin?
    (b) Why would a wet fiber be more easily twisted?
14. (a) In what weaves are linen yarns woven? (b) Name some fabrics.

13

WOOL AND HAIR

two natural protein fibers

Wool fiber and hair fiber are the natural hair growth of certain animals and are considered to be alike since they are both composed of *protein*.

HISTORY OF WOOL AND HAIR

Originally, wool was borne on wild species of sheep as a short, fluffy undercoat concealed by hair. When wild sheep were killed by primitive people for food, they used the pelts as body coverings. The fluffy undercoat probably became matted by usage, thus giving early man the idea of felting it into a crude cloth. It is believed that ancient shepherds in the first century A.D. discovered that Merino sheep could be bred to improve the fleece.

At first, wool was a very coarse fiber. Its development into the soft, fleecy coat so familiar on domesticated sheep is the result of long-continued selective breeding. The breeding of the animals and the production of the wool fiber into fabric are more costly processes than the cultivation of plant fiber and its manufacture. Consequently, wool fabrics are more expensive than cotton and linen. But wool provides warmth and physical comfort that cotton and linen fabrics cannot give. These qualities, combined with its soft resiliency, make wool desirable for apparel as well as for such household uses as rugs and blankets.

Hair fibers have all the qualities of wool and, in general, are even more expensive than wool. Vicuña is the world's costliest textile product and surpasses all other wool and hair fibers in fineness and beauty. These hairs are often mixed with wool, adding rather than detracting from the quality of any wool fabric in which they appear.

WOOL

The quality of the wool fiber is determined by the breeding, climate, food, general care, and health of the sheep.

Cold weather produces a hardier and heavier fiber. Excessive moisture dries out natural grease. Insufficient or poor food retards growth. Certain countries are suitable for large-scale sheep raising and consequently produce the greatest quantities of wool. The chief wool-producing countries are Argentina, Australia, the British Isles, India, South Africa, and the United States.

CLASSIFICATIONS FOR WOOL

Classification by Sheep

There are about forty breeds of sheep. Counting the crossbreeds, there are over two hundred distinct grades of sheep. Those that produce wool may be classified into four groupings according to the quality of the wool produced.

Merino Wool. Merino sheep produce the best wool (see Figure 13-1a). The variety originated in Spain and was so prized for its outstanding quality that during the Middle Ages it was a capital offense to export a Merino sheep from Spain. The staple is relatively short, ranging from 1 to 5 inches, but the fiber is strong, fine, and elastic and has good working properties. Merino fiber has the greatest amount of crimp of all wool fibers and has a maximum number of scales, totaling as many as 3,000 to the inch—two factors which contribute to its superior warmth and spinning qualities. Merino is used in the best types of wool clothing. The Ohio Merino, Austrian Silesian, and French Rambouillet are all varieties of Merino sheep. Other types are now found in Australia, New Zealand, South America, South Africa, and Spain.

Class-Two Wools. This class of sheep originated in England, Scotland, Ireland, and Wales. They helped make the British Isles famous for their fine wool fabrics. They are, however, no longer limited to that area and are now raised in many parts of the world. While not quite as good as the Merino wool, this variety is nevertheless a very good quality wool. It is 2 to 8 inches in length, has a large number of scales per inch, and has good crimp. The fibers are comparatively strong, fine, and elastic and have good working properties. Some of the better-known sheep of this variety include Bampton, Berkshire, Blackface, Cornwall, Devonshire, Dorset, Hampshire, Hereford, Exmoor, Kent, Norfolk, Shropshire, Southdown, Sussex, Oxford, Welsh Mountain, Wiltshire, Westmoreland, Irish, and Ryeland (Figure 13-1b, c, d).

Class-Three Wools. This class of sheep originated in the United Kingdom. The fibers are about 4 to 18 inches long, are coarser, and have fewer scales and less crimp than Merino and the class-two wools. As a result, they are smoother, and therefore have more luster. These wools are less elastic and resilient. They are nevertheless of good enough quality to be used for clothing. In fact, some of these sheep, such as Leicester, Cotswold, Cheviot, Harris, Lewis, and Shetland, have given their names to wool fabrics. (See Figure 13-1e.)

Class-Four Wools. This class is actually a group of mongrel sheep sometimes referred to as half-breeds. The fibers

Figure 13-1 *(a)* Merino ram produces class-one wool. *(Courtesy American News & Information Bureau)* *(b)* Blackface ewe produces class-two wool. *(Courtesy American Suffolk Sheep Society)* *(c)* Dorset ram produces class-two wool. *(Courtesy Continental Dorset Club)* *(d)* Southdown ewe produces class-two wool. *(Courtesy American Southdown Breeders Assn.)* *(e)* Cheviot ram produces class-three wool. *(Courtesy American Cheviot Sheep Society, Inc.)*

when a fiber or filament is straight, the light will reflect off the surface creating a luster.

are from 1 to 16 inches long, are coarse and hairlike, have relatively few scales and little crimp, and are therefore smoother and more lustrous. This wool is less desirable, with the least elasticity and strength. It is used mainly for carpets, rugs, and inexpensive low-grade clothing.

Classification by Fleece

Sheep are generally shorn of their fleeces in the spring, but the time of shearing varies in different parts of the world. In the United States, shearing takes place in April or May; in Australia, in September; in Great Britain, in June or July. Texas and California sheep are shorn twice a year because of the warm climate.

Sheep are not washed before shearing. Sometimes, they are dipped into an antiseptic bath, but this is done only when prescribed by law. Formerly, sheep were shorn with hand clippers; today the fleeces are removed in one piece by machine clippers, which shear closer as well as faster (see Figure 13-2).

A skilled worker can shear up to 200 sheep a day. Traveling by truck from Southwestern United States in the early spring, shearers work their way to the northern ranches and then south again.

Wool shorn from young lambs differs in quality from that of older sheep. Also, fleeces differ according to whether they come from live or dead sheep, which necessitates standards for the classification of fleeces.

Lamb's Wool. The first fleece sheared from a lamb about six to eight months old is known as *lamb's wool* and some-

Figure 13-2   A fleece just after shearing. (*Courtesy U.S. Department of Agriculture*)

times referred to as *fleece wool, or first clip.* This wool is of very fine quality; the fibers are tapered because the ends have never been clipped. Such fibers produce a softness of texture in fabrics that is characteristic only of lamb's wool. Because of its immaturity, however, lamb's wool is not as strong as fully developed wool of the same sheep.

Hogget Wool. Hogget (hogg or teg) wool comes from sheep twelve to fourteen months old that have not been previously shorn. The fiber is fine, soft, resilient, and mature, and has tapered ends. Hogget wool is a very desirable grade of wool and, because of its strength, is used primarily for the warp yarns of fabrics.

warp yarn is strongest.

Wether Wool. Any fleece clipped after the first shearing is called *wether wool*. This wool is usually taken from sheep older than fourteen months, and these fleeces contain much soil and dirt.

Pulled Wool. When sheep are slaughtered for meat, their wool is pulled from the pelt by the use of lime, by sweating, or by a chemical depilatory. Such wool fiber, called *pulled wool*, is of inferior quality for two reasons: (1) because sheep that are raised for meat generally do not have a good quality of wool, (2) because the roots of the fibers are generally damaged by the chemicals and the tension exerted in pulling.

Dead Wool. The wool fiber known as *dead wool* is sometimes mistaken for pulled wool. The term is correctly used for wool that has been recovered from sheep that have died on the range or have been accidentally killed. Dead wool fiber is decidedly inferior in grade; it is used in low-grade cloth.

Cotty Wool. Sheep that are exposed to severe weather conditions or lack of nourishment yield a wool that is matted or felted together and is hard and brittle. This very poor grade is known as *cotty wool*.

Taglocks. The torn, ragged, or discolored parts of a fleece are known as *taglocks*. These are usually sold separately as an inferior grade of wool.

WOOL PRODUCTS LABELING ACT

There has never been a sufficient supply of new wool stocks to take care of a steadily increasing demand for wool. To meet this situation, wool fibers have had to be recovered from old clothing, rags of all kinds, and waste from wool manufacturing; all are important sources. This wool is variously called salvaged, reclaimed, reworked, or remanufactured, but it is best known in the textile industry as *shoddy*. This term is misunderstood by the average consumer, who is inclined to believe that wool fabric containing remanufactured fibers is necessarily of inferior quality. This is not so.

The hardier, though less resilient, remanufactured fibers, when obtained from good original stock and combined with new wool from lamb, hogget, or wether fleeces, add durability to the soft new wool. Thus, remanufactured fibers contribute ability to withstand hard wear, although there is some sacrifice in warmth, softness of texture, and resiliency. They also make wool clothing available to consumers who cannot afford expensive wool fabrics.

To correct wrong impressions concerning the use of remanufactured wool, and also to protect consumers against unscrupulous practices, the U.S. government passed the Wool Products Labeling Act, which became effective in July, 1941. This act provides that every article of wool clothing must be labeled according to the type of wool used in its manufacture. The label must state: (1) the amount of wool fiber in the fabric, (2) the percentage by weight of new, or virgin, wool fibers, (3) the percentages of reprocessed fibers or reused fibers, (4) the percentage of each fiber other than wool, if such fibers constitute 5 percent or more of the total, (5) the aggregate of other fibers, and (6) the nonfibrous loading, filling, or adulterating substance.

New definitions of the types of wool fibers used in labeled garments were established by this act. Note that the law does not require labeling as to the type of sheep or the type of fleece from which the wool has come. The information on the labels is therefore of only limited value to the consumer.

Wool

The simple term "wool," according to government standards, must always mean new wool that has not been made up in any form of wool product. New wool comes directly from a fleece. It has never been previously spun, woven, felted, or worn.

The term "virgin wool" is now used by the textile industry to designate new wool from a sheep's fleece, but the term is too all-inclusive to serve as a criterion of quality. Although the term testifies to the fact that virgin wool does not contain remanufactured wool fibers, it can be used to identify the less desirable fibers of a fleece as well as a specially fine quality of wool. Virgin wool may also include pulled or dead wool, which may be of definitely inferior stock. One should not feel that a fabric labeled "100 percent new wool" is necessarily more serviceable than one containing any of the remanufactured wool fibers, for there are many different grades of new wool. It is important to remember that a high grade of reprocessed wool makes a more serviceable fabric than one having a low grade of new wool.

Reprocessed Wool

According to the government classification, reprocessed wool is fiber that has been reclaimed and remanufactured from unused wool materials. Such materials may come from combings and scraps of wool obtained during the manufacturing processes, from sample swatches, or from pieces of all-wool cloth from apparel manufacturing.

Reused Wool

The government gives the special classification of "reused wool" to fiber salvaged from all kinds of used consumers' goods.

MANUFACTURING PROCESSES

Preparation

Fleeces vary from 6 to 18 pounds in weight, average about 8 pounds each, and ultimately provide about 3 pounds of scoured wool. Since wool is sold according to the lowest grades in the fleece, it is often trimmed of the poorer quality edges, rolled up, tied, and packed in sacks weighing about 225 to 350 pounds. The trimmed skirtings are baled separately. In Australia, the fleece is separated at the time of shearing according to its quality. Superior wool comes from the sides and shoulders, where it grows longer, finer, and softer, and is treated as one fleece; wool from the head, chest, belly, and shanks is treated as a second fleece (see Figure 13-3).

Domestic wool reaches the mill in loosely packed bags; imported wool comes in tightly compressed bales. Each

Figure 13-3 One fleece produces various qualities of wool fiber (numbered 1 to 14 on the diagram), with number 1 yielding the softest, finest, and longest fibers.

The standard for wool grading in the United States is based upon the quality of wool produced by the Merino sheep because it yields the finest-quality wool in terms of diameter, scales, and crimp. For example, first-quality wool is identified as *fine* and is equivalent to the quality of wool that could be obtained from a full- to three-quarter-blood Merino sheep; second quality is equivalent to the kind of wool that could be obtained from a half-blood Merino. The poorest qualities are identified as *common* and *braid*; they are coarse, have little crimp, relatively few scales, and are somewhat hairlike in appearance.

The grading system on the world market is based upon the British numbering system, which relates the fineness, or diameter, of the wool fiber to the kind of combed, or worsted, yarn that could be spun from 1 pound of scoured wool. For example, the first in quality would be that wool which is fine enough for and capable of being spun from 1 pound of fiber into the highest wool yarn counts of 80s, 70s, and 64s (see page 304 for explanation of wool yarn count). The second in quality is fine enough to be capable of being spun into yarn counts of 62s, 60s, and 58s. The poorest grade is that wool which is capable of being spun into yarn counts of only 40s and 30s. An equivalent grading scale of the British and United States systems is shown in Table 13-1.

fleece contains different grades, or *sorts*, of wool, and the raw stock must be carefully graded and segregated according to length, diameter, and quality of the fiber. The raw wool or newly sheared fleece is called *grease wool* because it contains the natural oil of the sheep. When grease wool is washed, it loses from 20 to 80 percent of its original weight. The grease, known as *yolk*, is widely used in the pharmaceutical and cosmetic industries for lanolin compounds because it can be absorbed by the human skin.

Sorting and Grading. Wool sorting is done by skilled workers who are expert in distinguishing qualities by touch and sight. As many as twenty separate grades of wool may be obtained from one fleece if the sorting is especially rigid. Each grade is determined by type, length, fineness, elasticity, and strength.

Garnetting. Reprocessed and reused wool fibers are obtained by separately reducing the unused and used materials to a fibrous mass by a picking and shredding process called *garnetting*. The fibers are then put through a dilute solution of

Table 13-1

COMPARATIVE WOOL GRADING TABLE	
UNITED STATES SYSTEM	BRITISH SYSTEM
Fine (full- to three-quarter-blood)	80s, 70s, 64s
Half-blood	62s, 60s, 58s
Three-eighths-blood	56s
Quarter-blood	50s, 48s
Low-quarter-blood	46s
Common	44s
Braid	40s, 36s

sulfuric or hydrochloric acid, which destroys any vegetable fibers that may be contained in the raw stock. This process is known as *carbonizing*, and the resultant wool fibers are called *extracts*. The new staple ranges from $1/4$- to $1\,1/2$-inch lengths.

The quality and cost of reprocessed and reused wool fibers depend on the original stock from which they were obtained. A good grade of reprocessed wool may cost 5 times as much as a poor grade of virgin wool.

Scouring. The next step in preparing raw wool for manufacturing is a thorough washing in an alkaline solution; this process is known as *scouring*. The scouring machines contain warm water, soap, and a mild solution of soda ash or other alkali; they are equipped with automatic rakes, which stir the wool. Rollers between the vats squeeze out the water. If the raw wool is not sufficiently clear of vegetable substance after scouring, it is put through the carbonizing

bath of dilute sulfuric acid or hydrochloric acid to burn out the foreign matter.

For some consumers' goods, the term "naphthalated wool" is used, which means that the grease and dirt found in the fleece when originally sheared from the sheep's back have been removed by a series of naphtha baths followed by clear water to remove the naphtha. When wool has been thus treated by a cleansing agent, dyestuff penetrates better. For some purposes, wool is degreased by extracting the grease with a solvent, such as perchlorethylene. Excess solvent is evaporated off and recovered, and the wool is ready for further processing. This method is used both on stock and piece goods.

Drying. Wool is not allowed to become absolutely dry. Usually, about 12 to 16 percent of the moisture is left in the wool to condition it for subsequent handling.

Oiling. As wool is unmanageable after scouring, the fiber is usually treated with various oils, including animal, vegetable, and mineral, or a blend of these to keep it from becoming brittle and to lubricate it for the spinning operation.

Dyeing

If the wool is to be dyed in the raw stock, it is dyed at this stage. The advantage of stock dyeing has been described in Chapter 9. Some wool fabrics are piece-dyed, some are yarn- or skein-dyed, and some are top-dyed.

Blending

Wool of different grades may be blended or mixed together at this point (see Fig-

Figure 13-4   Various types of scoured wool are blended on a combination scale, which indicates the amount of each type of wool to be used in the blend. *(Courtesy The Wool Bureau, Inc.)*

ure 13-4). It is not uncommon for tag-locks and inferior grades of wool to be mixed with the better grades. The use of a mixture with a coarser grade of fiber is a legitimate practice if the purpose is to make a hardier product and a less expensive one, provided the label on the finished goods indicates a true description of the raw materials used. In the manufacture of *Union* fabrics, a small amount of cotton is blended with raw wool. A greater amount of twist can be given to such yarns, with a resultant increase of strength in the fabric. Because of its crimp, Peruvian cotton is frequently mixed with raw wool stock. Such mixtures have a place in certain finished

goods, but the amount of cotton used must be indicated on the label.

Depending upon the kind of fabric ultimately desired, such man-made fibers as nylon, polyester, or acrylic may be blended with the wool. The wool contributes warmth, absorbency, body, drape, and hand. Discussions of the contributions of man-made fibers in such blends are presented in the appropriate later chapters.

Carding

The carding process introduces the classifications of *woolen yarns* and *worsted yarns*. Manufacturing processes from

Figure 13-5   Carded wool in fine spider-web form is being drawn from the cylinder (left) into wool sliver (right). *(Courtesy National Association of Woolen Manufacturers)*

this point on depend on whether the wool fiber is to be made into a woolen or worsted product (Figures 13-5 and 13-6).

In the manufacture of woolen yarns, the essential purpose of carding is to disentangle the fibers by passing the wool fibers between rollers covered with thousands of fine wire teeth. Incidentally, this action also removes some dirt and foreign matter from the fibers. As the wool fibers are brushed and disentangled by these wires, they tend to lie parallel, which would make woolen yarns too smooth. Since woolen yarns should be somewhat rough or fuzzy, it is not desirable to have the fibers too parallel. By use of an oscillating device, one thin film, or sliver, of wool is placed diagonally and overlapping another sliver to give a crisscross effect to the fibers. This permits the fibers to be disentangled and

somewhat parallel and at the same time provides a fuzzy surface to the yarn. After this carding process, the woolen slivers go directly to the spinning operation.

When the crimp and loft of the wool fiber is to be increased, as is sometimes desirable particularly for woolen carpet yarns, the carding process may include the use of the IWS Crimper to produce *programmed pile* (see page 82).

In the manufacture of worsted yarns, the essential purpose of carding is also to disentangle the fibers by passing the wool fibers between rollers covered with fine wire teeth. Since worsted yarns, however, should be smooth, the fibers are made to lie as parallel as this process will permit. Following this operation, the wool goes to the gilling and combing processes.

Gilling and Combing

The carded wool, which is to be made into worsted yarn, is put through gilling and combing operations. The *gilling* process removes the shorter staple and straightens the fibers. This process is continued in the combing operation, which removes the shorter fibers of 1- to 4-inch lengths (called *combing noils*), places the longer fibers (called *tops*) as parallel as possible, and further cleans the fibers by removing any remaining loose impurities.

The short-staple noils are not necessarily of poor quality. Combing noils may well be of good quality, depending on the original source of the wool. They may be used as filler for other types of wool fabrics; however, such fibers must be classified as reprocessed wool.

The long-staple tops, which are over 4 inches in length, excel in color, feel, and strength. They are used in the production of such worsted fabrics as serge, whipcord, gabardine, and covert.

Drawing

Drawing is an advanced operation which doubles and redoubles slivers of wool fibers. The process draws, drafts, twists, and winds the stock, making the slivers more compact and thinning them into slubbers. Drawing is done only to worsted yarns.

Roving

This is the final stage before spinning. Roving is actually a light twisting operation to hold the thin slubbers intact.

Figure 13-6   Diagram shows difference in the manufacture of woolen and worsted yarns.

Spinning

In the spinning operation, the wool roving is drawn out and twisted into yarn. Woolen yarns are chiefly spun on the mule spinning machine. Worsted yarns are spun on any kind of spinning machine—mule, ring, cap, or flyer. The two different systems of spinning worsted yarns are the English system and the French system.

In the English system (Bradford), the fiber is oiled before combing, and a tight twist is inserted. This produces smoother and finer yarns. The more tightly twisted yarn makes a stronger, more enduring fabric. In the French system, no oil is used. The yarn is given no twist; it is fuzzier, and therefore suitable for soft worsted yarns.

Figure 13-7 *(a)* Drawing of smooth worsted yarn produced from long-staple fibers. *(b)* Drawing of uneven woolen yarn with protruding short ends, produced from short-staple fibers.

The differences between woolen and worsted yarns are as follows (see also Figure 13-7):

WOOLEN YARN	WORSTED YARN
Short staple	Long staple
Carded only	Carded and combed
Slack twisted	Tightly twisted
Weaker	Stronger
Bulkier	Finer, smoother, even fibers
Softer	Harder
Uneven twisting	Even twisting

Yarn Count

The fineness or thickness of wool yarns is based on different systems for woolen and worsted. One pound of worsted yarn yielding 560 yards is identified as No. 1s. Ply yarns are numbered according to the number of the single yarn from which they are spun. Thus, 2/60s worsted means two-ply yarns of No. 60 singles, twisted together.

In woolens, the size of the yarn is based on two separate systems: the cut and the American run. The latter is more generally used.

The *cut system*, sometimes called the *Philadelphia* because of its use in that area, uses a base of 300 yards to the cut.

Thus, 1 pound of woolen fiber drawn out to 300 yards sets a standard for No. 1s.

In the *American run system*, sometimes called the *New England*, 1 pound of woolen yarn yielding 1,600 yards is identified as No. 1s.

Warping

The yarn that leaves the spinning frame is not of sufficient length to serve as warp yarn on the loom. It is first wound on bobbins or spools and placed on a large rack or frame called a *creel*. As in the warping operation explained in Chapter 5, the warp yarns on the bobbins or spools are evenly wound on the warp beam. They may be immersed in a solution of starch, gum, or similar compound to make them smooth and strong for weaving. In the production of better-quality wool fabrics, a hard-twisted two-ply yarn is frequently used for the warp yarn, as the plied construction gives greater strength.

Weaving Woolen Fabrics

Basically, the weaving process for wool resembles the process described in Chapter 5. The short, curly woolen yarns obtained in the carding process are made into woolen fabrics by using the plain weave, or sometimes the twill. The weave pattern is not always discernible because woolen fabrics often have a napped surface. The thread count of woolens is usually less than that of worsteds because the construction is not so compact.

Woolen fabrics are soft, fuzzy, and thick; they are warmer than worsted, but not as durable. Napping gives wool-

Table 13-2

DIFFERENCES BETWEEN WOOLEN AND WORSTED FABRICS		
	WOOLEN FABRICS	WORSTED FABRICS
Fiber	Short, curly fibers	Long, straight fibers
Yarn	Carded only; slack twist; weaker yarns	Carded and combed; tight twist; greater tensile strength than woolens; generally yarn-dyed
Weave	Indistinct pattern; usually plain weave, sometimes twill; thread count generally less than worsteds	Distinct pattern; chiefly twill weave, infrequently plain weave; more closely woven than woolens
Finish	Soft finish; fulling, flocking, napping, steaming; since napping can conceal quality of construction, woolens are easily adulterated	Hard finish; singed, steamed; unfinished worsteds are napped; adulteration more difficult as fillers would be easily discernible
Appearance and touch	Soft, fuzzy, thick	Flat, rough, harsh
Characteristics	Warmer than worsteds, not so durable; nap acts as a protective agent against shine; soft surface catches and holds dirt; stains easily removed	Wrinkle less than woolens, more durable; hold creases and shape; become shiny with use; feel harsh when next to skin; more resistant to dust
Uses	Generally less expensive than worsteds if poorer yarns are used; desirable for sportswear, jackets, sweaters, skirts, blankets, winter use	Costlier yarns; appropriate for tailored and dressy wear; spring and summer coats and suits, tropical suits; good for business wear
Typical fabrics	Tweed, homespun, flannel, broadcloth, shetland, cassimere	Gabardine, whipcord, serge, worsted cheviot, tropical worsted, Bedford cord

ens a soft surface, which acts as a protection against objectionable luster. But napping can conceal poor construction and the quality of the yarns used; therefore, woolens can be more easily adulterated than worsteds. The napped surface tends to catch and hold dirt, but stains can be easily removed. If poorer yarns have been used in woolens, the fabric is less expensive than worsted. Woolens are desirable for sportswear, jackets, sweaters, skirts, blankets, and similar general use. (See Table 13-2.)

Weaving Worsted Fabrics

The worsted yarns, which have been specially carded and combed, are woven into fine worsted fabrics with distinctive patterns, chiefly by means of the twill weave. The plain weave is infrequently used. The thread count of worsteds is higher than that of woolens because the finer yarn permits closer construction.

Worsted fabrics are flat, rough, and harsh when worn next to the skin. They are more durable than woolens and more resistant to dirt. They wrinkle less and hold creases and shape, but they become shiny with use.

Worsted fabrics are costlier than woolens. They are appropriate for tailored and dressy purposes, for spring and summer coats and suits, and for tropical suits. They are suitable for business wear.

Inspecting and Correcting Flaws

Prior to various wet- and dry-finishing processes, wool fabrics are *perched*, or examined, for defects, which are marked with chalk. Some flaws are corrected by *burling* with a kind of tweezers (called *burling irons*) to remove loose threads and push knots to the back of the cloth and by *specking* to remove specks, burrs, and other foreign matter. Mending and sewing may be required to correct minor catches and similar defects.

FINISHING WOOL FABRICS

Fulling

After the weaving process, woolen and worsted gray goods are placed in warm, soapy water and are pounded and twisted to make the wool fibers interlock. This application of heat, moisture, and pressure, followed by a cold rinse, is calling *fulling* (also *felting* or *milling*). Sometimes, chemicals are used to help moisten, soften, and lubricate the fibers so that matting will occur.

Fulling produces a desired shrinkage and gives the fabric additional thickness and a firmer, fuller texture. The longer the fulling operation, the greater the shrinkage, with consequent

Figure 13-8 Woven pieces are sewed end-to-end and fed into the fulling machine where, in moisture and heat, the cloth is tumbled and pounded. This shrinks fabric in length and width to give it body and evenness. *(Courtesy The Wool Bureau, Inc.)*

increase in the strength of the fabric (see Figure 13-8).

The fulling process and other finishing operations for woolens and worsteds yield *flock*, extremely short staple ranging from $1/8$- to $3/4$-inch lengths. Flock is felted into the poorer grades of woolens to add weight. It is also blended with other raw wool stocks. Other waste material reclaimed from fulling is termed *mungo*. This is the lowest grade of waste. It is used for blending and is combined with yarn for low-grade wool fabrics.

Crabbing

To set the cloth and the yarn twist permanently, wool fabric is passed over several cylinders that rotate in hot water and is then immersed quickly in cold water. The cloth is held firmly and tightly to avoid wrinkling. Repetition of the treatment with increased pressure results in setting the cloth and the finish.

Decating

Decating, or decatizing, is a shrinking treatment that is sometimes used instead of London shrinking (discussed on page 184. Decating, however, is faster and gives reasonable protection against further shrinking. There are two decating techniques, and the one that is used depends upon the luster desired in the finished fabric.

Dry Decating. If the luster is to be set, the fabric is wound under tension on a perforated roller that is then placed in a preheated boiler equipped with a vacuum system. Steam is first forced from the inside of the roller through the layers of fabric for two to three minutes; then the process is reversed. The fabric is then removed and cooled by air.

Wet Decating. If the luster is to be increased, the fabric, wound under tension on a perforated roller, is placed in hot water (140 to 212 degrees Fahrenheit) that is first forced through the roller and fabric and then reversed. The hotter the water or steam used, the more effective the process will be. The cloth is then removed, cooled with cold water or cold air, and dried.

London Shrinking

This is a superior preshrinking treatment given to better-quality wool fabrics. It is a cold-water process by which the cloth is interleaved with wet blankets, dried slowly for twenty-four hours, and then set under 3,500 pounds of pressure per square inch.

Additional Finishing Processes

Wool fabrics are also given the following finishing processes:

Shearing—cutting and shaving for a uniform surface

Singeing and steaming—for hard finish of worsted fabrics

Pressing—improving appearance and giving final shape to the cloth

Steaming, sponging—removing excess glaze

Napping or gigging—to raise a fuzzy surface

Piece dyeing—to impart color to the wool fabric

Tentering—for desired uniform width

Water repellency—for all-weather wear

Shrink-proofing—for stability

Permanent press—for ease of care and shape retention

Mothproofing—for durability

These finishes are fully discussed in Chapter 8.

UNFINISHED WORSTEDS

Unfinished worsteds have the durability and tailored appearance characteristic of worsted fabrics and the comfort, greater warmth, and freedom from luster characteristic of woolens.

The soft texture of unfinished worsteds is due to additional manufacturing processes, such as fulling, brushing, or napping. Since they require more processing, the term "unfinished" gives a wrong impression.

The napped surface in the unfinished worsted gives softness of texture, serves the functional purposes of napped fabrics, and gives the beauty found in woolens. In addition, the fabric possesses the durability of worsteds. With continued wear, however, the nap rubs off, and these areas show an objectionable luster or shine. Such consumers' goods can be renapped by a cleaning establishment, but this is generally avoided since the renapping can weaken the cloth. One can enjoy longer serviceability by selecting an unfinished worsted in a light color. Light colors, such as gray, do not show luster as readily as the darker shades.

EVALUATING WOOL FABRICS

It is apparent that the quality and characteristics of wool fabrics are dependent upon the kind of sheep, its physical condition, the part of the sheep from which the wool is taken, and the manufacturing and finishing processes applied to the fabrics. While it might appear that these factors present a complicated problem in discerning preferred wool fabrics, there is much information and evidence available to the consumer to help him make satisfactory selections.

While it is not required that the labels on wool fabrics mention the type of sheep wool, fabrics made of Merino wool are frequently identified by label and in advertisements because they are preferred for their softness, warmth, resilience, and fineness. It should be noted, however, that there are trademarks that are similar but not identical in spelling to Merino; such fabrics do not necessarily contain Merino wool.

Another wool fabric that may be readily identified is the Harris Tweed. Harris sheep produce a quality of wool particularly well suited for durable tweeds. Harris sheep, which are raised on the Outer Hebrides Islands, have a coarse but strong fiber, which is spun into yarn and woven on looms in the cottages of the members of the Harris Tweed Association. These tweeds are preferred for their quality of construction, durability, and exclusive designs. These fabrics are identified by the Association's symbol and the registered number of the particular bolt of cloth (see Figure 13-9).

The indication of the amounts of new, reprocessed, and reused wools is also helpful. The presence of reprocessed or reused wool in a fabric does not condemn it so long as the product is properly labeled and the consumer understands the limitations as well as the advantages of such wool fabrics. A fabric made of new or virgin wool may be of inferior quality if it is made of inferior grades or of extremely short staple. The yarns should be examined for fineness and crimp of fiber, as these factors have a direct relationship to the quality of wool.

*wool does not conduct heat
it works as an insulator*

Figure 13-9   Genuine Harris Tweed is always identified by a label such as this containing the registered number and the association symbol.

The identification of the fiber (or fibers) blended with the wool is also important. To consider the characteristics and contributions of these fibers to the blend, refer to the chapter that discusses each of them.

Strength.   As wool is the weakest of the natural textile fibers, the fabric may be made more durable by the use of selected grades of reprocessed or reused wool, although durability is gained at the expense of texture and resiliency. To determine whether temporary body (without strength) has been given by the use of flock, brush and whip the fabric vigorously. Then examine the surface and selvages for powdery particles, which are the sign of short staple. Also examine the structure of the fabric to determine whether it has been weakened by excessive napping.

Wool fabric is strengthened by the use of ply yarns. A hard-twisted two-ply yarn may be regarded as an assurance of durability. Tightly twisted single yarns also make a strong fabric.

Elasticity.   One might look upon wool's elasticity as a compensation for its relative weakness. Depending upon the quality of wool, the fiber may be stretched from 25 to 30 percent of its natural length before breaking. This characteristic reduces the danger of tearing under tension and contributes to free body movements. To preserve this natural elasticity, wool garments should be hung properly after wearing and allowed to relax sufficiently to regain their shape.

Resilience.   Because wool fiber has a high degree of resilience, wool fabric wrinkles less than some others; wrinkles disappear when the garment or fabric is steamed. Good wool is very soft and resilient; poor wool is harsh. When buying a wool fabric, grasp a handful to determine its quality. If the fabric retains the wrinkles and feels stiff, this may indicate a mixture with cotton or an inferior grade of reused wool.

Heat Conductivity.   As wool fibers are nonconductors of heat, they permit the body to retain a temperature close to the 98.6 degrees Fahrenheit required for health. Wool garments are excellent for winter clothing and are protective on damp days throughout the year. The scales on the surface of a fiber and the crimp in the fiber create little pockets of air that serve as insulative barriers and give the garment greater warmth. Low-twist yarns will also contribute to the warmth of the garment. Lightweight wool of sheer construction is comfortable for summer wear because of its thermostatic quality.

Drapability. Wool's excellent draping quality is aided by its pliability, elasticity, and resiliency. One of the outstanding competitive features that wool has over many man-made fibers is its superior drapability.

Absorbency. Initially, wool tends to be water-repellent. One can observe that droplets of water on the surface of wool fabrics are readily brushed off. However, once the moisture seeps between the scales of the fiber, the fiber's high degree of capillarity will result in ready absorption. Wool can absorb about 20 percent of its weight in water without feeling damp; consequently, wool fabrics tend to feel comfortable rather than clammy or chilly. Wool also dries slowly.

Cleanliness and Washability. Dirt tends to adhere to wool fabric. Unless thoroughly cleaned, wool retains odors. Consequently, wool requires frequent dry cleaning, or laundering if the fabric is washable. Extreme care is required in laundering. Wool is softened by moisture and heat, and shrinking and felting occur when the fabric is washed. Since wool temporarily loses about 25 percent of its strength when wet, wool fabrics should never be pulled or wrung while wet. They should be lifted and squeezed.

To control the possibility of shrinking or stretching when laundering a wool sweater or a similar garment, wash it in cold water with an appropriate detergent, such as Woolite. To dry the garment, roll it in a towel, squeeze gently to remove as much moisture as possible, then spread it out to its original shape on a towel or heavy cardboard.

Reaction to Bleaches. The household bleaches that contain sodium hypochlorite or other chlorine compounds are harmful to wool. However, a bleach containing hydrogen peroxide or sodium perborate, such as Snowy, may be safely used.

Shrinkage. Shrinkage is greater in woolens than in worsteds, but all fabrics made of wool are subject to shrinkage, depending upon the preshrinking treatment. If the fabrics are dry-cleaned, the shrinkage will be less. *Clorinated wools* are wools that have been subjected to shrink-proofing, but this treatment reduces the strength of the fabric.

The ultrathin polymer resin film, made by the basic Wurlan process, is an excellent wool-shrinkage-control technique. This process was developed by the U.S. Department of Agriculture and is used on fabrics by various wool manufacturers and processors under their own trademarks.

If fabrics have been preshrunk or treated for shrink-proofing, this fact should be stated on the identifying labels. These tags should also indicate whether residual shrinkage may be expected, and if it is expected, how much to expect, and how the garments should be cared for.

Effect of Heat. Wool becomes harsh at 212 degrees Fahrenheit and begins to decompose at slightly higher temperatures. It will scorch at 400 degrees Fahrenheit and will eventually char. However, it is not easily combustible—it will smolder but not flame when fire is removed. Wool has a plastic quality in that it can be pressed and shaped at steam temperatures, whether in fabric, as for slacks and jackets, or in felt, as for hats.

Effect of Light. Wool is weakened by prolonged exposure to sunlight.

Affinity for Dyes. Because of their high affinity for dyes, wool fabrics dye well and evenly. The use of chrome dyes assures fastness of color.

Resistance to Mildew. Wool is not ordinarily susceptible to mildew; but if left in a damp condition, mildew develops.

Resistance to Moths. Wool fabrics are especially vulnerable to moths. They should be protected in some manner, as discussed in Chapter 8.

Reaction to Alkalies. Wool is quickly damaged by strong alkalies. It is imperative to use a mild soap or detergent when laundering wool fabrics.

Reaction to Acids. Although wool is damaged by hot sulfuric acid, it is not affected by other acids, even when heated. This property permits wool to be carbonized without damage.

Resistance to Perspiration. Wool is weakened by perspiration. Garments should be dry-cleaned or washed with care to avoid deterioration and odor.

HAIR

Hair fibers that have the qualities of wool are obtained from certain kinds of animals throughout the world. The hair of these animals has been so adapted by nature for the climate in which they live that the cloth produced from the fiber gives warmth with light weight. Some of these animals are used primarily as burden carriers; others are bred for their fleeces, which produce the most expensive fibers in the textile industry.

These hair fibers are used alone or are combined with sheep's wool for construction into fabrics whose cost varies according to the amount and quality of the blend. The consumer must be careful to analyze descriptions of certain of these blends. Parts of the names of rare animals are sometimes used to convey false or nonexistent values to mixtures with other fibers. Such blends may contain insignificant quantities of the lowest grade of hair fibers that could not possibly add quality to the fabrics.

Camel's Hair

Camel's hair is a fine hair that is known to the American consumer chiefly in the form of high-quality coat fabrics. This textile fiber is obtained from the two-humped Bactrian camel, which is native to all parts of Asia (Figure 13-10a). The climate of the desert countries, where the camel is used as a burden carrier and as a means of transportation, is exceedingly hot during the day and extremely cold at night. This constant change has produced a protective hair covering that is a nonconductor of both heat and cold; it is also naturally water-repellent. In the spring, the year's growth of hair, which hangs from the camel in matted strands and tufts, falls off in clumps to make room for the new growth. Masses of hair that are shed throughout the year are also accumulated. The camel is sometimes plucked to obtain the down or underhair.

Camel's-hair fabrics are ideal for comfort, particularly when used for overcoating, as they are especially warm but light in weight. Camel's hair is characterized by strength, luster, and smoothness. The best quality is expensive when used alone. It is often mixed with wool, thus raising the quality of the wool fabric by adding the fine qualities of camel's hair. The price of a mixed cloth is naturally much less than that of a fabric that is 100 percent camel's hair.

In the textile industry, camel's hair is divided into three grades. Grade 1 is the soft and silky light-tan underhair found close to the skin of the camel. This is short staple, or noil, of from 1¼ to 3½ inches, but it is also the choicest quality. Formerly, it was the only true camel's hair used in the manufacture of apparel. In wool, noils represent the less valuable short staple; in the hair fibers, the short fibers are the prized product and are the only ones used in high-grade hair fabrics.

Grade 2 is the intermediate growth, consisting of short hairs and partly of coarse outer hairs, ranging from 1½ to 5 inches in length. Grade 3 consists entirely of coarse outer hairs measuring up to 15 inches in length and varying in color from brownish black to reddish brown. This grade has no value for apparel manufacture; it is suitable only for cordage and for low-quality rugs.

Mohair

Mohair is the hair of the Angora goat, native to the province of Angora, Turkey (Figure 13-10b). This species of goat is now raised in the United States, principally in Oregon, California, and Texas. Some domestic mohair, particularly the mohair obtained from Texas, is of excellent quality. Imported mohair is of long staple, 9 to 12 inches long, and represents a full year's growth. The domestic goat is shorn twice a year, yielding a shorter staple, from 8 to 10 inches. Imported mohair can be spun to a fineness of 60s in yarn count. The highest count possible for domestic fiber is 40s. The domestic fiber has a great amount of coarse, stiff hair, known as *kemp*, which does not process readily or allow thorough penetration of dye.

Mohair is a smooth, strong, and resilient fiber. It does not attract or hold dirt particles. It absorbs dye evenly and permanently. Its fine silklike luster permits interesting decorative effects. Mohair fiber is more uniform in diameter than wool fiber. Under the microscope, mohair shows almost no scales; its indistinct scales do not project from the shaft, as is characteristic of wool fiber. Mohair, therefore, does not shrink or felt as readily as wool.

When mohair is used in pile fabrics, the naturally strong fiber combined with the strength of the pile weave makes an especially durable and serviceable fabric. Mohair fabrics are wrinkle-resistant and do not mat readily because of the natural resiliency of the fiber. The fabric can also be made mothproof. Because mohair is very resilient and is stronger than wool or the other hair fibers, it is used to great advantage in quality floor coverings, in better grades of upholstery materials and drapery materials, and in summer suitings.

Figure 13-10   *(a)* Camels. *(Courtesy American Museum of Natural History) (b)* Angora goat. *(Courtesy Arthur Ambler) (c)* Llamas. *(Courtesy S. Stroock & Co., Inc.) (d)* Alpaca. *(Courtesy New York Zoological Society) (e)* Vicuña. *(Courtesy S. Stroock & Co., Inc.)*

Cashmere

The Cashmere goat is native to the Himalaya Mountain region of Kashmir, India, and China. The fleece of this goat has long, straight, coarse outer hair of little value; however, the small quantity of underhair, or down, is made into luxuriously soft woollike yarns with a characteristic highly napped finish. This fine cashmere fiber is not sheared from the goat but is obtained by frequent combings during the shedding season. The microscope reveals that cashmere is a much finer fiber than mohair or any wool fiber obtained from sheep. The scales are less distinct and are farther apart; the fiber appears to be made of sections placed within each other.

Cashmere first became familiar in the beautiful soft, light cashmere shawls for which India has been famous. Today, it is used for such garments as sweaters, sports jackets, and overcoats. Cashmere is desirable because it is soft, lighter in weight than wool, and quite warm; however, because it is a soft, delicate fiber, fabrics produced from cashmere are not as durable as wool.

Llama

The llama is allied to the camel in species, having many of the characteristics of that animal, but being about one-third in size (Figure 13-10c). The llama is the traditional burden carrier in the higher parts of the Andes Mountains in South America, primarily Bolivia and Peru, and has not been bred for its fleece. Its hair fiber is generally coarse and brownish in color and is valued because it may be mixed with the hair of the alpaca, an animal of the same species that is raised for its fleece alone. Some noils are obtained from the undercoat of the llama.

When llama is part of a blend of fibers, it gives exquisite natural colors. Llama mixtures have a characteristic high insulative property with little weight and are used for high-quality coat fabrics, as they embody the essential qualities of wrinkle resistance, color fastness, and extreme durability.

Alpaca

In the higher regions of the Andes, 14,000 feet above sea level, is found another fleece bearer, the alpaca, a domesticated animal that resembles the llama and is related to the camel (Figure 13-10d). The fiber is valued for its silky beauty as well as for its strength. The hair of the alpaca is stronger than ordinary sheep's wool, is water-repellent, and has a high insulative quality. The staple is relatively long, ranging from 6 to 11 inches; yet it is as delicate, soft, and lustrous as the finest silk.

Alpaca consists of two varieties of fiber: soft, woollike hair, and stiff beard, or outer hair. Of the many colors obtainable, ranging from white to brown and black, the reddish brown variety is considered the most valuable.

A more highly selected type of alpaca is the *suri*—a superbreed just as the Merino is the highest type of sheep. The fiber of the suri is sought by manufacturers of outer apparel because the staple is longer, silkier, and finer, and has curl throughout its length. A crossbreed, with the alpaca as sire and the llama as dam, produces the *misti*. Another crossbreed, the *huarizo*, is the result of breeding a llama sire and an alpaca dam.

Vicuña

The rare animal whose fiber makes the world's most costly and most exquisite cloth, surpassing all others in fineness and beauty, is found in an almost inaccessible area of the Andes Mountains, at altitudes between 16,000 and 19,000 feet. The vicuña, one of the wildest of animals, is less than 3 feet high and weighs

75 to 100 pounds (Figure 13-10*e*). A single animal yields only ¼ pound of hair; thus forty animals are required to provide enough hair for the average coat. To preserve the species, the vicuña is now under the protection of the Peruvian and Bolivian governments. Attempts to domesticate this animal have not been very successful but are still being made in Peru. The fiber of the vicuña is the softest and most delicate of the known animal fibers; yet it is strong for its weight, is resilient, and has a marked degree of elasticity and surface cohesion. It is the most expensive fiber used in suitings and overcoat fabrics of tan to orange-brown.

Guanaco

The guanaco, native to southern Argentina where it is both wild and domesticated, is related to the llama and alpaca. The fiber is extremely soft and silky. It is also light, resilient, and warm, and the color is a honey beige. Because of these characteristics and its limited availability, it is expensive. It generally is blended with wool, frequently lamb's wool, so as not to mask the fiber's soft texture.

Angora

The Angora rabbit produces long, fine, silky white hair that is clipped or combed every 3 to 4 months. The finest angora comes from France, Italy, and Japan. The Angora rabbit is also raised in many other parts of the world, including the United States. The fiber's smooth, silky texture makes it difficult to spin, and the fibers tend to slip out of the yarn and shed from the fabric; nevertheless, the fiber is desired for its texture, warmth, light weight, and pure white color, although it is sometimes dyed in pastel shades. Angora rabbit hair is used primarily for items such as sweaters, mittens, baby clothes, and millinery.

REVIEW QUESTIONS

1. What are the advantages of wool fabrics?
2. Name the classification of fleeces according to quality.
3. What countries supply the world with wool?
4. Explain the United States government classifications of wool.
5. What qualities are found in fleece wool?
6. (a) How are grease and dirt removed from the fleece? (b) What by-product is obtained from the grease?
7. Name six differences between woolens and worsteds.
8. Name three woolen fabrics and three worsted fabrics.
9. What are unfinished worsteds?
10. How would you judge quality in wool fabrics?
11. What finishing processes are used for woolens?

12. Which finishing processes are used for worsteds? Why?
13. How do worsteds compare with woolens as to appearance and touch?
14. (a) Which type of wool fabric is warmer: woolen or worsted? Why? (b) Which is stronger? Why? (c) Which is higher in price? Why?
15. (a) How can the crimp be permanently increased in wool fibers? (b) What is its primary application?
16. Discuss the properties of wool in terms of (a) strength or durability, (b) warmth, (c) absorbency.
17. Discuss the care of wool fabrics in terms of (a) cleaning and washing, (b) shape retention, (c) moth protection.
18. What information should you look for in determining the quality of wool fabrics?
19. Differentiate among mohair, cashmere, and angora hair.
20. Why might some camel's-hair coats be inexpensive?
21. Compare llama, alpaca, vicuña, and guanaco fiber.

14

SILK

another natural protein fiber

Silk is the very fine strand of fiber that is a solidified *protein* secretion produced by certain caterpillars to encase themselves in the form of cocoons.

HISTORY OF SILK

The possibility of making cloth from the filament that the silkworm spins into a cocoon was first discovered in China about 2600 B.C. Legend tells us that a cocoon accidentally dropped into a cup of tea that a Chinese princess was having in her garden. The hot liquid softened and loosened the fiber, which the princess pulled and drew away from the cocoon as a continuous strand. Another story cites Empress Si-Ling-Chi as the first producer of silk fiber, from which she made a silk robe for her husband. From antiquity until the more recent es-tablishment of the Chinese Republic, she was venerated as the Goddess of the Silkworm.

The Chinese who first cultivated the silkworm and developed a silk industry endeavored to keep the source of the raw material secret. Their silk fabrics were highly prized. Caravans carried silks into the Near East where they were traded for hundreds of years. It is believed that silk was introduced into Europe by Alexander the Great in the fourth century B.C. As the desire for silk fabrics expanded, the interest in its production also increased. About three thousand years after its original discovery, the secret was stolen out of China.

A large silk industry eventually developed in southeastern Europe and subsequently spread westward because of the Moslem conquests. Spain began to produce silk in the eighth century. Italy began silk production in the twelfth century and was the leader for 500 years. In the sixteenth century, France became the rival of Italy in the production of silk fabrics of excellence and beauty.

Attempts have been made to cultivate the silkworm in the United States, but they have not succeeded commercially because of the higher labor and production costs in this country. The silk industry is an important one, however, because the United States has become the greatest importer and consumer of silk. That part of the industry that manufactures raw silk into fabrics closely touches the lives of American consumers. The possession of silk fabrics has always represented an ideal of luxury to Americans, perhaps more than to the inhabitants of other countries. Silk will probably always be prized by the consumer even though some man-made fibers now have qualities that were formerly possessed only by silk.

SILK-PRODUCING COUNTRIES

When farmers in the Asiatic countries first raised silkworms, the many diseased worms and defective cocoons resulted in poor grades of finished goods. The farmers were raising silkworms only as an additional means of support. Japan was the first country producing silk in large quantities to use scientific methods in cultivating the silkworm on farms as well as in factories. Japan has therefore always ranked highest in the production of fine silk, although satisfactory types are made in other silk-producing countries—China, India, Italy, Spain, France, Austria, Iran, Turkey, Greece, Syria, Bulgaria, and Brazil. The cultivation of the silkworm requires extreme care and close supervision, and the reeling of the filament from the cocoons can be undertaken only by skilled operators whose training is the result of many generations of experience.

CULTIVATION OF COCOONS

Since the discovery, so many years ago, that the fiber, or filament, composing the cocoon of the silkworm can be unwound and constructed into a beautiful and durable fabric, silkworms have been bred for the sole purpose of producing raw silk. The production of cocoons for their filament is called *sericulture*. Experiments have proved that the cocoon of the *Bombyx mori*, a species of moth, produces the finest quality of raw silk. In sericulture, all four stages of the life cycle of this moth are important, because some of the better cocoons must be set aside to permit full development, thus supplying eggs for another hatching. Under scientific breeding, silkworms may be hatched three times a year; under natural conditions, breeding occurs only once a year. The life cycle is as follows (see also Figure 14-1):

1. The egg, which develops into the larva or caterpillar—the silkworm
2. The silkworm, which spins its cocoon for protection, to permit development into the pupa or chrysalis
3. The chrysalis, which emerges from the cocoon as the moth
4. The moth, of which the female lays eggs, so continuing the life cycle

Figure 14-1

Within three days after emerging from the cocoons, the moths mate, the female lays 350 to 400 eggs on numbered cards, and the moths die. Based upon Louis Pasteur's discovery that the insect is subject to a hereditary infection, the moths are then examined microscopically. The cards of eggs from moths that have been infected are burned. By this

careful, scientific regulation, Japan has not only protected and fostered sericulture but has developed into the leading producer of silk fiber.

Each healthy egg hatches into what is called an *ant*. It is a larva about $1/8$ inch in length. The larva requires careful nurturing in a controlled atmosphere for approximately twenty to thirty-two

Figure 14-2 *(a)* Silkworms feeding on mulberry leaves. *(b)* Close-up of silkworm eating a mulberry leaf. *(Courtesy The Japan Silk Association, Inc.)*

days. During this period, the tiny worm has a voracious appetite. It is fed 5 times a day on chopped mulberry leaves (see Figure 14-2). After four changes of skin, or moltings, the worm reaches full growth in the form of a smooth grayish-white caterpillar about $3\frac{1}{2}$ inches long. Its interest in food ceases. It shrinks somewhat in size and acquires a pinkish hue, becoming nearly transparent. A constant restless rearing movement of the head indicates that the worm is ready to spin its cocoon. Racks, clusters of twigs, or straw are provided for this purpose (Figure 14-3).

Of importance to the silk industry is the small opening under the caterpillar's jaws, called the *spinneret*. The silkworm begins to secrete a proteinlike substance through its spinneret, and with a bending motion, the filament is spun around the worm in the form of the figure eight (see Figure 14-4). The silkworm is hidden from view within twenty-four hours; in three days, the cocoon is completed. It is about the size and shape of a peanut shell. The filament is in the form of a double strand or *fibroin*, which is held together by a gummy substance called

Figure 14-3 *(a)* Silkworms on a cocooning apparatus. *(b)* Cocoons on cocooning apparatus. *(Courtesy The Japan Silk Association, Inc.)*

sericin, or *silk gum.* The liquid substance hardens immediately on exposure to the air. If left undisturbed, the chrysalis inside the cocoon develops into a moth within two weeks. To emerge, the moth must break through the top of the cocoon

Figure 14-4   Close-up of silkworm spinning the cocoon around itself. *(Courtesy The Japan Silk Association, Inc.)*

Figure 14-5   Removing the cocoons from nests in preparation for stoving. *(Courtesy International Silk Guild)*

by secreting an alkaline liquid that dissolves the filament. As this cutting through damages the cocoon so that the filament cannot be unwound in one long thread, the life cycle is terminated at this point by a process known as *stoving*, or *stifling*. The cocoons are heated to suffocate the chrysalis, but the delicate silk filament is not harmed (Figure 14-5).

FILATURE OPERATIONS

The cocoons that are raised by silk farmers are delivered to a factory, called a *filature*, where the silk is unwound from the cocoons and the strands are collected into skeins. Some cocoons are scientifically bred in such factories.

Sorting Cocoons

The cocoons are sorted according to color, size, shape, and texture, as all these affect the final quality of the silk (Figure 14-6). Cocoons may range from white or yellow to grayish, depending on the source and the type of food consumed during the worm stage. Cocoons from China are white; Japanese cocoons

are creamy white and yellow; Italian cocoons are yellow.

Softening the Sericin

After the cocoons have been sorted, they are put through a series of hot and cold immersions, as the sericin must be softened to permit the unwinding of the filament as one continuous thread. Raw

Figure 14-6   Sorting cocoons. *(Courtesy International Silk Association, Inc.)*

silk consists of about 80 percent fibroin and 20 percent sericin. At this time, only about 1 percent of the sericin is removed, because this silk gum is a needed protection during the further handling of the delicate filament.

Reeling the Filament

The process of unwinding the filament from the cocoon is called *reeling.* The care and skill used in the reeling operation prevent defects in the raw silk. As the filament of a single cocoon is too fine for commercial use, three to ten strands are usually reeled at a time to produce the desired diameter of raw silk thread. The cocoons float in water, bobbing up and down, as the filaments are drawn upward through porcelain eyelets and are rapidly wound on wheels or drums while the operator watches to detect flaws. As the reeling of the filament from each cocoon nears completion, operators attach a new filament to the moving thread. Skilled operators have an uncanny ability to blend the filaments, while always retaining the same diameter of the rapidly moving silk strand. The sericin acts as an adhesive. It aids in holding the several filaments together while they are combined to form the single thread. On old-style reeling machines at high speed, an operator could handle five to seven threads, and on the newest models, twenty-five threads.

The usable length of the reeled filament is from 1,000 to 2,000 feet, approximately a quarter of a mile long. The remaining part of the filament is used as valuable raw material for the manufacture of spun silk.

The term "reeled silk" is applied to the raw silk strand that is formed by combining several filaments from separate cocoons. The diameter of the silk fiber is so fine that an estimated 3,000 cocoons are required to produce a yard of silk fabric. The silk filaments are reeled into skeins, which are packed in small bundles called *books*, weighing 5 to 10 pounds. These books are put into bales, weighing about 133.33 pounds. In this form, the raw silk is shipped to all parts of the world (Figure 14-7).

MANUFACTURE OF SILK YARNS

From the filature, the books of reeled silk are put through the following manufacturing processes.

Silk Throwing

Reeled silk is transformed into silk yarn —also called silk thread—by a process known as *throwing*. The term is derived from the Anglo-Saxon word "thrawn," meaning "to twist." Persons engaged in this work are called *throwsters*. Silk throwing is analogous to the spinning process that manufactures cotton, linen, or wool fibers into yarn. Unlike those fibers, the manufacture of silk yarn does not include the processes for producing a continuous yarn by carding, combing, and drawing out. The raw silk skeins are sorted according to size, color, and length or quantity, then soaked in warm water with soap or oil. This softening of the sericin aids in handling the thread. After mechanical drying, the skeins are placed on light reels from which the silk is wound on bobbins.

During this winding operation, single strands may be given any desired amount of twist. If two or more yarns are to be doubled, they are twisted again

Figure 14-7 *(a)* Reeling silk cocoons. *(Courtesy The Japan Silk Association, Inc.) (b)* Skeins of reeled silk. *(c)* Books of reeled silk. *(Photos Courtesy The Central Raw Silk Association of Japan)*

in the same direction or in a reverse direction, depending on the kind of thread to be made. To equalize the diameter, the thread is run through rollers. The thread is then inspected and packaged and is ready for shipment to manufacturers for construction into fabric.

Kinds of Thrown Silk Threads. Several kinds of silk yarns, or threads, are used in the manufacture of silk goods. The type of yarn and the amount of twist depend on what the weaver desires.

Singles. Usually, three to eight strands of silk filaments are twisted together in one direction to form a yarn called a *single*. Loose-twist singles, having two or three twists per inch, are used primarily for the filling yarns in many silk fabrics. Hard-twist singles, having a much greater number of twists per inch, are used in the sheer fabrics (see Figure 14-8*a*).

Tram. Tram is used only as a filling yarn. Usually, two to four untwisted singles are combined with only a slight twist of about three to five turns per inch. The number of turns may be increased for especially heavy silk fabrics. Tram is rarely twisted more than five turns to the inch, except in such fabrics as radium and taffeta, which use a special hard-twisted tram of about thirty turns per inch (Figure 14-8*b*).

Voile. This yarn is used for such sheer crepes as voile. It is composed of three untwisted singles combined with thirty-five to forty S turns per inch (Figure 14-8*c*).

Figure 14-8 Types of thrown silk yarns. "Turns" means turns per inch.

Georgette or Crepe de Chine. This yarn is composed of two untwisted singles combined with a very hard S or Z twist of seventy to seventy-five turns per inch. The result is a very fine, strong, elastic yarn used for warp yarns and for such sheer fabrics as georgette or crepe de chine (Figure 14-8d).

Organzine. Organzine is used primarily for warp yarns. It is composed of two or more singles, each of which has sixteen Z turns per inch. These singles are then combined by twisting them around each other in the opposite S twist, twelve to twenty turns per inch, which causes them to interlock more tightly, resulting in a firmer, stronger yarn (Figure 14-8e).

Grenadine. This yarn is composed of three to five singles, each given a twist of about thirty-six Z turns per inch, then combined by being twisted around each other in the opposite S direction, twenty-five to thirty-five turns per inch. Although these yarns have a high twist, they are nevertheless fine and are used for such sheer fabrics as organdy and grenadine (Figure 14-8f).

Two by Two (Grenadine Type). Each of two pairs of untwisted singles is twisted about thirty-six Z turns per inch, then twisted around the other twenty-five to thirty-five turns in the S direction. These yarns are consequently much like the grenadine yarns but are heavier. Their weight, body, and high twist make them desirable for crepe fabrics (Figure 14-8g).

Compensene S. This yarn is made of each of two pairs of untwisted singles. One pair is twisted together forty to forty-five S turns per inch; the other is twisted the same number of Z turns per inch. These twisted pairs are then twisted around each other five S turns per inch. The opposing directions of these twists prevent kinking but give elasticity. These yarns are often used for knitted fabrics (Figure 14-8h).

Crepe. Some crepe fabrics are made of crepe yarns. These yarns are composed of each of two pairs of untwisted singles. One pair is twisted sixty to eighty-five turns per inch in the S direction; the other is twisted the same number of turns per inch in the Z direction. They are then twisted around each other two and one-half to five S turns per inch (see Figure 14-8i).

Yarn Count of Thrown Silk. The size or the yarn count of silk threads is based on a system of weight known as *denier*. A denier represents a weight of 5 centigrams—that is, 0.05 or $1/20$ gram. The standard length of a raw silk skein is 450 meters. A 450-meter skein weighing $1/20$ gram contains a 1-denier thread, which is an extremely fine thread. To find the denier of 450 meters of silk thread weighing 70 centigrams (the usual weight of skeins from Japan), divide 70 centigrams by 0.05, or $1/20$, gram. The result is 14. The denier is expressed as 13/15 to allow for variation in the diameter of the thread.

In the laboratory, the denier size of a silk thread is obtained by a different method of figuring. The weight of a 450-meter skein is multiplied by 20 because 20 denier equals 1 gram (since 1 denier equals $1/20$ gram). For example, if the 450-meter skein weighs 2.16 grams, multiplying this weight by 20 gives 43.2

denier, which is expressed as 42/44 denier, to allow for variation.

The most common size of raw silk from Japan is 13/15 denier, which is as fine as a 350s cotton yarn. In the spring crop, a 13/15 denier requires four to five cocoons to a thread, whereas the summer and autumn crops require five to six cocoons to the thread. As each cocoon comprises two filaments, a 13/15 denier may contain eight to ten or ten to twelve filaments, depending on the season. The greater the number of cocoons used, the coarser the thread and the higher the denier.

Degumming

Thrown silk threads still contain some sericin that must be removed in another soap bath to bring out the natural luster and the soft feel of the silk. As much as 25 percent of the weight is lost by the degumming process. When the gum has been removed, the silk fiber or fabric is a creamy white color, beautifully lustrous, and luxuriantly soft.

Degumming may take place after the silk thread is thrown in order to prepare it for yarn dyeing, or it may be done in any finishing process after the fabric is woven. For example, the tightly twisted yarns used for crepe effects still contain sericin. A small amount of sericin is sometimes left in the yarn or in the fabric to give the finished product added strength or a dull finish. Ecru and souple are examples of silk fabrics from which sericin has been partially removed.

Spun Silk

Short lengths of inferior silk filaments obtained from waste material are not used in producing reeled silk. After the short lengths have been carded and combed, they are spun together much as cotton, linen, or wool yarns are spun. Spun silk threads are soft, but they are less lustrous than reeled silk and are not as strong or elastic. Spun silk fabric tends to become fuzzy after wearing because the yarn is made of short staple.

There are several sources of staple silk: (1) pierced cocoons, the result of breeding moths that have emerged from their cocoons; (2) double cocoons, the result of two cocoons having been spun by two silkworms too close together (sometimes called *douppioni silk*); (3) floss, brushed from cocoons before reeling; (4) frison, the coarse and uneven silk fiber at the beginning and end of each cocoon; (5) scrap, the machine waste left from reeling, throwing, and the like.

Spun silk is less expensive than reeled silk. Although spun silk has less strength and elasticity than reeled silk because of the shorter staple used, it possesses all the general characteristics of reeled silk. Tub silk fabric, for example, is made of spun silk, yet it gives good service when the quality of the fiber is good. Spun silk is used for shantung and pile fabrics; for dress trimmings, linings, elastic webbing, and sewing silk; for summer wash silks, velvets, umbrella fabrics, and insulative materials.

The waste derived from the processing of spun silk yarn is also used. The Trade Practice Rules of the Federal Trade Commission require that such fiber be labeled as *waste silk*, *silk waste*, *noil silk*, or *silk noil*. For obvious reasons, the last two designations are most frequently used. Silk noil may be reprocessed into spun yarn and woven into

textured fabrics for draperies, upholstery, and sportswear. These fabrics are
dull, rough, have a cottonlike appearance, but are generally more resilient.

Yarn Count of Spun Silk. The method of
determining the size of spun silk thread
is similar to that used for cotton yarn. In
cotton, the term "2/60s" signifies a two-
ply yarn consisting of two single strands
twisted together, each having a yarn
count of 60.

In spun silk, a two-ply yarn is indicated by the figures "60s/2." Although
this term appears to be only the reverse
of the cotton term, it does not mean the
same. In spun silk, 60s/2 means that two
yarns with a separate yarn count of 120
have been doubled, producing a ply yarn
with a new count of 60.

FINISHING SILK FABRICS

As with other textiles, silk fabrics may
be given a variety of finishes. There is
one finish, though, that is unique to silk.
It is weighting.

Weighting

The amount of weight that silk loses in
the degumming process is an appreciable
factor in manufacturing costs because
the manufacturer buys silk by weight.
As is customary in any business, the
price of the finished product must offset
this loss; therefore, silk has always been
an expensive fabric. The weighting of
silk fabric with metallic substances to
make up for the weight lost by degumming is an accepted practice in the silk
industry. This procedure lowers the cost
of silk to the consumer.

Weighted silk is less compactly
woven than unweighted silk and less silk
is used in the construction of the cloth.
In other words, weighting rather than
compact construction can give firmness
and body to a silk fabric. Weighting is
done during the dyeing process. To
weight colored silks, stannic chloride is
used, followed by treatment with sodium
phosphate. Black silks are weighted with
metallic mordants, such as iron salt and
logwood.

A small amount of metallic weighting, correctly applied to a fabric that is
well woven to hold the weighting, is not
considered injurious. In addition to low-
ering the cost, it is claimed that weighting gives silk crispness, luster, and
firmer body and feel. When weighted silk
is pleated, the crease is retained.
Weighted silk, however, loses the natural elasticity of the silk fiber and is subject to deterioration when exposed to
sunlight, perspiration, and dry cleaning. When the fabric is not properly constructed, threads shift. If the fabric is
not woven sufficiently wide to allow for
natural shrinkage, there is an unsatisfactory amount of shrinkage.

Taffeta is a commonly used fabric
that is usually heavily weighted, because today there is little demand for
pure-dye taffeta. Weighted taffeta is apt
to crack and split at the places subjected to the strain of wear and folded
for a length of time. (Rayon and acetate
taffeta do not contain any metallic
weighting.) Because the consumer cannot determine the percentage of weighting in a silk fabric, the Federal Trade
Commission ruled in 1938 that weighted
silk must be labeled, and the percentage
of weighting must be indicated.

Additional Finishing Processes

There is a variety of other finishes applied to silk fabrics to enhance their appearance, hand, or serviceability. The major finishes are as follows:

Singeing—for smoothness

Bleaching—very little is required for silk that is completely degummed

Stiffening—for body

Embossing—if such patterns as moiré are desired

Calendering—for enhancing luster

Ciréing—for body and luster

Water repellency—for use as rainwear

Steaming—for raising pile weaves

Wringing and stretching—for softening the fiber and increasing the luster

Pressing and lustering—for removing wrinkles from finished fabric with heated rollers, then soaking in dilute acid to develop luster

For more detailed information the reader is referred to Chapter 8.

PURE-DYE SILK

As silk is weighted during the dyeing process, the term "pure-dye silk" indicates that weighting was not added at that time. According to the Federal Trade Commission rulings, pure-dye silk is defined as a fabric made exclusively of silk fibers containing "no metallic weighting whatsoever." But the use of such water-soluble substances as starch, glue, sugar, or gelatin in the dyeing and finishing processes is allowed. Such foreign substances are limited to 10 percent for white or colored silks and 15 percent for black silks. Well-constructed pure-dye silk requires a greater amount of silk thread than weighted silk because pure-dye silk is usually more compact. Thus it is generally superior, having the qualities of elasticity and durability, because the natural elasticity of the silk fiber has not been lessened, and its great natural strength has been retained.

WILD SILK

The silkworms that hatch from a wild species of moth, the *Antheraea mylitta*, live on oak leaves instead of mulberry leaves that form the food of the cultivated species. This coarser food produces an irregular and coarse filament that is hard to bleach and hard to dye. The tannin in the oak leaves gives wild silk its tan color, and the silk is commonly woven with the naturally colored thread; it is rarely dyed except in solid shades. Wild silk is less lustrous than cultivated silk, as only a low percentage (about 11 percent) of sericin is removed in the degumming process. Wild silk fabrics are durable and have a coarse, irregular surface. They are washable and are generally less expensive than pure-dye silk. Typical fabrics are *rajah*, *shantung*, *tussah*, and *pongee*.

The standard wild silk thread differs from the standard reeled silk thread in size, as it is made from eighteen cocoons. It averages 32/34 denier.

TSUMUGI SILK

There are several varieties of silk fabrics made in various parts of Japan that are produced by hand in cottage industry. One of the somewhat better known is tsumugi silk. It is made in central Honshu, the large main island of Japan. Tsumugi is characterized by its yarn-dyed striped or plaid patterns. It has a somewhat coarse, homespun quality and handsome appearance.

EVALUATING SILK FABRICS

In spite of its high cost, silk has been one of the most popular fabrics because of its unique properties. Soft, supple, strong, and lighter in weight than any other natural fiber, silk is prized for its lightness with warmth, sheerness with strength, and delicacy with resiliency.

Strength. Silk is the strongest natural fiber. The continuous length of the filaments in thrown yarns provides a factor of strength above what is possible with short natural fibers. The smoothness of the silk filament yarns reduces the problem of wear from abrasion. The inherent strength of silk along with its fine diameter and lightness has made it a highly desirable fiber for sheer yet durable fabrics. The strength of silk fabric is also affected, of course, by its construction as well as its finish.

Spun silk yarn, though strong, is weaker than thrown silk filament yarns. The quality of spun silk depends upon the source of the staple. Douppioni and pierced-cocoon silk are generally stronger than the other silk staple, which tend to be less uniform.

Elasticity. While silk is an elastic fiber, its elasticity varies, as may be expected of a natural fiber. Silk fiber may be stretched from $1/7$ to $1/5$ its original length before breaking. It returns to its original size gradually and loses little of its elasticity. This characteristic means less binding and sagging, thus contributing to the wearer's comfort. It should be kept in mind that the elasticity of the yarn and the fabric is affected by the kind of yarn used (thrown or spun), the construction of the fabric, and the finish that it is given.

Resilience. Silk fabrics retain their shape and resist wrinkling rather well. This is particularly true of the fabrics made from pure-dye silk and from wild silk. Fabrics that contain a large percentage of weighting or are made from short-staple spun silk have less resilience.

Heat Conductivity. Like wool, silk is a protein fiber; therefore, it is also a nonconductor of heat. Because silk prevents body heat from radiating outward, it is desirable for winter apparel, including scarves. Thin silk fabrics are also comfortably warm when used for lingerie, pajamas, robes, and linings. The warmth-giving quality is lessened by weighting because the metallic content causes the fabric to become a conductor of heat.

A question often raised is why silk is used for summer fabrics when it is a nonconductor of heat. The answer is that silk, being fine and strong, may be made into very fine yarns and woven into very sheer fabrics. This permits the body heat and the air to pass freely through the open construction of such cloth.

Drapability. Silk has a pliability and suppleness that, aided by its elasticity and resilience, give it excellent drapability. (See Figure 14-9.)

Absorbency. The good absorptive property of silk also contributes to its comfort in a warmer atmosphere. Silk fiber can generally absorb about 11 percent of its weight in moisture, but the range varies from 10 percent to as much as 30 percent. This property is also a major factor in silk's ability to be printed and dyed easily.

Cleanliness and Washability. Silk is a hygienic material because its smooth surface does not attract dirt. When dirt does gather, it is given up readily by washing or dry cleaning. Care should be exercised in laundering silk—always use a mild soap. Wringing or strong agitation in the washing machine should be avoided, as silk weakens slightly when wet.

All silks water-spot easily, but subsequent washing or dry cleaning will restore the appearance of the fabric, unless it has a special finish. Taffeta, for example, may be given a finish that could be permanently stained by water. Dry cleaning is preferable for weighted silks, but wild-silk and spun-silk fabrics may be washed.

Reaction to Bleaches. Strong bleaches containing sodium hypochlorite will deteriorate silk. A mild bleach of hydrogen peroxide or sodium perborate may be used with normal caution.

Shrinkage. Because of the straightness of the filament, smooth-surfaced silk

Figure 14-9 Silk is used to best advantage for styles where draping is very important, such as for these kimonos. Women in this Japanese department store are being taught to arrange a kimono. *(Courtesy Japan Trade Center, N.Y.)*

fabrics have only a normal shrinkage, which is easily restored by ironing. Crepe effects shrink considerably in washing, but careful ironing with a moderately hot iron will restore the fabric to its original size.

Effect of Heat. Silk is somewhat sensitive to heat. It will begin to decompose at 330 degrees Fahrenheit; therefore, it should be ironed while damp with a warm iron.

Effect of Light. Continuous exposure to light weakens silk faster than either cotton or wool. Raw silk is more resistant to light than degummed silk, and weighted silk has the least light resistance. Silk drapery and upholstery fabrics should be protected from direct exposure to the light.

Resistance to Mildew. Silk will not mildew unless left for some time in a damp state of under the extreme conditions of tropical dampness.

Resistance to Moths. Silk is not attacked by moths.

Reaction to Alkalies. Silk is not as sensitive as wool is to alkalies, but can be damaged if the concentration and temperature are high enough. Use mild soap in lukewarm water when laundering.

Reaction to Acids. Concentrated mineral acids will dissolve silk faster than wool. Organic acids do not harm silk.

Resistance to Perspiration. Silk fabrics are damaged by perspiration. The silk itself deteriorates, and the color is affected, causing staining. Garments worn next to the skin should be washed or otherwise cleaned after each wearing.

Affinity for Dyes. Silk has a very good affinity for dyes. It readily absorbs basic, acid, and direct dyes. Prints on silk are taken so well that the color on the back of the fabric often differs only slightly from the face.

Dyed silk is colorfast under most conditions, but its resistance to light is unsatisfactory. The resistance of weighted silk is particularly poor; therefore, silk is not recommended for window curtains. Pure-dye silks may be redyed by the consumer, provided a suitable commercial dye is used and the directions on the container are followed.

REVIEW QUESTIONS

1. (a) Name the silk-producing countries. (b) What is the cultivation of silk called?
2. Describe the life cycle of the silkworm.
3. What process in the production of silk is analogous to the spinning process for other fibers?
4. Describe the degumming process and its effects on various types of silk fabrics.
5. What is the difference between weighted silk and pure-dye silk?
6. (a) Why is silk weighted? (b) What are the advantages of weighting? (c) What are the disadvantages?
7. What is spun silk?
8. (a) How does wild silk differ from cultivated silk? (b) How does the difference affect the consumer?
9. Why are most wild-silk fabrics tan in color?
10. Name some fabrics usually made from wild silk.
11. For what purpose is pongee most desirable?
12. What finishing processes are given to silk fabrics?
13. Why is silk not recommended for window curtains?

14. For what purpose would you select silk rather than other fabrics? Why?

15. List the essential qualities of silk, and show the effects of each quality on finished goods.

SUGGESTED ACTIVITY

Make a chart comparing the properties of the natural fibers: cotton, linen, wool, silk.

15

RAYONS: THREE BASIC VARIETIES

the regenerated cellulosic fibers

A rayon fiber is composed of pure cellulose, the substance of which the cell walls of such woody plants as trees and cotton are largely comprised (see Figure 15-1). We are already familiar with cellulose in the form of such products as paper.

Rayon fibers are made from cellulose that has been re-formed, or *regenerated*; consequently, these fibers are identified as *regenerated cellulosic fibers*.

HISTORY OF RAYONS

The production of a fiber such as rayon, the first of the man-made fibers, had been prophesied as long ago as 1664 by Robert Hooke, the English naturalist. He believed that it was possible to make an "artificial glutinous composition, much resembling, if not full as good, nay better, than that excrement, or whatever other substance it be out of which the silkworm wire-draws his clew." In 1710, René A. de Réaumur, the French scientist, suggested the possibility of making silk filaments out of gums and resins; for example, threads of varnish.

One hundred and thirty years later, in 1840, an apparatus was invented that drew synthetic filaments through small holes. In 1855, Georges Audemars, a Swiss chemist, discovered how to make cellulose nitrate. This was the first step toward the nitrocellulose process of making rayon. Almost thirty years later, in

Figure 15-1 Wood pulp and cotton are the sources of pure cellulose used to produce rayon fiber. (*Courtesy American Viscose Corp.*)

1884, Count Hilaire de Chardonnet produced the first synthetic textile fibers from nitrocellulose. He became known as the "father of rayon." Chardonnet obtained the original French patent and won the financial support that built the world's first rayon factory. These and other chemists of their day, as well as those who are constantly experimenting today on new fibers, have been guided by a desire to produce beautiful, smooth, light, supple fabrics with just the right amount of luster—the characteristics for which silk has long been noted—at a price within the income of every consumer.

Man-made textile filaments were officially recognized in 1925, when the Federal Trade Commission permitted the use of the name "rayon" for yarns obtained from cellulose or its derivatives. As the production and types of man-made fibers had increased and been given various trademarks, the Federal Trade Commission ruled again in 1937 that any fiber or yarn produced chemically from cellulose must be designated as *rayon*.

Over the period of the next fifteen years, however, confusion developed among garment manufacturers, and particularly among consumers, because there were as many as four different types of rayon with some similar and some different properties. Some rayons would fade faster than others; some would dry more quickly than others; some would stick to the iron and melt, others would iron nicely. The cause of this lay in the fact that there were basically two groups of rayons: one consisting of regenerated pure cellulose, the other of a cellulose compound. These different compositions gave different properties. The Federal Trade Commission therefore ruled that as of February 9, 1952, there would be two categories of cellulosic fibers: rayon and acetate. All fabrics and garments containing rayon and/or acetate must now be labeled as such and the percent of content of each fiber indicated. The rules also incorporated the first official designation of rayon and acetate products as man-made rather than synthetic. In the chemist's terminology, rayon and acetate are not synthetic because natural materials—cotton linters and wood pulp —are used in their manufacture, rather than chemical elements.

BASIC METHOD OF PRODUCING RAYON FILAMENT

The natural process by which the silkworm transforms the cellulose of mulberry trees into two fine filaments is simulated in the process of making rayon.

A liquid substance of cellulose is forced through a metal cap or nozzle about the size of a thimble. This nozzle is called a *spinneret* because it performs the same function as the silkworm's spinneret (see Figure 15-2). The cap is usually made of a platinum-rhodium alloy because that metal is not affected by acids or alkalies; it is perforated with small holes that are almost invisible to the naked eye. Through each of the tiny holes, a filament is extruded, which is solidified by a liquid bath as it comes from the spinneret. This is similar to the hardening by air of the raw-silk substance spun by the silkworm. The number of holes in the spinneret ranges from 1 to 20,000, and filaments of equal

Figure 15-2 The spinneret that forms the spinning solution into filaments. *(Courtesy American Viscose Corp.)*

size are simultaneously produced. In a subsequent operation, these filaments are combined by twisting to make any required diameter of rayon yarn.

TYPES OF RAYON

Although Chardonnet produced the first man-made textile fibers from nitrocellulose over ninety years ago, the nitrocellulose process is no longer a factor in the world production of rayon. Today there are three principal methods of making rayon. The fibers differ in important characteristics because the methods differ in specific features of manufacture.   These rayons—viscose, cuprammonium, and high wet-modulus—are classified as regenerated rayons because the original raw material (cellulose) is changed chemically into another form, which is then changed (regenerated) into cellulose again. These changes produce the final product — purified cellulose in fiber form.

VISCOSE RAYON

THE VISCOSE PROCESS

Viscose rayon is made from cotton fiber or wood pulp usually obtained from spruce, hemlock, and pine trees. The chemical process of dissolving wood pulp was first discovered in 1840 by F. G. Keller, a noted German weaver. The viscose method of using wood pulp to manufacture rayon was developed in 1892, more than fifty years later, by C. F. Cross and E. J. Bevan, both English scientists. The first viscose manufacturing plant in the United States was established in 1910.

In the viscose process, wood chips or cotton fibers are treated to produce sheets of purified cellulose that resemble white blotters. The cellulose sheets are then soaked in caustic soda, producing sheets of alkali cellulose. This substance is broken up into fluffy white flakes or grains called *cellulose crumbs*, which are aged for two or three days under controlled temperature and humidity. Liquid carbon disulfide is then added. This turns the cellulose into cellulose xanthate, a light-orange substance that is still in crumb form. The cellulose xanthate crumbs are dissolved in a weak solution of caustic soda and transformed into a thick viscous solution called *viscose*, resembling honey in color and consistency (see Figure 15-3). If the rayon is to be delustered, titanium dioxide is added at this point. The viscose is aged, filtered, and vacuum-treated to remove air bubbles, as they would cause the filament to break. It is then forced through the holes of the spinneret into sulfuric

Figure 15-3 (a) To regenerate the cellulose for the viscose rayon process, cellulose sheets are soaked in caustic soda to produce alkali cellulose. (b) Alkali cellulose crumbs are poured into a vat to be soaked in carbon disulfide, thus forming cellulose xanthate. (c) The cellulose xanthate crumbs are removed from the vat to be dissolved in weak caustic soda. (Courtesy American Enka Co.)

acid, which coagulates the cellulose of the soluble cellulose xanthate to form pure regenerated cellulose filaments.

Controlled variations in certain characteristics of viscose rayon are possible. It has been noted that the luster can be regulated from *bright* to *semidull* or *dull*, depending upon the amount of delustering agent that is added to the viscose solution before extrusion through the spinneret. Dyes may be added to the solution to produce solution-dyed filaments which have a high degree of color permanency. Variations in the chemical composition of the coagulating bath cause different rates of coagulation on the inside and the outside of the fiber that result in variations in the thickness of the skin of the fiber; this in turn provides a *latent crimp* that will emerge when the fiber is immersed in water. The diameter of the fiber may be varied to give a thick-and-thin effect by changing the pump pressure and drawing off the filaments as they are extruded. The shape of the spinneret holes may be varied to change the appearance of the fiber. The strength, or *tenacity*, of the fiber may be increased by inducing thicker skin and even all-skin and by aligning the molecules through stretching to produce medium-tenacity fiber and the high-tenacity rayon for such purposes as tire cord. These variations in production techniques have increased the versatility of rayon and have made viscose the major type of rayon used.

YARN PRODUCTION

Upon extrusion from the spinneret, the viscose rayon fibers are processed by one of several methods into filament or spun staple yarns (Figure 15-4).

Processing

There are three methods of processing the viscose rayon into filament as the fiber is extruded.

Pot, or Box, Spinning. The filaments are removed from the coagulating bath by being passed over a series of godet wheels. The resultant slight tension on the fibers causes a certain amount of molecular alignment and consequent strengthening of the filaments. The fibers are led through a funnel moving up and down in a covered cylinder called a *Topham box*, which whirls around and builds by centrifugal force a hollow cake of filament against the cylinder's wall. This action also gives the filaments a slight uniform twist. After the cake is removed, it is thoroughly washed, treated to remove any trace of residual chemical substances, bleached, rinsed, dried, and wound on spools.

Spool Spinning. The filaments may be drawn from the coagulating bath over guides and rollers and wound on perforated spools. A washing solution is forced through the spools' holes to cleanse filaments that are then bleached, rinsed, dried, and wound on cones or spools or put in skeins (Figure 15-5).

Continuous Process. Upon extrusion from the spinneret, the filaments may be carried in one continuous process over the godet wheels through a series of reels as they are washed, purified, bleached, dried, twisted, finished, and wound onto the desired package for the particular desired use. (This process is not included on the schematic shown in Figure 15-4.)

Filament Yarns

The rayon filament yarns are processed in a manner similar to thrown silk yarns. The filaments can be thrown, or twisted, as indicated in the pot and continuous spinning processes, or they may be thrown after being received in spool form.

The count of rayon yarn is expressed in denier, the unit of weight explained in Chapter 14. The denier of rayon yarn is controlled by the number and the size of holes in the spinneret. The number of denier required to weigh one skein of yarn, 450 meters long (the standard length), is the denier that indicates the size of the yarn in that skein. Because the sizes of yarns differ according to the purposes for which the yarns are intended, the weights of the skeins differ even though the skeins are of the standard length. The finer the yarn, the less

Figure 15-4 Production of viscose rayon yarn. *(Courtesy American Enka Co.)*

the skein weighs, and the lower the figure that expresses its weight in denier.

Monofilament Yarns. The monofilament yarns are composed of a single filament. The viscous solution is extruded through a spinneret with only one hole. Spinnerets, each with a different-sized hole, are used, depending on the denier of yarn desired. Monofilament yarn is used for a variety of products, including hosiery. The term "monofil" is applied to a type of monofilament yarn used in the millinery industry as a substitute for horsehair, which has limited use because of its short length.

Multifilament Yarns. The multifilament yarns are composed of more than one filament, usually a great many twisted together. These filaments are extremely fine, supple, pliable, and stronger than monofilament yarns of the same denier.

They are used for a wide variety of fabrics including sheers. The continuous-filament yarns may be used to produce smooth fabrics or creped-surface fabrics, depending upon the amount of twist given to the yarns.

Viscose rayon multifilament yarns to be used for apparel and upholstery fabrics are composed of 10 to 980 filaments, which may vary from 1 to 6 denier each. Thus, when 40 or more filaments are combined, the yarns will vary from 40 to 240 denier. A yarn designated as 100/40 would be 100 denier and be composed of 40 filaments (see Figure 15-6a).

Spun Yarns

The filament yarns can be adapted for other effects by reducing them to short lengths, usually 1 to 6 inches, and spinning the staple similarly to the spinning of cotton or wool. The counts of spun rayon yarns conform to the base of the system used; for example, count No. 1 would be 1 pound drawn 840 yards on the cotton system, 1,600 yards on the woolen system, and 560 yards on the worsted system. In each of these systems, of course, the higher the count, the finer the spun yarn (see Figure 15-6*b*).

Both conventional and direct spinning methods are used.

Conventional Spinning. Filaments ranging from 1.5 to 50 denier each may be gathered from the spool spinning process into a group, or *tow*, of 600 to 250,000 filaments. The tow may then be precision-cut while wet into predetermined lengths, washed, purified, bleached, rinsed, and dried. As the staple dries, it shrinks somewhat and develops a degree of crimp that facilitates later processing into yarn.

Some rayon fiber manufacturers process the tow through washing, purifying, bleaching, rinsing, drying, and then dry-cutting into predetermined staple lengths. This method has the disadvantage of producing uncrimped staple, but it permits production of staple as needed from stored tow. It also permits fiber processors, such as yarn manufacturers, to cut as much staple as they may need (Figure 15-7).

Depending upon the kind of yarn desired, the staple must be spun on a cot-

Figure 15-5 (*a*) The filaments of spool-spun viscose rayon are twisted and wound on cones. (*b*) In spool spinning, the coagulated viscose is drawn over guides and rollers and wound on a revolving spool. (*c*) Spools of viscose pass through the tunnel drier after being bleached and rinsed. (*d*) The pot-spun yarn is washed by pumping the washing solution through the hollow cake from the center to the outside. (*Courtesy American Enka Co.*)

Figure 15-6 *(a)* A cake of long-filament rayon yarn. *(b)* Staple fibers from which spun yarn is made. *(Photos Courtesy FMC Corporation)*

ton, woolen, or worsted system. The process conforms to the description of these methods of opening, breaking, carding, combing, and so forth, as described in Chapters 3 and 13.

Such spun rayon yarns have a different character from the filament rayon yarns. According to the amount of twist inserted in the spinning process, spun rayon yarn can be made stronger, less lustrous, and adaptable to napping and other finishes, producing fabrics that resemble wool, linen, or cotton. Such short-staple rayon can also be combined with any of the other fibers to make effective and useful fabrics. This blending would not be possible with the long rayon filament. Thus, spun rayon provides new finishes and a variety of low-priced fabrics that formerly were made only from natural fibers.

Direct Spinning. A more economical method of producing spun yarn is to reduce the filaments in the tow to staple without disturbing the parallelism of the fibers. This eliminates the need for opening and breaking, and since the fibers

Figure 15-7 The operating sequence of a staple cutter is as follows: (A) Reel of tow; (B) Top pull roll under spring pressure; (C) Bottom pull roll; (D) Adjusting screw for top pull roll; (E) Adjusting screw for top tension roll; (F) Top tension roll; (G) Bottom tension roll; (H) Bed knife adjusting screw; (I) Bed knife with hardened insert; (J) Rotating cutterhead, with eight fly knives making a shearing cut across the fiber; (K) Discharge chute with flanged outlet for air suction. *(Courtesy Taylor, Stiles & Co.)*

Figure 15-8 *(a)* The photograph of the Pacific Converter shows tows (left) being combined and passed under cutter roll (center), then through draft and shuffling sections (center) to diagonal roll (right), then crimped (right) and into coiler can (right). *(b)* Schematic of the Pacific Converter. *(Courtesy Warner and Swasey Co.)*

are of desired length and have no foreign matter or neps, the carding and combing operations are also unnecessary. There are three basic methods of accomplishing this:

1. The tow may be processed through such machines as the Pacific Converter (other machines are the Greenfield and the Campbell), which cuts the filament into either uniform or varied lengths of up to 6 inches. This method permits blending with other fibers and produces a crimped sliver, as described in the schematic in Figure 15-8. The sliver is then passed along for further processing into cotton, woolen, or worsted-type yarn of high quality with excellent uniformity of evenness and count.

Figure 15-9   The schematic diagram shows how the Turbo Stapler reduces tow to sliver in one machine by the Perlok principle. This action takes place in the breaking zone and may be described as a modified, controlled-stretch breaking process. To understand the process, visualize a single fiber-end as it leaves the intermediate nip rolls. It passes between the breaker bars and approaches the front roll nip, being carried under practically no tension by adjacent fibers. As it enters the front rolls, tension is suddenly applied and a break occurs in the area of stress concentration created by the abrasive breaker strips. This fiber, now reduced to staple length, is rapidly carried through the front rolls. The original end, from which it came, is again carried toward the front rolls, and the process repeats. Each end in the tow is exposed to the same process, but the breaks occur at different, perfectly random times. There are, therefore, no coterminal fibers, and evenness and parallelism are excellent. (*Courtesy Turbo Machine Co.*)

2. The tow filaments may be broken into staple by the Perlok process. The technique is the same as that described on page 86 for the production of high-bulk yarn. Figure 15-9 indicates the movement of the tow through the breaking zone where tension is applied suddenly between the break bars and the front rolls, which causes the individual filaments to break at their weakest points. This results in random breakage of the fiber into staple without disturbing their parallelism. The process is repeated as the staple is moved along to a crimper, where it emerges as crimped sliver. The sliver is then spun into yarn using any one of the desired spinning systems.

3. Another technique of reducing tow to staple is based upon the Perlok process but uses the Direct Spinner (Figure 15-10). This method is in much less use because the staple and yarn produced have certain limitations, as will be noted in the following description.

Tow is fed from one set of rolls onto a conveyor belt, then to a second set of rolls moving at a higher rate of speed. The tension created by this difference in speed and the grip exerted by the faster rolls cause the random breakage of the

HEAT STRETCH	CUTTING	DEBONDING
Heat stretched tow and relaxed tow enter simultaneously to form a proportionate blend. Speed of the infeed rolls may be varied to provide controlled stretch.	A driven helix blade cutter, acting against a revolving anvil, cuts continuous tow into uniform or variable lengths as desired.	The cut sheet passes between two sets of deeply fluted rolls that flex the fibers separating all of the individual ends after cutting.

SCHEMATIC OF DIRECT SPINNING BASED ON PERLOCK PROCESS

POSITIVE NIP	SHUFFLING	FORMING SLIVER	CRIMPING AND COILING
Three sets of nip rolls, separated by two shuffling sections, draft the fibers extending them lengthwise without strain to form a thinner sheet.	A serpentine action takes place when the fibers are passed between fluted rolls and a leather apron, producing further fiber separation.	After passing through the third draft roll section, the cut sheet is lifted from the apron and rolled diagonally upon itself, forming a continuous sliver of staple fiber.	Crimping rolls at the delivery end of the apron crimp the sliver imparting added strength. A ball bearing coiler head lays the sliver into the can ready for further processing.

Figure 15-10   *(Courtesy Warner and Swasey Co.)*

fibers at their weakest points. The fibers are then drafted into sliver form and directly spun in the conventional manner. However, with this procedure, it is not possible to blend the staple with other fibers. It may also be noted that the staple does not have any crimp.

Since the filaments are stretched to the breaking point and the fibers are then twisted into yarn without having sufficient opportunity to relax, direct-spun yarns will have a high rate of shrinkage in the wet-finishing processes. This disadvantage may be turned into an advantage, especially when such yarns are used to produce novelty nubby effects in fabrics, creped surfaces, or compact constructions.

TRADEMARKS OF VISCOSE RAYON

Many companies manufacture viscose rayon. All utilize the same basic principle of producing regenerated cellulose fiber by the viscose process and any of the several methods of spinning the fiber. These manufacturers have registered trademarks for their respective viscose rayon fibers and yarns in order to identify and promote their products. Trademarks identify variations in production that affect certain characteristics of the fibers and yarns, such as dull, staple, crimp, solution-dyed, or high tenacity. While the retailer and the consumer will find fabrics and garments advertised, labeled, or tagged with these trademarks, all viscose rayon of the same type has relatively similar quality and properties. Acquaintance with these names helps not only in recog-

nizing the textile as viscose rayon but also in being alert to special characteristics. In this regard, Table 15-1 should be of assistance.

Table 15-1

VISCOSE RAYON TRADEMARKS				
TRADEMARK	MANUFACTURER	TYPE	SPECIAL CHARACTERISTICS	USES
Avicolor	FMC Fibers Division	Multifilament, staple	Solution-dyed	Apparel, carpets
Avicron	FMC Fibers Division	Multifilament		Carpets
Aviloc	FMC Fibers Division	Multifilament	High tenacity	Industrial fabrics
Avisco	FMC Fibers Division	Multifilament, staple		Apparel, carpets, industrial fabrics
Briglo	American Enka Co.	Multifilament	Bright luster	Apparel, carpets, industrial fabrics
Coloray	Courtaulds North America, Inc.	Staple	Solution-dyed	Apparel, carpets, industrial fabrics
Dynacor	American Enka Co. and FMC Fibers Division	Multifilament	Improved adhesion	Tire cord
Englo	American Enka Co.	Multifilament	Dull	Apparel, carpets
Enka Rayon	American Enka Co.	Multifilament, staple		Apparel, carpets, industrial fabrics, tire cord
Enkrome	American Enka Co.	Multifilament, staple	Acid dyeable	Apparel, carpets
Fibro	Courtaulds North America, Inc.	Staple		Apparel, carpets, industrial fabrics
I. T.	American Enka Co.	Staple	Improved tenacity	Apparel, carpets, industrial fabrics
Jetspun	American Enka Co.	Multifilament	Solution-dyed	Apparel, carpets, industrial fabrics
Kolorbon	American Enka Co.	Staple	Solution-dyed	Apparel, carpets
Krispglo	American Enka Co.	Multifilament	Flat	Apparel
PFR	FMC Fibers Division	Staple	Permanent fire-retardant	Apparel
Purilon	FMC Fibers Division	Staple		Industrial fabrics
Rayflex	FMC Fibers Division	Multifilament		Industrial fabrics
Skyloft	American Enka Co.	Multifilament	Bulked natural or solution-dyed	Apparel, carpets, industrial fabrics

Table 15-1

	VISCOSE RAYON TRADEMARKS *(Continued)*			
TRADEMARK	MANUFACTURER	TYPE	SPECIAL CHARACTERISTICS	USES
Softglo	American Enka Co.	Multifilament	Semidull	Apparel, carpets
Super Rayflex	FMC Fibers Division	Multifilament	High tenacity	Industrial fabrics
Super White	American Enka Co.	Staple	Bleached, optically brightened	Apparel
Suprenka	American Enka Co.	Multifilament	High tenacity	Industrial fabrics
Suprenka Hi Mod	American Enka Co.	Multifilament	Super-high tenacity, low shrinkage, low elongation	Industrial fabrics
Suprenka M	American Enka Co.	Multifilament	Super-high tenacity, high elongation	Industrial fabrics
Suprenka MS	American Enka Co.	Multifilament	Super-high tenacity, high elongation	Industrial fabrics
Suprenka 2000	American Enka Co.	Multifilament	High tenacity	Industrial fabrics
Suprenka 6000	American Enka Co.	Multifilament	Super-high tenacity	Industrial fabrics, tire cord
Tyrex	American Enka Co. and FMC Fibers Division	Multifilament	Super-high tenacity	Industrial fabrics, tire cord

FINISHING PROCESSES

The many types of yarn that can be made from viscose rayon permit the production of a wide variety of fabrics. Spun rayon yarns can be made into fabrics resembling cotton, linen, or wool; rayon filament yarns can be made into fabrics resembling silk. To enhance the appearance of these fabrics and to improve their serviceability, they can be given various finishes. The most common finishes are as follows:

Calendering—for smoothness

Embossing—for decorative effects

Napping (spun rayons only)—for softness and warmth and to improve resemblance to wool

Stiffening—for body

Preshrinking—for greater dimensional stability

Water repellency—for resistance to water and rain

Wrinkle resistance—for better shape retention

Flame retardancy—for fire protection

These finishes are discussed in greater detail in Chapter 8. Printing and dyeing procedures are discussed in Chapters 10 and 9, respectively.

DECORATIVE EFFECTS

Viscose rayon is often combined with other textile fibers to produce novel and decorative effects. This can be accomplished by combining different types of yarns as well as by using such techniques as cross-dyeing. Viscose rayon can also be given a moiré finish, but it is not permanent and will come out with washing or dry cleaning.

EVALUATING VISCOSE RAYON FABRICS

In studying each of the natural fibers, cotton was rated highly for its economy and versatility. It was shown that linen excelled cotton in certain qualities, such as strength, luster, absorbency, cleanliness, and crispness. With respect to warmth and resiliency, wool and silk rank first.

The development of a man-made fiber possessing many of the above-mentioned prized qualities of the natural fibers is a tribute to human ingenuity. If the supply of natural fibers were insufficient or even nonexistent, man-made fibers could fully meet the situation.

Variations in the properties of viscose rayons are directly dependent upon the kind of fiber desired. Similar viscose rayon fibers have similar properties. Of course, the type of yarn that is used, as well as how the material is constructed, will contribute to the ultimate properties of the fabrics. The following discussion represents, in general, the properties of viscose rayon.

Strength.   Viscose rayon is about half as strong as silk. It is also weaker than cotton and linen, but stronger than wool. Yet, although viscose rayon is weaker than most natural fibers, it produces fairly durable, economical, and serviceable fabrics whose smoothness of surface favorably withstands the friction of wear.

Strength combined with sheerness of construction is possible in rayon fabrics by means of multifilament yarns. High-tenacity yarns afford a lightness with strength that surpasses silk.

Smooth-surfaced rayon fabrics are unusually slippery; therefore, the seams of rayon garments will slip unless the French seam or the flat-fell seam is used. Also, when cut on the bias, loosely constructed rayon fabrics may slip.

Elasticity.   Viscose rayon has greater elasticity than cotton or linen but less than wool or silk. Therefore, while viscose rayon fabrics have some inherent extensibility, undue strain might cause them to sag and even burst. High-tenacity rayon is generally less elastic than regular rayon.

Resilience.   Viscose rayon lacks the resilience natural to wool and silk and creases readily; but it should be remembered that the resistance of a fabric to creasing depends on the kind of yarn, weave, and finishing process. For example, the extremely fine filaments used in multifilament rayons have a greater resistance to creasing, and any of the crepe surfaces produced by tightly twisted yarns also resist creasing. Fabrics treated with one of the better patented crease-resistant finishing processes are highly resistant to creasing. Also, a soft surface produced by napping, typical of spun rayon, has some degree of crease resistance because of the softness and flexibility of the short staple, which recovers easily from wrinkles. Crimped staple offers increased resilience to spun yarn.

Drapability. Viscose rayon possesses a marked quality of drapability because it is a relatively heavyweight fabric. The filament can be made as coarse as desired, depending on the holes in the spinneret; and the yarn can be made heavy without the use of metallic filling, thus producing body substance in the fabric. Higher tenacity rayons are stiffer and do not have the good draping quality of regular viscose rayons.

Heat Conductivity. Viscose rayon is a good conductor of heat and is therefore appropriate for summer clothing. Spun rayon fabrics, however, are adaptable to winter apparel because they can be napped. The fuzzy surface provides some insulation, although the warmth will certainly not be as great as can be provided by wool or silk.

Absorbency. Viscose rayon is one of the most absorbent of all textiles. It is more absorbent than cotton or linen and is exceeded in absorbency only by wool and silk. The combination of high heat conductivity and high absorbency of rayon makes it very suitable for summer wear.

One limitation in this regard, however, is that rayon loses up to 70 percent of its strength while it is wet and therefore cannot take too much strain when it is wet. Also, as viscose rayon absorbs moisture from the air, there is a tendency to sag; but as the humidity reduces, the fabric shortens. This presents a disadvantage for its utilization in curtains.

Cleanliness and Washability. Because of its smoothness, viscose rayon fiber helps to produce hygienic fabrics that shed dirt. Some viscose rayon fabrics wash easily (see Figure 15-11); and depending on the finish that may be given to them, they will not become yellow when washed or dry-cleaned. White viscose rayon remains white and therefore needs no bleaching. Since viscose rayon temporarily loses strength when wet, it must be handled with care when washed. When laundered, a mild soap and warm water should be used. The garments should be squeezed, not wrung, to remove the water. When in doubt about whether a garment should be washed, it is safer to dry-clean it, because viscose rayon dry-cleans very well.

Reaction to Bleaches. It has been mentioned that white viscose rayon does not normally discolor. However, with prolonged exposure to sunlight, certain finishes or blends with such fibers as cotton may show some discoloration. Household bleaches containing either sodium hypochlorite (such as Clorox), sodium perborate (such as Snowy), or hydrogen peroxide may safely be used. However, it is always advisable to be careful of the amount of bleach used as well as the temperature of the water.

Figure 15-11 Demonstration of the washability of Avicron viscose rayon. *(a)* Cotton tuft before washing. *(b)* Cotton tuft after washing. *(c)* Avicron tuft before washing. *(d)* Avicron tuft after washing. *(Courtesy FMC Fibers Division)*

Shrinkage. Viscose rayon fabrics tend to shrink more than cotton fabrics of similar construction. Crepe weaves and knitted fabrics always shrink more than flat-woven fabrics because of the nature of the construction. Spun viscose rayon fabrics shrink more with repeated laundering than fabrics made of the filament yarns. Spun viscose rayon fabrics can be given a shrink-resistant finish, such as Sanforset, which makes them suitable for apparel that must be frequently washed. When spun viscose rayon is blended with wool, the great amount of shrinkage characteristic of the wool is reduced.

Effect of Heat. Since viscose rayon is a pure cellulosic fiber, it will burn in much the same manner as cotton. Napped or pile viscose rayon fabrics are susceptible to flash burning and must therefore be flameproofed. Application of heat at 300 degrees Fahrenheit causes viscose rayon to lose strength; above 350 degrees Fahrenheit, it begins to decompose. When ironing, it is wise to use either a moderately hot iron on a dampened fabric or a steam iron.

Effect of Light. Viscose rayon has generally good resistance to sunlight, though prolonged exposure of intermediate-tenacity rayon results in faster deterioration and yellowing.

Affinity for Dyes. Viscose rayon fabrics absorb dyes evenly. Colored viscose rayons have a high resistance to sunlight; they withstand strong light better than silk. This property makes them especially adaptable for window curtains. Of course, over a period of time, viscose rayon fabrics will fade. To overcome this, pigmented rayon, in which the dyestuff is put into the spinning solution thus becoming an integral part of the fiber, has been developed. Pigmented, or solution-dyed viscose rayon, is absolutely fast to light, washing, atmospheric gases, perspiration, crocking, and dry cleaning. Trademarks for pigmented viscose rayon yarns include Jetspun and Coloray. Solution-dyed rayons are not produced in large quantities and are not widely used because there is not a large sustained demand for specific shades.

Resistance to Mildew. Like cotton, viscose rayon has a tendency to mildew.

Such fabrics, therefore, should not be allowed to remain damp for any length of time.

Resistance to Moths. Moths are not attracted to cellulose. Consequently, mothproofing treatments are not necessary for viscose rayon.

Reaction to Alkalies. Concentrated solutions of alkalies disintegrate viscose rayon. A mild soap and lukewarm water is therefore recommended when laundering such garments.

Reaction to Acids. Viscose rayon reacts to acids in a manner similar to cotton. Being pure cellulose, the fabric is disintegrated by hot dilute and cold concentrated acids.

Resistance to Perspiration. Viscose rayon is fairly resistant to deterioration from perspiration. The color, however, is not usually as resistant as the fabric and will fade if not solution-dyed.

CUPRAMMONIUM RAYON

THE CUPRAMMONIUM PROCESS

The cuprammonium process of making rayon was first developed by L.H. Despaisses in France in 1890. However, the process was abandoned a few years later because it could not compete commercially with the more economical viscose process. It was subsequently successfully revived in Germany in 1919 by the J.P. Bemberg Co., AG, as a result of the invention and application by Dr. E. Thiele and Dr. E. Elsaesser of a *stretch-spinning*

technique, which produced very fine denier fibers with a soft hand and high flexibility. In 1926 the American Bemberg Corp. began production of cuprammonium rayon in Elizabethton, Tennessee.

The cuprammonium process uses purified cellulose obtained from cotton linters or, more usually, wood pulp. The pulp is mixed with copper sulfate and ammonia at low temperatures. The name "cuprammonium" is derived from these two substances. Caustic soda and stabilizing agents are added to maintain the solution's equilibrum and control its cellulose content. The solution is filtered for impurities and deaerated, prior to extrusion through the spinneret for further treatment, to form pure regenerated cellulose filaments and yarn (see Figure 15-12).

YARN PRODUCTION

Upon extrusion from the spinneret, the cuprammonium solution is processed into multifilament yarns.

Processing

The two methods of spinning cuprammonium rayon are by conventional reel spinning and continuous spinning.

Conventional Reel Spinning. As the solution is pumped through large-sized holes of the spinneret, it passes into a glass funnel where most of the ammonia and about one-third of the copper sulfate is removed, causing the solution to coagulate into filaments. On its way through the funnel, the filaments are uniformly stretched to finer diameters. As the fila-

Figure 15-12 Flow chart of the manufacturing process of cuprammonium rayon yarn. *(Courtesy American Viscose Corp.)*

ments leave the funnel, they enter a bath of mild sulfuric acid that hardens them as its reaction removes the remaining ammonia and copper salt, leaving filaments of pure cellulose. The yarn is then wound on reels and subsequently washed, rinsed, lubricated, and dried.

The stretch-spinning feature of the cuprammonium process produces fine yarn that can be given a great amount of twist. For its weight, it has greater elasticity than viscose rayon filament. The fine threads can be woven into the sheerest of fabrics. The high twist contributes to drapability.

Continuous Spinning. A technique for continuous spinning was introduced in 1944 with the development of a continuous machine by Dr. Hugo Hofmann. The cuprammonium solution is pumped through 120 spinning funnels, forming two banks of 60 parallel filaments. These filaments are passed through a solution of hot sulfuric acid in a pretreatment pan where they contract to approximately one-third their original diameter and are ultimately converted into cellu-

losic fiber. The banks of filaments are passed from the pretreatment pan through an acid trough for further purification and then into water to wash off the acid. The filaments are then lubricated or sized, dried, oiled, wound on spools or skeins, and conditioned in controlled humidity for a few days. This method is more economical than other methods because it requires no handling of the filaments from the spinneret through the winding machine.

As has been indicated, cuprammonium rayon is produced in multifilament form only. These yarns may be twisted or untwisted because, unlike viscose rayon, cuprammonium filaments are not separated; they adhere to each other unless subjected to relatively high friction. Cuprammonium yarn generally ranges from 40 to 900 denier and has from 30 to over 700 filaments each. The most popular deniers for fabrics are 50 to 100.

Variations in certain characteristics of cuprammonium rayon are possible. Dyes may be added to the solution to produce solution-dyed yarns. Techniques have been developed to produce novelty filament yarns having smooth, slub, and nubby effects. The finer deniers are suitable for a wide range of apparel, such as dresses, blouses, and sportswear. The heavier deniers are used for interesting textural effects for upholstery and related fabrics.

FINISHING PROCESSES

The finishes that are applied to cuprammonium rayon fabrics are fewer than for viscose rayon. For example, since cuprammonium rayon comes only in multifilament form, it is never napped. The fine filaments make the fabrics extremely pliable and the amount of sizing is therefore limited. The most common finishes are as follows:

Calendering—for smoothness

Dyeing—for fibers that are not solution-dyed

Printing—for decorative effects

Stain resistance—for ease of care

TRADEMARKS OF CUPRAMMONIUM RAYON

Cuprammonium rayon is sold under any one of several trademarks, as shown in Table 15-2. The fibers are all chemically the same—that is, they are all made from cellulose and have the same chemical properties. Variations in certain physical properties, such as solution-dyed effects and slub effects, can give the fabrics a unique appearance. These variations may be identified by the respective trademarks.

EVALUATING CUPRAMMONIUM RAYON FABRICS

Cuprammonium yarn has a subdued luster and a soft hand, giving it a silklike appearance and feel. But because it is a cellulosic fiber, many of its other properties are quite similar to those of viscose rayon. Since it can be produced in extremely fine deniers, cuprammonium yarn is very suitable for triple sheer, fancy sheer, and chiffon fabrics as well as heavier-weight cloth.

Strength. Cuprammonium rayon is about as strong as regular viscose filament yarn but is weaker than intermediate- and high-tenacity viscose rayons. The production of thick-and-thin, slub, and nubby effect multifilament yarns makes it possible to produce textured fabrics, usually made of spun yarns. Such cuprammonium yarns have relatively good wearing qualities because they are made of filament rather than staple yarns; they have a smoother surface that results in less friction and provides greater abrasion resistance. However, like viscose, cuprammonium rayon loses up to 70 percent of its strength when it is thoroughly wet.

Elasticity. Cuprammonium rayon yarns are generally slightly less elastic than viscose yarns. They therefore tend to sag less but, on the other hand, cannot take undue strain.

Resilience. A desirable characteristic of cuprammonium rayon is its fair degree of resilience. It does not wrinkle too easily; rumpled fabrics tend to smooth out and wrinkles will iron out nicely.

Table 15-2

CUPRAMMONIUM RAYON TRADEMARKS				
TRADEMARK	MANUFACTURER	TYPE	SPECIAL CHARACTERISTICS	USES
Bemberg	Bemberg Industries	Multifilament	Reel-spun	Apparel, carpets
Cupioni	Bemberg Industries	Multifilament	Entangled slub	Apparel, carpets
Cuprel	Bemberg Industries	Multifilament	Texturized	Apparel, carpets
Cupracolor	Bemberg Industries	Multifilament	Solution-dyed	Apparel, carpets

Drapability. Cuprammonium rayon is especially suitable for drapery fabrics because the numerous fine filaments make the material extremely pliable.

Heat Conductivity. Cuprammonium rayon is a good conductor of heat and is therefore appropriate for summer clothing. Its ability to be produced in very fine denier and woven into lightweight, sheer fabrics makes it highly desirable for warm-weather apparel.

Absorbency. Cuprammonium rayon is slightly less absorbent than viscose rayon under normal conditions, but it is equally absorbent under more humid conditions. Therefore, cuprammonium fabrics, particularly lightweight ones, tend to be relatively comfortable in warm, humid weather.

Cleanliness and Washability. Depending upon the construction of the garment, apparel made of cuprammonium rayon may be laundered, though some shrinkage may occur. The smooth surface of cuprammonium yarn tends to shed dirt. However, the relatively high absorbency may result in easy staining unless such

fabrics are given a spot-resistant finish. A mild soap and warm water should be used. Since cuprammonium rayon temporarily loses strength when wet, the garments should be handled with care to avoid wringing, pulling, or other great stress. Of course, cuprammonium fabrics may be dry-cleaned.

Reaction to Bleaches. White cuprammonium rayon normally remains white. Bleaches are therefore unnecessary unless it has discolored because of the fibers blended with it or yellowed because of excessive heat. Under such circumstances, the ordinary household bleaches may be used with usual care.

Shrinkage. Cuprammonium rayon will shrink when laundered, but shrink-resistant finishes reduce this effect. Less shrinkage will occur if cool water is used.

Effect of Heat. Heat of 300 degrees Fahrenheit causes cuprammonium rayon to weaken, scorch, and begin to decompose. Exposure to flame will cause it to burn like paper. When ironing, it is wise to use either a moderately hot iron on a dampened fabric or a steam iron.

Effect of Light. Much like cotton, cuprammonium rayon has generally good resistance to deterioration by sunlight.

Affinity for Dyes. Cuprammonium rayon has a good affinity for dyes; it takes dyes evenly and prints very well. It holds color well but, over a period of time, it will fade. However, solution-dyed cuprammonium rayon has excellent color-fastness.

Resistance to Mildew. Like cotton and viscose rayon, cuprammonium rayon will mildew when allowed to remain damp for any length of time. It should therefore be treated the same as cotton for removing mildew odor and stain.

Resistance to Moths. Being a cellulosic fiber, cuprammonium rayon is not attacked by moth larvae.

Reaction to Alkalies. Cuprammonium rayon is unaffected by mild alkalies. Mild soaps and detergents are therefore safe to use. However, strong alkali solutions cause swelling, loss of strength, and ultimate deterioration.

Reaction to Acids. Hot dilute and cold concentrated mineral acids, such as sulfuric and nitric acids, destroy cuprammonium rayon. Milder organic acids, such as citric acid, will cause tendering, and the fabric should be rinsed after exposure to them.

Resistance to Perspiration. Cuprammonium rayon has good resistance to perspiration. This contributes to its usefulness for garments worn next to the skin, particularly in warm weather.

Since color may fade, however, solution-dyed cuprammonium is preferable.

HIGH WET-MODULUS RAYON

Several properties of viscose and cuprammonium rayon represent limitations, particularly for their use as substitutes for cotton. The most significant limitation is their wet strength: both of these rayons lose up to 70 percent of their strength while wet. The tensile strength of a fiber is identified as its *tensile modulus*—the relative amount of pulling force that it can endure before breaking.

In 1960, commercial production was initiated for a rayon that approximated the natural strength of cotton and retained most of that strength, even when wet. It was consequently identified as a *high wet-modulus rayon*. Subsequently, it also became known as a *modified rayon*.

There are two varieties of this type of rayon in commercial production: Zantrel and Avril. While both are cellulosic and have basic characteristics similar to high-grade cotton, they do differ from each other in certain respects.

ZANTREL RAYON

The development of Zantrel originated with the research of a brilliant Japanese scientist, Dr. Shozo Tachikawa. In 1938 he began experimentation in his own laboratory to produce man-made cotton, and by 1951 he had made considerable progress. However, because his laboratory techniques were impractical for commercial production, a European textile firm, CTA, subsequently acquired an option to the patents and adapted Tachikawa's laboratory techniques to commercial production. By 1958, CTA had developed a process for the manufacture of the fiber, identified as *Z-54*.

A license to produce the fiber in the United States was obtained in 1959 by the Hartford Fibers Co. Commercial production, begun in 1960 under the trademark of *Zantrel*, was subsequently acquired by the American Enka Co. It is now produced under the trademark of Fiber 700. Yarns and fabrics containing Fiber 700 that meet construction and performance standards set by American Enka Co. may be identified by the trademarks Zantrel and Zantrel 700.

METHOD OF MANUFACTURE OF ZANTREL (FIBER 700) RAYON

The production of Zantrel fiber requires the use of much highly specialized, costly equipment. Treatment of the purified cellulose requires different chemical compositions, concentrations, and temperatures, as well as much greater critical control of the process than is required for the viscose or cuprammonium rayons.

The objective of the process is to control the cellulose molecular length and arrangement in the fiber, for the longer the chain of molecules and the more longitudinally parallel they can be made to each other the stronger the fiber will be. The individual molecules, or monomers, of cellulose are formed into long-chain polymers. Upon extrusion from the spinneret, controlled stretching orients these polymers so that they tend to straighten out and lie parallel to each other. Where these cellulose polymers become parallel, they tend to group into bundles forming chemical bonds along the length of the fiber. The object is to achieve a desired amount of such orientation and bonding. This organization of fairly long-chain molecules into connecting groups, or bundles, forms a microfibrillar structure resembling that of cotton.

The similar structures of Zantrel high wet-modulus fiber and cotton fiber account for the difference between this type of rayon and the viscose and cuprammonium rayons. The long-chain molecular structure has a greater number of and stronger chemical bonds between the molecules, which are arranged into fibrils that are compactly spaced and rather uniform in size and distribution. This structure inhibits such swelling agents as water and alkalies from readily penetrating between the cellulose molecules and thereby weakening the chemical bonds that hold the structure together. There is, then, much less loss of strength in Zantrel when it is wet than occurs in viscose and cuprammonium rayons, which are composed of small bundles of shorter cellulose molecules, irregularly distributed and with consequently fewer and weaker chemical bonds.

YARN PRODUCTION

Zantrel fiber, which is produced in 1.0, 1.5, and 3.0 denier, is cut into staple ranging from $1\frac{1}{4}$- to 2-inch lengths. It may be processed into yarn on any of the conventional spinning systems. It may also be spun in blends with cotton or other man-made fibers.

FINISHING ZANTREL RAYON FABRICS

The finishing processes given to Zantrel and Zantrel blend fabrics vary with the composition of the fabric and its desired end use. Listed below are some typical finishes:

Singeing—for a clear, smooth surface

Bleaching—for whiteness

Resin impregnation—for wrinkle resistance and wash and wear care

Compressive shrinkage—for greater dimensional stability

Calendering—for smoothness

Plissé—for crinkle-textured effects

These finishes are more fully discussed in Chapter 8. Wrinkle-resistant resin treatments need only a light application to Zantrel fabrics to obtain the desired results, and the fabrics are not weakened by the finish as much as is cotton. Fabrics of 100 percent Zantrel are not mercerized. However, blends of Zantrel and cotton may be mercerized to give improved luster and strength to the cotton.

EVALUATING ZANTREL RAYON FABRICS

Zantrel fabrics fall into the price range of combed cotton. They have a natural, soft luster and smooth, soft hand. The quality of the fabric will, of course, be affected by such factors of yarn and fabric construction as were previously considered. The following characteristics and performances may be expected of Zantrel fabrics.

Strength. Zantrel high wet-modulus rayon is approximately as strong as such cotton as Upland, and it is considerably stronger than either regular viscose or cuprammonium rayon. A major feature is its relatively high wet strength. Zantrel loses some strength when wet but not as significantly as do viscose and cuprammonium rayons. (Zantrel 700 is somewhat stronger but is better suited for certain industrial uses than for apparel.)

The abrasion resistance of Zantrel fabrics is somewhat lower than that of similar cotton fabrics. Fabrics of 100 percent Zantrel are therefore not well suited for apparel that is expected to be hard-wearing, such as children's clothes or workclothes.

Elasticity. Zantrel is less elastic than viscose or cuprammonium rayon but slightly more elastic than cotton. In this regard, Zantrel fabrics tend not to sag but rather to hold their dimension.

Resilience. Fabrics of Zantrel have some natural wrinkle resistance that is slightly better than viscose or cuprammonium rayon. This may be enhanced without great loss of strength by the application of a wrinkle-resistant resin finish.

Drapability. Fabrics of Zantrel fiber are highly drapable. They have a markedly better drape than either viscose or cuprammonium rayon, as well as having a supple, firm hand.

Heat Conductivity. Being a cellulosic fiber, Zantrel is a good conductor of heat. It has a cool, comfortable feel and is suitable for warm weather.

Absorbency. Due to its molecular structure, Zantrel is a little less absorbent than viscose or cuprammonium rayon or cotton. Nevertheless, it is sufficiently absorbent to feel comfortable in warm, humid weather. Since Zantrel does not swell as much as those rayons when wet, there is less tendency to distort or sag.

Cleanliness and Washability. Because Zantrel rayon fiber is round and has a smooth surface, it tends to shed dirt and stay cleaner than the rougher cellulosic fibers. Zantrel fabrics are completely washable. However, since Zantrel loses some strength when wet and does not have abrasion resistance that is as good as cotton, reasonable care should be taken in laundering it to avoid heavy rubbing action, pulling, or twisting. Soaps and detergents used for cotton may also be used for Zantrel fabrics. Wash and wear characteristics may be imparted by using an appropriate resin finish, which has a less weakening effect on Zantrel than occurs on cotton or on viscose or cuprammonium rayon.

Reaction to Bleaches. Many household bleaches, such as those containing sodium hypochlorite, are not too effective on Zantrel fabrics, though they may be used. The most desirable bleaches are sodium chlorite and paracetic acid, which are generally used commercially.

Shrinkage. Like other cellulosic fibers, Zantrel will shrink. However, Zantrel fabrics can be given a compressive-shrinkage finish, such as Sanforized, so that the residual shrinkage may be as little as 1 percent.

Effect of Heat. Zantrel fabrics begin to scorch at 400 degrees Fahrenheit and burn at 465 degrees Fahrenheit. These fabrics have a greater resistance to damage by heat than do cotton or the other rayons. Pressing may therefore be readily done with a hot iron and a damp cloth. When Zantrel does ignite, it burns in the same manner as other cellulosic fibers.

Effect of Light. Zantrel has good resistance to light, similar to that of other cellulosic fibers. For most apparel and decorative purposes, this is quite adequate. However, since prolonged exposure will weaken the fiber, it is not suitable for such outdoor purposes as awnings.

Affinity for Dyes. Zantrel rayon can be readily colored with a wide range of dyes. Fabrics that have been vat-dyed have generally good all-around colorfastness.

Resistance to Mildew. Like other cellulosic fibers, Zantrel will be damaged by mildew. Damp conditions should be avoided.

Resistance to Moths. Being a cellulosic fiber, Zantrel is not attacked by moths.

Reaction to Alkalies. One of the desirable features of Zantrel is its good resistance to alkalies. This characteristic makes it possible to mercerize fabrics blended of cotton and Zantrel rayon to obtain increased luster and strength in the cotton as well as an increased dye level in the blend.

Reaction to Acids. Zantrel reacts to acids in a manner similar to that of the other cellulosic fibers. Hot dilute acids or cold concentrated weak acids will disintegrate the fiber.

Resistance to Perspiration. Zantrel is fairly resistant; however, it is deteriorated by acid perspiration.

ZANTREL RAYON FIBER BLENDS

Zantrel fiber is readily blended with a wide variety of other fibers because it can be easily spun on any conventional system and reacts favorably to the usual finishing and dyeing techniques. It can be blended with cotton, triacetate, nylon, polyester, and acrylic fibers. Depending upon the blend percentage, Zantrel may impart a crisp or lofty hand and a luster ranging from that of high-grade cotton to silk. A blend of 40 percent Zantrel and 60 percent carded cotton, for example, will produce a fabric that has a hand as good as or superior to that of 100 percent combed cotton and has the sheen of Pima cotton.

AVRIL RAYON

After several years of research and development, in 1961 the American Viscose Corp. (which subsequently became a division of the FMC Corp.) began commercial production of its high wet-modulus rayon fiber identified as *Fiber*

40. The fiber is sold as Fiber 40 to processors and, when the yarns and fabrics produced from this fiber are processed and finished according to FMC's quality control standards, the product is marketed as *Avril rayon.*

METHOD OF MANUFACTURE OF AVRIL (FIBER 40) RAYON

Like other high wet-modulus rayon fibers, Avril is produced from purified cellulose by means of techniques modified from the basic viscose process, which provides greater control of the molecular structure of the fiber. The long-chain cellulose molecules are arranged lengthwise, relatively parallel to each other, thereby forming bonds in a microfibrillar structure that has a relatively low number of spaces between the molecules for water to penetrate.

The fiber is produced in 1.0, 1.25, 1.5, and 3.0 denier. It is almost round and more closely resembles cuprammonium rayon in shape and smoothness than do any of the other rayons.

YARN PRODUCTION

The fiber is cut into staple lengths of $1^1/_4$, $1^9/_{16}$, and 2 inches, depending upon the kind of yarn and the other staple with which it is to be blended. Conventional spinning systems, such as for rayon, are used to produce the desired yarn.

FINISHING AVRIL RAYON FABRICS

These fabrics are finished in the same manner as viscose rayon or cotton. Since Avril is whiter than cotton, bleaching is generally not required unless a higher level of whiteness is desired. Other finishes include the following:

Resin impregnation—for wrinkle resistance and wash and wear care

Compressive shrinkage—for greater dimensional stability

Calendering—for smoothness

Schreinering—for increased luster

Plissé—for crinkle-textured effect

Fabrics of Avril/cotton blended yarns may also be mercerized to enhance their appearance.

EVALUATING AVRIL RAYON FABRICS

Avril fabrics have a silky, lustrous appearance and a soft hand. They have been used in a variety of lightweight as well as heavier weight fabrics. Judgment of performance may be based upon the following characteristics.

Strength. The strength of Avril rayon is about equal to Pima cotton and greater than Zantrel. When wet, Avril loses some strength. It remains, of course, much stronger than viscose or cuprammonium rayon. Avril fabrics also have satisfactory abrasion resistance. They may therefore be expected to give good service in a variety of apparel from dresswear and sportswear to underwear and sleepwear.

Elasticity. Avril has very little elasticity, approximating that of cotton. Fabrics of Avril will not sag, which is an advantage in dress goods and draperies.

Resilience. Avril has better resilience than viscose or cuprammonium rayon. Its resilience approximates that of Zantrel. When treated with a wrinkle-resistant finish, the resilience of Avril is also considerably improved with little loss of strength.

Drapability. Avril fabrics have a good hand with good draping quality. They have been found suitable for draperies as well as women's apparel.

Heat Conductivity. Like similar cellulosic fibers, Avril is a good conductor of heat and is therefore quite well suited for warm-weather apparel.

Absorbency. Avril rayon is as absorbent as viscose rayon. It is interesting to note, though, that despite the higher wet-modulus (strength) of Avril over Zantrel, Avril is more absorbent. This relatively high absorbency makes Avril well suited for a wide variety of apparel that may be comfortably worn in warm, humid weather. Avril can also be used for towels and sheets.

Cleanliness and Washability. Avril rayon fiber has a smooth surface with a round to oval shape; therefore, it sheds dirt easily. On the other hand, its absorbency of water-borne substances may cause spotting. It launders readily, however, and is resistant to damage by soaps as well as to the machine washing action. Avril fabrics do not become harsh from repeated washings. Wash and wear finishes contribute to their easy care with much less loss of strength than occurs with cotton or viscose and cuprammonium rayons.

Effect of Bleaches. With reasonable care, bleaches of sodium hypochlorite or sodium chlorite may be safely used. Hydrogen peroxide should not be used at home since special care must be given.

Shrinkage. Like other cellulosic fibers, Avril will shrink when wet. However, it can similarly be given a compressive-shrinkage finish so that it will have a residual shrinkage of less than 1 percent.

Effect of Heat. Avril fabrics scorch and flame at about the same temperature as viscose rayon. When pressing fabrics of Avril, the iron should be set at "rayon" and the fabrics should be damp.

Effect of Light. Avril, like other cellulosic fibers, has good resistance to light.

Affinity for Dyes. Avril fabrics can be dyed in a full range of shades with a wide variety of dyes used for other cellulosic fibers. However, the fastness varies with the dye. Vat dyes, for example, provide good colorfastness.

Resistance to Mildew. Being a cellulosic fiber, Avril will be attacked by mildew unless kept in a dry condition.

Resistance to Moths. Avril is not attacked by moth larvae.

Reaction to Alkalies. Avril has very good resistance to damage by alkalies. Consequently, fabrics blended of Avril rayon and cotton may be treated with caustic soda for mercerized and plissé finishes.

Reaction to Acids. Hot dilute acids or cold concentrated weak acids will destroy Avril fiber.

Resistance to Perspiration. While Avril is fairly resistant, it is affected by acid perspiration.

AVRIL RAYON FIBER BLENDS

Avril may be effectively blended with cotton to produce dimensionally stable fabrics. Avril contributes strength, improved luster, a soft hand, and an appearance of combed cotton to the blend. Resin-treated blends for wrinkle resistance and wash and wear care are stronger than similarly treated 100 percent cotton fabrics.

Blends of Avril and other man-made fibers have produced favorable results. For example, when blended with viscose rayon, Avril generally adds comfort (due to its absorbency and draping quality), good appearance, pleasant hand, and strength.

COMPARISON OF HIGH WET-MODULUS RAYONS

Table 15-3 is for the reader's general guidance. It is a summary composite based upon information supplied by the producers and evaluations of performance of the high wet-modulus rayon fibers as described in the literature. The reader is reminded that variations do exist within each trademark as well as within each blend combination, type of yarn, fabric weight, construction, and finishing operation. These factors will affect the performance of all the fibers. It is also possible that any future changes in either the chemical or the physical compositions of these fibers may alter their performance.

Table 15-3

COMPARISON OF PROPERTIES—THE HIGH WET-MODULUS RAYON FIBERS		
	ZANTREL	AVRIL
Strength	Fair; similar to Upland cotton	Good; approximates Pima cotton
Abrasion resistance	Fair	Fair
Elasticity	Little	Little
Resilience	Fair (improved with resin treatment, little strength loss)	Fair (improved with resin treatment, little strength loss)
Absorbency	Good	Superior
Laundering care	Avoid heavy rubbing, twisting; household bleaches not too effective	Avoid heavy rubbing or twisting; bleaches may be used with care
Household bleaches	Not very effective	Only sodium hypochlorite or sodium chlorite safely effective
Shrinkage	Shrinks unless preshrunk	Shrinks unless preshrunk
Ironing temperature	At cotton setting	At rayon setting
Resistance to light	Good	Good
Resistance to mildew	Damaged	Damaged
Reaction to alkalies	Good resistance	Good resistance
Reaction to acids	Poor resistance	Poor resistance
Resistance to perspiration	Fair	Fair
Colorfastness	Good	Good

REVIEW QUESTIONS

1. (a) What is the source of rayon? (b) What natural fiber does rayon resemble chemically?
2. (a) What are the different types of rayon? (b) Distinguish between types of rayon and rayon trademarks.
3. Compare the basic differences in manufacture of each of the major types of rayon.
4. Compare the characteristics of the several types of rayon in terms of (a) durability, (b) serviceability, (c) care.
5. (a) How are multifilament yarns made? (b) What are their main characteristics?

6. (a) What are spun yarns? (b) What are their main characteristics?
7. Describe how spun yarns are made by the conventional spinning methods.
8. Describe how spun yarns are made utilizing the Perlok breakage techniques and each of the two direct-spinning methods.
9. What is meant by the description of a rayon yarn (a) of 150/30; (b) of 30s, cotton system; (c) of 40s, woolen system; (d) of 40s, worsted system?
10. (a) What is the advantage of solution-dyed rayon? (b) Identify three such rayons by trademark.
11. What major finishes are applied to rayon fabrics?
12. What characteristics would fabrics made of blends of regular rayon and each of the natural fibers have?
13. Name and describe (a) five fabrics made of filament rayon and (b) five fabrics made of spun rayon.
14. (a) Name the high wet-modulus rayon fibers. (b) How is their structure different from the viscose and cuprammonium rayons?
15. What properties do the high wet-modulus rayon fibers have in common?
16. What properties do the high wet-modulus fibers have that are similar to the other cellulosic fibers?
17. In what respects do the high wet-modulus rayons differ from each other?

SUGGESTED ACTIVITY

Obtain advertisements and/or labels with rayon trademarks for fabrics or garments and identify the type of rayon used.

16

ACETATE AND TRIACETATE

the cellulose acetate fibers

The cellulose acetate fibers differ from rayon in that they are not pure cellulose products; they are chemical compounds of cellulose and have their own unique properties. In fact, the various types of cellulose acetate fibers also differ from one another.

HISTORY OF CELLULOSE ACETATES

Cellulose acetate was developed in England during World War I by Henri and Camille Dreyfus as a nonflammable lacquer for the fabric used on the wings and fuselage of aircraft. In 1918 they perfected a technique for spinning the substance into lustrous filaments of "artificial silk." Subsequently, the fiber was produced by British Celanese, Ltd. Commercial production was begun in the United States in 1924 by the Celanese Corp. of America under the trademark of Celanese. Much later, other manufacturers in this country produced this type of fiber under their respective trademarks. All of these became generally referred to as *acetate* fiber according to the Federal Trade Commission ruling of 1952.

More recently, the Celanese Corp. of America undertook the production of a variation of this chemical synthesis. This product, a cellulose triacetate, is marketed by the Celanese Fibers Marketing Co. under the trademark of Arnel.

ACETATE

THE ACETATE PROCESS

Cotton linters or wood chips are converted into sheets of pure cellulose. The cellulose is steeped in glacial acetic acid and aged for a period of time under a controlled temperature. After aging, it is thoroughly mixed with acetic anhydride. A small amount of sulfuric acid is then added as a catalyst to facilitate a reaction producing a thick, clear liquid solution of cellulose acetate. After further aging, this *dope*, as it is called, is mixed

Figure 16-1 Flow chart of the manufacturing process of acetate. *(Courtesy FMC Corp.)*

with an excess of water, causing the cellulose acetate to precipitate as white flakes. The flakes are dried, dissolved in acetone, and filtered several times to remove impurities. The result is a clear, white spinning solution of the consistency of syrup (see Figure 16-1).

If delustered yarn is required, titanium dioxide, a delusterant, is added at this stage to produce the desired degree of brightness: bright, semidull, or dull. This has no effect on the characteristics or properties of acetate other than on the luster. The variation in the amount of luster given to acetate increases its versatility. Acetate fibers not only have various degrees of sheen; they can also simulate as well as blend with other fibers, thereby providing a wider use of acetate.

A flame-retardant component may be added to the dope. Sayfr and Acele FLR are such forms of flame-retardant acetate fibers.

Dyestuff may also be added to the spinning solution. Solution-dyed acetate, which has excellent colorfastness, is identified by such trademarks as Celaperm and Chromspun.

After the delusterant has been added, the spinning solution is forced through a spinneret and into a cabinet of heated air that evaporates the acetone and solidifies the filament (see Figure 16-2). It is then ready for winding on spools, cones, or bobbins. No washing or bleaching is required as the solution was cleaned and filtered before it passed through the spinneret.

Further variations in the acetate filaments may be obtained by varying the shape of the spinneret holes. Normally, as the solution is pumped through round holes, the cellulose acetate coagulates into filaments with irregular cross-sectional shapes. However, when the solution is extruded through oblong holes, it produces flat, ribbonlike filaments that are highly reflective and impart a sparkle when woven into cloth. One variation, Estron 50, is extruded to produce doughnut-shaped filaments that give bulk, resilience, and added luster to the fabric. If greater bulk and covering

Figure 16-2   Acetate solution is forced under pressure through a spinneret and then falls in fine streams down a tall spinning shaft. The streams solidify into filaments in the warm air of the shaft. These filaments are drawn out of the shaft at the bottom and twisted together to form a single strand of yarn. (*Courtesy Eastman Chemical Products, Inc.*)

power are desired, as well as a stiffer, crisper hand, Y-shaped filaments, such as Celacloud and Estron 10, may be produced (Figure 16-3).

YARN PRODUCTION

After the acetate filaments have been formed, they are processed into filament, textured, or spun yarns, and there are variations within each of these types.

Filament Yarns

A wide variety of acetate yarns can be made in many different deniers depending on the number, size, and shape of the holes in the spinneret.

Monofilament Yarns. The acetate solution may be extruded through a spinneret with one hole. This will produce a single, or monofilament, yarn. The denier of such a yarn can be regulated by the size of the hole in the spinneret. These yarns are not very strong but provide good body and smoothness.

Multifilament Yarns. The majority of acetate yarns are composed of two or more filaments extruded simultaneously from the same spinneret and then eventually twisted (thrown) around each other in a manner similar to silk yarns. The denier of the multifilament yarns is dependent on the denier of the individual filaments as well as on the number of filaments in the yarn. Multifilament yarns are stronger than monofilament yarns because of the greater number of filaments

Figure 16-3   (*a*) The round surface of Estron 50 acetate adds luster to fabrics. The hollowness of the fiber increases bulk and gives a more resilient hand. (*b*) The Y shape of Estron 10 acetate gives maximum bulk and covering power and contributes stiff, crisp hand to fabrics. (*Photos Courtesy Eastman Chemical Products, Inc.*)

and the amount of twist given to the yarns. They also have good drape.

Textured Yarns

These yarns are really variations of filament yarns wherein the filaments have been processed to develop permanent kinks or loops. Such yarns offer bulk or loft, have the appearance of spun staple yarns, possess a warm, dry hand, but retain the advantages of continuous-filament construction. One example is Loftura.

Spun Yarns

The relatively smooth, round acetate filaments can be reduced to staple, usually from 1 to 6 inches in length, and spun into yarns. The filaments in tow form may be cut by a staple cutter (the same as for rayon staple, page 341) and then spun on either the conventional cotton, woolen, or worsted system into yarns resembling one of these textiles; or they may be broken by the Perlok technique and spun into yarn by direct spinning on the Saco-Lowell or Pacific Converter system (as for rayon spun yarn, pages 341-344). Sometimes acetate staple is blended with other staples to obtain yarns and fabrics that will have characteristics of all the fibers used. These yarns are dull, fuzzy, and generally have the appearance and texture of natural fiber yarns.

TRADEMARKS OF ACETATE FIBERS

Acetate fibers are produced by many companies and each company has its own trademark. The better-known acetate fibers appear in Table 16-1.

FINISHING ACETATE FABRICS

Acetate fabrics can be given various finishes depending on the kind of yarn used and the effect desired. The more common finishes are listed below:

Embossing—for pattern or design

Moiréing—for permanent watermarking effect

Napping—on spun acetate for softness and warmth

Sizing—for stiffness and body

Heat setting—for crease and shape retention

Water repellency—for resistance to water and rain

Wrinkle resistance—for better shape retention

The characteristics of acetate are quite different from those of all the other fibers considered in the text thus far. One of the most unique of its characteristics is its thermoplasticity; that is, it can be softened by the application of heat and placed or pressed into a particular shape. This permits the permanent embossing and moiréing of acetate fabrics. Also, creases and pleats heat-set into acetate fabrics are relatively durable and are retained better than in cotton, linen, wool, silk, or rayon, although some amount of re-pressing is usually desirable.

Although acetate is not very absorbent, it does absorb some moisture. A water-repellent finish, such as Zelan, given to acetate fabrics makes them satisfactorily water-repellent.

Table 16-1

ACETATE TRADEMARKS				
TRADEMARK	MANUFACTURER	TYPE	SPECIAL CHARACTERISTICS	USES
Acele	E. I. du Pont de Nemours & Co.	Multifilament		Apparel, carpets, home furnishings
Acele FLR	E. I. du Pont de Nemours & Co.	Multifilament	Flame-retardant	Apparel, carpets, home furnishings
Avicolor	FMC Fibers Division	Multifilament	Solution-dyed	Apparel, carpets, home furnishings
Avisco	FMC Fibers Division	Multifilament		Apparel, carpets, home furnishings
Celacloud (Type F)	Celanese Fibers Marketing Co.	Staple		Apparel, carpets, home furnishings
Celafil (Type K)	Celanese Fibers Marketing Co.	Staple		Carpets, home furnishings
Celanese Acetate	Celanese Fibers Marketing Co.	Multifilament, staple, tow		Apparel, carpets, home furnishings
Celaperm	Celanese Fibers Marketing Co.	Multifilament	Solution-dyed	Apparel, carpets, home furnishings, industrial fabrics
Chromspun	Eastman Chemical Products, Inc.	Multifilament	Solution-dyed	Apparel, carpets, home furnishings
Estron	Eastman Chemical Products, Inc.	Multifilament	Varied cross sections, depending on use	Apparel, carpets, home furnishings
Estron SLR	Eastman Chemical Products, Inc.	Multifilament	Dull, resistant to sunlight and weathering	Carpets, home furnishings
Estron FR	Eastman Chemical Products, Inc.	Multifilament	Flame-resistant	Home furnishings
Sayfr	FMC Fibers Division	Multifilament	Flame-resistant	Apparel, home furnishings

EVALUATING ACETATE FABRICS

The properties of acetate fabrics will vary to some extent depending on the type of yarn used (filament, textured, or spun), on the type of fabric construction, and on the finish. Acetate has the following general properties.

Strength.   Acetate is not a strong fiber. It is weaker than any rayon and is, in fact, one of the weakest textile fibers. Acetate has poor abrasion resistance and is therefore not suited for garments that are expected to take hard wear.

Elasticity.   Acetate is more elastic than any rayon. However, its elasticity is limited, being much less than that of silk.

Resilience. Acetate is more wrinkle-resistant than any rayon; consequently, the fabric will tend to return to its original shape much better than will rayon after it is pulled or crumpled. After wearing, acetate garments should be carefully hung to permit the yarns to relax to their original shape.

Drapability. Acetate fabrics have good body and flexibility and therefore drape very nicely.

Heat Conductivity. Acetate does not have as high a rate of heat conductivity as rayon and therefore is warmer. Acetate is consequently more useful for linings and warmer clothing, particularly if it is spun acetate. Of course, filament yarns woven or knitted into sheer fabrics will result in cooler fabrics because of their greater porosity.

Absorbency. Acetate is not very absorbent. It absorbs only half as much moisture as the rayons. This represents both advantages and disadvantages. Acetate fabrics get wet mostly on the surface and will not become saturated; therefore, they dry quickly. This makes acetate very suitable for shower curtains, umbrellas, and raincoats. It is also suited for bathing suits, particularly at the seashore because salt air does not have any deteriorating effect on acetate. On the other hand, acetate is uncomfortable in warm, humid weather because of its low absorbency. Acetate garments, such as blouses and lingerie, worn next to the skin feel clammy and uncomfortable because they do not absorb perspiration or atmospheric humidity.

Cleanliness and Washability. Acetate fiber smoothness helps to produce hygienic fabrics that shed dirt and wash easily. They will not become yellow when washed or dry-cleaned.

Since acetate temporarily loses some strength when wet, such fabrics must be handled with care when washed. When laundered, a mild soap and warm water should be used. The garments should not be rubbed vigorously or wrung but should be handled gently and squeezed to remove the water. They will dry readily and should be hung so that the water will drip off.

When in doubt about the launderability of an acetate garment because of its tailoring or finish, it is always best to dry-clean it. Acetate garments dry-clean very well.

Effect of Bleaches. White acetate remains white, and acetate fabrics need not be bleached. If bleaching is desired, it should be done with a very mild solution of hydrogen peroxide or a very dilute solution of sodium hypochlorite, such as a dilution of Clorox, Rose-X, or the like.

Shrinkage. Acetate fabrics will shrink less than any rayon. Sometimes they are given a shrink-resistant finish.

Effect of Heat. Acetate is a thermoplastic fiber, but it gets tacky at about 350 degrees Fahrenheit. Acetate fabrics need less ironing than rayon fabrics. A warm iron will easily smooth out an acetate fabric, particularly if the fabric is a little damp. If the iron is too hot, it will melt the acetate causing it to stick to the iron and make the fabric stiff.

Effect of Light.   Acetate is more resistant to the effect of light than cotton or any rayon. Over a period of time, acetate will be weakened from exposure to light.

Resistance to Mildew.   Acetate is highly resistant to mildew. It is ideal for fabrics exposed to moisture, such as shower curtains.

Resistance to Insects.   Moths, carpet beetles, and similar insects will not attack acetate. Mothproofing of all-acetate fabrics is not necessary.

Reaction to Alkalies.   Concentrated solutions of alkalies disintegrate acetate.

Reaction to Acids.   Acetate is more resistant to acids than rayon, but it will be decomposed by concentrated solutions of strong acids.

Affinity for Dyes.   Since acetate fiber is not very absorbent, special acetate dyes were developed, but they are not as fast as one may wish. A full range of shades with moderate fastness to light and washing is available. The color is also affected by perspiration. Acetate's greatest weakness, however, is poor fastness to atmospheric gases. Grays and blues particularly will gas-fade badly and change color to pink, red, and purple. Inhibitors can be added during the finishing process to minimize this effect.

Solution-dyed acetate fibers do not have these disadvantages. They are colorfast to light, atmospheric fumes, perspiration, crocking, washing, and dry cleaning.

Resistance to Perspiration.   Acetate fabrics are fairly resistant to deterioration by perspiration, but the color will be affected if it has not been solution-dyed.

ACETATE FIBER BLENDS

Acetate fibers are sometimes blended with other fibers to reduce the price of a fabric or to obtain a desired combination of acetate properties with the properties of other fibers. Acetate yarns may be combined with other textile yarns in weaving fabrics for economy, cross-dyeing, or textural effects.

Acetate and Wool

Acetate will reduce the tendency of a fabric to shrink, felt, or pill when blended with wool. The combination provides good shape retention and holds creases well. Although such a fabric may be relatively inexpensive, it will not be as durable as an all-wool cloth.

Acetate and Rayon

Of all the fibers discussed thus far, acetate fibers are most frequently blended with rayon. Acetate adds shape retention to fabrics. Garments made of such fabrics tend to wrinkle less because of the resilience of acetate. Such fabrics when pleated or creased tend to hold their shape well because of the thermoplastic characteristic of acetate. The easy care of acetate/rayon blended fabrics usually means little ironing for garments that have been laundered. Such fabrics, however, have reduced absorbency because of the acetate. They also may tend to shine when pressed if not given sufficient care.

TRIACETATE (ARNEL)

METHOD OF MANUFACTURE

As early as 1914 and prior to the commercial production of cellulose acetate, fibers known chemically as *triacetate cellulose* were produced. They were, however, never fully exploited. Problems involving production, dyes, and finishes were not sufficiently pursued and solved.

With the advancement of chemistry and the development of advanced textile engineering techniques, the Celanese Corp. of America began commercial production of its triacetate cellulose fiber, *Arnel*, in 1954. The process of manufacturing Arnel is initially similar to the method of producing acetate except that triacetate cellulose is not reduced to diacetate cellulose (that is, acetate or cellulose acetate). After the cellulose triacetate solution is mixed with water, precipitated as white flakes, and then washed and dried, it is dissolved in a solution of methyl chloride with a small proportion of alcohol.

In its normal condition, Arnel is highly lustrous. To increase its versatility, it may be delustered by adding a delusterant to the spinning solution in a manner similar to the way acetate is delustered, so that either bright or dull fiber may be produced. Adding the delusterant has no effect on the properties of the fiber other than to dull it.

The solution will accept a black dyestuff. Therefore, if desired, a fast, black solution-dyed Arnel fiber may be obtained.

The solution is pumped through a spinneret into a cabinet of air that evaporates the solvent and solidifies the filaments. It is then ready for processing into yarn.

YARN PRODUCTION

The triacetate Arnel filaments are made into either multifilament or spun yarns.

Multifilament Yarns

Arnel multifilament yarns are produced in a wide variety of deniers. The denier of each fiber in the yarn is dependent on the size of the holes in the spinneret. The ultimate denier of each yarn is dependent on the number of fibers in the yarn.

Arnel multifilament yarns are made by twisting 15 to 160 filaments around each other. The subsequent denier of the thrown yarns ranges from 50 to 600 denier. The strength, texture, and draping quality of the yarns are dependent on the number of filaments, the denier of these filaments, and the amount of the twist in the yarns. The greater the twist, the stronger the yarn, but the higher the twist, the rougher or harder the yarn will feel. The lower the denier and the greater the number of filaments, the better the fabric will drape.

Innumerable variations are possible to obtain the desired effects. A special type of multifilament thick-and-thin yarn has been developed. This yarn varies in thickness throughout its length to give the impression of a spun slub yarn, but it has the general properties of multifilament yarns. The multifilaments may also be textured by the producer.

Spun Yarns

Filaments of Arnel triacetate (generally in the range of 2.5, 3, and 5 denier per fiber) may be gathered as tow and crimped and cut into any of the standard lengths desired. The staple can then be spun on the conventional system used for cotton, woolen, or worsted yarns to produce yarns resembling these textiles. Arnel tow may also be broken into staple on a Perlok system and processed by direct spinning into spun yarn as described for rayon staple processing on pages 341-344. One form of Arnel is produced as a flame-resistant staple for use in spun yarn form. Arnel staple may also be blended with other staple to obtain yarns and fabrics that will have characteristics of all the fibers used.

FINISHING ARNEL TRIACETATE FABRICS

Arnel fabrics can be given a variety of finishes depending on the effects desired. The most common finishes for Arnel fabrics are as follows:

Embossing—for pattern or design

Water repellency—for resistance to water and rain

Spot resistance—for resistance to water and oil stains

Sizing—for stiffness and body

Antistatic—for protection against electrostatic buildup and as a dust repellent

Heat setting—for wrinkle resistance and shape retention

Fabrics of Arnel can be given shallow and surface embossing patterns with heated engraved rollers. This technique can be used to obtain moiré and glazed effects. Such embossed patterns are durable to repeated home washings and to tumble drying. Where pressing is required to remove wrinkles, a light steam pressing will remove the wrinkles without reducing the shallow embossed texture.

Silicone resins, properly applied to Arnel triacetate fabrics, provide a durable water repellency. Such a finish also provides spot resistance against waterborne substances as well as a reduction in the spreading of oil stains when a cationic softener is used.

Sizing may be given to Arnel fabrics to provide stiffness, firmness, and body. The effectiveness of the sizing varies, depending on the technique used. For example, a silicone resin provides a durable finish that imparts the scroop, or rustle, desirable in taffeta. Some sizings help fabrics retain a very firm hand after repeated washings, but the cloth wrinkles easily and tears more easily than without such finishes.

Arnel fabrics have a tendency to develop static electricity when they are rubbed, as when worn. This may cause the fabric to crackle and cling undesirably. Also, the static electricity attracts and holds dust particles. Limited durable antistatic finishes have been developed. They are limited in that they greatly reduce the static behavior of the fabric, but are not absolutely antistatic, and the effectiveness of the finish is reduced by washing and dry cleaning.

Arnel is thermoplastic. Consequently, when properly heat-treated, Arnel fabrics may be heat-set so that they will retain their shape, creases, and

Figure 16-4 *(a)* Garments of knitted textured Arnel triacetate fabrics drape well and are shape retentive. *(b)* Woven arnel triacetate printed sport shirt provides good appearance and easy care. *(Photos Courtesy Celanese Fibers Marketing Co.)*

pleats after repeated washings. Although the type of yarn used and the construction of the fabric have some influence on the effectiveness of the heat-setting finish, Arnel fabrics of either multifilament or spun yarns, whether woven or knitted, generally retain their shape well when properly heat-set.

EVALUATING ARNEL TRIACETATE FABRICS

A wide variety of fabrics is being made of Arnel. Since these fabrics can be made of multifilament yarns and spun yarns and can be constructed in any of the standard manners, Arnel fabrics tend to look and feel like similar fabrics made of other textiles, such as cotton, wool, silk, rayon, and acetate. Arnel, however, lends its own distinctive properties to the finished fabric. As is true with other fibers, there are similarities between

certain properties of Arnel and various other individual fibers. But Arnel has its own combination of distinctive characteristics with its own advantages and disadvantages. The general properties of fabrics made of Arnel are given here.

Strength. Arnel is not a strong fiber. Its strength approximates that of acetate. Arnel has poor abrasion resistance, like acetate, and a much lower abrasion resistance than wool. Arnel is therefore not suited for garments that are expected to take hard wear.

Elasticity. Arnel can be stretched about the same as acetate and has a slightly better recovery to original dimension. However, its elasticity is limited, and it is much less elastic than silk.

Resilience. Arnel is the most resilient of the cellulosic fibers. It also has very good shape-retentive qualities. Arnel fabrics will not wrinkle easily even at high humidity, and any wrinkles that may develop from packing or wearing will fall out readily when allowed to hang properly for a reasonable period of time.

Drapability. Arnel fabrics have good body and flexibility and drape very nicely (see Figure 16-4*a* and *b*).

Heat Conductivity. Like acetate, Arnel does not have a high rate of heat conductivity and is therefore warmer than cotton, linen, or rayon. To compensate for this, finer yarns and sheerer construction are used, thus providing Arnel fabrics with year-round versatility.

Absorbency. Arnel is less absorbent than acetate. Since it does not absorb much water, Arnel is well suited for fabrics where some amount of water repellency is desirable. Also, because Arnel gets wet primarily on the surface rather than saturated within the fiber, fabrics made of Arnel dry rapidly when they are wet. On the other hand, the relatively low moisture absorbency of Arnel makes it uncomfortable when worn next to the skin in warm, humid weather. Sheerness of the fabric may counteract this characteristic to some extent.

Cleanliness and Washability. Under the microscope the appearance of Arnel fiber is similar to that of regular acetate. Being relatively smooth, the fibers tend to shed dirt. The fabric washes easily and has a high degree of shrink resistance. Arnel fabrics when wet are not weakened to the same extent as acetate and therefore can be safely home-washed and tumble-dried. All that is required for washing is reasonable care

and the use of ordinary soaps or detergents. Hot-water temperatures of not more than 160 degrees Fahrenheit may be safely used.

Since Arnel fabric lends itself so readily to home laundering and can be heat-set, garments made of Arnel may be sold as wash and wear. If proper heat-setting treatment has been given to the fabric, the garments will return to their original shape after laundering. They are likely to need little or no ironing if not wrung or crushed but allowed to dry while properly buttoned and carefully hung on a wooden hanger.

Shrinkage. Arnel triacetate fabrics are relatively stable; and since they absorb little water, they are not subject to shrinkage.

Effect of Bleaches. Arnel has good resistance to household bleaches containing sodium hypochlorite or hydrogen peroxide.

Effect of Heat. Triacetate is a thermoplastic fiber, but it gets tacky at about 570 degrees Fahrenheit. Fabrics made of Arnel triacetate have superior resistance to damage, such as glazing, even when ironed at high temperatures. No great precaution, therefore, need be taken when ironing is desired. If the construction of the garment does not permit laundering on account of padding or interlining, clothing made of Arnel may be safely dry-cleaned.

Effect of Light. Fabrics of Arnel lose some strength when exposed to sunlight but are generally more resistant to light than silk, rayon, acetate, and semidull nylon. This indicates that Arnel fabrics are suited for curtains and can be used for normal outdoor wear.

Resistance to Mildew. Arnel has extremely high resistance to deterioration by mildew. Arnel fabrics do not lose strength or become stained from mildew and are well suited for a variety of purposes where they might be exposed to damp conditions.

Resistance to Insects. Fabrics made of Arnel are resistant to attack from moths and carpet beetles. Mothproofing is not necessary.

Reaction to Alkalies. Arnel triacetate has a very high resistance to alkalies. Fabrics of Arnel will be weakened only by very strong solutions at very high temperatures. Ordinary household alkalies, such as strong soaps and ammonia, will have no harmful effect.

Reaction to Acids. In general, the effect of acids on Arnel is similar to their effect on acetate. Fabrics of Arnel are more resistant to acids than cotton, linen, silk, or rayon but would be decomposed by concentrated solutions of strong acids.

Affinity for Dyes. Dyes similar to those used for acetate may be used on fabrics of Arnel. But Arnel has a lower absorptive ability than acetate and does not take dyes as readily. Techniques have been developed, however, that result in more uniform color.

If properly treated, dyed fabrics made of Arnel are more resistant to fume- or gas-fading and crocking than acetate fabrics. In general, dyes that have good washfastness on acetate have

Figure 16-5 This pants suit is made of a blend of Arnel/nylon velour. *(Courtesy Celanese Fibers Marketing Co.)*

an even higher fastness on Arnel triacetate. Lightfastness, perspiration fastness, and resistance to wet bleeding are similar to acetate. To obtain good fastness in black, Arnel is also produced in solution-dyed black filament and staple form. Such fibers have a very high degree of fastness to all conditions.

Resistance to Perspiration. Fabrics of Arnel have good resistance to perspiration. Such fabrics are not easily deteriorated or discolored by perspiration if properly finished.

ARNEL TRIACETATE FIBER BLENDS

To obtain special styling and performance characteristics, blending of Arnel staple fiber with other fibers is sometimes advantageous. Processing and finishing characteristics, as well as the contribution to fabric performance, have a bearing on the selection of fibers and the percentages used in blends with Arnel.

Arnel is most often blended with cotton, wool, or rayon, less frequently with other fibers (see Figure 16-5).

Arnel and Cotton

Arnel provides easy care and shape retention when these fabrics are laundered. Arnel and cotton blended fabrics resist wrinkling and need little or no ironing. Cotton provides strength, abrasion resistance, and durability. Such fabrics are given greater absorbency by the cotton and are therefore less clammy and more comfortable in warm, humid weather.

This type of blend increases the styling properties and permits interesting cross-dyeing possibilities. Arnel/cotton blends have a cottonlike hand and appearance. To retain the intrinsic desirable properties of Arnel, such blends should not contain more than 30 percent cotton. Some blends contain 50 percent or more of cotton, permitting higher yarn counts; that is, finer yarns, which may be desirable where styling is the prime consideration. This greater amount of cotton will, however, decrease the desirable contribution of Arnel to the blend.

Arnel and Wool

A wide variation of blend proportions is possible and feasible with Arnel/wool blends. The Arnel provides wrinkle resistance and shape retention. The wool provides a fair amount of abrasion resistance, drape, resilience, and absorbency. Such blends will not be as warm as all-wool fabrics, which may be of advantage for use in mild weather.

Arnel and Rayon

Blends of up to 30 percent rayon and the remainder Arnel are satisfactory. Rayon provides absorbency and contributes to such styling features as textural effects and cross-dyeing. Arnel provides wrinkle resistance, shape retention, and easy care in handling and washing. However, such blends cannot take hard wear.

REVIEW QUESTIONS

1. (a) What types of yarn are made of acetate fiber? (b) How are they made?
2. (a) What types of yarn are made of Arnel triacetate? (b) How are they made?
3. (a) What variations are made in producing acetate filaments? (b) What characteristics do they give to the yarn?

4. Give three trademarks each of (a) regular acetate, (b) solution-dyed acetate, (c) special varieties of filament acetate, (d) textured acetate yarn.
5. Distinguish between triacetate and Arnel.
6. (a) What major finishes are applied to acetate fabrics? (b) How effective and durable are they?
7. (a) What major finishes are applied to Arnel fabrics? (b) How effective and durable are they?
8. Fabrics of Arnel triacetate are considered to be easy-care material. Why?
9. Name some fabrics (a) that could be made of acetate and (b) that could be made of Arnel. Name uses of each.
10. What would be the characteristics of fabrics that were made of blends of (a) acetate and wool, (b) acetate and rayon, (c) Arnel and cotton, (d) Arnel and wool, (e) Arnel and rayon?

SUGGESTED ACTIVITY

Obtain one advertisement or label identifying an acetate fabric, an Arnel triacetate fabric, a blend of acetate and another fiber, and a blend of Arnel and another fiber. Make a chart comparing the properties described on the labels. Evaluate this information.

17

NYLON

the polyamide fiber

The word "nylon" is a generic term that designates a group of related chemical compounds classified as *polyamides*. Nylon is not a trademark—it is a textile, just as cotton, linen, wool, silk, rayon, and acetate are textiles. As defined by the FTC, nylon "is a long-chain synthetic polyamide in which less than 85 percent of the amide linkages are attached to two aromatic rings." While this chemical definition may not be easily recognized by laypersons, it is evident that variations are possible and that there could be and are many varieties of nylon with certain differing properties.

HISTORY OF NYLON

Responsibility for the discovery or invention of nylon belongs to E. I. du Pont de Nemours & Co. More specifically, the credit belongs to Dr. Wallace H. Carothers and his staff of organic chemists of that company's chemical department. Realizing that there was a need for a more active program of research to provide new developments that would in-

sure the future growth of the company, Du Pont began a long-range program of chemical exploration in 1928. Deviating from the applied research previously conducted, this fundamental research aimed primarily to develop basic knowledge of chemical materials and processes. Dr. Carothers was interested in obtaining a better understanding of polymerization. He wanted to know how and why certain molecules join to form "giant" molecules, such as those that occur in cotton, silk, and rubber. After many months of research, one of Dr. Carothers's assistants discovered that one polymer, which looked like clear, heavy molasses when molten, could be drawn out into a long fiber. When it cooled, the fiber could be drawn out farther to several times its original length. This strand was strong, lustrous, and silky. The question naturally arose as to whether this would make a good textile fiber.

At this point, the experiments became practical. The Carothers group was working with a type of compound called *polyesters.* A great many were synthesized. Each was deficient in one or more vital textile properties. Attempting to find a better fiber, they mixed polyesters and polyamides, which are related to polyesters. They were not successful and therefore decided to discontinue the mixtures and concentrate on the polyamides. One of the chemists filled a container, fitted with the tip of a hypodermic needle, with a hot viscous polyamide solution. He squirted a stream of it into the air, and the stream cooled into a fine filament. After the lustrous fiber was drawn and tested, it was found to be strong and pliable and had such promise, that a large group of chemists and engineers were employed to make it a commercial success. During the next several years, research with a series of polyamides continued. In February 1935, one of these was made from hexamethylene diamine and adipic acid. This polymer was called *6,6* because each of these component chemical compounds contains six carbon atoms per molecule. This 6,6 polymer proved to be best at that time.

The name "nylon" was given to this material. (The name has no meaning. It was chosen because it was short, catchy, and hard to mispronounce.) The discovery was made public in 1938. Since nylon is proteinlike in composition, the fiber was said to be similar in certain of its properties to silk, wool, and hair. Furthermore, this new fiber had many wonderful properties of its own. On May 15, 1940, nylon hosiery went on sale throughout the country. After that, nylon began to be used for a wide variety of garments. Du Pont subsequently licensed other companies to use its patents to produce nylon 6,6, and later variations in techniques were independently

patented by others to produce this nylon.

Other experimentation with polyamides eventually led to the creation of other forms of nylon. In 1939 Schlak and Kleine of the I. G. Farben combine produced a German counterpart, nylon 6, from a polyamide called *caprolactum,* which contains 6 carbon atoms. Since then, other forms have been developed: examples are nylon 7 produced in the U.S.S.R., nylon 11 produced in Italy, and nylon 4, 8, 10, 6,10, and 6,12 produced in the United States. These nylons are all polyamides created from various raw materials in different ways, as found most economical by the producer. Chemically, they are similar but differ in molecular structure, which sometimes results in subtle differences in properties. Today, the major production in the United States is nylon 6,6 with less production of nylon 6, used primarily for carpeting and industrial fabrics. The major type produced in foreign countries is nylon 6.

METHODS OF MANUFACTURE

Nylon is actually a group of related chemical compounds. It is composed of hydrogen, nitrogen, oxygen, and carbon in controlled proportions and structural arrangements. Variations can result in types of nylon plastics, such as combs, brushes, and gears. We are here concerned with the production of nylon yarn. Since the two types of nylon that predominate the market are nylon 6,6 and nylon 6, we shall consider their basic methods of production, although variations in technique do exist among manufacturers (see Figures 17-1 and 17-3).

PRODUCTION OF NYLON 6,6

Figure 17-1 (Courtesy Celanese Fibers Marketing Co.)

HOW NYLON POLYMER 6,6 IS MADE

HOW A NYLON YARN IS MADE

FOUR ESSENTIAL STAGES IN PRODUCTION OF NYLON

A. PREPARATION OF THE NEW MATERIALS
B. CONDENSATION INTO A POLYMER
C. MELTING OF THE POLYMER CHIPS FOLLOWED BY EXTRUSION INTO FILAMENTS
D. COLD-DRAWING THE FILAMENTS

Nylon 6,6 Synthesis

By a series of chemical steps beginning with such raw materials as coal, petroleum, or such cereal by-products as oat hulls or corncobs, two chemicals called *hexamethylene diamine* and *adipic acid* are made. These are combined to form nylon salt. Then, since the nylon salt is to be shipped to the spinning mill, it is dissolved in water for easy handling. At the spinning mill, it is heated in large evaporators until a concentrated solution is obtained. The concentrated nylon salt solution is then transferred to an autoclave, which is like a huge pressure cooker. The heat combines the molecules of the two chemicals into giant chainlike ones, called *linear superpolymers*. This process gives nylon a molecular structure somewhat like wool and silk and is also the source of nylon's strength and elasticity. The linear superpolymer is then allowed to flow out of

Figure 17-2 Nylon polymer, pressed out on this huge casting wheel, is sprayed with water and solidified into a strip resembling ivory. *(Courtesy E. I. du Pont de Nemours & Co.)*

a slot in the autoclave onto a slowly revolving casting wheel. As the ribbons of molten nylon resin are deposited on the wheel, they are sprayed with cold water, which hardens them to milky white opaque ribbons. The ribbons are removed from the casting wheel to a chipper, which transforms them into flakes (see Figure 17-2).

Nylon 6 Synthesis

Beginning with coal, a series of chemical steps produces another complicated chemical called *cyclohexanone-oxime*, which converts to a substance called *caprolactum* when it is treated with sulfuric acid. Polymerization of the molten caprolactum is begun by gently heating it in a steam-jacketed stainless steel vessel as it is constantly mixed. It is then filtered and pumped to a polymerization kettle where, under carefully controlled

Figure 17-3

SCHEMATIC OF NYLON 6 PRODUCTION

Courtesy American Enka Corporation

steam heat and pressure, the caprolactum is stabilized as a superpolymer (Figure 17-4). The molten nylon 6 polymer is
then converted into chips in a manner
similar to that of nylon 6,6.

Spinning the Fiber

Nylon fiber can be made in several ways.
The most important of these methods is
the *melt process* that, depending upon
the denier of the filament desired, generally uses either the grid or extruder
spinning technique. In grid spinning,
nylon flakes from several autoclaves
are blended and poured into the hopper
of the spinning machine to insure uniformity in the final nylon yarn. Through
a valve in the bottom of the hopper, the
nylon flakes fall onto a hot grid, which
melts them. The molten nylon is pumped
through a sand filter to the spinneret, a
disk about the size of a silver dollar. The

Figure 17-4 Polymerization of the molten caprolactum under controlled stream heat and pressure
produces the stabilized superpolymer, nylon 6.
(Courtesy American Enka Co.)

spinneret has one or more holes, depending on the purpose for which the yarn is to be made. As the filaments come out of the spinneret and hit the air, they solidify. After they cool, the filaments converge, pass through a conditioner where they are moistened sufficiently to make them adhere together, and are given a few turns per inch to form a single thread and facilitate further handling.

Extruder spinning is primarily used for heavier denier yarns. The chips flow by gravity into a device that forces them by screw action through heated zones. The combined action of the heat and screw pressure melts the chips. The molten liquid is subsequently processed in the same manner as described for grid-spun yarn.

Variations in the ultimate appearance of the nylon filaments may be accomplished. It is possible to obtain a bright, lustrous nylon that can be used for satin or a semidull or dull nylon for curtains. Nylon may be delustered by a process similar to delustering rayon and acetate. The delusterants are titanium oxide, barium sulfate, zinc oxide, or zinc sulfate. When any of these chemical compounds are mixed with the polyamide solution, they will cause the nylon to be delustered. Although nylon is naturally white, the whiteness can be increased by adding an optical whitener to the molten polymer.

The nylon filaments are usually spun from round holes and have a round cross section; such fibers are smooth and slippery. The appearance and texture of the nylon filament can be altered by adjusting the shape of the holes of the spinneret. Nylon filaments may be spun to have a trilobal cross section. Antron, a nylon 6,6 fiber, and Enkaloft, a nylon 6 fiber, are of this form. They have a unique luster, a dry, pleasing hand, greater opacity, and can be printed with a sharper definition and clarity. Antron III nylon 6,6 and Enkalure II nylon 6 are forms of soil-hiding nylon fibers. Although they will hide soil, they will nevertheless get dirty. Their somewhat elongated trilobal, very smooth surfaces highly reflect light in such a way that sheen overcomes the darkened (dirty) areas. These yarns are crimped for appropriate applications, such as carpets.

Nylon filaments can also be produced so that they develop a permanent crimp. Crepeset is a 20-denier monofilament nylon 6 fiber that is permanently crimped. As the trademark implies, the fiber is extremely well suited for producing crepe fabrics that do not require a high twist. Such fabrics not only have a crepe appearance but, in addition, have a soft, luxurious texture not usually associated with crepes.

Another, Qiana nylon 6,6 fiber, highly resembles silk in its soft and supple hand. It is lightweight, drapes exceedingly well, and has excellent resistance to wrinkling. There are four types of this fiber with a total of seventeen variations produced for stretch, textured, self-bulking, and slub effect yarns.

Nylon filaments may be produced as *epitropics* or *conductive epitropics*. They contain minute particles of carbon powder embedded in their surfaces, thereby providing the ability to conduct electricity. Excellent antistatic properties can thus be produced in multifilament yarn with an extremely small amount of the carbon particles in a relatively few filaments of such yarn.

Drawing the Fiber

Up to this point, the chemical structure of the filaments is about the same as the flakes from which they were made. The filaments are opaque, have poor pliability, and are not very strong because of the random arrangement of the linear superpolymer molecules. This can be changed, however, by stretching, or cold-drawing, the filaments from 2 to 7 times their original length. The amount of stretching is dependent on the denier, elasticity, and strength desired. As the filaments are stretched, they become more and more transparent. The polyamide molecules straighten out, become parallelized, and are brought very close together. Up to a point, the nylon becomes stronger, more elastic, more flexible, and more pliable.

This elongation by cold-drawing, which is permanent, is accomplished by unwinding the yarn from one godet, or wheel, and winding it onto another godet that is rotating much faster. The speed of the second wheel determines the amount of cold-drawing; that is, if the nylon filament is to be stretched 4 times its original length, it is unwound from one godet and wound on another at a speed that will subject it to a four-fold stretch during the operation.

The yarn from the second godet is wrapped on a cylindrical tube called a *pirn*. A small amount of twist is normally inserted in the yarn as it is wound on the pirn so as to keep the filaments together and aid in the future processing of the yarn (Figure 17-5).

In conjunction with the drawing process, the nylon filaments may be textured. Draw-texturing at the production

Figure 17-5   Inspecting and wrapping pirns of nylon 6 filament for shipment. *(Courtesy American Enka Co.)*

stage places this important process under the control of the fiber producer and eliminates the additional subsequent step of texturizing by the yarn producers.

TYPES OF NYLON YARN

The diameter of the individual nylon filaments is determined by the rate of delivery from the pump to the spinneret, by the number of holes in the spinneret, and by the rate at which the yarn is drawn away from the spinneret. The size, or denier, of the yarn before drawing is determined by the diameter and number of filaments in the yarn. The denier of the yarn after drawing is determined by its original denier and the amount of cold-drawing. If it is drawn 3 times its original length, the stretched yarn will be one-third of its original denier. The individual filaments produced usually range from 1 to 15 denier.

Monofilament Yarns

Though single-filament, or monofilament, yarns of 7 denier are produced, 12-denier, 15-denier, or heavier yarns are more often manufactured. The monofilament yarns are used for hosiery and for industrial filters. These yarns are very fine and have little or no twist. Consequently, they are relatively weak nylon yarns. Heavier denier, strong monofilament yarns are also produced for various purposes.

In 1963 Du Pont introduced a new type of nylon monofilament yarn for hosiery under the trademark of Cantrece. It is a bicomponent fiber created by extruding nylon 6,6 and 6,10 solutions from a single spinneret to form the filaments adhering as one. It is a self-crimping yarn. Upon exposure to steam heat, Cantrece nylon develops a helical, or corkscrew, shape as a result of the different effects of the heat on the components of the fiber. The amount of crimp is dependent upon the temperature and rate of heating. The crimp provides greater resilience and superior fit as well as fit retention and comfort. The improved fit characteristic is said to increase the life of the hose, since there is less strain on the yarn.

In 1972, Monsanto Textiles Co. introduced a biconstituent nylon/spandex fiber called Monvelle. This monofilament is a straight, smooth, round fiber, one half of which is nylon to provide strength and transparency and the other half, spandex, to provide greater elasticity.

Multifilament Yarns

Multifilament yarns are made in both standard and high-tenacity forms. The number of filaments in each yarn varies according to the purpose of the yarn. The yarns generally range in denier from 20 to 210. Multifilament yarns are stronger than monofilament yarns because of the numerous filaments. The strength can be further increased by the amount of twist per inch given to the yarns.

Stretch Yarns

Nylon filaments can be processed to have a crimp or coiled characteristic. This gives yarns made of such nylon filaments the ability to be greatly stretched (like a spring) and come back to shape when the tension is released. These yarns are produced under several trademarks, of which one of the better known is Helanca. (See pages 75-82.)

Textured Yarns

Nylon filaments can also be processed to have a looped characteristic. Crimp-textured nylon is sometimes referred to as BCF nylon—that is, bulk continuous filament nylon. It is given a permanent crimp by the producer. Thrown yarns of these filaments have a texture and hand similar to yarns made of a staple fiber, such as cotton, but retain all the other characteristics of filament yarns. One of the best known of these textured yarns is Taslan, discussed on page 89, which is

Figure 17-6   Nylon staple and textured filament yarns such as Enkaloft nylon may be used for upholstery and carpeting. *(Courtesy American Enka Co.)*

used for sport shirts and similar apparel. Some textured filament yarns have a curly appearance that imparts a resilient, springy effect called *loft*. Examples of these are Cumuloft and Enkaloft, which are used for rugs (Figure 17-6).

Another type of textured nylon is Antron 24, which has the latent ability to increase in bulk when subjected to a hot wet-finishing process developed by Du Pont (see Figure 17-7). This yarn has very high covering power, unique luster, rapid deep-dye rates, luxurious hand, attractive texture, and resilience and durability. It is used for upholstery.

Spun Yarns

Nylon filaments may be cut about 1 to 5 inches in staple length. The individual filaments range in denier from 1.5 to 15. The staple is usually crimped and spun on a cotton system. These yarns are fuzzy and soft. They have lower tensile strength but greater abrasion resistance. They are not so elastic as the filament yarns and take longer to dry.

TRADEMARKS OF NYLON FIBERS

To identify and promote their respective products, manufacturers give trademarks to their nylon yarns that are found in advertisements and on labels or

Figure 17-7   *(a)* Close-up of untextured nylon filament yarn (bottom) and Cumuloft textured nylon filament yarn (top) showing the latter's curly, bulky appearance. *(Courtesy Monsanto Textiles Co.)* *(b)* Comparison of the bulk of Antron 24 nylon yarn before and after hot wet-finishing in a relaxed condition. *(Courtesy E. I du Pont de Nemours & Co.)*

BEFORE HOT-WET FINISHING

AFTER HOT-WET FINISHING

tags attached to garments and fabrics. Although the basic properties of these nylon yarns are similar, it is apparent that the characteristics of these yarns differ insofar as the type of nylon, cross section of the fiber, and yarn construction are concerned (see Table 17-1).

Table 17-1

NYLON TRADEMARKS				
TRADEMARK	MANUFACTURER	TYPE	SPECIAL CHARACTERISTICS	USES
Actionwear	Monsanto Textiles Co.	Multifilament	Producer-textured	Apparel
Anso	Allied Chemical Corp.	Multifilament, staple		Household furnishings, carpets
Anso-X	Allied Chemical Corp.	Multifilament, staple		Household furnishings, carpets
Antron	E.I. du Pont de Nemours & Co.	Multifilament, staple, tow	Multilobal	Apparel, carpets, household furnishings
Astro Turf	Monsanto Textiles Co.	Monofilament	Flat, ribbonlike	Sportsfields, industrial fabrics
Ayrlyn	Rohm & Haas Co.	Monofilament, multifilament		Apparel, carpets, household furnishings
Barbara	Sauquoit Fibers	Multifilament	Non-torque stretch	Apparel
Beaunit Nylon	Beaunit Corp.	Multifilament	Multilobal	Carpets, household furnishings, industrial fabrics, tire cord
Blue "C"	Monsanto Textiles Co.	Multifilament	Types vary according to desired purpose	Carpets, household furnishings, industrial fabrics, tire cord
C-Cadon	Monsanto Textiles Co.	Multifilament	Types vary according to desired purpose	Apparel, carpets, household furnishings
Cadon	Monsanto Textiles Co.	Multifilament	Types vary according to desired purpose	Apparel, carpets, household furnishings
Camalon	Camac Corp.	Multifilament		Apparel, carpets, household furnishings
Cantrece	E.I. du Pont de Nemours & Co.	Monofilament, multifilament	Bicomponent	Apparel
Caprolan	Allied Chemical Corp.	Monofilament, multifilament, staple	Types vary according to desired purposes	Apparel, carpets, household furnishings, industrial fabrics, tire cord

Table 17-1

NYLON TRADEMARKS *(Continued)*

TRADEMARK	MANUFACTURER	TYPE	SPECIAL CHARACTERISTICS	USES
Captiva	Allied Chemical Corp.	Multifilament		Apparel
Cedilla	Fiber Industries, Inc.	Multifilament	Bulked in manufacture	Apparel, carpets, household furnishings
Celanese Nylon	Fiber Industries, Inc.	Multifilament	Types vary according to desired purposes	Apparel, carpets, household furnishings, industrial fabrics, tire cord
Chadolon	Chadbourn Industries	Monofilament, multifilament		Apparel
Cordura	E.I. du Pont de Nemours & Co.	Multifilament		Industrial fabrics
Courtaulds Nylon	Courtaulds North America, Inc.	Multifilament		Apparel
Crepeset	American Enka Co.	Monofilament	Textured crepe effect built in during manufacture. Antistatic property available.	Apparel
C-Cumuloft	Monsanto Textiles Co	Multifilament	Textured	Carpets, household furnishings
Cumuloft	Monsanto Textiles Co	Multifilament	Textured	Carpets, household furnishings
Diane	Sauquoit Fibers	Multifilament	Stretch	Apparel
Du Pont Nylon	E.I. du Pont de Nemours & Co.	Monofilament, multifilament, staple, tow	Types vary according to desired purposes	Apparel, carpets, household furnishings, industrial fabrics, tire cord
Enkaloft	American Enka Co.	Multifilament, staple	Textured multi-lobal, differential dyeing	Carpets, household furnishings
Enkalure	American Enka Co.	Multifilament	Soil hiding	Apparel, carpets, household furnishings
Enkalure II	American Enka Co.	Multifilament, staple	Multilobal, improved soil hiding	Carpets, household furnishings
Enkalure III	American Enka Co.	Multifilament, staple	Antistatic	Piece-dyed, printed jersey
Enka Nylon	American Enka Co.	Monofilament, multifilament, staple	Type 6, properties vary with desired purpose	Apparel, carpets, household furnishings, industrial fabrics, tire cord

Table 17-1

TRADEMARK	MANUFACTURER	TYPE	SPECIAL CHARACTERISTICS	USES
		NYLON TRADEMARKS *(Continued)*		
Enkasheer	American Enka Co.	Monofilament	Modified torque	Apparel
Formelle	Rohm & Haas Co.	Multifilament	Color-spun	Apparel, carpets, household furnishings
Hanover Nylon	Hanover Mills, Inc.	Monofilament, multifilament		Apparel, industrial fabrics
Hazel	Sauquoit Fibers	Monofilament	Stretch	Apparel
Industrial Wire & Plastic Nylon	Industrial Wire & Plastics Co.	Monofilament	Flat, round	Apparel, household furnishings, industrial fabrics
Monvelle	Monsanto Textiles Co.	Monofilament, multifilament	Biconstituent nylon/spandex	Apparel
Multisheer	American Enka Co.	Multifilament	Stretch	Apparel
MX 108	Shakespeare Co.	Monofilament	Opaque, round	Industrial fabrics
NM 1000	Monofilaments, Inc.	Monofilament	Clear, melt-dyed	Apparel, household furnishings, industrial fabrics
NM 1200	Monofilaments, Inc.	Monofilament	Clear, melt-dyed	Apparel, household furnishings, industrial fabrics
NM 1400	Monofilaments, Inc.	Monofilament	Clear, melt-dyed	Apparel, household furnishings, industrial fabrics
Nypel Nylon	Nypel, Inc.	Monofilament		Industrial fabrics
Nytelle	Firestone Synthetic Fibers Co.	Monofilament, multifilament	Types vary according to desired purposes	Apparel, industrial fabrics, tire cord
Phillips 66 Nylon	Phillips Fibers Corp.	Multifilament	Types vary according to desired purposes	Apparel, carpets, household furnishings, industrial fabrics
Qiana	E.I. du Pont de Nemours & Co.	Monofilament		Apparel, household furnishings
Recall	Fiber Industries, Inc.	Monofilament, multifilament		Apparel
Ruvea	E.I. du Pont de Nemours & Co.	Monofilament	Ribbonlike	Apparel, household furnishings, industrial fabrics
S-3	Shakespeare Co.	Monofilament	Clear, melt-dyed	Industrial fabrics

Table 17-1

NYLON TRADEMARKS *(Continued)*				
TRADEMARK	MANUFACTURER	TYPE	SPECIAL CHARACTERISTICS	USES
Shareen	Courtaulds North America, Inc.	Monofilament, multifilament		Apparel
Shoeflex	Shakespeare Co.	Monofilament	Clear, melt-dyed	Industrial fabrics
Sooflex	Shakespeare Co.	Monofilament	Clear, melt-dyed	Industrial fabrics
Soo Valley Nylon	Shakespeare Co.	Monofilament	Round	Industrial fabrics
Source	Allied Chemical Corp.	Multifilament, staple		Household furnishings
Star Nylon	Star Fibers, Inc.	Staple		Apparel, household furnishings, industrial fabrics
Stryton	Phillips Fibers Corp.	Multifilament	Undulating, variable cross section	Apparel, household furnishings
Sunlon	Nylon Engineering	Multifilament, staple	Textured, nontextured, solution-dyed	Household furnishings, industrial fabrics
Super Bulk	American Enka Co.	Multifilament	High bulk	Household furnishings
Superflex	Shakespeare Co.	Monofilament	Clear, melt-dyed	Industrial fabrics
Synflex-N	Wall Industries	Monofilament		Household furnishings
Tajmir	Alrac Corp.	Monofilament, multifilament, staple	Nylon 4; moisture-related behavior similar to cotton	Apparel
Ultron	Monsanto Textiles Co.	Multifilament		Apparel
Variline	American Enka Co.	Multifilament	Thick-and-thin diameter variations	Apparel, household furnishings
Vylor	E.I. du Pont de Nemours & Co.	Monofilament		Industrial fabrics
Wellon	Wellman, Inc.	Staple		Apparel, household furnishings, industrial fabrics
Wellstrand	Wellman, Inc.	Staple	Heavy-denier nylon/polyester monofil	Household furnishings, industrial fabrics
X-static	Rohm & Haas Co.	Multifilament	Antistatic modified	Apparel, household furnishings
Zefran	Dow Badische Co.	Multifilament, staple		Apparel, household furnishings

Figure 17-8   Nylon filament yarn being wound from a creel onto a warp beam. *(Courtesy American Enka Co.)*

FINISHING NYLON FABRICS

Nylon fabrics can be given various finishes:

Heat setting—for permanent shape

Embossing—for pattern or design

Moiréing—for shimmer effect

Molding—for shaping fabrics

Nylonizing—for increased absorbency

Water repellency—for added protection against water

Antistatic finish—for reduction of electrostatic buildup

An outstanding feature of nylon is that it is thermoplastic; consequently, a nylon fabric or garment can be heat-set by subjecting it to a high degree of heat while being held in a particular shape. After being heat-set, the fabric or garment will always retain its shape, creases, or pleats, and require little or no ironing. Washing, dry cleaning, or wear will not cause loss of shape. Properly done, heat setting prevents nylon fabrics from shrinking.

Since nylon is thermoplastic, the application of a hot embossing roller will cause the nylon to melt in conformity with the embossing pattern. This results in a permanent finish that cannot be removed by wearing, washing, or dry cleaning. The same principle applies to nylon moiré. As with thermoplastic acetate, nylon moiré is permanent.

Because nylon is thermoplastic, fabrics made of nylon may also be *thermoformable*, which means that they can be molded into shapes by the application of pressure and heat. The fabrics may have a woven, knitted, or lace construction that has been only partially drawn in the manufacturing process. When such a fabric is preheated and then pressed in a heated mold, the drawing operation is, in effect, completed and the fabric is heat-set to the desired permanent shape. Examples of such products are hats, brassieres, and swimsuits.

Raised designs may also be created on nylon fabrics by printing the background area with phenol, which causes the treated nylon to shrink and the untreated areas to pucker.

Nylon is not very absorbent, which is a disadvantage for shirts and lingerie. To overcome this, nylon fabrics may be treated by a process known as Nylonizing. The technique utilizes nylon 8, which is more absorbent than other forms of nylon, to coat other nylon fabrics for improved absorbency.

Nylon fabrics may also be treated with a water-repellent finish, which makes them ideal for rainwear and for shower curtains.

EVALUATING NYLON FABRICS

Because nylon fabrics are produced in such a wide variety, they can be made to appear similar to cotton batiste and plissé, to the texture of linen, to jersey for sweaters, and to silk, rayon, or acetate shantung and velvet. The properties of these fabrics depend on the type of nylon, the cross section of fiber, whether the fabric is made of multifilament or spun yarn, and how the fabric is constructed.

Although there are basic properties that all nylons share, the consumer should maintain an awareness of their variations when selecting or caring for nylon fabrics.

Strength. Nylon is produced in both regular and high tenacity strengths. Although one of the lightest textile fibers, it is also one of the strongest. It is surpassed in strength only by aramid and glass. Its strength competes with the more recently developed forms of high-tenacity viscose rayon and the high wet-modulus Avril and Zantrel rayons, as well as with polyester fibers.

The strength of nylon will not deteriorate with age. These advantages make nylon desirable for sheer hosiery, curtains, blouses, and dress fabrics. Nylon not only has great tensile strength with light weight, it is also tough and pliable. Nylon has the highest resistance to abrasion of any fiber. It can take a tremendous amount of rubbing, scraping, bending, and twisting without breaking down. Spun nylon yarn has even a higher abrasion resistance than filament nylon, which makes it desirable for socks and upholstery.

Elasticity. Nylon is one of the most elastic fibers that exists today, though it does not have the exceptional elastic quality of spandex fibers. After being stretched, nylon has a strong natural tendency to return to its original shape. Like any other textile, nylon has its own limit of elasticity. If stretched too much, it will not completely recover its shape.

In addition, the type of yarn and the construction of the fabric may contribute to the behavior of the garment. For example, spun nylon is not so elastic as filament nylon. Knitted spun nylon fabrics, such as those used in sweaters, will sag more easily than knitted filament nylon fabrics, such as those used in tricot.

Of course, such stretch nylon yarns as Helanca and Agilon (discussed on pages 75–82) have exceptional elasticity. These yarns have given rise to a wide variety of stretch garments that retain their shape and comfortably conform to the contours of the body.

Resilience. Nylon has excellent resilience. Nylon fabrics retain their smooth appearance, and wrinkles from the usual daily activities fall out readily. Pile fabrics, such as velvets and rugs, keep a neat uncrushed appearance.

Heat Conductivity. Nylon fabrics may or may not conduct heat well. The warmth or coolness of a nylon garment depends on the weave of the fabric and on the type of yarn used. The smoothness, roundness, and fineness of nylon filaments permit the manufacture of very smooth low-denier yarns, which can be packed very closely when weaving the fabric. If nylon fabric is woven compactly, it will not be porous. The tight construction will not permit air to circulate through the fabric, and the heat and moisture of the body will not readily pass through it but will build up between the fabric and the body; so, the wearer will feel very warm. Such fabrics are good for winter apparel, such as windbreakers, but are not suitable for summer garments.

On the other hand, these fine nylon filament yarns may be woven into extremely thin, lightweight, sheer fabrics. These materials are very porous and permit the circulation of air. Consequently, they are cool and can be used for summer blouses and curtains.

Spun nylon yarn will produce warm fabrics. These yarns are composed of thousands of short, crimped fibers twisted together, which provide millions of tiny dead-air spaces that act as insulators. This insulation makes spun nylon fabrics warm and therefore useful for such apparel as sweaters and winter socks.

Drapability. Fabrics of nylon filament yarn have excellent draping qualities (see Figure 17-9). Lightweight sheers may have a flowing quality, medium-weight dress fabrics can drape very nicely, and heavier-weight Jacquards also drape well.

Absorbency. Nylon does not absorb much moisture. Fabrics made of nylon filament yarns will not readily wet through the material—most of the water remains on the surface and runs off the smooth fabric, which therefore dries quickly. Such fabrics are useful for raincoats and shower curtains. Spun nylon fabrics, however, will not dry quickly. Droplets of water tend to cling to the sides of the thousands of staple fibers, clogging the air spaces and relatively increasing the drying time for spun nylon fabrics. Nylon's low absorbency has a disadvantage in that the fabric feels clammy and uncomfortable in warm, humid weather unless it is a nylon 8 or a nylon 4 variety, such as Tajmir nylon,

Figure 17-9   Because of its excellent draping qualities, Qiana nylon is suitable for evening clothes of many styles. *(Courtesy E. I. du Pont de Nemours & Co.)*

which has moisture-absorption properties similar to cotton. Sometimes a hydrophilic (water-attracting) finish is used on nylon 6 or 6,6 fabrics.

Cleanliness and Washability.   Because of nylon's smooth surface, dirt and stains often come clean merely by using a damp cloth. If the yarn has an antistatic component in it (such as does X-static nylon) or if the fabric has an antistatic finish, then dirt particles are less likely to be attracted and cling, and the garment will stay cleaner longer. Otherwise, a fabric softener with antistatic properties, such as Downy or Sta-Soft, could be used in laundering. To wash nylon garments by hand or washing machine, use warm water (about 100 degrees Fahrenheit) and a detergent or soap with a water softener.

White nylon fabrics should always be separated from colored fabrics before washing because the nylon will pick up color (even from the palest pastels) and develop a dingy gray appearance that is extremely difficult to remove. Garments should be thoroughly rinsed to obtain thorough removal of soil particles and drip-dried to obtain maximum freedom from wrinkling.

Nylon filament fabrics dry very quickly. They need little or no ironing because the garments are usually heat-set to retain their shape, pleats, or creases.

Spun nylon has a tendency to pill, or form balls, on the surface of the fabric.

To minimize this, such fabrics should not be rubbed. They should be washed gently, preferably by hand. Brushing with a soft brush will reduce the pilling.

Effect of Bleaches. With proper care, nylon fabrics retain their whiteness and should not need bleaching. However, if the nylon does become yellow or gray due to either the finish on the fabric or the absorption of color from other fabrics in the same water, a good, common household bleach may be used with reasonable care.

Shrinkage. Nylon has good dimensional stability and retains its shape after being wet.

Effect of Heat. Like acetate, nylon will melt if the iron is too hot; therefore, the iron should be set at the proper heat level. Special care must be taken with fabrics made of nylon 6 because it has a lower melting point (420 degrees Fahrenheit) than nylon 6,6 (480 degrees Fahrenheit). One can identify the type of nylon by its trademark, as shown in Table 17-1.

Effect of Light. Bright nylon is more resistant to the effects of sunlight than most other fibers. Dull nylon will deteriorate a little more quickly than bright nylon; however, even dull nylon has good resistance to light.

Resistance to Mildew. Mildew has absolutely no effect on nylon. Mildew may form on nylon, but it will not weaken the fabric.

Resistance to Insects. Moths and other insects will not attack nylon because it has no attraction for them.

Reaction to Alkalies. Nylon is substantially inert to alkalies.

Reaction to Acids. Nylon is decomposed by cold concentrated solutions of such mineral acids as hydrochloric, sulfuric, and nitric acids. A boiling dilute 5 percent solution of hydrochloric acid will destroy nylon.

Affinity for Dyes. Nylon 6 has greater affinity for dyes than nylon 6,6 and can be more easily dyed with a wider range of dyes. Both types of nylon retain their color and have good resistance to fading. Nylon 4 has excellent dyeability.

Resistance to Perspiration. Nylon fabrics are resistant to perspiration. The color, however, may be affected.

NYLON FIBER BLENDS

The consumer uses many textile products that do not possess all the properties he would like them to have. He would, for example, prefer overcoats with sufficient warmth but less weight; cool, light summer clothes that would not lose their fresh, clean appearance on hot sticky days; fabrics that would wash readily, dry quickly, and not lose their shape. Textile designers and engineers are producing new fabrics to meet such needs. These combine or blend two or more fibers to give the desired properties to the fabrics.

Nylon and Cotton

When properly combined with cotton, nylon adds strength, which allows the development of unusually fine textures not possible to obtain from cotton alone. Nylon provides smoothness, silkiness, and dirt rejection. It also reduces the weight of the fabric and increases its wrinkle resistance. The cotton gives softness and moisture absorption. This combination permits the weaving of fabrics that are soft, supple, and extremely serviceable. If the combination is not properly balanced, the cotton may shrink, causing the fabric to pucker. Also, the nylon fibers may cut the cotton fibers. A blend of at least 17 percent high-tenacity nylon staple with cotton will produce very durable fabric.

Nylon and Wool

The proper combination of nylon and wool will produce a lighter-weight fabric with greater durability. Such a fabric will retain the hand, drape, and warmth of wool as well as the elasticity, resilience, and shape retention of nylon. The properties of the fabric will be in direct proportion to the amount used of each of the two fibers. A blend of 10 to 15 percent nylon and the remainder wool is considered satisfactory.

Nylon and Silk

In this combination, the silk improves the hand and provides moisture absorption. The nylon improves the stability or shape retention, as well as the elasticity and strength.

Nylon and Rayon

In this blend, the nylon gives wrinkle resistance and strength. The rayon gives suppleness, drape, and moisture absorption. Such a combination makes possible a fine-quality fabric of extremely light weight. As with cotton, if the combination is not properly balanced, the rayon may shrink, causing the fabric to pucker. Also, an improper blend of nylon and rayon may result in the nylon fibers cutting the rayon fibers. Like cotton, rayon staple blended with high-tenacity nylon staple can produce fabrics with 70 percent longer wear than all-rayon fabrics if the nylon is blended in a proportion of at least 17 percent. This blend is desirable for garments classed wash and wear.

Nylon and Acetate

The acetate in such a blend provides a luxurious hand and the nylon gives light weight and strength. As with cotton or rayon, improper blending may result in the nylon cutting the acetate fiber, and in some fabrics puckering may occur. Also, neither nylon nor acetate absorbs much moisture. Such fabrics may feel clammy and uncomfortable in warm and humid atmospheres.

Nylon and Arnel Triacetate

A blend of 15 percent nylon and 85 percent Arnel triacetate in gabardines for shirts, slacks, and fabrics for outerwear is a satisfactory combination. The nylon provides strength to give good durability. Fabrics of this blend hold their creases and pleats and shape well. They can be laundered easily and need little or no ironing. Garments made of such a blend are among those classed as wash and wear type.

REVIEW QUESTIONS

1. Who was responsible for discovering nylon?
2. (a) What is nylon? (b) May any company manufacture it?
3. (a) What are the major differences between nylon 6,6 and nylon 6? (b) For what is each used primarily?
4. How does Antron nylon differ from regular nylon 6,6?
5. (a) What is Cantrece nylon? (b) What is its outstanding feature?
6. What is Nylonizing?
7. What is meant by thermoformable nylon fabrics?
8. What types of yarns can be made of nylon? Describe them.
9. Why are some nylon fabrics warm while others are cold?
10. Why do some nylon fabrics dry faster than others?
11. What advantage does heat setting give to nylon garments?
12. Is nylon damaged (a) by mildew, (b) by moths?
13. What is the reaction of nylon (a) to alkalies, (b) to acids, (c) to perspiration?
14. (a) What are the properties of a nylon/cotton fabric? (b) What are its disadvantages?
15. What are the outstanding properties of a nylon/wool fabric?

18

ARAMID

the aromatic polyamide fiber

Aramid fibers are chemically related to the nylon polyamides. The chemical difference is that whereas nylon has *less than* 85 percent of the amide linkages attached directly to two aromatic rings, the aramid classification is based upon its having *at least* 85 percent of the amide linkages attached directly to two aromatic rings as a long-chain synthetic polyamide. This accounts for significant differences in properties between aramid and nylon as well as other fibers. Furthermore, the definition of aramid accommodates variations in types and therefore in properties within the group itself.

HISTORY OF ARAMID

While researchers at E. I. du Pont de Nemours & Co. were working on variants of nylon, they produced a fiber in the late 1950s that had certain properties—particularly heat resistance—that were significantly different from those of other types of nylon as it was then defined. The differences were considered so important

that the company began a market development program in the early 1960s and promoted its product under the trademark of *Nomex* nylon fiber in 1963. Commercial production got under way in 1967, and demand for the highly flame-resistant fiber grew for industrial use and protective garments and uniforms. The Flammable Fabrics Act, as amended in 1967, gave further impetus to interest in the fiber's use for such consumer products as apparel and sleepwear.

Du Pont research in this area of nylon variants also resulted in another type of fiber, which it experimentally designated as Fiber B. The development of Fiber B resulted in the production of another fiber which had certain unique properties, for example, that it was 5 times stronger than steel fiber of equal weight. This new fiber was named *Kevlar.*

By this point, Du Pont was convinced that it had created a group of fibers that was so significantly different in chemical composition and properties from the originally defined nylon, that in

1971 the company petitioned the U.S. Federal Trade Commission for the designation of a new generic classification. The FTC responded by taking the matter under advisement and issuing a temporary identification of DP-01. Subsequently, the commission issued a decision establishing the generic classification of *aramid*, effective January 11, 1974. By this time, Du Pont had developed four types of aramid: Nomex, Kevlar, Kevlar 29, and Kevlar 49.

METHOD OF MANUFACTURE

The raw materials for the manufacture of aramid fibers are principally derived from petroleum and natural gas, which contain the essential elements of hydrogen, nitrogen, oxygen, and carbon. These form certain chemical compounds which ultimately produce a long-chain polymer that is extruded through a spinneret as an aromatic polyamide filament. Through variations in the molecular composition and production, different forms of the several types of aramid are produced. The specific methods of production cannot be given, since the manufacturer is reluctant to divulge information for proprietary reasons.

FORMS AND TYPES OF ARAMID YARNS

The several aramids may be generally classified into two groups: those for the broadly described industrial purposes and those for consumer uses. However, there is overlapping in the two groups. The Kevlar aramid varieties are applicable principally to industrial uses. The original Kevlar aramid fiber is produced in filament form and is used for tires and industrial hose and belting. Kevlar

29 is produced in filament form and is used for cables, parachutes, and reinforcement tapes. Kevlar 49 is manufactured as filament yarn and staple roving and is used for plastic reinforcement for aerospace applications, boat hulls, and canoe and related constructions.

Depending upon the type, Nomex aramid is applicable to industrial and consumer uses. It is produced in several forms of fibers and as *fibrids*, which are very short fiber particles. Fibrids and fibers are processed into Nomex paper for electrical insulation in transformers and motors; this paper is also formed into honeycomb structures for such applications as airplane construction (Figure 18-1). Nomex aramid fibers are applicable to a wide variety of uses, from protective clothing for fire fighters, industrial workers, military aviators, and race-car drivers, to hospital pajamas and robes, to filter bags for air-pollution control, to upholstery fabrics and carpets for aircraft and ships. It is the Nomex aramid fiber types that we will consider here, since they are the textiles that are the more commonly used for fabric construction and are more directly related to consumer applications.

Figure 18-1 Honeycomb of Nomex aramid fibrils used for structural body support in airplanes. (*Courtesy E. I. du Pont de Nemours & Co.*)

Filament Yarns

Nomex aramid fiber is extruded in monofilament and multifilament forms. The yarns produced of these filaments come in a variety of numbers of filaments and are available in a range of deniers. The variations of the types available can be observed by the following:

Type 430 is a bright fiber of a natural off-white color. It is produced in 200-denier yarns of 100 filaments and 1,200-denier yarns of 600 filaments.

Type 431 is a bright fiber of off-white color specifically designed with electrical insulative properties. It is produced in 200-denier yarns of 100 filaments.

Type 432 is a regular grade fiber that is solution-dyed as olive green. It is also produced in 200-denier yarns of 100 filaments.

Type 433 is similar to type 432 except that it is solution-dyed as sage green.

Type 434 is also similar to type 432, but it is solution-dyed as international orange.

Spun Yarns

Nomex aramid fiber is also processed as tow and staple for manufacture into spun yarn on either the cotton or worsted system. There are several types based upon color, denier, and staple length. The different types, as follows, reflect the satisfaction of end product need.

Type 450 is a bright fiber which comes in dyeable and nondyeable varieties. It is produced as tow of 120,000 denier, 2.0 denier per filament, and 126,000 denier, 1.5 denier per filament. It is also produced as staple of 1.5 and 2.0 inches in length, 1.5 or 2.0 denier per fila-ment, and of 3.0 inches in length, 2.0 denier per filament.

Type 451 is the same in all respects as type 450 except that it is solution-dyed as olive green.

Type 452 is produced as tow of 126,000 denier, 1.5 denier per filament, and as staple of 1.5 and 2.0 inches in length, 1.5 denier per filament. It is solution-dyed as sage green.

Type 453 is the same in all respects as type 452 except that it is solution-dyed as international orange.

Type 454 is a 10 denier per filament dyeable staple which is cut to lengths suitable for processing on carpet yarn spinning systems.

FINISHING ARAMID FIBERS

Fabrics made of Nomex aramid can be given the following finishes:

Antistatic—for reduction of electrostatic buildup

Heat setting—for dimensional stability

Oil repellency—for protection against permanent staining

Water repellency—for protection against water absorption

Water absorbency—for improved wicking and comfort

Friction from rubbing or ordinary wear will cause electrostatic buildup in fabrics of Nomex aramid fiber. This will cause particles of dust, dirt, etc., to cling to the material. The fabric may tend to cling to itself or to other fabrics that facilitate such mutual attraction. Upon touching a metallic object, wearers could experience a very mild electric shock that, while harmless, may be disconcerting. This can be reduced significantly by treatment with appropriate antistatic finishes. There are both durable and nondurable antistatic finishes, and one should endeavor to ascertain the type used.

Not all aramid fibers are thermoplastic, thus they vary in their response to heat setting. Fabrics of Nomex aramid can be heat-set to obtain permanent shape retention.

Nomex aramid will absorb oil. Fabrics of Nomex aramid can therefore be stained. However, they can be treated with an oil-repellent finish. Although some oil may cling to the material, it may be readily removed with laundering or dry cleaning.

Like nylon, Nomex aramid does not absorb much water. Depending upon its ultimate use, fabrics of such yarn may be given a water-repellent finish for greater protection. One such suitable finish is Zepel.

The addition of a substance like *Avitex DN* will cause a fabric to wick water more readily. When such a finished fabric is part of a garment, the wicking of body moisture provides greater comfort to the wearer.

EVALUATING ARAMID FABRICS

The properties among the aramid fibers vary in certain significant ways. The particular combination of properties of each kind of aramid fiber provides uniqueness and restricts its use. This has been observed in reference to the industrial and consumer uses of them.

The salient features of each aramid fiber are considered here with reference to the fiber's application.

As has been previously noted, Kevlar is 5 times stronger than steel fiber of equal weight. It also has 50 percent more stretch resistance and greater flexibility. It has better fatigue resistance than polyester, but less than that of nylon 6,6. It has excellent resistance to dimensional change in weather and moisture conditions. It also has very good resistance to high temperatures. These properties indicate that Kevlar aramid fiber is particularly suitable for cord for radial tires but is, nevertheless, limited for other applications and is not appropriate for consumer fabrics.

Kevlar 29 also has high strength and stretch resistance. Fabrics made of this fiber have excellent tensile and tear strength, high impact resistance, and good dimensional stability. Its properties make it most suitable for industrial fabrics.

Nomex aramid fiber has characteristics which are suitable for both industrial and certain kinds of consumer fabrics. We shall concentrate on these properties. Of course, it should be kept in mind that the properties of the fabrics will also be influenced by the nature of the yarn (filament or spun), the construction and compactness of the fabric, and the finishes applied.

Strength. Nomex aramid filament fiber is stronger than regular tenacity, lighter nylon as well as the heavier high wet-modulus rayons. It is also, in general, stronger than the polyester fibers of the same weight. This strength does not deteriorate with age. Yarns of Nomex aramid staple also provide relatively high tensile strength.

Nomex aramid fiber has excellent properties for fabrics that are needed to provide a high degree of durability to wear. It has very good flexing ability, that is, it will withstand many flexings before the fibers crack and break causing the fabric to eventually wear and tear. It is favorably comparable with nylon and polyester—and can be used where fabrics are to be subjected to considerable repeated twisting and bending. The tear strength of Nomex fabric is also very high. Nomex is also highly resistant to wear from rubbing; its abrasion resistance is similar to that of nylon and polyester and is superior to that of cotton, wool, or acrylic fibers. These characteristics indicate the suitability of Nomex for such purposes as specialized work garments and sportswear, as well as carpeting.

Elasticity. Adequate information regarding the elastic properties of Nomex aramid fiber is not available.

Resilience. Nomex is resilient. Fabrics made of the fiber hold their shape.

Heat Conductivity. Nomex is not a good conductor of heat. It is adaptable for consumer garments and other purposes, since coolness or warmth of a fabric will be influenced by whether it is made of filament or spun yarn and by the nature and compactness of the construction of the fabric itself. As has been previously described for such fibers as nylon, spun yarns will produce warmer fabrics than filament yarns; open, loose, or sheer construction will produce cooler fabrics; different combinations of these elements will produce various degrees of heat conductivity or retention. Since Nomex is available in both filament and spun yarn form, variations in fabric heat conductivity are possible. However, this property is a secondary consideration for its use. When consideration is being given to its use because of its primary attributes, it is reasonably adaptable to the requirements for heat conductivity.

Drapability. While there is only limited information available, it appears that Nomex can lend itself to fabric construction that has reasonably adequate drapability for the purposes intended.

Absorbency. Nomex aramid fiber does not absorb much moisture and will tend to dry quickly.

Cleanliness and Washability. Garments of Nomex can generally be laundered by conventional home-laundering methods, including tumble drying and drip drying. Ordinary dirt and soil wash out quite satisfactorily. However, in order to retain the maximum flame resistance of Nomex, such articles should be washed separately so as to avoid pickup and adherence of the more commonly flammable lint deposits of fibers from other types of materials. Garments can be conventionally ironed with no concern about heat deterioration.

However, home laundering is inadvisable for clothing that is intended for use in areas where explosive hazards exist, since the antistatic finish on the fabric may be removed in the process and cannot be satisfactorily replaced by home methods. Cleaning such garments requires either commercial laundering or dry cleaning with specific preparation to treat them properly with an aqueous antistatic solution.

Most dirt and stains can be removed satisfactorily from fabrics of Nomex aramid, as in the case of cotton and polyester blends, for example. But for heavily soiled garments, particularly those soiled with grease or oil, dry cleaning is necessary in order to remove the stains and, importantly, thereby to preserve the flame-resistant objective of Nomex. In fact, such stains should be given a spot-cleaning treatment first to facilitate removal. Effective dry-cleaning solvents include perchlorethylene and Valclene, a Du Pont product.

Effect of Bleaches. Common bleaching agents such as hydrogen peroxide, sodium chlorite, and sodium hypochlorite used in the ordinary manner may be effectively used without having any harmful effect upon Nomex aramid fiber.

Shrinkage. Properly finished fabrics of Nomex are dimensionally stable, and one should expect size and shape retention under ordinary conditions of washing in water of 140 to 180 degrees Fahrenheit. Changes in the relative humidity of the atmosphere and immersion in water at normal temperatures have virtually no effect on Nomex fabrics.

However, under more drastic conditions there will be some effects. When immersed in boiling water, Nomex will immediately shrink about 1.25 percent, and repeated immersions for periods of five minutes or more will result in an ultimate total shrinkage of about 3.75 percent. Also, when exposed to dry air at a temperature of 500 degrees Fahrenheit, Nomex will quickly shrink about 1 percent in a few seconds. An additional 0.7

percent shrinkage will occur within ten minutes of continued exposure; thereafter, there is essentially no further shrinkage. This relatively low shrinkage reaction to heat, which can be readily accommodated in garment manufacture, is another significant factor in the suitability and usefulness of Nomex aramid fiber for fabrics that are required to be exposed to high heat conditions.

Effect of Heat. We have just considered the stability of Nomex to wet and dry heat. Beyond that, it is particularly resistant to flame (see Figure 18-2). Nomex does not melt or drip when subjected to flames, as is common for some other synthetic fibers. It has extremely low flammability. At temperatures above 700 degrees Fahrenheit the fiber does shrink, pucker, and char in proportion to the heat intensity. Any flame that is produced as a result of oxidation self-extinguishes when the heat is removed

Figure 18-2 Firefighter's turnout coat made of Nomex aramid fiber provides good protection against flames. (*Courtesy E. I. du Pont de Nemours & Co.*)

from the fiber. This flame-resistant property is an inherent characteristic of Nomex and laundering or dry cleaning will not significantly affect it.

It should be noted that oils, resins, or sizings on fabrics of Nomex or other fibers which support combustion and are blended with Nomex in fabrics will burn, flame, or create hot drips. Obviously, this would reduce the safety protection afforded by the use of Nomex.

For flash-fire protection, garments made of two layers of fabric of Nomex have been found to provide protection against second-degree burns from flames at a temperature of 2500 degrees Fahrenheit for a vital period of approximately ten seconds, when the greatest initial danger and damage generally occurs (see Figure 18-3). For greater protection, other models of fire-protective garments include aluminized fabrics of Nomex.

Effect of Light. Nomex aramid fiber is degraded by exposure to light. Tested under severe conditions, it was found that it loses 50 percent of its strength during fifty hours of exposure to direct, strong sunlight or artificial light and turns to a bronze color. This discoloration appears to act as a barrier that tends to reduce the rate of loss of strength.

While fabrics of Nomex are not likely to be ordinarily exposed to such stringent conditions, it is advisable to take light degradation into consideration when its use is contemplated. This is particularly important when the strength of Nomex is a critical factor. In such instances, precautions should be taken to protect the fiber from direct exposure to both sunlight and artificial light.

Figure 18-3   In this demonstration, gasoline was splashed over a uniform of Nomex aramid fiber and ignited. The uniform protected the wearer from burns. *(Courtesy E. I. du Pont de Nemours & Co.)*

Resistance to Mildew. Nomex has excellent resistance to mildew.

Resistance to Insects. Moths, beetles, and other insects will not attack Nomex because it has no food value for them.

Reaction to Alkalies. Nomex is substantially resistant to alkalies. It has good resistance to alkalies at room temperature. It will be degraded by a strong alkali, such as sodium hypochlorite, at elevated temperatures for long periods of exposure.

Reaction to Acids. The resistance of Nomex aramid fiber to both strong mineral and organic acids is superior to that of nylon. However, it will lose strength from prolonged exposure to hydrochloric, nitric, and sulfuric acids at elevated temperatures.

Affinity for Dyes. Nomex staple fiber can be dyed to a wide range of colors, but a carrier and pressurized equipment are required. As noted on page 399, it is produced in certain solution-dyed types.

Resistance to Perspiration. Nomex is resistant to degradation by perspiration.

NOMEX ARAMID FIBER BLENDS

The value of blending Nomex aramid fiber with another fiber or fibers would be primarily to enhance the flame-resistant properties of a fabric. To be sufficiently effective and still gain possible combined advantages of Nomex with those that other fibers might contribute, Nomex would best be blended only with other fibers that have an inherent flame-resistant characteristic in their composition. Such fibers would include certain cellulosic fibers, such as PFR rayon and Acele FLR acetate; certain polyesters, such as Dacron D-489 (FLR); and certain modacrylics, such as SEF.

The properties that rayon and acetate fibers would contribute have been previously discussed. The contributing characteristics of the other fibers are considered in subsequent chapters.

REVIEW QUESTIONS

1. How does aramid compare in composition with that of nylon?
2. What are the several kinds of aramid fibers and for what purposes are they used?
3. How do the several types of Nomex aramid yarns differ?
4. What are the major finishes that can be given to fabrics of Nomex aramid fiber?
5. Compare the strength of Kevlar and Nomex aramid fibers.
6. Summarize the wearability and durability of Nomex aramid fiber.
7. Review the general procedures for the cleaning and pressing of fabrics of Nomex, noting any particular precautions that may be desirable to take.
8. What is the major characteristic of Nomex aramid fiber?
9. What is the effect of light on Nomex?
10. Will Nomex aramid fiber be damaged by (a) mildew, (b) insects?
11. Describe the reaction of Nomex to alkalies.
12. Summarize the reaction of Nomex to acids.

SUGGESTED ACTIVITY

Obtain samples of fabrics made of nylon; Nomex aramid; flame-resistant rayon, acetate, polyester, and modacrylic; and flame-retardant treated cellulosic materials. Compare their resistance to flaming and disintegration. Note whether they flame at all, if so to what extent, and how long it takes each to disintegrate.

19

POLYESTER

the terephthalate fiber

Polyester fibers are long-chain polymers produced from elements derived from coal, air, water, and petroleum. As defined by the FTC, these fibers are chemically composed of "at least 85 percent by weight of an ester of a substituted aromatic carboxylic acid, including but not restricted to substituted terephthalate units and para substituted hydroxybenzoate units." While it is difficult for the average layperson or consumer to comprehend this technical definition, it is apparent that there are variations in the compositions and therefore in the properties of polyester fibers.

HISTORY OF POLYESTERS

The groundwork for the development of polyester fibers was laid by Dr. W. H. Carothers in his experiments with giant molecular structures. Seeing more immediate promise in the polyamides, he ultimately concentrated his research on them and, as a result, developed nylon. However, Dr. Carothers had published

research information on polyesters, and after studying his works, British research chemists decided to examine the possibilities of polyesters. During the period from 1939 to 1941, investigations were conducted in the laboratories of the Calico Printers Association, Ltd., by J. R. Whinfield, J. T. Dickson, W. K. Birtwhistle, and C. G. Ritchie. The work resulted in the development of a polyester fiber known in England as *Terylene*.

In 1946 E. I. du Pont de Nemours & Co., the company under whose auspices Carothers had engaged in the initial research, purchased the exclusive rights to produce this polyester fiber in the United States. Under the temporary name of Fiber V and in essentially the same chemical form, Du Pont conducted intensive development work. By 1951, the company was commercially producing this fiber, which is called *Dacron* (pronounced day'kron).

Subsequently, other companies became interested in polyester fiber. In 1958, Eastman Chemical Products, Inc., announced its own version of polyester, which is called *Kodel;* it is produced by its affiliate, Tennessee Eastman Co. The following year, the Celanese Corp. of America obtained licenses to use certain patents owned by Du Pont and entered the market with a polyester called *Fortrel,* which is now manufactured by the Celanese affiliate, Fiber Industries, Inc. In 1966, American Enka Co. announced its *Enka* polyester fiber and Chemstrand Co., now Monsanto Textiles Co., introduced its *Blue "C"* polyester fiber. (Because the Blue "C" trademark is used for other kinds of Monsanto fibers, the full generic fiber identification beyond this trademark must be noted to avoid confusion among that company's fibers.) The following year, the American Viscose Division of FMC Corp. introduced its Fiber 200 polyester with the trademark *Avlin,* and Hoechst Fibers, Inc., an outgrowth of an alliance between Hercules, Inc., and Farberwerke Hoechst AG, presented its *Trevira* polyester fiber. Since then, additional companies have joined the polyester competition.

The polyester fibers produced by these companies may be primarily divided into two varieties: PET (polyethylene terephthalate) and PCDT (poly-1,4-cyclohexylene-dimethylene terephthalate). Most of the production is PET. Modification of each of these varieties is engineered to provide specific properties. It is also possible to produce other variants of polyester.

METHODS OF MANUFACTURE

Generally, each company produces only one variety of polyester, though there are likely to be modifications under such specific trademarks as Dacron 51, a bright, high-tenacity PET polyester fiber. (The reference to a number indicates the particular modification of that variety of polyester fiber.) One exception is Kodel polyester, which is produced as a Kodel 400 series (a PET variety) and a Kodel 200 series (a PCDT variety).

It is interesting to note that the same polyester used to produce a PET fiber is also made in thin, transparent film form. It is marketed under the trademark Mylar and used as a protective coating over metallic yarns, such as Lurex. Mylar is also used for magnetic tape for recording purposes.

PET Polyester

The process of manufacture of PET polyester fiber is similar to that of nylon, but the chemicals used are different (see Figure 19-1). The principal raw material is ethylene obtained from petroleum. The ethylene is oxidized to produce a glycol monomer dihydric alcohol that is then combined with another monomer, terephthalic acid, in an autoclave at a high temperature in a vacuum. Polymerization takes place with the aid of catalysts. The clear, colorless, molten polyester then flows from a slot in the vessel onto a casting wheel and forms into a ribbon as it cools to a porcelainlike hardness. The polymer is then cut into very small chips, dried to remove all traces of moisture, and blended for uniformity in preparation for spinning into yarn.

PCDT Polyester

The original PCDT polyester fiber is Kodel, which is now designated as the Kodel 200 series. This form of polyester is made by condensing terephthalic acid with 1,4-cyclohexane-dimethanol to form the tongue twister, poly-1,4-cyclohexy-lene-dimethylene terephthalate; hence, the convenient abbreviation PCDT polyester. As for PET polyester, PCDT is processed for melt spinning.

Spinning the Fiber

The molten polymer is rigorously maintained in an airtight condition, as oxygen will affect its stability. The spinning technique is similar to that used for nylon fibers. The viscous melt is extruded through a spinneret, and the filaments are subsequently drawn into the desired polyester fiber. Variations in the production process depend upon the desired end results.

Polyester is normally a bright fiber, but it may be made semidull or dull by the addition of a delusterant. A flame retardant may be added to the solution, as is done to produce such fibers as Dacron D-489 (FLR) polyester. Generally, the shape of the spinneret holes is round, but this may be altered to affect the appearance and hand of the fiber. Certain additives may be included in the melt to alter the fiber's affinity for certain dyes.

Drawing the Fiber

Upon extrusion from the spinneret, the polyester filament does not have all the desired characteristics because of the random arrangement of the superpolymer molecules. The fibers are therefore drawn, or elongated, with the aid of godet wheels, in the same manner as nylon fibers are drawn. The temperature conditions and the extent to which the fibers are drawn depend upon the pro-

perties desired. The polyester fibers are usually drawn to 5 times their original length (which results in a fiber denier that is one-fifth the original denier upon extrusion from the spinneret). If higher-tenacity fiber is to be produced, the filaments are drawn to a greater extent, as this increases the linear molecular orientation of the fiber. As they emerge from the drawing process and meet cold air, the filaments solidify.

Generally, the PET polyester filaments are drawn hot because this procedure produces more uniform fibers. However, when heavier deniers are desired, the monofilaments may be drawn at room temperature because the poor heat conductivity of the fiber results in irregularities in thick filaments that are drawn hot. PCDT (Kodel 200 series) polyester fibers are drawn at a higher temperature because of their higher melting point.

During the drawing process, the fibers may be textured. Draw-texturing is increasingly significant in the production of polyester fiber. It saves steps, time, and production costs, and it gives the fiber producer greater quality control over the finished fiber (pages 73–74).

TYPES OF POLYESTER YARN

The diameter of the polyester yarn is determined by (1) the rate of extrusion of the filaments from the spinneret, (2) the number of spinneret holes and therefore the number of filaments, and (3) the rate of drawing of the filaments. The yarns come in a wide range of deniers and staple lengths. The yarns are produced as monofilament, multifilament, and spun (see Figure 19-1).

MANUFACTURING PROCESS OF POLYESTERS

PROCESSING FILAMENT YARN

PROCESSING STAPLE FIBER

DRIER

MELT HOPPER

POLYMER POLYETHYLENE TEREPHTHALATE

DRIER

MELT HOPPER

CRIMPER

DRAW ROLLERS

CUTTER

TEXTURING YARN

UNDRAWN YARN

SPINNING HEAD

SPINNING HEAD

POST TREATING HEATER

FEED ROLL

STAPLE FIBER

SPINDLE

FEED ROLLERS

FALSE TWIST HEATER

FILAMENT YARN

FEED ROLL

DRAW TWIST MACHINE

(TEXTURED YARN)

OPENING – FIBERS OR BLEND OF FIBERS (NATURAL OR MAN-MADE) START THEIR TRIP THROUGH THE MILL IN THE OPENING ROOM. FIBERS ARE MIXED TOGETHER IN THIS MACHINE.

CARDING – FIBERS MUST BE STRAIGHTENED AND MUST POINT IN THE SAME DIRECTION. IN THE CARDING PROCESS. THE FIBER IS FORMED INTO A ROPE LIKE STRAND CALLED *SLIVER*.

KNITTING – ANOTHER WAY OF MAKING FABRIC IS KNITTING. KNITTED FABRIC IS USED IN HOSIERY, UNDERWEAR, SWEATERS, SKIRTS AND WOMEN'S SUITS. KNITTING DIFFERS FROM WEAVING IN THAT ONE YARN CAN FORM THE ENTIRE FABRIC. A SERIES OF LOOPS OF YARN ARE HOOKED TOGETHER. A KNITTING MACHINE IS SHOWN HERE, WITH CLOTH COMING OUT THE BOTTOM CENTER.

DRAWING – THE DRAWING FRAME DRAWS OUT SEVERAL SLIVERS AND CONDENSES THEM INTO ONE AGAIN. FORMING A NEW SLIVER THAT GOES INTO A ROVING FRAME.

ROVING – IN THE ROVING PROCESS THE STRAND OR SLIVER IS STRETCHED MORE. REDUCED IN SIZE AND SLIGHTLY TWISTED TO GIVE STRENGTH BEFORE IT GOES TO THE SPINNING MACHINE.

MACHINE

WEAVING – LOOMS ARE THE MACHINES THAT MAKE YARN INTO FABRIC. THE PROCESS IS CALLED WEAVING. IN PLAIN WEAVING, THE CROSSWISE YARNS PASS OVER AND UNDER THE LENGTHWISE YARNS. THERE ARE SEVERAL TYPES OF LOOMS FOR WEAVING VARIOUS TYPES OF FABRIC.

WARPING – SEVERAL THINGS MUST BE DONE TO THE YARN THAT RUNS LENGTHWISE BEFORE IT CAN BE WOVEN INTO FABRIC. THE YARN IS WOUND ON A LARGE BEAM. DIPPED INTO BOILING STARCH TO GIVE PROTECTIVE COATING. THE YARN CAN NOW BE WOVEN INTO FABRIC.

SPINNING – YARN IS MADE IN THE SPINNING STAGE. THE ROVING IS STRETCHED INTO THIN YARN AND TWISTED TO ADD MORE STRENGTH.

Figure 19-1 *(Courtesy Celanese Fibers Marketing Co.)*

Filament Yarns

Filament yarns are produced of PET polyester. They are made in monofilament and multifilament forms. The direction and amount of twist per inch are determined by the desired end use. The variety of characteristics of the yarns is also predetermined.

Bright, regular-tenacity polyester yarn is one popular type. It has good light resistance, as well as stretch and sag resistance. It can be used for sheer, lightweight fabrics, such as tulle, voile, and organdy, and is very suitable for curtains. Another very popular type is the regular-tenacity, semidull yarn. It is used for a wide variety of apparel, including dresses and lingerie. A duller version is used for shirts and blouses.

Another type produced is a semidull polyester containing an additive that gives it an affinity for basic dyes, thereby giving the yarn greater versatility for use in fabrics that can be cross-dyed. Sometimes the PET polyester is treated with an optical brightener so that the fabric made of this type of yarn will have a permanent white character. To impart more drapability, softer hand, and greater luster, the yarn may be made of filaments that are trilateral, or trilobal. Polyester yarns, which are resistant to various chemicals, seawater, and microorganisms, are made of a bright, high-tenacity fiber for such industrial purposes as conveyor belts, ropes, netting, and sails. High-tenacity polyester filament yarns are available for tire cord.

Textured Yarns

Textured polyester yarns are produced of PET multifilaments. They are given a texturizing either in conjunction with the drawing process or subsequently as part of the throwing and texturizing process in producing the finished yarn. *Taslan* polyester fiber is one example.

Spun Yarns

Spun yarns are made of staple or of cut, crimped tow of either PET or PCDT polyester fiber (see Figure 19-2). The staple is produced in a wide range of deniers and lengths according to the desired end uses. The staple may be bright, semidull, or dull. The fiber may be polished to reduce the crimp and increase the luster. It may be regular-, mid-, or high-tenacity. It may be round or trilateral for increased sheen. The staple may be spun directly into yarn or blended with other staple, such as cotton, wool, or rayon and then spun into yarn.

The type of fiber cut into staple depends upon the ultimate end use. PCDT (Kodel 200 series) polyester fiber is particularly suited to staple and spun yarn purposes. It has great resilience, exceptional bulking ability, and good resistance to pilling. Unless the product is labeled as being made of some type of Kodel 200 polyester, the consumer should assume that PET polyester is used and must rely upon the proper choice of fiber and/or yarn made by the product manufacturer.

Semidull, regular-tenacity polyester staple may be spun on either the cotton or wool system, depending upon the ultimate yarn desired. Finer yarns are used for summer suitings that require both unusual resiliency and dimensional

Figure 19-2 *(a)* Polyester tow bands of up to 1,000,000 denier are broken by stretching and restretching the broken tow to reduce the staple to desired relatively uniform length, then crimped and formed into staple sliver. *(b)* The flow diagram depicts the process. *(Courtesy Turbo Machine Co.)*

stability to prevent puckering and change in shape during humid weather. Heavier yarns made of this staple may be used for outerwear and for knitted fabrics because of their exceptional shape retention and stretch resistance.

Semidull, regular-tenacity polyester may also be spun on the worsted or rayon (modified cotton) system. These yarns are used for winter-weight and spring-weight fabrics. Such fabrics include finished worsteds like sharkskin, gabardine, and Bedford cord, as well as such napped unfinished worsteds as flannel and serge. Still heavier weights may be made of bright, regular-tenacity fiber and spun on a woolen or modified worsted system for pile fabrics.

Regular-tenacity polyester staple containing an optical brightener may be spun into yarn for such products as men's knitted underwear. Mid-tenacity polyester is very suitable for blending with cotton and high wet-modulus rayon fibers for spun yarn for such purposes as men's shirting fabrics.

Bright, trilateral, polished staple may be spun into yarn to be used to make carpets or upholstery fabrics. Trilateral, polished, basic-dyeable staple is also available for such purposes as upholstery fabrics.

A variety of staple polyesters called conductive epitropics has also been developed. These polyesters contain tiny particles of carbon powder embedded in the surface of the fiber. The carbon particles give the fiber the ability to conduct electricity, which provides antistatic protection. Remarkably small quantities of the fiber are needed to be blended with non-epitropic fibers to provide excellent antistatic effects. It is also expected that epitropic fibers will be developed for other purposes, such as heat conductivity.

A variety of high-tenacity polyester staple is available for spun yarns required for sewing threads, belts, ropes, fire hoses, and various other industrial purposes.

Polyester staple is also produced for fiberfill, rather than yarn. It is lightweight and has excellent resilience and loft, which provides comfort and insulation. Since it is also nonallergenic, it is used for pillows, quilting, and sleeping bags (see Figure 19-3).

TRADEMARKS OF POLYESTER FIBERS

As illustrated in Table 19-1, there are many polyester yarns produced by many manufacturers. Most of them manufacture several types. Each usually produces either PET or PCDT polyester fiber. One company, Eastman Chemical Products, Inc., produces both. Every manufacturer has its own registered trademarks which appear on labels and tags for its products. Within the groups of variations of the types of polyesters, the properties are essentially similar. The difference in quality among polyesters depends upon the quality control of the fiber and yarn production, as well as the fabrication of the final product.

Figure 19-3 (a) Fiberfill polyester staple is used as insulation that contributes warmth with light weight to ski jackets. (*Courtesy Beaunit Fibers*) (b) Polyester fiberfill gives warmth and light weight to the quilt. (*Courtesy Celanese Fibers Marketing Co.*)

Table 19-1

POLYESTER TRADEMARKS				
TRADEMARK	MANUFACTURER	TYPE	SPECIAL CHARACTERISTICS	USES
Avlin (Fiber 200)	FMC Fibers Division	Multifilament, staple		Apparel, household furnishings
Blue "C"	Monsanto Textiles Co.	Multifilament	Types vary according to desired purpose	Apparel, household furnishings, industrial fabrics, tire cord
Dacron	E.I. du Pont de Nemours & Co.	Multifilament, staple, tow	Types vary according to desired purpose	Apparel, household furnishings, industrial fabrics, tire cord
Dacron D-489 (FLR)	E.I. du Pont de Nemours & Co.	Staple	Flame-retardant	Apparel, household furnishings, industrial fabrics
Diane	Sauquoit Fibers	Multifilament	Textured	Apparel
Ektafill	Eastman Chemical Products, Inc.	Staple	Fiberfill	Household furnishings
Encron	American Enka Co.	Multifilament, staple	Types vary according to desired purpose	Apparel, household furnishings, industrial fabrics, tire cord
Encron MCS	American Enka Co.	Staple	Modified cross section	Apparel, household furnishings
Enkalure II	American Enka Co.			Household furnishings
Enka Polyester	American Enka Co.	Multifilament, staple	Types vary according to desired purpose	Apparel, household furnishings, industrial fabrics, tire cord
Esterweld	IRC Fibers Co.	Multifilament		Industrial fabrics
Fortrel	Fiber Industries, Inc.	Multifilament, staple, tow	Types vary according to desired purpose	Apparel, household furnishings, industrial fabrics, tire cord
Fortrel 7	Fiber Industries, Inc.	Tow		Apparel, household furnishings
Goodyear Polyester	Goodyear Tire & Rubber Co.	Multifilament		Tire cord
Hanover Polyester	Hanover Mills, Inc.	Monofilament, multifilament		Apparel, household furnishings, industrial fabrics
Hystron	Hoechst Fibers, Inc.	Multifilament, staple, tow	Varieties have high tenacity, low pilling	Apparel, household furnishings, industrial fabrics

Table 19-1

POLYESTER TRADEMARKS *(Continued)*				
TRADEMARK	MANUFACTURER	TYPE	SPECIAL CHARACTERISTICS	USES
IRC Polyester	IRC Fibers Co.	Multifilament		Industrial fabrics, tire cord
Kodel 200	Eastman Chemical Products, Inc.	Multifilament, staple	Types vary according to desired purpose; PCDT variety	Apparel, household furnishings, industrial fabrics
Kodel 400	Eastman Chemical Products, Inc.	Staple	Types vary according to desired purpose	Apparel, household furnishings
MX6020	Shakespeare Co.	Monofilament	Round; regular, medium, and low shrinkage	Industrial fabrics
MX6020H	Shakespeare Co.	Monofilament	Round; hydrolysis-resistant; regular, medium, and low shrinkage	Industrial fabrics
Newton Polyester	Newton Filaments, Inc.	Multifilament		Industrial fabrics
NM3100	Monofilaments, Inc.	Monofilament	Clear, melt-dyed	Apparel, household furnishings, industrial fabrics
Polar Guard	Fiber Industries, Inc.	Multifilament, tow		Apparel, industrial fabrics
Quintess	Phillips Fiber Corp.	Multifilament		Apparel, household furnishings
Soo Valley Polyester	Shakespeare Co.	Monofilament		Industrial fabrics
Spectran	Monsanto Textiles Co.	Staple		Apparel
Star	American Enka Co.	Multifilament	8-pointed, reflection-reducing	Apparel
Strialine	American Enka Co.	Multifilament	Varied thick-and-thin diameter; color contrast dyeing	Apparel, household furnishings
Trevira	Hoechst Fibers, Inc.	Multifilament, staple, tow	High-tenacity tow	Apparel, household furnishings, industrial fabrics
Wellene	Wellman, Inc.	Staple		Household furnishings, industrial fabrics
Zefran	Dow Badische Co.	Multifilament		Apparel, carpets

FINISHING POLYESTER FABRICS

Several finishes can be given to polyester fabrics to increase their usefulness. Among the most important are:

Heat setting—for permanent shape retention

Compressive shrinking—for increased shrink resistance

Calendering—for smoothness and reduced pilling

Singeing—for improved hand and reduced pilling

Embossing—for design and luster

Shearing—for smooth, even pile or nap

Water and soil repellency—for comfort and ease of care

Antistatic finish—for reduction of electrostatic buildup

Fabrics made of PET polyester yarn should be given compressive shrinking and heat setting to obtain dimensional stability to subsequent finishing processes and washing. This is particularly important for polyester blends with cotton and rayon. Fabrics made of polyester spun yarn can be effectively stabilized in normal dyeing and finishing operations. PCDT polyester fabrics need not be initially heat-set because they are inherently stable. Both forms of polyester fabrics can be permanently pressed since they are thermoplastic and hold their shape exceedingly well. Blends of polyester and wool may be fulled, crabbed, and decated to improve compactness and dimensional stability.

Stabilized fabrics made of either polyester filament yarn or spun yarn have excellent wrinkle resistance and recovery from wrinkling. Essentially permanent creases can be pressed into them at the ordinary ironing temperature for rayon (about 275 degrees Fahrenheit) and remain sharp even after the fabric is washed. Such creases, however, can be ironed out if desired. This means that such garments as suits made of polyester staple will hold their shape and press in abnormally damp weather and even when wet.

Singeing has been found to be an effective method for reducing the pilling of spun yarn fabrics. While some types of polyester yarns are inherently pill-resistant, singeing does yield a firmer hand. Careful control of the speed of the fabric movement and the height of the flame is maintained merely to remove fuzz and yet prevent melting of the fibers in the fabric, which will cause loss in fabric strength.

Calendering also improves the pilling resistance by flattening the fiber ends and smoothing the surface. It also provides increased luster and better covering power by reducing the size of the fabric pores.

Fabrics made entirely of polyester filament yarns can be preshrunk in finishing as much as 20 percent. Consequently, such fabrics will not shrink to any significant extent thereafter. It is therefore also possible to produce cloth with very little porosity. Since polyester is hydrophobic and therefore will not absorb moisture, polyester fabrics serve excellently for such purposes as raincoats.

When polyester staple is blended with another fiber, such as cotton, into yarn, fabrics of such yarn can be given a water-repellent finish which could be highly effective. Sometimes such a fabric is given a water- and soil-repellent finish. This is particularly helpful since polyesters do absorb oil, causing stains which are very difficult to remove. Finishes such as Scotchgard and Zepel are highly effective.

Shallow embossing, including schreinering, may also be applied to polyester and cotton blends to increase luster.

Polyester fabrics are subject to the accumulation of static electricity. Where this would prove objectionable, polyester fabrics can be treated with antistatic agents. The electrostatic property of polyester fabrics attracts lint, dust particles, hair, and similar substances. It therefore becomes difficult to keep dark fabrics looking neat and to prevent light fabrics from looking dingy. Such fabrics also cling to the body as the static electricity builds up. Consequently, several antistatic finishes have been developed. Some provide temporary protection; others are durable finishes. The consumer should carefully read the labels identifying such finishes to determine the maximum benefits that the finish has given the fabric.

EVALUATING POLYESTER FABRICS

The two major forms of polyester (PET and PCDT) have certain differences between them. These differences are principally in mechanical attributes rather than chemical. In general, the consumer may assume that the polyester being used is PET unless the fiber is identified as a Kodel 200 variety. Since Kodel polyester fiber comes in the two forms, 400 and 200, care instructions should be observed. It should be expected that the manufacturer will use the form of polyester better suited to the product.

It has been noted that polyester fiber is produced in both filament and staple form and that each form has certain properties that affect the appearance and performance of the finished fabric. Furthermore, some polyester filament and staple have properties designed for general consumer use while others are designed for industrial use. Within these two categories, there are further variations in properties. Therefore, while the ultimate user may be able to distinguish between fabrics of filament and spun yarn, one is not likely to be able to determine the particular type of polyester used in order to anticipate the precise properties and the performance of the fabric. One must rely upon the manufacturer's ability to make the proper polyester fiber selection. Within this framework, the consumer may expect a certain range of characteristics and certain standards of performance of the polyester fabrics purchased. Some of these are general, others are specific.

Strength. As a group, polyester fibers may be characterized as relatively strong fibers. The PET polyesters are, in general, stronger than the PCDT Kodel 200 series polyesters.

Fabrics of regular-tenacity PET polyester filament yarns are very strong and durable. The high-tenacity PET polyester filament yarns used for tires and industrial purposes are extremely strong; some types are the strongest of all textiles except glass, aramid, and certain highly specialized, exotic fibers not commonly used for consumer products. The staple fibers also vary in strength depending on the type of fiber.

In general, PET polyester staple ranges from high tenacity, which is stronger than nylon staple, to regular tenacity, which is about equal to or slightly weaker than nylon staple.

The abrasion resistance of polyester fiber is exceptionally good, being exceeded only by nylon among all of the commonly used fibers. However, the abrasion resistance of low-pilling types, including those of PCDT polyester is of a lower order that is generally similar to wool.

In summary, the tensile strength and abrasion resistance of polyester fiber are very good, and the fiber will provide relatively good service. PET polyester is superior in this regard to PCDT Kodel 200 series polyester.

Elasticity. Polyester fibers do not have a high degree of elasticity, although PCDT polyester is more elastic than PET polyester. In general, polyester fiber is characterized as having a high degree of stretch resistance, which means that polyester fabrics are not likely to stretch out of shape too easily. This property makes polyester suited for knitted garments; sagging and stretching that would ordinarily occur are reduced. Fabrics of polyester fiber have good dimensional stability.

Resilience. Polyester fiber has a high degree of resilience. PCDT polyester is more resilient than PET polyester. Not only does a polyester fabric resist wrinkling when dry, it also resists wrinkling when wet. For example, a suit of polyester will keep its pressed appearance after many wearings, even after exposure to rain or moist, humid weather.

Absorbency. Polyester is one of the least absorbent fibers. This low absorbency has two important advantages. Polyester fabrics will dry very rapidly since almost all the moisture will lie on the surface rather than penetrate the yarns. Fabrics of polyester fiber are therefore well suited for water-repellent purposes, such as rainwear. Furthermore, this low absorbency means that polyester fabrics will not stain easily. Most substances that would stain other fabrics lie on the surface and can be wiped or washed off easily. (One limitation, though, is polyester's affinity for oil, which stains and is extremely difficult to remove.)

Fabrics of low absorbency generally have the disadvantage of being clammy and uncomfortable in humid weather because they will not absorb perspiration or atmospheric moisture. As a result, an absorbent fiber such as cotton is often blended with the polyester staple.

Cleanliness and Washability. Since polyester fibers generally are smooth and have a very low absorbency, most stains lie on the surface and can easily be washed by hand or machine. Strong soaps are not needed. However, oil stains are more stubborn and under certain circumstances cannot be entirely removed. Some polyester fibers, such as Spectran, do have built-in superior stain release and less redisposition of soil during laundering.

Fabrics of polyester filament yarn dry very quickly. Those of spun yarn dry comparatively rapidly if wrung out well. There is essentially no water shrinkage of polyester fabrics; therefore, shirts, blouses, and even slacks made entirely of polyester (including the sewing thread) may be safely laundered.

When ironing polyester fabrics, it is best to use a moderately hot iron as for rayon. Excessive heat will cause polyester to melt. (Burning tobacco will quickly melt holes in such fabrics. Certain resins are being used to coat the material, thus minimizing this danger.) Actually, little ironing is needed even after long wear or after being completely wet, because garments made of polyester hold their shape and creases after being heat-set. Furthermore, the wrinkle resistance of polyester is extremely good (see Figure 19-4).

Fabrics of spun polyester yarn that have a tendency to pill should be washed gently and brushed with a soft brush while drying in order to disentangle the fiber ends and straighten them out. Since PCDT polyester is, in general, weaker than PET polyesters, Kodel 200 fiber ends in spun yarns tend to break off rather than hold the pilling. Fabrics of Kodel 200 spun yarns therefore do not have as much pilling.

Heat Conductivity. Fabrics of polyester fiber are better conductors of heat than fabrics made of acrylic fibers (discussed in Chapter 20). In general, polyester filament fiber is round. This results in a smoother yarn woven into fabrics with fewer air spaces and less insulation. When the filaments are textured, there is an increase in loft and therefore some amount of insulation. Polyester staple fiber is crimped and this does provide greater insulation in the yarns and fabrics. But a fabric of polyester spun yarn would not be as warm as a fabric made of the acrylics, silk, or wool; it would be warmer than if made of cotton, linen, or rayon. One of the reasons for the apparent greater warmth of polyester is its

Figure 19-4 Polyester filament yarn may be woven into sheer, durable, easy-care fabrics. *(Courtesy Celanese Fibers Marketing Co.)*

low absorbency. However, polyester fiberfill is crimped to provide bulk and insulative properties.

Drapability. Fabrics of polyester filament yarn have satisfactory draping qualities. The trilobal filament type is more supple and imparts better drapability. Staple polyester can produce spun yarn that is more flexible and softer, thereby imparting the draping quality. Drapability of fabrics of blended polyester staple will depend upon the type and proportion of blend in the yarn as well as the fabric construction.

Effect of Bleaches. Fabrics of polyester may be safely bleached because polyester has good resistance to deterioration by household bleaches. If the polyester has an optical brightener, no bleaching is necessary.

Shrinkage. As has been indicated, polyester fabrics shrink as much as 20 percent during wet-finishing operations and they are generally heat-set in later treatments. Consequently, finished polyester woven and knitted fabrics will not shrink. They have excellent dimensional stability.

Fabrics of polyester blends should be properly treated for permanent press so as to prevent the nonpolyester component from shrinking. Also, garments should be sewn with polyester thread to avoid puckering.

Effect of Heat. Depending upon the type, polyester will get sticky at 445 to 455 degrees Fahrenheit. Therefore, if ironing is needed, it should be done at lower temperatures such as those used for ironing rayon. At temperatures in the range of 482 to 554 degrees Fahrenheit, polyester will melt and flame but will self-extinguish when heat or flame is removed unless the fabric has a finish which burns or supports combustion. Since sparks, burning cigarette ashes, and the like will easily melt holes in polyester fabrics, appropriate care should be exercised.

Effect of Light. Polyester has good resistance to degradation by sunlight. Fabrics of polyester are therefore well suited for outdoor use. Over a prolonged period of exposure to direct sunlight, however, there will be a gradual deterioration of the polyester fiber. When exposed to sunlight behind glass, polyester shows a considerable increase in resistance to sunlight; it has a marked superiority over most other fibers under these conditions and is therefore very well suited for curtains.

Resistance to Mildew. Polyester fabrics are absolutely resistant to mildew. They will not be stained or weakened. Should mildew form on the fabric, it would be due to the finish; but mildew should readily wash off the fabric without any deterioration to it. However, there may be some discoloration.

Resistance to Insects. Polyester is unaffected by moths, carpet beetles, silverfish, or other insects.

Reaction to Alkalies. At room temperature, polyester has good resistance to weak alkalies and fair resistance to strong alkalies. This resistance is reduced with increased temperature. At boiling temperatures, it has poor resistance to weak alkalies and dissolves in strong alkalies.

Reaction to Acids. Depending upon the type, polyester has excellent-to-good resistance to mineral and organic acids. Highly concentrated solutions of a mineral acid, such as sulfuric acid, at relatively high temperatures will result in degradation.

Affinity for Dyes. Polyesters can be dyed with appropriate disperse, azoic, and developed dyes at high temperatures, producing a good range of shades that have good-to-excellent washfastness and fair-to-good lightfastness. Some polyesters are modified to take basic dyes. Solvent dispersion-dye techniques using hydrocarbon solvents, such as perchlorethylene, or ammonia may enhance dye reactions. Pigment colors have a tendency to crock and rub off.

Resistance to Perspiration. Polyester has no significant loss of strength from continued contact with either acid or alkaline perspiration.

POLYESTER FIBER BLENDS

Polyester fiber has been successfully blended with many other fibers. Various effects and combinations of properties are derived from these blends depending on the fibers used and on the percentages in the blends. One of the most important characteristics that polyester provides is its high degree of shape retention for garments that require little or no ironing after they are washed.

Polyester and Cotton

For satisfactory wash and wear purposes, fabrics for rainwear, tailored clothing, dress shirts, and sport shirts should have a blend of at least 65 percent polyester with the cotton. Polyester will provide wrinkle resistance and shape retention. Cotton will provide absorbency and consequent comfort. However, unless properly constructed and properly cared for, a fabric of a polyester and cotton blend may pucker and lose its shape if the cotton should shrink or if cotton thread is used in sewing. Polyester and cotton blends are well suited for fabrics to be given a permanent press finish. The polyester not only contributes its own inherent shape-retentive qualities but also retains its strength, thereby reducing the total potential strength loss from finishing that an all-cotton fabric would have.

Where greater absorbency and softer hand are desired, a 50/50 blend is preferable, but there will be a corresponding strength loss of as much as 20 percent as well as a slight loss in resil-

ience. A 50/50 blend of polyester and cotton is also satisfactory for effective permanent press finishes.

On the other hand, blends of as much as 80/20 of polyester and cotton, respectively, will have a somewhat stiffer, slicker hand. Strength, wrinkle resistance, and shape retention will be increased but absorbency will be reduced.

Polyester and Wool

In combination with wool, polyester provides outstanding wrinkle resistance and crease retention, so that wet or dry, the shape retention is improved according to the proportions used. The greater abrasion resistance of polyester also provides longer wear. The wool contributes good draping quality and elasticity. The wool also reduces the hazard of melted holes due to burning tobacco. The greater the proportion of wool, the less pilling there is likely to be.

Blends of polyester and wool generally range from 65 percent polyester and 35 percent wool to 60/40, 55/45, and 50/50, respectively. For lightweight, shape-retentive summer suiting, 65 percent polyester and 35 percent wool is a satisfactory blend. For optimum benefits of both fibers, a 60/40 blend of polyester and wool, respectively, appears to be generally best for medium worsteds. A blend of 55 percent polyester and 45 percent wool is suitable for year-round garments. Where greater warmth is desired, a 50/50 blend for woolens is preferable.

Polyester and Rayon

In a blend with viscose rayon, polyester gives greater resiliency, shape retention, and durability. Viscose rayon provides absorbency and variety of color and texture. For satisfactory wash and wear service, a blend of at least 55 percent polyester with the rayon is desirable.

A blend of 65 percent polyester and 35 percent high wet-modulus rayon provides a strong, durable, and serviceable fabric. The fabric has a good hand and drapes well. The rayon again provides the absorbency that polyester lacks. The strength and durability of such blends are comparable with blends of polyester and Pima cotton and have the advantage of greater resilience and shape retention.

Polyester and Arnel Triacetate

Since both fibers are thermoplastic, fabrics made of polyester and Arnel will have excellent shape retention and provide good wash and wear service. But they will have low absorbency and are likely to feel clammy in humid weather. Polyester is important because it adds strength to the blend, since Arnel is a weak fiber. The fabric will pill unless it is made of PCDT Kodel 200 polyester and/or fine-count yarn.

A suitable blend of 50/50 is satisfactory. However, this blend produces a yarn weaker than a similar blend of polyester and any cellulosic fiber.

Polyester and Nylon

Nylon contributes strength and abrasion resistance. Polyester contributes outstanding wrinkle resistance. Such a combination offers stability, easy laundering, quick drying, and resistance to damage from mildew and insects. The fabric will be clammy to the skin, however, in warm, humid weather. Since both fibers are thermoplastic and neither is very absorbent, any combination in the blend will provide good wash and wear characteristics. Care should be taken to avoid pilling of fabrics with this type of blend.

REVIEW QUESTIONS

1. (a) What is Dacron? (b) May any company produce or imitate it? Why?
2. What forms of polyester are there? Explain their differences.
3. Discuss the washability and general care of fabrics made of polyester.
4. How does the strength of polyester compare to that of other fibers?
5. How is polyester affected (a) by mildew, (b) by moths?
6. What reaction has polyester (a) to alkalies, (b) to acids, (c) to perspiration?
7. Discuss the possible value of polyester fabrics and blends for summer wear.
8. What are the outstanding properties of a polyester/wool blend?
9. What blends of polyester and cotton are satisfactory? Discuss the merits of these blends.
10. What blends of polyester and rayon are satisfactory? Discuss their merits.

20

ACRYLIC

the polyacrylonitrile fiber

Basically, acrylic is a type of plastic. According to the definition set forth by the FTC, an acrylic fiber is "any long-chain synthetic polymer composed of at least 85 percent by weight of acrylonitrile units." This definition classifies a group of chemically related fibers and accounts for similarities in some of their properties. However, there are differences in their specific chemical compositions, molecular structures, physical appearance, and methods of production.

HISTORY OF ACRYLICS

The clear liquid acrylonitrile was first made in Germany in 1893 by Moureau, but it remained a laboratory curiosity. Interest was revived in the late 1920s with the granting of a variety of German patents. Dr. Carothers's discovery of the fiber-forming properties of linear superpolymers spurred researchers everywhere to investigate the fiber-forming possibilities of a host of polymers. Experiments by H. Rein of I. G. Farbenindus-

trie resulted in his publication in 1938 of successful methods of dissolving the polymer in a variety of aqueous solutions. But it was the research at Du Pont that produced the first acrylic fiber, initially called Fiber A and subsequently named *Orlon*. In 1944 a "semiworks" was built under the auspices of the Research Section of Du Pont's Acetate Division. Until August, 1945, the development of Orlon acrylic fiber was concerned primarily with its possible aid in the war effort, but was not brought to fruition before World War II ended. By early 1946, Orlon looked promising enough for commercialization. Process development continued, and in October, 1948, Du Pont built a plant near Camden, South Carolina, capable of producing $6^{1}/_{2}$ million pounds of yarn a year. Production of Orlon acrylic fiber started in May, 1950.

Following the lead of Du Pont, the Chemstrand Corp. (now known as Monsanto Textiles Co.) developed another acrylic fiber, which they named *Acrilan*. A plant was built in Decatur, Alabama; and operations, with a capacity of 30 million pounds annually, were started late in 1952.

For many years, the American Cyanamid Co. manufactured acrylonitrile for use by other companies in the manufacture of such products as acrylic fibers. The company eventually decided to experiment in the production of its own acrylic fiber. After much experimentation, it produced, in 1953, a fiber tentatively designated as X-51 at its pilot plant in Stamford, Connecticut. After spending fifteen years on research, the American Cyanamid Co. began commercial production in 1958 of its own acrylic fiber, *Creslan*, in a new plant near Pensacola, Florida.

The development of *Zefran* acrylic fiber was begun in 1949. Research in the laboratories of the Dow Chemical Co. was concerned with polymers and particularly with polyacrylonitriles. One of the problems associated with polyacrylonitriles had been their low affinity for dyes and the limited fastness of the colors. After several years of intensive research, a chemical alloy with acrylonitrile was produced having properties similar to those of acrylic fibers plus superior dyeing properties. This fiber could be dyed with a wide variety of dyes including those used for natural fibers as well as those used for man-made fibers. This not only meant greater affinity for dyes but also greater possibilities for blending this new fiber with a wide array of other fibers without being hampered by dyeing problems frequently encountered with blending. Satisfied that they had a desirable product which was commercially feasible, the Dow Chemical Co. established the trademark of that fiber as Zefran. Dow introduced its new fiber as a nitrile alloy in 1958, thereby differentiating its composition as well as its properties from the other acrylonitrile fibers. Upon establishment of the Federal Trade Commission's ruling in 1960, Zefran was classified as an acrylic fiber. It is now manufactured by the renamed Dow Badische Co. in Williamsburg, Virginia. Subsequent to its development of Zefran, Dow introduced another acrylic fiber under the trademark of *Zefkrome*. However, that trademark was later dropped in favor of the identification Zefran for all its fibers.

The variations of acrylic fibers and their subvarieties now produced require some individualized consideration of each trademarked variety produced in the United States.

ORLON ACRYLIC

METHOD OF MANUFACTURE

The manufacture of Orlon acrylic resin is the result of complicated chemical synthesis (Figure 20-1). Acrylonitrile may be made from acetylene or from ethylene; both are petroleum derivatives. When the ethylene is treated with hypochlorous acid, a chlorohydrin is formed. The chlorohydrin is reacted with sodium hydroxide to form ethylene oxide. Hydrocyanic acid is added to the ethylene oxide, producing cyanoalcohol, which is dehydrated to yield acrylonitrile. The acrylonitrile is then polymerized into polyacrylonitrile resin, a long-chain linear polymer. The polyacrylonitrile is dissolved in a suitable solvent, such as dimethylformamide, and extruded through a spinneret. By adding a delusterant, such as the one used for nylon, Orlon acrylic is made semidull.

Figure 20-1   Flow chart of the manufacturing process of Orlon acrylic fiber. (*Courtesy of E. I. du Pont de Nemours & Co.*)

After coagulation, the filaments are oriented and stabilized by stretching.

Variations in the basic process that have been developed to meet specific needs change the fiber both in appearance and in certain properties.

FORMS AND TYPES OF ORLON ACRYLIC YARNS

After orientation and stabilization, the Orlon acrylic filaments are shipped as tow or cut into staple lengths for spinning into yarn. The fibers are identified according to type and have particular characteristics suitable for particular purposes. These varieties provide Orlon acrylic fibers with considerable flexibility in application to serve numerous consumer uses.

Type 21 is designed for use in bulky knits and in hand-knitting yarns. It is a bicomponent acrylic fiber with a reversible, permanent crimp. The components,

each having different shrinkage potential, are extruded together and adhere as one fiber. When treated with heat and moisture in later finishing processes, one component shrinks more than the other and causes a permanent random-spiral crimp. The crimp enhances the loft, bulk, and covering power of the yarn, giving it a warm, soft, pleasing hand. The elasticity and resilience of the yarn are also considerably increased while still retaining the inherent crease-retentive property of the fiber. The crimp may be described as reversible—that is, the fiber has the ability of decreasing its crimp, thus elongating the fiber when wet and recovering its spiral crimp when dry. This unique characteristic provides excellent retention of its built-in elasticity in knitted fabrics after repeated laundering.

Type 23 is another bicomponent acrylic fiber designed for bulky, mid-bulky, and other knit outerwear of two-ply yarns. It has a nonreversible crimp.

Type 24 is a 9.0-denier bicomponent with nonreversible crimp designed for bulky hand-knits and knit outerwear. It is stock, top, or skein dyeable. The tow is converter processible.

Type 28 is produced as 4.5- and 8.5-denier acid-dyeable, bright, low-crimp, surface-modified staple. It is designed to provide unique surface effects in knitwear when blended with other types of Orlon acrylic fiber.

Type 30 is a 15-denier flame-retardant bicomponent carpet staple.

Type 31 is a blend of homo- and bicomponent staple averaging 7.0 denier. It is designed for making yarns via the woolen spinning system for use in athletic hose.

Type 32 is a staple designed for use in sliver knit-pile fabrics. It is available in 3, 4.5, and 6 denier.

Type 33 is a blend of bicomponent and homofiber carpet staple of 15 denier. It contains a flame retardant.

Type 34 is a blend of homo- and bicomponent staple of 2.7 denier designed for making yarns on the cotton spinning system for use in circular-knit piece goods.

Type 37 is a 14-denier basic-dyeable worsted-length staple designed for craft rug yarns.

Type 39 is a blend of semidull 2- to 6-denier staple, averaging 4.2 denier, and lengths of $1\frac{1}{4}$ to $2\frac{1}{2}$ inches for woolen system spinning.

Type 39A is a blend of semidull 1.5- to 3-denier staple, averaging 2.5 denier, and lengths of $1\frac{1}{2}$ to $2\frac{1}{2}$ inches for woolen system spinning.

Type 39B is a blend of semidull 3- to 10-denier staple, averaging 6.5 denier, and lengths of $1\frac{1}{4}$ to $2\frac{1}{2}$ inches for woolen system spinning.

Type 42 is a standard semidull, color-sealed black staple and tow acrylic fiber. Semidull staple blends of 60 percent regular-shrinkage and 40 percent high-shrinkage fiber are also available.

Type 43 is produced in 3 and 6 denier and is designed for fine-gauge and bulky knitwear uses where a soft, luxurious hand is desired.

Type 44 is an acid-dyeable, semidull acrylic fiber produced in staple and tow forms. It is designed to permit cross-dyed styling when blended with basic-dyeable types. It is available in 3 and 6 denier.

Type 72 is a 1.5-denier, $1\frac{1}{2}$-inch staple designed for blending with cotton for use in lightweight apparel fabrics.

Type 74 is an acid-dyeable staple available in 3 and 6 deniers of $1\frac{1}{2}$- and 2-inch lengths. It is designed to extend styling flexibility in cotton system spinning for circular knits, pile, broadwovens, and hosiery.

Type 75 C.S. Black is available in 3, 4.5, and 6 deniers of $1\frac{1}{2}$- and 2-inch staple lengths. When used in combination with Type 74 and other fibers, three-color styling can be obtained.

Type 75 is a 2.5-denier, regular-shrinkage staple which is used for cotton system spinning.

Type 75B is a staple blend of deniers averaging 5.25, for use in deep-pile fabrics and in blends with rayon or cotton for broadwoven outerwear fabrics.

Type 321 is a staple designed for use in premium pile fabrics. It is available in 3 denier.

Blanket fiber is a staple blend of semidull deniers averaging 3.7, designed for the manufacture of blankets of 100 percent Orlon acrylic fiber from yarns made on the woolen spinning system.

Sandbag fiber is available as semi-dull 5.2-denier, 3-inch staple.

As indicated above, Orlon acrylic fibers are produced in a variety of homofil and bicomponent forms to serve particular objectives. The yarns produced from them may be sold under any one of several Du Pont certification marks of consumer serviceability appropriate to the use for which the yarn was made. Sayelle is the certification mark for spun yarns of 100 percent Orlon Type 21 bicomponent fiber. Nomelle yarn is made of 100 percent homofil Orlon Type 43 acrylic fiber and has a very soft, luxurious hand. Wintuk refers to a variety of yarns made from combinations of certain Orlon bicomponent and homofil acrylic fibers; it has great crimp and loft. Nandel is a relatively fine-denier fasciated yarn of Orlon acrylic staple of 100 denier or less. The texture of the yarn varies from soft and supple to crisp and firm, according to the desired hand, and has high pill and fuzz resistance.

Spun Yarn

The Orlon acrylic filaments range from 1.5 to 10 denier. The tow is usually processed through the Pacific Converter, the Turbo Stapler (Figure 20-2), or through the Turbo Poly Breaker (page 410). The cut staple ranges from 1.5 to 5 inches, depending on the type of yarn to be made. The staple is crimped and spun on a cotton or wool system into fuzzy yarns. The more twist in the yarn, the finer, smoother, and harder the yarn will be. The less twist in the yarn, the thicker and softer the yarn will be. Spun yarns of Orlon acrylic with a low twist have the hand of cashmere. Soft spun Orlon acrylic yarns, however, are fuzzy and have a tendency to pill, or form little balls on the fabric surface.

Figure 20-2   The Turbo Stapler is designed especially to process acrylic fibers in tow form. It heat-stretches, breaks, and crimps the tow into even slivers as shown. (Details of photo continued on p. 426.)

Figure 20-2 *(continued)* *(a)* Tow is fed through an overhead creel and delivered to the stapler as a band up to 9 inches wide. It is controlled for proper width and centering as it passes around two bars, each with single quick-knob adjustment as shown. *(b)* Tow passes through the first set of nip rolls at left, and around four snub rolls that are moving at the same speed. Tow then passes through two 10- by 14-inch heater plates. Next, the tow moves through the four intermediate snub rolls and around the intermediate nip rolls. The intermediate section operates at a higher speed than the infeed rolls in order to develop tension on the tow passing through the draw zone. This stretch zone is the heart of the high-bulk yarn. *(c)* The heater plates are individually thermostatted in two zones for each plate. Temperature is continuously indicated at each of these four points. Plates automatically close when machine starts and open when machine stops. Top plate hinges back as shown for ease of cleaning. Pressure between plates is adjustable. *(d)* As tow leaves the intermediate nip rolls, it passes between the breaker bars. The intermediate rolls at left are moving at a slower speed than the front rolls at right. The breaker bars, which are rotating at an intermediate speed, have an abrasive strip in each groove. The fibers in the tow are broken as they pass through this zone and the tow becomes sliver. *(e)* Close-up of breaker bars. *(f)* Close-up of crimper. Degree of crimp is controlled by two calibrated knobs. *(Courtesy Turbo Machine Co.)*

High

Orlon [...] ay be spun
into [...] gy yarns
called [...] arns pro-
duce [...] ics with
a luxu[...] lon acryl-
ic crim[...] led with
other fi[...] r stretch
as well [...] For fur-
ther dis[...] 2.

Fasciated

Orlon acr[...] ucted
into a rot[...] sed of
such disco[...] laid
parallel to [...] to-
gether by s[...] und
the bundles [...] den-
tified as Na[...]

FINISHING OF

Several finish[...] n
acrylic fabrics [...] -
ness. Among the[...]

Heat setting—f[...]

Water repellenc[...]
against water [...]

Antistatic finish—[...]
trostatic buildup [...]

An outstandi[...]
acrylic is that a fa[...]
of it can be given a[...]
being subjected to a [...] degree of heat.
If properly heat-set, the fabric will retain its shape as well as its creases or
pleats. Nor will washing, dry cleaning,
or wearing cause the garment to lose its
shape.

Orlon acrylic is not a particularly
absorbent textile. To make it less absorbent, it may be treated with a water
repellent, such as Syl-mer or Zelan. This
process makes the fabric desirable for
rainwear and children's playclothes.

EVALUATING ORLON ACRYLIC FABRICS

The properties of fabrics made of Orlon
acrylic depend on the type of fiber used
as well as how the material is woven,
knitted, or finished. The several types of
Orlon acrylic provide for flexibility in
application due to differences in their
properties. Therefore, fabric and garment performance should be evaluated
in terms of these particular characteristics as well as general properties common to all Orlon acrylic fibers.

Strength.   Orlon acrylic fiber is of moderate strength, but it is the weakest of the
acrylic fibers. Compared with the natural fibers, it is weaker than all with the
exception of wool. Since Orlon acrylic is
used primarily as a replacement for
wool, its greater strength is an advantage. The abrasion resistance of Orlon
acrylic is good and compares favorably
with that of wool.

Elasticity.   Like the other acrylics, Orlon has little stretch. The low stretchability makes it useful for knitted wear,
since it is not likely to stretch unduly.
Most of the stretch that does exist is due
to the mechanical crimp put into the fiber. The additional random-spiral crimp
of some types of Orlon acrylic provides
good extensibility without straining the
fiber, thus providing freedom of movement without developing sag.

Resilience. Orlon acrylic fiber has very good resilience and therefore will not wrinkle easily. Fabrics of Orlon acrylic staple are not as lively in springing out from a creased position as polyester or wool, but they are still good in this respect. High resilience makes Orlon acrylic desirable for men's slacks and suits as well as for women's dresses.

Heat Conductivity. Like all acrylics, Orlon does not conduct heat rapidly; therefore, fabrics of orlon acrylic can be warm. The fiber is dog-bone in shape, which provides overlapping and bulk (with little weight). As a result, fabrics of Orlon staple have approximately 20 percent greater insulating power per ounce of fiber than wool fabrics. Since an ounce of Orlon acrylic is thicker than an ounce of wool fabric, it is possible to obtain an Orlon fabric that, while being as thick and as warm as wool, is about 20 percent lighter in weight. The warmth of the yarns can be increased by bulking through the use of special types of Orlon acrylic and by blending with the high-shrinkage type Orlon.

Drapability. The drapability of Orlon acrylic varies with the type of fiber. Generally speaking, it provides satisfactory draping qualities (Figure 20-3).

Absorbency. Orlon, like the other acrylics, has low absorbency. Nevertheless, fabrics made of Orlon acrylic staple will take on quite a bit of water on account of the staple's adsorbency: the tendency for water droplets to cling to the surface of the individual fibers. Since these water droplets get into the air spaces between the fibers and evaporate slowly, fabrics of Orlon acrylic spun yarn dry slowly, although not as slowly as wool fabrics.

This low adsorbency gives the fabric the advantage of resisting stains. Many substances that are ordinarily absorbed by other fibers merely remain on the surface of fabrics made of Orlon acrylic yarns and can be easily removed by wiping, washing, or dry cleaning.

Cleanliness and Washability. These fabrics do not soil or stain easily, and washing or dry cleaning quickly renews their freshness. A mild soap should, however, be used in laundering since strong soaps will damage them. If desired, any ordinary cleaning fluid and household bleach may be safely used.

Soft, bulky Orlon acrylic yarns will pill. To reduce this tendency, such garments as sweaters should be laundered

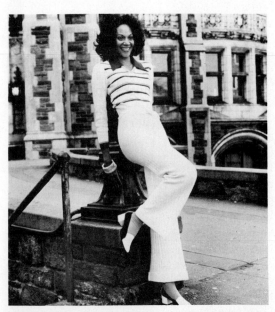

Figure 20-3 Garments knitted of acrylic yarns, such as this of Orlon, can be warm, comfortable, drapable, and shape retentive. (*Courtesy E. I. du Pont de Nemours & Co.*)

while turned inside out, with as little rubbing as possible. After rinsing through mild suds and then lukewarm water, squeeze out the water, turn the garment right side out, spread it on a towel, and gently brush it with a very soft brush while drying. The tendency of Orlon acrylic to pill is reduced when it is blended with most other fibers. Tightly spun yarns of Orlon acrylic will not pill readily because they are harder smoother, and not too fuzzy.

Sweaters of some types of Orlon acrylic require special attention. They can be washed in a machine or by hand with equally satisfactory results. White sweaters should be washed with only white articles to avoid developing a dingy appearance caused by pickup of dye particles; colored sweaters can be laundered with other colored garments. Neither white nor colored sweaters should be washed in the same load with lint-shedding fabrics. Sweaters trimmed with sequins or other delicate materials should be washed by hand and air-dried. Of course, such sweaters can also be dry-cleaned.

When laundering sweaters of Orlon acrylic fiber by hand, use warm water (100 degrees Fahrenheit) with a detergent or soap and a water conditioner, such as Calgon. Wringing or twisting the garment while washing or rinsing should be avoided. The sweater should be rinsed thoroughly in clear, warm water until all the soap or detergent has been removed. A final rinse in fresh water containing a fabric softener, such as Sta-Puf or Nu-Soft, will maintain the soft texture of the sweater. The sweater should be rolled in a clean white towel and the excess water squeezed out—never wrung or twisted. The garment should

then be bunched and spread out loosely on a flat surface (but not a towel) to dry. The sweater will appear larger in this condition, but as it dries, the reverse crimp in the fiber will cause the yarns to shorten and the garment will return to its original size. Bulky sweaters will take longer to dry than thinner sweaters.

When machine laundering sweaters of Orlon acrylic fiber, the washer should be set for a 5- to 8-minute agitation cycle or at the delicate or knit setting at a high water level using warm water (100 degrees Fahrenheit). Any household detergent or soap and a water conditioner may be used. The sweater should be spun-dried and then must be tumble-dried at a low or medium temperature setting for about 30 minutes. Before the garment is removed from the dryer, it should be tumbled for about 5 minutes using the cold-temperature setting (although some dryers have special wash and wear cycles that are suitable). Remove the garments immediately after cooling. Garments that have been machine washed should not be drip-dried or flat-dried.

Effect of Bleaches. Fabrics of Orlon acrylic yarn may be safely bleached with any of the household bleaches.

Shrinkage. The discussion regarding the various types of Orlon acrylic fiber shows that some will shrink in processing and that this characteristic is utilized in obtaining desired effects, such as high-bulk yarns and pile fabrics. However, once the finished product reaches the consumer, it may be expected to have excellent dimensional stability since the Orlon acrylic fiber will have practically no further shrinkage.

Effect of Heat. Orlon acrylic fiber gets tacky at 455 degrees Fahrenheit, which is slightly above that of nylon. At higher temperatures, it will melt.

Fabrics of orlon acrylic should be ironed with a moderately warm iron; in fact, they may be ironed while dry. Old creases may be removed, and new ones added. Since fabrics of Orlon acrylic yarn may be heat-set, it is often unnecessary to press them, but some ironing may be desired to smooth the cloth.

Effect of Light. Orlon acrylic has outstanding resistance to light. Its extreme resistance to such degradation makes it especially useful for fabrics that will be exposed to sunlight for an extended period of time.

Resistance to Mildew. Mildew may form on the surface, but it will have no effect on fabric of Orlon acrylic yarn. It may be easily wiped off.

Resistance to Insects. Orlon acrylic is unaffected by moths or their larvae or by carpet beetles.

Reaction to Alkalies. Orlon acrylic has fair-to-good resistance to weak alkalies.

Reaction to Acids. Orlon acrylic is exceedingly resistant to strong mineral acids as well as organic acids.

Affinity for Dyes. Some types of Orlon acrylic fibers are specific to acid dyes and some to basic dyes, which can provide interesting cross-dyed effects. Orlon acrylic can be dyed in a wide range of colors and hues. The colors have satisfactory fastness to washing and light.

Resistance to Perspiration. All indications are that fabrics of Orlon acrylic yarn are not readily deteriorated by perspiration, but the color may be affected.

ORLON ACRYLIC FIBER BLENDS

Orlon acrylic has many desirable properties that may be imparted to fabrics containing other fibers as well, depending on the relative amount of each fiber used.

Orlon Acrylic and Cotton

In combination with cotton, Orlon acrylic adds light weight and body. The cotton contributes strength and absorbency. The fabric is wrinkle-resistant, retains its shape well, and provides easy care. A blend of 80 percent or more of Orlon acrylic with cotton will provide the general characteristics of a wash and wear fabric, such as is used for sport shirts.

Orlon Acrylic and Wool

One of the outstanding characteristics of Orlon acrylic is its bulk, so that when the staple is blended with wool, the resulting fabric is lightweight and yet warm. It also has a soft hand but there may be some pilling. Fabrics of this combination have very good crease retention and wrinkle recovery. These blends are washable. Where there is a good proportion of Orlon acrylic, the fabrics seldom need pressing. A good blend for a wash and wear tailored garment should have 60 percent or more Orlon acrylic with the wool, though too much acrylic makes the fabric too bulky. Such a blend will also be stronger than an all-wool fabric.

Orlon Acrylic and Silk

Orlon acrylic and silk provide interesting cross-dyed and textured effects. Such blends have outstanding hand and excellent stability. In addition to the good appearance, the combination gives long wear. Orlon acrylic contributes easy-care qualities and shape retention; the silk contributes absorbency and strength. The fabric is very resilient and may be warm, depending on its weight.

Orlon Acrylic and Rayon

To the versatility of rayon, Orlon acrylic adds wrinkle resistance and stability. New and unusual surface and dye effects, including cross-dyes, are possible. It provides a dry, warm, and soft hand. A wash and wear blend should have at least 70 percent Orlon acrylic with the rayon.

Orlon acrylic blended with high wet-modulus rayon provides a stronger fabric with the same general properties as that of a blend with regular rayon. A blend could therefore have a lower proportion of Orlon acrylic fiber.

Orlon Acrylic and Acetate

Orlon acrylic and acetate together in a fabric provide a soft, luxurious feel and excellent drapability. It also has excellent shape retention and good resilience. The fabric launders easily with mild soap and warm water, dries rapidly, and is easy to iron. Orlon acrylic provides greater resistance to sunlight. Neither Orlon acrylic nor acetate is particularly absorbent, which presents a disadvantage in warm, humid weather. Such blends will be warm and clammy.

Orlon Acrylic and Nylon

The strength and abrasion resistance of nylon combined with the luxurious hand and covering power of Orlon acrylic produce attractive, warm, strong fabrics. Similar qualities of Orlon acrylic and nylon, such as wrinkle resistance, crease retention, and easy care, are increased when these fibers are combined. Such fabrics will not be very absorbent.

Orlon Acrylic and Polyester

Orlon acrylic improves the hand of a fabric when combined with a polyester fiber, giving better body comfort and warmth. The polyester fiber contributes even greater wrinkle resistance, especially under humid conditions (Figure 20-4). A 50/50 blend will provide good

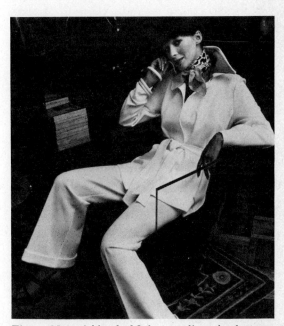

Figure 20-4   A blend of Orlon acrylic and polyester fibers can produce fabrics that drape well, are shape retentive, and washable. (*Courtesy E. I. du Pont de Nemours & Co.*)

wash and wear characteristics. Such a fabric will generally wear well because of the strength of the polyester fibers and the good abrasion resistance of Orlon acrylic; however, it is likely to pill if care is not exercised.

ACRILAN ACRYLIC

METHOD OF MANUFACTURE

The processing of Acrilan is similar to Orlon acrylic (see Figure 20-5). Natural gas and air are combined to form ammonia. Ammonia and natural gas are combined to produce hydrocyanic acid. Natural gas at elevated temperatures produces acetylene that, when combined with hydrocyanic acid, produces acrylonitrile. Then the acrylonitrile is

polymerized. This polyacrylonitrile in powder form is dissolved by a suitable solvent and passed through spinnerets, and unlike Orlon acrylic fiber (which is extruded into air, where it hardens), Acrilan fiber is formed in a coagulating bath to produce continuous filaments. The fibers, produced in semidull, bright, or solution-dyed varieties, are then washed, stretched, and crimped.

FORMS AND TYPES OF ACRILAN YARNS

Acrilan acrylic fiber is produced in tow and staple forms. The fiber is normally produced in 2 to 15 denier and in many types having built-in characteristics suitable for particular purposes (Figure 20-6).

Type 16 is the basic variety. It is produced in bright and semidull staple

Figure 20-5 Production of Acrilan acrylic fiber. *(Courtesy Monsanto Textiles Co.)*

Figure 20-6 Acrilan acrylic fiber emerging from the spinneret. *(Courtesy Monsanto Textiles Co.)*

and tow forms. It has a high level of whiteness and a pleasing hand. Yarns made of this type have good loft, are warm, but have a tendency to pill. They are used for a wide variety of fabrics for apparel and such home furnishings as drapery and upholstery.

Type 25 is a semidull high-strength acrylic fiber used for industrial purposes, such as sandbags. It has resistance to sunlight, weathering, and soil burial that is superior to that of nylon, polyester, or polypropylene.

Type 26 is produced as bright and semidull staple for carpets. It has high resilience and good abrasion resistance. It has excellent whiteness and can be dyed to light, bright pastel shades. This acrylic is generally blended with other fibers, such as certain modacrylics, and meets U.S. surface flammability standards.

Type 36 is acid-dyeable and resistant to cationic dyes. It is used primarily for blending with Type 16 for cross-dyeing to achieve such color stylings as color-and-white, tone-on-tone, and two-color (can include heathers) for apparel. It is semidull and is available as staple and tow.

Type 37 is a producer-colored bright staple. It is excellent for deep-pile, particularly sliver-knit, fabrics.

Type 38 is a solution-dyed semidull staple used primarily for sewing thread and such industrial purposes as tie strings and sandbags.

Type 49 is a bicomponent bright staple for carpets. It is acid-dyeable and resistant to cationic dyes. It is used primarily with cationic-dyeable carpet Type 90 or 94 for piece-dyed color-and-white, tone-on-tone, and two-color cross-dyed effects. It has good resistance to abrasion, excellent resilience, and good flame retardancy. This acrylic fiber may be blended with certain modacrylics.

Type 57 is a bicomponent produced in staple and tow forms. Its helical crimp imparts high bulk and cover. It is used (frequently in blends with Type 16) for hand-knitting yarns, sweaters and other knits, and specialty pile fabrics.

Type 77 is similar to Type 16 but is designed for use in pile and fleece fabrics. It is produced as bright staple.

Type 80 is similar to Type 16 but is designed for use in blankets. It is produced as semidull, variable-cut staple.

Type 81 is also similar to Type 16 but is designed for spinning on the wool system for apparel. It is produced as semidull, variable-cut staple.

Type 82, another variety similar to Type 16, is designed for blankets. It is produced as a semidull, variable-denier, variable-cut staple.

Type 88 is a solution-dyed, bright staple. It is used for such industrial applications as awnings and pennants and in blends for apparel. It has superlative resistance to degradation by such factors as sunlight and weathering but is very soft.

Type 90 is produced as bright, midluster, and semidull staple for carpets, particularly for plush styles with pinpoint tufts. It has good abrasion resistance and high resilience. It is antistatic under normal conditions and meets U.S. surface flammability standards. It may be blended with certain modacrylics.

Type 94 is a bicomponent bright staple used for carpets. It has good abrasion resistance, high resilience, and is virtually antistatic. It meets U.S. surface flammability standards. It may be blended with certain modacrylics.

Type 98 is a solution-dyed staple used for carpets. It is extremely colorfast, has good abrasion resistance, high resilience, and is antistatic. It meets U.S. surface flammability standards and may be blended with certain modacrylics.

Spun Yarns

Acrilan acrylic staple is spun into yarn on cotton or wool systems. Tow is usually processed through the Pacific Converter, Turbo Stapler, or Turbo Poly Breaker and spun, as appropriate, into yarn.

High-Bulk Yarns

Several of the fiber types discussed above are used to produce various kinds of bulk yarns, and the properties and textural effects will vary with the type of fiber.

FINISHING ACRILAN ACRYLIC FABRICS

Fabrics of Acrilan may be finished similarly to Orlon acrylic. The principle finish is heat setting, which will permit semipermanent creases. Care must be taken in the process because dry heat in excess of 300 degrees Fahrenheit for more than a few minutes will yellow the fiber. With proper precautions, fabrics of Acrilan will be bulky and silky.

EVALUATING ACRILAN ACRYLIC FABRICS

Acrilan fabrics are made of various types of filament, spun, and high-bulk yarns. The characteristics of the fabrics depend on the type of fiber used and the kind of yarn produced, as well as the fabric construction and finish. The following properties of Acrilan acrylic fiber should be considered when judging Acrilan fabrics.

Strength. Acrilan is of moderate strength. It is slightly stronger than Orlon but weaker than the other acrylic fibers. Compared with those natural fibers with which it is sometimes blended, Acrilan is weaker than cotton but stronger than wool. It is also stronger than rayon and acetate. Its durability lies largely in the fact that it has good abrasion resistance as well as very good resilience.

Elasticity. Acrilan has little stretchability. This low elastic characteristic makes it particularly suitable for knitted wear and for garments where retention of shape is desired.

Resilience.   As has been stated, Acrilan has very good resilience. It will not wrinkle easily and therefore is good for dresses, suits, and slacks. Some types are also used for rugs.

Heat Conductivity.   Acrilan is similar in insulating value to the other acrylic fibers. In some forms, it is almost as warm as wool but lighter in weight. Thus, Acrilan can provide warmth with light weight. This combination makes Acrilan particularly suitable for blankets as well as for winter wear. It is cooler in filament form, since there is less bulking and insulative quality.

Drapability.   The drapability of Acrilan varies with the type and form of the yarn as well as the fabric construction. However, it is generally quite satisfactory.

Absorbency.   Like the other acrylic fibers, Acrilan has little absorbency. Nevertheless, Acrilan, like Orlon acrylic yarns, have quite a bit of adsorbency and dry slowly because the water that gets trapped between the fibers evaporates slowly. This low absorbency gives Acrilan the advantage of resisting stains. Watery or oily substances, which stain other textiles, are not readily absorbed into fabrics of Acrilan. They lie on the surface and can be easily removed by wiping, washing, or dry cleaning.

Cleanliness and Washability.   It is relatively easy to keep Acrilan acrylic fabrics clean, and they may be dry-cleaned readily. Laundering is also no problem, although it is preferable to use a mild soap or detergent. Since Acrilan fabrics may be heat-set, it is often unnecessary to iron them, although some pressing with a moderately warm iron to smooth the cloth may be desired. Too hot an iron or heat for too long a period will cause yellowing.

Effect of Bleaches.   Acrilan has good resistance to bleaches and, therefore, household bleaches may be used.

Shrinkage.   Fabrics of Acrilan, when properly finished, have excellent dimensional stability. The consumer can expect virtually no further shrinkage.

Effect of Heat.   Acrilan shrinks when exposed to a temperature of 455 degrees Fahrenheit. At higher temperatures, it shrivels and decomposes.

Effect of Light.   Acrilan has good resistance to the effect of sunlight, although not as good as Orlon acrylic. Compared with other fibers, it is one of the most light-resistant textiles, and this indicates its value for outdoor uses.

Resistance to Mildew.   Like the other acrylic fibers, Acrilan is wholly resistant to mildew. Any mildew that forms on the surface can be easily removed, and there will be no damage to the fabric.

Resistance to Moths.   Acrilan is unaffected by moths. Together with its warmth and loft, Acrilan is, in this respect, well suited for both garments and rugs. This provides a particularly good advantage over wool.

Reaction to Alkalies. Acrilan has good resistance to weak alkalies. Its resistance decreases as the strength of the alkali, the temperature, and the length of immersion increase.

Reaction to Acids. Acrilan has good resistance to strong mineral acids as well as to organic acids.

Affinity for Dyes. Since some types of Acrilan are solution-dyed, they need not be dyed again and do have excellent colorfastness. Other types are dyed by a variety of dyes as appropriate to each type in a wide range of colors, which generally have good fastness to light and water.

Resistance to Perspiration. Acrilan is resistant to perspiration.

ACRILAN ACRYLIC FIBER BLENDS

Acrilan is readily adaptable to blending with other fibers. The chief blends are with cotton, wool, rayon, and acetate (see Figure 20-7).

Acrilan Acrylic and Cotton

In combination with cotton, Acrilan adds warmth, light weight, and wrinkle resistance. The cotton provides strength to the fabric. The fabric can be laundered and pressed easily.

Acrilan Acrylic and Wool

The primary value of blending Acrilan and wool is to provide the same warmth as an all-wool fabric but with less

Figure 20-7 Acrilan acrylic fiber being measured for blending with other fibers, such as cotton, wool, rayon, or acetate *(Courtesy Monsanto Textiles Co.)*

weight. The combination also provides a resilient, wrinkle-resistant fabric that nevertheless tends to retain creases and pleats. Acrilan will also add strength, but too much of this fiber in the blend will make the fabric too bulky.

Acrilan Acrylic and Rayons

Various surface and color effects are possible by blending Acrilan and viscose rayon. The Acrilan provides greater resilience and shape retention. Such a fabric will also be warmer than an all-rayon fabric. Acrilan blended with a high wet-modulus rayon will provide similar results, but it will be stronger due to the greater strength (both wet and dry) of the modified rayon.

Acrilan Acrylic and Acetate

A combination of Acrilan and acetate produces a soft, warm fabric with good draping qualities, good shape retention, and resilience. The fabric can be easily laundered or dry-cleaned.

Acrilan Acrylic and Nylon

The strength of nylon and the warmth of Acrilan together can produce a blend that is also resilient and stable.

CRESLAN ACRYLIC

METHOD OF MANUFACTURE

Creslan acrylic fiber is produced from a copolymer containing a high percentage of acrylonitrile. After polymerization, acrylonitrile copolymer is dissolved in a solvent, filtered, and deaerated to form a spinning solution. A delustering agent may be added. The spinning solution is extruded through a spinneret into an aqueous bath from which it emerges as filaments which are washed to remove the solvent and stretched to impart fiber properties. They are also crimped and treated with an antistatic to aid textile processing. Creslan acrylic fiber is produced in bright and semidull varieties as tow or staple. Modification of the method of manufacture of Creslan fiber permits the production of low-, medium-, and high-shrinkage varieties for staple use.

FORMS AND TYPES OF CRESLAN ACRYLIC YARNS

Several types of Creslan acrylic fibers are manufactured with certain characteristics suitable for particular pur-

poses. The fiber is produced in 1.5 to 15 denier for staple cut in various lengths ranging from $1\frac{1}{2}$ to $7\frac{1}{2}$ inches. Tow is produced in 3 and 5 denier. All types are crimped.

Type 61 is produced as bright or semidull and in tow or staple form. It is the basic type and is spun into yarn on all systems for a wide variety of uses.

Types 61, 61B, 61BF and 61BF-2 Carpet Staple are variations of the basic variety and are spun on the woolen or worsted system, depending upon the texture of yarn desired.

Types 61BC and 61BC-2 staple are also variations of the basic variety and are spun on the cotton system.

Type 61BB is produced as bright and semidull staple of variable lengths. It is specifically designed for yarn to be spun on the woolen system for blankets.

Type 67 is a semidull staple to be spun on the cotton system for double knits.

Type 68B is a semidull staple to be spun on the woolen or worsted system for apparel.

Type 68 (bicomponent) is produced as tow for processing into yarn on a worsted or a modified synthetic system. It has good bulking properties.

Types 83, 84, and 85 are bicomponent bright acrylic fibers produced as tow or staple for carpet yarns produced on the woolen, worsted, or modified synthetic system. They have good loft and resilience.

Type 94 is an acid-dyeable staple that may be bright or semidull. It is spun on the cotton system.

Type 94 (bicomponent) is produced as semidull tow. It has good loft and resilience and is spun into yarns on the worsted or modified synthetic system.

Type 96 (bicomponent) is produced as an acid-dyeable bright or semidull staple for spinning on the cotton system.

Type 98 is a fibrillated Creslan acrylic for specialized purposes.

Spun Yarns

Creslan acrylic staple is spun into yarn for apparel, blankets, and rugs. Versatility in the production and application of these spun yarns is due to the variations provided in the types produced, as noted above. Tow is processed on the Pacific Converter, Turbo Stapler, or Turbo Poly Breaker for spinning into yarn.

Bulk Yarn

Low-, medium-, and high-shrinkage varieties of Creslan staple may be blended and then spun into yarn. Subsequent immersion of such a yarn in boiling water results in hardly any shrinkage in the low-shrinkage fibers but a great deal in the high-shrinkage fibers. This results in a lightweight, spongy, bulky yarn.

FINISHING CRESLAN ACRYLIC FABRICS

Fabrics of Creslan may generally be given the same kinds of finishes given to fabrics of other acrylic fibers. Like the other acrylic fibers, Creslan is thermoplastic. Fabrics and garments of Creslan fiber can be permanently heat-set. This is a major finishing treatment given to such products. They can be given pleats, creases, or any shape, heated under carefully controlled conditions, and thereafter retain the desired shape through repeated wearing, washing, and dry cleaning. Proper finishing es-tablishes dimensional stability and enhances the aesthetic qualities inherent in Creslan.

EVALUATING CRESLAN ACRYLIC FABRICS

The properties of fabrics of Creslan will depend on the properties of the fiber itself, the type of spun yarn used, and the construction of the fabric. The use of the Creslan trademark is controlled by the American Cyanamid Co. through its quality testing program, which requires that fabrics meet certain standards in order to carry the name of its acrylic fiber. The performance of such fabrics is based upon a few general characteristics.

Strength. As compared with Orlon and Acrilan, Creslan staple fiber has from equal to above equal strength. It is, however, weaker than Zefran acrylic fiber. On the other hand, Creslan filament is stronger than any of these staple, and the serviceability of Creslan fiber will vary with the type. Compared with all fibers, generally, Creslan is of moderate strength. Its resilience adds good abrasion resistance to its strength. Fabrics of Creslan, therefore, give good wear.

Elasticity. Creslan has very little stretchability whether in staple or filament form. Fabrics of Creslan will resist stretching and sagging.

Resilience. Creslan fiber has excellent resilience, and fabrics of Creslan will not wrinkle easily. Wrinkles that may form due to crushing will tend to fall out readily, contributing to a neat appearance.

Heat Conductivity. Like other acrylic fibers, Creslan does not conduct heat rapidly. In filament form, the fibers can be made into yarns for fabrics that can feel comfortable but not warm next to the skin. On the other hand, the crimp plus potential shrinkage of the staple can produce spun yarns of various bulk and loft to provide warmth. Creslan is about 25 percent lighter than cotton and about 10 percent lighter than wool. Consequently, yarns of Creslan acrylic are relatively lightweight. Summer fabrics can be light and cool. Winter fabrics of Creslan can provide adequate warmth for such outerwear as sweaters, jackets, and coats.

Drapability. Creslan fiber has a good, pleasant hand, and the fabrics have good draping quality.

Absorbency. Generally speaking, Creslan is about the least absorbent of the acrylic fibers. Its wicking action, or adsorbency, accounts for its comfort when worn next to the skin. The low absorbency gives fabrics of Creslan the property of resisting stains. Such fabrics dry fairly rapidly when wet.

Cleanliness and Washability. All fabrics made of Creslan can be easily laundered with any mild soap in warm water. They may be safely put into automatic washers and dryers, and the fabrics tend to resist pilling. Strong soaps containing much alkali will cause yellowing, particularly if the water is very hot.

Fabrics of Creslan may be safely dry-cleaned. They have good dimensional stability. If properly constructed and finished, they will retain pleats and shape after washing or dry cleaning. If ironing is desired, these fabrics may be pressed while damp with a warm iron, as used for nylon.

Effect of Bleaches. Fabrics made of Creslan that are of Type 61 have a built-in extra whiteness and should not require bleaching. When bleaching is desired for any kind of fabric containing Creslan, sodium chlorite is recommended for the best results.

Shrinkage. When properly finished, fabrics of Creslan acrylic have excellent dimensional stability and do not shrink or pull out of shape.

Effect of Heat. Creslan staple gets tacky and sticks at temperatures of 400 to 440 degrees Fahrenheit, while Creslan filament sticks at temperatures of 430 to 460 degrees Fahrenheit. These temperatures indicate that fabrics of Creslan may be safely ironed, if need be, at temperatures about those used for nylon fabrics. Higher temperature will cause Creslan to react as do other thermoplastic fibers: it will shrivel and melt.

Effect of Light. Creslan has excellent resistance to degradation by sunlight. It is therefore very well suited for fabrics for apparel and home furnishings that are likely to have lots of exposure to the sun (though colors may still fade, depending upon the dye used).

Resistance to Mildew. Creslan acrylic is absolutely resistant to deterioration by mildew.

Resistance to Moths. Creslan is unaffected by moths and their larvae or by carpet beetles.

Reaction to Alkalies. Creslan acrylic has fair resistance to alkalies. Exposure to alkalies at high temperatures will cause yellowing. Higher concentrations and higher temperatures will cause more severe damage.

Reaction to Acids. In general, Creslan has excellent resistance to acids. There is a tendency to bleach when the acid concentration is high.

Affinity for Dyes. Staple Creslan fiber can be dyed with a variety of dyes, depending upon the type. This provides versatility in dyeing, including cross-dyeing applications, with a wide range of colors of generally good fastness to light, washing, and crocking.

Resistance to Perspiration. All indications are that fabrics of Creslan are not readily deteriorated by perspiration.

CRESLAN ACRYLIC FIBER BLENDS

Fabrics are presently available in blends of Creslan with cotton, wool, mohair, and rayons, all of which have a wide range of differences in hand, texture, appearance, and application.

Creslan Acrylic and Cotton

This blend may be expected to provide a relatively durable, serviceable fabric. A properly blended fabric that meets the established quality standards will retain the desirable wrinkle-resistant, shape-retentive, and wash and wear characteristics of Creslan. The cotton will contribute strength and absorbency. The blended fabric will be light-weight and comfortable.

Creslan Acrylic and Wool

Depending upon the kind of yarn and the kind of finish used, fabrics of Creslan and wool may have textures ranging from soft to crisp. They provide good drape and are shape retentive and wrinkle-resistant. Depending upon the fabric and garment, they may be washed and should need only light pressing.

Creslan Acrylic and Mohair

This blend provides a silky, luxurious hand and good draping qualities. Both fibers contribute resilience. Creslan adds the qualities of shape retention and easy care; mohair contributes strength.

Creslan Acrylic and Rayons

Blends of Creslan and viscose rayon provide a comfortable fabric. The rayon provides absorbency; Creslan contributes resilience, shape retention, and easy care. For greater durability and service, a blend of Creslan acrylic fiber and a modified rayon should prove a good combination.

ZEFRAN ACRYLIC

METHOD OF MANUFACTURE

It is important to observe that Dow Badische Co. manufactures all of its fibers—nylon, polyester, and acrylic—under the trademark of Zefran.

Precise information concerning the production of Zefran acrylic cannot be given since the manufacturer is reluctant to divulge information concerning the manufacturing processes or the raw materials used. All that can be stated is that Zefran acrylic fiber is a nitrile-acrylic alloy produced with somewhat the same general procedure used in the manufacture of acrylic fibers with modifications whereby a dye-receptive polymer is grafted to the acrylonitrile molecule. The copolymer alloy is extruded from the spinneret as white, bright, or semidull tow. It is also produced as precolored tow. All tow is stretched, crimped, and cut into staple lengths as desired.

FORMS AND TYPES OF ZEFRAN ACRYLIC YARNS

Zefran acrylic staple is produced in lengths of $1\frac{1}{8}$ to 6 inches and 2 to 15 denier and in several types with certain characteristics for particular purposes. All are crimped and can be processed into spun and high-bulk yarns on conventional textile equipment. These yarns contribute good wrinkle recovery, press retention, and dimensional stability to fabrics. They impart a pleasing hand and, like the other acrylics, are nonirritating and nonallergenic.

Type 100 series is a special-dyeable, bright staple used for carpets.

Type 200 series is a basic-dyeable staple produced as bright or semidull. There are several subtypes designed specifically for apparel, carpets, and other uses. They can be spun on the appropriate systems.

Type 400 series is producer-colored staple. The shorter, semidull, low-denier staple is spun on all systems and is designed for apparel uses; the longer, bright, higher-denier staple is spun on the woolen or worsted system for carpet yarn. One example is Type A404, which is used for pile knits. Another is Type A405, a producer-colored staple which has greater resilience, tenacity, toughness, and stiffness than the above Zefran acrylic fibers. It is designed for double-knit yarns.

Type 500 series is a semidull staple produced for industrial fabrics such as awnings and beach umbrellas. Fibers in this series are the hardest and strongest of the Zefran acrylic fibers and have excellent resistance to degradation by sunlight, weather, and industrial fumes. They can be spun on all systems.

Spun Yarns

Since Zefran acrylic fiber can be made in all these varieties and can be spun on all these systems to produce a wide range of yarns—from smooth to fuzzy—all can be produced in intimate blends with cotton, rayon, or wool.

High-Bulk Yarns

The crimp imparted to Zefran acrylic fiber is sharp and durable and provides loft and resilience. The fiber may be spun into yarns that are high in bulk and low in weight. Fabrics of Zefran acrylic can be thick and resilient, having more warmth or insulating value than comparable fabrics of cotton, rayon, or wool.

FINISHING ZEFRAN ACRYLIC FABRICS

Various finishes have been and are being developed for fabrics of Zefran acrylic. Such fabrics may be either dyed or printed in a wide variety of colors. They may be napped to give a soft, warm hand and heat-set to retain pleats, creases, and shape in fabric or garments.

In addition, Dow Badische Co. has established certifications applicable to its carpet fiber. Zefwear is a wear performance guarantee for Zefran acrylic carpet fiber which assures a minimum of five years of wearability, exclusive of tears, burns, cuts, damage due to improper use, or improper cleaning agents or maintenance methods. If the carpet has been properly installed and maintained but loses 10 percent of its pile fiber, it will be replaced free of all charges.

Zefstat is an antishock guarantee for Zefran acrylic carpet fiber. Such carpet, properly installed and maintained according to Dow Badische's instructions, will be certified as shockproof to humans for its useful life. Replacement free of all charges will be made should the carpet fail to perform according to the guarantee.

EVALUATING ZEFRAN ACRYLIC FABRICS

The principal properties of the types of Zefran acrylic fiber are generally similar. However, the variations that do exist are significant in the ultimate performance of the fabrics.

Strength. Zefran acrylic fiber is stronger than any of the other acrylic staple fibers. When compared with the natural fibers, it is weaker than cotton, linen, or silk but stronger than wool. The fiber has very good abrasion resistance and can be used to produce relatively durable fabrics.

Elasticity. The elasticity of Zefran acrylic approximates the low elasticity of Acrilan. This characteristic makes it suitable for garments that are required to hold their shape, such as knitted wear.

Resilience. Zefran acrylic fiber has excellent resilience. Fabrics of this fiber have an extremely high rate of wrinkle recovery. This characteristic makes Zefran acrylic highly desirable for blends.

Heat Conductivity. Zefran acrylic has a high rate of heat conductivity. The cross sectional shape is somewhat round and so the fibers lack the natural bulking characteristics of an acrylic fiber like Orlon. But Zefran acrylic fiber can be permanently crimped to provide sufficient bulk in yarn form, producing the desirable insulative effect. In fact, fabrics of Zefran acrylic yarn can be produced that will be warmer than comparable fabrics of wool. These fabrics will also be lighter in weight than wool, though not quite so lightweight as fabrics of some of the other acrylic fibers.

Drapability. Fabrics of Zefran acrylic yarn have a pleasant, soft hand and provide satisfactory draping qualities.

Absorbency. Zefran acrylic is slightly more absorbent than any of the other acrylic fibers. It is, however, much less absorbent than any of the natural fibers and some of the man-made fibers. This means that, while fabrics of Zefran acrylic will dry more slowly than fabrics of most acrylic fibers, they will dry faster than cotton, wool, or rayon.

The greater absorbency of Zefran acrylic compared with the other acrylic fibers is due to its alloy composition. The grafted copolymer in the fiber's molecular structure provides some additional absorbency. This greater absorbency not only provides greater comfort in humid weather but also reduces the tendency which the fabric has to develop static electricity.

Cleanliness and Washability. Although fabrics of Zefran acrylic are made of spun yarns and have varying degrees of fuzz that catch and hold dirt, the fiber has the advantages of cleanliness and washability. It develops less static electricity than most other acrylic fibers and consequently does not easily attract or hold dust particles on its surface. Also, fabrics of Zefran acrylic yarn have excellent wrinkle recovery and excellent shape retention. Creases placed in fabrics of Zefran acrylic yarn stay in extremely well after repeated washing and require no ironing. This makes the yarn highly suitable for wash and wear garments. For best results, the garment should be made entirely of Zefran acrylic yarn. When washing these fabrics, it is best to use a mild soap, though hot water may be safely used. Such fabrics may also be safely dry-cleaned.

Effect of Bleaches. Ordinary household bleaches may be safely used on fabrics of Zefran acrylic yarn.

Shrinkage. Properly finished fabrics of Zefran acrylic yarn have very little residual shrinkage. Such fabrics also have good dimensional stability.

Effect of Heat. Zefran acrylic has a sticking temperature of 490 degrees Fahrenheit. Consequently, if ironing is desired, fabrics of Zefran acrylic yarn may be safely ironed at temperatures of up to 350 degrees Fahrenheit, which is higher than for fabrics of other acrylic fibers. When subjected to flame or excessive heat, Zefran acrylic fiber will fuse and shrink away.

Effect of Light. Zefran acrylic is highly resistant to degradation by sunlight. Along with other desirable properties, this indicates that it is very suitable for drapery and upholstery fabrics.

Resistance to Mildew. Zefran acrylic is wholly resistant to mildew and is undamaged even when hung or stored under damp conditions.

Resistance to Insects. Fabrics of Zefran acrylic are unaffected by moths or other insects. As with the other acrylic fibers, this offers a decided advantage over wool.

Reaction of Alkalies. Zefran acrylic is resistant to weak alkalies. Although it will turn yellow when subjected to strong hot alkalies, it may be safely subjected to mercerizing conditions when blended with cotton.

Reaction to Acids. Zefran acrylic has excellent resistance to acids of up to 40 percent concentration.

Affinity for Dyes. Because of its composition, Zefran acrylic takes dyes better than most other acrylic fibers. Satisfactory dyes are available for essentially all colors and end uses. Vat dyes generally provide good-to-excellent lightfastness and excellent washfastness. Acid, basic, sulfur, direct, and acetate dyes may be used, but their colorfastness is not generally as good. Such dyes may be necessary when Zefran acrylic is blended with fibers that require specific dyes to obtain certain colors.

Zefran acrylic fiber may be precolored in the manufacturing process in a wide range of good shades. The process produces excellent colorfastness.

Resistance to Perspiration. There is no indication that perspiration will deteriorate Zefran acrylic, but the color may be affected.

ZEFRAN ACRYLIC FIBER BLENDS

Zefran acrylic has been blended to a limited extent with cotton, rayon, and wool. Development of blends continues. The following results have been achieved.

Zefran Acrylic and Cotton

Zefran acrylic and cotton blends provide comfortable, durable fabrics that will wash easily, dry fairly rapidly, and need little or no ironing. Zefran acrylic provides shrink resistance, resilience, and shape retention. Cotton increases the absorbency and lowers the cost of the fabric.

Zefran Acrylic and Wool

A blend of 50 percent Zefran acrylic and 50 percent wool has twice the wrinkle recovery of an all-wool fabric and almost as much wrinkle recovery as an all-Zefran acrylic fabric. Due to the Zefran acrylic, garments of such a blend show excellent dimensional stability after repeated home washings. They show no appreciable shrinkage and need little ironing. They are warm, comfortable to wear, and do not pill. Zefran acrylic fiber also provides greater strength, and the combination provides good abrasion resistance, making a durable fabric.

Zefran Acrylic and Rayon

A major contribution of Zefran acrylic in a blend with rayon is wrinkle recovery and dimensional stability. A blend of 50 percent Zefran acrylic with 50 percent rayon will have 3 times the wrinkle recovery of an all-rayon fabric and actually be more resilient than an all-wool fabric. Zefran acrylic fiber will also provide greater strength. Rayon will provide greater absorbency and contribute to the comfort of such a fabric. Such a blend may be classified among the wash and wear fabrics.

Zefran Blend CR-4

Dow Badische Co. has developed several trademarked blends for carpet manufacture. Zefran Blend CR-4 is one of separately stock-dyed Zefran acrylic and Zefran nylon staple fibers blended for high performance and aesthetics for commercial carpets. The fibers are intimately blended and parallel spun. The nylon provides the strength and abrasion resistance; the acrylic provides the soft, woollike texture.

Zefran Blend ZK-3

This is a blend of precolored Zefran acrylic and modacrylic staple which is spun on woolen and worsted systems in several counts and ply combinations for contract (commercial) carpet manufacture. This blend allows for a wide variety of textures and color effects.

Zefran Blend H-52

This is a blend of Zefran acrylic, BCF (bulk continuous filament) nylon, and modacrylic fibers for contract and residential carpeting. The blend provides a coarse, highly textured, handmade look. The nylon provides the strength and abrasion resistance. All the fibers contribute the resilience, woollike texture, and color effects.

COMPARISON OF ACRYLIC FIBERS

Table 20-1 is a summary composite based on information supplied by the producers of these fibers and on evaluations of the performance of the acrylic fibers as described in the current literature. The reader is reminded that variations do exist within each trademark as well as blend combination, type of yarn, fabric weight, construction, and finish and that these factors will affect the performance. It is also possible that future changes in the chemical and physical compositions of these fibers may alter their performance.

Table 20-1

COMPARISON OF PROPERTIES OF THE ACRYLIC FIBERS				
PROPERTY	ORLON	ACRILAN	CRESLAN	ZEFRAN
Strength	Fair	Fair	Fair to good	Good
Abrasion resistance	Fair	Fair to good	Fair	Good
Elasticity	Low; good extensibility for Sayelle	Low	Low	Low
Resilience	Very good	Very good	Excellent	Excellent
Absorbency	Little	Little	Little	Little
Laundering care	Varies; requires care, use mild soap or detergent; may pill	Launders readily; some pilling may occur	Easy care with mild soap; relatively pill-resistant	Easy care with mild soap; fair resistance to pilling
Ironing temperature	Moderately warm	Moderately warm	Moderately warm	At rayon setting or slightly higher
Shrinkage	Virtually none	Virtually none	Virtually none	Virtually none
Household bleaches	All safe	All safe	Requires sodium chlorite; some types have built-in whiteness	All safe
Resistance to light	Excellent	Very good	Excellent	Very good
Resistance to mildew	Wholly resistant	Wholly resistant	Wholly resistant	Wholly resistant
Reaction to alkalies	Fair-to-good to weak alkalies	Good to weak alkalies	Fair to weak alkalies	Fair to weak alkalies

Table 20-1

	COMPARISON OF PROPERTIES OF THE ACRYLIC FIBERS *(Continued)*			
PROPERTY	ORLON	ACRILAN	CRESLAN	ZEFRAN
Reaction to acids	Very resistant	Very resistant	Excellent resistance; tendency to bleach	Excellent resistance
Resistance to perspiration	Good	Good	Good	Good
Colorfastness	Good	Good; excellent for solution-dyed types	Good	Good

REVIEW QUESTIONS

1. What is an acrylic fiber?
2. Give the trademarks for the acrylic fibers. Which companies produce each one?
3. Differentiate between an acrylic trademark and a certification mark.
4. Identify by name and characteristics the three certification marks of Orlon acrylic fiber.
5. Compare the strength of the various acrylic fibers with each other and with other fibers.
6. Compare the elasticity of the various acrylic fibers with each other and with other fibers.
7. Discuss the washability and general care of fabrics made of acrylic fibers.
8. What general types of yarns can be made from each of the acrylic fibers?
9. Discuss the reactions of each of the acrylic fibers (a) to acids, (b) to alkalies, (c) to perspiration.
10. Discuss the affinity for dyes and the colorfastness of each of the acrylic fibers.
11. What are the general properties of acrylic fibers that tend to improve blends?
12. How are each of the acrylic fibers affected (a) by mildew, (b) by moths, (c) by other insects?

SUGGESTED ACTIVITY

Obtain advertisements for Orlon, Acrilan, Creslan, and Zefran acrylic fibers. Identify similar properties cited and note any properties cited as individual to a particular fiber.

21

MODACRYLIC

the modified acrylic fiber

As the identification implies, modacrylic fibers are modified acrylic fibers consisting of acrylonitrile in combination with other polymers. Consequently, there are differences in production and in certain properties between acrylics and modacrylics.

HISTORY OF MODACRYLICS

The Carbide and Carbon Chemicals Co. started experimenting with super-polymers in 1934. The company contributed much to the present knowledge of these substances, but it was not until 1949 that *Dynel*, a partly acrylic staple fiber, was developed. The first commercial plant started production of 5 million pounds annually in July, 1950. Since then, the company's name has been changed to the Union Carbide Chemicals Co., a division of Union Carbide Corp., and the production and the use of Dynel have expanded.

In an effort to diversify its position in textile fibers, Eastman Chemical Products, Inc., a subsidiary of Eastman Kodak Co., also entered the acrylic fiber field. After due experimentation, the company announced the production of its own modified acrylic fiber, *Verel*, in March, 1956. Commercial production of Verel was begun in 1958 at newly developed facilities of the company's corporate associate, Tennessee Eastman Co., which also manufactures acetate fibers at Kingsport, Tennessee.

Until 1960, both Dynel and Verel were identified by their manufacturers as acrylics. Under the ruling of the Federal Trade Commission, they were reclassified as *modacrylics* and are now sold under that identification.

In response to evolving consumer requirements and the amended Flammable Fabrics Act (see page 212), Monsanto Textiles Co. joined the modacrylic production competition in 1972, when it introduced its *SEF* modacrylic fiber. The development of this fiber was an outgrowth of its experience with its Acrilan acrylic fiber, which had already been on the market for twenty years. Monsanto also produces Elura modacrylic fiber which, since it is used exclusively for wigs, is not discussed in detail in this chapter.

Similarly, Du Pont developed its Orlon modacrylic fiber which it began market testing in 1973.

DYNEL MODACRYLIC

METHOD OF MANUFACTURE

Dynel modacrylic fiber is produced from such basic substances as natural gas, salt, ammonia, and water. These are chemically combined to form two basic ingredients: acrylonitrile, which is the clear liquid used to produce acrylic and modacrylic fibers, and vinyl chloride, which is a gas used to produce vinyl plastics. When acrylonitrile and vinyl chloride are combined under pressure and heat, they copolymerize and form a white powdery resin. This resin is dissolved in acetone (the basic ingredient of nail polish removers), producing a viscous solution similar in appearance to that of acetate. It is then passed through spinnerets into a water bath from which it emerges as a tow, or group of continuous filaments. The tow is dried, stretched, and annealed (Figures 21-1 and 21-2).

FORMS AND TYPES OF DYNEL MODACRYLIC FIBERS AND YARNS

Dynel modacrylic fiber may be sold in tow form or cut into staple and crimped (Figure 21-3). It is generally produced as a semidull fiber, but it is also produced in several solution-dyed colors in the 3-denier weight. There are four types of Dynel fiber that can be processed into sliver for pile fabrics, into spun yarn for flat fabrics, or into such molded apparel as hats.

Figure 21-1   Flow chart of the manufacturing process of Dynel modacrylic. *(Courtesy Union Carbide Chemicals Co.)*

Figure 21-2 Dynel modacrylic emerges from the spinning bath as groups of endless fibers called tow. (*Courtesy Union Chemicals Co.*)

Figure 21-3 Dynel modacrylic tow is cut to length, them crimped and sent by conveyor to the balers. (*Courtesy Union Carbide Chemicals Co.*)

Type 150 is produced as uncrimped tow in a limited range of deniers. It is used for such specialty applications as wigs and hairpieces.

Type 180 is made in staple form in a variety of deniers. It has a wide array of uses from air filters to luxury furlike coats.

Type 183 is a controlled-high-shrinkage fiber produced in 3-denier tow or staple. It is used to produce high-bulk yarn and pile for furlike fabrics.

Type 297 is produced as a bright staple, solution-dyed fiber specifically engineered for carpet use. It has excellent resilience and stain resistance. It also has good abrasion resistance and weatherability.

FINISHING DYNEL MODACRYLIC FABRICS

Dynel may be finished somewhat like the acrylic fibers. The outstanding feature is heat setting, which molds a fabric or gar-ment into permanent shape and also permits permanent creases and pleats. These shapes are resistant to change due to wetting and are relatively permanent until the shaping temperature is again equaled or excelled.

The highly thermoplastic characteristic of Dynel gives it a thermoformable quality. Fabrics of Dynel modacrylic yarn, for example, may be permanently molded into hats. Wigs of Dynel may be given permanent settings.

The thermoplastic quality of Dynel is utilized in its dyeing. At temperatures above 205 degrees Fahrenheit, the fiber softens and the dyestuff penetrates to become an integral part of the fiber. The color thus becomes fixed in the fiber when it is cooled. During this process, however, the fiber becomes dull. Since the color of dull fiber is not as fast to light as lustrous fiber, Dynel must be semidecated with steam to restore its luster and this must be followed by slow cooling to avoid setting creases.

EVALUATING DYNEL MODACRYLIC FABRICS

The manner in which the yarn is spun, the construction of the cloth, as well as the intrinsic properties of the Dynel fiber are all important factors in evaluating the fabric.

Strength. Dynel high-shrinkage fiber is the strongest of the several types. All Dynel modacrylics are stronger than the other modacrylics. Although Dynel modacrylic is weaker than cotton, linen, or silk, it is 2 to 3 times as strong as wool. It is also stronger than regular rayon, acetate, triacetate, and the acrylics, but it is weaker than nylon. Dynel also has good abrasion resistance that assures long wear. This property makes Dynel very desirable for blending with other fibers that are not as strong.

Elasticity. Like the acrylic fibers, Dynel has very little stretchability, and the high-shrinkage type is even less elastic. This contributes to the dimensional stability and shape retention of fabrics of Dynel modacrylic yarn.

Resilience. Dynel, particularly the type used for carpets, is highly resilient, thus assuring lasting loft (springiness) and softness. This resilience and loft make possible fabrics with a pleasant and permanent nap that will not pill. Dynel is therefore a desirable fiber for blankets and such fabrics as flannel. Because of the high degree of resilience of Dynel, fabrics made of this fiber bounce back into shape. They do not wrinkle easily, and any wrinkles that may form fall out readily. Fabrics of Dynel hold their shape well even in damp weather.

Heat Conductivity. Dynel is a soft, bulky, warm fiber similar in insulating value to the acrylic fibers. It is about as warm and heavy as wool. The insulative property of Dynel produced in different deniers of various textures makes it very suitable for pile, furlike fabrics.

Drapability. The drapability of Dynel modacrylic fabrics varies with the type and denier of the fibers. They may produce soft, flexible fabrics of good draping quality for skirts and drapes. On the other hand, they may produce slightly pliable or stiff materials for hats and for radio speaker grilles.

Absorbency. Dynel is the least absorbent of the modacrylic fibers. In fact, it is one of the least absorbent textile fibers. This has certain disadvantage, such as making a garment uncomfortable in warm, humid weather. But it has the advantage of resistance to staining. Such stains as catsup, coffee, mustard, or ink come out in washing, leaving no trace.

Cleanliness and Washability. Fabrics of Dynel can be washed or dry-cleaned. They lose very little strength while wet and are not damaged by strong soaps or detergents. Dynel fabrics resist shrinking and retain their shape in washing and dry cleaning. The water temperature should, however, be below 160 degrees Fahrenheit; otherwise, the fabric will become harsh. Dynel is one of the fastest drying fibers. Even heavily napped and knitted fabrics are relatively quick-drying. Although fabrics of Dynel modacrylic yarn can be washed in automatic washing machines, extreme agitation should be avoided as napped fabrics may pill.

Effect of Bleaches. Household bleaches may be safely used on Dynel modacrylic fabrics.

Shrinkage. Properly finished fabrics of Dynel have very good dimensional stability and normally will not shrink. However, when subjected to high temperatures, such as boiling water, Dynel fabrics could shrink unless held under tension. For this reason, fabrics of Dynel should be washed with water that is not too hot.

Effect of Heat. Dynel softens on application of heat and shrinks at about 260 degrees Fahrenheit. Fabrics of Dynel need little ironing. When ironing is desired, the iron should be warm or set at "rayon."

Although Dynel will melt and burn, it will not support combustion; it will stop burning when the flame is removed (unless the dyestuff is flammable).

Effect of Light. Although Dynel is not as resistant as Verel to the effect of sunlight, it has good resistance to deterioration by light. Dynel has about the same resistance as cotton to the effect of light. Over an extended period of time it darkens and weakens. It is satisfactory for use as curtains and draperies.

Resistance to Mildew. Like the acrylic fibers, Dynel modacrylic is wholly resistant to mildew.

Resistance to Insects. Dynel is not damaged by moths, carpet beetles, or other insects. Together with its warmth, this provides a particularly good advantage over wool. Dynel may therefore be safely used for rugs as well as clothing.

Reaction to Alkalies. Dynel has high resistance to strong alkalies. Common household cleaning alkalies, such as soap, ammonia, lye, and detergents, have no effect on Dynel. This resistance to such corrosive chemicals makes Dynel useful in industrial plants for clothes, gloves, filters, and the like.

Reaction to Acids. Dynel is extremely resistant to acids. In some industrial operations, work clothing of Dynel modacrylic is regularly washed in sulfuric and other strong acids to remove chemical contaminants.

Affinity for Dyes. Dynel modacrylic can be dyed in a full range of light to dark colors with excellent fastness to fumes, crocking, washing, and good fastness to light. Almost the entire range of acetate dyestuffs, many of the direct dyes, and certain vat dyes can be used. As a result, dyestuffs can be selected to match nearly any color and withstand nearly every type of service required of the finished fabric.

As has been mentioned, solution dyeing is sometimes used in the production of Dynel. This technique is employed to produce such colors as black, brown, and gray for Dynel fibers that are to be used to make furlike fabrics. These dyes have excellent fastness to all conditions.

Resistance to Perspiration. Dynel is absolutely resistant to deterioration from perspiration.

DYNEL MODACRYLIC FIBER BLENDS

Dynel has been found to be an excellent blending fiber. It works well with other staple fibers and contributes worthwhile properties to fabrics.

Dynel Modacrylic and Cotton

In a blend of Dynel and cotton, Dynel contributes softness, warmth, and resistance to shrinkage. Cotton contributes strength. Together, the blend provides a durable, comfortable, launderable fabric. A satisfactory blend should contain 25 to 50 percent Dynel.

Dynel Modacrylic and Wool

A combination of Dynel and wool provides a warm, resilient, wrinkle-resistant fabric. The Dynel contributes shape retention and greater strength. The bulking power of Dynel contributes shape retention and greater strength. The bulking power of Dynel also means that more warmth is possible with less weight. The wool also reduces the tendency of Dynel to glaze and harden from a hot pressing iron or other application of heat. A satisfactory blend should have about 35 percent Dynel.

Dynel Modacrylic and Rayon

To a rayon blend, Dynel contributes warmth, light weight, resilience, and shape retention. Rayon provides the needed absorbency for greater comfort. There should be a proportion of 25 to 30 percent Dynel for satisfactory results.

Dynel Modacrylic and Acetate

In combination, Dynel and acetate produce fabrics that are richly textured, warm, and resilient. They retain their shape and creases, and they drape well. Such a fabric, however, will have low absorbency. For satisfactory results, a combination of 25 to 30 percent Dynel with the rest acetate is desirable.

Dynel Modacrylic and Nylon

In a combination of Dynel and nylon, Dynel provides warmth, and nylon provides strength, abrasion resistance, and elasticity. Such a blend produces a resilient, wrinkle-resistant, shape-retentive fabric that launders easily and dries relatively fast.

Dynel Modacrylic and Acrylic

One of the most outstanding of the successful Dynel blends is the furlike fabric of Dynel modacrylic and Orlon acrylic made for women's coats. The original version of this blend was Borgana, a blend of Dynel modacrylic and Orlon acrylic in the pile on a knit backing of 100 percent Dynel. Both fibers provided resistance to stretching and shrinking. Orlon acrylic contributed the softness, and Dynel was responsible for the luster and body.

As a result of Borgana's success, other similar fabrics were produced. Some used the same fiber combination. One used pile of Dynel modacrylic and Orlon acrylic on a cotton back, and there were other combinations. The better known of these fabrics are O'llegro, Andante, Mutation, Glanara, Bakella, Dynasty, and Cloud No. 9. Their popularity has sprung from their ability to fill a long-felt need in the moderate- to better-priced coat field; that is, to provide warm, durable garments resembling expensive fur coats but at prices more people can afford.

VEREL MODACRYLIC

METHOD OF MANUFACTURE

The Tennessee Eastman Co., manufacturer of Verel, is reluctant to disclose its method of manufacture beyond the fact that it is composed of acrylonitrile and certain modifiers that are polymerized. The viscous solution is forced through a spinneret, and it coagulates as the solvent is removed. The filaments, which may be either bright or dull, are gathered into tow and then treated to make the fiber resistant to shrinking or stretching. The tow, composed of filaments of 2, 3, 5, 8, 12, 16, 24, and 40 denier, is then crimped and cut into staple.

FORMS AND TYPES OF VEREL MODACRYLIC YARNS

There are three basic types of Verel modacrylic fiber: Regular, Verel III, and Verel R. Regular Verel is produced in several types, and each type has a different degree and permanence of crimp to serve particular spinning processing and textural needs. The crimped types are as follows.

Regular

Type A is the general-purpose Verel fiber for normal textile processing. Having a high level of crimp with good crimp retention, it is used in scatter rugs, draperies, and other applications where spun yarns are required. Type A is also used in pile fabrics when high crimp is desirable.

Type B has the same number of crimps per inch as Type A but has a lower degree of crimp permanence. It can be electropolished more readily than Type A. It is used in pile fabrics where good crimp at the base of the pile is desired along with ease of electropolishing of the fiber tips.

Type CA is used in floor coverings. The crimp level and crimp retention are similar to Type A.

Type C was the original guard-hair type of fiber for pile fabric use. It has moderate crimp with ease of electropolishing. It has been discontinued in favor of Type D except in certain special instances where the high crimp of Type C is necessary.

Type D is the basic guard-hair type of fiber designed to simulate the outer, longer hair of fur for pile fabric use. It has low crimp with low crimp permanence and is very easily electropolished. Type D is not completely stabilized in manufacture and as a result has 10 to 15 percent hot-water shrinkage.

Type F is a combination of Type D and Type A. This fiber has a crimp level similar to Type A, with low crimp permanence and ease of crimp removal resembling Type D. Also like Type D, this fiber has 10 percent to 15 percent hot-water shrinkage. Type F is generally used for guard hair and in rugs where electropolishing is employed.

Type HB has extremely high crimp permanently set in the fiber. This type of Verel is used in paint rollers, in blends for piece-dyed carpeting, and in creating special pile fabric effects.

Verel III

Verel III is a high-shrink fiber having approximately 35 percent hot-water shrinkage. It is normally supplied in 3-denier bright-luster filaments. This modacrylic fiber is used in bulk yarns, pucker fabrics, and fabrics of extremely tight construction.

Verel R

Verel R has a ribbon cross section and was developed primarily for pile fabrics where increased luster and sparkle in the finished fabric is desired. Verel R is available in most of the above types and in several deniers.

Since Verel is produced only in staple form, it can be made only into spun yarns on the cotton or wool system.

FINISHING VEREL MODACRYLIC FABRICS

Fabrics of Verel may be given finishes similar to those of acrylic fibers. They may be dyed and may be napped to be given a very soft, luxurious, warm hand. Interesting textural effects can be obtained with the proper use of the appropriate type of Verel fiber. Fabrics of Verel may be heat-set to retain pleats, creases, and overall shape in garments.

EVALUATING VEREL MODACRYLIC FABRICS

All fabrics made of Verel are constructed from spun yarns. The spun yarn used to produce the fabric has a contributory effect on the characteristics of the fabric as well as on its construction. Even the type of Verel will have an effect on the characteristics of the fabric. The following properties, however, can be generally expected from fabrics of Verel.

Strength. Verel is of moderate strength. It is weaker than Dynel but compares favorably with the acrylics. Comparing Verel with the natural fibers, it is about twice as strong as wool but weaker than cotton, linen, or silk. Verel is stronger than regular rayon, acetate, and Arnel triacetate, but is weaker than nylon. Fabrics of Verel have fairly good abrasion resistance.

Elasticity. The elasticity of Verel is comparable with Dynel and the acrylic fibers. It has very little stretchability, and there tends to be a moderate amount of recovery when it has been stretched. Fabrics of Verel therefore have good dimensional stability and shape retention.

Resilience. Verel modacrylic has good resilience. Wrinkles tend to fall out easily, and wrinkles that persist will iron out readily at the "low" or "rayon" setting.

Heat Conductivity. Like the acrylic fibers, Verel does not conduct heat readily. In addition to its low heat conduction due to its chemical composition, Verel fibers have the added characteristic of having either a dog-bone or a flat cross section. This gives Verel fibers an overlapping quality that produces high bulk with relatively few fibers, which consequently makes fabrics lightweight.

Also, the spun characteristic of Verel yarns provides air pockets among the staple that contribute insulation to the fabric. Like Dynel modacrylic, it is suitable for warm, pile fabrics.

Drapability. The drapability of fabrics of Verel depends upon the type of that fiber used and the denier and crimp of the yarn. The draping quality may be good.

Absorbency. Although Verel is less absorbent than either the natural fibers or rayon, acetate, Arnel triacetate, or nylon, it has some absorbency. In fact, it is much more absorbent than the acrylics and the other modacrylics. Fabrics of Verel will dry more slowly than fabrics of acrylic and other modacrylic fibers.

Cleanliness and Washability. Fabrics of Verel may be washed or dry-cleaned by the conventional methods without difficulty. Verel has a tendency to pill, and the fabric should not be unduly rubbed. Soft brushing will reduce any pilling.

Verel is a thermoplastic fiber, and fabrics of Verel tend to retain their shape. Pleats and creases tend to stay in the fabrics after washing, and little ironing is needed.

Effect of Bleaches. Verel has an excellent white color and should not be bleached because such treatment causes the fiber to discolor.

Shrinkage. Properly finished fabrics of Verel modacrylic will not shrink—they have good dimensional stability. Regular Verel fiber has very little shrinkage even at high water temperatures, and garments tend to retain their size and shape.

Effect of Heat. Like Dynel modacrylic fiber, Verel will not support combustion. It will, however, stick at temperatures above 356 degrees Fahrenheit. If ironing is done at a low setting, fabrics of Verel will iron easily. If the iron is too hot, such fabrics will stiffen and glaze.

Effect of Light. Verel is highly resistant to degradation by sunlight. This makes Verel well suited for drapery and similar home furnishing uses.

Resistance to Mildew. Verel is wholly resistant to mildew and can be safely used in damp climates.

Resistance to Insects. Verel is unaffected by moths, carpet beetles, or other insects. This characteristic, along with its warmth and resilience, makes it suitable not only for clothing but also for rugs.

Reaction to Alkalies. Verel has good resistance to alkalies; however, excessive exposure to alkalies will cause discoloration. It is therefore best not to use strong soaps or other household cleaning agents.

Reaction to Acids. Verel modacrylic has excellent resistance to acids.

Affinity for Dyes. Three classes of dyes—basic, acetate, and neutral-dyeing premetalized dyes—are considered the most effective for dyeing Verel in a wide range of colors from bright pastels to blacks and navies. Basic dyes are generally used when brighter shades are required, as for specialty fabrics. Acetate dyes may be used for brighter shades, in some cases, than can be obtained with premetalized dyes; but colorfastness is generally somewhat less. Neutral-dyeing premetalized dyes provide the best all-around lightfastness and washfastness.

The affinity of Verel for this variety of dyestuffs permits a multitude of dyeing effects including cross-dyeing when Verel is blended or combined with other fibers.

Resistance to Perspiration. All indications are that fabrics of Verel are not readily deteriorated by perspiration. The color may, however, be affected.

VEREL MODACRYLIC FIBER BLENDS

Verel has properties that make it very suitable for blending with other fibers. Some very desirable results can be accomplished.

Verel Modacrylic and Cotton

One of the important factors in determining the percentages of fibers in a blend of Verel and cotton is the cost. Cotton is relatively inexpensive and, therefore, the greater the amount of Verel in the blend, the more expensive the fabric. Fabrics containing up to 25 percent Verel are within reasonable price range.

To this type of blend, Verel contributes a soft, pliable hand with good drapability. Verel also provides dimensional stability, so that the fabric will not wrinkle easily, will resist shrinkage, and will retain its shape. Cotton contributes greater absorbency and additional strength. Fabrics of a Verel and cotton blend are used for underwear, children's sleepers, sport shirts, and outer garments.

Verel Modacrylic and Wool

A blend of Verel and wool produces a warm fabric but light in weight due to the lightness and bulkiness of Verel fiber. Verel also provides greater strength, good shape retention, and wrinkle resistance. The thermoplastic characteristic of Verel also tends to hold creases and pleats in fabrics of such blends. Wool provides body and elasticity. Verel modacrylic/wool blends are particularly well suited for flannels.

Verel Modacrylic and Rayon

Verel has been satisfactorily blended with viscose rayon. Verel provides wrinkle resistance and shape retention. Rayon provides absorbency, coolness, and comfort.

Verel Modacrylic and Acetate

Since both acetate and Verel are thermoplastic, such a blend can produce fabrics and garments with good wash and wear characteristics. In addition to the wrinkle-resistant and shape-retentive characteristics of both fibers, acetate can reduce the bulk of the fabric, while Verel can add strength. One disadvantage of such a blend is the relatively low absorbency of both fibers, which would cause the fabric to be somewhat uncomfortable next to the skin in humid weather.

SEF MODACRYLIC

METHOD OF MANUFACTURE

Proprietary restrictions prevent the disclosure of the method of production of SEF modacrylic fiber. However, the manufacturer indicates that it is a modification of its Acrilan acrylic fiber. SEF is produced in 3-, 5-, and 8-denier semibright tow which is cut into various uniform staple lengths.

FORMS AND TYPES OF SEF MODACRYLIC YARNS

There is one type of SEF modacrylic fiber and, as noted, it is produced as a semibright staple. The staple is spun into yarn on either the cotton or woolen system.

FINISHING SEF MODACRYLIC FABRICS

Fabrics of SEF may be given finishes similar to those of acrylic and other modacrylic fibers. They may be napped to provide a very soft, warm, luxurious hand with good drapability similar to that of Acrilan. Fabrics of SEF take dyes very well and at a relatively low cost when compared with other modacrylics. They can be dyed at the boil or under pressure, which is generally not possible for fabrics of the other modacrylics. Like other thermoplastic fibers, fabrics of SEF can be heat-set to hold their shape and creases.

EVALUATING SEF MODACRYLIC FABRICS

Since there is just one type of SEF fiber, all fabrics made of that fiber will have the same properties insofar as their composition is concerned. Variations will of course occur, depending upon the kind of yarn, fabric construction, and finishes given.

Strength. SEF is, in general, of moderate strength; however, it is the weakest of the modacrylics. Its strength closely resembles that of Acrilan acrylic fiber. Its abrasion resistance is good.

Elasticity. The elasticity of SEF is low, though a little higher than that of the other modacrylics. When stretched, the fabrics have good recovery. Fabrics of SEF therefore have good dimensional stability and shape retention.

Resilience. SEF modacrylic has very good resilience. Fabrics of SEF do not crush or look mussed; wrinkles tend to fall out easily.

Heat Conductivity. As a modacrylic, SEF does not conduct heat well. This property is enhanced when SEF is spun into staple yarn which has air pockets which increase its insulative properties.

Drapability. Fabrics of SEF have very good drapability, generally superior to that of the other modacrylics. It closely resembles similar fabrics of Acrilan acrylic fiber.

Absorbency. SEF has low absorbency, falling between that of Dynel and Verel modacrylics. Fabrics of SEF may feel uncomfortable in humid weather. On the other hand, they are reasonably water-repellent and dry quickly.

Cleanliness and Washability. Fabrics of SEF modacrylic will wash and dry-clean easily, though excessive rubbing should be avoided to prevent possible pilling. SEF has excellent resistance to staining by oils, cosmetics, food, and beverages, which wash out readily in warm water.

Since SEF is a thermoplastic fiber, fabrics of SEF tend to retain their shape. Pleats and creases stay in the fabrics and little ironing is needed.

Effect of Bleaches. Fabrics of undyed SEF modacrylic have a very good natural whiteness which can be readily retained with ordinary household bleaches.

Shrinkage. SEF has excellent resistance to shrinkage. Fabrics have excellent dimensional stability.

Effect of Heat. Like the other modacrylics, SEF will not support combustion. It will char when subjected to flame but will not drip. Properly constructed and finished fabrics of SEF will self-extinguish when the flame is removed. This inherent property is not impaired by most household softeners, hand builders, water repellents, or repeated laundering.

Shrinkage and yellowing from excessively hot ironing is less than that of the other modacrylics. Actually, little ironing should be needed and a warm iron should be adequate.

Effect of Light. Like the other modacrylics, SEF has very good resistance to degradation by sunlight.

Resistance to Mildew. SEF is also wholly resistant to mildew degradation.

Resistance to Insects. SEF is not attacked by moths, carpet beetles, or other insects.

Reaction to Alkalies. Fabrics of SEF modacrylic have good resistance to weak alkalies and moderate resistance to strong, cold alkalies.

Reaction to Acids. SEF is extremely resistant to most acids.

Affinity for Dyes. Fabrics of SEF dye well with cationic dyestuffs in a full range of selected colors—from light, bright pastels to black—with good colorfastness properties. Disperse dyes also take well; fastness to light of selected colors is fair.

Resistance to Perspiration. Resistance to degradation by perspiration appears to be very good. Some colors may, however, be affected.

SEF MODACRYLIC FIBER BLENDS

Like the other modacrylics, SEF has properties that make it suitable for blending with other fibers. SEF was originally oriented toward fabrics of 100 percent SEF because of its outstanding flame-retardant characteristic in combination with its hand, drape, shrink resistance, and good tensile properties, which produce fabrics that meet the flammability-resistant requirements for children's sleepwear and other products. SEF may ultimately be used in blends with other fibers. Some blends would reduce the flame-retardant properties. In general, it may be expected that blends similar to those with acrylics or other modacrylics will have similar characteristics.

COMPARISON OF MODACRYLIC FIBERS

Table 21-1 is a summary composite based on information supplied by the produc- ers of these fibers and on evaluations of the performance of the fibers as de- scribed in the literature dealing with modacrylic fibers. The reader is re- minded that variations do exist within each trademark as well as blend combi- nation, type of yarn, fabric weight, con- struction, and finish and that these fac- tors will affect the performance. It is also possible that future changes in the chemical and physical compositions of these fibers may alter their perform- ance.

Table 21-1

COMPARISON OF PROPERTIES OF THE MODACRYLIC FIBERS			
PROPERTY	DYNEL	VEREL	SEF
Strength	Moderate; strongest of the modacrylics	Moderate	Moderate
Abrasion resistance	Good	Good	Good
Elasticity	Very little	Very little	Little
Resilience	Good to very good	Good to very good	Very good
Drapability	Satisfactory to good	Good	Very good
Absorbency	Very little; least of the modacrylics	Little; more than other modacrylics or acrylics	Little; more than acrylics
Laundering care	Excellent, but extreme agitation or rubbing could cause pilling	Excellent, but extreme agitation or rubbing could cause pilling	Excellent, but extreme agitation or rubbing could cause pilling
Ironing temperature	Needs little ironing; use rayon setting	Needs little ironing; use rayon setting	Most resistant to heat
Household bleaches	Safe	Some discoloration may occur	Safe
Shrinkage	None, provided water is not too hot	None	None
Flame resistance	Very good; difficult to ignite, self-extinguishing	Very good; difficult to ignite, self-extinguishing	Very good; difficult to ignite, self-extinguishing

Table 21-1

COMPARISON OF PROPERTIES OF THE MODACRYLIC FIBERS *(Continued)*			
PROPERTY	DYNEL	VEREL	SEF
Resistance to light	Very good	Very good	Very good
Resistance to mildew	Wholly resistant	Wholly resistant	Wholly resistant
Resistance to insects	Excellent	Excellent	Excellent
Reaction to alkalies	Highly resistant	Resistant; excessive exposure will cause discoloration	Good resistance to weak alkalies; moderate resistance to strong, cold alkalies
Reaction to acids	Extremely resistant	Extremely resistant	Extremely resistant
Resistance to perspiration	Excellent	Excellent	Excellent
Colorfastness	Excellent	Excellent	Good

REVIEW QUESTIONS

1. How do modacrylics differ in composition from acrylics?
2. What are the trademarks for the modacrylic fibers?
3. How do they differ from each other?
4. In what respects are they similar?
5. How do the several types of each of the basic modacrylics differ?
6. For what are these modacrylics best used?
7. What are the outstanding features of modacrylics?
8. What limitations do you see in modacrylics?
9. What blends are considered best for these modacrylics?
10. What features do these blends have?

SUGGESTED ACTIVITY

Obtain advertisements for each modacrylic discussed and identify similar properties cited; note any properties cited as individual to a particular modacrylic.

22

SPANDEX

the elastomeric fiber

Spandex is an elastomeric fiber—that is, it has superior elasticity. Spandex fibers are capable of being stretched from about five to over seven times their length and returning immediately to their relaxed state upon release of tension. Yet, the elastic characteristic of spandex should not be confused with the elasticity of stretch nylon or rubber yarns. Spandex is different in both composition and properties from either of these. It may be described as being molecularly composed of a chainlike arrangement of soft, stretchable segments of polyurethane (the substance described on pages 217–218, which is used for foam laminating fabrics) linked together for reinforcement by hard segments. There is some degree of variation among the several spandex fibers.

HISTORY OF SPANDEX

For many years the only elastic substance that was available for use in ap-

parel was rubber, and prior to 1930, yarn was cut from sheets of rubber. This method was replaced when a technique was developed for extruding liquid latex into a finer, round rubber yarn. To make the yarn suitable for garments, the rubber thread was covered by winding around it two layers of such yarns as cotton or rayon. These yarns were known by such names as *Lastex*, a trademark of the U.S. Rubber Co. (now Uniroyal Inc.).

This type of yarn has several limitations: it is relatively coarse and heavy, and while the textile wrapping of such yarn may be dyed, the rubber thread does not take dyes readily and therefore shows, or "grins through," when the yarn is stretched. The properties of these yarns are also affected by the particular properties of the textile plied around the rubber. In terms of serviceability, rubber has a relatively limited flex life and inadequate abrasion resistance. In addition, rubber is not too desirable for use next to the skin because it is deteriorated by oils, such as natural body oils, and various cosmetic and suntan lotions.

In 1947 the Heberlein Patent Corp. introduced *Helenca* stretch yarn, which is made from nylon filament. This was the first elastic yarn made entirely of a textile. Other similar stretch yarns soon followed. (See Chapter 4.) However, none of these are truly elastomeric yarns because the fibers themselves do not stretch materially—their stretchability is dependent upon the straightening out of the coil, curl, or crimp of the filaments. Furthermore, the amount of stretch is about one-quarter to one-half that of rubber. These stretch yarns do not have the ability to resist pulling, nor do they have the restraining power of rubber. While they have excellent stretch and form-fitting characteristics for such purposes as socks, tights, lingerie, and blouses, they lack the holding power needed for such apparel as support hose and foundation garments.

This interest in elastic fibers was also pursued in another direction. Pioneer work done in the Du Pont laboratories led to the creation in 1947 of an experimental elastomeric textile identified as *Fiber K*. After much developmental effort, the fiber was introduced to the trade for evaluation in April, 1958. It was tested for the next year and a half by foundation garment manufacturers. This led to its commercialization as the first spandex fiber and the adoption by Du Pont of the *Lycra* trademark in October, 1959. The fiber met with some initial resistance from buyers who were skeptical about its alleged stretch and holding power. However, the effective sales promotion overcame resistance and the

claims were proven. Having achieved good consumer acceptance, Du Pont began full-scale production of Lycra spandex fiber in Waynesboro, Virginia, in 1962.

The interest in spandex fiber then quickly grew. It was recognized as desirable and in some respects superior to both rubber thread and stretch yarns. In 1963, Globe Manufacturing Co., which had been a producer of extruded latex thread in Fall River, Massachusetts, introduced its *Glospan* spandex fiber. It developed two forms of this fiber. More recently, it produced *Cleerspan*, a nearly transparent spandex fiber. In 1964, *Numa* spandex fiber was introduced. It is manufactured by Ameliotex, Inc., of Rocky Hill, New Jersey.

Other companies also joined the competition with the production of spandex fibers under the names of *Vyrene*, *Spandelle*, *Blue C*, *Fiber 32*, *Durospun*, and *Unel*. They ultimately discontinued manufacture of these fibers for various reasons.

METHODS OF MANUFACTURE

In this highly competitive field, the specifics of the manufacture for each of the several spandex fibers are closely guarded by the respective producers. The chemistry and processing are generally described as being very complicated. All spandex fibers are segmented polyurethane and formed through spinnerets either by melt extrusion or by solvent spinning. Variations among the methods of manufacture include the use of delustering agents, optical whiteners, and dye receptors.

Spinning the Fiber

By way of explanation of production, the following general processing information for Numa spandex fiber is presented. It is basically produced by wet-spinning a solution of a segmented polyurethane in an appropriate strong solvent (some typical strong solvents used with polyurethanes are dimethylformamide, dimethylacetamide or dimethylsulfoxide). In general, the first step involves the preparation of a segmented polyurethane structure by the reaction of a glycol with a diisocyanate to form a so-called prepolymer, followed by chain extension of the prepolymer with diols or diamines to yield a high molecular weight polymer. It is called *segmented* because the completed polymer is made from a block copolymer in which reasonably long segments, or chains, of a flexible structure (the so-called glycol soft segments) are joined to shorter chains of a stiff structure (diisocyanate hard segments) through urethane linkages.

In the second step, a solution of the urethane polymer is blended with various delustering pigments and stabilizing additives, filtered, and stored in spinning tanks. The third step involves extrusion of this so-called spinning dope through multihole spinnerets into a water-solvent coagulation bath to form a multifilament yarn which is thoroughly washed to remove and recover all traces of solvent, then dried and wound on disposable cardboard tubes after application of a lubricant. The solvent and water are recovered and recycled, resulting in both an economical and pollution-free process. The final step before shipment of the finished product to the consumer involves inspection, testing, and packaging of the tubes of Numa multifilament spandex yarn.

TRADEMARKS OF SPANDEX FIBERS

The spandex fibers are produced as multifilaments that are coalesced, or fused together, at points of contact giving the appearance of monofilaments. Manufacturers of multifilament spandex claim that this type provides greater flex life, suppleness, and draping quality. They also state that the multifilament type is less subject to damage from stitching because the needle passes between the filaments. (See Table 22-1.)

The fibers are, in general, delustered and white. One exception is Cleerspan spandex, which is nearly transparent. Garments made with it achieve a high degree of transparency. Consequently, they appear to be lighter than garments made with the other spandex fibers. The near transparency is particularly suited for support hose and pantyhose. The transparency virtually eliminates grin-through when used for covered yarns.

The deniers of the fibers range from 40 to 3,360. As a reference point, 70 denier is similar to the denier of nylon used for many fabrics. When 70-denier yarn is stretched 300 to 400 percent, the yarn reduces in diameter to almost 15 denier, which is the typical size for most women's nylon hosiery yarn.

FORMS OF SPANDEX YARNS

Spandex fibers are made into several forms of yarn depending upon the functions to be served. The factors that determine the selection of the form of yarn

Table 22-1

SPANDEX TRADEMARKS				
TRADEMARK	MANUFACTURER	TYPE	SPECIAL CHARACTERISTICS	USES
Cleerspan	Globe Manufacturing Co.	Multifilament	Nearly transparent, irregular coalesced filaments	Hosiery
Glospan S-1	Globe Manufacturing Co.	Multifilament	Dull, white, irregular coalesced filaments	Foundation garments, swimsuits
Glospan S-5	Globe Manufacturing Co.	Multifilament	Dull, white, irregular coalesced filaments. Greater stretch, less holding power than S-1	Hosiery
Lycra	E.I. du Pont de Nemours & Co.	Multifilament	Dull, white, irregular coalesced dog-bone filaments	All purposes
Numa	Ameliotex, Inc.	Multifilament	Dull, white, irregular coalesced filaments	All purposes

include the desired amount of elasticity, power, hand, fabric sheerness, and styling, the yarn's resemblance to the other fibers in the fabric in which it will be used, and fabric end use.

Bare Yarns

The extruded, fused multifilaments and the monofilament spandex may be used without being covered. These bare yarns are utilized where lighter, sheerer, more supple, and more elastic fabrics are desired. Bare spandex yarns are more economical due to the elimination of the covering operation and the greater fabric yield that results from cutting smaller garments with a higher stretch level.

Bare yarns are incorporated into raschel power-net and circular-knit fabrics for foundation garments and swimwear. They may also be used for support hosiery and sock tops.

Covered Yarns

Spandex fiber is covered by wrapping yarn of any other fiber around it, which is the method originally used to cover rubber for apparel use. The stretch of spandex is limited by the extent to which the spiral of the cover yarn can be pulled. Covered spandex yarns also have the appearance and hand of the yarn used for covering. Covered yarns are used for raschel power-net and circular-knit fabrics, as well as other fabrics that require stretch and good holding power, such as for foundation garments, swimwear, and support hose.

Core-Spun Yarns

The core-spun technique is somewhat similar to that for producing covered spandex yarn. By application of a conventional cotton or wool spinning system, a roving of covering fiber (or a blend of fibers) is twisted to form a sheath of staple fiber around the spandex core that is held under tension and subsequently relaxed. The hand and texture of the yarn is determined by the covering staple, and the elasticity is limited by the length to which the twisted sheath may be extended. The spandex core of such yarns may be as little as 5 to 15 percent of the total fiber content, but it will provide more stretch and holding power than thermoplastic stretch yarns of similar diameter.

Core-spun yarns are claimed to have greater versatility and application than the above-mentioned spandex yarns. Consequently, they are being utilized in a wide variety of woven as well as knitted fabrics, including dresses, blouses, slacks, suits, sportswear, coats, uniforms, and raincoats.

Intimate Blend Spun Yarns

Much interest has been expressed regarding yarns spun of spandex fibers blended with inelastic fibers. As a textile fiber, spandex has many properties that make it suitable for blending. Its superior stretch characteristic has resulted in considerable experimentation in the development of blends of spandex staple with other fiber staple. These include blends of 4 to 30 percent spandex that is spun with other fibers into staple yarn. These blends provide sufficient elasticity and holding power for woven and knitted fabrics.

Biconstituent Yarns

Monofilament yarn of a biconstituent composition, such as Monvelle nylon/spandex fiber, is also available. The purpose is to combine the desirable properties of each component, which in the instance cited would be the strength and transparency of nylon and the superior stretch and recovery of spandex.

FINISHING FABRICS CONTAINING SPANDEX

The most common finishes given to fabrics containing spandex fiber are as follows:

Bleaching—for whiteness

Semidecating—for improved hand

Calendering and pressing—for smoothness of the fabric

Dyeing and printing—for producing decorative effects

Heat setting—for dimensional stability

Water repellency—for rainwear

Spandex fibers are inherently white; bleaching is therefore done only when the other fibers used in the yarn or fabric require it. However, since spandex fibers are yellowed by chlorine, a reducing bleach that does not contain chlorine should be used. Optical whiteners may be used safely.

Semidecating, calendering, and pressing are done under careful conditions without tension and at appropriately low temperatures to avoid possible loss of elasticity.

Heat setting is done under carefully controlled conditions to maintain the required degree of elasticity of the spandex fiber and to impart dimensional stability to the fabric. The degree of elasticity is reduced, but if properly done, heat setting can maintain a level of elasticity appropriate for the particular end use of the fabric.

Spandex fibers have very low absorbency. However, blended fabrics containing other fibers that are absorbent may be treated with a water repellent.

EVALUATING FABRICS CONTAINING SPANDEX

Fabrics are never made entirely of spandex fiber. As has been indicated, spandex yarns are frequently made in combination with other fibers. These yarns are generally incorporated with other yarns in fabrics. When bare spandex yarns are used, they are always utilized in conjunction with other yarns in fabrics. The form, amount, and arrangement of spandex yarns used in fabrics depend upon the type and construction of the garment, the fabric weight, and the amount of stretch and holding power desired. In fact, the primary purpose of using spandex is to obtain elasticity with holding power.

When considering the performance and care of fabrics containing spandex, attention must be given to the other fiber used with it to comprise the yarn, to the composition of the other yarns used, and to the fabric's construction and finish. In addition, some consideration should be given to the particular spandex fiber used. While many of the properties of these fibers are similar, certain differences do exist among them.

Strength.   Spandex fiber does not reach the breaking point until after the fiber has been stretched to its maximum length. This point is not usually reached in general use and wear. The strength of the various spandex fibers is quite adequate. The great flexibility of spandex fibers further adds to their serviceability and durability. In comparison with rubber, spandex is far superior in break strength and flex life. The abrasion resistance of the various spandex fibers is good, thereby contributing to their good wearing characteristics.

Elasticity.   Elasticity is the prime characteristic of spandex along with its holding power. Spandex fibers may be stretched from 500 to above 700 percent—that is, five to over seven times the relaxed state before breaking. This is almost as much as rubber yarn, which may be stretched to a maximum of about 750 percent. Also, the restraining force, or power, of spandex is about twice that of rubber that has been stretched 100 percent (or twice its length). Spandex is almost twice as elastic as the stretch nylons and exceeds their holding power by about six times.

The most elastic spandex fibers are Glospan S-5 and Cleerspan, which have a

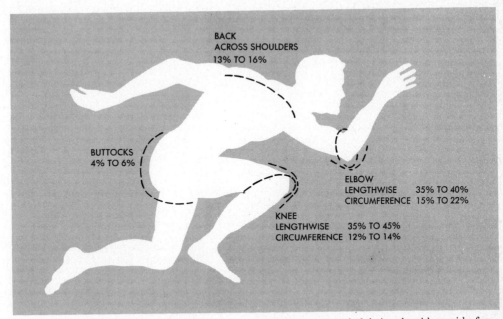

Figure 22-1 For comfort and freedom of body movement, stretch fabrics should provide for the amounts of skin extension shown.

maximum elongation of 725 percent. However, their power is lower than the others. They are therefore better suited for support hosiery and garments that are to provide light control. Glospan S-1 spandex has an elongation range of 550 to 625 percent. Lycra spandex has an elongation range of 500 to 600 percent. Numa spandex can stretch 600 to 700 percent. The extent of elongation is affected by yarn denier and other inherent properties of the particular fiber. In general, the heavier the denier, the less stretch can be expected. All the spandex fibers have instant and almost complete elastic recovery that is substantially retained along with their holding power, over extended periods of repeated washing and wearing.

The great elasticity of spandex far exceeds the requirements for comfort and power in apparel. As a base of reference, a study by the textile industry reveals that body movements require the following amounts of skin extension (see also Figure 22-1):

Back (across the shoulders)—13 to 16 percent

Elbow (lengthwise)—35 to 40 percent

Elbow (circumference)—15 to 22 percent

Knee (lengthwise)—35 to 45 percent

Knee (circumference)—12 to 14 percent

Buttock—4 to 6 percent

Standards of stretchability have been established from these figures. For stretch that is sufficient to provide comfort and freedom of body movement, stretchability of 25 to 30 percent with a recovery loss of no more than 2 to 5 percent is recommended. This amount of *comfort stretch* is suitable for a wide variety of apparel, such as blouses, shirts, and jackets, as well as such home furnishings as slipcovers and upholstery.

For sufficient power to provide support, stretch of 30 to 50 percent with a recovery loss of no more than 5 to 6 percent is recommended. This amount of *power stretch* is suitable for support hose, foundation garments, skiwear, swimwear, and other athletic apparel, as well as for industrial uses. Depending upon the end use of the fabric, the power stretch may be more than 50 percent, in which case a greater amount of spandex fiber must be incorporated into the fabric.

It is apparent that spandex fibers can readily satisfy many needs. Adequate and proper performance depends upon the yarn structure, fabric construction, and garment manufacture.

Resilience. Spandex fibers are highly flexible and resilient. This property of rapid shape recovery imparts a flat, neat appearance to fabrics.

Heat Conductivity. Spandex is not a good conductor of heat. Some degree of heat buildup may be expected when wearing clothes made of Spandex.

Drapability. The light weight and pliability of spandex fibers contribute good draping qualities to fabrics.

Absorbency. Spandex fibers have a very low absorbency—lower than even the polyester fibers. Therefore, for comfort next to the skin, the spandex should be covered, core spun, or blended with fibers that will provide the desired absorbency.

Cleanliness and Washability. All spandex fibers are unaffected by dry-cleaning solvents. They are also machine washable with the usual household soaps and detergents, but the temperature of the water should be about 100 to 120 degrees Fahrenheit, depending upon the particular spandex fiber. Higher temperatures may reduce the elasticity of the spandex. Clothing containing spandex may be machine-dried at temperatures usually between 140 and 160 degrees Fahrenheit. In general, these conditions are also satisfactory for the other fiber in the fabric. It is highly desirable to refer to the washing instructions that are attached to the garments.

Effect of Bleaches. All the spandex fibers are white, though the degree of whiteness varies. Under certain conditions, yellowing may occur. Fibers used in conjunction with spandex in the fabric may discolor and bleaching may be desired. However, the several spandex fibers differ in their reaction to bleaches. Treatment must be given accordingly.

Lycra spandex is yellowed by bleaches of calcium hypochlorite (also known as bleach powder), sodium hypochlorite, and hydrogen peroxide. Under certain conditions of concentration, these bleaches will also weaken the fiber. Sodium chlorite, a bleach used commercially, will degrade and discolor Lycra spandex. A safe, effective bleach is one that contains sodium perborate, such as Snowy.

Glospan and Cleerspan may be safely bleached with any household bleach.

However, the commercially used sodium chlorite bleach will affect their properties.

Numa may be safely bleached with household chlorine bleach, hydrogen peroxide, or sodium perborate. Strong chlorine bleaches, such as sodium chlorite and sodium hypochlorite, cause yellowing and should not be used.

A question may arise concerning the ill effect of the chlorine in swimming pools on swimwear containing spandex. The answer is that pools are usually treated with calcium hypochlorite. If this solution is of a proper level, it is not likely to be strong enough to degrade the fiber performance, particularly if the water temperature is not above 80 degrees Fahrenheit. Furthermore, the fiber is usually well hidden or covered and possible yellowing is not likely to be noticeable (see Figure 22-2).

Effect of Seawater. Since we are considering the important place that spandex fiber has in swimwear and other related uses, it is important to emphasize that it is unaffected by seawater.

Shrinkage and Growth. Spandex fibers will not shrink from exposure to water; however, some do shrink upon exposure to certain temperatures (discussed below). On the other hand, a garment may have a small loss of elastic recovery as it used. This gradual extension is known as *growth*. The amount of growth may not be too significant, particularly if taken into consideration during garment construction.

Effect of Heat. Exposure to heat has varied effects on the spandex fibers.

Figure 22-2   Spandex is lightweight, elastic, and resists deterioration by chlorine in pools and by seawater. This swimsuit is made of 69% acrylic rotofil yarn, 7% spandex, and 24% nylon. *(Courtesy E. I. du Pont de Nemours and Co.)*

Generally, excessive exposure to heat should be avoided. As a rule, ironing should be done quickly and with a warm iron.

Lycra spandex yellows and loses elasticity and strength at over 300 degrees Fahrenheit. It sticks at 347 degrees Fahrenheit and melts at 446 degrees Fahrenheit.

Glospan and Cleerspan retain good dimensional stability when exposed to heat. They stick at 420 degrees Fahrenheit.

Numa sticks at about 437 degrees Fahrenheit and melts at about 511 degrees Fahrenheit.

Effect of Light. Light and other atmospheric conditions have varying effects upon the several spandex fibers. However, no really serious damage may be expected to occur in the normal use of spandex for dress or sportswear.

Lycra spandex has initial good resistance to light, but over a prolonged period of time, it will lose some strength and yellow slightly. Fumes of oxides of nitrogen will also cause yellowing.

Glospan, Cleerspan, and Numa spandex have very good resistance to degradation by sunlight. Although there is no loss of physical properties, they do discolor slightly. They also have good resistance to gas fumes.

Resistance to Mildew. The spandex fibers have good to excellent resistance to damage by mildew.

Resistance to Insects. As may be expected, spandex fibers are unaffected by insects.

Reaction to Alkalies. Reactions of spandex fibers to alkalies vary, but all are affected.

Lycra and Numa spandex have moderate resistance to most alkalies. Glospan and Cleerspan are rapidly deteriorated by hot alkali.

Reaction to Acids. Reactions of spandex fibers to acids also vary. Lycra spandex has good resistance to most acids, though some discoloration may occur. Glospan and Cleerspan are resistant to cold dilute acids. Numa is unaffected by weak acids.

Affinity for Dyes. The spandex fibers have a good affinity for many classes of dyes, including disperse, acid, chrome, and other dyes. While the colors are good, colorfastness ranges from poor to fair on continued exposure to light, washing, and seawater. The degree of fastness depends upon the dye used and the technique of application.

Resistance to Perspiration. Indications are that all the spandex fibers have good resistance to degradation by perspiration.

Resistance to Oils. An important attribute of all of the spandex fibers is their high resistance to body oils, cosmetics, and suntan lotions. This is a particularly important advantage over rubber for use in such garments as girdles and swimwear.

COMPARISON OF SPANDEX FIBERS

Table 22-2 is for the reader's general guidance. It is a summary composite based on information supplied by the producers of these fibers and on evaluation of the performance of the fibers as described in the literature dealing with spandex fibers. The reader is reminded that variations do exist in blend combinations, types of yarn, fabric weights, constructions, and finishes and that these factors will affect the performance. It is also possible that future changes in the chemical and physical compositions of these fibers may alter their performance.

Table 22-2

COMPARISON OF PROPERTIES OF THE SPANDEX FIBERS				
PROPERTY	LYCRA	GLOSPAN	CLEERSPAN	NUMA
Strength	Satisfactory; excellent flex life	Satisfactory; excellent flex life	Satisfactory; excellent flex life	Satisfactory; excellent flex life
Abrasion resistance	Good	Good	Good	Good
Elasticity (approximate)	520 to 600%; slight growth with use	S-1, 600%; S-5, 725%; slight growth with use	725%; slight growth with use	500 to 600%; slight growth with use
Resilience	Excellent	Excellent	Excellent	Excellent
Absorbency	Practically none	Practically none	Practically none	Practically none
Laundering care	Hand or machine washable with household soaps or detergents	Hand or machine washable with household soaps or detergents	Hand or machine washable with household soaps or detergents	Hand or machine washable with household soaps or detergents
Ironing temperature	Quickly with warm iron (low setting)	Use warm iron	Use warm iron	Use warm iron
Shrinkage	None to water below boiling point	None to water	None to water	None to water
Household bleaches	Sodium perborate; others may yellow and weaken	Any household bleach; sodium chlorite degrades	Any household bleach; sodium chlorite degrades	Any household bleach; strong solutions of sodium chlorite or sodium hypochlorite yellows
Effect of heat	Yellows and loses elasticity above 300°F; melts at 446°F	Good dimensional stability. Sticks at 420°F	Very good dimensional stability. Sticks at 420°F	Good dimensional stability. Sticks at 437°F; melts at 511°F
Resistance to light	Good, but loses some strength and yellows slightly after prolonged exposure	Very good, but will discolor slightly	Very good, but will discolor slightly	Very good, but will discolor slightly
Seawater	Not harmful	Not harmful	Not harmful	Not harmful
Resistance to mildew	Good	Good	Good	Good
Reaction to alkalies	Good resistance to most alkalies	Rapidly deteriorated by hot alkalies	Rapidly deteriorated by hot alkalies	Good resistance to most alkalies
Reaction to acids	Good resistance to most acids; some discoloration may occur	Resistant to cold dilute acids	Resistant to cold dilute acids	Unaffected by weak acids

Table 22-2

COMPARISON OF PROPERTIES OF THE SPANDEX FIBERS *(Continued)*				
PROPERTY	LYCRA	GLOSPAN	CLEERSPAN	NUMA
Affinity for dyes	Good for wide variety; colorfastness poor to good, depending upon dye and technique	Good for wide variety; colorfastness poor to good, depending upon dye and technique	Good for wide variety; colorfastness poor to good, depending upon dye and technique	Good for wide variety; colorfastness poor to good, depending upon dye and technique
Resistance to perspiration	Good	Good	Good	Good
Resistance to oils	Good	Good	Good	Good

REVIEW QUESTIONS

1. Name each of the spandex fibers and its manufacturer.
2. What is spandex fiber?
3. Compare the elastic properties of spandex to those of (a) stretch nylon, (b) rubber, (c) stretch cotton.
4. Explain what is meant by (a) comfort stretch, (b) power stretch.
5. How much stretch is needed for comfort over various parts of the body?
6. Describe the different forms of spandex yarns and indicate their characteristics and uses.
7. What finishes may be given to fabrics containing spandex fibers?
8. What limitations do you consider spandex fibers to have?
9. Describe and illustrate the appearance of each spandex fiber.
10. Compare the properties of the spandex fibers.

SUGGESTED ACTIVITY

Obtain advertisements for at least three spandex fibers. Identify similar and unique properties claimed for each fiber.

23

POLYPROPYLENE

the olefin fiber

Olefins are a family of polymers that may be generally described as *paraffins*, a group familiar to the consumer as wax. While it is possible to develop an infinite variety of fibers from this paraffin group, polypropylene has been developed furthest for consumer acceptance.

HISTORY OF POLYPROPYLENE

By using high-pressure techniques in the 1930s, research in polymer chemistry led to the polymerization of a form of polyethylene in England. Ultimately, this led to the independent initial development of polymerization of polyethylene under low-pressure techniques in Germany, by Professor Ziegler, and in the United States, by the Phillips Petroleum Co. This provided the basis for commercial production of another form of polyethylene plastic from which the flexible plastic products such as the familiar squeeze bottle are now made.

Subsequent research led to the development of varieties of polyethylene and also revealed the possibility of a wide variety of related olefins. The basis for controlling the molecular arrangements of these olefins was established in Italy by Professor Giulio Natta who, with Ziegler, received the Nobel Prize in 1963 for his explanation of the polymerization of polypropylene. Professors Natta and Ziegler also filed the first patent applications for the manufacture of polypropylene fibers. Production was begun at the Montecatini Co. in Italy, in 1951, under the trademark of *Meraklon*.

Meanwhile, several American companies were engaged in research and development, and limited production of polyethylene monofilament. These fibers had certain common disadvantages and greater attention was turned to the development and commercial production of polypropylene fiber, which has a higher melting point, greater resilience and strength, as well as a lighter weight. The first commercial production of polypropylene resin was done in the United States in 1957 by the Hercules Powder Co., Inc. This company later acquired facilities at Covington, Virginia, for the manufacture of its polypropylene fiber, *Herculon*, thus becoming the first completely integrated manufacturer in the United States from raw material to finished fiber.

Another company moving in this direction was Reeves Brothers, Inc., one of the first producers of polypropylene fiber under the trademark of *Reevon*. By a series of mergers and corporate reorganizations, this company became a part of Alamo Industries, Inc., which announced, in 1965, the new trademark of *Marvess* to identify its polypropylene fiber. This trademark is licensed by Alamo to other companies that meet certain quality standards.

By this time, these and other producers, such as U.S. Rubber Co. (Uniroyal Inc.), established plants capable of producing millions of pounds of polypropylene fiber. In an effort to compete with better-established man-made fibers, producers began promoting polypropylene before certain of its limitations (subsequently to be resolved) were overcome. As a result, consumer reaction was skeptical and acceptance was slow. However, it is expected that, with continued improvements and sound consumer education, polypropylene fiber will find a good market for such diverse products as rope, rugs, sweaters, hosiery, slacks, and other apparel.

METHOD OF MANUFACTURE

The production of polypropylene fiber varies among the manufacturers. In fact, individual manufacturers have variations in their processes to achieve certain properties, such as dyeability, light stability, heat sensitivity, and shape of the filament cross section.

The basic procedure, as illustrated in Figure 23-1, is to polymerize propylene gas with the aid of an appropriate metal compound, such as titanium chloride, in a diluent. The polymer formed from the propylene is slurried in the diluent to decompose the catalyst, and is then filtered, purified, and reduced to powder form as polypropylene resin. Additives may be included in the resin to stabilize the relatively low inherent heat and light degradation properties of polypropylene.

The resin is melted and extruded through a spinneret in filament form. The filaments are then treated and drawn to get the proper crystallinity and molecular orientation in order to obtain such desired characteristics as strength, abrasion resistance, elasticity, resilience, and shrinkage. For example, the greater the amount of drawing, the higher the tensile strength and the lower the elasticity of the fiber. The fiber may be heat-set to alter its shrinkage, elasticity, and flex-resistance characteristics.

Polypropylene may also be extruded in sheet form for various uses. The sheets may be fibrillated, or slit, to form monofilaments or bundles of multifilaments. This technique of producing filaments is considerably cheaper than extrusion through a spinneret. The sheets are slit into predetermined, very narrow ribbons by scribing, cutting, perforating, or other suitable technique.

FORMS AND TYPES OF POLYPROPYLENE YARNS

As has been stated, polypropylene fiber is produced in a variety of forms and in a wide range of deniers. Some are non-

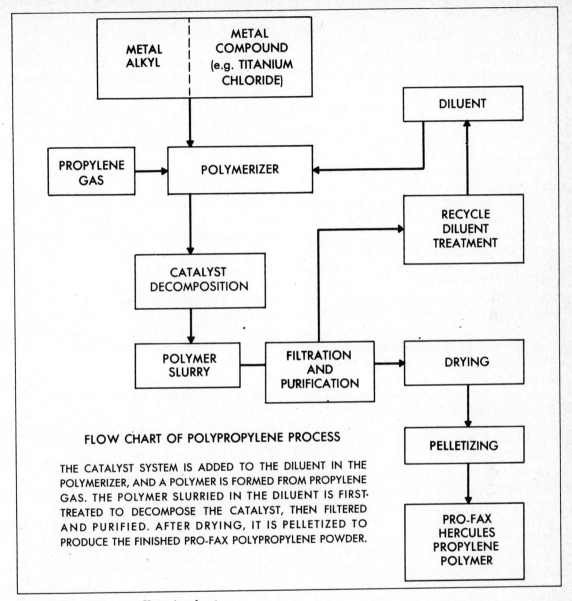

FLOW CHART OF POLYPROPYLENE PROCESS

THE CATALYST SYSTEM IS ADDED TO THE DILUENT IN THE POLYMERIZER, AND A POLYMER IS FORMED FROM PROPYLENE GAS. THE POLYMER SLURRIED IN THE DILUENT IS FIRST· TREATED TO DECOMPOSE THE CATALYST, THEN FILTERED AND PURIFIED. AFTER DRYING, IT IS PELLETIZED TO PRODUCE THE FINISHED PRO-FAX POLYPROPYLENE POWDER.

Figure 23-1 *(Courtesy Hercules, Inc.)*

dyeable white, some are nondyeable pigmented, others are completely dyeable. They are produced in bright and semibright forms. Some are highly stabilized to resist degradation by sunlight; some are highly heat-stabilized. The fibers may be crimped or uncrimped. The texture and appearance may vary, depending upon the fiber cross section. Some of the fibers are designed to be suitable for specific products (such as rugs), others for wearing apparel, others for industrial purposes. Many of these characteristics are tentative as manufacturers improve their products and develop new types.

The polypropylene fibers are produced in monofilament, multifilament, bicomponent tow, and staple form. These, in turn, are made into several forms of yarn.

Monofilament Yarns

The monofilament yarns are produced from individual filaments, and the range of denier is very wide. The yarns are used for such purposes as automobile seat covers, outdoor furniture webbing, and radio grille fabrics.

Multifilament Yarns

Polypropylene multifilament may be produced as straight or bulked (BCF) yarn of about 17 to 420 filaments, ranging from about 165 to 3,750 denier. The straight multifilament yarn is used for both general apparel and industrial purposes, depending upon the type of polypropylene fiber.

Fibrillated Yarns

Polypropylene sheets may be slit into various narrow widths as required. The fibrillated strands may be used individually, as for monofilament yarn, or they may be twisted together, as for multifilament yarn. The properties of fibrillated yarn are essentially the same as those of monofilament or multifilament. They are used for such purposes as backing on carpets, rope, twine, and netting.

Spun Yarns

Polypropylene filaments may be cut into staple and subsequently spun on a conventional cotton or wool system with very slight modification either into 100 percent polypropylene into spun yarn blended with other fibers. Polypropylene tow may be processed on a Pacific Converter into spun yarn. Yarns of spun polypropylene staple have been found to be relatively pill-resistant and can be used for a wide variety of apparel.

Bulk and Textured Yarns

Multifilament polypropylene fiber may be crimped or textured. The crimped multifilaments are thrown into yarn. This type of yarn is being used for carpets. It shows much promise for this purpose because polypropylene has good resistance to abrasion, soiling, staining, and pilling, as well as being virtually static-free. The yarn is bulky and has a soft, pleasant hand.

TRADEMARKS OF POLYPROPYLENE YARN

To identify and promote their respective products, the manufacturers have given trademarks to their polypropylene yarns as shown in Table 23-1. Although certain basic properties are similar, it is apparent from the foregoing discussion that the characteristics of the yarns differ insofar as the type of polypropylene fiber, its cross section, and the yarn construction are concerned.

FINISHING POLYPROPYLENE FABRICS

Much work remains to be done in developing finishing techniques for fabrics containing polypropylene fiber. Polypropylene is resistant to water and a wide variety of chemicals. Some finishes, such as water and stain repellents, are unnecessary. In blends with other fibers, such

Table 23-1

POLYPROPYLENE TRADEMARKS				
TRADEMARK	MANUFACTURER	TYPE	SPECIAL CHARACTERISTICS	USES
Amco Polypropylene	American Mfg. Co.	Monofilament, multifilament (fibrillated)	Flat	Industrial fabrics
American Polypropylene	American Mfg. Co.	Monofilament, multifilament (fibrillated)	Flat	Industrial fabrics
Chadolene	Tennessee Fibers, Inc.	Multifilament, (fibrillated)	Flat	Apparel, home furnishings, industrial fabrics
Concorde Polypropylene	Concorde Fibers, Inc.	Multifilament	Textured, dyed	Home furnishings
Diamond	Metlon Corp.	Monofilament	Flat	Apparel, home furnishings
DLP Polypropylene	Thiokol Chemical Corp.	Monofilament, multifilament	Round or flat, regular and high tenacity	Apparel, home furnishings, industrial fabrics
Fibergras	Patchogue-Plymouth Co.	Multifilament		Home furnishings
Fibrilawn	Fibron, Inc.	Multifilament, (fibrillated)		Home furnishings, industrial fabrics
Fibron	Fibron, Inc.	Multifilament (fibrillated)		Home furnishings, industrial fabrics
Goldcres	Shuford Mills, Inc.	Monofilament, multifilament (fibrillated)	Flat	Apparel, home furnishings, industrial fabrics
Herculon	Hercules, Inc.	Multifilament, staple, tow	Some bulked	Apparel
Herculon II	Hercules, Inc.	Multifilament	Bicomponent	Apparel
Herculon IV	Hercules, Inc.	Multifilament	Bulk continuous filament (BCF), soil hiding	Carpets
Lo-Pic	Fibron, Inc.	Monofilament	Flat	Home furnishings, industrial fabrics
Lustreloft	Fibron, Inc.	Multifilament (fibrillated), staple	Flat	Home furnishings, industrial fabrics

Table 23-1

POLYPROPYLENE TRADEMARKS *(Continued)*				
TRADEMARK	MANUFACTURER	TYPE	SPECIAL CHARACTERISTICS	USES
Marvess	Phillips Fibers Corp.	Multifilament, staple, tow		Apparel, home furnishings, industrial fabrics
Marvess III	Phillips Fibers Corp.	Multifilament	Modified cross section, high luster, solution-dyed	Home furnishings
Marvess CG	Phillips Fibers Corp.	Staple	Heavy denier, solution-dyed	Home furnishings
Montrel	Wellington Synthetic Fibres, Inc.	Multifilament	Low shrinkage, high modulus	Home furnishings, industrial fabrics
Olefin (Waltrich)	Waltrich Plastics Corp.	Monofilament		Apparel, home furnishings, industrial fabrics
Olefin (Indian Head)	Indian Head Yarn & Thread Co.	Multifilament (fibrillated)	High modulus, flat	Industrial fabrics
Oletex	Poncar Plastic Corp.	Multifilament		Industrial fabrics
Parapro	Wall Industries, Inc.	Multifilament		Home furnishings
Polyloom	Chevron Chemical Co.	Multifilament (fibrillated)	Flat	Home furnishings, industrial fabrics
Polywrap	Indian Head Yarn & Thread Co.	Multifilament (fibrillated)	High modulus, flat	Industrial fabrics
Poncar	Poncar Plastic Corp.	Multifilament		Industrial fabrics
Pro-Tuft	Bemis Co., Inc.	Monofilament	Flat	Industrial fabrics
Shurti	Shuford Mills, Inc.	Multifilament (fibrillated)	Flat	Industrial fabrics
Tytite	Indian Head Yarn & Thread Co.	Multifilament (fibrillated)	Flat	Industrial fabrics
Unifil	Wall Industries, Inc.	Monofilament		Home furnishings
Vectra	Vectra Corp.	Multifilament, staple		Apparel, home furnishings, industrial fabrics
Voplex	Voplex Corp.	Multifilament	Round or flat	Industrial fabrics
Wall Polypropylene	Wall Industries, Inc.	Monofilament		Industrial fabrics
Waltrich Polypropylene	Waltrich Plastics Corp.	Monofilament		Industrial fabrics
WSF PP	Wellington Synthetic Fibres, Inc.	Monofilament	Round, high tenacity	Industrial fabrics

chemical finishes as mercerizing may be applied if heat conditions permit. Heat sensitivity is a problem because it is generally recommended that polypropylene not be subjected to temperatures above 250 degrees Fahrenheit. Also, many types of polypropylene are nondyeable. Printing is also a problem.

Mechanical finishes, such as napping, will enhance the soft texture and warmth of the fabric. Other finishes, such as embossing and heat setting, require caution.

Producers are optimistic that these problems will ultimately be solved.

EVALUATING POLYPROPYLENE FABRICS

Polypropylene is the lightest of all textile fibers and therefore provides more fiber per pound for greater area coverage. It has many inherent properties that could also make it popular for fabrics. However, the fiber's heat and light sensitivity and its poor dyeability factor are handicaps. Since manufacturers produce many types of polypropylene fibers with variations of characteristics to try to overcome these limitations, and since developmental work continues, all-inclusive statements of performance are not possible. However, some generalities may be drawn from information provided by the producers based upon tests under laboratory conditions and from limited evaluations based on performance in daily consumer use and care.

Strength. The range of the strength of polypropylene fibers is quite wide, but in general, it is comparable to that of nylon and the polyesters. (There are indications that continued developmental research may result in different types of polypropylene that are stronger than any existing fibers.) The strength and generally good abrasion resistance of polypropylene fiber make it durable and serviceable for both consumer and industrial uses.

Elasticity. Polypropylene fibers are less elastic than nylon fibers. Over a period of time, constant stress on the yarn results in a certain amount of permanent elongation.

Resilience. Polypropylene fiber has good resilience. This property contributes to its suitability for rugs as well as apparel. However, it is a general characteristic that the greater the strength of polypropylene fibers, the less resilient they are.

Heat Conductivity. One of the great advantages of polypropylene is its superior light weight. This characteristic combined with its ability to be crimped and otherwise treated to form bulky, lightweight yarns gives polypropylene very good insulating qualities. Very comfortable and warm blankets and sweaters can be made of such yarn.

Drapability. Since polypropylene can be produced in various cross sections and is lightweight and sufficiently pliable to be processed into a variety of yarns, it may be expected that fabrics of polypropylene will drape satisfactorily.

Absorbency. Polypropylene is practically nonabsorbent. While this presents severe limitations in terms of comfort when worn next to the skin, as well as for dyeing and printing, the lack of absorbency does provide certain advantages. Polypropylene cannot be saturated with water; consequently, it acts as its own water repellent. It also resists soiling and staining by such substances as grease, cosmetics, fruit juices, soft drinks, coffee, and eggs. These substances tend to stay on the surface of the fiber and can be readily removed with water and a detergent or other household cleaner.

Cleanliness and Washability. Polypropylene fabrics can be washed or dry-cleaned easily. Soil tends to remain on the surface and can be readily removed from fabrics. There is no loss of strength when wet, and any soap, detergent, or cleaning agent may be safely used. Since polypropylene is heat sensitive, however, warm rather than hot water is recommended. Fabrics of polypropylene are dimensionally stable, shape retentive, and quick-drying. Again, when being washed or dried, the fibers should not be exposed to high temperatures, as shrinkage could occur. Although polypropylene fabrics may be dry-cleaned, the common dry-cleaning solvent perchlorethylene could affect dimensional stability.

Effect of Bleaches. Polypropylene has good resistance to degradation by various bleaches at temperatures below 150 degrees Fahrenheit. Loss of strength begins when the fabrics are subjected to bleaching solutions above that level. This is another reason why the water temperature should not be too high when laundering.

Shrinkage. Polypropylene is unaffected by water and will not shrink. However, depending upon the type, it does begin to shrink when subjected to temperatures of 212 degrees Fahrenheit (boiling) and above.

Effect of Heat. Reference has already been made to the heat sensitivity of polypropylene. Because they are thermoplastic, polypropylene fabrics can be heat-set to a desired shape—in fact, they are moldable. However, depending upon the type of polypropylene, the fibers shrink and then soften at temperatures above 265 degrees Fahrenheit, and they melt at temperatures above 325 degrees Fahrenheit.

To overcome this handicap, some types of polypropylene have heat stabilizers to reduce their sensitivity. However, they have not been as successful as desired. They tend to break down when exposed to certain conditions and chemicals in finishes and certain other conditions in the use and care of the fabrics.

Effect of Light. Polypropylene is deteriorated by exposure to direct sunlight. The ultraviolet light causes the breakdown. To overcome this, light stabilizers have been added to certain types of polypropylene. This technique has had limited success because these stabilizers, like the heat stabilizers, tend to break down.

Resistance to Mildew. Polypropylene is wholly resistant to mildew.

Resistance to Insects. Polypropylene is not attacked by moth larvae, beetles, or other insects.

Reaction to Alkalies. Polypropylene has excellent resistance to alkalies.

Reaction to Acids. Polypropylene has excellent resistance to most acids (Figure 23-2).

Affinity for Dyes. The greatest handicap of polypropylene fiber is its dyeing difficulty. To overcome this, some types are pigmented before extrusion; however, this method only provides limited colors. Some types are modified to take specific dyes; but here again, a complete color range is lacking. Attempts to vary conventional dyeing techniques have had some effect, but the colors are generally not fast to washing, to dry cleaning, or to light. Surface pigment binders have provided some washable and dry-cleanable dark colors, but these tend to crock.

Continued research promises to overcome these difficulties. For instance, premetallized acid dyes and disperse dyes similar to those used for nylon show promise. Certain of the latter have shown good fastness to washing, to dry cleaning, and to light.

Resistance to Perspiration. Polypropylene is a relatively chemically inert fiber. It therefore will not be deteriorated by perspiration.

POLYPROPYLENE FIBER BLENDS

Polypropylene fiber has been successfully blended with cotton, wool, and rayon, but more evaluation is needed to determine the optimum blend proportions. The chief values of polypropylene in blends would be to lower the yarn cost, to reduce the yarn weight, to improve the yarn bulk and therefore warmth, to contribute strength and durability, as well as to add shape retention and enhance cleaning and drying properties.

Figure 23-2 Polypropylene fiber is sufficiently inert to be used as carpet for this chemical laboratory. *(Courtesy Hercules, Inc.)*

REVIEW QUESTIONS

1. What is meant by the designation, olefin?
2. Describe the basic procedure for producing polypropylene fiber.
3. Name five polypropylene trademarks and their manufacturers.
4. In what ways may the various types of polypropylene fibers differ?
5. Describe the characteristics that are generally common to all polypropylene fibers.
6. What limitations do the polypropylene fibers have?
7. What are the most favorable properties of polypropylene fibers?
8. What kinds of yarns can be made of polypropylene fibers?
9. What characteristics do polypropylene fibers contribute to blends?
10. What is fibrillated yarn?

24

SARAN

the polyvinylidene chloride fiber

"Saran" is a generic term that refers to a particular type of plastic fiber that is a linear copolymer of vinylidene chloride and vinyl chloride. Some variation in its chemical composition is possible.

HISTORY OF SARAN

The chemical compound vinylidene chloride was discovered in 1838. It is a clear, colorless liquid that boils at 90 degrees Fahrenheit. Although chemists since 1922 had observed that it could easily polymerize, it was not until 1936 that further research was conducted. At that time the Dow Chemical Co. began a research program, probably spurred by the successful results of other companies' research with polymers, which ultimately resulted in 1940 in the commercialization of its fiber, saran.

The relatively low cost of the raw materials from which this fiber was made and certain of its other desirable features attracted the attention of several companies. Since the designation *saran* had not been registered as a trademark, other companies also used the term, and it became recognized as a general identification for this fiber. Subsequently, each company registered its particular saran trademark.

METHOD OF MANUFACTURE

The raw materials used to produce vinylidene chloride are ethylene, which is derived by cracking natural petroleum, and chlorine, which is electrolyzed from seawater. Ethylene is treated with chlorine to produce trichlorethane, which in turn is treated with lime to produce unpolymerized vinylidene chloride. The vinylidene chloride is then copolymerized with a small quantity of vinyl chloride to produce a powdered resin. The resin is melted and extruded through a spinneret into a water-cooling bath. While still being cooled, it is drawn out 400 percent to improve its crystallinity and molecular orientation, thereby increasing its strength in a manner similar to nylon.

The longitudinal appearance of the fiber is smooth and straight. The cross section may be round, flat, or oval. The natural color of saran is pale gold or straw. It may be delustered to a translucent or to an opaque appearance by the addition of a delusterant such as titanium dioxide. The fiber may be solution-dyed, but the colors are not bright because the natural color of saran tones down the hue.

FORMS AND TYPES OF SARAN YARNS

Saran may be made in monofilament, multifilament, and staple forms, though its use as a monofilament predominates. Some manufacturers produce a few types frequently associated with the shape of the fiber.

Monofilament Yarns

These yarns are made in a wide variety of diameters. Some companies express the thickness of the yarns in denier, others in terms of a decimal part of the inch. In denier, monofilament saran yarn is produced in 70 to 1,100; in inches, in a range of 0.005- to 0.05-inch diameters. It is used for a wide variety of purposes, such as window screens, handbags, millinery fabrics, and trimmings. Saran is also produced in rattanlike monofilament strips. This form is readily adapted to fabrics used for seat covers in automobiles, buses, and railroad cars, as well as for outdoor furniture.

Multifilament Yarns

The production of saran multifilament yarns is more limited. They are used for brocades and other fabrics. The amount of twist given to each of the following yarns varies depending on the desired ultimate result. Examples of saran mul-

tifilament yarns are 750 denier, of 50 filaments; 1,200 denier, of 100 filaments; 3,000 denier, of 300 filaments.

Staple

Saran staple fiber has been produced in 2- to 40-inch lengths in three forms: straight, crimped, and curled. The fiber deniers range from 10 to 70. Although saran staple may be used for a wide variety of purposes, including outerwear, rugs, and linings, it has not received much acceptance for consumer use, though it has been used for such industrial purposes as filter cloths.

TRADEMARKS OF SARAN FIBERS

Several companies produce saran fibers. Their basic quality is the same, since they are all generally made of the same substances in the same way. The important differences among the yarns produced are dependent on whether they are monofilament, multifilament, or staple, and on the denier of the fibers and the amount of twist in the yarns. For example, Saran, produced by S.E. Polymers, Inc., may be either monofilament, multifilament, or staple. Saran (Amtech), produced by Amtech, Inc., is monofilament.

Velon, produced by Firestone Plastics Co., Inc., is another saran trademark. Velon is also made in plastic sheet form for plastic tablecloths and similar protective coverings. *Saran Wrap* is another trademark for a very thin, clear sheet form used for wrapping foods and other items. It is produced by the Dow Badische Co.

Except for the plastic sheets, these companies produce only the fibers and yarns. The ultimate fabrics are woven by other companies. The quality of saran fabric depends further on the construction as well as on the type of yarn used.

FINISHING SARAN FABRICS

Saran is a thermoplastic fiber and can be permanently shaped at relatively low temperatures. Saran fabrics can therefore be molded into any desired shape. They can also be embossed in both deep and shallow patterns. Lamination of saran fabrics to other substances, such as polyurethane foam, vinyl film, paper, rayon, or cotton can be accomplished by bonding the heat-sensitive saran. Another method of laminating is by using appropriate adhesives.

Saran fabrics can be dielectrically sealed, eliminating the need to stitch the fabrics together. This results in a stronger bond and less likelihood for tearing at these points as well as in greater impermeability.

Chemical finishes are generally not used for saran. It is inert to many chemicals, and it is inherently water-repellent. It cannot be dyed by conventional means, and printing can be done only with pigment resins.

EVALUATING SARAN FABRICS

Saran has some valuable properties as a textile. It also has some definite limitations.

Strength. The strength of saran fiber varies with its diameter. Generally, the finer filaments are stronger than the coarser ones. Saran is weaker than any natural fiber except wool. It is weaker than most man-made fibers; it is stronger than regular viscose or cupram-monium rayon, acetate, and Arnel triacetate. Woven saran fabrics do have excellent abrasion resistance.

Elasticity. Saran has a fair degree of stretchability. Its return to original shape is more gradual as the amount of initial stretch is increased. The elasticity of saran has contributed to its use for seat covers and for upholstery used in outdoor furniture.

Resilience. Saran is a rather stiff fiber. While it is rather resistant to crushing, heavy compression could permanently deform the fiber and thereby reduce its resilience.

Heat Conductivity. Saran fabrics are not good conductors of heat but are easily affected by it. The heat conductivity of saran can be reduced by bulking the fiber.

Drapability. Saran is a rather stiff fiber. Finer diameters, of course, are more pliable, but saran is not generally considered to have a draping quality.

Absorbency. Saran is one of the least absorbent of all textiles, having virtually no absorbency. It is similar in this respect to polypropylene. Saran cannot be used for such garments as underwear, shirts, blouses, and dresses, since they would not absorb perspiration or atmospheric moisture and therefore would be uncomfortable. On the other hand, saran fabrics, being virtually waterproof, are suitable for outerwear, such as raincoats, and for outdoor furniture. Tablecloths are another use for saran.

Cleanliness and Washability. Saran fabrics may be easily cleaned by merely wiping them with a damp cloth. Fabrics of saran will wash both quickly and easily.

Laundering should be done by hand in lukewarm water. It must be remembered that saran fabrics should be kept away from heat when being dried because of their tendency to melt. Ironing is generally not needed, but if ironing is desired, a wet press cloth and an iron set as low as possible should be used. Saran fabrics may be dry-cleaned. However, perchlorethylene, a common dry-cleaning solvent, should not be used.

Effect of Bleaches.   Saran has good resistance to staining. Therefore, it does not generally need bleaching, though saran has good resistance to damage by any of the usual bleaches.

Shrinkage.   Saran is unaffected by water and will shrink only at temperatures above 168 degrees Fahrenheit.

Effect of Heat.   Saran also loses strength at its shrinking temperature. It softens at 240 to 320 degrees Fahrenheit, depending upon the type. It melts at about 340 to 350 degrees Fahrenheit. This places a serious limitation on saran fabrics. They cannot be easily ironed, and cigarette sparks are dangerous because they will melt holes in the saran fabric.

Effect of Light.   Exposure to sunlight over a long period of time will tend to darken saran fabrics slightly, but there is no appreciable loss of strength. This shows its value as an outdoor fabric.

Resistance to Mildew.   Saran fabrics are wholly resistant to deterioration from mildew.

Resistance to Insects.   Saran is unaffected by moths or other insects.

Reaction to Alkalies.   Saran has good resistance to most alkalies; however, it is discolored by hot solutions of sodium hydroxide and ammonium hydroxide.

Reaction to Acids.   Saran has good-to-excellent resistance to acids. This resistance to acids as well as alkalies makes saran very suitable for industrial filter cloths.

Affinity for Dyes.   Saran cannot be dyed readily because it is nonabsorbent. Such dyes as disperse dyes can be used, but the fastness properties are poor because saran can neither absorb the dyes well nor hold them subsequently.

However, by adding the desired color to the solution before the saran filaments are spun through the spinnerets, it is possible to obtain the extensive variety of colors. These colors, being inside the fibers, are very fast and will not wash out or fade.

Resistance to Perspiration.   Saran is very resistant to perspiration.

REVIEW QUESTIONS

1.   What is saran? How is it produced?
2.   What are the leading trademarks and manufacturers of saran fiber?
3.   What kind of yarns can be made of saran?
4.   For what purpose is saran most suited? Why?
5.   What are the chief advantages and limitations of saran?

25

GLASS

a transformation into fiber

Although ordinary glass is a hard and inflexible mineral substance, it can be made into fine, translucent textile fibers that have the appearance and feel of silk.

HISTORY OF GLASS FIBER

The idea of making yarns and fabrics from glass is hundreds of years old. During the Renaissance, artisans were drawing out a "spun glass" of fine glass strands or rods for decorative purposes on goblets and vases. There followed many efforts to produce glass filaments for textile purposes. Fine glass strands were drawn by hand for decorative purposes on textiles as early as 1713 by the French physicist, René-Antoine Ferchault dé Reaumur, and in 1822 by the British inventors, Alexander and David Gordon.

In 1842, production was reported of glass filaments and glass fabric made by Louis Schwabe, a Manchester silk weaver and supplier to Queen Victoria and the French Court. He produced glass fil-aments by extruding molten glass through small orifices, which may have been the first use of spinnerets for the modern technique of spinning man-made and synthetic fibers.

In 1893, Edward Drummond Libbey exhibited a glass dress, lampshades, and other articles of woven glass at the World's Columbian Exposition in Chicago. The fabric was made of bundles of glass fibers woven together with silk threads. The experiment was spectacular but of no practical value, since the fabric was too stiff to be creased, folded, or draped.

Some progress was made during the early 1900s when several patents were issued in Germany and in England on various processes for drawing glass fibers. These fibers were relatively coarse, and the cost was high. During World War I, however, Germany suffered a shortage of asbestos and developed a somewhat primitive method of producing filaments of glass fibers from heat-softened glass rods. These fibers were used for insulating purposes.

It was not until 1931 that experiments were started in the United States to produce glass fibers that were finer, more pliable, and lower in cost. At that time, the Owens-Illinois Glass Co. and the Corning Glass Works started to develop a method of drawing out glass from the molten state through very fine orifices into pliable filament form. For several years, work progressed in development of filament and staple yarns. By 1938, sufficient progress was made to indicate a promising future for glass fiber for practical textile purposes. The two companies merged to form the Owens-Corning Fiberglas Corp. Their textile product is registered under the trademark of *Fiberglas*.

Other companies became very much interested in this new product, particularly after World War II when competition began to develop in the promotion of what was, and is still, frequently referred to as "fiber glass." Of course, each company also attached its own trademark to the product.

Figure 25-1   Raw materials are melted in a bucket to form molten glass, which is drawn through platinum bushings at the bottom of the furnace. *(Courtesy PPG Industries, Inc.)*

METHODS OF MANUFACTURE

There are two major methods of producing glass fiber yarns. Both begin with accurate batch formulation of selected silica sand, limestone, soda ash, and borax (or other ingredients depending on the ultimate purpose of the fiber) in an electric furnace. From the precisely controlled furnace, the molten glass at a temperature of about 2500 degrees Fahrenheit flows to marble-forming machines that turn out small glass marbles about five-eighths of an inch in diameter. These marbles permit visual inspection of the glass for the purpose of eliminating impurities that would interfere with subsequent operations or lower the desired uniform quality of the fibers. The marbles are then remelted in small electric furnaces and extruded through spinnerets.

Another method eliminates the marble operation but maintains quality control. The molten glass is extruded directly from the bottom of the furnace through spinnerets (Figure 25-1). The kind of fiber desired—continuous or staple—determines the process that will follow (Figure 25-2).

GLASS FIBER PRODUCTION

AUTOMATIC MIXING OF
NINE RAW MATERIALS:
SILICA SAND
LIMESTONE
BORIC ACID
CLAY
FLUORSPAR
DOLOMITE
SODIUM SULPHATE
AMMONIUM SULPHATE
COAL

SUPERFINE PRODUCTION   YARN PRODUCTION

MELTING FURNACES

MOLTEN GLASS   MOLTEN GLASS

PLATINUM
BUSHING
200 TO 1200
HOLES

FOR INSULATION BLANKETS
FILAMENTS ARE SPRAYED
WITH BINDER AND
BLOWN INTO AIRY MASS

FILAMENTS

BINDER
APPLICATOR

MASS SETTLES ON
CONVEYOR BELT

FOR YARN
HIGH-SPEED WINDERS GATHER
FILAMENTS ONTO TUBES

TUBES ARE THEN TAKEN
FOR WINDING INTO YARN

DRIED AND PRESSED INTO BLANKETS

Figure 25-2 Method of glass fiber production is dependent upon end use. (*Courtesy PPG Industries, Inc.*)

Figure 25-3 A typical platinum bushing has been highly magnified in this photo. It contains hundreds of tiny openings through which molten glass is drawn from the furnace to form filaments hundreds of times thinner than human hair. (*Courtesy PPG Industries, Inc.*)

Continuous-Filament Process

This process produces continuous filaments of indefinite length having exceptional brilliance. Molten glass flows downward through temperature-resistant metal-alloy bushings (spinnerets) that have two hundred or more small openings (see Figure 25-3). The strand of multiple filaments is carried to a high-speed winder. Since the winder revolves at a much faster rate (more than 2 miles a minute) than the stream flow from the melting chamber, the tension attenuates the glass while it is still molten, and thus draws out the fibers in parallel filaments to a fraction of the diameter of the openings, and a binder is applied. After winding, the filaments are twisted and plied to form yarns by methods similar to those used for making other continuous-filament yarns (Figure 25-4).

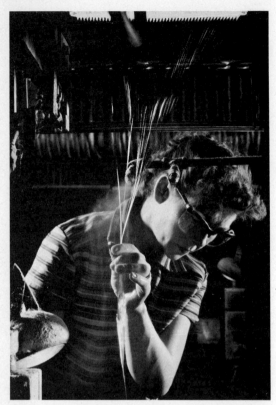

Figure 25-4   More than 200 fine, continuous glass fiber filaments are shown coming from the melting tank through white hot bushings (above the operator). These fibers are being guided together into a high-speed winder on the floor below, where they are twisted into a single thread. (*Courtesy PPG Industries, Inc.*)

These yarns are used for such fabrics as curtains and draperies.

Staple-Fiber Process

The staple-fiber process produces fibers that have long-staple characteristics. As the molten glass flows through small holes in the temperature-resistant bush-

ing, jets of compressed air literally jerk the thin stream of molten glass into fine fibers varying in length from 8 to 15 inches. The fibers fall through a spray of lubricant and a drying flame onto a revolving drum on which they form a thin web. This web of staple fibers is gathered from the drum into a sliver. The sliver is then made into yarn by methods similar to those used to make cotton or wool yarn. The yarn thus produced is used primarily for tapes and fabrics for industrial purposes where insulation is needed.

Another method of producing staple glass fiber is the rod-drawing process. It is a modern version of the old technique of drawing strands from glass rods. As the ends of the rods are melted, drops of glass fall away drawing off glass filaments after them onto a speedily revolving cylinder where they are wound parallel to each other. Sideways movement of the cylinder causes a web of sliver to be formed. The sliver is then processed into spun yarn. Alternatively, the staple may be thrown off the cylinder continuously onto a stationary sieve where it forms a sliver for processing into spun yarn.

The staple fiber may be sprayed with a binder and conveyed through an oven with controls that determine the thickness of the web. In the oven, the fiber mass is compressed to the desired thickness and the binder is cured, permanently binding the fibers. Rolls of the glass staple web may be run through facing or coating equipment for various industrial uses.

Rovings of glass filaments may be chopped into staple for use as reinforcement of plastics.

FORMS AND TYPES OF GLASS YARNS

Glass fiber is produced in a wide range of fine diameters. They can be so fine as to be seen only through an electron microscope. A more common diameter filament extruded from 1 cubic inch of molten glass could be so fine as to be drawn to a length of 380 miles.

The fineness of the fiber contributes greatly to its flexibility. One form, produced by PPG Industries, Inc., is finer than human hair, and its hollow center provides lighter weight and greater insulative properties (see Figure 25-5).

Manufacturers produce various types of glass fiber for different end uses. Some are for home furnishings; others are being developed for apparel. They vary in fineness and flexibility to provide a range of textures and styles. Fiberglas Beta is such a fiber, which is produced by Owens-Corning Fiberglass Corp.

A newer technique, *Microdyne*, developed by PPG Fiber Glass Division, can produce as many as 6,000 filaments at once in a broad range of sizes from extremely fine to coarse. The glass fibers may be used for a wide variety of purposes, such as drapery, tires, and reinforced plastics (Figure 25-6).

Some types of glass fiber can resist heat up to 13,000 degrees Fahrenheit and withstand forces encountered at speeds of 15,000 miles per hour. These are used as filament windings around rocket cases, nose cones, exhaust nozzles, and heat shields for aerospace equipment.

Some types of glass fiber, such as Aero Rove, are impregnated into various plastics to contribute strength to the fiber. These are used for such diverse

Figure 25-5 These unique PPG glass fiber filaments have been magnified several times to show the hollow cross section. These fibers give lighter weight and greater insulation to products in which they are used. *(Courtesy PPG Industries, Inc.)*

products as boat hulls and seats, fishing rods, and wall paneling. Other types of glass fiber are used for reinforcing electrical insulation. Some types are used as batting for heat insulation in refrigerators and stoves.

Glass fibers are made into three types of yarn: multifilament, spun, and textured.

Multifilament Yarns

Continuous-filament yarns have numerous strands that are produced in a wide range of diameters. The individual strands may measure 0.00025 inch (about 0.25 denier) and may number as many as 1,800. The yarn thickness generally ranges from about 0.0026 inch, or 26 denier, to over 0.055 inch, or 22,320 denier. These yarns are used for a wide variety of purposes, from draperies to cord.

Spun Yarns

Various diameters of glass fiber yarn are made from staple. These yarns are used for industrial purposes, such as conveyor belts and electrical-braid insulation.

Textured Yarns

Different types of textured glass fiber yarns have been produced. An air-bulking process, similar to the technique used to make Taslan, disarranges and loops the filaments giving the yarn a rough texture. It looks and almost feels like wool or mohair. A process of expanding individual strands or groups of glass fibers permits the weaving of Aerocor into openwork casements, producing a fabric that looks like wool or linen. In flat weaves it looks like linen.

Novelty-structure yarns made of thick-and-thin and other types of uneven-surfaced filaments provide further textural effects. These are intended to offer additional styling effects at a lower production cost.

TRADEMARKS OF GLASS FIBER YARNS

Trademarks of glass fibers that are produced by several companies for various purposes are presented in Table 25-1.

Figure 25-6 *(a)* Cross section of tie cord of glass fiber imbedded in a resin. *(b)* Single glass filament (magnified 4,500 times) showing the sizing as it coats the individual fiber. *(c)* Impact sample of glass filament reinforced with polypropylene (magnified 600 times) showing the fractured surface due to poor adhesive between resin and glass. *(Courtesy PPG Industries, Inc.)*

Table 25-1

GLASS FIBER TRADEMARKS				
TRADEMARK	MANUFACTURER	TYPE	SPECIAL CHARACTERISTICS	USES
Activa	Owens-Corning Fiberglas Corp.	Multifilament		Home furnishings
Aero Rove	Kaiser Glass Fiber	Multifilament		Plastics
Beta	Owens-Corning Fiberglas Corp.	Multifilament		Home furnishings, industrial fabrics
Fiberglas	Owens-Corning Fiberglas Corp.	Multifilament, staple	Chopped and milled fiber, mat, roving, woven roving, yarn	Home furnishings, industrial fabrics, plastics, tire cord
Fiber glass	Johns-Manville Corp.	Multifilament	Chopped and milled fiber, mat, roving, yarn	Home furnishings, plastics
Fiber glass	Kaiser Glass Fiber	Staple	Chopped fiber, roving, woven roving	Plastics
Fiber glass	PPG Industries, Inc.	Staple	Mat and chopped fiber, roving	Home furnishings, industrial fabrics, tire cord
HI	Ferro Corp.	Multifilament, staple		Plastics
NUF	Ferro Corp.	Monofilament, multifilament	Mat, strand	Industrial fabrics, plastics
Ply-Mat	Johns-Manville Corp.	Monofilament, multifilament		Plastics
Trianti	PPG Industries, Inc.	Multifilament	Extremely fine filaments; very soft, drapable	Home furnishings
Uniroving	Ferro Corp.	Multifilament, tow	Roving yarn	Industrial fabrics, plastics
Unistrand	Ferro Corp.	Multifilament, tow	Chopped, roving yarn	Plastics
Vitro-Flex	Johns-Manville Corp.	Multifilament	Chopped strand, mat	Home furnishings, plastics
Vitron	Johns-Manville Corp.	Multifilament	Woven roving	Home furnishings, plastics
Vitro-Strand	Johns-Manville Corp.	Multifilament	Milled fiber	Plastics

FINISHING GLASS FIBER FABRICS

A basic finishing operation for all glass fiber fabrics is to subject the cloth to high temperatures. This releases the stresses that may be present in the yarns as a result of twisting and weaving. This treatment provides the fabrics with such desirable qualities as wrinkle resistance, greater durability, and good hand. They may then be treated in a number of ways. Color may be applied with the aid of a binder to hold the dye to the surface of the cloth. The fabric may be coated with a protective agent to improve its abrasion resistance. For marquisettes, the finish is regulated to produce a crisp yet flexible fabric.

A patented process called Coronizing is also available. This process combines a heat-setting treatment with the application of finishing resins. The heat setting relaxes the fibers, permanently crimps the yarns, and sets the weave, giving the fabric a soft hand, good drape, and wrinkle-proof qualities. The finishing resins provide abrasion resistance, launderability, and water repellency. Better color retention and the use of pastel shades are possible with the aid of this process.

Other finishes given are an antistatic finish, a corrosion-resistant finish for industrial purposes, and a strengthening treatment for heavy-duty fabrics, such as awnings and tarpaulins. The strengthening treatment involves a technique whereby the fabric is given a resinophobic coating that inhibits resinous materials from adhering to the glass yarns. Then the fabric is coated with a resin. However, since the resin will no longer adhere to the glass yarns, it coagulates in the interstices of the fabric. This increases the tear and bursting strength of the glass fabric.

EVALUATING GLASS FIBER FABRICS

Most glass fiber fabrics for consumer purposes have been made of filament yarns. Since all glass fiber is produced in the same general manner from similar ingredients, the fiber used for similar purposes has similar properties. In fact, the designation of glass fiber is more frequently expressed as fiber glass. As has been mentioned, this term is often interchanged with the Owens-Corning trademark Fiberglas.

Strength. Glass fiber is the strongest of all textiles. Some types are stronger than equivalent diameters of stainless steel. However, because glass cuts into glass as the yarns slide and rub over each other and are flexed, the filaments roughen and break and the fabric becomes hairy. This will also occur when glass fiber draperies, for example, rub against rough objects such as window sills or radiators. This poor abrasion resistance can be overcome to some extent by Coronizing.

Elasticity. Glass fiber is virtually inelastic. Being the least elastic of all textiles has obvious disadvantages for clothing; but when used for draperies and curtains, such fabrics will not stretch or sag out of shape.

Resilience. The lack of elasticity has no effect on the flexibility and wrinkle resistance of glass fiber fabrics. With the aid of certain finishes, glass fiber fabrics have good wrinkle-resistance qualities.

Heat Conductivity. As with ordinary glass, yarns made of glass fiber are good conductors of heat. Yet, when glass fiber is in staple form, the thousands of fibers form cells of trapped air. These dead air spaces act as excellent insulation and make glass fiber staple batting very effective as an interlining in jackets and coats. (The same principle is applied to insulate refrigerators and stoves.)

Drapability. The fine glass fibers have excellent flexibility and pliability and can be woven into fabrics of excellent draping quality, particularly when given the proper finish. Consequently, they are excellent for curtains and draperies. Glass fiber fabrics can be easily sewed by hand or by machine with good-quality mercerized cotton thread, using a sharp needle, a long stitch, and low tension.

Absorbency. Glass fiber is not absorbent—a property that represents both advantages and disadvantages. Being nonabsorbent, these fabrics are water-repellent and, in general, unaffected by water. This quality makes glass fiber unsuitable for clothing worn next to the skin because perspiration and humidity make the fabric uncomfortable.

Cleanliness and Washability. The glass fiber fabric's smoothness makes it a clean fabric. Dirt and dust do not cling as readily to such fabrics as to rough materials. The cleaning of these fabrics is simple and quick. They may be wiped clean with a damp cloth. If complete immersion in water is desired, the temperature of the water and the soap or detergent used are immaterial, since these factors will not affect glass fiber fabrics. No strenuous agitation of the fabrics is necessary because the dirt comes off easily. The cloth will dry just as fast as the water will evaporate off the surface. If the fabrics are hung properly while wet, ironing is unnecessary.

Effect of Bleaches. Glass fiber is unaffected by bleaches; bleaching is in fact unnecessary since this fiber does not discolor.

Shrinkage. Glass fiber is dimensionally stable. It will not shrink because it is unaffected by water.

Effect of Heat. Glass fiber is highly resistant to heat and will not burn. The types available for general consumer use begin to lose strength at about 600 degrees Fahrenheit, and they soften above 1350 degrees Fahrenheit.

Effect of Light. Sunlight has no effect on glass fiber fabrics. This makes them useful for outdoor purposes, such as awnings, as well as for such decorative fabrics as curtains and draperies.

Resistance to Mildew. Glass fiber is unaffected by mildew, but the binder or resin used to finish or size such a fabric may be attacked by mildew.

Resistance to Insects. Moths and other insects do not attack glass fiber.

Reaction to Alkalies.   Glass fiber is resistant to most alkalies.

Reaction to Acids. Glass fiber is damaged only by hydrofluoric and hot phosphoric acids.

Affinity for Dyes. Since glass fiber is not absorbent, it cannot take dyes by ordinary methods. Coronizing provides good fastness. A technique for glass yarn dyeing has been developed to give the yarn desired color depth as in other textile fibers. Special methods are used to bind the color to the surface of the fabric. Another procedure adds color to the molten glass before fibers are formed, providing a limited number of colors.

Resistance to Perspiration. Glass fiber is unaffected by perspiration.

REVIEW QUESTIONS

1. How are glass fiber yarns made?
2. Discuss the strength and abrasion-resistant qualities of glass fiber.
3. What desirable qualities does Coronizing give to glass fiber fabrics?
4. Discuss the general care required for fabrics made of glass fiber.
5. How do the elasticity and resilience of glass fiber compare to those of other fibers?
6. How is glass fiber affected (a) by sunlight, (b) by heat?
7. How is glass fiber affected (a) by alkalies, (b) by acids, (c) by perspiration, (d) by mildew?
8. What are some of the used (a) of glass fiber filaments, (b) of glass staple fibers?
9. Differentiate between Fiberglas, fiber glass, and glass fiber.

26 COMPARATIVE CHARACTERISTICS

summary of fiber qualities

To make a satisfactory textile choice for a particular use, one must understand not only the separate and combined properties of the various textile fibers but also comparative merits of the fibers.

The commercial value of any fiber depends largely on the extent to which it possesses certain characteristics, such as tensile strength, elasticity, fineness, cohesiveness, and sufficient length—all of which facilitate the process of spinning fibers to yarn to produce satisfactory fabrics for the consumer. The effectiveness of finishes and the care of fabrics depend upon such properties as the effect of heat, reaction to alkalies and acids, and affinity for dyes. The consumer is also concerned with serviceability, performance, and ease of care. Therefore, consideration must be given to such factors as absorbency, cleanliness and washability, effect of bleaches, shrinkage, resilience, drapability, and resistance to mildew and perspiration.

The choice, then, is a matter of selecting the fabric of the fiber or combination of fibers that offers the most desirable properties and will best satisfy the particular purpose for which the fabric or garment is intended. But this kind of determination has become increasingly difficult with the greater number of fiber groups and the variations within each group. Consideration is given here to the general properties of each group, classified by the Federal Trade Commission in accordance with the Textile Fiber Products Identification Act, such as acrylics, polyesters, spandex, and so on. The wide variations of properties existing within each group do indeed make specific and precise statements difficult, if not impossible. Reasonable comparisons among the groups are given here.

LENGTH

To form a yarn, fibers are made to lie parallel and are then twisted. If the fibers are long, there will be fewer ends protruding from the surface of the twisted yarn. Fewer surface ends result in a smoother fabric, which has less attraction for dirt particles. The smooth surface also helps to give an attractive luster to the finished cloth. Short fibers cause more surface ends and more points of potential separation, thus making a relatively weaker fabric.

The expression "The longer the fiber, the stronger the yarn" is true only when fibers within a single group are compared; for example, two or more wool fibers or two or more cotton fibers. Comparing wool with cotton reveals that wool fiber, though longer than cotton fiber, is not stronger.

Long-staple yarns within each group of fibers produce stronger, smoother, more serviceable fabrics that cost more than the less durable fabrics made from short-staple yarns (see Figure 26-1). In wool, for example, the short-staple fiber is used in the manufacture of woolens, and the longer staple is reserved for worsteds. Worsteds are considered more serviceable. A similar distinction is found in every textile fiber.

Man-Made Fibers. The length is dependent on the ultimate use of the fiber, as well as on engineering problems in its production. The long, or continuous filament, fiber is used to produce smooth-surfaced fabrics. The staple, or short fiber filament, is used for soft, fuzzy fabrics.

Viscose and cuprammonium rayon, acetate, triacetate, nylon, the polyesters, acrylics, polypropylene, spandex, saran, and glass fiber are produced in both staple and continuous filament forms. The length is dependent on the ultimate use of the fibers and on the convenience of handling.

Figure 26-1 The longer fibers produce the smoother yarns; the shorter fibers produce more surface ends, which results in fuzzier yarns.

Silk. Raw silk fiber from cultivated cocoons is the longest of natural fibers. It consists of a continuous fiber that varies in length from 1,200 to 4,000 feet. It produces a smooth, lustrous fabric.

Shorter broken and cut silk fibers are also available. These are reduced to convenient staple length for spun silk yarns to produce coarser, rougher, and textured fabrics.

Linen. The flax fiber is longer than the cotton fiber and the wool fiber, ranging from 12 to 20 inches. This length accounts for the absence of lint in linen fabrics.

Wool. The length of the average woolen staple varies from 1 to 3 inches. Worsted yarns are made of 3- to 8-inch staple fibers.

Man-Made Fibers in Staple Form. The fibers in this group generally range from

$^1/_2$- to 6-inch lengths and are frequently made to resemble wool yarns. They are also sometimes spun to resemble cotton yarns and are sometimes blended to produce various effects and properties.

Cotton. Cotton fiber is the shortest of all the fibers, varying from $^1/_2$- to $2^1/_2$-inch lengths. The bulk of the domestic cotton crop ranges from $^3/_4$- to $1^1/_2$-inch lengths.

LUSTER

Luster is produced by the reflection of light from a smooth surface. A lustrous effect adds to the attractiveness of the fabric and, in some cases, may be absolutely necessary, depending on the purpose of the fabric. While luster may not be desired, as in napped or crepe surfaces, an appropriate lustrous effect is generally a desirable quality.

Degrees of luster are obtained in several ways. The use of long-staple yarns produces a smooth surface that has a natural luster. Caustic soda in the mercerizing process is a chemical method of producing luster. The satin weave and certain finishing processes also are used for this purpose.

The luster of a fiber has an important effect on its ultimate use. A fabric such as satin is expected to have a high luster and is therefore made of a highly lustrous fiber, while a fabric such as flannel is expected to be dull and is therefore made of a dull fiber. The following is the sequence of the fibers according to luster.

Lustrous Man-Made Fibers. This group includes viscose, cuprammonium, and high wet-modulus rayons as well as acetate, Arnel triacetate, nylon, aramid, polyesters, acrylics, Verel modacrylic, polypropylene, and glass fiber. These fibers can be produced with a very high luster, which is referred to as *bright*. However, luster can be controlled to a great extent, and some of these fibers are produced in lesser degrees of luster.

Silk. The luster of silk depends on the amount of surrounding sericin, or gum, that is removed from the surface of the filaments. The degree of luster is generally high.

Linen. The luster of the flax fiber is apparent at all times. This characteristic is helpful in identifying the fiber.

Semidull Man-Made Fibers. This group includes Zantrel high wet-modulus rayon, Dynel and SEF modacrylics, and saran. These fibers have a semidull or soft luster. When otherwise appropriate, the semidull appearance of these fibers makes for compatible blending with cotton, wool, or other staple fibers.

Cotton. Cotton generally does not have much natural luster. The degree of luster varies, however, with the type of cotton: the better the quality, the higher the luster.

Wool. Wool has crimp and a serrated, scaly surface. Better-quality wool has more crimp and scales, which, in turn, reduce the amount of luster possible. The best wool, therefore, does not have natural luster.

Some fibers that belong to the wool group show some degree of luster; these are the hair fibers, such as mohair, vicuña, camel's hair, alpaca, and cashmere.

Spandex. Spandex is produced as a dull fiber so that it will become as inconspicuous a part of the fabric as possible.

STRENGTH

Fibers differ in their resistance to tearing apart when subjected to tension. Therefore, the serviceability and durability of a fabric are not determined by the length of staple alone. Tensile strength is a prime necessity in fibers if the resultant fabric is to withstand the strain of wear. The ability of a fiber to resist wearing away by friction or rubbing, referred to as abrasion resistance, is another aspect of durability. Yet, it does not follow that tensile strength and abrasion resistance go together. The relative strengths of the fibers are as follows.

Glass Fiber. Glass is by far the strongest of all textile fibers. Its tensile strength exceeds that of stainless steel of an equivalent diameter, yet its abrasion resistance is not high.

Nylon, Aramid, Polyesters, Polypropylenes, and High Wet-Modulus Rayons. These textiles are all relatively strong. There is much overlapping of tensile strengths among the groups of fibers as well as among the fibers within these groups. Polypropylenes and polyesters do not lose strength when wet, and nylon weakens only about 10 percent when wet. The high wet-modulus rayons also have some temporary loss of strength when wet.

Abrasion resistance varies. For example, regular nylon staple is one of the highest abrasion-resistant fibers but does not possess the greatest tensile strength.

Silk. This fiber has long been known as the strongest of the natural fibers. Considering the extremely small diameter of the fiber (varying from 0.001 to 0.005 inch), silk is one of the strongest of textile fibers. The breaking strength of raw silk is equivalent to nearly one-third the breaking strength of the best iron wire of the same size.

Linen. Flax fiber, which is second in strength to silk, is especially durable. Linen gains strength when wet.

Cotton. This natural fiber has good strength. When wet, its strength may increase temporarily by as much as 30 percent. Cotton may be permanently strengthened by mercerization.

Acrylics. In general, the acrylics are weaker than cotton, though there is a fairly wide range of strengths among them. For instance, some types of Creslan and Zefran are stronger than the modacrylics, while the other acrylics are weaker. Acrylic fibers generally lose about 20 percent of their strength while wet and should therefore be treated with reasonable care. These fibers have good abrasion resistance.

Modacrylics. The modacrylics compete favorably with the acrylic fibers. The modacrylic fibers have the advantage of not losing any appreciable strength when wet. They also have good abrasion resistance.

Saran. The strength of saran has been demonstrated by a man standing on a suspended window screen made of this fiber. Since saran is virtually nonabsorbent, it is not weakened by water.

Viscose Rayon. Viscose and cuprammonium rayons are approximately equal in strength; however, since it is possible to produce some varieties of viscose rayon of greater than usual strength (known as medium- and high-tenacity rayons), viscose rayon is rated above cuprammonium. The strength of rayon fiber is conditioned by its moisture content. When wet, viscose rayon loses from 40 to 70 percent of its natural strength; but this strength is completely regained when the fiber is dry. Viscose rayon is, therefore, not considered a weak fiber because it is judged by its natural strength when dry, which is one-half to one-third that of silk.

Cuprammonium Rayon. The strength characteristic of cuprammonium rayon, whether wet or dry, is similar to that of ordinary viscose rayon. Cuprammonium, however, is not produced in medium- or high-tenacity forms.

Acetate. Acetate is a relatively weak fiber. It has relatively low tensile strength as well as low abrasion resistance. Furthermore, acetate may temporarily lose up to 45 percent of its strength when wet.

Wool. Wool has the lowest tensile strength of the natural fibers; however, because its springiness and resilience ac-

tually increase its wearing strength, it is rated above some of the other fibers. While wet, wool may temporarily lose as much as 25 percent of its strength.

Arnel Triacetate. The tensile strength of Arnel closely approximates that of wool. When wet, Arnel temporararily loses up to one-third of its strength. Arnel does not have good abrasion resistance.

Spandex. When compared to other fibers, spandex fibers have low tensile strength. However, the point of stress is reached only after the fiber exceeds its maximum point of elasticity. In normal use, this point is not readily reached; therefore, tensile strength is not usually a matter of concern. The abrasion resistance of spandex fibers is quite good.

ELASTICITY

Elasticity means that when the fiber is elongated or stretched, on release of tension, it will tend to return to its original length. Consequently, the less stress that is necessary to stretch the fiber and the more nearly it returns to its original length, the more elastic it is. The greater the elastic quality, the more the fiber will resist tearing. This elasticity contributes not only to the strength of a fiber but to the strength of a fabric as well. Elasticity permits materials to drape well on the body. Because elastic fibers do not break as easily as inelastic ones, this quality also facilitates the spinning process.

Spandex. Spandex fibers are by far the most elastic textile, being almost as elastic as rubber. They can be stretched from 500 to 700 percent, which is almost twice as much as that of the specially processed stretch nylons. Spandex returns to its original condition readily upon release of tension. Spandex also has the restraining or holding power so desirable for support and foundation purposes.

Nylon. Nylon has a high degree of elasticity. It has the ability to return readily to its original shape after a great deal of stretching. This is one of the characteristics that has made nylon an excellent fiber for women's hosiery.

Polypropylenes. Polypropylenes have fairly good elasticity. However, polypropylenes generally tend to lose the ability to relax to their original length if the tension is retained too long.

Wool. Wool is one of the most elastic fibers, certainly the most elastic of the natural fibers. It can be stretched to about 30 percent of its original length without breaking.

Saran. Saran can stretch up to 30 percent of its original length before breaking, and it returns to its original size slowly.

Silk. Silk is the second most elastic of the natural fibers. With too much strain, however, it will never recover its original size.

Arnel Triacetate. Arnel triacetate is much less elastic than silk, yet it does have good recovery to its original dimension after tension is released.

Acetate. Acetate has about the same stretchability as triacetate but has slightly less recovery.

Acrylics and Modacrylics. These fibers have relatively little elasticity. However, there are variations among them in the amount of stretchability and recovery that can be expected.

Polyesters. These fibers have even less elasticity than acrylics and modacrylics.

Viscose Rayon. Rayons are not considered to be elastic fibers. Comparatively, however, viscose rayon is the most elastic of the rayons.

Cuprammonium Rayon. Cuprammonium has less stretchability and recovery than that of viscose rayon.

High Wet-Modulus Rayons. These rayons are even less elastic than cuprammonium rayon.

Cotton. Cotton has very little natural elasticity. The elasticity in certain cotton fabrics is added by special processing, such as slack mercerization.

Linen. Linen is the least elastic of the natural fibers.

Glass Fiber. Glass fiber is inelastic, but this should not be confused with flexibility. Glass fiber is quite pliable due to the fineness of the fiber.

RESILIENCE

Resilience means that the fiber can be compressed or crushed and, on release of pressure, will tend to return to its original shape. When a fiber is resilient, it can be spun or twisted into springy yarns and the resultant fabric is also resilient.

This quality causes the fabric to be wrinkle-resistant, with the resistance varying according to the degree of elasticity inherent in the fiber. Resilience also contributes to the abrasion resistance of a fabric. Some fibers have both elasticity and wrinkle resistance, but it is possible for a fiber to have none or little of either. It is also possible for a fiber not to have one quality, such as stretchability, but to have the other quality of wrinkle resistance.

Fibers that are not inherently resilient can be given a degree of resilience by reducing them to short staple. Short-staple yarns contribute softness to a fabric and help to make it somewhat wrinkle-resistant, but some strength is sacrificed. A chemical finish can be used to obtain wrinkle resistance, but this method may also affect the strength of the fiber.

While it is difficult to establish an absolute range for the fibers, the following generalities are adequate for average consumer needs.

Spandex. Spandex has excellent resilience, flexibility, and pliability. It is also very springy, reacting much like rubber.

Man-Made Polymer Fibers. Nylon, aramids, polyesters, acrylics, modacrylics, and polypropylenes have very good to excellent resilience that varies with the type of fiber in each group. The resilience can be enhanced by texturing or by crimping the fibers.

Saran. The polymer saran has very good resilience. However, it can be deformed by bending and by adding heavy pressure.

Arnel Triacetate. Arnel has a resilience rivaling that of nylon. Fabrics of Arnel hold their shape very well and resist wrinkling that normally occurs from much wear or packing. The wrinkles that might occur generally tend to hang out.

Acetate. Acetate has good resilience, but not equal to that of triacetate.

Glass Fiber. Glass fibers are surprisingly resilient, which is due to their extreme fineness and consequent flexibility. Excessive flexing or heavy creasing pressure will, however, cause the fibers to crack and break.

Wool and Silk. These are the most resilient natural fibers. The resilience of wool varies with its quality, and the better grades are very resilient. Pure silk is also very resilient, and the wrinkles that develop in silk fabrics tend to hang out. Weighted silks are much less resilient.

Rayons. These are the least resilient of the man-made fibers. The high wet-modulus rayons are a little more resilient than cuprammonium rayon. The fineness to which cuprammonium rayon can be spun makes it possible to achieve more resilience than viscose rayon.

Cotton. Cotton lacks appreciable resilience. While special finishes reduce this disadvantage, the durability of the fabric is also reduced.

Linen. Linen is relatively brittle, and sharp creasing will crack the fibers. It is the least resilient of the major fibers and requires special finishes to improve its resilience.

HEAT CONDUCTIVITY

The ability of a fiber to conduct heat has great significance in textiles. The degree of heat conductivity determines whether fabrics are suitable for winter or for summer use.

In addition to the heat conductivity inherent in the fiber, the kind of yarn, fabric formation, and finish will also affect this quality. When a fabric is loosely constructed, for example, it has air spaces, which have an insulative property. The captive air pockets contained in a napped surface add warmth to a fabric. These are the more important considerations concerning the warmth or coolness of a fabric along with the following generalities about the heat conductivity of the fibers themselves.

Linen.   The flax fiber is the best conductor of heat. Linen fabric is therefore most suitable for summer apparel, as it allows the heat of the body to escape easily and quickly.

Cotton.   Cotton fiber is a good conductor of heat. Cotton fabrics are also suitable for summer clothing. The surface of the cloth has much to do with the degree of heat conductivity.

Rayons.   Being cellulosic fibers, the rayons are also good conductors of heat. Cuprammonium rayon is not only an inherently good conductor of heat, it also lends itself to sheer and therefore cool fabrics because the yarn can be made extremely fine. High wet-modulus rayons are likewise good conductors, making cool, comfortable fabrics. Viscose rayon is a good conductor, but it may not be as cool as cuprammonium since the yarns produced may not be as fine.

Arnel Triacetate.   The triacetate cellulose Arnel is not as good a conductor of heat as the pure cellulosic fibers. Also, being less absorbent, it feels warmer and is less comfortable in warm weather.

Acetate.   Acetate is a poor conductor of heat. Because it does not absorb much moisture, it has a tendency to feel warm and clammy on warm, humid days.

Nylon.   Nylon fabrics seem to have the peculiar property of being cold in winter and warm in summer. Actually, this is dependent on whether filament or staple is used and on the construction of the fabric. The spun staple nylon has thousands of air pockets that act as an excellent insulator; therefore, the staple nylon fabrics will be warm. The warmth or coolness of the filament fabrics is dependent on the porosity of the weave and on the amount of moisture in the air and on the body, for nylon reacts to moisture in the same way as acetate does.

Aramids.   Aramid fibers are not good conductors of heat. Fabrics of the fiber will, however, vary in warmth or coolness depending upon whether the fiber used is filament or staple and how compactly the fiber is constructed. Since the fiber has low absorbency, its feeling of warmth is increased by atmospheric humidity.

Polyesters.   The polyester fibers are promoted for summer-weight fabrics, particularly in blends with more absorbent fibers. While they are fair heat conductors, the polyesters can be crimped to add bulk and insulation to fabrics. They also have been found to provide excellent warmth as fiberfill for sleeping bags and quilts.

Silk. Silk is a natural protein fiber and therefore a nonconductor of heat. It may be used for winter clothing. Silk is generally thought of as a cool, summer fabric; however, the coolness of a silk garment for summer wear is directly dependent on its lightness in weight and the sheerness of the fabric: the lighter and sheerer the fabric, the cooler; the heavier the fabric, the warmer.

Wool. Wool is very warm for two reasons: it has a scaly surface that provides air pockets for insulation, and it is composed of a protein, which is a nonconductor of heat.

Acrylics and Modacrylics. These fibers have a low rate of heat conductivity. They are also relatively lightweight and, when crimped, provide considerable insulation. This lightweight bulk produces very warm fabrics. The dog-bone shape of some acrylic and modacrylic fibers contribute additional bulk and insulation for their relatively light weight. Fabrics of these fibers are warmer than wool fabrics of equal weight.

Polypropylenes. The polypropylenes are low conductors of heat and have the lightest weight of all textile fibers. When they are crimped, they provide excellent lightweight bulk for warm fabrics.

Glass Fiber. This fiber is unique in regard to heat conductivity. While glass filaments conduct heat, the staple acts as an excellent insulator because of the thousands of air pockets it traps. For this reason, glass staple batting is used for insulating refrigerators, stoves, and houses.

Spandex. Spandex is not a good conductor of heat. However, because it is usually blended in small amounts with other fibers, this does not become a significant factor.

Saran. Saran is also a low conductor of heat.

DRAPABILITY

The drapability of a fabric, or its ability to hang and fall into graceful shape and folds, is dependent upon the finish, construction, the kind of yarn used, and the fibers in the yarn. The other factors being equal, the pliability and springiness of the various fibers will contribute different amounts of drapability.

Wool and Silk. These natural protein fibers have excellent draping qualities.

Cotton and Linen. These natural cellulosic fibers do not have good draping quality; linen, however, has the better drape of the two, which is partially due to its longer fibers and greater body.

Rayons. These fibers have only fair drapability, and the long, fine filament forms produce the most drapable fabrics.

Acetate and Arnel Triacetate. These fibers generally have body and draping qualities that are better than the rayons.

Nylon. These fibers can produce fabrics of softness, body, and suppleness, which provide superior drape. The trilobal types of nylon, such as Antron and Qiana, have excellent draping qualities.

Aramid. The Nomex aramid fiber has adequate drapability for its purposes.

Polyesters. The polyesters have fair drapability. Some types, such as the trilobal Dacron, are better in this respect than others.

Acrylics and Modacrylics. These fibers provide fair drapability, but this quality varies with the type.

Polypropylenes. These fibers are now considered to have only fair drapability. However, their stage of development is such that a further period of observation is required.

Spandex. Spandex fibers have excellent pliability and contribute to the drape of the fabric in which they are combined.

Saran. This is a relatively stiff fiber and therefore does not drape well. The fabric is used for upholstery, but it is not used for draperies or apparel.

Glass Fiber. Glass fibers can be produced in such fine diameters that they may be extremely flexible. Consequently, glass fiber can have very good draping quality. However, on account of certain limitations (which may be ultimately overcome), glass fiber is not used for apparel, though it is quite well suited for curtains and draperies.

ABSORBENCY

The quickness with which a fabric absorbs moisture and gives it up again in evaporation has an important bearing on health and comfort. Textile fibers vary in their natural absorptive capacity, but absorbency may be increased by fabric construction or by a finishing process. A loosely constructed fabric or one with a napped surface, for example, is more absorptive than a smooth-surfaced fabric.

Wool. Wool fibers absorb moisture quickly and hold a large amount, allowing it to evaporate slowly. In fact, wool can absorb up to 20 percent of its weight in water without feeling damp, and 50 percent of its weight in water without dripping. When wet, wool does not stick to the body and so is ideal for outerwear on cold, damp days.

Silk. Silk fiber absorbs moisture readily and, like wool, can hold much water without feeling wet.

Rayon. The absorbency and drying qualities of both viscose and cuprammonium rayons are closely akin to those of silk, and the high wet-modulus rayons fall into the same range of absorbency. Because rayons absorb moisture readily, they tend to feel wet and heavy when the air is humid.

Linen. Linen absorbs moisture more quickly and dries more quickly than cotton. For this reason, coupled with its strength and hygienic characteristics, it is excellent for towels and handkerchiefs.

Cotton. Cotton absorbs water rather well but does not dry very quickly.

Acetate. Acetate does not absorb much moisture: only 14 percent of its weight at a 95 percent relative humidity. On warm, humid days, the moisture therefore clings to the surface of acetate, and it feels uncomfortable. Although acetate clings to the body and feels warm and clammy, it dries quickly.

Arnel Triacetate. The absorbency of Arnel is slightly lower than that of acetate under normal temperatures and humid conditions. However, Arnel absorbs more moisture under higher humid conditions, which accounts for its somewhat greater comfort than acetate. Fabrics of Arnel also dry quickly.

Nylon. Nylon absorbs about half as much moisture as acetate. It also feels very clammy and uncomfortable on warm, humid days. Filament nylon garments dry very rapidly, often in one hour; staple nylon yarn dries more slowly. Water droplets cling to the surfaces of the short pieces of nylon fiber and have difficulty evaporating from within the central portion of the yarn. Garments made of spun nylon yarn may take twenty-four hours to dry.

Aramid. Nomex aramid fiber is slightly more absorbent than nylon.

Acrylics. While the acrylics are less absorbent than nylon, the range of their absorbency is quite close. Water does tend to cling to the surface of the acrylic fibers and this adsorbency results in water penetrating between the fibers of the yarn, causing such fabrics to dry slowly.

Modacrylics. There are differences in absorbency among the modacrylic fibers. Verel is more absorbent than the acrylics, but Dynel is much less absorbent; in fact, Dynel has absorbency similar to that of the polyesters. SEF is a little less absorbent than Verel.

Polyesters. These fibers have very little absorbency. Therefore they do not stain easily and are relatively water-repellent.

Spandex. Spandex fibers are even less absorbent than the polyesters.

Polypropylenes and Saran. These fibers are virtually nonabsorbent. Moisture tends to lie on the surface. They resist staining and may be considered to be water-repellent.

Glass Fiber. Glass fiber is not absorbent.

CLEANLINESS AND WASHABILITY

The consumer is interested in knowing what textiles are hygienic, how long a garment may be expected to remain clean, and whether it will require special care when laundering or dry cleaning is necessary. The fibers that show smooth surfaces under the microscope produce fabrics that are easy to launder; thus garments made of linen, silk, and rayon wash easily. A napped surface on any one of these materials makes it necessary to give the garment more care in washing. The fact that a fiber does not absorb much water does not imply that the fiber is unhygienic. Actually, such fibers usually do not absorb dirt particles and have relatively smooth surfaces. The water then washes the dirt off the surface, and the fiber dries quickly.

Glass Fiber.   A fabric made of glass filament yarn may be cleaned either by rinsing in water or by wiping with a damp cloth. Neither dirt nor water affects glass fiber because both remain on the surface.

Polypropylenes.   Since the polypropylene fibers are virtually nonabsorbent, they do not stain or attract dirt readily and surface soil may be easily wiped off. Fabrics may be washed in any household detergent, or they may be dry-cleaned. However, because polypropylenes are generally heat sensitive, very hot water and other sources of heat must be avoided.

Spandex.   Dirt and stains also tend not to soil spandex fibers easily. They are not harmed by the usual soaps, detergents, or dry-cleaning fluids. However, they are very heat sensitive and must be handled accordingly with care.

Saran.   Saran may get dirtier a little more easily than the above-mentioned fibers because dirt can get imbedded into its slightly softer surface. However, it does wash easily, but the water should not be too hot.

Polyesters.   The polyesters are smooth-surfaced fibers that do not get dirty easily. They may be dry-cleaned or laundered with a soap or a detergent. Most stains wash out readily. Heat-set garments made of polyesters do not lose their shape or permanent creases after washing. These garments also dry very quickly and do not shrink. Some types of polyesters have a tendency to pill.

Nylon.   Nylon filament is also a smooth-surfaced fiber that does not get dirty readily. It may be laundered easily with a soap or a detergent. Fabrics made of nylon filament may be heat-set so that they will retain their shape and creases or pleats after washing. Staple nylon launders easily also but takes longer to dry. Nylon staple pills very easily.

Aramid.   Garments of Nomex aramid fiber can be laundered by conventional methods including tumble drying and drip drying. When they are heavily soiled, particularly with grease or oil, dry cleaning is desirable. Clothing can be ironed easily.

Acrylics and Modacrylics.   All of the acrylic and modacrylic fibers have approximately equal degrees of cleanliness. Since they are usually made into fuzzy, soft yarns, they can get dirty easily; however, fabrics of these fibers wash readily and retain their shape, creases, and pleats. They all have good wash and wear characteristics and may also be readily dry-cleaned. Some types of these fibers pill badly, others pill moderately, and some special types have relatively good pill resistance.

Silk.   Silk makes a hygienic material because of its smooth surface and absence of short fiber, which cause it to shed dust and to give up dirt readily. If handled properly, silk can be washed easily, unless it is given special finishes that require dry cleaning.

Acetate and Arnel Triacetate. These fibers are not as smooth as silk, but they can be easily dry-cleaned. They may also be laundered with a mild soap in warm water.

Linen. Because of the smooth surface of its fiber, linen gives up stains readily and affords little adhering surface for particles of dirt. Bacteria do not thrive on linen. Linen launders well. Its softness is enhanced by repeated washings.

Cotton. The short cotton fiber produces a fabric with a relatively rougher surface than that of linen, silk, or rayon, and therefore soils easily. Nevertheless, cotton fabric is considered a hygienic material because it can be cleaned easily. Since cotton is stronger when wet, it withstands rough handling and boiling temperatures.

High Wet-Modulus Rayons. These rayons do not soil as easily as cotton or the other rayons. They do lose some strength when wet and require more careful handling than cotton. However, they retain considerably more strength than the other rayons when wet. If desired, they can also be dry-cleaned.

Viscose and Cuprammonium Rayons. These rayons must be dry-cleaned for best results. Laundering must be done with care, particularly the spun rayons that have a shrinkage problem.

Wool. The scaly surface of the epidermis of wool fiber attracts dust, bacteria, and dirt particles. Consequently, wool fabric requires frequent dry cleaning, or washing if the nature of the fabric permits it. Felting occurs when wool is washed improperly. A wool garment should not be rubbed or handled like a cotton one.

REACTION TO BLEACHES

Sometimes fabrics are bleached to get them whiter or to remove stains. When a bleach is used, it should be put into the water and be thoroughly mixed before the garment is added. This will prevent the possibility of damaging the fabric with a bleach that is too concentrated.

Most white man-made fibers do not usually turn gray or yellow. Sometimes, however, the finish on the fabric may cause the discoloration. It is therefore a good idea to wash garments first without a bleach to determine whether one is necessary.

Cotton and Linen. The natural cellulosic fibers cotton and linen may be safely bleached by using normal care with the ordinary household bleaches containing sodium hypochlorite. For more careful treatments, sodium perborate and hydrogen peroxide bleaches may be used.

Wool and Silk. The natural protein fibers wool and silk must be bleached with care. Hydrogen peroxide is the safest bleach for them.

Viscose and Cuprammonium Rayons. These man-made cellulosic fibers may be bleached with mild solutions of sodium hypochlorite. For safer results, hydrogen peroxide may be used.

High Wet-Modulus Rayons. Unlike the other rayons, the high wet-modulus rayons require individual treatments. Avril may be bleached with sodium hypochlorite. Zantrel should not be bleached with the usual household bleaches; it requires the commercial type of sodium chlorite or paracetic acid.

Acetate and Arnel Triacetate. These fibers must be bleached with care in a mild solution of sodium hypochlorite or hydrogen peroxide.

Nylon, Polyesters, Saran, and Glass Fiber. These fibers must also be bleached with care, although most bleaching agents can be used. These include the household bleaches containing sodium hypochlorite, sodium perborate, or hydrogen peroxide.

Aramid. Such common bleaches as hydrogen peroxide, sodium chlorite, and sodium hypochlorite may be safely and effectively used on fabrics of aramid fiber.

Acrylics. With the exception of Creslan, the acrylics can also be safely bleached with any of the household bleaches. Creslan requires sodium chlorite.

Modacrylics. The modacrylics require individual, different treatments. Dynel and SEF may be bleached with any household bleach. On the other hand, bleaches cause the excellent whiteness of Verel to discolor.

Polypropylenes. These fibers may be bleached with the usual household bleaches, but their heat sensitivity requires that the water temperature never be above 150 degrees Fahrenheit and preferably lower.

Spandex. The spandex fibers require various individual treatments. Hydrogen peroxide may be safely used for fabrics containing Numa spandex fiber. Any household bleach may be safely used for fabrics containing Glospan; sodium perborate bleach is safe for Lycra.

SHRINKAGE

Shrinkage caused by water varies from considerable to none, depending upon the fiber. Fibers which are susceptible to this shrinkage may be given special finishes which significantly reduce the residual shrinkage that may occur from laundering or other exposure to water.

Wool. Wool shrinks more than any other fiber, though some finishes reduce its shrinkage potential and a few make it shrink-proof.

Cotton, Linen, and the Rayons. The cellulosic fibers cotton, linen, and all the rayons shrink considerably when wet. Shrink-resistant finishes are available to control this.

Silk and Acetate. Silk and acetate tend to shrink somewhat, though not as much as the fibers mentioned above.

Other Man-Made Fibers. Arnel triacetate, nylon, aramid, polyesters, the acrylics and modacrylics, spandex, polypropylene, saran, and glass fiber do not normally shrink when wet if the yarns and fabrics have been properly constructed and processed. Polypropylene, however, will shrink when it is exposed to moderately hot temperatures, and aramid will shrink slightly when immersed in boiling water.

EFFECT OF HEAT

Heat affects different fibers in different ways and at different temperatures. Some fibers scorch and flame; others melt and flame or shrink. Some fibers are self-extinguishing; others are completely noncombustible. Some appropriate fire-retardant and protective finishes are available.

Cotton. Cotton is highly resistant to degradation by heat. It scorches at about 300 degrees Fahrenheit but does not burn until the temperature is 475 degrees Fahrenheit.

Linen. The reaction of linen to heat is similar to that of cotton. Because of the greater natural stiffness of linen, it should be very damp when ironed and the iron should be hotter than ordinarily used for cotton.

Wool. Although wool will start to decompose at 266 degrees Fahrenheit, it does not flame. It will support combustion at 572 degrees Fahrenheit. Wool should be pressed with a steam iron, or a very damp pressing cloth should be used with an ordinary iron.

Silk. Silk is less resistant to heat than wool. It will decompose at about 330 degrees Fahrenheit.

Rayons. All of the rayons decompose at temperatures of about 300 to 350 degrees Fahrenheit and then flame and burn in a manner similar to cotton. The lower scorching temperatures of the rayons require the use of a cooler iron than for cotton.

Acetate. Acetate will stick to the iron at about 350 degrees Fahrenheit. At 500 degrees Fahrenheit it will melt; then it will char, sputter, and flame. A cooler iron should be used for acetate than for rayon. Cigarette sparks and glowing embers falling on acetate fabrics will melt holes in the fabric on contact.

Arnel Triacetate. Arnel is a little more resistant to heat, melting at 572 degrees Fahrenheit. Heat-treated Arnel will stick to an iron at temperatures only above 482 degrees Fahrenheit. The fabrics will also be damaged by glowing embers.

Nylon. Nylon is more sensitive to heat than triacetate. One of the major differences between nylon 6,6 and nylon 6 is their comparative heat sensitivity. Both yellow when exposed to a temperature of 300 degrees Fahrenheit, but nylon 6 melts at about 420 degrees Fahrenheit; nylon 6,6 sticks at 445 degrees Fahrenheit and melts at about 480 degrees Fahrenheit. For purposes of safety, it is advisable to iron nylon in the same manner as acetate. Nylon garments may be commercially heat-set to retain their shape after washing or dry cleaning without further pressing or ironing. As with acetate fabrics, cigarette sparks and glowing embers will melt holes on contact.

Aramid. Aramid is highly resistant to heat. For example, Nomex aramid fiber will resist flames up to 700 degrees Fahrenheit, at which point it will shrink away, pucker, and char. It is self-extinguishing. It can be ironed in the ordinary manner without fear of damage.

Polyesters.   Each of the polyester fibers has a different sticking and melting temperature. Furthermore, variations exist among the types of each polyester. In general, they react at temperatures somewhat similar to nylon 6,6 with melting temperatures ranging from 455 to 500 degrees Fahrenheit. Being thermoplastic, these fibers can be heat-set.

Acrylics.   The acrylic fibers also vary in the way they are affected by heat. Acrilan, for example, shrinks at 487 degrees Fahrenheit. Sticking temperatures for the acrylics range from 400 to 490 degrees Fahrenheit, and they melt at higher temperatures. These fibers can also be heat-set.

Modacrylics.   The modacrylic fibers will not support combustion. However, Dynel will shrink considerably at 260 degrees Fahrenheit, and it will melt at higher temperatures. Verel is a little more heat-resistant, but it will stick at about 390 degrees Fahrenheit and will melt above that temperature. SEF is very heat-resistant but will melt at high temperatures. All can be heat-set.

Spandex.   There is wide variation in the effect of heat on spandex fibers. Lycra yellows and degrades above 300 degrees Fahrenheit and melts at 466 degrees Fahrenheit. Glospan and Cleerspan become sticky at 420 degrees Fahrenheit. Numa sticks at about 437 degrees Fahrenheit and melts at about 511 degrees Fahrenheit. All spandex fibers can be heat-set.

Polypropylenes.   The polypropylenes are among the most heat sensitive of all fibers, which is one of their major disadvantages. Added heat stabilizers have shown some limited success. In general, polypropylene fibers will shrink progressively at temperatures above 212 degrees Fahrenheit, and they will melt above 325 degrees Fahrenheit. Polypropylene fibers can be heat-set.

Saran.   Saran fibers are also heat sensitive. They stick at about 210 degrees Fahrenheit and melt above 340 degrees Fahrenheit. Saran is self-extinguishing when the flame is removed.

Glass Fiber.   Temperatures must be extremely high to damage glass fiber. It begins to lose some strength at 600 degrees Fahrenheit and softens above 1350 degrees Fahrenheit. Obviously, ironing not only will not affect glass fiber, it is actually a waste of time.

EFFECT OF MILDEW

Mildew often attacks textiles, particularly where there is dampness. Mildew stains and deteriorates fabrics and leaves a musty odor.

Nylon, Aramid, Polyester, Acrylic, Modacrylic, Polypropylene, Saran, and Glass Fibers.   These fibers are wholly resistant to mildew. If any of these fibers ever appears to get moldy, it is actually the finish on the fiber and not the fiber itself that is mildewing. Such mildew will wash off readily leaving no stains or damage.

Spandex.   These fibers have good-to-excellent resistance to mildew.

Arnel Triacetate.   Arnel is highly resistant to mildew.

Acetate.   Acetate has good resistance to mildew, but discoloration will develop.

Wool.   Wool has good resistance to mildew, but it will succumb after a period of time.

Silk.   Silk has good resistance to mildew but eventually will be damaged under extreme conditions of dampness and darkness.

Cotton, Linen, and Rayons.   All these fibers will definitely be attacked by mildew.

EFFECT OF LIGHT

Textiles are constantly exposed to the outdoors and light. Some need to be very resistant to degradation by sunlight.

Cotton.   Cotton loses strength in sunlight and has a tendency to yellow.

Linen.   Linen is much more resistant to light than cotton.

Wool.   Wool loses strength. Its dyeing properties, however, are improved on exposure of the fiber to sunlight.

Silk.   Silk will be deteriorated more quickly than cotton or wool.

Rayons.   Viscose, cuprammonium, and high wet-modulus rayons lose strength after a long period of exposure.

Acetate.   Acetate will lose some of its strength, but it will not lose as much as viscose rayon.

Arnel Triacetate.   Arnel also loses some strength from exposure to sunlight but less than acetate.

Nylon.   Prolonged exposure to sunlight deteriorates nylon. Bright nylon is more resistant to sunlight than is the semidull or dull nylon. Ultraviolet absorbers may be incorporated during the production of nylon to overcome this problem.

Aramid.   Aramid is deteriorated and discolored by prolonged exposure to both direct sunlight and artificial light.

Polyesters.   Polyester fibers have good resistance to sunlight, but they will lose strength after prolonged exposure.

Acrylics.   The resistance to sunlight degradation varies from very good to excellent among the various types of acrylic fibers.

Modacrylics.   Dynel and SEF have good resistance to sunlight but deteriorate from prolonged exposure. Verel, however, has superior resistance.

Spandex.   Some spandex fibers will discolor from exposure to sunlight, but their resistance in general is good to very good. They may, however, gradually lose elasticity and strength.

Polypropylenes.   One of the disadvantages of polypropylenes is their susceptibility to deterioration by sunlight. To overcome this, light stabilizers are sometimes incorporated into the solution during production. However, these stabilizers may themselves break down under certain conditions.

Saran. Saran darkens slightly in sunlight, but it is not deteriorated. As a result, it is used a great deal for window screens and outdoor furniture.

Glass Fiber. Sunlight and outdoor exposure do not affect glass fiber.

REACTION TO ALKALIES AND ACIDS

A knowledge of the reaction of textile fibers to alkalies and acids is important, as alkalies destroy animal fibers; and acids, even in a weak solution, destroy vegetable fibers. For example, chemical tests for determining the fiber content of fabrics are made by noting the disintegration of wool and silk when exposed to a strong alkali, and there is a similar reaction when cotton and linen are exposed to acids. Good results in the bleaching, finishing, and dyeing processes depend on the reaction of the fibers to alkali or acid chemical agents. Not only is this reaction important in testing and manufacturing, it also closely touches the consumer when the care of fabrics is considered.

This reaction to alkalies and acids is most important to the consumer when fabrics are washed. Proper soaps and detergents should be selected for laundering the various kinds of textiles.

Cotton. Cotton is destroyed by concentrated inorganic acids—such as hydrochloric, hydrofluoric, sulfuric, and nitric—and is damaged when such acids are in dilute solutions. It is not injured by alkalies even in hot, strong solutions. Strong soap may be used for washing cotton.

Linen. The reaction of linen to acids is similar to that of cotton. Linen is not readily damaged by alkalies; however, strong soap should not be rubbed on the fabric as it will turn linen yellowish.

Wool. Dilute acids do not injure wool, but concentrated acids destroy it. Wool is quickly destroyed by strong alkalies. It dissolves if completely immersed in a boiling alkali. A neutral or mild soap must be used for wool.

Silk. The organic acids—acetic, tartaric, stearic, and formic—have little effect on silk. Weak inorganic acids also have little effect, but strong solutions injure silk. A dilute solution of nitric acid produces a bright yellow color in silk, and this reaction identifies silk from wool when testing.

Silk is destroyed by strong alkalies; strong soap should be avoided when washing silk. Compared with wool, silk is more resistant to alkalies but less resistant to strong acids.

Rayons. All the rayons react to acids in the same manner as cotton—they are disintegrated by hot dilute acids and cold concentrated acids. Viscose and cuprammonium rayons are also weakened by alkalies, and strong solutions deteriorate them. High wet-modulus rayons, however, have good resistance to alkalies, and they have the advantage over the other rayons in that they can be mercerized without serious deterioration.

Acetate. Strong acids will destroy acetate. Acetate will, however, withstand solutions of organic acids as strong as 28 percent. Acetate is easily affected by alkalies, especially if the water is very hot. Mild soaps and lukewarm water should therefore be used when laundering acetate.

Arnel Triacetate. Acids and alkalies have the same effect on Arnel that they have on acetate. Care should be taken to use mild soaps and lukewarm water when laundering fabrics of Arnel.

Nylon. Nylon is affected by concentrated solutions of the strong mineral and organic acids. Alkalies, however, have virtually no effect on nylon.

Aramid. Aramid has outstanding resistance to both strong mineral and organic acids, but some strength will be lost from prolonged exposure to hydrochloric, nitric, and sulfuric acids at elevated temperatures. It also has good resistance to alkalies, though it will be degraded by a very strong alkali at elevated temperatures after prolonged exposure.

Polyesters. Polyesters have good resistance to most mineral acids, although a concentrated solution of sulfuric acid will decompose them. They also have good resistance to weak and strong alkalies; however, they will be disintegrated by strong alkalies at boiling temperatures.

Acrylics. The acrylic fibers have good-to-excellent resistance to mineral acids. They generally have fair-to-good resistance to weak alkalies but will be weakened by stronger alkali solutions.

Modacrylics. The modacrylic fibers are extremely resistant to acids. Dynel and

Verel are highly resistant to alkalies, but Verel will become discolored from excessive exposure. SEF has good resistance to weak alkalies but moderate resistance to strong, cold alkalies.

Spandex. There is a wide range of reactions of spandex fibers to alkalies and acids, depending upon the particular fiber, the kind of alkali or acid, as well as its strength and temperature. In general, the spandex fibers have poor-to-good resistance to most alkalies and acids.

Polypropylenes. The polypropylenes are among the most resistant textiles to alkalies and acids, being relatively inert.

Saran. Saran has fair resistance to concentrated sulfuric acid and good resistance to others. It is unaffected by most alkalies, but it is affected to a limited extent by sodium hydroxide and ammonium hydroxide.

Glass Fiber. The only acids to affect glass fiber are hydrofluoric and hot phosphoric acids. It is also damaged by hot solutions of weak alkalies and cold solutions of strong alkalies.

AFFINITY FOR DYES

The readiness with which a fiber absorbs and retains dye affects the appearance and serviceability of a fabric. Affinity for dyes is usually determined by the porosity of a fiber.

Cotton. Cotton has affinity for direct dyes, reactive dyes, certain azoic dyes, and sulfur and vat dyes in a reduced state. The fastness of direct dyes is improved by the aftertreatments that are sometimes given. Mercerized cotton absorbs and retains dyes better than cottons that are not so treated.

Linen. Linen fibers have a poor affinity for dyes. The hard, nonporous surface of the fiber and its natural gum content (pectin) do not allow even penetration of the dyestuff. A more favorable reaction can be induced by removing the pectin by a strong bleaching process, but this may entail some sacrifice in the durability of the fabric. For this reason, unbleached linens are preferable when extreme whiteness of a fabric is not a primary consideration.

Wool. Wool has a very high affinity for dyes. Wool fabrics dye well and evenly.

Silk. Silk has excellent affinity for acid, basic, and some direct and reactive dyes.

Rayons. The several kinds of rayon have affinities for the same dyes as cotton, but they usually dye to a deeper shade. Dull rayon, however, does not pick up dye as readily as bright or semidull rayon. The dyestuff is absorbed evenly, and the material is consequently dyed successfully. Some rayons are solution-dyed and have excellent fastness.

Acetate. Acetate can be colored with disperse, acid, basic, and azoic dyes. However, some colors, such as grays and blues, tend to gas-fade and turn red or purplish. Excellent fastness can be obtained by solution dyeing.

Arnel Triacetate. Arnel has good affinity for the same dyes as used for ace-

tate. Its resistance to gas-fading and crocking is generally somewhat better than that of acetate, if properly dyed. Black solution-dyed Arnel has excellent fastness.

Nylon. Nylon dyes fairly well when acetate dyes are used, and the colors are generally fast. It can also be solution-dyed.

Aramid. Aramid has poor dyeability. Nomex aramid staple can be dyed with the aid of a carrier in pressurizing equipment. Certain colors are obtained by solution dyeing.

Polyesters. Polyester fibers can be dyed with disperse and developed dyes at high temperatures. For some types, cationic dyes may be used.

Acrylics. A wide variety of dyes is used for acrylics depending upon the color, the kind of acrylic fiber, and the particular type. No single dye can be used for all acrylics. Creslan and Zefran acrylic fibers are also produced in solution-dyed or precolored form and have superior fastness.

Modacrylics. The modacrylics can be colored with disperse and cationic dyes. Some vat dyes can be used on Dynel; Verel can be dyed with premetalized and basic dyes. Disperse dyes can be used for SEF modacrylic fiber.

Spandex. The spandex fibers take a wide variety of dyes well. These include disperse, chrome, premetalized, and some selected acid and basic dyes. This is one of the great advantages of using spandex rather than rubber.

Polypropylenes. One of the major limitations of the polypropylenes has been their lack of affinity for dyes. Consequently, the fibers are frequently pigmented during manufacture. Some have dye receptors added during production to facilitate dyeing with disperse dyes and certain vat, sulfur, and azoic dyes.

Saran. Saran can be dyed only by including the color before the fiber is actually extruded.

Glass Fiber. A special technique is used that causes the dye to stick to the surface of glass fiber.

REVIEW QUESTIONS

1. How may a knowledge of textiles help the consumer?
2. What is the sequence of development of fiber into fabric?
3. What practical significance does the quality of absorbency have in apparel?
4. Explain how length of staple affects the quality of a fabric.
5. What quality of acetate makes it desirable as a lining material?
6. (a) Why is elasticity important in textiles? (b) How may elasticity in textile fabrics be improved?
7. What qualities of linen make it suitable for (a) towels and handkerchiefs, (b) summer apparel, (c) draperies?
8. What qualities of silk make it suitable for (a) women's dresses, (b) neckties, (c) ribbons?
9. Why is cotton used so extensively for infants' wear?
10. What qualities of rayon make it a poor fiber to use for (a) sewing thread, (b) stockings, (c) winter underwear?
11. What specific qualities do spun rayon fabrics have that are not found in filament rayon fabrics?
12. What properties may wool fabrics be expected to have?
13. How does a napped surface affect the hygienic quality of a fabric?
14. Why does a cotton bathing suit feel cooler than a woolen one?
15. Why does a fabric of nylon filament yarn dry faster than one of nylon spun yarn?
16. What single characteristic do all the acrylic fibers have that is of great advantage to the consumer and homemaker?
17. Why is the use of saran limited?
18. Which textiles will be damaged quickly by cigarette sparks?
19. Which textile would be considered best for curtains? Why?

20. Compare the warmth of wool, acrylic, and polypropylene fabrics.
21. Compare the elasticity of wool, silk, nylon, and spandex.
22. Compare the launderability of the various textiles.

SUGGESTED ACTIVITIES

1. Obtain as many samples of fabrics as you can, and cut them into small square pieces, 3 by 3 inches. Mount them on small cards. Determine the fiber content of each sample, and record your data on the card. Give all possible uses for each fabric. Give the reasons for your answers in terms of the basic qualities of the fibers.
2. Observe carefully the various contents of your home furnishings, and make a record of every item that uses any textile fibers. Add the name of the fiber used, indicating if this is a guess or the result of observation and analysis. Give reasons for each answer.

27

MINOR TEXTILES

vegetable, mineral, and man-made fibers

The textile industry uses other fibers in addition to those already studied. Each has its field of usefulness. Some have qualities that make them suitable for purposes that none of the fibers previously discussed could fulfill satisfactorily. Others can be used as acceptable substitutes or even adulterants, as long as the finished goods fulfill the purpose for which they are intended and the selling price is in line with the value of the product.

VEGETABLE FIBERS

Jute

Jute is a natural fiber obtained from a tall plant of the same name. It is grown throughout tropical Asia, chiefly in India and Bangladesh, for commercial uses. The plant is easy to cultivate and harvest. The fiber is obtained by retting, similarly to flax. The fine, silklike fiber is easy to spin but is not durable, as it deteriorates rapidly when exposed to moisture. Jute is the cheapest textile fiber and is used in great quantities. Because of its lack of strength, jute is difficult to bleach and can never be made pure white. It can be converted into a woollike fiber by treatment with a strong caustic soda.

Though jute is often used as an adulterant with other fibers, it can be easily recognized when tested for its marked sensitivity to mineral acids. Concentrated mineral acids readily dissolve jute. Dilute mineral acids rot it quickly. It is especially weak in salt water. Jute is used as a substitute for hemp, as binding threads for carpets and rugs, as rug cushions, as a filler with other fibers, and as a linoleum base. It is made into coarse, cheap fabrics, such as novelty dress goods and heavy cotton bagging.

Kapok

Kapok is a natural fine, white hairlike fiber obtained from the seed capsules of plants and trees grown in Java, Kalimantan (formerly Borneo), Sumatra, and Central America. It is sometimes called *silk cotton* because its luster is almost equal to that of silk. Kapok resembles cotton in general appearance but is always of shorter average staple—less than 1 inch. Under the microscope, kapok can be easily distinguished from cotton, as it appears to be a hollow tube with very thin walls and frequent folds but no twist.

The smooth texture and weakness of kapok prevents its being spun into yarn, but it is felted for use in mattresses, cushions, upholstered furniture, and life preservers. Kapok is buoyant, but with continued use has a tendency to mat and become lumpy. This condition can be improved if bedding articles in which kapok has been used are aired and put in the sun at frequent intervals. Kapok is resistant to vermin and is especially resistant to moisture, drying quickly when wet. It is adaptable for articles that are constantly exposed to moisture. Kapok is also used for soundproofing in airplanes and for insulating material in refrigerator cars and trucks.

Ramie

Ramie is a natural woody fiber resembling flax. Also known as *rhea* and *China grass*, it is obtained from a tall shrub grown in Southeast Asia, China, Japan, and southern Europe. The fiber is stiff, more brittle than linen, and highly lustrous. It can be bleached to extreme whiteness. Ramie lends itself to general processing for textile yarns, but its retting operation is difficult and costly, making the fiber unprofitable for general use. When combed, ramie is half the weight of linen, but much stronger, coarser, and more absorbent. It has per-

manent luster and good affinity for dyes; it is affected little by moisture. Ramie is used as filling yarn in mixed woolen fabrics, as adulteration with silk fibers, and as a substitute for flax. The China-grass cloth used by the Chinese is made of ramie. This fiber is also useful for rope, twine, and nets.

Hemp

Some thirty varieties of hemp, another tall plant with a natural woody fiber, are grown in nearly all the temperate and tropical countries of the world. All these varieties resemble one another in general appearance and properties, but only those having fibers of high tensile strength, fineness, and high luster have commercial value. Hemp must pass through a retting process and subsequent manufacturing operations similar to those used for flax. It resembles flax closely, and its fiber is easily mistaken for linen. Hemp is harsh and stiff and cannot be bleached without harm to the fiber. As hemp is not pliable and elastic, it cannot be woven into fine fabrics. Manila hemp, which is very strong, fine, white, and lustrous, though brittle, is adaptable for the weaving of coarse fabrics. Hemp is durable and is used in rug and carpet manufacturing. It is especially suitable for ship cordage as it is not weakened or rotted by water. Central American hemp is chiefly used for cordage.

Sisal

Sisal is a natural fiber obtained from the leaves of a plant that resembles cactus, grown in Africa, Central America, the West Indies, and Florida (see Figure

Figure 27-1   The strong sisal fiber, obtained from the leaves of the agave, has long been used for rope. Now, however, it is receiving competition from polypropylene fiber. *(Courtesy CIBA Review)*

27-1). The best supply is produced in Yucatan, where it is known as *henequen*. The smooth, straight fiber is light yellow in color. Sisal is used for the better grades of rope, for twine, for the bristles of inexpensive brushes, and as a substitute for horsehair in upholstering. Sisal may be mixed with hemp, but it should not be used for ship cordage because it disintegrates in salt water.

Coir

This natural coarse brown fiber is obtained from the husk of the coconut. It is stiff but elastic. Because of its resem-blance to horsehair, it is used for stuffing upholstered furniture. Coir is also suitable for cordage, sailcloth, and coarse mattings.

Pina

Pina, or pineapple fiber, is obtained from the large leaves of the pineapple plant grown in tropical countries. This natural fiber is white and especially soft and lustrous. In the Philippine Islands, it is woven into pina cloth, which is soft, durable, and resistant to moisture. Pina is also used in making coarse grass cloth and for mats, bags, and clothing.

Alginate Fibers

Interesting research has been conducted with seaweeds. British scientists at Leeds University have derived jellylike calcium alginate from certain forms and extruded it into multifilament fibers. They are flameproof and are used to some extent instead of asbestos for theater curtains in England.

The calcium alginate fibers have a dry strength comparable with that of viscose rayon. However, considerable strength is lost when wet, and the fibers could ultimately disintegrate if care is not exercised. This characteristic has resulted in some interesting applications. For instance, alginate yarns have been used as scaffolding to help support other yarns in the manufacture of lightweight, sheer, and lacy fabrics. After these fabrics have been constructed, they are washed with soap and water to disintegrate the alginate yarns, leaving the desired design or gossamer effect not attainable by the usual methods of fabric construction.

The alginate fibers have also been used in medical applications for dressings. They have been found to hasten blood coagulation and to facilitate healing when placed over wounds. Alginate fiber dressings have also been used by dentists as packing to stop bleeding; as healing progresses, the dressings eventually break down and disappear.

MINERAL FIBERS

Metallic Yarns

Any of the ductile metals, such as gold, silver, copper and even the cheaper alloys, can be drawn out into fine filaments. These are used to ornament fabrics. Metallic threads are made round or flat and may be twisted with any of the major textile fibers. Sometimes, base metals are drawn out as fine wires and are covered with the more costly metals. Thus, silver thread may have a core of copper covered with a layer of silver; similarly, gold thread may consist of gold-plated copper wire. Brunsmet stainless steel filament fiber and Brunslon, a blend of nylon and stainless steel staple, have been introduced by Brunswick Corp.

Metal threads are elongated to an extremely fine diameter and are used in the millinery trade and as decoration in the form of fringe and braid, as well as for woven and embroidered patterns on tapestries, brocades, and upholstery fabrics. Fine metal threads are used in fabrics for evening dresses, handbags, and ecclesiastical robes.

These metal yarns, however, have many limitations. Some, such as gold or silver, are very expensive. All are heavy.

Frequently they make the fabrics too stiff to drape well. Silver threads tarnish, and all fabrics containing metal threads pose a cleaning problem.

To overcome these disadvantages, special types of metallic yarns have been developed. One technique of producing these yarns is to sandwich with the aid of an adhesive a layer of metal (usually aluminum foil) between two extremely thin layers of clear polyester film called *Mylar*. When a silver color is desired, the adhesive holding the polyester film to the aluminum is clear; when gold or some other color is desired, pigments are added to the adhesive or printed on the film before laminating. Such a thread can not only have a metallic gleam, but can also be in any color. This foil type of metallic yarn woven into a fabric resists bleaching, mercerizing, vat-dyeing operations, and many other wet-finishing processes that are required to finish fabrics that also contain other fibers which may require such processing.

Another technique of producing metallic yarns is to expose a layer of Mylar polyester film to aluminum vapor under high vacuum, so that the layer of Mylar becomes coated with aluminum particles. This metallized film is then sandwiched between two layers of clear Mylar film. Color is imparted to the adhesive as described in the above-mentioned process. The metallized type of metallic yarn is, however, brighter and more lustrous. It also is better suited for some types of looms and offers a greater yield of yardage per pound because it is lighter in weight.

Some metallic yarns are made of aluminum foil bonded between two layers of cellulose acetate butyrate film. Others

Figure 27-2 Lurex, with cross section showing metal layer sandwiched between two layers of Mylar film. *(Courtesy Dow Badische Co.)*

Figure 27-3 *(a)* Asbestos rock is manufactured into *(b)* asbestos fiber. Note the similarity of asbestos fiber to *(c)* cotton fiber. *(Courtesy Johns-Manville Corp.)*

are made of aluminum covered with a polyolefin. The selection of metallic yarn used in combination with other textiles depends upon the economy involved as well as its compatibility with the other textiles for general care purposes. Usually, these metallic yarns are very flexible, drape very well, and give good service.

These metallic yarns are produced by several companies. Essentially they employ the same methods of production, using one of the two basic techniques described above. Each company produces the yarn under its own trademark. Some of the better known are Durastron, Lurex, Metlon, and Reymet (Figure 27-2).

Asbestos

Asbestos is a natural fiber obtained from varieties of rocks found in Italy, South America, and Canada. It is a fibrous form of silicate of magnesium and calcium, containing iron, aluminum, and other minerals (see Figure 27-3). The soft, long, glossy white fibers are pressed into sheets; and the best quality can be spun into yarn. Chrysolite asbestos is the most valuable for the latter purpose, as it has a fine, long staple that has strength and flexibility. Asbestos yarns are always made as ply yarns to increase their tensile strength. Asbestos will not burn, but it will melt at a sufficiently high temperature. Asbestos is acidproof and rustproof. Asbestos is now made in greatly advanced types of fire-fighting suits and fire-resistant fabrics, and in fireproof materials of many types—theater curtains, draperies, shingles, tiles, auto brake lining, andiron holders, and partitions. It is spun around copper wire and wrapped around pipes and joints of high-pressure steam engines. Inferior grades are used for soundproofing.

Ceramic

Ceramics are a group of fibers introduced in 1966. An outstanding characteristic of ceramic fibers is high heat resistance, which makes them particularly well suited for rocket applications. The American Viscose Division of FMC Corp. manufactures its ceramic filament fiber under the trademark of Avceram; the Carborundum Co. introduced its ceramic filament fiber as Fiberfrax.

Slag Wool

Molten lead or iron can be processed into the form of fibers, which are used as felt and packing material for insulative purposes in the building trades. This by-product of the blast furnace is light in weight; it is fireproof, heatproof, sound-proof, verminproof, moistureproof, and rotproof.

Carbon

Thomas A. Edison initially experimented with carbon filaments in the development of the electric light bulb. However, it was the later jet and rocket propulsion requirements of very high strength and heat resistance that caused its development into fibers from rayon precursor filaments. Thornel and Magnamite are trademarks for such high modulus fibers. Variations are used for other high-strength, flexible purposes, such as shanks for golf clubs.

REVIEW QUESTIONS

1. For what purposes are the minor natural fibers generally used?
2. Name five minor fibers, and give one use for each.
3. Why is jute never available in a pure white color?
4. Why is kapok always felted, never woven?
5. How does kapok differ from cotton?
6. Compare ramie with linen.
7. Why is hemp suitable for cordage?
8. (a) How are metals threads made? (b) For what purposes are they used?
9. Describe the qualities of asbestos and its uses.
10. (a) What by-product of the steel industry is used as insulative material? (b) Name four of its qualities.
11. (a) What is the source of alginate fibers? (b) What are they used for and why?
12. (a) What are the most significant characteristics of carbon fibers? (b) Identify a trademark for one. (c) For what are such fibers used?

28

RUGS AND CARPETS

textile floor coverings

Floor coverings have been made from textile fibers for more than 5,000 years. Throughout civilization, rugs and carpets have formed a part of the history and culture of races and nations. Early kings and conquerors included valuable rugs among their treasures and trophies, and many of these famous pieces have retained values that in some cases are inestimable. Priceless handmade carpets and rugs woven hundreds of years ago in the Far East are exhibited today in museums as representative of the patient labor and creative art of weavers whose skills have been passed on through many generations.

Well-chosen rugs or carpets serve as a colorful foundation for the decorative plan and color scheme of all rooms in the modern home. As floor coverings are among the most expensive items in a house-furnishings budget, careful consideration must be given to fiber, color, decorative character and design, size, and construction to obtain the best value for any price level.

RUG CONSTRUCTION

The terms "rug" and "carpet" are used synonymously, but the form or the size in which these coverings are manufactured differs. Rugs may vary in shape as well as in width and length. In general, certain size standards are maintained that in the large rugs have been adapted to standard sizes of rooms. The term "broadloom" does not refer to quality but describes a type of carpet woven all in one piece on a loom wide enough to produce the width desired.

The factors that account for differences in price are the type, quality, and quantity of fiber used, as well as the amount of twist in the yarn, the number of plies in the yarn, and the basic method of construction. Carpets may be woven, tufted, formed (nonwoven), or knitted. Weaving is the slowest and most expensive method of construction; tufting is the most rapid and least expensive.

Some rugs are coated on the back with a plastic binder, latex foam, vinyl

Figure 28-1 The roll of carpeting shown has been coated on the back with latex. *(Courtesy American Carpet Institute, Inc.)*

foam, or urethane foam (see Figure 28-1). They are sometimes referred to as *patent-backed*, which is an inexpensive method of providing firmness, body, and resilience. This technique contributes flexibility in laying the rug because patent-backed rugs can be cut in any direction without fraying the edges or unraveling the yarns, and the edges do not require binding. This feature permits the patent-backed broadloom to be fitted easily to irregularly shaped areas. Also, holes caused by damage or wear can be cut out and matched pieces put in their places.

Rug Composition

Floor coverings are made from various kinds of fibers—cotton, silk, wool, rayons, acetate, nylon, polyesters, acrylics, modacrylics, polypropylenes, and blends of these fibers, as well as mohair, jute, hemp, or grass straw. The wool fiber had

been the most popular natural fiber for rugs because wool offered the advantages of extreme softness, resiliency, absorbency to shock and noise, and, particularly, resistance to wear when the right fibers and construction have been used. Wool rugs, however, have become the most expensive type, and are susceptible to attack by moth larvae and other insects.

Rugs of man-made fibers are not damaged by these insects. The nylon, polyester, acrylic, modacrylic, and polypropylene fibers have varying degrees of softness and resilience (as related earlier in the text). Nylon is extremely durable. The polyester and acrylic fibers wear rather well but there is some tendency to pill, though manufacturers claim to have minimized this problem. Indications are that polypropylene gives less pilling difficulty. Polypropylene also builds up much less static electricity; after standing or walking on polypropylene carpets, fewer irritating shocks will occur when metal objects are touched. Sometimes metallic strands, such as Brunsmet stainless steel, are incorporated into the construction to conduct off the electrostatic charge which is generated by friction (Figure 28-2).

The man-made fibers are not particularly absorbent, and polypropylene is the least absorbent. Rugs made of these fibers therefore resist staining. Spilled substances, such as ink, soda, mustard, and the like, can be wiped off readily without leaving a stain. One great disadvantage of rugs constructed of nylon, polyester, acrylic, modacrylic, and polypropylene fibers is that, since these fibers are thermoplastic, a burning cigarette or any other very hot object will melt a hole at the point of contact. Of all

Figure 28-2   Plainwoven fabric of polyester/cotton blend with one-half of one percent Brunsmet stainless steel fiber to serve as electrical conductor, thereby eliminating static electricity. It is used in hospital operating rooms, laundries, mills, etc. *(Courtesy Brunswick Corp.)*

fibers used for rugs, rayon is the least durable and least resilient; and it had been the least expensive until the introduction of polypropylene.

Ultimately, the choice of a rug will depend on its attractiveness, its construction, its serviceability, and its cost. The consumer must weigh the relative merits of these factors in making his choice.

Types of Surface Appearance and Texture

The surface appearance and texture of a rug is affected by its construction. There are several types.

Cut Pile.   When the pile is cut and the yarn is untwisted, a soft, plush effect is achieved. When the cut pile is made of tightly twisted yarns, the surface has a harder, frieze texture. Examples are Ax-

minster, chenille, Oriental, velvet, Wilton, and tufted broadlooms (Figure 28-3).

Uncut Pile.   When the pile is uncut to retain the loops, a pebbly, harder texture is obtained. Examples are Brussels, tapestry, and tufted broadlooms.

Combination Cut and Uncut Pile.   Attractive surface-texture effects are obtained by combining cut and uncut pile in interesting patterns. This may be done on woven and tufted broadlooms.

Sculptured.   The pile may be woven in different heights to form either a definite or a random pattern, which provides uneven but interesting and attractive patterns. This textural effect is also referred to as *carved* and *multilevel.* Combination cut and uncut pile may be utilized in this construction in woven and tufted broadlooms.

Flat.   This construction exists in novelty and special-purpose rugs made from miscellaneous fibers. These rugs do not have any pile and, ordinarily, they

Figure 28-3   High cut pile of a tufted broadloom of 50/50 blend crimped polyester and viscose rayon staple. *(Courtesy American Enka Co.)*

can be used on either side. Examples are grass rugs and hooked rugs. Another type of flat rug is the needlepunched fibrous carpet, which resembles felt.

Methods of Construction

Carpets are made by several techniques. In most instances, a pile construction is obtained.

Woven Rugs. Until fairly recently, woven carpets of several types were the most common. They are constructed of pile woven perpendicularly to the warp and backing yarns.

Tufts are the cut loops of surface yarns held in the small squares that are discernible on the reverse side of the rug. *Pitch* expresses the number of warp threads crosswise of the loom to each 27 inches of width. *Wires* refer to the number of tufts to the inch in the warp, or lengthwise, direction.

The construction of the rug is indicated by the closeness of the tufts in each direction—that is, by the pitch and wires. The number can usually be determined by counting the rows of tufts on the back of the rug. Compact construction of the tufts, represented by a high number of pitch and wires, indicates a dense pile, showing that a greater quantity of fiber has been used, resulting in a more durable product. Density of construction is considered the most important factor in determining the durability of floor coverings.

Additional crosswise yarns are used to bind the pile to the backing of the rug. The number of yarns used is indicated by the term "shot." In a two-shot construction, one crosswise yarn can be seen to be between each row of tufts; the other crosswise yarn behind the row. In the three-shot contruction, there are two crosswise yarns between each row of tufts and a third yarn in back. The three-shot construction requires additional yarn and more loom operations. It is more expensive but more durable.

Axminster. Before the advent of the tufted rug, the most popular type of rug had been the Axminster. There is no limit to the number of colors that may be used in Axminster design; fifty colors have not been uncommon. The *spool Axminster* has been the most widely made. The colored yarns are wound on separate loom spools and each is placed in correct position as indicated by the design. The spools are fitted in an overhead roller and provide an endless supply of yarn to form the pile, which is produced by inserting the yarn as tuft loops with a needle stitch rather than a shuttle.

The *gripper Axminster* uses a different technique for yarn color selection. The spools of colored yarn are carried on a creel behind the loom and are operated by a Jacquard mechanism. As an appropriate colored thread is determined by the mechanism, a gripping device grasps that yarn and pulls it forward.

The *gripper-spool Axminster* combines the gripper device with the overhead spool system rather than using the Jacquard mechanism.

A fourth type of Axminster, *chenille*, is discussed separately below.

Weeks are required to set the yarns for an Axminster design; but, once the design is arranged, the 9 by 12 size may be woven in only an hour or two. Only soft-twisted yarn is used for the Axminster, as the weave is not tight enough to permit the use of hard-sur-

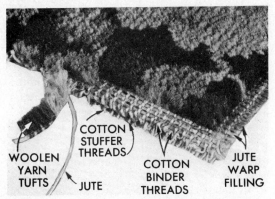

Figure 28-4   Axminster construction shown in detail. *(Courtesy Mohawk Carpet Mills, Inc.)*

WOOLEN YARN TUFTS — **JUTE** — **COTTON STUFFER THREADS** — **COTTON BINDER THREADS** — **JUTE WARP FILLING**

faced yarn. The surface closely resembles the hand-knotted carpet, but the Axminster can be easily distinguished from any other type because it can be rolled only in its lengthwise direction. The stiff jute fibers used in the backing form pronounced ridges on the reverse side. The better-quality Axminster has a deep pile, some flexibility in its backing, and as many as 70 tufts to the square inch. The less expensive grades have fewer tufts, low pile, and a very rigid back (Figure 28-4).

Chenille.   Chenille is the most expensive of the domestic types, and it offers the widest range of possibilities with respect to depth of pile, design, colorings, and width. Chenille may be constructed as wide as 30 feet without a seam, and can be made as a single unit to fit irregularly shaped areas. It can be produced with a pile up to a full inch in height. This height, when supported by a heavy cushion back, gives a luxuriously soft and resilient quality to the carpet as well as remarkable durability.

The woven chenille construction requires two separate loom operations.

First, soft- or hard-twisted yarns are woven into a blanket containing cotton warp threads. Actually, this blanket is composed of vertical soft- or hard-twisted yarns bound together by the cotton warp. Another machine cuts this filling halfway, producing furry strips that are held together by the cotton yarns in the center. This strip, which resembles a caterpillar, is pressed into V-shaped form; and the separate ends are tied together, forming a continuous chain. This chain is subsequently used on the second loom as a filling for the final weaving of the chenille rug. A well-constructed chenille uses a fine-quality wool and a densely packed high pile, which results in the durability characteristic of this weave (Figures 28-5 and 28-6).

Smyrna rugs resemble chenille, as they are made with a chenille fur. But the fur is twisted into a round yarn instead of the V shape of the chenille. A shot of fiber filling makes the Smyrna rug reversible—the pattern and pile are alike on both sides. It has a shorter pile than the chenille.

Wilton.   Wilton is an expensive weave to manufacture, ranking next to chenille. It is always woven on a Jacquard loom and is considered one of the best of all machine-made rugs. In weaving the Wilton, the surface yarn is held in trays called *frames.* Each frame holds spools wound with yarn of the same color. If there are six full colors in the pattern of a Wilton, there must be six frames. In a six-frame Wilton, only one of the six pile yarns apppears on the surface at a time. The other five lie underneath, constituting hidden value in the form of added resiliency and quality. The number of frames in a Wilton varies from two to six,

Figure 28-5   Chenille construction shown in detail. (*Courtesy Mohawk Carpet Mills, Inc.*)

indicating the thickness of its fiber cushion and the number of separate colors in its design. A method known as *planting* makes it possible to add, in small areas, more colors than are indicated by the number of frames.

The pile effect of the Wilton is produced by looping the surface yarns over wires that have razor-sharp knives at the ends. When the wires are withdrawn, the knives cut the pile. The Wilton is made with soft- or hard-twisted yarns.

Figure 28-6   (*a*) Hand tufting is done in chenille weaving by using a steel comb. The comb brings up the surface yarns in the fur through strong cotton-catcher warp threads as four shuttle motions weave the heavy backing yarn to the base of the fabric. (*b*) Chenille fur, or hairy caterpillar, is made from woolen blanket cloth. The cloth shown has been partly cut so that the warp of the caterpillar may be seen. (*Courtesy Mohawk Carpet Mills, Inc.*)

Figure 28-7 Worsted Wilton construction shown in detail. *(Courtesy Mohawk Carpet Mills, Inc.)*

When closely woven, the worsted Wilton offers maximum durability together with fineness of texture and delicacy of design even though it has a short pile (see Figure 28-7). The finest grade of worsted Wilton is woven with six frames, with a three-ply yarn. It has 13 wires to the inch, a three-shot construction, and about 115 tufts to the square inch. Lower grades are woven with a smaller number of frames, have 10 wires to the inch, a two-shot construction, and as few as 60 tufts to the square inch.

The soft-twist Wilton has a more luxurious feel than the hard-twist Wilton because of its greater softness and depth of pile. It is made with at least two and a half frames and has $7\frac{1}{2}$ to $9\frac{1}{2}$ wires to the inch and a pitch of 214 (Figure 28-8).

A better grade of woolen Wilton made from unusually heavily twisted woolen yarns with large and firm tufts is

Figure 28-8 Woolen Wilton construction shown in detail. *(Courtesy Mohawk Carpet Mills, Inc.)*

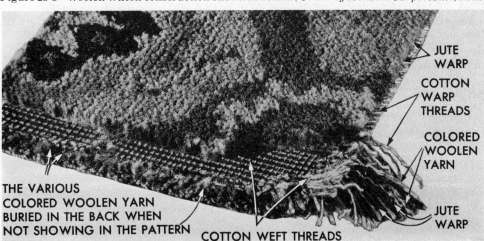

called *Saxony*. These yarns produce a luxurious depth of pile with large, loose tufts and a coarse design. The rug is especially durable in spite of its extreme softness.

Brussels. The Brussels was the first type of carpet woven on a Jacquard loom. It is woven like a Wilton except that the wires used to make the surface loops do not have any cutting ends. As the wires are withdrawn, the pile is left as upright loops instead of cut pile. Hard-twisted yarns are used for the pile, producing a very durable product. The best-quality Brussels is usually woven with five frames and has 9 wires to the inch and a pitch of 256.

Velvet. The velvet construction is the simplest pile weave. Its pile is woven over wires having cutting ends that produce the cut tufts as the wires are withdrawn. All the fiber lies on the surface of velvet carpet, with no buried yarns in the backing (Figure 28-9). Only one yarn is used, and it must be uniform and of good quality throughout to absorb the dye evenly when printed. The common method of producing a pattern on velvet rugs is by printing the design after the rug has been constructed. Sometimes, yarns that have been printed before weaving are used. The velvet rug is inexpensive, as it is the fastest type to weave. It is made on an ordinary loom. Twisted yarns are used to produce what is known in the trade as hard-twisted velvets. For firmness, jute yarns, sized with glue, are used as stuffing warp yarns. The better-quality velvet rug has a deeper pile; its density should range from 56 to 80 tufts to the square inch.

Figure 28-9   Velvet construction shown in detail. *(Courtesy Mohawk Carpet Mills, Inc.)*

Tapestry. The construction of the tapestry rug is similar to that of the velvet except that the wires used to form the pile do not have any cutting ends. Thus an uncut pile is left when the wires are withdrawn. Because of its resemblance to the Brussels type, the tapestry rug is sometimes termed *tapestry Brussels*. This is a misnomer. The term attempts to attribute to the tapestry rug the superior construction of the Brussels, which is made on a Jacquard loom with a two- to five-frame construction. The tapestry rug is made on an ordinary loom and requires only one warp yarn. A good grade should have 8 wires to the inch and a pitch of 8. The tapestry rug is not intended for heavy or long wear. It does not have the softness of other rugs, nor does it have delicate or distinct designs. It is intended to satisfy the demand for an inexpensive yet reasonably sturdy product.

Sheen-type or American Oriental. The name "American Oriental" is frequently used for the sheen-type or luster-type domestic rugs that are produced by the

Wilton, Axminster, or velvet weave. The sheen in the domestic product is obtained by washing or brushing the wool rugs in a chlorine solution or by using man-made or synthetic fibers, which imparts the characteristic luster of the imported Oriental rug. The patterns are faithful reproductions and in many cases are woven through to the back, as in the genuine Oriental. When made of good-quality yarns, the American Oriental gives satisfactory wear.

Tufted.   Tufted carpet represents a process of construction that can be utilized to simulate woven-pile rug construction at a much lower cost of production. The technique has become widely adopted by rug manufacturers, and over 90 percent of today's rugs are produced by this method.

The backing is constructed first. It may be woven, generally of jute, kraftcord, or cotton. A woven nylon scrim with the yarn covered in polyurethane foam has been introduced under the trademark Chemback. (The backing may also be made of a nonwoven material, such as Loktuft, which is primarily composed of Marvess polypropylene fiber.) The newer backing media have added to the tufting technique such advantages as less dependence on uncertain foreign export conditions, reduction in manufacturing problems and costs, greater dimensional stability of the carpet, greater stability and inertness of the backing material during finishing operations, and greater resistance to bacteria and mildew.

The tufts are inserted in the interstices between the backing yarns by a machine that simultaneously punches thousands of tufting needles through them. To secure the tufts permanently in place, the backing is then coated with a layer of latex. A second backing is sometimes added to enhance the body and hand as well as to improve the dimensional stability (see Figure 28-10).

Carpet production is much faster by tufting than by the weaving techniques. Whereas a carpet loom may produce at the rate of about $2\frac{1}{2}$ inches per minute, a tufting machine produces at about 75 inches per minute (Figures 28-11 and 28-12).

The tufting technique is extremely versatile. A wide variety of textures and patterns can be achieved with the tufting process. The pile can be cut, uncut, or sculptured, or it can be a combination of these. All kinds of color combinations and multicolor combinations are also possible (Figure 28-13).

Among the versatile productions of tufted carpets is the *shag* (see Figure 28-14). This has a long pile of more than 1 inch, possibly over 2 inches. The pile tends to lay in a somewhat random fash-

Figure 28-10 Tufted Construction. *(Courtesy American Carpet Institute, Inc.)*

Figure 28-11 Creel rack shown is used for carpet tufting machine. *(Courtesy American Carpet Institute, Inc.)*

ion rather than stand erect. It tends to crush but can be somewhat restored with a special brush to raise the pile.

A variation or offshoot of tufting pile through a backing which is subsequently coated with latex or vinyl, is a technique whereby the backing is first coated and then the pile is inserted into the vinyl coating. The process is faster and uses less yarn since the pile does not go through the backing. The technique locks the yarns permanently in place, increases carpet density, and is said to improve wearing qualities and ease of maintenance, as well as form an impervious barrier to moisture.

Rivet Head. In 1972, Stanley Sharrock, an aeronautical engineer from Vienna, Austria, introduced a new technique for producing carpets, the Blackburn Rivet Head Carpet System (see Figure 28-15).

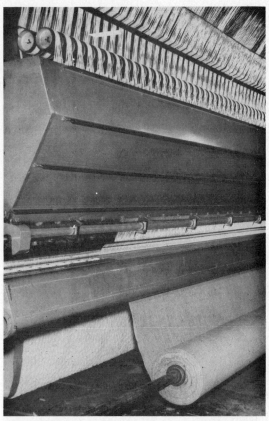

Figure 28-12 Tufting machine in operation shows the tufting yarns at the top being guided down to be needlepunched through the backing fabric coming off the roller at the front. The fabric is seen as it is fed off toward the rear of the machine. *(Courtesy Allied Chemical Corp.)*

Figure 28-13 Variations in pile height give tufted carpeting a sculptured effect. *(Courtesy Allied Chemical Corp.)*

Figure 28-14   Shag carpet of continuous filament nylon pile tufted through a web of nylon staple needlepunched to a secondary polypropylene backing. The primary nylon web backing of the same fiber and color of the pile gives the carpet the appearance of a greater pile density than there actually is. (*Courtesy Thiokol Fibers Div.*)

Figure 28-15   Schematic diagrams of the Rivet Head carpet construction technique. (*a*) A tuft of yarn is advanced horizontally to the position shown at (1), being pushed to this position by the advancing roller (2). The needle unit and cutter are linked through cams shown at the top of the diagram (3). Through linking mechanism (4), the tuft of yarn is cut to length by a cutter unit (5) which allows it to fall into delivery tube (6). The rocker arm (4) not only operates the yarn cutting phase, but also opens a compressed air supply (7) which applies a low pressure (0.5 lb/in²) to project the tuft or yarn down tube (6) to the reception chamber (8) of the tubular insertion needle. This chamber is vertical and is tapered at its base to a precise minimal diameter (9). This is the segment which penetrates the primary backing (10). (*b*) The precut tuft of yarn is inserted into the base fabric through the needle while a plunger holds it there as the needle withdraws. (*Courtesy Modern Textiles Magazine*)

The pile is formed by moving a predetermined length of yarn by means of a hollow needle through the base or backing fabric. A very short length of the pile does not pass through; rather, it remains protruded through the base fabric. When the hollow needle is withdrawn, the constrictive action of the backing causes the end to bloom, or spread out, like a mushroom, or more appropriately, a rounded rivet head. To lock the rivet heads in place, a latex mist is sprayed onto the back as the pile carpet emerges from the machine. The elimination of the linking strand joining each tuft saves about 10 to 15 percent yarn.

Pile height is determined by the length of the yarn passed by the hollow needle through the backing. Pile density is determined by the closeness of the needle thrusts. Design can be obtained by transferring the designer's colored grid pattern to an electronically controlled device which can operate the hollow needles for each of the several colored yarns needed.

Durcam. A more recent development (first announced in 1973) is the Durcam machine, which can produce a patterned carpet similar to spool Axminsters. However, the pile height cannot be greater than $9/16$ inch. The tapestrylike pattern may be produced with up to fifteen different colored yarns. The pattern construction is governed by magnetic tape and an electronic decoder device. Essentially, the machine cuts individual yarns into short lengths and bends them into U-shaped tufts which are pressed at the bend to a burlap backing which is coated with a plastic glue—that is, a polyvinylchloride plastisol. The cost of production is much less than for Axminster because less yarn is used and the equipment is less expensive, even less than for some carpet printing equipment.

Colourtuft. Another technique recently introduced for producing yarn-dyed patterned carpets is accomplished on the Colourtuft machine. Using multineedlebars and an individual needle selection system, differently colored pile yarns can be inserted along the same row of tufts. Almost any multicolored design can be produced in high and loop pile. In addition to a semishag style, it is expected that a semiplush construction that will resemble a good-quality Wilton in appearance and pattern will also become available.

Omnipoint. Another variation of the tufting technique is produced by the Omnipoint machine, which has two needlebars that can be shifted horizontally to form zigzag tufted rows which eliminate undesirable tuft rowing. As a result, a consolidated design appearance is achieved. The first needlebar, with a straight yarn-feed, tufts the basic field. The second bar, with either one color or two alternating color yarns fed through the patterning device, actually sews the pattern directly into the basic field. With the use of three different colored yarns, it is possible to obtain up to seven distinctly textured hues. An infinite variety of pile heights can be obtained by a photoelectric scanning system that controls the thrust of the tufting needles.

Needlepunched. Carpets are produced in both flat and pile form by needling fibrous webs. The flat carpets are manufactured in a needlepunching manner for producing nonwoven fabrics as described on pages 162–166. They are generally made of a thermoplastic polymer, such as polypropylene. These flat needled carpets are harsh and stiff but suitable for outdoor and indoor uses where traffic is heavy, pile is not needed, and resistance to moisture and/or staining is desired.

The technique for producing pile needled carpet was originally done on a Dilo needlepunching machine. The pile may be in the form of either plush (cut-type) or modified loop. Preneedled web without a substrate, or backing, is fed into the machine equipped with forked needles (rather than the barbed needles which are used for producing nonwoven flat fabrics). If plush, or cut type, pile is desired, the forked needles push fibers from the body of the fabric through the surface so that one or both ends of the protruded fibers come out completely, forming a cut-pile appearance. If a loop pile is desired, the forked needles' thrusts are reduced in depth to push fibers from the body of the fabric through the surface sufficiently so that the ends of the fibers do not protrude; instead, small loops of the caught fibers protrude. Such factors as type of fiber, fiber length, depth of needle penetration, closeness of the needles, and fabric weight affect the specific fabric appearance.

Another type of needlepunched carpet is produced from *Tultrim*, based upon the Cambrelle heterofil nylon fabric (Figure 28-16). The fabric, composed either entirely of heterofil or a blend of heterofil and homofil (conventional) thermoplastic fibers, is passed through a special type of needle loom which imparts a design to the surface of the fabric. The carpet is strong, durable, and resilient. When produced of appropriate fibers, it has low flammability characteristics.

Stitch-bonded. The stitchbonding technique for producing carpets is done on a Schusspol machine, which is based upon the Mali technique (see pages 154–157). The Schusspol constructs in one operation a backing fabric, which may include a foam substrate, and stitches a loop pile onto the surface of the fabric. The loop pile may be up to almost $1/2$ inch in height. If desired, the pile can be produced in cut form by adding a cutting device to the machine. Although the machine is expensive, ultimate savings are great not only in basic fabric construction but also in pile yarn, since it is located entirely on the surface of the fabric and thereby saves on the amount of yarn needed.

Knitted. Knitted carpets are made by using three sets of needles to loop together the backing yarn, the stitching yarn, and the pile yarn in a single operation similar to that of hand knitting. A coat of latex is applied to the back to give additional body. A second backing is often added for greater dimensional stability.

The pile is usually uncut, but cut pile can be obtained with modifications in the knitting machine. Sculptured surfaces are also possible. Solid, tweed, and multicolored patterns can also be achieved.

Hooked. Hooked rugs from the southern and New England states and from Canada are popular as throw rugs for bedrooms and halls. These are hand-

Figure 28-16 *(a)* Sheathed-core bicomponent fibers meld together to form a sturdy, stable Cambrelle fabric which could be needled and tufted to produce such fabrics as carpet backing. *(b)* Tultrim backing made of Cambrelle heterofil nylon melded fabric showing comparison of "before (top) and after (bottom)" needle-punching. *(Courtesy ICI Fibres, England)*

made of twisted rags sewed together, usually in colonial patterns. They are also produced commercially in room and small sizes in cotton, wool, and nylon.

Flocked.   Flocked carpets are produced for wall coverings and automotive and commercial uses. While the base fabric is frequently made of jute, it could be of any appropriate composition. The fabric is coated with a suitable adhesive and then flocked by any one of several methods (see pages 260–262). Such carpets are said to have good abrasion resistance depending upon the type of flock used, the height of the flock, and the quality of the adhesive. The tenacity of the adhesive and the extent to which the flock is imbedded into it affect the resistance of the flock to being dislodged or pulled out.

Tile Types.   Carpet can be produced in rectangular pieces of about 1 square foot. These may be made by a variety of methods, such as tufted, cut, or uncut pile, including shag and nonwoven fibrous fabric. These squares have their own backing and do not need padding. They are a relatively inexpensive, convenience item which the consumer can easily lay alone, and they are particularly suited for small and irregular areas. Serviceability and durability are limited and dependent upon composition and construction, both of which have much variation as indicated by the variety of carpet construction discussed here.

Grass.   A wirelike grass that grows wild in the northeastern section of the United States is used for grass rugs. Grass rugs are woven with a plain weave that shows on one side. A pattern applied by stencil appears on the other side. Colored warp threads can be used to form geometric designs. Grass rugs are always varnished to preserve their surface.

Sisal.   Sisal fiber imported from Central America and the West Indies can be made into rugs. The chief use of this fiber is for twine and rope, but its durability makes it adaptable for floor coverings. Sisal fiber is obtained from the leaf of the agave plant. It is twisted into strands and woven similarly to any of the fiber rugs.

ORIENTAL RUGS

Very few of the Oriental rugs produced before 1795 are on the commercial market today, but many are displayed in museums. These older Oriental rugs are valuable because of their age, beauty, and intricacy of design. Those made in the last hundred years are accepted as "old Orientals," and although scarce, are still obtainable.

Oriental rugs are classified according to the country and the section from which they originated. They are divided into six groups: Persian, Turkish, Caucasian, Turkoman, Indian, and Chinese. These groups can be subclassified according to their weave and also by the method of looping or knot tying that is characteristic of Oriental rug construction. Only two kinds of knots are used for the many kinds of Oriental rugs made throughout Europe and Asia. The Persian, or Senna, knot is more of a twist or wrapping; the Turkish, or Ghiordes, knot is a real knot as understood today.

The largest class of Oriental rugs has a pile surface composed of tufts.

Each tuft is made separately by means of the knot formed by strands looped around the warp yarns. When the quality of an Oriental rug is being judged, consideration should be given to coloring, design, depth of pile, quality of the yarn, age, condition, and fineness of texture. The number of knots to the square inch may vary from 50 to 500.

The consumer may find it difficult to distinguish between the imported Oriental and the machine-made domestic product. It may be helpful to remember that the reverse side of the Oriental always shows the entire pattern in detail and that the pile is produced by rows of knots, which can be easily seen by separating the pile. The back should also be examined to see whether the entire pattern has the same colors on the reverse side as are on the face of the rug and to check the number of knots to the square inch.

In the genuine Oriental, the fringe of the rug is never sewed on; it is always an extension of the warp threads. In proportion to size, the Oriental is always heavier than the domestic. Experienced rug merchants distinguish the two by examining the dyed portion of the pile nearest the knot. Oriental rugs use natural dyes, which usually fade to a lighter shade of the original color. The domestic rug uses aniline dyes, which fade to different hues.

Persian. Wool rugs from the Middle East are frequently referred to as *Persian rugs*. Perhaps the reasons for this are the use of the Persian knot and the designs, colors, luxuriousness of the pile, beauty, durability, and overall quality of rugs which had come from Persia at one time. They had become world-renowned and had thus dominated the Oriental rug market. Today, most of this type of rug comes from Iran and to a lesser extent from such other countries as Armenia and Turkey.

There are a number of different kinds of Persian rugs. Each is named after its geographic location of production. There are subtypes depending upon the type of weave used and the resultant design. They demonstrate a high degree of creative ability, skill, and artistic achievement. Depending upon quality, they are relatively expensive.

Indian. Rugs made of wool, wool-and-silk, and all-silk utilizing the Persian knot are made in Kashmir. These rugs resemble Persian rugs in some of their motifs, color, and sheen, which is particularly beautiful when silk is used. Quality is again dependent upon closeness of the knots per inch, the design, the number and quality of colors used, the height of the pile, and the luxuriousness of the hand.

Small-sized rugs imported from other parts of India are made from felted goat's hair and embroidered by hand with bright wool threads similar to the work found in crewel fabrics. They are known as *Numdah rugs*. They are inexpensive and adaptable for general household use as they can be easily washed. Another rug imported from India, called a *drugget*, is woven with the wool of wire-haired sheep. Jute is used in its backing. It is usually highly colored and should be dry-cleaned instead of washed.

Chinese. Antique Chinese rugs were made with the Persian, or Senna, knot, making possible a large number of knots to the inch and a close shearing of the pile. Later, rugs were made with large, coarse designs and a deep pile. In more recent years, Chinese rugs have been made in plain colors as well as in the floral and dragon patterns characteristic of Chinese design. The pile of Chinese rugs is unusually deep, making these rugs remarkably durable.

RUG COLORATION AND DECORATION

At one time, the conventional method of obtaining color and design in rugs was to use yarn-dyed pile. Today, color and design are imparted to carpets by a variety of methods similar to those used for garment and home-furnishings fabrics. In addition to yarn dyeing, printing and piece dyeing are the general methods used. While the methods are identified here, expansion on these procedures is provided in Chapters 9 and 10. Certain modifications are, of course, made in these methods to accommodate the particular needs of the carpet fabrics being processed.

Yarn Dyeing

Yarns to be used for the carpet pile may be dyed prior to looming. They may be package-dyed (sometimes with the aid of hypodermic-type needles penetrating cross-wound yarn on spools). The yarns may also be space-dyed by the knit-deknit dyeing technique whereby the yarn is loosely knitted into tubular form and then roller- or vigoreaux-printed, sprayed, jet-striped, or otherwise colored. After the color is set, the yarn is unraveled onto a spool. Skein space-dye-

ing may be accomplished with the aid of spray bars to provide randomized variously colored yarns.

The yarn may be warp-printed at the rate of 150 to 400 yarns at once. Roller printing is the most common method, but spray or jet may be employed. The latter differs from the spray technique in that jet uses a more viscous paste with a more concentrated dye ejection and is sometimes followed by padding to obtain greater color penetration.

Printing

Designs may be printed onto carpet by flatbed or rotary screens. Warp may also be printed immediately prior to tufting. Automated block printing is also used. In the latter instance, a *deep-dye* technique used is an alteration from the method used for flat fabrics; the carpet has the pile down, and the print blocks which have the dye liquor in the design are lifted toward the pile to immerse it into the color of the pattern.

TAK dyeing, which is a form of controlled scattered color distribution, may be considered to be a type of printing since the entire carpet is not dyed and the pattern is repeatable. The appearance of a random multicolor effect has attracted much favorable attention.

Polychromatic dyeing has likewise increased in use. Patterns may be varied by regulating the amount and fineness of the jet sprays and their placement. Differential-dyeable pile yarns may be used to multiply the pattern possibilities.

Transfer printing is also being used for carpets. Multicolored designs are transferred with the aid of heat from rolls of printed paper directly onto the carpet surface. No wet processing is used. The method is rapid and the prints are reasonably durable.

Piece Dyeing

There are several different systems for dyeing carpet. They may be either batch or continuous in operation and applied to all types of carpet, from needlepunched to shag. Differentially dyed yarns may be used in the fabric to enhance the coloring possibilities. The techniques are becoming more versatile and more efficient, thereby resulting in greater consumer interest and larger consumer market, as well as greater consumer satisfaction and value.

CARE OF RUGS

The appearance and the life of a rug depend on the amount and kind of attention it receives. Dirt and grit must be removed frequently; otherwise, dirt works into the recesses of the pile and into the backing, soon cutting the yarn fibers and finally producing worn areas. A carpet sweeper, or vacuum cleaner, should be used on carpets for a few minutes every day—surely twice a week—cleaning in the direction of the pile, not against it.

When sweeping a new pile-surfaced rug, loose pieces of the pile, or fuzz, are likely to come off. This is caused by the excess short fibers worked in during manufacturing operations. It does not necessarily indicate defects. When ends of tufts appear above the surface of a new rug, clip them level with the surface.

A new wool rug or one recently returned from storage should always be swept and brushed gently because the wool in the rug is in a dry condition, not having had sufficient opportunity to absorb its natural intake of moisture. The constant absorption of moisture from the atmosphere, so important for the healthful condition of a rug, keeps it resilient and resistant to wear.

Constant pressure on a rug flattens the tufts or slants them in one direction. The position of the rug or the furniture should be changed so that the wear may be distributed instead of concentrated in a particular area. This helps to prevent the uneven shading that occurs when sections of a rug show localized wear. An important safeguard in the care of a rug is to place a cushion backing under it to absorb the constant impact. Any stains should be removed promptly. Many spots can be easily removed when fresh. Removal is difficult when a stain has set. The rules for the removal of spots and stains from general textile fabrics apply as well to textile floor coverings. (See Chapter 29.)

Moths and carpet beetles may damage wool rugs. Keeping the rug clean and providing a healthful circulation of air reduces this danger. For this reason, some people do not put their rugs away during the summer months, letting them remain on the floor for the frequent cleanings so essential for long and serviceable wear. Rugs that are cleaned frequently with a vacuum cleaner are never attacked by moths. If a damaged area is regular in form, this is an indication that the attacking insect is not the moth but the tow bug, which is likely to be found in overstuffed upholstered furniture.

Curling of the corner of a rug can be remedied by applying a hot iron on a damp cloth to both face and back of the corner. The curling is usually caused by constant tripping or by some similar unusual strain.

REVIEW QUESTIONS

1. What basic properties of textile fibers are required for floor coverings?
2. What are the two main classifications of floor coverings?
3. What identifying characteristics distinguish Persian and Chinese rugs?
4. How does the Brussels carpet differ from broadloom?
5. Describe the Wilton construction. How does a worsted Wilton differ from a woolen Wilton?
6. (a) How can humidity affect floor coverings? (b) How is this indicated to the owner? (c) What remedy is available?
7. Describe the Axminster carpet, indicating how to distinguish it from other carpets.
8. (a) What are the advantages of a chenille carpet? (b) What are the disadvantages?
9. Compare the imported Oriental with the domestic product.
10. Why is patent-back construction important in carpet production?
11. What are some precautions to take in caring for floor coverings?
12. Under what conditions may a wool rug be left on the floor in summer?
13. Describe the tufting process.
14. Why have tufted carpets become the predominant type of rug?
15. Compare the attributes of the man-made fibers for rugs.
16. How do these characteristics compare with wool?
17. How are knitted rugs made?
18. What are hooked rugs?
19. What are sculptured carpets?
20. What is rivet head carpet construction?
21. What is needlepunched carpet?
22. What are the several methods of giving color and design to rugs and carpets?

29

FABRIC CARE

service, economy, and appearance

The care of garments and other products made of fabrics has always been a concern of consumers. Such care is reflected in economy, the household budget, serviceability, and appearance. Assistance has been provided to consumers through the Federal Permanent Care Labeling Rule, which primarily deals with matters of laundering and dry cleaning.

In addition, there are other care procedures which consumers should observe in order to get the greatest use and satisfaction from textile products. Textile products should not only be carefully selected, they should also be given proper care throughout their service. This care includes (1) frequent brushing and airing, (2) clean storage when not in use, (3) immediate mending when damaged by tearing, (4) stain removal before washing or further use, (5) intelligent choice of cleaning method—washing or dry cleaning, (6) frequent laundering when the fabric is washable, (7) proper method of laundering for type of fabric, (8) proper ironing or pressing.

PERMANENT CARE LABELING

As the variety of fibers, fiber blends, yarns, fabric constructions, and finishes multiplied, consumers became more confused and uncertain about the characteristics or properties of the products reaching them. Some producers and manufacturers provided labels or hangtags to aid the consumers in identifying their products' properties and in caring for them in an appropriate manner so as to retain their claimed characteristics for a reasonable period of time. However, the continued innovations by all facets of the textile industry made matters more complex for the consumers; it made it increasingly difficult to make value judgments. Furthermore, even when labels accompanied products, consumers frequently either were unable to match these products after use with the correct, removed care labels or had lost or discarded them. Thus, a combination of pressures developed from consumer interest groups and voluntary initiative among some sectors of the textile industry for the use of care labels that would be permanently attached to textile products. These pressures ultimately caused the Federal Trade Commission to establish the Permanent Care Labeling Rule, which became effective July 3, 1972.

Coverage and Exemptions

The Permanent Care Labeling Rule covers items made wholly or partly from a textile product. However, articles of wearing apparel composed wholly of genuine fur, leather, or suede, and those composed primarily of genuine fur, leather, or suede and only partially of textile products (e.g., leather coats with textile linings), are *not* covered by the rule. Articles of wearing apparel consisting primarily of textile products, even though some portions are genuine fur, leather, or suede (e.g., textile coats with fur or leather trim or pocket linings), *are* covered by the rule. Since the Federal Trade Commission has no jurisdiction over foreign producers, the domestic companies handling imported products are required to attach labels. Of course, the importers may establish independent contractual requirements with their foreign suppliers so as to have the foreign producers provide the labels.

Three types of merchandise specifically exempted from the rule are handwear (e.g., gloves), headwear (e.g., hats), and footwear (e.g., sneakers, but not hosiery); additionally, products which do not require laundering or dry cleaning are exempted. There are also two classes of merchandise *eligible* for exemption: articles whose "utility or appearance would be substantially impaired by an attached label" (e.g., see-through blouses) and articles "intended to be sold at retail for $3.00 or less and which are completely washable under all normal circumstances." However, this stipulation requires that application to and approval from the commission must be obtained prior to marketing the product.

Supplemental rules are promulgated from time to time for purposes of clarification and necessary adjustment. For example, the Federal Trade Commission has ruled that remnants labeled by the *manufacturer* (not the retailer) as 10 yards or less are eligible for exclusion from the labeling rule.

Label Permanency and Placement

The Permanent Care Labeling Rule states that textile products requiring labels must have appropriate care instructions which are permanently legible. These labels must be affixed in a manner that will assure permanent attachment for the length of the product's useful life. The labels may be sewn, glued, or in any other appropriate manner attached to the product. The care instructions may be woven, printed, or in any other appropriate manner inscribed. They may be placed directly on the product, rather than on a label.

The label must be so placed that it is readily available to the consumer at the time of purchase. If this should not be possible and the label is hidden from view, then the care instructions must also be either on the package or on a visible insert in the package. The purpose is to protect comsumers and help them make value judgments when buying.

Instructions and Law Labeling

The care instructions should be clear, specific, and sufficient. For example, if the instructions state that the item is washable, it should not be assumed that it is also dry cleanable; rather, the label should state that the item should not be dry-cleaned, if that is the case. Or, if a product is machine washable but not machine dryable, the label should either so state or provide suitable instructions for proper drying. The rule assumes that the care information is correct, and the consumer may therefore also make that assumption. (See Table 29-1.)

The commission is aware of the possibility of low labeling—that is, providing care instructions that are safe but not necessarily the best or most economical. The intent of the rule is to aid the consumer and provide protection against unnecessary economic hardship. For example, if the products are known by the manufacturer and/or retailer to be dry cleanable but have not been tested for launderability, they should not simply be labeled "Dry Clean Only"; rather, they should be tested for alternative methods of care and then labeled accordingly.

Testing and Responsibility

There is implied in the rule, that reasonably complete testing of the product is made before care instructions are established. Advanced testing is not specifically required. However, without it, reputations and business may suffer; and litigations may be instituted either by the individual consumer or by an interest group as a class action.

Care labeling requires consideration of performance characteristics of all of the product's components, including the methods used to join them together. The product must perform as a unit. The responsibility for the performance of the product and its care instructions rests with the producer, retailer, or whoever is responsible for the product and/or its finishes and applies the care instructions. If the retailer specifies to his supplier the instructions to be put on the product, then he assumes the responsibility. Affixed care instructions imply a warranty that those instructions will not reduce the use and enjoyment of the item. There is also the implied warranty that the product will perform satisfactorily if the care instructions are followed.

Although a fairly complete testing approach is implied, no test procedures or standards were initially developed. These matters were left to the industry. Standardization of testing methods and criteria for satisfactory and unsatisfactory performance in all textile categories need to be established. Shrinkage, for example, needs to be defined and delimited. In one garment, such as a shirt, shrinkage of more than 1 percent would be unsatisfactory; but 2 percent might be tolerated in another garment, such as a dress. Here, the issue is not shrinkage alone, but shrinkage *out of fit*. The performance tests should include emphasis on consumer experience and reaction if the rule is to be met in the spirit of its intent. What may ultimately be needed are definitions, testing procedures, and standards, possibly set forth by the industry and made compulsory. Industry, as well as the consumer, could thereby be well served.

It is important to note that the Permanent Care Labeling Rule makes no reference to the correctness or accuracy of the care instructions. Nor are there any punitive statements in it. The Federal Trade Commission is not required to test the claims nor to maintain surveillance over those claims. However, according to the Federal Trade Commission Act itself, under Section 5, which deals with unfair and deceptive trade practices, the commission has full power to take necessary steps for controlling action.

CARE OF FABRICS

In addition to the care prescribed on labels for garments, there are several practices that should be utilized to preserve the good appearance of garments, to protect them against deterioration, and to extend their usefulness.

Brushing and Airing

The frequent brushing of garments, especially those having napped surfaces, removes the kind of dirt that starts as dust. The accumulation of dust particles soils the fabric (even when the soil is not readily discernible) and eventually causes deterioration.

When a garment is not washable and does not require frequent dry cleaning, its life can be prolonged and its appearance kept bright and attractive by brushing. To offset the absorption of perspiration in such garments, they should

Table 29-1

CONSUMER CARE GUIDE FOR APPAREL		
	WHEN LABEL READS:	IT MEANS:
MACHINE WASHABLE	Machine wash	Wash, bleach, dry, and press by any customary method including commercial laundering and dry cleaning
	Home launder only	Same as above but do not use commercial laundering
	No chlorine bleach	Do not use chlorine bleach. Oxygen bleach may be used
	No bleach	Do not use any type of bleach
	Cold wash Cold rinse	Use cold water from tap or cold washing machine setting
	Warm wash Warm rinse	Use warm water or warm washing machine setting
	Hot wash	Use hot water or hot washing machine setting
	No spin	Remove wash load before final machine spin cycle
	Delicate cycle Gentle cycle	Use appropriate machine setting; otherwise, wash by hand

Table 29-1

CONSUMER CARE GUIDE FOR APPAREL *(Continued)*		
	WHEN LABEL READS:	**IT MEANS:**
	Durable press cycle Permanent press cycle	Use appropriate machine setting; otherwise, use warm wash, cold rinse, and short spin cycle
	Wash separately	Wash alone or with like colors
NONMACHINE WASHING	Hand wash	Launder only by hand in lukewarm (hand comfortable) water. May be bleached. May be dry-cleaned
	Hand wash only	Same as above, but do not dry-clean
	Hand wash separately	Hand wash alone or with like colors
	No bleach	Do not use bleach
	Damp wipe	Surface clean with damp cloth or sponge
HOME DRYING	Tumble dry	Dry in tumble dryer at specified setting—high, medium, low, or no heat
	Tumble dry Remove promptly	Same as above, but in absence of cool-down cycle remove at once when tumbling stops
	Drip dry	Hang wet and allow to dry with hand shaping only
	Line dry	Hang damp and allow to dry
	No wring No twist	Hang dry, drip-dry, or dry flat only. Handle to prevent wrinkles and distortion
	Dry flat	Lay garment on flat surface
	Block to dry	Maintain original size and shape while drying
IRONING OR PRESSING	Cool iron	Set iron at lowest setting
	Warm iron	Set iron at medium setting
	Hot iron	Set iron at hot setting
	Do not iron	Do not iron or press with heat
	Steam iron	Iron or press with steam
	Iron damp	Dampen garment before ironing
MISCELLANEOUS	Dry-clean only	Garment should be dry-cleaned only, including self-service
	Professionally dry-clean only	Do not use self-service dry cleaning
	No dry-clean	Use recommended care instructions. No dry-cleaning materials to be used

This care guide was produced by the Consumer Affairs Committee, American Apparel Manufacturers Association, and is based on the Voluntary Guide of the Textile Industry Advisory Committee for Consumer Interests.

be frequently aired, outdoors if possible. If this is not possible, hang clothes for a time outside the closet in a well-aired room. Frequent brushing with a clothes-brush that has soft but firm bristles is necessary to keep wool garments in good condition. Hang them on wide-shoul-dered hangers in a closet where clothes are not packed tightly together. Oc-casional airing is also necessary to prolong the life of wool fiber. Clothes hanging in a closet should always be but-toned, and zippers should be closed.

Storing

Clothing that is not in daily use should be protected from deterioration by storage in dustproof containers in which a moth preventive for wools is used. No useful purpose is served if the garment is stored without careful brushing and airing, because the accumulated dirt damages the stored articles. For long storage, garments should be washed or dry-cleaned and stored immediately, pre-ferably in sealed containers.

If newly purchased linens are to be stored for a while, they should be washed to remove any possible sizing. Any resi-due of starch in new or used stored linens may cause mildew. If white linens are wrapped in blue paper, and the ends of the package are sealed to exclude light and air, the linens will not turn yellow during storage.

Mending

A torn fabric should be mended before further use. Makeshift repair with a pin tends to cause longer tears or frays that are more difficult to mend. The mended portion will be less noticeable if it is repaired before the surrounding yarns are further damaged.

Stain Removal

Successful removal of stains from fab-rics depends on the basic principle of not allowing the spot or stain to become set. A stain should be removed at the first possible opportunity because it may be more easily dissolved when fresh. Dif-ferent fibers require different methods and different stain removers. Use of an incorrect remover may damage or even destroy the fiber content of a fabric. Knowledge of the nature of the stain makes possible the immediate use of the appropriate method and removal agent. Hot water should never be used on an unknown stain. The heat will set the stain, making it more difficult to remove. If the stain is known to be of a nongreasy nature, sponging with cold water may be all that is necessary. On the other hand, a greasy stain requires the use of carbon tetrachloride or some other dry cleaner, such as benzine, gasoline, turpentine, or denatured alcohol.

Kinds of Stain Removers. No single chemical can be used to remove all spots from the many different kinds of fibers. For example, since acids destroy cotton and linen, they cannot be used to remove stains from these fibers. Similarly, alka-lies cannot be used on silk and wool. Vis-cose or cuprammonium rayon can be treated like cotton. Acetate requires special care, as it dissolves in acetone, acetic acid, and chloroform.

Water, Alkalies, and Acids. Acids and alkalies should be used only as mild solu-tions. When using a mild acid such as vinegar, any possible damage that might occur to the fabric must be counteracted by applying a weak alkali, such as a solution of bicarbonate of soda or ammonia water, to neutralize the acid. The fabric should be thoroughly rinsed in clear water. If an alkali solution is necessary, it should be followed immediately with a mild acid solution (such as lemon juice, vinegar, or a dilute solution of acetic acid) to neutralize the action of the alkali. The fabric should be well rinsed.

Many man-made fibers, such as the polyesters, acrylics, modacrylics, polypropylenes, and saran are not very absorbent, and fabrics of such fibers do not readily stain. Removal of stains generally requires merely wiping with a damp cloth or washing with a mild soap in warm water.

Bleaching Agents. Various bleaching chemicals are commonly used to remove stains. But such chemicals must be used carefully because they extract color and weaken the cloth. Household bleaches of chlorine solutions (sodium hypochlorite) should be used only on cottons, linens, and rayons—never on silk or wool. If a stain is to be removed with a bleaching chemical, the fabric should be stretched over a bowl of hot water and fastened around the edge of the bowl. The bleaching agent should be dropped on the stained area with a medicine dropper. This application must be followed immediately with a thorough rinsing. The entire procedure must be done quickly so that the bleaching agent will not remain too long on the material and cause undue weakening of the fabric. To prevent weakening, a few drops of oxalic acid or sodium thiosulfate (photographer's hypo) will neutralize the action of any

chlorine bleach that may remain in the fabric. If a bleaching agent is used on a colored fabric, the dipping method is advisable to avoid unequal distribution of any subsequent loss of color.

Sodium perborate and oxalic acid are effective in removing iron rust, metal stains, and some ink stains from all types of fabrics. These chemicals are the least harmful of all bleaches, but they must be used quickly to prevent abstraction of the dye. For white woolens, sodium perborate is particularly effective and harmless. For the removal of mildew, ink, iron rust, dye stains, iodine, grass stains, and fruit stains, a solution of one teaspoon of sodium hydrosulfite in a glass of water is one of the most effective bleaches. But the liquid must be used quickly, and the fabric should be well rinsed. Otherwise, the color is destroyed and the fabric is weakened.

Hydrogen peroxide may be used on all kinds of fabrics. It is a mild bleach, but it can be made more effective by the addition of a little ammonia. Oxalic acid and sodium hydrosulfite cannot be used on weighted silk.

Solvents. Where a stain is known to be of a greasy nature, the use of a solvent alone is sufficient. Grease stains are easily removed by the following solvents: carbon tetrachloride, benzine, turpentine, Stoddard solvent, gasoline, ether, acetone, alcohol. With the exception of ether, acetone, alcohol, and colored gasoline, these solvents will not change the color of the material. Sponging is generally most effective. The solvent should be applied on the wrong side of the fabric. The absorbent cloth underneath the stain will draw the dissolved grease and solvent from the fabric.

For fresh grease spots or slight oil stains, a sprinkling of talcum, powdered chalk, or magnesium carbonate (magnesite) rubbed into the stained area and left for while, will absorb the grease. When the absorbent powder is subsequently brushed off, the stain will be entirely removed. Butter stains can be removed in this manner, but they must first be heated to melt the butter before they can be fully absorbed.

A general chemical stain remover has become available. One is sold under the trademark of Texize K2r. It comes both in a tube and an aerosol spray can, and it may be safely used on wool, silk, and various man-made fibers. However, it should not be used for the cellulosic fibers of cotton, linen, or rayon. Texize K2r will remove spots and stains made by most foods, beverages, grease, oil, alcohol, shoe polish, grass, and cosmetics, as well as most ball-point and stamp pad inks. A thin layer of this remover should be worked into the dry, stained area of the fabric, and after the substance has completely dried to a chalky white, it should be vigorously brushed away.

Methods of Stain Removal. There are several techniques for applying stain removers. They require care and are best applied when the stain is not too large.

Dip Method. When the entire fabric can be immersed in the stain remover, the best method is dipping. This is the most convenient method if the spot is large, or if there are many spots on an all-cotton or all-linen fabric.

Steam Method. Stains on wool, silk, or any colored fabric may be removed by steaming. The stained area is saturated with steam by spreading the cloth over a bowl partly filled with hot water into which a small amount of the appropriate removal agent has been placed.

Drop Method. Small drops of a removal agent can be applied by means of a medicine dropper, glass rod, or orange stick.

Sponge Method. Sponging is the most frequently used method of stain removal, but if it is not done with care, it will not be effective. An absorbent cloth or a blotter should be placed underneath the stain to absorb the removal agent as well as the stain. The blotter also prevents further spreading of the wet area. Both the sponging cloth and the absorbent material should be renewed whenever they show the slightest tinge of the stain. The stained portion of the fabric must not be soaked with the cleaning fluid, and the fabric must not be harshly rubbed. Apply small quantities of the fluid with a soft cloth using light strokes in a circular direction from the outer rim of the stain toward its center. Feather the edges of the stain to prevent formation of a ring, which indicates an improper method of sponging, an excessive amount of cleaning fluid, or lack of sufficiently quick evaporation. Rapid evaporation can be obtained by blowing on the fabric or by placing it in front of an electric fan or dryer. To prevent a ring, hold the fabric over the spout of a steaming kettle until the area is damp. Then iron immediately (see Table 29-2).

Application of Stain and Soil Repellents

There are a number of stain and soil repellents which can be purchased,

Table 29-2

REMOVAL OF STAINS FROM FABRICS MADE OF NATURAL FIBERS

KIND OF STAIN	TYPE OF FABRIC	PROCEDURE AND REMOVAL
Acid	All	Neutralize with ammonia
Adhesive tape	All	Harden with ice cubes; rub off with fingers, then carbon tetrachloride or kerosene
Airplane glue	All	Apply acetone or nail polish remover followed by alcohol
Alcoholic beverages	All	Soak in cold water immediately followed by white vinegar, then rinse with cold water
Alkali	All	Neutralize with vinegar
Blood	Cotton, linen	Soak in cold water, then in dilute ammonia; wash
	Silk, wool	Sponge with cold water
Butter	All	Sponge with naphtha or carbon tetrachloride
Candle wax	All	Scrape away, then sponge with benzine
Chewing gum	All	Apply ice; soak in cold water; sponge with carbon tetrachloride or ether
Chocolate	Cotton, linen	Soak in cold water; wash with hypochlorite bleach
	Silk, wool	Soak in cold water; wash in hydrogen peroxide
Coffee	Cotton, linen	Soak in cold water; wash
	Silk, wool	Soak in cold water, then in hydrogen peroxide
Egg	Cotton, linen	Soak in cold water; wash
	Silk, wool	Soak in cold water; sponge with carbon tetrachloride
Fruit	All	If fresh, pour boiling water through stain; if stubborn, bleach with hypochlorite or hydrogen peroxide
Grass	All	Sponge with alcohol, then with soap and water
Ice cream	All	Sponge with gasoline or carbon tetrachloride
Iodine	All	Soak in alcohol or boil in solution of sodium thiosulfate (photographer's hypo)
Ink (writing)	Cotton, linen	If fresh, soap and water. If dried, sponge with bleach, then sponge with oxalic acid, then wash, or put in sweet milk and let turn sour
	Silk, wool	Sponge with hydrogen peroxide, then with oxalic acid or skim milk
Ink (ball point)	All	Let stand 10 to 15 minutes in detergent suds, rinse. If stain remains, use petroleum jelly or sodium hydrosulfite, then sponge with carbon tetrachloride. Some inks dissolve in glycerine followed by shampoo
Iron rust	Cotton, linen	Sponge with oxalic acid, rinse well; or spread with salt, moisten with lemon juice, and place in sun

Table 29-2

KIND OF STAIN	TYPE OF FABRIC	PROCEDURE AND REMOVAL
Lipstick	Cotton, linen	Rub with lard until stain is soft, scrape off grease, wash in hot suds
	Silk, wool	Sponge with alcohol or carbon tetrachloride
Mildew	Cotton, linen	Sponge with hypochlorite bleach
Milk or cream	All	Sponge with benzine or carbon tetrachloride
Mustard	Cotton, linen	Apply warm glycerine; wash with suds and hydrosulfite bleach
Oil	All	Wash in soap and water or sponge with carbon tetrachloride
Paint	All	Wash in soap and water and sponge with carbon tetrachloride or with turpentine on wrong side of stain (latex and acrylic paints wash out if not dried)
Perspiration	All	Sponge with peroxide and ammonia
Rubber	All	Sponge with carbon tetrachloride
Rust	All	Sponge with lemon, vinegar, or oxalic acid
Shellac	All	Sponge with denatured alcohol
Scorch	All	If light, dampen and place in sunlight or sponge with hydrogen peroxide
Sugar	All	Sponge with hot water
Tar	All	Moisten with carbon tetrachloride or with benzine. Scrape off, then sponge residue with same solvent
Tea	Cotton, linen	Soak in borax solution, rinse; or keep stain moist with lemon juice, then expose to sun for day or two
Urine	All	Varies. Sponge with soap and water or with salt solution, then apply dilute ammonia or hydrogen peroxide briefly and rinse
Varnish	All	Sponge with equal parts alcohol and benzine
Petroleum jelly	All	Sponge fresh stains with carbon tetrachloride, or spread talcum. Let stand, then brush
Water spot	Silk, wool	Hold in steam until damp, then iron damp

usually in aerosol containers, by the consumer and which are useful for protecting fabrics against permanent staining and soil retention, as well as for providing a reasonable degree of water repellency. Proper selection and application of such products can increase the service life of the fabric and reduce cleaning costs. The sprays vary in effectiveness of application with the various textile fibers, stains, and durabilities. Generally, they are sufficiently flame-resistant. Among the better-known products are Hagerty Fabric Guard, Protege

Tissu Scotchgard Fabric Protector, Royal Guard Suede & Fabric Protection, Scotchgard Fabric Protector, and Shirlo Magic Guard.

Application should be made only on new or freshly and thoroughly cleaned fabrics. The material should be colorfast. (Colorfastness can be tested by spraying the repellent on a hidden portion, such as a hem, and then rubbing the sprayed fabric while still wet with a white, absorbent cloth. If any color comes off onto the white cloth, the fabric should not be treated.) After the fabric has been sprayed and is thoroughly dried, the finish should be sprinkled with a few drops of water. If the drops bead up and remain on the surface of the fabric, then it has been sufficiently treated. If the drops are absorbed, then the fabric should be sprayed again.

Dry Cleaning

If the care information on a fabric or garment advises dry cleaning, that advice should be followed. Though dry cleaning is more expensive than washing, it pays to have a garment dry-cleaned rather than take a chance on washing and thereby ruining it. If acetate is dry-cleaned at home, the cleaning fluid must not contain alcohol, chloroform, strong acetic acid, or acetone. Any of these destroy acetate—particularly acetone, which is the solvent used in the acetate process.

When leaving the item with the dry cleaner, leather and plastic parts, such as belts, should be removed, as these could be damaged by certain commercial dry-cleaning fluids. The dry cleaner should note the kind of fibers used in the product so as to use appropriate dry-cleaning agents. If there are stains, he should be advised as to their nature so as to use the proper solvents.

Laundering Methods

When a fabric is known to be washable, frequent and prompt washing is desirable, particularly of clothing worn next to the skin. If such garments are not washed after each use, they are more difficult to clean, and the body perspiration that they have absorbed causes the fabric to deteriorate while awaiting cleaning. In general, fine underwear and brightly colored outer garments and household linens should be laundered at home. Knowledge of how to wash fragile and dainty white garments as well as dyed fabrics is essential for good results.

Just knowing that a fabric is washable is not enough information for good results in laundering. The consumer must be acquainted with the proper method of washing each type of garment and fabric. Some fabrics may be subjected to hard laundering, which includes boiling and the use of strong soaps, without too great a strain on their durability. It may be done at home as well as in commercial laundries, where it is customary to use strong substances for bleaching purposes and for sanitary reasons.

Before any attempt is made to wash clothes, colored fabrics should be separated from white ones, and heavy workclothes from fine and delicate pieces, as different washing methods are necessary. Bad stains must be removed before the fabrics are immersed in hot water. Slightly soiled clothes that do not require soaking should be washed in water not over 115 degrees Fahrenheit.

Extremely hot water tends to set dirt spots and minor spots or stains that may not have needed special treatment. Clothes that are very soiled should be soaked in warm, soapy water for about ten minutes.

A good-quality household soap or detergent should be dissolved in a washing machine or in a tub of hot water. Soft water will lather quickly, resulting in a more thorough cleaning. If the water is hard, the soap tends to curd because there is a high concentration of iron, calcium, magnesium, and aluminum salts in hard water. Any of the good commercial water softeners may be used to precipitate these soap-destroying metals in the water. Hard water can be softened by the use of washing soda, or sal soda (hydrated sodium carbonate). Some detergents contain water softeners, which are described on the packages.

REVIEW QUESTIONS

1. In what way does the label on a garment help in caring for the garment?
2. (a) Why should most clothes be placed on hangers when not in use? (b) Why are knitted garments an exception? (c) How should knitted clothes be kept?
3. Why is a firm brush recommended for brushing clothing?
4. Why should garments not be crowded in a clothes closet?
5. Why should white garments be separated from colored ones before laundering?
6. Give illustrations of what is meant by "needed repairs." Give reasons for attending to these without delay.
7. (a) Why should clothes be given a rest? (b) How does this apply to wool clothes?
8. Why should a stain or spot be removed as soon as it is discovered?
9. What are the principle features of the Permanent Care Labeling Rule?

SUGGESTED ACTIVITIES

1. For your next buying trip to a retail store, prepare a list of questions that you consider important enough to ask the salesperson to make certain that your selection of the clothing item is a prudent one.
2. Cut six advertisements from a newspaper, and circle all the textile terms that have taken on new meaning for you since studying textiles. Explain how familiarity with these textile terms has proved helpful to you recently.

GLOSSARY OF STANDARD FABRICS

COTTON FABRICS*

Airplane Fabric. Plain weave. Closely woven, desized, durable medium-weight and lightweight fabric originally used in the manufacture of airplane wings and parts. Made of combed and mercerized yarns; usually in square weave. Many fabrics go under this name. Most important is fancy, irregular broken weave.

Armure. Drapery fabric with a small woven design, usually on a rep foundation. Can be either Jacquard or dobby weave. Pattern is made by floating warp threads over the surface, giving a raised effect.

Backing or Back Cloth. Gray goods, usually printcloth, used to take up surplus dye and to reinforce fabric on the printing machine.

Balloon Cloth. Plain weave. Of finest Pima yarns. High thread count. The extremely fine yarns give the fabric luster. Usually mercerized. When used for balloons, given a special coating. Also used for dresses, shirts, typewriter ribbons.

Batiste. Plain weave. A sheer, soft-finished fabric of the lawn family. Comes in various grades from coarse to very fine. Generally woven of combed yarns, but occasionally of carded. Often given high mercerization; bleached, dyed, or printed. Sometimes embroidered.

Beach Cloth. A strong, coarse fabric of plain weave, heavy yarns, and low thread count. Has the appearance of crash. There are a number of versions of this fabric.

Bedford Cord. A carded yarn, wale, or cord material. Two-ply warp yarns and heavier single or ply yarns used as a backing. These heavy yarns are caught at intervals in the weaving of the fabric. Single yarns sometimes used in cheaper versions; the effect of the cord is obtained in the weaving. Wale runs in warp. Can be napped in back, bleached, dyed, or printed. Often the face of the fabric is given a suede finish.

Bengaline. Rib effect in filling with a high luster. Has somewhat the appearance of grosgrain. For draperies and dresses.

Bird's-eye (Diaper Cloth). Fabric woven on a dobby loom of carded yarns in tiny geometric designs that look like the eye of a bird, or in diamond effect. Heavier filling yarns are loosely twisted, making the fabric absorbent.

Blanket Cloth. Plain or twill weave, 60 × 80 inches and over. Thick, soft filling yarns, heavily napped both sides. Often yarn-dyed in plaids or stripes.

Book Cloth. Coarse, plain-weave printcloth or sheeting. Dyed, heavily sized, often pyroxylin coated or embossed.

Box-loom. Fabrics made with right-hand and left-hand twist in filling, notably box-loom crepe. Such fabrics as ginghams and plaids are also made on box-looms.

The glossary of cotton fabrics is based upon material prepared by The Cotton Textile Institute, Inc.

Broadcloth. Plain, closely woven fabrics of either carded or combed yarns with a fillingwise rib effect. Originally a poplin or adapted from a poplin construction, broadcloths are of lighter weight with a finer rib. Ribs are made by using finer warp yarn and medium filling. Many more warp threads than filling. Better broadcloths are combed ply yarns and have high thread counts of 144 × 76. Coarser fabrics often have both ply and single carded yarns.

Brocade. Basic weave is satin. Elaborate lustrous design woven on a Jacquard loom. Has a raised appearance, usually on a filling-faced satin ground but often on twill or rep. The design is on the surface only. Multicolored yarns used.

Brocatelle. A heavier version of brocade. Woven on a Jacquard loom with two, three, four, or more shuttles. Ordinary warp yarns but fewer twists in filling yarns. Has extra backing threads. The floating warp yarns over the backing yarns make the design stand out in relief.

Bunting (Cheesecloth, Gauze, Tobacco Cloth). Loose, open, plain weave of printcloth yarns with low thread count. Cheesecloths range from 25 to 55 inches in width. Tobacco cloths are 36 inches and over in width but somewhat lower thread count than cheesecloth. Bunting may be dyed or printed. Gauze may be specially treated as for bandages.

Calico. A low-count or medium-count cotton printcloth with special designs called calico designs. Many early American designs are in use.

Cambric. Originally linen, now cotton printcloth or lightweight sheeting construction. Given special sizing and calendered finish.

Canton Flannel. Warp-face twill flannel with a heavy, soft filling and lighter warp than filling yarn. Has a long nap on one side only. Comes unbleached or bleached. For men's workgloves, infants' wear, linings.

Challis. Plain or twill weave, printed or dyed. Given a soft finish and very slight nap.

Chambray. Pattern is formed by the use of colored yarn warp and natural or white filling. This gives a tiny check or mottled effect. There are endless variations of this fabric, such as stripes and satin stripes. The end-to-end chambrays are woven with alternate colored and natural or white yarns in warp and all natural or white yarns in filling, or vice versa. Many novelties on the market.

Chenille. Fluffy or fuzzy faced fabric made with a cotton warp yarn and a cotton chenille filling yarn that has a fuzzy pile protruding from all sides. Some imitations made by tufting, using no chenille yarn.

Cheviot. A strong twilled fabric woven with a colored stripe or check.

Chiffon. A sheer voile with a dull finish; of fine, hard-twisted yarns. Often dyed or printed.

Chintz. A printcloth or high-count fine sheeting with bright, attractive floral or geometric designs, both large and small. Often given a permanent or semipermanent glaze; then known as glazed chintz. For draperies, slipcovers, dresses.

Clokay. A plain-woven fabric with an embossed surface of some geometric pattern. Rather compact weave. Embossed design is permanent if the fabric is laundered only in lukewarm water with a mild soap.

Corduroy. A ribbed pile fabric with a high, soft luster. Made with extra filling threads or extra warp threads. In weaving, the extra filling yarns form loops or floats over the ground threads. After weaving, the loop threads are cut on a special machine. Threads are then brushed, forming a pile.

Cottonade. Generally a three-harness, left-hand, warp-face twill of coarse yarns. Comes mostly in dark stripes on a solid or medium-dark ground. Durable finish.

Coutil. A strong three-harness herringbone or reverse-twist twill weave of high count. For suits, corsets, and other purposes requiring a durable fabric.

Covert. A medium-weight or medium-lightweight fabric with warp-face left-hand twill. Usually of two-ply warp yarns and single or two-ply filling. Mixed yarns, such as natural and color in warp and matching color alone in filling. Has a mottled appearance. Often made with slack-twisted single yarns consisting of two rovings, one white and one color in warp and all color in filling.

Crash. Name given to fabrics having coarse, uneven yarns in both plain and twill weaves. Usually sheeting, osnaburg, or twill-weave construction with a special finish. Used for toweling and drapery purposes. In lighter weights, used for suits and dresses.

Crepe. Has a pebbly or crinkled surface produced by use of special crepe yarns. Can be either crepe, granite, or plain weave. Generally, mixed-twist crepe yarns used in both warp and filling; occasionally crepe yarns used only in the warp or the filling. Mostly woven on a box-loom.

Cretonne. Generally a medium or heavy sheeting or osnaburg printed in bold, bright designs. Used for draperies and other household articles.

Crinoline. Cheesecloth, tobacco cloth, or loosely woven sheetings given a stiff starched or plastic finish. Gives a firm appearance and feel.

Damask. Design, woven on Jacquard loom, on both sides of the fabric. Usually given a lustrous, smooth finish when used for tablecloths and a soft or lustrous finish for draperies or upholstery.

Denim. A durable fabric of the twill family. Usually of single hard-twisted yarns with colored warp and natural or white filling.

Dimity. A sheer white, dyed, or printed fabric of plain weave with a spaced rib made with warp cords. This rib may be single, double, or in groups. Comes also in checks and other novelty versions. Coarser small-check dimities are known as pajama checks.

Dobby. Woven on a dobby loom. All material with small figures, such as dots and geometric designs; floral patterns woven in the fabric, such as certain shirtings, huck towels, diaper cloth, certain dress goods, drapery and upholstery fabrics. Can be dyed, bleached, or yarn-dyed in many colors.

Dotted Swiss. Generally a voile or lawn construction woven with either clip spots or swivel dots. The clip spot is the more popular version. The fabric is given a crisp, clear finish, which may be permanent or semipermanent. Often yarn-dyed dots are woven on a white ground, or a dark ground has white dots. Many imitations on the market, e.g. pigment and flock dots.

Drill. A durable fabric of medium weight. Usually, three-harness warp-face twills made of carded sheeting yarns. Comes in various weights and thread counts ranging from 60×36 to 80×48. When dyed, known as khaki, tickings, silesia, herringbones. One thread goes over two filling yarns, then under one.

Duck. Covers a wide range of fabrics. It is one of the most durable fabrics made. A closely woven, heavy material. The most important fabrics in this group are known as *number duck*, *army duck*, and *flat* or *ounce duck*. Number and army ducks are always of plain weave with medium or heavy ply yarns; army ducks are the lighter. Ounce ducks always have single warp yarns woven in pairs and single or ply filling yarns. Other variations of these fabrics are sail duck, belt duck, hose duck, tire duck (such as breaker, cord, chafer), wide and narrow duck, biscuit duck, harvester duck, oil-press duck, wagon duck, enameling duck, boot duck, canvas, and so on. Generally of ply yarns in warp and yarns of various sizes and weights in filling. Thread counts range from 54×40 to 72×40.

Duvetyn. Sheeting napped on one side similar to suede cloth but with longer nap.

Éponge (also Ratiné). A loosely woven fabric of plain weave, with a rough, nubby appearance. This is obtained by the use of ratiné yarns; that is, one heavy and two fine, twisted together at different tensions, thus forming a knotty ply yarn. In less expensive versions, ordinary yarn is used in the warp with ratiné yarn in the filling. Can be bleached, dyed, or printed, and given a high luster or other finishes.

Express Stripe. Warp-face twill with a woven stripe. A durable fabric. An even number of unbleached and blue yarns are used in the pattern, forming a stripe.

Friezette. An uncut loop or pile ribbed fabric similar to a heavy rib or rep. Of heavy yarns, usually mixed in color.

Gabardine. A distinctive steep-diagonal warp-face twill of carded or combed yarns. Twill is to the left if made with all single yarns, and to the right when ply warp and single filling are used. Thread counts range from 110×76 to 130×80.

Gauze. *See also* Cheesecloth. Usually bleached; often specially treated, as when used for bandages. Better cheesecloths are also used for less expensive infants' items under various trademarks.

Gingham. Plain-weave, medium-weight, or lightweight fabrics. Can be either combed or carded yarns. Usually woven on a box-loom. Colored and white yarns or multicolored yarns form the pattern. Same number and variation of yarns in the warp as in the filling, forming squares, plaids, and similar patterns. Strange to say, a solid-color gingham is called a novelty gingham. Endless variations in color and design. Tissue ginghams are sheer ginghams made with lighter-weight yarns.

Glazed Chintz. Generally a printcloth or percale or a lightweight sheeting having bright, attractive floral or geometric designs. The fabric has a semipermanent or permanent glaze finish. Sometimes calendered or given a plastic finish. Fine twills are also used for this purpose.

Granite (also Mummy, Momie Cloth). Although this fabric has the appearance of crepe with a crinkled surface, it is not made with crepe yarns but with ordinary yarns and is woven on a dobby loom. Can be bleached, dyed, or printed.

Grosgrain. Plain-weave fabric similar to poplin but with a heavier rib effect and coarser, lower thread count. Made with single or ply filling.

Hickory Cloth. Resembles ticking somewhat, but of lighter weight and not so firm a weave.

Holland. Usually a low-count printcloth or high-count cheesecloth, heavily sized and glazed. Occasionally, sheeting constructions are used.

Hopsacking. Made of yarns about the same weight as osnaburg in a loose and low thread count. Sometimes made with spiral yarns. It has a soft texture and is of the homespun family of cottons. Sometimes made with fine warp and heavier filling. Many versions of this fabric.

Huck. Small-figured dobby weave used for towels. Has a rough surface. Comes bleached or with yarn-dyed striped border.

Indianhead. A porous fabric of a plain weave. The yarn is somewhat thick. The fabric feels wiry, resembling butcher linen but not as stiff or as lustrous.

Jaspé. A durable, narrow woven stripe made on a dobby loom with multicolored threads or with different shades of the same color. Has a shadow effect. Sometimes printed versions are shown in the market. Often small dots are woven into the fabric. Used for draperies and slipcovers.

Jeans. Three-harness warp-face twills of lightweight sheeting yarns. One warp thread goes over two or more filling threads, then under, moving one pick higher for each return filling thread. Sometimes made in chevron or herringbone versions.

Kasha Cloth. Flannel with napped face and mottled color. Usually tan or brown. An unbleached soft-filled sheeting. Mixed yarns are used with sized warp yarns that take dye and filling yarns with natural wax that do not take dye. When bale-dyed, has a mottled appearance.

Khaki. Tan or dusty colored warp face twill; softer and finer than drill. Name derived from East India word meaning earth color.

Lawn. Sheer and medium-sheer plain-weave fabrics made with lightweight yarns and medium to high count. Can be bleached, dyed, or printed. Also known as batiste or organdy, depending on the finish.

Linene (Osnaburg). A plain weave made of low-grade cotton, medium or heavy coarse yarns. Low thread count. When made of waste mixed with low-grade cotton, it is known as part-waste osnaburg; when of short-staple, low-grade white cotton, known as clean osnaburg. Woven with colored stripe and check effects, known as crash toweling. Comes in both wide and narrow widths and in innumerable variations in weight and thread count. Known also under the names of drapery crash, hopsacking, suiting. Has a number of uses.

Longcloth. Also known as *fineplain*. A plain-weave, closely woven, high-count fabric. The weight is between a printcloth and lawn. Generally combed finer yarns, and with more threads to the square inch than percales. A few are made of printcloth yarns.

Madras. Usually woven in stripes, cords, dobby, and Jacquard. Mostly all white, but in a number of cases done with a patterned warp and white filling, such as white and color warp, or color-and-color warp and white filling, or vice versa. Often a stripe is woven in solid colors. A number of variations of the above.

Marquisette. Lightweight open-mesh fabric of low thread count. Can be either a gauze or leno weave. Made with ply or single yarns. Dots and figures can be woven in. Either combed or carded. Generally the ply yarns are combed. Can be bleached, dyed, or printed.

Matelassé. Woven on a box-loom. A real matelassé is a double warp-face fabric, stitched together in warp and filling. Face of cloth has a fine warp and filling, the back a fine warp and heavy filling. Other matelassé crepes are made by interlacing crepe yarns with ordinary yarns in warp and filling, or in filling only. Comes in dobby or Jacquard designs. Has a slightly quilted appearance.

Moiré. A fabric with a compact plain weave with a shimmering effect on the surface. The finish is permanent provided the fabric is washed with luke-warm water, a mild soap, and no bleach.

Moleskin. Mostly a right-hand filling-face twill with a soft, smooth, shiny face. High thread count, usually many more fine filling threads and fewer heavier warp threads. Generally a napped back.

Monk's (Druid's) Cloth. Basket weave, a variation of the plain weave. Made with heavy rough yarns. Can be a 1×1, 2×2, 4×4, or 8×8 thread; the best known is the 4×4. These four threads in warp and filling are placed flat together and woven over and under in a plain weave; the resulting appearance is that of a basket.

Muslin. Coarse type of cotton fabric made of carded yarns; of various thread counts up to 140. Gray printcloth and lightweight sheetings known as unbleached muslins.

Nainsook. Plain weave. Mostly fine combed-yarn lawns, given a soft finish and light luster. Comes bleached and sometimes dyed.

Netting. A lightweight or heavy open-construction fabric made by knotting or twisting yarns together, thereby forming geometric patterns such as squares or hexagons. Ranges in weight from very sheer to very heavy fabrics, from fine nets to fishing or laundry nets.

Oilcloth. Sheetings or printcloth that are printed, bleached, or dyed, and given a special linseed oil and pigment preparation.

Organdy. Plain weave. A sheer, transparent lawn of lightweight yarns. Slightly lower construction than ordinary lawns. The filling is slightly finer than the warp yarns. Fewer filling than warp threads. Comes in many variations, such as permanent crinkles, leno effects, embroidery, plain or crinkled mixtures, clip spots. Bleached, dyed, or printed. Stiff finish, either starched or permanent stiff starchless finish.

Outing (Domett) Flannel. Can be either plain or twill weave. Lightweight or medium-weight soft-filled single yarn with nap on both sides. Mostly yarn-dyed. Woven in stripes, plaids, or checks. Sometimes bleached or piece-dyed, and occasionally printed. Domett is generally white with a longer nap.

Oxford. A plain weave of medium or heavy weight. Made with a variety of yarns. The majority of oxfords are of combed yarns, with heavier filling than warp yarns. Cheaper grades are mixed carded and combed yarns, and sometimes all carded yarns. Two warp yarns, placed flat next to each other, are woven over and under one heavier filling thread. Usually mercerized. A number of variations of this weave are on the market. For shirtings, dresses, and similar purposes.

Pajama Check. A lightweight or medium-weight plain weave fabric with small-sized or medium-sized cord checks. Usually carded yarns. One of the dimity family.

Percale. Plain weave of medium-weight yarn. Fabric in the printcloth group. Thread count 80 × 80 and over. Usually given a firm finish. Can be bleached, dyed, or printed.

Percaline. In the lightweight, low-count printcloth or lawn group with a bright, soft finish. Usually mercerized. Made in both fine and cheap versions. Used for the lining of furs.

Picolay. A compact fabric with a plain weave. The cloth is embossed with a diamond pattern to resemble diamond piqué. With careful laundering, the design is permanent.

Piqué. Has a warp or filling wale or cord, usually warp. Can be of carded or combed yarns. It is woven on a dobby loom or with a dobby motion. A heavy stuffer yarn is used in back of the cloth; this heavy yarn is caught at intervals by a filling thread. Groups of fine warp yarns are woven on the surface over the back stuffer yarn, forming a rib. Many of the cheaper versions are woven without this stuffer yarn. Other versions of piqué are irregular or novelty wales, woven dots, bird's-eye, diamond, square, ladder effects.

Plissé. A plain-weave crepe or crinkled fabric that has been specially treated. The plain fabric, which can be printcloth, lawn, or lightweight sheeting, is bleached, dyed, or printed, then covered with a gum in the desired pattern—stripe, check, floral, or geometric. The fabric is then passed through a caustic soda bath. The soda crinkles or crepes the fabric, leaving the gummed sections plain. When the gum is washed off, the crinkled pattern is revealed.

Plush. Plain-weave fabric with occasional twill or novelty versions. A deep velvetlike pile woven on a cam loom in what is known as a velvet weave. Many plushes are made on a Jacquard loom in patterns with many colored yarns. The ground yarns are generally two-ply carded. The double fabric is woven face to face and the warp yarns severed on the loom. Generally piece-dyed, and occasionally printed.

Pongee. Plain-weave fabric adapted from the early silk fabric of that name. Generally combed yarns. More and heavier filling yarns than warp. Schreinered to have a silklike finish.

Poplin. Has a heavier rib effect than broadcloth. Heavier filling than warp yarns, and more threads in the warp than filling. Printcloth yarns mostly. Combed yarns in the better cloths. Many mixtures made. Poplin comes in many variations, such as slubs, nubs, and yarn-dyed checks and stripes. Mainly dyed solid colors or printed. Often given special finishes, such as water-repellent, fire-retardant, mildewproof.

Printcloth. Carded cloth made with same yarns as cheesecloth, but with more warp and filling threads to the inch. Most printcloths are made in narrow widths up to 40 inches. Given a range of finishes, thus producing cambric, muslin, lawn, longcloth, and printed percales.

Rep. Plain weave. Has a rib running across the fabric. The rib stands out more than in broadcloth or poplin. Usually given a high luster, although not always. Rib produced by heavy warp ends or extra floating filling. Also formed by using two warp beams with slack and tension warp ends. Two slacks are woven as one, and the tension is woven plain.

Sateen. A satin weave. Usually woven so that the surface is smooth and the finish lustrous, resembling satin. Can be either a strong warp-face sateen or a softer filling-face sateen. Often, though not always, filling sateens have a softer finish than warp sateens. Either carded or combed yarns.

Scrim. A durable plain weave. Generally ply yarns and low thread count. Somewhat similar to voile but a much lower thread count. Cheesecloth with a stiffening finish is often referred to as scrim. Comes in many variations. Usually has a selvage. Generally carded, but a few combed varieties on the market.

Seersucker. A plain weave. Usually a medium-weight or medium-heavyweight fabric with a woven crinkled stripe, check, or plaid. Yarn-dyed or bleached, occasionally overprinted. The woven crinkle is made by alternating slack tension in warp yarns. Not to be confused with plissé.

Shantung. Plain weave. Has a rib effect formed by slub yarns. Certain parts of the yarn are not given the usual number of twists. These places form the slub in the rib.

Sheetings. Plain weave. Mostly carded but occasionally combed yarns in all weights: light, medium, and heavy. Generally about the same number of yarns in warp as in filling, but often warp yarns are heavier than filling. Sheetings come in both wide and narrow widths. Yarn sizes range from 10s to 29s.

Silesia. Generally a lightweight twill lining with a calendered glaze.

Suede Cloth. Sheeting napped on one side to resemble leather suede.

Tapestry. A closely woven yarn-dyed figured material with two or more sets of warp and filling, often plied. Woven on a Jacquard loom. Comes in both fine and coarse versions. The reverse side is smooth.

Terry Cloth. A fabric having uncut loops on both sides. Woven on a dobby loom with terry arrangement. Various sizes and numbers of yarns used in picks and ends, forming different versions of terry cloth. Can be woven on Jacquard loom to form designs. Can be yarn-dyed in different colors to form patterns. Bleached, piece-dyed, even printed.

Tickings. A variety of fabrics is known by this name. The main weave is a closely woven, strong yarn twill. Spaced, colored, and natural or white yarns repeated in the warp, and all natural or white in the filling, forming a stripe. Several color combinations used, as blue and white, brown and white, red and white. Heavy warp-face sateens as well as heavy sheetings are printed and sold as tickings. Jacquard damask tickings woven in lovely damask effects also sold for this purpose, as well as other fabrics, such as drills.

Velveteen. Pile construction on plain or twill background. Short cut, dense pile. Quality varies with background and density of pile. May have sheen if mercerized cotton is used.

Venetian. Durable warp-face eight-harness sateen of fine reverse-twist yarns.

Voile. A soft yet firm, sheer fabric of plain weave. Generally made of combed hard-twisted single yarns, although ply yarns are also used. About the same number of yarns in warp as in filling. Occasionally dots are woven in, and a crisp finish given the fabric; then it is sold as dotted swiss.

Whipcord. Serviceable fabric with prominent steep-twill effect. Often mercerized and preshrunk. Generally a left-hand warp twill. Many finished with slight nap on back of cloth. Some woven in solid colors, others have mixed warp and solid matching color filling.

Wigan. Usually made of printcloth or lightweight sheetings. Dyed in dark colors and starched and calendered. Used mostly for interlinings.

LINEN FABRICS*

Art Linen. Closely woven round-thread linen, used chiefly for embroidery, generally in the plain weave. Bleached, unbleached, and colors. Also used for dresses and table linens.

Bisso Linen. Fine, sheer linen; sometimes called *altar linen.* Made of wiry yarns. Has a crisp feel. Used for altar cloths.

Cambric. Fine, closely woven fabric with a high thread count. Plain weave; white and colors. Used chiefly for handkerchiefs.

Canvas. Many fabrics come under this heading. Two principal types: (1) Open-mesh canvas used for embroidery; made of hard-twisted yarns; very durable. Most popularly known in this group is Java canvas. (2) Close-woven canvas made from coarse hard-twisted yarns in the plain weave; in various weights. Finishes range from heavily sized to soft.

Crash. A relatively coarse fabric made of uneven slack-twisted yarns. Made in various qualities; plain weave. Used for towels, suitings, dresses, depending on the weight.

Damasks. In satin weave as well as the Jacquard pattern. Two types: single damask and double damask. Single damask has a five-shaft satin construction; thread count ranges from 100 to 200 to the square inch; if given a high thread count, is more durable than double damask. Double damask is more lustrous because of the longer float of the eight-shaft construction; reversible because the design is made on both sides; thread count ranges from 165 to 400 to the square inch.

Handkerchief Linen. Same as linen cambric. Sometimes called *linen lawn* or *linen batiste.* Plain weave, often corded.

Huckaback. Coarse fabric, having rough surface. Variations in weave; may have small figures. Color range from semibleached to white.

Sheeting. Firmly constructed plain-weave cloth. Used industrially. Closer construction used for bed linens. May be unbleached or white.

Toweling. General name that covers all types of linen woven in special widths for towels. Some are terry, huckaback, crash, bird's-eye, glass.

WOOL AND HAIR FABRICS*

Alpaca. The lower grades of alpaca were originally used as linings, and the better grades for fine dress goods. The fabrics sometimes being sold as alpaca merely resemble an alpaca fabric in finish; the use of the term for such fabrics is incorrect.

Astrakhan. Rough fabric with closely curled face resembling astrakhan lamb's pelt. Often made with cotton warp or cotton back.

Batiste (Wool). Lightweight wool fabric in plain weave similar to plain cambric. Should be all wool unless otherwise described.

Bedford Cord. Vertically ribbed fabric of substantial construction used for severe wear. Rib is pronounced

*The glossary of linen fabrics is based upon material prepared by the Linen Trade Association.

*The glossary of wool and hair fabrics is based upon material furnished by the Associated Wool Industries.

and runs in same direction as warp. Originally an all-wool fabric, now also made of other fibers. Term describes weave rather than material.

Bengaline. A thin fabric made generally of silk and wool, usually with a relatively inconspicuous rib running at right angles to the warp. The name does not denote any particular fiber blend.

Bolivia. A soft, plushlike fabric of wool, usually containing some special hair fiber, such as alpaca or mohair. The term is properly applied only to an all-wool product, closely woven and of fine stock.

Bouclé. A fabric woven from curled or specially twisted yarn in such a way as to produce small loops on the surface, giving a kinky appearance. The curled nap does not cover the entire surface but occurs at intervals, distinguishing it from astrakhan. Usually made in coating weights but also in lighter weights for dress goods.

Broadcloth. A fine wool fabric openly woven and then fulled to achieve uniform texture. The surface is then napped, closely sheared, and polished. The term originally was applied only to wool fabrics, but it is also applied to a cotton fabric used principally for men's shirtings. Not only is the fiber content of these fabrics wholly dissimilar but also the construction, finish, and use, so that they cannot be confused.

Camel's Hair. In undyed form, camel's hair is light tan. Fabrics that merely have this distinctive color cannot be correctly called camel's hair. The best grade is very expensive, and even then camel's hair is sometimes mixed with sheep's wool or other fibers.

Candlewick. A soft woolen dress fabric made in imitation of the candlewick bedspread, with tufted patterns similarly constructed.

Cashmere. A real cashmere fabric is woven only from the hair of the Cashmere goat. It is of fine close twill weave and extremely soft. The total amount of cashmere hair available is strictly limited.

Cassimere. (Not to be confused with cashmere.) Cassimere is a woolen fabric closely woven with a plain twill weave, and fulled. Most unclassified woolen fabrics are referred to as cassimeres.

Challis. A lightweight sheer fabric of all wool or of silk and wool. Sometimes made with a woven pattern but more often printed with designs after weaving. The designs are commonly of the type found in silk goods. Challis is made of fine yarn; it is very thin, light in weight, and soft and pliable.

Cheviot. Rough, somewhat harsh woolen fabric, woven from finer yarns than used in typical tweeds. Usually in plain colors or herringbones but may be in other fancy patterns. Woven from woolen yarns except for more expensive cheviots made from worsted yarns, generally in high colors, and referred to as worsted cheviots.

Chinchilla. A thick, heavily napped fabric with a close curled surface in imitation of chinchilla fur. The tufts are close together, covering the entire surface. Generally dyed in the piece in solid colors. Used for women's and children's coats and hats.

Covert. Twill fabric made from highly twisted woolen or worsted yarns, usually of two colors, which give it a speckled appearance. Closely woven with a fine,

smooth face. Used largely for men's topcoats and women's coats or tailored suits.

Crepe (Wool). Wool crepe is a lightweight worsted fabric with a more or less crinkly appearance, obtained by using warp yarns that are tightly twisted in alternate directions. The term is often applied to lightweight worsted fabrics for women's wear that have little or no crepe surface.

Doeskin. A very close and compact wool fabric with exceptionally smooth face. The weave is similar to a satin, but the smooth finish generally obliterates any trace of the weave on the face.

Flannel. A fulled and napped woven fabric, made generally of woolen yarn but sometimes with worsted yarn used in the warp or filling. Usually woven with a twill weave, which may be obscured by the nap. Counts range from 56×30 to 86×52; distinguished for its softness. Used for bathrobes, skirts, men's suits and trousers. Cotton flannel or flannelette is not dissimilar in appearance.

Fleece. Wool fabric with deep, soft nap. Term properly applied to flat woven or knit woolen fabrics as well as to those woven on the pile principle. The long nap or pile provides many air spaces, resulting in a fabric with high insulative properties.

Gabardine. A firm, hard-finished worsted fabric in the twill weave with a fine diagonal wale.

Homespun. A coarse and loosely woven woolen material made to simulate homemade cloth—in effect, a coarse, rough tweed. Yarn is usually heavy and contains coarse wool fiber unevenly spun.

Hopsacking. A rough open-weave woolen fabric made of coarse yarn, usually in a basket weave. Used for novelty effects.

Jersey. Elastic knitted fabric made from either woolen or worsted yarn. The rib is clearly discernible on one side of the fabric.

Kersey. A medium-weight woolen fabric, well fulled in the finishing, with a napped and closely sheared surface that obscures the weave. Used extensively for military and civil uniforms.

Mackinaw. A heavy woolen fabric, heavily fulled or felted, sometimes napped, with the result that no weave is apparent on the surface. In general construction, the same as melton except that the latter is usually made in plain colors, whereas mackinaw cloth is commonly woven with large distinctive plaids or color effects. Usually made of the coarser wools.

Melton. Well-fulled or felted overcoating fabric with smooth finish and close-cropped nap. Generally in plain colors. Coarser meltons similar to mackinaw cloth, but sometimes made of fine, soft wools to produce smooth coating fabric with finish similar to broadcloth.

Mohair. Yarns and fabrics of mohair are bright and lustrous. Warp yarns of cotton or worsted generally used in flat mohair fabrics. Mohair pile fabrics used in automobiles and for upholstery usually have pile introduced as warp, but in such fashion that the special system of threads is not subjected to severe tension.

Nun's Veiling. A fine, lightweight plain-weave woolen fabric, very soft and thin, originally for veils but now used for women's and children's dresses. Plain colors.

Plaid Back. A type of construction used in overcoatings. The face may be finished like melton, fleece, or similar fabrics. The back is a fancy or tartan plaid.

Poplin. Originally a fabric having a silk warp and a filling that consisted of a wool yarn heavier than the silk, thus producing a ribbed surface something like a rep.

Rabbit's Hair. Rabbit's hair is used in combination with other fibers. It is soft and lustrous. In the better fabrics, enough hair may be present to justify the use of the term.

Ratiné. A rough, pebbly woolen fabric the surface interest of which is obtained by the use of novelty yarns with a fancy twist.

Saxony. A term applied to certain flannels and to smooth woolen fabrics made from fine wools similar in nature to Saxony wools.

Serge. A fabric with a diagonal twill and a smooth finish. The twill is visible both on the face and on the back; counts range from 48 × 34 to 62 × 58. Dark blue is the color most commonly used, but other plain colors are made for certain purposes.

Sharkskin. A term descriptively applied to wool fabrics woven in a 2 and 2 right-hand twill, with a 1 and 1 color arrangement of yarns in the warp and filling. This combination of weave and color results in color lines running diagonally to the left, opposed to the direction of the twill lines, and a distinctly sleek appearance and feel that suggests the texture of the skin of the shark. Modifications of this design are often loosely designated as sharkskin.

Sheers. General classification for thin, lightweight women's-wear fabrics. Usually woven from worsted yarns, although some woolen fabrics are sufficiently thin to be classified as sheers.

Shetland. The term is now applied to fabrics made of wool with the characteristics of Shetland Islands wool. Shetlands are extremely soft. The herringbone weave is common.

Snow Cloth. Fabrics designed for outdoor winter use. May be meltons, kerseys, heavy flannels, and similar fabrics. Often indicates these fabrics have been given water-repellent finish.

Suede. A fine soft fabric with closely clipped nap made to imitate suede leather.

Tropical Weights. Lightweight suitings of woolen or worsted, usually the latter, used for men's and less frequently for women's summer suits. The weave should be firm but open, as the fabric is especially designed for hot-weather wear.

Tweed. A term broadly applied to the sturdier types of fabrics made of the coarser grades of wool. Tweed fabrics originally derived their interest from the color effects obtained by mixing stock-dyed wools. More recently the term includes monotones, which derive their interest from weave effects. The most popular weaves for tweeds are the plain, the twill, and variations of the latter.

Velour. A smooth, sleek fabric with a closely cut pile face. The upright pile, which yields in any direction, gives the fabric an exceedingly smooth feel.

Vicuña. Short, soft, exceedingly fine hair fiber, very valuable because of the limited supply. It is rarely used by itself, although a few vicuña coats are manufactured each year. Sometimes mixed with wool to produce special soft coating fabrics. The term and certain derived and coined names have been much misused.

Whipcord. Sturdy wool fabric with pronounced diagonal wale, closely woven and smooth-finished. Used for riding habits and other garments subjected to hard wear; in heavier weights for upholstery.

SILK FABRICS

Bengaline. A ribbed fabric having cotton or wool yarns for the filling and silk for the warp. Similar to poplin but having a heavier ribbed effect. Used for coats, suits, dresses.

Broadcloth. A fine, smooth, closely woven fabric in plain colors or in woven stripes; also known as silk shirting. It has a plain weave. Used for shirts and dresses.

Brocade. Most figured silk fabrics in a Jacquard weave are known as brocades. The pattern is raised above the general surface of the fabric. Used mainly for elaborate evening wear.

Brocatelle. Similar to brocade but usually heavier with a pronounced raised design. Used primarily for upholstery and draperies.

Canton Crepe. Characterized by a heavy filling and a finer warp. Heavier than crepe de chine, having pronounced crinkle and greater durability. Used chiefly for dresses.

Chiffon. A transparent sheer fabric in a plain weave. Extremely light in weight but very strong. It usually has a soft finish. Used for evening dresses, lingerie, blouses, and scarves.

China Silk. A very soft, extremely lightweight silk made in a plain weave, used chiefly for linings. Irregularities of threads, caused by the extreme lightness and softness of China silk, are characteristic of the fabric.

Crepe. Fabric with a crinkled effect, produced either by the use of tightly twisted yarns or by the method of weaving.

Crepe-back Satin or Satin Crepe. Satin weave with a crepe-twist filling. As the fabric is reversible, interesting effects can be obtained by contrasting the surfaces. Used for dresses, blouses, linings.

Crepe de Chine. Soft but strong; lighter in weight than canton crepe. Has a fine crinkled effect produced by alternately twisted filling yarns. Popular for dresses, lingerie, blouses, and scarves.

Crepe Meteor. Similar to georgette in construction on the reverse side. Satin construction on its face, thus showing more luster than any of the flat crepes. Light in weight, drapes well, has a soft feel and finish.

Damask. Reversible figured silk fabrics woven on the Jacquard loom. Pattern flatter than in brocade. Used for upholstery and draperies; the lighter weights, for dresses and lingerie.

Ecru Silk. Thrown silk with a small amount of sericin removed.

Faille. A silk fabric of the grosgrain type. In plain weave with flat ribs in the filling. Has good body and wears well if not too loosely constructed. Usually slightly lustrous finish. Used for dresses, coats, and handbags.

Faille Crepe. Lighter weight than faille with creped filling. Used for dresses.

Faille Taffeta. Stiff and crisp with a fine cross-ribbed appearance. Used for dresses and coats.

Flat Crepe. Similar to crepe de chine but with a flatter surface.

Foulard. A lightweight silk fabric with a soft finish. Made with a twill weave. Usually printed with small figures on dark and light backgrounds. Suitable for dresses, robes, and scarves.

Georgette. Highly creped sheer silk fabric, chiefly for dresses and blouses.

Gloria Silk. A very closely woven, lightweight cloth generally constructed of plain weave, but sometimes of twill or satin. Made with silk warp and a cotton, worsted, or nylon filling. Much used as an umbrella cloth.

Grosgrain. A fine cross-ribbed fabric of close texture having a heavy filling, which is sometimes made of cotton yarns. Ribs are rounder than in faille; heavier than in poplin. Used chiefly for ribbons and trimmings.

Habutai. Similar to China silk but heavier. A closely woven, pure-dye fabric. Used for lampshades, dresses, blouses, lingerie, curtains.

Lamé. Silk in which metal threads form the pattern or the background. Used chiefly for evening wear.

Marquisette. Very sheer silk fabric in the gauze weave. Sometimes called *silk gauze*. Used for evening dresses and trimmings.

Matelassé. A fabric having a raised figured pattern in a blistered, quilted effect. Woven on a Jacquard loom. Used for dresses and blouses.

Merveilleux. An all-silk or silk-and-cotton mixture in twill weave. Used as lining in men's outer apparel.

Moiré. Watermark designs embossed on plain-weave fabrics that have crosswise ribs.

Mousseline de Soie. Sheer, transparent silk in a plain weave. Similar to chiffon but with a more open texture and a stiffer finish produced by the use of sizing. Used chiefly for evening dresses.

Ottoman. Heavy plain-weave fabric with wide, flat crosswise ribs that are larger and rounder than in faille. Filling may be cotton, silk, or wool. Used for dress-coats, suits, trimmings.

Pongee. Also called *tussah silk*. Made from wild silk. Has a rough, uneven texture. Generally is in its natural colors of cream to light brown, but may be dyed. Used for dress goods and household decoration.

Radium. A lustrous, supple fabric having the drapability of crepe and the crispness of taffeta. Plain weave. Used for women's dresses, slips, negligees, blouses, linings, draperies.

Satin. Silk fabric with a highly lustrous surface and usually a dull back. Made in different weights according to its uses, which vary from lingerie and dress goods to drapery and upholstery fabrics. May be made with a cotton back. Sometimes double-faced for use as ribbon.

Shantung. Low in luster, heavier and rougher than pongee. A plain weave in which irregular (slub) filling yarns are used. Sometimes used to describe a heavy grade of pongee made in China.

Souple Silk. Silk dyed in the skein, only part of the sericin being removed.

Surah. A soft, strong silk with a twill weave. Used for dresses and scarves.

Taffeta. A smooth, closely woven fabric in a plain weave. Often weighted to produce its characteristic crispness. Sometimes has a moiré pattern. Used for dresses, suits, coats, and lingerie.

Velvet. Silk velvet has a silk pile and a silk back. Some velvets are made with a silk pile and a rayon or cotton back. *Transparent velvet* is a sheer velvet having a rayon pile and a silk back. *Panne velvet* has a special luster that is produced by pressing the pile in one direction.

FABRICS OF MAN-MADE FIBERS

The foregoing fabrics are also made of man-made fibers, blends of man-made and natural fibers, and combinations of yarns of which some are of man-made fibers and others of natural fibers. In addition, there are other fabrics of man-made fibers, blends, and yarn combinations that have different characteristics from those of the natural fiber fabrics (though sometimes with similar names) e.g., alpaca crepe, bark crepe, fur fabrics, linen-textured rayon, romaine crepe, sharkskin, tricotine.

INDEX